REA's Test Prep Books Are The Best!

(a sample of the <u>hundreds of letters</u> REA receives each year)

" Great refresher book... I looked at the others, but [the REA book] is concise, well-written, and easy to follow. I recommend it to all people who are taking the GRE test. "

A GRE Test-Taker from Texas

" What I found in [REA's] book was a wealth of information sufficient to shore up my basic skills in math and verbal... The practice tests were challenging and the answer explanations most helpful. It certainly is the *Best Test Prep for the GRE!* "

Student, Pullman, WA

" I am writing to thank you for your test preparation... Your book helped me immeasurably, and I have nothing but praise for your GRE preparation. "

Student, Benton Harbor, MI

" Your book was such a better value and was so much more complete than anything your competition has produced — and I have them all! "

Teacher, Virginia Beach, VA

" Compared to the other books that my fellow students had, your book was the most useful in helping me get a great score. "

Student, North Hollywood, CA

(more on next page)

(continued from front page)

" You don't really have to study your boring, cumbersome textbook. Just use this book instead and you have a guaranteed A+. "

Student, Singapore

" Your *Fundamentals of Engineering Exam* book was the absolute best preparation I could have had for the exam, and it is one of the major reasons I did so well and passed the FE on my first try. "

Student, Sweetwater, TN

" I used your book to prepare for the test and found that the advice and the sample tests were highly relevant... Without using any other material, I earned very high scores and will be going to the graduate school of my choice. "

Student, New Orleans, LA

" An excellent book for practicing review questions. The best thing about the book is that it's updated and the information is accurate. "

Student, Chicago, IL

" I really appreciate the help from your excellent book. Please keep up the great work. "

Student, Albuquerque, NM

" If you want more in-depth review for the exam, you should...look into the new study guide published by REA in C++. "

Student, Cerritos, CA

(more on back page)

The Very *Best* Coaching & Study Course for the

GRE® GENERAL TEST

GRE is a registered trademark

Pauline Alexander-Travis, Ph.D.
Assistant Professor of Reading
Southwestern Oklahoma State University
Weatherford, OK

David Bell, Ed.D.
Professor of Education
Arkansas Technical University, Russellville, AR

James W. Daley, M.A.
Educational Consultant
New York, NY

Anita Price Davis, Ed.D.
Professor Emerita of Education
Converse College, Spartanburg, SC

Lucille M. Freeman, Ph.D.
Associate Professor of Educational Administration
University of Nebraska at Kearney

Leonard L. Gregory, Ph.D.
Associate Professor of Educational Administration
University of Nebraska at Kearney

Alexander Kopelman, M.B.A.
Educational Consultant
New York, NY

Lutfi A. Lutfiyya, Ph.D.
Associate Professor of Mathematics
University of Nebraska at Kearney

James S. Malek, Ph.D.
Chairperson and Professor of English
DePaul University, Chicago, IL

Marcia Mungenast, B.A.
Educational Consultant
Private Test Preparation Instructor
Upper Montclair, NJ

Donald E. Orlosky, Ed.D.
Chairperson of Educational Leadership Department
University of South Florida, Tampa, FL

Jerry R. Shipman, Ph.D.
Professor and Chairperson of Mathematics
Alabama A&M University, Normal, AL

Ricardo Simpson-Rivera, M.S.
Visiting Scientist
Oregon State University, Corvallis, OR

Research & Education Association
Visit our website at:
www.rea.com
GRE test updates at: **www.rea.com/GRE**

To Our Readers:

Educational Testing Service and the Graduate Record Examinations Board are revising the GRE General Test gradually through 2009 and beyond. As these incremental changes are announced, you can count on REA to keep you up to speed at *www.rea.com/gre*.

Research & Education Association

61 Ethel Road West
Piscataway, New Jersey 08854
E-mail: info@rea.com

The Very Best Coaching and Study Course for the GRE® GENERAL TEST

Published 2008

Copyright © 2003, 2002, 1999 by Research & Education Association, Inc. All rights reserved. No part of this book may be reproduced in any form without permission of the publisher.

Printed in the United States of America

Library of Congress Control Number 2002108375

ISBN-13: 978-0-87891-445-6
ISBN-10: 0-87891-445-5

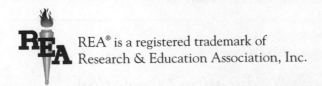

REA® is a registered trademark of Research & Education Association, Inc.

CONTENTS

SIX GRE CBT PRACTICE TESTS

ABOUT RESEARCH & EDUCATION ASSOCIATION

Founded in 1959, Research & Education Association is dedicated to publishing the finest and most effective educational materials—including software, study guides, and test preps—for students in middle school, high school, college, graduate school, and beyond.

REA's Test Preparation series includes books and software for all academic levels in almost all disciplines. Research & Education Association publishes test preps for students who have not yet entered high school, as well as high school students preparing to enter college. Students from countries around the world seeking to attend college in the United States will find the assistance they need in REA's publications. For college students seeking advanced degrees, REA publishes test preps for many major graduate school admission examinations in a wide variety of disciplines, including engineering, law, and medicine. Students at every level, in every field, with every ambition can find what they are looking for among REA's publications.

REA's series presents tests that accurately depict the official exams in both degree of difficulty and types of questions. REA's practice tests are always based upon the most recently administered exams, and include every type of question that can be expected on the actual exams.

REA's publications and educational materials are highly regarded and continually receive an unprecedented amount of praise from professionals, instructors, librarians, parents, and students. Our authors are as diverse as the fields represented in the books we publish. They are well-known in their respective disciplines and serve on the faculties of prestigious high schools, colleges, and universities throughout the United States and Canada.

We invite you to visit us at *www.rea.com* to find out how "REA is making the world smarter."

ACKNOWLEDGMENTS

In addition to our authors, we would like to thank John Paul Cording, Vice President, Technology, for his editorial review; Larry B. Kling, Vice President, Editorial, for his overall guidance which brought this publication to completion; Pam Weston, Vice President, Publishing, for setting the quality standards for production integrity and managing the publication to completion; Teresina Jonkoski, Associate Editor, for coordinating revisions for this edition; Brian Walsh, M.A., Instructor, Faculty of Arts and Sciences, Rutgers University, and Craig Pelz for their editorial contributions; Christine Saul and Ilona Bruzda, Senior Graphic Artists, for designing the cover; and Wende Solano for her typesetting services.

GRE CBT STUDY SCHEDULE

This study schedule will help you become thoroughly prepared for the GRE General CBT. Although the schedule is designed as a 12-week study program, if less time is available it can be compressed into a six-week plan by collapsing each two-week period into one. Be sure to set aside enough time each day for studying purposes. If you choose the 12-week program, you should plan to study for at least one hour per day. If you choose the six-week program, you should plan to study for at least two hours per day. Depending on your personal time schedule, you may find it easier to study during the weekend. Keep in mind that the more time you devote to studying for the GRE CBT, the more prepared and confident you will be on the day of the exam.

Week	Activity
1	Read and study our introduction to the GRE CBT on the following pages.
2	Take and score REA Practice Test 1 to determine your strengths and weaknesses. (Be sure to record your scores on the Scoring Worksheet to track your progress.) Any area in which you score low will require that you thoroughly review the relevant review sections. For example, if you obtain a low number of correct answers on the Verbal Section, then you will need to carefully study each part of the Verbal Review when you get to that section. Your performance on the Quantitative and Analytical Writing sections should be treated in the same manner, and you should study their corresponding reviews.
3	Study the Quantitative Review. Complete the practice drills and check your answers. Always be sure that you are comfortable with the material you just covered before continuing to the next week's agenda.
4	Study the Verbal Review. Be sure to complete all drills and check your answers for each section of the review. Don't neglect the targeted vocabulary list we provide. You may wish to make flash cards to help learn words that are new to you.

Week	Activity
5	Study the Analytical Writing Review. Carefully examine every suggestion and example and make sure you understand it.
6	Review any areas of the Verbal, Quantitative, and Analytical Writing reviews in which you may have a need for improvement. Brush up on these skills before the coming week, when you will take the second Practice Test.
7	Take REA Practice Test 2. After scoring the exam, record your score on the Scoring Worksheet and measure your progress. Make sure to thoroughly review all of the explanations to the questions you answered incorrectly. This will help you gain confidence in areas where you're underperforming. Then, go over the relevant review material.
8	Take REA Practice Test 3. Score the exam and record your score on the Scoring Worksheet to record your progress. Then, thoroughly review all of the explanations to the questions you answered incorrectly. Restudy the reviews of the areas in which you are weak.
9	Take REA Practice Test 4. Score the exam and record your score. Again, thoroughly review all of the explanations to the questions you answered incorrectly. Study the reviews of the areas in which you still show weakness.
10	Take REA Practice Test 5. Score the exam and record your score. Continue to thoroughly review all of the explanations to the questions you answered incorrectly. Restudy the subject areas in which you are still weak.
11	Take REA Practice Test 6. Score the exam and record your score. Review the explanations to the questions you answered incorrectly. Restudy the areas in which you are still weak.
12	Use this time to cover any areas in which you still need help by continuing to study the reviews. You may benefit by retaking Practice Test 1.

GOOD LUCK ON THE GRE GENERAL CBT!

CHAPTER 1:
Scoring High
on the GRE CBT

The GRE CBT Computer Screen
At a Glance*

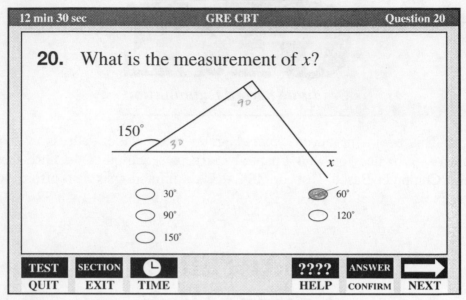

20. What is the measurement of *x*?

- ○ 30°
- ○ 90°
- ○ 150°
- ◉ 60°
- ○ 120°

TEST	SECTION	🕐		????	ANSWER	⟶
QUIT	EXIT	TIME		HELP	CONFIRM	NEXT

GETTING AROUND - You will use a mouse to navigate the GRE CBT computer screen. In addition, there are a few buttons you'll have to click on to get where you're going. Let's take them in the order in which they appear along the bottom of your screen.

Test Quit - Click here to end the test.

Section Exit - Click this button to move on to the next section of the exam—that is, if there is one—before your time expires. Don't plan on using this button, however. If you finish before the clock runs out, you probably should have spent more time on the section.

Time - Use this button to turn the on-screen clock on or off. When you start getting down to the wire (with about five minutes left in a section) the clock will start blinking and seconds will be added to the display.

Help - Here's another one you should avoid if you can. You see, the clock won't stop because you didn't memorize the directions. Learn how to take the test *before* you take the test.

Next - When you're sure about your answer choice, click here.

Confirm - After clicking NEXT, click here to move on to the next item.

* GRE CBT software for the Analytical Writing Section runs like a standard word-processing program minus the grammar and spell-check features.

CHAPTER 1

SCORING HIGH ON THE GRE CBT

ABOUT THIS BOOK

This book—produced expressly for readers without access to computers—provides you with a paper-based representation of the GRE General Computer-Based Test, or CBT. REA's printed tests also afford you excellent preparation if you're planning to take the paper-based GRE General Test.

Unlike its former incarnation as a fully computer-*adaptive* test, or CAT, the GRE General CBT contains a non-adaptive essay component, which graduate schools had been championing for years.

Inside this book you'll find topical reviews and six full-length true-to-format practice exams that will equip you with the information and strategies you'll need to master the GRE General CBT. Our practice tests contain every type of question that you can expect to encounter on the actual exam. Following each REA model test, we provide an answer key with detailed explanations designed to help you confidently grasp the test material and benchmark exactly what constitutes top-scoring performance.

ABOUT THE TEST

The GRE General CBT is required by graduate and professional schools, as it is considered a crucial component for admission to a graduate program. Applicants for graduate school submit GRE CBT test results together with other undergraduate records as part of the admission process. The test examines your verbal, quantitative, and analytical writing abilities. These are skills that have been found to contribute to successful achievement in a graduate program. The exam does not test prior knowledge of data or facts specific to any field of study.

The computer-based GRE contains three distinct sections with various types of questions:

- **Analytical Writing Ability:** One 45-minute "Present Your Perspective" task, and one 30-minute "Analyze an Argument" assignment.

- **Quantitative Ability:** One 28-question section containing arithmetic, algebra, geometry, quantitative comparison, and data interpretation questions.

- **Verbal Ability:** One 30-question section containing analogies, antonyms, sentence completions, and reading comprehension questions.

Following this introduction are extensive reviews with test strategies, numerous examples, and suggested studying techniques for attacking all three sections of the test.

The Quantitative and Verbal sections of the GRE General CBT consist entirely of multiple-choice questions contained in timed sections. Each question in the Verbal section presents five answer choices, while the Quantitative Comparison section presents four answer choices. The "Present Your Perspective" task of the Analytical Writing section gives you a choice of two essay questions, whereas the "Analyze an Argument" assignment consists of only one essay you have to evaluate. The test contains a trial section, which is neither identified nor counted toward your score. So don't let it concern you. The purpose of the trial section is to test new questions for future exams. For practical purposes, our test-preparation book has omitted the trial section and presents only the counted and scored sample sections for each practice exam.

CAT VS. CBT: WHAT'S THE DIFFERENCE?

While you can take all three sections of the GRE General Test on the computer, that is not to say that the entire test is *adaptive*; clearly, it contains a non-adaptive essay component. "CBT" simply means that you will take the test on a computer. Then again, portions of two parts of the GRE General—the Quantitative and Verbal sections—*are* adaptive. This means that the software picks which questions to pose next based on your performance on the earlier items. Thus, the test customizes itself to your level of ability. A correct response is followed by a more difficult question, and an incorrect response is followed by an easier question. Difficult questions increase your score in greater increments than moderate or easier questions. For the Analytical Writing section, the computer presents you with essay questions without considering your performance on other sections of the test. All essay tasks have the same level of difficulty.

On a traditional paper-based test—including the paper-based GRE General Test itself—every examinee sees questions in a fixed sequence. Because of the adaptive nature of two parts of the GRE General and the large pool of available questions, different test-takers are asked different questions. The test items have been designed to meet content and difficulty specifications that allow for an equitable comparison of scores.

Pros and Cons of Computer-Based Testing

There are several advantages to computer-based testing. First, you will receive your unofficial scores for the Quantitative and Verbal sections on the day you take your test, rather than several weeks later. Second, the CBT is offered much more frequently than its paper-and-pencil predecessor, and you can register closer to the administration date. Third, you may choose to take the test in the morning or afternoon. In addition, the testing venue is quieter and more orderly than traditional testing locations. Finally, there are fewer questions on the GRE CBT than on traditional paper-and-pencil tests.

Unfortunately, there are also some important disadvantages to the CBT. People who are unfamiliar with computers may find the testing environment intimidating. While no computer skills are required, an unusual environment may have a psychological impact on your preparedness. In addition, you must answer the questions in the order in which they are presented. You cannot skip a question and return to it later—or return to an earlier question to change your answer, as you could on a paper-and-pencil test. This is significant because it eliminates the important test-taking strategy of answering the easier questions first and returning to the more difficult questions if you have time. Finally, in the computer-adaptive sections, the majority of the questions you encounter will be challenging to you.

Taking the CBT

The CBT testing environment is based on a point-and-click interface. You will be presented with a question, and you will use a mouse to choose your answer. Once you have chosen your answer, you will click on the on-screen "Answer Confirm" button to verify your choice. When you have confirmed your answer, the computer will select the next question. In the computer-adaptive sections, the first question asked in each multiple-choice section will be of medium difficulty. Subsequent questions will be more or less difficult depending on your answer to the preceding question. The adaptive software will adjust throughout the test until it matches your ability level.

The computer will also give you your essay questions. You'll then word-process your answer*. The computer software used for the essay sections is specially designed in order to ensure fairness for all examinees. It contains the following functions: inserting text, deleting text, cut and paste, and undoing the previous action. There won't be a spell- or grammar-checking feature.

---

* The hand-writing option is not available at CBT centers. Visit www.gre.org for details.

At any time during the test, you may choose to quit an individual section, or the entire test. You may wish to exercise this option if you feel that you are ill-prepared for the exam. However, you must not take this decision lightly. Once you quit a section or the entire test and confirm your desire to do so, you will be unable to reverse your decision. Note that you will not be able to take the GRE CBT again for 30 days, *even if you do not complete the exam.*

When you complete the exam, the computer will instantaneously give you unofficial scores for the multiple-choice sections. Your official score report, which includes the score for the Analytical Writing section, will be mailed to you within 10 to 15 days of the test date. If you have hand-written your essays it may take up to six weeks until you receive your scores due to possible shipping and handling delays.

Should I take paper-and-pencil practice exams?

The practice exams in this book will provide you with the best possible *printed* version of the type of test you will be facing. Our model tests have been calibrated to provide a score that is comparable to what you would achieve on a CBT. Consequently, the written tests necessarily contain extra questions, and the testing time is 15 minutes longer than the CBT.

Who administers the test?

The test is administered by the Educational Testing Service under the direction of the Graduate Record Examinations Board, which, though independent, is affiliated with the Association of Graduate Schools and the Council of Graduate Schools.

Is there a registration fee?

Yes, there is a registration fee. All costs are listed in the information bulletin. There is a basic registration charge, and special services sometimes require extra fees. The fees for the GRE can be waived or reduced if you meet the criteria for financial assistance. Consult the ETS bulletin for further information on all fees and options for financial assistance.

When and where is the test given?

Test locations and dates are listed in the *GRE Information and Registration Bulletin*, which is provided upon request by ETS. For more information, or to get an information bulletin, see your college advisor, or contact ETS as detailed here:

Graduate Record Examinations
Educational Testing Service
P.O. Box 6000
Princeton, NJ 08541-6000
Phone: (609) 771-7670
Website: http://www.gre.org

In addition, students with special needs may wish to consult the bulletin in order to arrange for convenient testing accommodations.

HOW TO USE THIS BOOK

What do I study first?

Remember that the GRE General CBT is designed to test knowledge that has been acquired over a long period of time. Therefore, your best preparation is to take the sample tests provided in this book, which will acquaint you with the types of questions, directions, and, of course, the overall format of the GRE General. It will also help you establish a time frame in which each section must be completed. Read over the book and its suggestions for test-taking, take one of our practice tests to determine your area(s) of weakness, and then go back and focus your study on any specific problem area(s). Brushing up on the areas in which you tested well will also improve your total test score. We strongly recommend that you follow the Study Schedule in the front of this book to best utilize your time.

When should I start studying?

It is never too early for you to start studying for the GRE CBT. The earlier you begin, the more time you will have to sharpen your skills. Do not procrastinate! Cramming is not an effective way to study, since it does not allow you the time needed to learn the test material.

FORMAT OF THE GRE GENERAL

All of the questions in the Quantitative and Verbal sections of the GRE CBT will be in multiple-choice format. Some of the questions will have five options lettered A through E, and some will have only four options. The Analytical Writing section consists of two separate essay questions. Be aware that there is a time limit for each section, so you should keep track of the time as you take each test section. Our practice tests will help you greatly in this respect.

Section	Number of Questions	Minutes
1 Analytical	1 "Present Your Perspective" task 1 "Analyze an Argument" task	75
2 Quantitative	14 quantitative comparisons 14 mathematical problems	45
3 Verbal	10 antonyms, 7 analogies, 7 sentence completions, 6 reading comprehension	30
4 Trial Section	Not included for preparation purposes	30

Total 3 hours

<u>*Approximate Number of Questions Per Section*</u>
Analytical Writing   =   2
Quantitative   =   28
Verbal   =   30
Total Questions   =   *60*

Note: The Analytical Writing sections will always come first; the order of the two sections will vary in different exams.

SECTIONS OF THE GRE CBT

ANALYTICAL WRITING SECTION

This section tests your ability to construct and analyze arguments. You find two essay questions in this part: one asks you to address an issue from your perspective(s), the other wants you to evaluate the reasoning of someone else's argument. Here are the details:

1) **"Present Your Perspective on an Issue":** You will have a choice between two topics. You have to show your ability to articulate a complex idea clearly and effectively. While you can address the issue from any perspective you wish, you have to support your argument with relevant, cogent reasons and examples and construct a well-written and focused essay.

2) **"Analyze an Argument"**: This item requires you to critique an argument by discussing how plausible you find it. Rather than agreeing or disagreeing with it you will have to examine the soundness of the argument's claims and the evidence provided.

QUANTITATIVE ABILITY SECTION

Quantitative Ability is designed to measure your understanding of basic math skills and concepts, and the ability to solve problems of a quantitative nature. This section does not normally require any mathematical knowledge beyond the high school level. The mathematics section can be broken down into broad areas of arithmetic, geometry, data analysis, and algebra. In detail, the sections look like this:

1) **Algebra:** These questions involve factoring and simplifying, relations and functions, and equations and inequalities. Required skills include the ability to solve first- and second-degree equations, inequalities, and simultaneous equations. Word problems also fall under this section, as well as basic algebraic skills applicable to problem-solving.

2) **Arithmetic:** These questions involve such operations as addition, subtraction, multiplication, and division. These operations are to be performed on real numbers and radical expressions. This area also covers percents, estimations, absolute values, and properties of numbers.

3) **Geometry:** Geometry deals with the properties of circles, triangles, parallel lines, rectangles, and polygons. Area, volume, perimeter, angles, and the Pythagorean Theorem are also included. Simple coordinate geometry is also tested by these questions, including intercepts, slope, and graphing.

4) **Data Analysis:** Data analysis includes descriptive statistics, interpreting data given in graphs or tables, probability, determining if enough data is given to solve a problem, and choosing appropriate data for problem solution.

VERBAL ABILITY SECTION

Verbal Ability will measure your effectiveness at solving a problem hinging on your command of the English language. This involves understanding, analyzing, and discerning relationships between or among words or groups of words. The verbal ability section contains four types of items: antonyms, analogies, sentence completion, and reading comprehension.

Here are the details:

1) **Antonyms:** These questions measure strength of vocabulary and your ability to make a transition from a word to its most likely opposite.

2) **Analogies:** These questions test your ability to recognize relationships among words and to recognize when they parallel each other. A pair of words is given and you are asked to determine which, among the five answer choice sets, is most like the original pair.

3) **Sentence Completion:** These questions measure your ability to recognize which words or phrases best stylistically and logically complete a sentence.

4) **Reading Comprehension:** These questions require you to analyze a written passage from several perspectives, and to read with thorough understanding and insight. You will encounter six types of reading comprehension questions. They primarily focus on the main idea, explicitly stated information, the author's implied ideas, applications of the author's ideas to other scenarios, the author's reasoning, logic, or persuasive technique, and the attitude or tone of the passage. There are four passages on the general test, two of which are longer and yield seven or eight questions, and two shorter passages followed by three or four questions. Each of these passages is drawn from four different areas of study: the social sciences, the humanities, and physical and biological studies.

ABOUT THE REVIEW SECTIONS

Our reviews are written to help you understand the broad concepts behind GRE General CBT questions. They will prepare you for the test by helping you survey what you need to know. Our reviews are accompanied by drills and numerous examples to help reinforce the subject matter. By using the reviews in conjunction with the practice tests, you will be able to substantially sharpen your test-taking skills.

ANALYTICAL WRITING REVIEW

Our Analytical Writing Review helps you gauge your essay-writing skills. It offers suggestions about how to prepare and pre-plan your essay, as well as how to effectively use the English language. You will also find an extensive writing skills review.

QUANTITATIVE ABILITY REVIEW

REA's Quantitative Ability Review includes refreshers with several examples to help familiarize you with basic math and its properties. Refreshers are provided for arithmetic, algebra, and geometry, as well as quantitative comparisons, and mastering data interpretation.

VERBAL ABILITY REVIEW

Strategies and tips for improving performance are provided in REA's Verbal Ability Review, as are the directions for each subset. Sentence completion, reading comprehension, analogies, and antonyms are covered.

SCORING THE PRACTICE EXAMS

Our scoring conversion table will give you a rough approximation of how you will score on the Quantitative and Verbal sections of the GRE CBT. Use the following method to calculate your scaled score:

First, compare your Answer Sheet to the Answer Key. Mark each response as correct or incorrect. Then, total the number of correct responses for each section of the GRE. Place each section's total of correct responses on its corresponding space on the Scoring Worksheet (which you'll find at the front of this book). Next, add together the scores from your two Verbal sections to obtain a Verbal subtotal (e.g., Reading Comprehension score plus Sentence Completion scores equals your total Verbal Raw Score); do likewise with your scores on the two Quantitative sections for a Quantitative subtotal. You will now have computed two separate raw scores for these two parts of the GRE. Then, convert the raw scores to scaled scores. At this point you'll need to make allowances for the computer-guided weighting and number-crunching that ETS does and the fact that relative percentile rankings are bound to shift over time. But to get a *rough* idea of where you stand in the GRE General Test score universe, use these benchmarks:

In the **Verbal** section, raw scores of approximately 60 to 76 embrace the top range of performance, from roughly 650 to a perfect 800. For the **Quantitative** section, the equivalent range in performance would have a top of 60 and a bottom of 47. Again, such scoring approximations fail to take into account the adaptive nature of both sections, and indeed the only way to derive true equivalencies is to simulate completely the environment of the CBT. Keep a record of your scores so you can track your progress. Doing so will enable you to gauge your progress and to discover weaknesses in particular sections.

The Analytical Writing section will be scored separately. To estimate how well your essays will score read the annotations and analyses of each sample essay in the practice exams. Remember that this section is designed to test your ability to write and analyze complex arguments. Make sure you understand what graders are looking for so you can evaluate your own practice essays.

SCORING THE GRE CBT

When will I receive my score report and what will it look like?

One of the advantages of computer-based testing is that scores for the Quantitative and Verbal sections should be available immediately. Approximately two weeks after you take the exam, you will receive your official score report in the mail. This report will include your score for the Analytical Writing section. If you have hand-written your essays the report may take up to six weeks to reach you due to possible processing delays. The results are mailed to the address you supply on the test form, and approximate dates for when you should receive your results are given in the information bulletin. Separate scores for each of the three sections will be reported. Score recipients will receive a copy of your essay responses, as well as short score descriptions. In addition, score recipients will be provided with the percentile ranks of all three sections to indicate your score's position in relation to all other students who have taken the test in the prior three-year period. In both the Quantitative and Verbal measure, a maximum score of 800 can be obtained. A minimum of 200 is possible, but at least one question must be answered in order to receive a score of 200. If no questions are answered, then no score can be given. Use our scoring table at the end of this chapter to score your performance on these two sections of our practice tests.

How will my essays be scored?

When you take the GRE CBT, two trained readers will score each essay on a 6-point scale. They will assign scores on the basis of the overall quality of your essays, emphasizing critical thinking and analytical writing rather than grammar and mechanics. The top score for your essays is six, the lowest possible score is zero. If the two assigned scores differ by more than one point, a third GRE reader will be called in to determine the score. The final scores of the two essays are then averaged and rounded up to the nearest half-point. Only one score will be reported in the Analytical Writing section.

The scoring system for both the "Present Your Perspective on an Issue" and the "Analyze an Argument" essays are identical. The 6-point scale looks like this:

6—Outstanding
5—Strong
4—Adequate
3—Limited
2—Seriously Flawed
1—Fundamentally Deficient
0—Illegible, Off-Topic
NR— Blank or Nonverbal

Readers come from a variety of academic disciplines throughout the United States. Every one of them has experience in teaching and grading writing-extensive courses. All of them have undergone extensive training and passed a certification test demonstrating that they can apply the same consistent scoring standards as other readers to every essay question. To become familiar with each essay topic, they review topic notes, read pre-scored sample essays, and practice scoring before reading your actual GRE essays.

STUDYING FOR THE GRE CBT

It is critical that you choose the time and the place for studying that works best for you. Some students may set aside a certain number of hours every morning to study, while others may choose to study at night before going to sleep. Other students may study during the day, while waiting on a line, or even while eating lunch. Only you can determine when and where your study time will be most effective. But be consistent and use your time wisely. Work out a study routine and stick to it.

When you take the written practice tests, try to make your testing conditions as much like the actual test as possible. Turn your television and radio off, and sit down at a quiet table free from distraction. Make sure to time yourself by setting a timer for $3\frac{1}{4}$ hours.

As you complete each practice test, score your test and thoroughly review the explanations to the questions you answered incorrectly; however, do not review too much at once. Concentrate on one problem area at a time by reviewing the question and explanation, and by studying the review until you are confident that you completely understand the material.

You should carefully study the reviews that cover your areas of difficulty, as this will build your skills in those areas.

GRE CBT TEST-TAKING TIPS

Computer-based testing has eliminated many of the traditional test-taking strategies, like answering the easier questions first and returning to the more difficult questions later. The GRE CBT moves inexorably forward; there's no turning back to second-guess yourself. New strategies have evolved, however, that take the place of traditional ones. The most important of these strategies are listed here:

- **Use Your Time Wisely**
  Keep in mind that this is a timed test, and check your progress regularly. As with any standardized test, you should not spend too much time on any one question. If you do not know the answer to a question, try to make an educated guess by eliminating as many of the answer choices as possible, and move on to the next question. You will be given scratch paper at the testing center to be used on the mathematical and analytical sections. Drawing diagrams can be very helpful in working out complex mathematical problems. What seems like an extra step may actually save you precious time.

- **Answer Every Question in Each Section**
  Because the number of questions answered is calculated into your overall score, it is in your best interest to answer every question. If you are running out of time, you will be better served by guessing, even random guessing, than by leaving the last questions unanswered.

- **Pay Particular Attention to the First Questions of Each Section**
  The adaptive testing engine makes major score adjustments based on your answers to the first few questions of each section, and uses subsequent questions to "fine-tune" your score. While you should not spend an undue amount of time on these questions, you should be aware that they are potentially more important than later questions: treat them accordingly.

- **Use the "Answer Confirm" Button with Care**
  It is very easy to get into the habit of choosing an answer and automatically clicking on the "Answer Confirm" button. This is a poten-

tially dangerous tendency. Be absolutely sure that you have clicked on the appropriate answer choice before confirming.

- **Pre-plan Your Essay**
  Before you start writing take some time to outline your essay. This will help you work more efficiently. You can concentrate on the content of your essay instead of thinking about what to write next.

- **Make Effective Use of Break Periods**
  You will generally be given an optional 10-minute break between test sections. Use this time to rest and take a well-deserved break.

HOW TO BEAT THE CLOCK

Here's how to make the clock work *for* you instead of *against* you:

- **Memorize the test directions for each section of the test.** Let's be blunt: Reading directions on the day of the exam is a waste of time. Commit them to memory and get right to answering the questions.

- **Pace yourself.** Work steadily and quickly. Be sensitive to the point of diminishing returns as you address each item: Every question is worth answering, but no question is worth puzzling over as the clock ticks down.

THE DAY OF THE TEST

BEFORE THE TEST

On the day of the test, you should wake up early (after a decent night's rest, it is hoped) and have a good breakfast. Make sure that you dress comfortably, so that you are not distracted by being too hot or too cold while taking the test. Also, plan to arrive at the test center early. This will allow you to collect your thoughts and relax before the test, and will also spare you the stress that comes with running late.

Before you leave for the test center, make sure that you have your authorization voucher or admission ticket, and one form of identification containing a recent photograph and signature. Acceptable forms of ID include passports, driver's licenses, national ID cards, or military ID cards. Expired IDs, Social Security cards, employee IDs, credit cards, and letters prepared by a notary are all unacceptable forms of identification. Without proper identification, you will not be admitted into the test center and you will lose your registration fee. If you do not have a valid ID or if you are taking the GRE outside your country of citizenship, contact ETS.

If you would like, you may wear a watch to the test center; however, watches with alarms, calculator functions, flashing lights, beeping sounds, etc., will not be allowed. You also cannot bring calculators, slide rules, or any written material such as dictionaries, textbooks, or notebooks. In addition, you will not be permitted to have briefcases or packages in your testing room. Drinking, eating, and smoking are prohibited.

DURING THE TEST

When you arrive at the test center, you will be assigned a seat. If you need to use the rest room, you may leave the testing room, but you will not be allowed to make up any lost time. Procedures will be followed to maintain test security.

Once you enter the test center, follow all of the rules and instructions given by the test supervisor. If you do not, you risk being dismissed from the test and having your GRE scores cancelled.

AFTER THE TEST

When you have completed the last section of the GRE, you must wait until the supervisor collects all test-taking materials before you will be permitted to leave. Then, go home and relax!

To Our Readers

This book features the best available paper-and-pencil practice tests for the computer-based GRE General Test, portions of which are adaptive. Because of the printed format, our model tests contain more questions than the actual test in order to provide a score that is roughly comparable to what your score would be on the GRE CBT. It is also important to bear in mind that the GRE CBT moves inexorably forward. Thus, unlike in our printed tests, *there's no turning back once you commit to your response.* Despite format differences, our tests will give you an accurate idea of your strengths and weaknesses, provide guidance for further study, and enable you to master the GRE General. Good luck!

SCALED SCORES AND PERCENTS BELOW*

Raw Score	Verbal Score	% Below	Quantitative Score	% Below
72–76	800	99		
71	790	99		
70	780	99		
69	760	99		
68	750	98		
67	740	98		
66	720	96		
65	710	96		
64	700	95		
63	690	94		
62	680	93		
61	660	91		
60	650	89	800	98
59	640	88	800	98
58	630	86	790	98
57	620	85	780	97
56	610	84	770	95
55	600	82	750	92
54	590	80	740	90
53	580	78	730	89
52	570	75	720	87
51	560	73	700	83
50	550	71	690	81
49	540	68	680	79
48	530	65	670	77
47	520	63	650	72
46	510	60	640	71
45	500	57	630	68
44	490	55	620	65
43	480	52	600	61
42	470	49	590	59
41	460	45	580	56
40	450	43	560	52
39	440	40	550	49
38	430	37	540	46
37	420	34	530	44
36	420	34	510	39
35	410	31	500	37
34	400	28	490	34
33	390	26	480	32
32	380	24	460	27
31	370	22	450	26
30	360	18	440	23
29	360	18	430	21
28	350	17	410	18

(Table continues on next page)

SCALED SCORES AND PERCENTS BELOW*
(Table continues from previous page)

Raw Score	Verbal Score	% Below	Quantitative Score	% Below
27	340	15	400	16
26	330	13	390	14
25	330	13	380	13
24	320	11	360	10
23	310	10	350	9
22	300	8	340	8
21	290	7	330	7
20	280	6	310	5
19	270	4	300	4
18	260	3	290	3
17	250	3	280	3
16	240	2	260	2
15	230	1	250	1
14	220	1	240	1
13	210	1	230	1
12	200	0	210	0
11	200	0	200	0
10	200	0	200	0
9	200	0	200	0
8	200	0	200	0
0-7	200	0	200	0

*Percent of examinees scoring below the scaled score is based on the performance of those who took the test in a recent multi-year period. This table is applicable only to the practice tests in this book. It will give you a rough equivalency that you can use to judge how well you'll score on the GRE CBT.

Score Level Description for the Analytical Writing Assignment

Score Levels 6 and 5.5

The essays are well-focused and well-organized. They develop and support complex ideas with logical and highly persuasive examples. There is a superior understanding of sentence structure, grammar, and vocabulary with few, if any, errors.

Score Levels 5 and 4.5

The essays provide a generally insightful analysis of complex ideas. They support main arguments with sound and well-chosen reasons. They are generally well-focused and display fluent use of language including effective sentence variety, appropriate vocabulary, and grammar.

Score Levels 4 and 3.5

The writer provides a competent analysis of complex ideas with the support of relevant examples. The essays show a sufficient control of language. Sentence structure, grammar, and mechanics are satisfactory but there may be minor errors.

Score Levels 3 and 2.5

The essays display some ability of critical thinking and writing. There is at least one of the following flaws: limited analysis, development, or organization; weak control of language; sentence structure and grammar. At times the essays lack clarity.

Score Levels 2 and 1.5

At this level, the essays display serious deficiencies in analytical writing skills, resulting in incoherence. The content lacks analysis, there is little development, and there are severe errors in language, grammar, and sentence usage.

Score Levels 1 and 0.5

There are fundamental deficiencies in the essays that result in incoherence. The content is confusing and irrelevant, there is little or no development and severe errors make the essays incoherent.

Score Level 0

The essays cannot be evaluated because they are merely attempts to copy the assignments, are in a foreign language, or are no text whatsoever.

SCORING WORKSHEET FOR PRACTICE TESTS

Tests	Verbal Sections		Quantitative Sections	
	Reading Comprehension	Sentence Completion	Data Sufficiency	Problem Solving
Test 1				
Test 2				
Test 3				
Test 4				
Test 5				
Test 6				

Tests	Total Raw Score	Scaled Scores	Percentiles
Test 1			
Test 2			
Test 3			
Test 4			
Test 5			
Test 6			

GRE
Graduate Record Examination

CHAPTER 2:
Quantitative
Review

CHAPTER 2

GRE QUANTITATIVE REVIEW

OVERVIEW OF THE QUANTITATIVE ABILITY SECTIONS

The Quantitative Ability sections are designed to measure basic mathematical skills and evaluate your ability to think quantitatively and apply mathematical concepts. To do well on these sections you must have a working knowledge of arithmetic, algebra, and geometry. You must also be able to read and solve word problems.

There are three basic types of Quantitative Ability questions: quantitative comparison, discrete quantitative, and data interpretation. Each Quantitative Ability section consists of 28 questions in the following format:

14 quantitative comparison

10 discrete quantitative

4 data interpretation

HOW TO PREPARE FOR THE QUANTITATIVE ABILITY TEST

The best way to begin your preparation is to review basic arithmetic, algebra, and geometry. These skills alone, however, will not necessarily win you a good score. This is because GRE questions usually demand more than just working through a formula or calculation. Instead, they require you to look at a problem and determine which math concepts are needed to solve it. The hardest part of a GRE question is usually not the math involved, but figuring out what to do.

TRAINING YOUR THINKING

GRE questions tend to follow predictable patterns. By studying the types or questions that appear often on the GRE, you can gain insight into the way the test is constructed. You can learn to recognize certain types of problems and the kinds of solutions they require. You can become familiar with the ways that certain skills and concepts are most likely to be applied. You can learn to spot shortcuts. Soon you will discover that many questions that look complicated are really quite simple. With the proper perspective, you can learn to work rapidly and efficiently and use your math skills to their fullest advantage.

USING THIS REVIEW

This Review is designed to give you the skills and strategies that you need in order to do well on the Quantitative Ability test. The first part of the Review consists of Refresher courses in arithmetic, algebra, and geometry. Each Refresher provides a review of basic concepts plus strategy tips on how to use these concepts.

As you work through the Refresher sections, you will notice boxes labeled TEST BREAKER. TEST BREAKERS show you how the concept you are reviewing may be applied on the actual test. TEST BREAKERS are strategy tips that will help you save time, avoid traps, and zero in on what the test makers are looking for. When you come to a TEST BREAKER, you will probably find it helpful to mark it with a highlighter pen. This way, you can review these strategies frequently so they become a part of your thought patterns.

Once you have worked through the Refresher sections, you are ready to master the basic problem types. The next three sections of this Review show you how to approach quantitative comparison questions, discrete quantitative questions, and data interpretation questions. You will learn specific strategies for dealing with each type of question, along with practice questions called EXAMPLES. You will also see how the arithmetic, algebra, and geometry concepts—as well as TEST BREAKERS—are used in these questions.

The final section of this Review should be used after you have taken a practice test. This section will show you how to evaluate your answers and use your insights to coach yourself.

A WORD OF ENCOURAGEMENT

If you have been away from math for several years, you may feel overwhelmed by the amount of material that you need to know. Keep in mind, however, that all of the basic skills are things that you once learned. You would not have even made it into college if you had not passed arithmetic, algebra, and geometry! As you work through the Refresher sections, you should find your "missing math skills" coming back into memory. Spend extra time on those concepts that you seem to have trouble with. If you still need additional help, find a textbook or review book that specifically addresses the content area you are weak in.

Always keep in mind that *you can improve your GRE Quantitative Score*. People have been known to increase their scores by 50, 100, or even *200* points with the help of good coaching. By carefully following the methods outlined in this Review, you can gain the skills, insight, and confidence you need to see this test not as an obstacle, but as an opportunity to shine. Good luck!

ARITHMETIC REFRESHER

This section is one of the most important for you to study. Arithmetic skills are required to solve just about every type of GRE math problem, and many of the strategies needed to solve difficult problems are based on arithmetic concepts. Also, remember that you won't be able to use a calculator when you take this test—so if your basic arithmetic is rusty or slow, practice!

In addition to the basic operations (adding, subtracting, multiplying, and dividing), the arithmetic topics that you will need to know include these: properties of numbers, fractions, decimals, percents, averages, ratios, proportions, powers, and roots. You will not need to know conversions of measurements from one unit to another or from one system to a another. You also will not need to know negative exponents or imaginary numbers.

COMMON SYMBOLS

Some standard symbols that appear on the GRE are listed here. You will find some additional symbols listed in the Geometry Refresher.

SYMBOL	DEFINITION
$=$	is equal to
$\neq$	is not equal to
$<$	is less than
$>$	is greater than
$\leq$	is less than or equal to
$\geq$	is greater than or equal to

PROPERTIES OF NUMBERS

An **integer** is any of the whole numbers {1, 2, 3,...} or their opposites {–1, –2, –3,...} or 0. Integers can be represented on a number line:

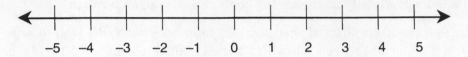

Numbers to the right of 0 on the number line are **positive numbers** and numbers to the left of 0 are **negative numbers**. (The number 0 is neither positive nor negative.) Numbers commonly referred to as fractions or decimals fall between the integers on the number line. For example, ½ would fall between 0 and +1; –6.37 would fall between –6 and –7. Numbers on the number line increase in value from left to right.

TEST BREAKER

Always remember that negative numbers get *smaller* in value as they move away from 0. This means that –9 is smaller than –8, and –10 is smaller than –1.

Operations with Positive and Negative Numbers

To add numbers with the same sign, add the numbers and keep the same sign in the answer.

Examples:

$$7 + 8 = 15; \qquad -2 + (-3) = -5$$

To add numbers with unlike signs, subtract the number with the smaller absolute value from the number with the larger absolute value. Then take the sign of the larger number.

Examples:

$$-8 + 9 = +1; \qquad 7 + (-10) = -3; \qquad -4 + 2 = -2$$

To subtract positive and negative numbers, remember that the subtraction sign changes the sign of the number being subtracted. Once you change the sign, just add the numbers according to the above rules.

Examples:

$$-6 - (+7) = -6 + (-7) = -13; -9 - (-2) = -9 + 2 = -7$$

To multiply and divide positive and negative numbers, multiply or divide as usual, then sign the answer according to these rules:

Product or quotient of two positive numbers is positive.

Product or quotient of two negative numbers is positive.

Product or quotient of a positive number and a negative number is negative.

Examples:

$$6 \times (-7) = -42; \qquad -5 \times (-4) = +20; \qquad -4 \div 2 = -2$$

Absolute Value

The absolute value of a number is its distance from 0 on the number line. The symbol for absolute value is | |. So the absolute value of −5, which is written |−5|, is 5, because −5 is five units away from 0 on the number line. The absolute value of +5, written |+5|, is also 5.

This leads to an important rule about absolute value: The absolute value of a number is always positive. You may find it helpful to think of absolute value as the numerical value of a number, regardless of whether the number is positive or negative.

Odds and Evens

Determination of evenness or oddness flows from simple definitions: Numbers that can be divided evenly by 2 are even; numbers that cannot be divided evenly by 2 are odd. Zero is considered an even number.

TEST BREAKER

You should know the rules for adding and multiplying even and odd numbers. If you forget a rule, just think of an example; what works for one pair of numbers will be true for the rest. The important thing is that you *think* about these rules and learn how to apply them, because they often show up in the more difficult GRE questions.

ADDITION	MULTIPLICATION
even + even = even	even × even = even
odd + odd = even	even × odd = even
even + odd = odd	odd × odd = odd

Prime Numbers

Whole numbers that can be divided evenly by only themselves and 1 are called **prime numbers**. An exception is 1, which is *not* a prime number. (Also remember that 0 is not a prime number.) The number 2 is the smallest prime number and the only even prime. The next eight prime numbers are 3, 5, 7, 11, 13, 17, 19, 23.

Divisibility, Factors, and Multiples

If a number can be divided evenly by another number, the first number is said to be divisible by the second number.

Examples:

$24 \div 4 = 6$;   24 is divisible by 4

$75 \div 3 = 25$;   75 is divisible by 3

Any number that can divide another number evenly with no remainder is said to be a factor of that number. The factors of a number are all those numbers that can divide it evenly.

Example:

The factors of 75 are 1, 3, 5, 15, 25, and 75.

The prime factors of a number are all those factors that are prime numbers. In the above example, the prime factors of 75 are 3 and 5. A whole number can always be written as a product of its prime factors:

$75 = 3 \times 5 \times 5$

A multiple of a number is that number multiplied by any non-zero number. For example, some multiples of 4 are 4, 8, 16, 72, 244, 400.

TEST BREAKER

Properties of numbers come up *a lot* on the GRE. These questions usually involve little or no math—you just have to know the definitions.

PRACTICE DRILL 1

1. List all the positive integers between –2.5 and +7.9.

   No Zero! 1 2 3 4 5 6 7

2. List all the odd multiples of 5 that are less than 40.

   5 15 25 35

3. Perform the indicated operations:

   (A) $-9 + (+7) =$ –2   (B) $5 + (-5) =$ 0

   (C) $2 \times (-8) =$ –16   (D) $-6 \times (-3) =$ 18

   (E) $-77 \div 11 =$ –7   (F) $35 \div 5 =$ 7

   (G) $|-6| + |-4| + |2| =$ 12   (H) $|3 - 1| + |4 - 8| =$ ✗ 6

   2 –4

4. List all of the prime numbers that are greater that 5 but smaller than 48.   7 11 13 17 19 23 29 31 37 41 43 47

5. Write 98 as a product of its prime factors.

   2 3 5 7 11 13 17 14 2 × 49

FRACTIONS

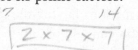

2 × 7 × 7

For any $^x/_y$, x is defined as the numerator and y is defined as the denominator. The fraction bar indicates division. Thus, in the fraction $^2/_5$, the numerator is 2 and the denominator is 5. The meaning of the fraction is "2 divided by 5."

Equivalent fractions are fractions that have the same value.

Examples:

$$\frac{2}{3} = \frac{4}{6}; \qquad \frac{20}{28} = \frac{5}{7}; \qquad \frac{50}{20} = \frac{5}{2}$$

Adding and Subtracting Fractions

You can add or subtract fractions with the same denominators by adding or subtracting the numerators.

Examples:

$$\frac{1}{7} + \frac{3}{7} = \frac{1+3}{7} = \frac{4}{7}$$

To add or subtract fractions with different denominators, you must first find the lowest common denominator (LCD) of the different denominators. To find the lowest common denominator, write the prime factors of the denominators.

Example:

$$\frac{1}{6}+\frac{3}{10}$$

$$6 = 2\times 3$$

$$10 = 2\times 5$$

Cross out any prime factor in the second denominator that already appears in the first denominator. Then multiply the remaining factors.

$$6 = 2\times 3$$

$$10 = 2\times 5$$

$$LCD = 2\times 3\times 5 = 30$$

Once you have found the lowest common denominator, convert the fractions into equivalent fractions having the lowest common denominator as a denominator. Then you can add or subtract the fractions by adding or subtracting the numerators.

$$\frac{5}{30}+\frac{9}{30}=\frac{14}{30}=\frac{7}{15}$$

Multiplying Fractions

To multiply fractions, multiply the numerators and then multiply the denominators.

Example:

$$\frac{2}{5}\times\frac{3}{7}=\frac{2\times3}{5\times7}=\frac{6}{35}$$

Dividing Fractions

To divide fractions, invert the numerator and denominator of the divisor (fraction after the division sign) and then multiply.

Example:

$$\frac{2}{5}\div\frac{3}{4}=\frac{2}{5}\times\frac{4}{3}=\frac{2\times4}{5\times3}=\frac{8}{15}$$

Mixed Numbers

A **mixed number** consists of an integer and a fraction. For example, $2\frac{1}{2}$. To change a mixed number to a fraction, express the integer as a fraction with the same denominator as the fractional part. Then add the fractions.

Example:

$$2\frac{1}{2} = \frac{4}{2} + \frac{1}{2} = \frac{5}{2}$$

Once you have changed a mixed number to a fraction, you can then add, subtract, multiply, or divide as with any other fraction.

$$4\frac{1}{3} + \frac{2}{5} = \frac{13}{3} + \frac{2}{5} = \frac{71}{15}$$

TEST BREAKER

As the denominator of a fraction gets larger, the value of the fraction gets smaller, providing that the numerator stays the same.

Examples:

$$\frac{1}{3} > \frac{1}{4}; \qquad \frac{3}{7} > \frac{3}{11}; \qquad \frac{10}{19} > \frac{10}{30}$$

DECIMALS

Every number is actually a decimal, because our number system is based on place value relative to a decimal point. According to common usage, however, the word "decimal" has come to mean a number that has a written decimal point: 0.2, 1.89, 0.003, 3.8, 131.07. Numbers such as 19, 105, and 12,998 can become "decimals" simply by writing them 19.0, 105.0, and 12,998.0.

Adding and Subtracting Decimals

To add or subtract decimals, write the numbers in a vertical column and line up the decimal points. Write in zeros if necessary. Add or subtract the numbers as usual, then place the decimal point of the answer in line with the decimal points in the numbers being added or subtracted.

Examples:

$$89.7 + 8.32 = \quad \begin{array}{r} 89.70 \\ + \ 8.32 \\ \hline 98.02 \end{array} \qquad 75.6 - 0.03 = \quad \begin{array}{r} 75.60 \\ - \ 0.03 \\ \hline 75.57 \end{array}$$

Multiplying Decimals

To multiply decimals, multiply the numbers as usual. Then place the decimal point in the answer according to the *total* number of decimal places in the numbers being multiplied.

Example:

$$45.1 \times 0.3 = \quad \begin{array}{r} 45.10 \\ \times \ 0.30 \\ \hline 13.53 \end{array}$$

Dividing Decimals

Set up the division problem as usual. Move the decimal point in the divisor (outside number) to the right until the divisor shows no decimal part. Move the decimal point in the other number (dividend) the same number of decimal places, adding zeros if necessary. Divide the numbers, then place the decimal point in the answer above the decimal point in the dividend.

Example:

$$6.25 \div 2.5 =$$

$$2.5\overline{)6.25} \rightarrow 25\overline{)62.5}^{\ 2.5}$$

Fractions and Decimals

To convert a fraction into a decimal, divide the denominator into the numerator.

Example:

$$\frac{4}{5} = 4 \div 5 = 0.8$$

You will notice that some fractions, such as $\frac{1}{3}$, never divide evenly, but continue to repeat the same digit in the quotient over and over again:

$$\frac{1}{3} = 0.333333333\ldots$$

Such a quotient is called a repeating decimal. The bar over the 3 indicates that this digit repeats: $^1/_3 = 0.\overline{3}$

To convert a decimal into a fraction, first determine the denominator by counting the number of decimal places to the right of the decimal point. If there is only one decimal place, the denominator will be tenths, because the first place after the decimal point is the tenths place; if there are two decimal places, the denominator will be hundredths, because the second decimal place is the hundredths place; if there are three decimal places, the denominator will be thousandths, because the third place is the thousandths place, and so on. The digits to the right of the decimal point make up the numerator.

Examples:

$$0.4 = \frac{4}{10}; \qquad 0.17 = \frac{17}{100}; \qquad 0.621 = \frac{621}{1000}$$

PERCENTAGES

Percent means "part of 100." So 5% means 5 parts of 100; 25% means 25 parts of 100, and so on.

To change a percent to a fraction, remove the percent sign and write the number over 100.

Example:

$$65\% = \frac{65}{100}$$

To change a fraction to a percent, write the fraction as an equivalent fraction with the denominator 100. Then take the numerator as the percent.

Example:

$$\frac{3}{4} = \frac{75}{100} = 75\%$$

To change a percent to a decimal, simply remove the percent sign and move the decimal point two places to the left.

Examples:

$65\% = 0.65;\ 4\% = 0.04$

To change a decimal to a percent, move the decimal point two places to the right and add a percent sign.

Examples:

$0.78 = 78\%;\ 0.02 = 2\%$

Word problems involving percent will be covered in the Mastering Discrete Quantitatives section.

PRACTICE DRILL 2

1. Add.

   (A) $\dfrac{1}{3} + \dfrac{1}{8} =$ $\dfrac{\overset{3}{11}}{24}$

   (B) $\dfrac{2}{5} + \dfrac{1}{7} =$ $\dfrac{\overset{5}{19}}{35}$

   (C) $\dfrac{1}{5} + \dfrac{2}{5} =$ $\dfrac{3}{5}$

2. Multiply or divide.

   (A) $\dfrac{5}{6} \div \dfrac{1}{9} =$ $\dfrac{5}{\underset{2}{6}} \cdot \dfrac{\overset{3}{9}}{1} = \dfrac{15}{2} = 7\dfrac{1}{2}$

   (B) $\dfrac{7}{8} \times \dfrac{4}{7} =$ $\dfrac{\overset{2}{28}}{56} = \dfrac{2}{4} = \left(\dfrac{1}{2}\right)$

   (C) $\dfrac{1}{4} \times \dfrac{2}{3} =$ $\dfrac{2}{12} = \dfrac{1}{6}$

   (D) $\dfrac{99}{121} \div \dfrac{33}{11} =$ $\dfrac{3}{11}$

3. Express as a fraction.

   (A) $6\dfrac{1}{4}$ $\dfrac{25}{4}$

   (B) $4\dfrac{2}{3}$ $\dfrac{14}{3}$

   (C) $1\dfrac{3}{5}$ $\dfrac{8}{5}$

4. Perform the indicated operation.

   (A) $2\dfrac{1}{5} + 1\dfrac{1}{5}$ $2\dfrac{2}{5}$

   (B) $\dfrac{3}{8} \times 1\dfrac{4}{7}$ $\dfrac{11}{7}$ $\dfrac{33}{56}$

   (C) $\dfrac{5}{4} \div \dfrac{3}{13}$ $\dfrac{13}{3}$ $\dfrac{65}{12} = 5\dfrac{5}{12}$

0.006
7.3
18
420
.0.438

5. Express each percent first as a fraction or mixed number and then as a decimal.

(A) 76% $\frac{76}{100} = \frac{38}{50} = \frac{19}{25}$ .76   (B) 20% $0,2$ $\frac{1}{5}$ $\frac{20}{100}$

(C) 150% $1\frac{50}{100} = 1.50$ (D) 3% $\frac{3}{100}$ $0,03$

6. Add or subtract.

(A) 7.88 − 0.7 2.18 (B) 55.09 + 839.8 894.89

(C) 0.7 + 0.62 1.32 (D) 101.17 − 0.114 101.056
114

7. Multiply. 7.33

(A) 0.006 × 7.3 0.438 (B) 17.5 × 1.1 19.25
1.1
75
1750
19.25

(C) 0.8 × 0.152 0.1216
.8

8. Divide.

5⟌230   (A) 23 ÷ 0.5 46 (B) 8.4 ÷ 0.02 $4,200$
4⟌21.6   (C) 2.16 ÷ 0.4 5.4 420.0. 2⟌840.0

9. Express each decimal as a fraction.

(A) 0.07 $\frac{7}{100}$ (B) 0.12 $\frac{12}{100}$

(C) 0.8 $\frac{8}{10}$ (D) 0.331 $\frac{331}{1000}$

10. For each pair, indicate which fraction is larger.

(A) $\frac{1}{19}, \frac{1}{12}$ (B) $\frac{7}{19}, \frac{14}{34}$

(C) $\frac{99}{100}, \frac{99}{1000}$

11. Compute.

200   (A) 90% of 400. 360 (B) 180% of 400. $400 + 320 = 720$
160
(C) 50% of 500. 250 (D) 200% of 4. 8

12. Express

(A) 1.65 as a percentage. 165% (B) 0.7 as a fraction. $\frac{7}{10}$

(C) $-\frac{10}{20}$ as a decimal. -0.5 (D) $\frac{4}{2}$ as an integer. 2

AVERAGES, RATIOS, AND PROPORTIONS

Averages

The average of a set of numbers is the sum of all the numbers in the set divided by the number of elements in the set.

Example:

Find the average of {3, 6, 7, 9, 10}

$$\frac{3+6+7+9+10}{5} = \frac{35}{5} = 7$$

Another name for average is mean or arithmetic mean. Two other terms that are related to average sometimes appear in GRE problems, and it is important that you know what they are:

Median is the middle value in a set containing an odd number of data items; in a set containing an even number of items, median is the average of the two middle values.

Mode is the value that appears most often in a data set.

Example:

For the set {2, 3, 3, 4, 5, 6, 6, 6, 8},

5 is the median and 6 is the mode.

TEST BREAKER

Some GRE questions simply ask you to compute an average, but more difficult questions require you to apply the concept of average. For example, if you are told that the average of 10 numbers is 61, you should know that the sum of the numbers must be 610.

Ratios and Proportions

A ratio compares two numbers. A ratio can be written as a fraction or as two numbers separated by a colon:

Example:

The ratio of 2 to 3 is $\frac{2}{3}$ or 2:3.

A proportion describes two ratios that are equal.

Example:

5 is to 6 as 10 is to 12

$$\frac{5}{6} = \frac{10}{12}$$

PRACTICE DRILL 3

1. Find the mean, median, and mode of the following set:

   {4, 4, 6, 6, 6, 7, 9, 15, 15, 16}

2. What is the sum of five numbers if the average of the numbers is 51?

3. Write each ratio as a fraction.

   (A) 5:9

   (B) 7 is to 8

   (C) 10 is to 100

   (D) 1:2

4. Determine the missing term in each proportion.

   (A) $\dfrac{3}{8} = \dfrac{x}{16}$

   (B) $\dfrac{15}{x} = \dfrac{1}{3}$

5. Find the mean salary for four company employees who make

   (A) $\dfrac{\$5}{hr}$.

   (B) $\dfrac{\$8}{hr}$.

   (C) $\dfrac{\$12}{hr}$.

   (D) $\dfrac{\$15}{hr}$.

6. Find the mean length of four fish with lengths of

   (A) 7.5 in.

   (B) 7.75 in.

   (C) 8.5 in.

   (D) 8.25 in.

7. For this series of observations find the mean, median, and mode.

   500, 600, 800, 800, 900, 900, 900, 900, 900, 1000, 1100

POWERS AND ROOTS

An exponent is a number that raises another number to a power. For any positive integer exponent n, raising a number to the nth power means multiplying the number by itself n times.

Examples:

$$5^4 = 5 \times 5 \times 5 \times 5; \qquad a^3 = a \times a \times a$$

To "square" a number means to raise it to the second power. To "cube" a number means to raise it to the third power

It is important to remember that any number raised to the zero power equals 1.

Examples:

$$2^0 = 1; \qquad x^0 = 1; \qquad 10^0 = 1$$

It is also important to remember that raising a negative number to an even-numbered power will produce a positive number, while raising a negative number to an odd-numbered power will produce a negative number.

Examples:

$$(-2)^2 = 4; \qquad (-2)^3 = -8; \qquad (-2)^4 = 16; \qquad (-2)^5 = -32$$

TEST BREAKER

You probably know common squares from the multiplication tables. However, there are some not-so-common squares and higher powers that you should memorize, because knowing them will save you valuable time on the test.

$2^3 = 8$	$3^3 = 27$	$11^2 = 121$	$15^2 = 225$
$2^4 = 16$	$3^4 = 81$	$12^2 = 144$	$16^2 = 256$
$2^5 = 32$	$4^3 = 64$	$13^2 = 169$	$20^2 = 400$
$2^6 = 64$	$5^3 = 125$	$14^2 = 196$	$25^2 = 625$

TEST BREAKER

When a decimal or fraction of value less than 1 is raised to a power, the result is always a number *smaller* than the original number—and the larger the power, the smaller the result.

Examples:

$$\left(\frac{1}{16}\right)^2 = \frac{1}{256} \qquad (0.5)^3 = 0.125$$

Roots

The symbol $\sqrt{\ }$, which is known as a radical sign, means "positive square root of." A radical sign with a positive integer n written in the upper-left corner means "nth root of." For example $\sqrt[3]{\ }$ means "cube root of." The root of a perfect square, cube, or higher power is always a rational number; the root of a non-perfect square, cube, or higher power is irrational. Remember that the nth root of 1 always equals 1.

TEST BREAKER

Certain irrational square roots are used so often on the GRE that you should memorize their approximate value.

$$\sqrt{2} = 1.4$$
$$\sqrt{3} = 1.7$$
$$\sqrt{5} = 2.2$$

Rules for Powers and Roots

1. $a^n \times a^m = a^{n+m}$ Example: $x^2 \times x^3 = x^5$

2. $\dfrac{a^n}{a^m} = a^{n-m}$ Example: $\dfrac{a^3}{a^2} = a^{3-2} = a^1$

3. $(a^n)^m = a^{nm}$ Example: $(3^2)^3 = 3^6$

4. $\left(\dfrac{a}{b}\right)^n = \dfrac{a^n}{b^n}$ Example: $\left(\dfrac{2}{3}\right)^2 = \dfrac{4}{9}$

5. $(ax)^n = a^n x^n$ Example: $(5x)^2 = 25x^2$

6. $\sqrt{\dfrac{a}{b}} = \dfrac{\sqrt[n]{a}}{\sqrt{b}}$ Example: $\sqrt{\dfrac{49}{81}} = \dfrac{7}{9}$

7. $\sqrt{ab} = \sqrt{a} \times \sqrt{b}$ Example: $\sqrt{16y^2} = 4y$

PRACTICE DRILL 4

1. Without performing calculations, write each value.

   (A) 3^3 27

   (B) 25^2 625

   (C) 2^6 64

   (D) 13^2 169

   (E) 15^2 225

   (F) 4^3 64

2. Which is larger?

   (A) $\left(\dfrac{1}{4}\right)^2$ or $\sqrt{4}$?

3. Perform the indicated operation.

   (A) $x^6 \times x^2 =$ x^8

   (B) $\left(\dfrac{4}{7}\right)^2 =$ $\dfrac{16}{49}$

   (C) $\sqrt{\dfrac{1}{64}} =$ $\dfrac{1\cdot1}{8\cdot8} = \dfrac{1}{8}$

   (D) $(y^3)^4 =$ y^{12}

4. Which is larger?

   (A) $\sqrt{5}$ or $\dfrac{5}{2}$

5. Simplify the following expressions.

   (A) -3^{-2} -9

   (B) $(-3)^{-2}$

   (C) $\dfrac{-3}{4^{-1}}$ -4

ALGEBRA REFRESHER

The algebra required for the GRE is basic. About the hardest thing you will have to do is solve a quadratic equation—and you won't have to do that very often. However, you will have to be good at applying the basics, because some algebra is required to solve all but the most straight-forward arithmetic and geometry problems. In addition, you can find many shortcuts by quickly recognizing algebraic patterns.

The algebra skills that you will need to know include: understanding absolute value; evaluating algebraic expressions; solving first-degree (linear) equations; solving second-degree (quadratic) equations; and solving simultaneous equations. You should bear in mind that a number of GRE questions ask you to do nothing more than evaluate an algebraic expression or solve an equation. By learning and applying the rules presented in this section, you are almost certain to get these questions right.

ALGEBRAIC EXPRESSIONS

There are three basic things that you can do to transform an algebraic expression. You can: rearrange it; factor it; or multiply it out. In order to do these things quickly, you should memorize the following properties and formulas.

Associative Property

$$(a + b) + c = a + (b + c)$$

$$(ab)c = a(bc)$$

The associative property enables you to group numbers any way you like as you add or multiply them. This property is useful when you want to rearrange an algebraic expression.

Distributive Property

$$ab + ac = a (b + c)$$

$$ab - ac = a (b - c)$$

This property is essential when you want to find a common factor in an expression. By reversing the above process, you can multiply out an expression.

Difference of Squares

$$a^2 - b^2 = (a + b) (a - b)$$

TEST BREAKER

Difference of squares appears so often in the GRE that you should learn to recognize it in every possible form. Usually a difference of squares involves variables, but it may consist of only numbers.

Examples:

$$x^2 - y^2 = (x + y) (x - y)$$

$$x^2 - 4 = (x + 2) (x - 2)$$

$$9 - y^2 = (3 + y) (3 - y)$$

Binomial Squares

$$(a + b)^2 = a^2 + 2ab + b^2$$
$$(a - b)^2 = a^2 - 2ab + b^2$$

Binomial squares is the most common pattern that you are likely to find on the GRE. Like difference of squares, binomial squares can involve variables, numbers, or a combination of numbers and variables.

Examples:

$$(x - 2)^2 = x^2 - 4x + 4$$
$$(3 + a)^2 = 9 + 6a + a^2$$

Multiplying Binomials:

$$(a + b)(c + d) = ac + ad + bc + bd$$

Example:

$$(x + 5)(x - 1) = x^2 - x + 5x - 5 = x^2 + 4x - 5$$

If you forget the formula for multiplying binomials, just remember to multiply each term in the second binomial by each term in the first.

Factoring Trinomial Expressions

If a trinomial is a perfect square, you can use the formula shown above for binomial squares. If a trinomial is not a perfect square, you must find factors that will multiply to produce the trinomial. This process requires a bit of trial and error, but with practice you can learn to spot likely factors quickly.

Examples:

$$a^2 - 5a + 4 = (a - 4)(a - 1)$$
$$x^2 + x - 6 = (x + 3)(x - 2)$$
$$n^2 + 8n + 15 = (n + 5)(n + 3)$$

PRACTICE DRILL 5

Use the associative property to complete each statement.

1. $(x + y) + 7 =$

2. $3(nm) =$

Use the distributive property to complete each statement.

3. $3(a + b) =$ $3a + 3b$

4. $5ax + 10a + 45 =$

Factor each expression.

5. $9x^2 - y^2 =$ $9(x+y)(x-y)$

6. $4x^2 + 4x + 1 =$

7. $a^2 - 3a + 2 =$

Multiply.

8. $(k + 9)(k - 8)$ $k^2 - 72$

9. $(3ab + 2)^2$ $9a^2b^2 + 4$

10. $(6x + 1)(6x - 1)$

EQUATIONS

An equation tells you that two quantities are equal. When an equation contains one or more variables, you are often asked to solve the equation for a particular variable. In order to do this, you must remember the following rules:

1)   You can add or subtract the same number from both sides of an equation.

2)   You can multiply or divide both sides of an equation by the same number.

Linear (First Degree) Equations

A linear equation is one in which the highest power of any variable is one. For example: $x + y = 3$; $3n = -10$; $a + b + c = 15$. You can solve a linear equation for a particular variable by isolating that variable on one side of the equation. You do this by applying the rules stated above.

Example:

Solve for x: $11 + x = 2x$

Subtract x from both sides of the equation:

$11 + x - x = 2x - x$; $11 = x$

Example:

Solve for c in terms of a: $2c - a = 10$

Add a to both sides of the equation:

$2c - a + a = 10 + a$; $2c = 10 + a$

Divide both sides of the equation by 2:

$$c = \frac{10}{2} + \frac{a}{2}; \ c = 5 + \frac{a}{2}$$

Quadratic Equations

A quadratic equation is an equation in which at least one variable is raised to the second power. In order to solve a quadratic equation for a particular variable, you must first set one side of the equation equal to 0.

Example:

$x^2 + 3x = 4$

Subtract 4 from both sides of the equation:

$x^2 + 3x - 4 = 4 - 4$; $x^2 + 3x - 4 = 0$

Next, you must factor the non-zero side of the equation:

$x^2 + 3x - 4 = (x + 4)(x - 1) = 0$

Finally, you must set each factor equal to 0, and solve for the variable.

$(x + 4) = 0$; $x = -4$

$(x - 1) = 0$; $x = 1$

The two solutions are $x = -4$ and $x = 1$.

Simultaneous Equations

Simultaneous equations are two or more equations that contain the same variables. Simultaneous equations on the GRE tend to be simple.

The easiest way to solve them is to first solve one equation for one variable, then substitute that value into the second equation to solve for the second variable. (If you have three equations and three variables, simply repeat the process with the third variable.)

Example:

$$x - y = -1; 3x = 9 + y$$

Solve for x.

$$x = y - 1$$

Substitute.

$$3(y-1) = 9 + y$$
$$3y - 3 = 9 + y$$
$$3y = 12 + y$$
$$2y = 12$$
$$y = 6$$

Plug into x.

$$x = y - 1; x = 6 - 1; x = 5$$

The answers are $x = 5$ and $y = 6$.

PRACTICE DRILL 6

Solve for the variable.

1. $3x + 2 = 15$

2. $4b - 1 = 3b + 2$

3. $m - 3m + 1 = -7$

4. $x^2 - 10x + 25 = 0$

5. $x^2 - 6x - 16 = 0$

6. $y^2 = 9$

Solve for x in terms of r.

7. $5r + 2x = 20$

8. $x = 3x + 2r$

9. Solve for x and y.

   $x^2 - y^2 = 20$

   $x + y = 10$

10. Solve for a, b, and c.

    $a + 1 = 9$

    $a^2 + b = c + 8$

    $c + a = 12$

11. Solve, justifying each step.

    $3x - 8 = 7x + 8$

12. Solve the equation.

    $2(x + 3) = (3x + 5) - (2x - 5)$

13. Solve the following equations by factoring.

    (A) $2x^2 + 3x = 0$ (B) $y^2 - 2y - 3 = y - 3$

    (C) $z^2 - 2z - 3 = 0$ (D) $2m^2 - 11m - 6 = 0$

14. Solve for x and y.

    $x + 2y = 8$

    $3x + 4y = 20$

GEOMETRY REFRESHER

Most geometry problems on the GRE can be solved with basic knowledge of lines, angles, triangles, rectangles, parallelograms, and circles. Some problems will require knowledge of solids and coordinate geometry. You will not have to work with proofs on this test.

While you do not need to know a great deal of geometry, what you need to know is essential. Because the same formulas tend to be used over and over again, failure to memorize a basic principle can cost you not just one question, but several.

COMMON SYMBOLS

SYMBOL	DEFINITION
‖	is parallel to
⊥	is perpendicular to
∠	angle
$\overline{AB}$	line segment AB (any letters can be used)
∟	right angle

LINES AND ANGLES

A line in geometry is defined as a straight line. A line can be named by a single letter or by two points on the line.

Examples:

line *l*; line segment $\overline{MN}$.

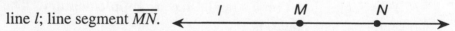

A line segment is all the points on a line between and including two points; for example, $\overline{MN}$.

The bisector of a line segment divides the line segment into two equal parts.

Example:

$\overline{LM}$ bisects $\overline{AB}$; $\overline{AM} = \overline{MB}$

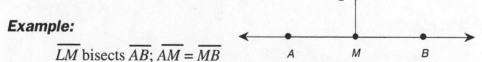

An angle is formed when two straight lines meet at a common point, which is called the vertex of the angle. An angle can be named in three ways:

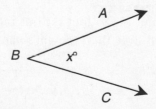

47

1)   by a small letter written inside the angle: $\angle\, x$

2)   by the capital letter at the vertex: $\angle\, B$

3)   by the three letters that form the angle, with the vertex letter in the middle: $\angle\, ABC$.

The bisector of an angle divides the angle into two equal parts. For example: $\angle\, ABC = \angle\, CBD$.

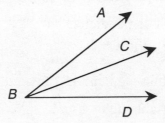

Special Angles

An **acute angle** is greater than 0° but less than 90°. An **obtuse angle** is greater than 90° but less than 180°. A **right angle** is a 90° angle. An angle of 180° is a **straight line**.

Two angles that form a straight line are **supplementary**. The sum of two supplementary angles is 180°.

Two angles that form a right angle are **complementary**. The sum of two complementary angles is 90°.

Vertical angles are formed when two lines intersect. Vertical angles are equal.

Example:

$\angle\, a = \angle\, c; \qquad \angle\, b = \angle\, d$

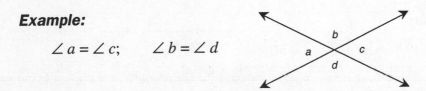

Parallel Lines

Two lines in the same plane that do not intersect are parallel. If two lines are parallel to a third line, then they are parallel to each other.

Example:

Line *l* is parallel to line *m*; line *m* is parallel to line *n*; therefore, line *l* is parallel to line *n*.

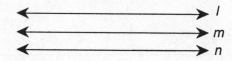

A line that passes through two or more parallel lines is called a transversal. Parallel lines cut by a transversal form equal angles as shown.

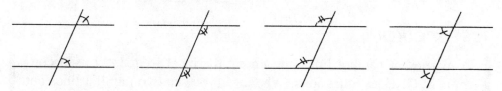

1) Corresponding angles are equal.

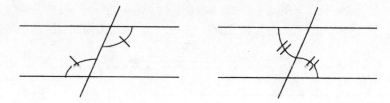

2) Alternate interior angles are equal.

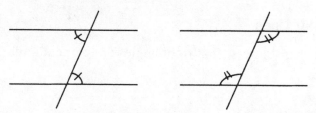

3) Same side interior angles are supplementary.

Parallel lines cut by a transversal form supplementary angles as shown.

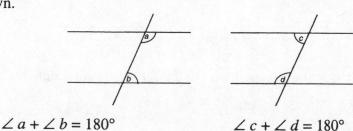

$\angle a + \angle b = 180°$ $\angle c + \angle d = 180°$

4)   Same side exterior angles are supplementary.

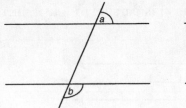 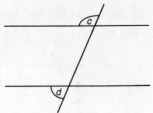

$\angle a + \angle b = 180°$ $\angle c + \angle d = 180°$

5)   Alternate exterior angles are equal.

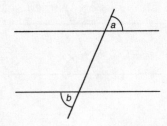 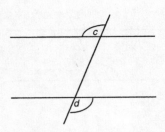

$\angle a = \angle b$ $\angle c = \angle d$

TEST BREAKER

Properties of parallel lines are among the most frequently used concepts in GRE test questions. Whenever you see two parallel lines cut by a transversal, you should immediately look for pairs of angles that are equal or supplementary.

Perpendicular Lines

Two lines that intersect at right angles are perpendicular.

Example:

$AB \perp MN$

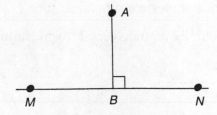

Two lines that are perpendicular to the same line are parallel.

Example:

$m \perp l$ and $n \perp l$; therefore, $m \parallel n$

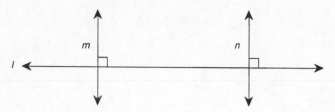

TRIANGLES

A triangle is a three-sided figure. Triangles are named according to their vertices.

Example:

triangle *ABC*

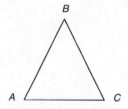

Special Triangles

An **equilateral triangle** has three equal sides and three equal angles.

An **isosceles triangle** has two equal sides. The angles opposite the two equal sides are equal.

A **right triangle** has one right angle. The longest side, which is opposite the right angle, is called the **hypotenuse**. The other two sides are called **legs**.

Formulas:

The sum of the angles of a triangle is 180°.

The sum of the lengths of any two sides must be greater than the length of the third side.

Area: $A = \frac{1}{2}bh;$ where $b = $ base and $h = $ height, drawn perpendicular to the base.

Pythagorean theorem: For a right triangle, the square of the length of the hypotenuse is equal to the sum of the squares of the other two sides.

Example:

$$a^2 + b^2 = c^2$$

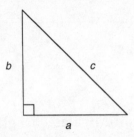

PRACTICE DRILL 7

1. Determine the measures of the missing angles in each figure.

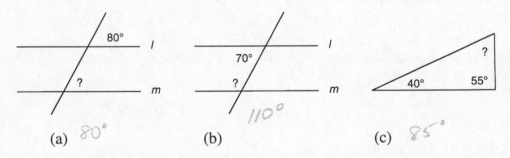

(a) $80°$ (b)   (c) $85°$

2. For each triangle, determine the length of the missing side.

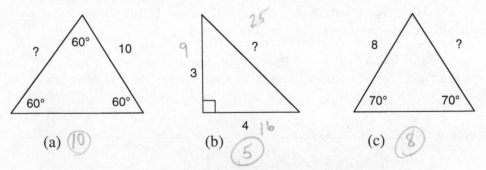

(a) 10 (b) 5 (c) 8

3. Find the area of a triangle with base 12 and height 14.

    $6 \cdot 14 = 84$

4. In the figure, we are given line AB and triangle ABC. The measure of $\angle 1$ is five times the measure of $\angle 2$. Determine the measures of $\angle 1$ and $\angle 2$.

$$7x = \frac{180}{7}$$

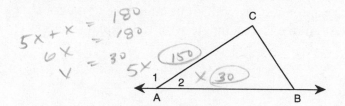

$5x + x = 180$
$6x = 180$
$x = 30$

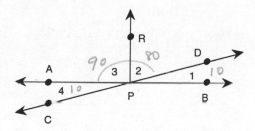

5. We are given straight lines *AB* and *CD* intersecting at point *P*. *PR* $\perp AB$ and the measure of $\angle APD$ is 170°. Find the measures of $\angle 1$, $\angle 2$, $\angle 3$, and $\angle 4$.

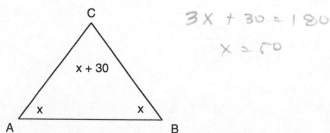

6. The measure of the vertex angle of an isosceles triangle exceeds the measurement of each base angle by 30°. Find the value of each angle of the triangle.

$3x + 30 = 180$
$x = 50$

PARALLELOGRAMS AND RECTANGLES

A **parallelogram** is a four-sided figure in which opposite sides are parallel. In a parallelogram, opposite sides are equal and opposite angles are equal.

Example:

$AB = CD$ and $AC = BD$;

$\angle A = \angle D$ and $\angle B = \angle C$

A **rectangle** is a parallelogram with right angles. The diagonals of a rectangle are equal. (A **square** is a rectangle with four equal sides.)

Example:

$AC = BD$

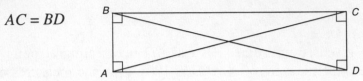

Formulas:

Area: $A = lw$; where l = length and w = width

Perimeter: $P = 2l + 2w$; where l = length and w = width

CIRCLES

A **circle** is a set of points equidistant from one point, called the center. A circle is named by the letter of its center.

Example:

circle O

A line passing through the center of a circle connecting two points on the circle is called a **diameter**.

A line from the center of the circle to any point on the circle is called a **radius**. The radius is $\frac{1}{2}$ the diameter.

A **tangent** is a line that intersects a circle at one point.

The **circumference** is the distance around a circle. An **arc** is a portion of the circumference. An arc is named by its two endpoints. The measure of an arc is the measure of its **central angle** (an angle whose vertex is at the center of the circle). The measure of an arc is measured in degrees. The length of an arc is a portion of the circle's circumference.

Example:

> AB is a diameter; OA and OB are radii; line l is a tangent; MB is an arc; $\angle BOM$ is a central angle.

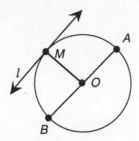

Formulas:

The degree measure of a circle is 360°.

Area: $A = \pi r^2$; where r = radius

Circumference: $C = \pi d$ or $2\pi r$; where d = diameter, r = radius

Length of an Arc: Arc $AB = (x/360) \times 2\pi r$; where x = the measure of arc AB, r = radius

TEST BREAKER

It is essential that you know the approximate value of π, which is 3.14 or $^{22}/_{7}$.

INSCRIBED FIGURES

An angle drawn inside a circle with its vertex lying on the circle is called an **inscribed angle**. The measure of an inscribed angle is half the measure of its intercepted arc.

A figure drawn inside a circle with all of its vertices lying on the circle is inscribed in the circle.

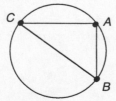

A circle drawn inside a figure with each side of the figure tangent to the circle is inscribed in the figure.

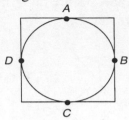

SOLIDS

A **solid** is a three-dimensional figure.

A **rectangular solid** has six faces that are rectangles.

A **cube** is a rectangular solid in which all edges are equal because all faces are squares. The surface area of a cube of edge length a is $S = 6a^2$.

Example:

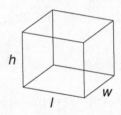

Formulas:

Volume: $V = l \times w \times h$; where l = length, w = width, and h = height.

Surface area: The sum of the areas of all the faces.

COORDINATE GEOMETRY

Coordinate geometry describes points on a graph called a **coordinate plane**. The coordinate plane has a horizontal **x-axis** and a vertical **y-axis**. The point where the two axis intersect is 0. Points are named (x, y) according to an x-coordinate (distance from 0 horizontally) and a y-coordinate (distance from zero vertically). An x-coordinate to the right of 0 is positive and to the left of 0 is negative; a y-coordinate above 0 is positive and below 0 is negative.

Examples:

point $A = (2, -5)$

point $B = (-2, 1)$

Formulas:

Distance: $d = \sqrt{(x_1 - x_2)^2 + (y_1 - y_2)^2}$

Midpoint: $MP = \left(\dfrac{x_1 + x_2}{2}, \dfrac{y_1 + y_2}{2} \right)$

Slope: $\dfrac{y_1 - y_2}{x_1 - x_2} \quad (x_1 \neq x_2)$

PRACTICE DRILL 8

1. Determine the missing angle or length.

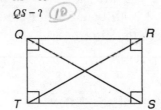

$AB \parallel CD$
$AD \parallel BC$

$RT = 10$
$QS = ?$ (10)

$KL \parallel NM$
$KN \parallel LM$

a.   b.   c.

2. Find the area and circumference of circle O if $AB = 6$. Then determine the length of arc AC.

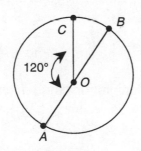

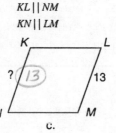

$A = \pi r^2$

$A = \pi \cdot 9$

$A = 3.14 \cdot 9$

$A = 28.26$

$C = d\pi$

$C = 6 \cdot 3.14$

$C = 18.84$

$\dfrac{9.42}{3} \cdot 2$

$3.14 = 6.28$

3. Name the coordinates of each point.

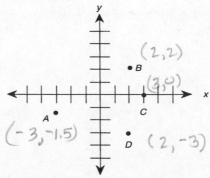

$(2,2)$
$(3,0)$
$(-3,-1.5)$
$(2,-3)$

4. Draw a circle inscribed in an equilateral triangle.

5. Determine the volume and surface area of a cube with an edge of 4 cm.

    $4 \cdot 4 \cdot 4 = 64 (cm^3)$ $16 \cdot 6 = 96 (cm^2)$

6. What are the dimensions of a solid cube whose surface area is numerically equal to its volume?

MASTERING QUANTITATIVE COMPARISONS

Quantitative comparison questions test your ability to determine quickly the relationship between two quantities. By looking at a question for about 30 seconds, you are expected to determine if one quantity is larger than the other; if both quantities are equal; or if you cannot determine a relationship from the information given.

UNDERSTANDING THE DIRECTIONS

The directions that appear at the beginning of each Quantitative Comparison section are printed below. An easy-to-read interpretation of the directions follows. You should learn the directions now, so you won't have to spend time reading them when you take the test.

Numbers: All numbers used are real numbers.

Figures: Position of points, angles, regions, etc. can be assumed to be in the order shown; and angle measures can be assumed to be positive.

Lines shown as straight can be assumed to be straight.

Figures can be assumed to lie in a plane unless otherwise indicated.

Figures that accompany questions are intended to provide information useful in answering the questions. However, unless a note states that a figure is drawn to scale, you should solve these problems NOT by estimating sizes by sight or by measurement, but by using your knowledge of mathematics (see Example 2 on the following page).

Directions: Each of the questions consists of two quantities, one in Column A and one in Column B. You are to compare the two quantities and choose

A   if the quantity in Column A is greater;
B   if the quantity in Column B is greater;
C   if the two quantities are equal;
D   if the relationship cannot be determined from the information given.

Common
Information: In a question, information concerning one or both of the quantities to be compared is centered above the two columns. A symbol that appears in both columns represents the same thing in Column A as it does in Column B.

	Column A	**Column B**	**Sample Answers**
Example 1:	2×6	$2 + 6$	● ⒝ ⒞ ⒟ ⒠

Examples 2–4: refer to $\triangle PQR$.

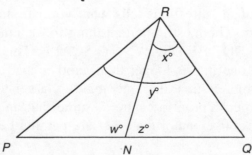

Example 2:   *PN*   *NQ*   Ⓐ Ⓑ Ⓒ ● Ⓔ

(since equal measures cannot be assumed, even though *PN* and *NQ* appear equal)

Example 3:   *x*   *y*   Ⓐ ● Ⓒ Ⓓ Ⓔ

(since *N* is between *P* and *Q*)

Example 4:   *w + z*   180   Ⓐ Ⓑ ● Ⓓ Ⓔ

(since *PQ* is a straight line)

THE ESSENTIALS

The most important directions, which appear last, are:

Compare the quantities in Column A and Column B. Mark choice (A) if the quantity in Column A is greater, choice (B) if the quantity in Column B is greater, choice (C) if the two quantities are equal, and choice (D) if you cannot determine a relationship from the information given.

NEVER MARK (E) BECAUSE THERE ARE ONLY FOUR CHOICES.

Interpreting Diagrams

The first part of the directions tells what you can and cannot determine from a diagram. The most important thing to remember is that GRE DIAGRAMS MAY NOT BE DRAWN TO SCALE. This means that you cannot assume that one line is longer than another just because it looks longer, and you cannot assume that one angle is larger than another just because it looks larger. You also cannot assume that an angle is a right angle because it looks like one or that lines are parallel because they look parallel.

What you can determine from a diagram is that straight lines are straight and closed figures are closed. You can also assume that angles and vertices lie in the order stated—for example, angle *C* will always lie between angles *B* and *D* in figure *ABCD*.

Interpreting Conditions

The last part of the directions tells you that information pertaining to quantities A and/or B will appear centered across the two columns just above the problem number. Very often, this information will be in the form of a condition. Conditions are restrictions placed on the values of variables. Conditions may be very specific, such as $x = 3$, or more general, such as $x > 0$. In some cases, restrictions are specific about what a variable cannot be, but open-ended about what it can be—for example, $n \neq 0$.

While you can't go too far wrong with a specific condition such as $x = 3$, general conditions can be tricky. The most common mistake is to assume that a condition is more restrictive than it actually is. For example, the condition $x > 0$ means that x is positive. The temptation is to assume that x is a positive whole number—when x can just as easily be a fraction, decimal, mixed number, or even a radical.

SKILLS AND STRATEGIES

Avoiding Unnecessary Calculations

You can save a lot of time on quantitative comparison questions by avoiding unnecessary calculations. One way to do this is to keep in mind that you are looking for a relationship between two quantities, not a specific answer. Once you are sure of that relationship, you can stop working the problem—even if there are additional calculations that you could do.

Example:

Column A	Column B
$6 + \sqrt{16}$	$4 + \sqrt{49}$

Solution: Taking the square roots, you get

$$6 + 4 \qquad \text{and} \qquad 4 + 7$$

You don't have to finish the addition to see that the quantity in Column B is greater.

The above example illustrates another strategy for avoiding unnecessary calculations: eliminate any quantity that appears in both columns. You can do this by using addition, subtraction, multiplication, or division.

As in an equation, a quantity that appears on both sides can be eliminated because it affects both sides equally and does not change the relationship.

An important strategy for avoiding unnecessary arithmetic calculations is: look for trends and generalizations. For example, consider this TEST BREAKER from the Arithmetic Refresher: "As the denominator of a fraction gets larger, the value of the fraction gets smaller, providing that the numerator stays the same." Properties of numbers can also provide valuable trends and generalizations.

The following example shows how several of the above strategies can be used to solve a problem.

Example:

Column A	Column B
9	$9 - \dfrac{1}{10} + \dfrac{1}{11} - \dfrac{1}{12} + \dfrac{1}{13}$

Solution: The worst thing you can do (in terms of time) is to add up all the fractions. Instead, begin by subtracting 9 from both columns. This leaves you with 0 in Column A and four fractions in Column B:

$$0 \qquad \underbrace{\underbrace{-\dfrac{1}{10} + \dfrac{1}{11}}_{negative} + \underbrace{-\dfrac{1}{12} + \dfrac{1}{13}}_{negative}}_{negative}$$

Next, look at the first two fractions in B. You know that adding a positive number and a negative number produces a number with the same sign as the number with the larger absolute value. According to the TEST BREAKER above, the absolute value of $-\frac{1}{10}$ is greater than the absolute value of $\frac{1}{11}$—so adding $-\frac{1}{10}$ and $\frac{1}{11}$ will produce a negative number. Now look at the last two fractions. Because the absolute value of $-\frac{1}{12}$ is greater than that of $\frac{1}{13}$, adding these will also produce a negative number. The sum of two negative numbers is always negative, so the sum or all four fractions must be negative. Because 0 is larger than any negative number, the answer is A.

You can often avoid unnecessary algebra calculations by transforming algebraic expressions. In fact, whenever you see an algebraic expression, you should immediately think, "How can this expression be transformed?" You will recall that the three basic ways of transforming an algebraic expression are factoring, rearranging, and multiplying out.

Example:

$$32m = 24n$$

Column A	Column B
$4m$	$3n$

Solution: By factoring $32m = 24n$, you obtain $8(4m) = 8(3n)$.

Since 8 appears on both sides of the equation, you can divide by 8 to eliminate it. The answer is C, because $4m$ and $3n$ are equal.

Example:

Column A	Column B
$(3\sqrt{5}+2)(3\sqrt{5}-2)$	41

Solution: By now you should recognize a familiar algebraic pattern in Column A—only this time, it's all numbers: By difference of squares, $(3\sqrt{5}+2)(3\sqrt{5}-2) = (3\sqrt{5})^2 - 2^2 = 45 - 4 = 41$. Clearly, the answer is C.

Backing Up Your Answers

You can improve your ability to solve quantitative comparison questions by learning to back up your answers. Backing up your answers means justifying your conclusions with specific rules and formulas. This strategy is important, because it prevents you from relying on hunches. While it is true that hunches are sometimes right, hunches on the GRE tend to match attractive wrong answers.

Example:

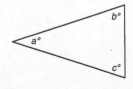

The average of b and c is 80°.

Column A	Column B
a	30°

Solution: Say to yourself, "I know that $(b + c)/2$ by the definition of average. Therefore, $b + c = 160°$. I also know that $a + b + c = 180°$, because that is the sum of the angles of a triangle. If $b + c = 160°$, $a = 20°$. Since 30° is larger than 20°, the answer is *B*."

Using "If...Then" Reasoning

Similar to backing up your answers is using "if...then" reasoning. "If...then" reasoning trains you to think logically in order to reach a conclusion.

Example:

$$\frac{3}{8} < \frac{x}{24}$$

Column A	Column B
x	8

Solution: Say to yourself, "If x were equal to 8, then $x/24$ would equal $8/24$, or $1/3$. Since $1/3$ is smaller than $3/8$, x must be greater than 8." The answer is A.

When the Answer is D

Quantitative comparison questions have D for an answer when the relationship between the two quantities is ambiguous or when the information provided in a problem is insufficient. You can improve your chances of doing well on these questions by learning to recognize problems that usually have D for an answer as well as problems that never do.

When the Answer is Never D

The answer is never D when a problem contains only numbers and no variables, because an exact relationship can always be determined. The answer is also never D when all variables are defined absolutely—for example, $x = 3$.

Always...Or Sometimes?

Before you choose A, B, or C as the answer to a quantitative comparison question, you must ask yourself, "Is this relationship ALWAYS true?" If you spot an exception, or if you realize that the relationship is true in some cases but not in others, you know that the answer is D.

Example:

$$n + m = 5$$

Column A	Column B
m	n

Solution: By trying a few different numbers for m and n, you can see the ambiguity. For example, if $m = 2.5$ and $n = 2.5$, the answer is C, but if $m = 5$ and $n = 0$, the answer is A. Thus, the answer is D.

Apples and Oranges

You have probably heard the expression, "You can't compare apples and oranges." What this means is that you cannot compare dissimilar items, because there is no basis for the comparison. "Apples and oranges" show up on the GRE as problems in which there is not enough information to determine a relationship between the two quantities.

Example:

x cans of Diet Cola cost \$15.00

Column A	Column B
The cost of y cans of Diet Orange	$15\dfrac{y}{x}$

Solution: The formula in Column B is tempting, because it tells the cost of y cans of Diet Cola. However, the quantity in Column A is Diet Orange—which is totally unrelated to Diet Cola. Thus, the answer is D.

The Dead-End Problem

A potential hazard on the GRE is the dead-end problem. A dead-end problem provides you with a lot of information and looks logical—until you get close to a solution. Then you find that a vital piece of information is missing or that you have a set of conclusions that do not relate to each other. The danger is that you will think that you have made a mistake and try to solve the problem again—a waste of valuable time.

Example:

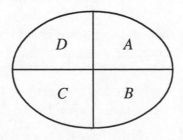

Gardens A and B each contain 50 plants.
The average number of plants in Garden B
and Garden C is 65.

Column A	Column B
The average number of plants in Gardens *C* and *D*	45

Solution: By definition of average, you know that the total number of plants in Gardens *B* and *C* is 130. This means that the number of plants in Garden *C* is 80. However, as you try to compute the average number of plants in Gardens *C* and *D*, you realize that you have no numerical information about Garden *D*. You've reached a dead end—so the answer is D.

MASTERING DISCRETE QUANTITATIVES

Discrete quantitative questions may be straight-forward arithmetic, algebra, or geometry problems, or they may be problems that require a combination of mathematical skills. Discrete quantitatives show a wide range of difficulty.

A simple direction line precedes the questions and pertains to all the remaining questions on the test. The directions state that you are to choose the best of five answer choices, which are labeled A through E.

SKILLS AND STRATEGIES

When to Calculate? When to Estimate?

Unlike quantitative comparison questions, which ask you to determine a relationship, discrete quantitative questions require a specific answer. This means that you will use estimation less frequently. However, there are times when estimation can be used effectively. These guidelines will help you know when to consider using estimation:

1) Estimate when the answer choices show a wide enough range that the correct answer is likely to be obvious.

2) Estimate when the math needed to calculate the answer is extensive enough that you would have to spend a lot of time on the problem without estimation.

3) Estimate when you have worked through part of the problem and have some idea of what the answer might be.

4) Estimate when you are running out of time, and you feel that an intelligent guess is your best bet.

Example:

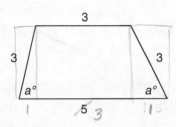

$1 + x^2 = 9$

$x^2 = 8$

What is the area of the figure shown above?

(A) $4\sqrt{2}$ (B) $8\sqrt{2}$

(C) $12\sqrt{2}$ (D) 12

(E) 16

Solution: Start out by dividing the figure into smaller, more familiar figures. The figure divides easily into a rectangle and two identical right triangles. You know that the bottom leg of each right triangle must be 1, because the base of the rectangle is 3 and the total base of the figure is 5.

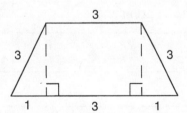

Now is the time to use estimation. You know that the vertical leg of each right triangle must be smaller than 3, because the hypotenuse is the longest side of a right triangle. However, this leg must also be greater than 2, because the sum of two sides of any triangle must be longer than the third side. So the length of the leg is some number between 2 and 3. This means that the area of the rectangle is between 6 and 9, and the area of each right triangle is between 1 and 1.5. Thus, the total area of the figure is between 8 and 12. Now look at the answer choices. Answer (A) is less than 8; answers (C), (D), and (E) are greater than or equal to 12. The correct answer is (B).

WORD PROBLEMS

You probably remember word problems from junior high school math classes. Word problems describe a situation and then ask you to apply mathematical principles in order to solve a problem.

Recognizing Keywords: Translating Sentences Into Equations

The most difficult part of solving a word problem can be knowing how to set up the necessary equations. You can do this more easily if you learn to recognize keywords. Keywords are words or phrases that tell how quantities in a problem are related. They provide clues that help you translate sentences into questions. Listed below are some common keywords and the type of mathematical action they indicate.

Keyword	Action
sum; more than; greater than	add
difference; less than; smaller than	subtract
of	multiply
half of	divide by 2
twice as much; twice as great	multiply by 2
half of	divide by 2
is; was; will be; total	equals

Example:

The difference between two positive integers is 15. The smaller number is $\frac{1}{6}$ of the larger number. What is the value of the smaller number?

(A) 1

(B) 3

(C) 9

(D) 12

(E) 18

Solution: The first sentence contains keywords *difference* and *is*. Assigning the variables x and y to the unknown numbers, you can write: $x - y = 15$.

The second sentence contains keywords *is* and *of*. This sentence becomes $y = (\frac{1}{6})x$

Solving the two equations by substitution, you obtain: $x = 18$ and $y = 3$. The correct answer is (B). Notice that the value for x appears as choice (E)—a potential trap for anyone who reads the problem carelessly.

Example:

An instant lottery awarded $500,000 worth of prizes to tickets bearing the letters J, K, and X. Each ticket marked J was worth twice as much as each ticket marked X, and each ticket marked K was worth $1\frac{1}{2}$ times as much as each ticket marked X. The number of people claiming prizes were as follows:

TICKET	NUMBER OF CLAIMS	
Letter J	50	$J = 2x = 1.5k$
Letter K	100	$a + 2a + 1.5a = 500,000$
Letter X	150	$4.5a = 500,000$

How much money did each person with a ticket marked X receive?

(A) $2,300   (B) $2,000 $50a + 300a + 150a$

(C) $1,740   (D) $1,250 $5\cancel{)}9)\overline{500\,044}$

(E) $670

Solution: This problem requires you to set up several equations, then solve them simultaneously. The first keyword is *was* followed by the phrase *twice as much*. These keywords relate the value of ticket J to that of ticket X. The correct equation is: $J = 2X$. The next keyword is another *was*, followed by the phrase *$1\frac{1}{2}$ times as much*. This equation relates the values of tickets K and X: $K = \frac{3}{2}X$. The keyword *total* is not stated in this problem, but it is understood to be the total amount of money awarded, which is $500,000. By using the information about how many people claimed prizes, you can relate the value of each type of ticket to the total amount of money:

$$50J + 100K + 150X = \$500,000$$

Substituting the values from the previous equations and solving for X:

$$50(2X) + 100(\tfrac{3}{2}X) + 150X = \$500,000$$

$$100X + 150X + 150X = \$500,000$$

$$400X = \$500,000$$

$$X = \$1,250$$

Common Types of Word Problems

The test example above is a variation on a type of word problem known as a "coin problem." In a coin problem, coins of different worth are combined to create a total amount of money. Other versions of coin problems involve different dollar bills, stamps, and tickets.

In addition to coin problems and their variations, there are other types of word problems that show up often on the GRE. You can increase your chances of getting word problems right by recognizing these common problem types and learning what kind of solutions they require.

Percent Problems

Mastering percent problems is extremely important, because many data interpretation questions are also written as percent problems. The three basic types of percent problems are:

1) What is p percent of n?

2) What percent of n is m?

3) m is p percent of what number?

Example:

What is 40% of 500?

Solution: Change the percent to a fraction or decimal, then multiply by the "of" number.

$$0.40 \times 500 = ? \qquad 0.40 \times 500 = 200$$

Example:

What percent of 50 is 35?

Solution: Write as a fraction the "is" number over the "of" number. Divide, then change the decimal to a percent.

$$\frac{35}{50} = ?\% \qquad \frac{35}{50} = 0.7 = 70\%$$

Be forewarned that the most common error in solving this type of problem is reversing the numbers on the top and bottom of the fraction. Always remember: "is over of."

Example:

6 is 30% of what number?

Solution: Write an equation in which you set the given number equal to the percent times the unknown. Change the percent to a decimal or fraction, then solve for the unknown.

$6 = 30\%$ of n;

$6 = 0.3n$;

$20 = n$

Percent problems that appear in the discrete quantitative section can be worded in a variety of ways, and it may take a little practice to learn to recognize the different problem types. It is also important to keep in mind that a percent problem may be but one step in a problem that requires other mathematical techniques as well.

Example:

An airport waiting room contains 80 people. If 15% of those people are not U.S. citizens, how many U.S. citizens are in the room?

(A) 12   (B) 56

(C) 68   (D) 70

(E) 85

Solution: If 15% of the people are not U.S. citizens, then 85% are U.S. citizens. Set up the problem: "What is 85% of 80?"

$(0.85)(80) = 68$

Notice that choice (A) is 15% of 80. This is an appealing trap for anyone who rushes to find the percent without carefully reading the problem.

Percent Increase or Decrease Problems

Percent increase or decrease problems ask you to express as a percent the change in value of a quantity. The rule for solving percent increase or decrease problems is:

percent change = difference in value/original value

Example:

What is the percent increase if the price of a magazine changes from $2.50 to $3.00?

$$\text{percent increase} = \frac{\$3.00 - \$2.50}{\$2.50} = \frac{\$0.50}{\$2.50} = 20\%$$

Example:

The number of students dropped from 700 to 630. What was the percent decrease?

$$\text{percent decrease} = \frac{700 - 630}{700} = \frac{70}{700} = 10\%$$

The most important thing to remember when solving a percent change problem is that you must compare the difference in value to the original value. You can be sure that other comparisons will inevitably appear as wrong answer choices.

Distance Problems

Distance problems are not difficult, and most of them can be solved by applying this formula:

rate × time = distance

The tricky part of a distance problem on the GRE can be the little "extras" involved, such as changing hours to minutes or calculating round trips.

Example:

Harry lives 10 km from the beach. If Harry averages 50 km/hr, how many minutes will it take him to drive to the beach and home again?

(A) 5   (B) 10

(C) 12   (D) 20

(E) 24

Solution: Applying the formula you obtain:

$$\frac{50 \text{ km}}{\text{hr}} \times t = 10 \text{ km}; \quad t = \frac{1}{5}\text{hr}$$

Changing hours to minutes, you obtain $\frac{1}{5} \times 60$ minutes = 12 minutes. Since 12 minutes is the time it takes to drive one way, the total driving time is 24 minutes—choice (E). Notice that choice (C) is waiting for you if you forget to calculate the round trip.

The Fence-Post Problem

The fence-post problem shows up on almost every GRE test. This type of problem describes a series of fence posts (or similar items) with a certain distance between each post, and with one post at each end. The problem then asks you to calculate the total distance between the first fence post and the last. The most common mistake is to multiply the distance between posts times the total number of posts, forgetting that there is a post at each end. Another mistake is to subtract both endposts and then multiply by the distance. The correct way to solve the fence-post problem is with this formula:

distance = (number of posts – 1) × (distance between posts)

Example:

A gardener plants a straight row of trees with 5 meters between each tree. If 15 trees are planted, what is the number of meters between the first tree and the last tree?

(A) 50   (B) 65

(C) 70   (D) 75

(E) 80

Solution: Apply the formula: $(15 - 1) \times 5 = 70$, which is choice (C). Notice that choices (B) and (D) are the answers you obtain if you make either of the common mistakes described above.

Working Backwards

The problem-solving strategies presented thus far are direct strategies—that is, they teach you to work directly from the given information to obtain an answer. Sometimes it is helpful to approach a problem indirectly, by working backwards from the answer choice. This is especially true for problems in which a direct method is not obvious.

Example:

A bank teller counted out $120 in cash. If each of the bills he counted was either a $5 bill or a $10 bill, which of the following cannot be the

24 = 5   12 = 10

number of $5 bills?

(A) 2   (B) 8

(C) 15   (D) 16

(E) 20

Solution: Look at the five answer choices. Does one answer look different from the rest? Choice (C) stands out because it is the only odd number in the group. Start by testing this choice: $15 \times \$5 = \$75$. Subtracting $75 from $120, you see that the remaining amount of money is $45. Since $45 is not a multiple of 10, it could not be made up of $10 bills. Thus, the number of $5 bills cannot be 15.

Eliminating Obvious Wrong Answers

A technique similar to working backwards is eliminating obvious wrong answers. In fact, you can combine these techniques by first eliminating obvious wrong answers and then working backwards from the remaining answer choices. Eliminating obvious wrong answers is a very useful strategy when you are running out of time and you want to make an intelligent guess on a problem that you do not have time for. By eliminating obvious wrong answers, you increase your odds of guessing correctly.

Example:

$$3 + \frac{1}{3} + \frac{1}{5} + 1\frac{1}{6} =$$

(A) $\dfrac{79}{20}$ (B) $\dfrac{91}{30}$

(C) $\dfrac{127}{35}$ (D) $\dfrac{71}{25}$

(E) $\dfrac{141}{30}$

Solution: The lowest common denominator for adding the fractions is 30—meaning that the sum of the numbers must have a denominator of 30 or a multiple of 30. This eliminates choices (A), (C), and (D), leaving you with a 50-50 chance of choosing correctly between (B) and (E). If you work the problem, you will find that the sum of the numbers is $^{141}/_{30}$.

Example:

What is the largest prime factor of 126?

(A) 2

(B) 3

(C) 7

(D) 23

(E) 63 = 3 · 21

Solution: Choice (E), 63, is not a prime number. This leaves you with four possible choices. Working the problem shows that 7 is the correct answer: $2 \times 3 \times 3 \times 7 = 126$.

MASTERING DATA INTERPRETATION

Data Interpretation questions test your ability to read information from graphs and tables and then apply that information to solve problems. Data Interpretation questions require basic arithmetic skills with an emphasis on percents and ratios. The first few questions usually require nothing more than a correct reading of the data and perhaps a simple calculation. The last questions are more difficult, usually requiring several steps and asking you to synthesize or interpret information.

All Data Interpretation questions are based on the same set of data, which is presented before the first problem. As in the Discrete Quantitative sections, you are given five answer choices, labeled (A) through (E). You are to choose the best answer.

SKILLS AND STRATEGIES

Before You Begin

It is not a good idea to spend too much time looking at the data before you begin answering the questions. However, there are a few things that you should take time to notice. As you look at the data, ask yourself the following questions:

1) In general, what does the entire data set describe?

2) What are the headings above each graph or table?

SALES AND EARNINGS FOR DEPARTMENT STORE X CLOTHING AND NONCLOTHING ITEMS

Total Earnings
(millions of dollars)

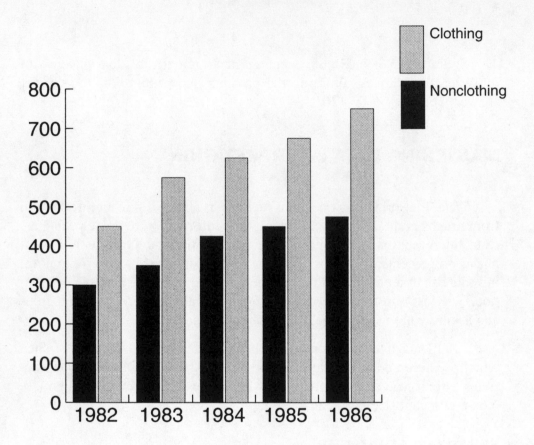

**Total Sales
(billions of dollars)**

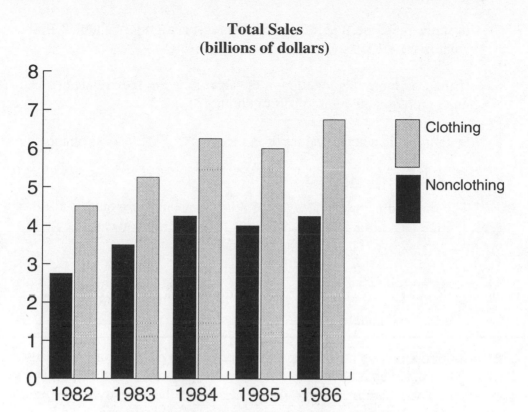

**DISTRIBUTION OF EARNINGS FROM
NONCLOTHING ITEMS, 1985**

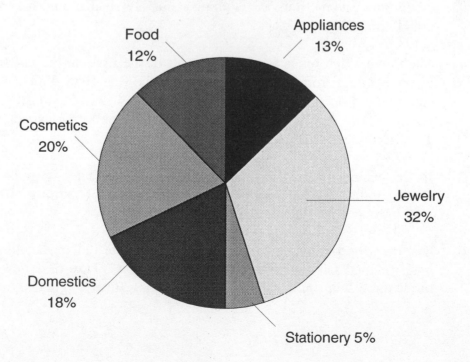

3) Is more than one type of data presented on a graph or table? If so, what is the difference?

4) If there is more than one graph or table, how are they related? Does one graph or table refer to part of another?

5) Is data given in actual values or in percents?

6) Is all data given in the same units?

The data on pages 76 to 77 is similar to what you would find on a typical GRE test. Look at the data and see how quickly you can answer the six questions above. Then read the explanation.

1) You can tell what the data is about by looking at the title. This data set describes the sales and earnings of Department Store X for both clothing and nonclothing items.

2) It is important to note the headings above each graph or table, because questions often refer to them. In this case, headings over the bar graphs are "Total Earnings" and "Total Sales." The heading over the circle graph is "Distribution of Earnings from Nonclothing Items, 1985."

3) The bar graphs present two types of data—for clothing items and nonclothing items. Bars for clothing items are shaded, and bars for nonclothing items are black.

4) The circle graph refers to a specific part of the first bar graph—that is, the earnings from nonclothing items for the year 1985. You can be sure that at least one question will ask you to use this relationship. A good tip is to draw an arrow from the circle graph to the part of the Total Earnings graph that it refers to.

5) In this example, data for total earnings and total sales is given in actual dollar amounts; data for the distribution of earnings from nonclothing items is given in percents.

6) The data for total earnings is given in millions of dollars, while the data for total sales is given in billions of dollars. Take time now to circle the words "millions" and "billions" above the two graphs.

Avoiding Traps and Pitfalls

By now you are probably aware of some of the traps and pitfalls that await you in data interpretation questions. An obvious pitfall is reading data from two graphs that have different units and forgetting to convert to common units. Another pitfall is reading percent data and thinking it is value data, or vice-versa. Other common mistakes include reading data from the wrong graph when two graphs are similar, or reading the wrong type of data, such as clothing items instead of nonclothing items. These mistakes can usually be avoided if you pay close attention to what you are doing.

Example: *[Refer to data at the beginning of this section.]*

In 1983, total earnings from nonclothing items were approximately what percent of total sales for nonclothing items?

(A) 1%   (B) 10%

(C) 5%   (D) 35%

(E) 100%

Solution: This is a classic "fall into the trap of using the wrong units" problem. Total earnings are given in millions of dollars, while total sales are given in billions of dollars. Failure to recognize this will cause you to calculate an incorrect percent. (The results of some common miscalculations are choices (A) and (E).) Using units correctly, you obtain

$350,000,000/$3,500,000,000 = 10%.

Using Estimation

You can use estimation to answer most data interpretation questions. In fact, you will notice that many questions use the words "approximate" or "approximately" when asking for an answer. This is important, because it means that you are *expected* to estimate. If you do not, you will probably spend longer on each problem than the test-makers intended.

There are many estimation techniques that you can use, but two are especially useful when solving data interpretation questions. One is using convenient percents, and the other is using convenient fractions.

Using Convenient Percents

Data is often given to you in the form of a percent. The percent may be a number that is inconvenient to work with, such as 24.2%. What you must do is find a percent close to the given percent that is easy to use. For example, 24.2% is very close to 25%, or $\frac{1}{4}$. Some other, similar, conversions include: percents between 45% and 55% become 50% or $\frac{1}{2}$; percents close to 33% become $\frac{1}{3}$; percents close to 100%, such as 97.5%, become 1.

Using Convenient Fractions

Among the most convenient fractions are $\frac{1}{4}$, $\frac{1}{3}$, $\frac{1}{2}$, $\frac{1}{5}$, and $\frac{1}{10}$. Other fractions with the same denominators are also easy to work with: for example, $\frac{2}{3}$, $\frac{3}{4}$, $\frac{4}{5}$, $\frac{7}{10}$. Data Interpretation questions often require you to form fractions from large and unwieldy numbers. Your goal should be to reduce the fraction to a convenient fraction close in value.

Example:

Find the ratio of 1,149 to 3,560.

Begin by rounding off both numbers to the nearest hundred, so that $\frac{1,149}{3,560}$ becomes $\frac{1100}{3600}$. Looking at this fraction, you can see right away that it is very close to $\frac{12}{36}$, which is equal to $\frac{1}{3}$.

Recognizing Keywords

Like word problems, Data Interpretation questions contain certain keywords that tell you what to do. The most important keywords for you to recognize are value, total, percent, percent increase or decrease, and ratio. *Value* always refers to a numerical amount, usually in dollars. This is an essential word to know, because many graphs and tables present data as percents, while the problem may ask you to use or find value. *Total* may refer to the heading of a graph, such as Total Sales, or it may be telling you to add several data items in order to arrive at a total. Like total, *percent* may refer to data that is already given in percents or it may be asking you to compute the percent. *Percent increase or decrease* is comparing the change in a value to the original value. *Ratio* is asking you to compare two data items, usually in the form of a fraction.

THREE STEPS FOR SOLVING DATA INTERPRETATION PROBLEMS

There are three basic steps involved in solving a Data Interpretation problem. Easier problems may require only one or two of these, but more difficult problems will require you to use all the steps at least once. The three basic steps are:

1) Read

2) Transform

3) Apply

The first step tells you to read necessary information from the appropriate graph or table. The second step tells you to transform, if necessary, the data into another form, such as changing a dollar value into a percent. The third step tells you to apply the data in some way, such as comparing it to another data item.

Example: *[Refer to data at the beginning of this section.]*

From 1982 to 1984, total sales from nonclothing items increased by approximately what percent?

(A) 55%   (B) 43%

(C) 39%   (D) 28%

(E) 15%

Solution: This is a clear example of "read and apply." First you must read the Total Sales graph to obtain nonclothing sales for 1982 and 1984:

1982 = $2.75 billion; 1984 = $4.25 billion

Next, you must apply this information to find the percent increase:

$$\% \text{ increase} = \frac{4.25 - 2.75}{2.75} = \frac{1.50}{2.75}$$

Using estimation, you can see that this fraction is slightly larger than $\frac{1}{2}$. Thus, the answer is (A).

Breaking a Question into Parts

Some of the more difficult data interpretation questions require you to read, transform, and apply a number of different data items. You can break a difficult question into manageable parts by following this strategy, for which you may want to use scratch paper:

1) Take account of words that tell you what information to read from graphs and charts.

2) Isolate phrasing that indicates the need to transform information.

3) Take note of words that tell you how information is going to be applied.

Example: *[Refer to data at the beginning of this section.]*

In 1985, the value of earnings from jewelry was approximately what percent of the value of earnings from both clothing and nonclothing items for the same year?

(A) 65%   (B) 50%

(C) 32%   (D) 30%

(E) 15%

Solution: Notice the words *value of earnings from jewelry* and *value of earnings from both clothing and nonclothing items*. The phrase *value of earnings from jewelry* indicates information that must be transformed from a percent to a dollar value. The word *both* tells you that you must compute a total for clothing and nonclothing items. Finally, the word *percent* tells you how to apply that information. Working the problem, you obtain:

Value of earnings from jewelry = 32% of $450 million, or ⅓ of $450 million = $150 million.

Total value earnings from clothing and nonclothing = $450 million + $675 million = $1,125 million.

$$\frac{\text{Earnings from jewelry}}{\text{total earnings}} = \frac{\$150}{\$1,125} = \text{approximately } 15\%.$$

So, the correct answer is (E).

A FINAL THOUGHT

A subtle difficulty of the Data Interpretation section is its placement on the test. These questions begin the last third of the Quantitative Ability section, a point at which you may be getting tired and may be feeling pressed for time. Yet because these questions are not at the end of the test, you may be worried about the last questions. Unless you really like numbers, the need to read and digest a lot of data and large numbers may seem overwhelming. This problem may be compounded if you have an aversion to fractions or percents.

The best way to deal with any or all if these feelings is to remember that the first few GRE CBT Data Interpretation questions are easy—most people get them right, and you probably will, too. Also remember that you won't have to make complicated calculations—estimating will be fine. If you find yourself bogging down over the last few questions, click on the best answers you can and move on.

YOU AS COACH—EVALUATING YOUR OWN PERFORMANCE

Now that you have worked through the Refresher sections and the Mastering Quantitative Comparison, Discrete Quantitative, and Data Interpretation sections, you are ready to take a practice test. Each of our written practice tests contains two Quantitative Ability sections. It is important that you take each Quantitative Ability section in exactly 30 minutes. Once you have taken a practice test, you are ready to evaluate your performance.

The best way to evaluate your performance is to note the types of questions that you got wrong and *why* you got them wrong. It is also helpful to look for a pattern in your timing—for example, if you lacked sufficient time to answer all the questions, did you tend to run out of time near the same question number in both sections?

The following chart will help you organize your test results. You should make a copy of the chart for each Quantitative Ability section that you take. Be sure to allow enough lines to list each wrong answer. Under the heading "Type of Question," you should describe the question both in terms of the math involved and the kinds of questions that have been described in this Review. For example, you might write "percent problem" or "distance problem" to describe a word problem. You might write "apples and oranges" to refer to a type of quantitative comparison problem described in this Review. Or you might write "geometry—parallel lines and angles" to describe a geometry problem. Under the heading "Reason," you should tell why you got the problem wrong. Typical reasons might include: ran out of time; did not know how to do the problem; did not know specific formula; careless mistake; fell into a trap.

EVALUATING WRONG ANSWERS

Test Number _____ Section Number _____

Total Number of Wrong Answers _____

1–15: Quantitative Comparison

Question #	Type of Question	Reason

16–20: Discrete Quantitative

Question #	Type of Question	Reason

21–25: Data Interpretation

Question #	Type of Question	Reason

26–30: Discrete Quantitative

Question #	Type of Question	Reason

Once you have completed the chart, analyze your data. Do many of your wrong answers appear in a particular section, such as Data Interpretation? Are you obviously weak in a particular mathematical subject area, such as geometry? Do you seem to get a lot of word problems wrong? Do you miss a lot of questions because of errors in calculations? Or do your wrong answers seem to include a little of everything?

The easiest wrong answers to correct are those for which you did not know a specific rule or formula. Chances are, the rule or formula is included in one of the Refresher sections. Look it up and LEARN IT!

If you made more than one or two careless mistakes—such as adding 2 + 2 and getting 5—you are probably working too fast. You don't want to dwell on a problem, but you should take a few seconds to check your work as you go along. Your problem may also be one of concentration—especially if you did something unthinkingly, such as marking choice (E) for a question that has only four choices. Learn to focus your mind on what you are doing and not be distracted by nervousness or too much clock-watching.

An important part of analyzing your data is to look at the questions you did not have time for. Were any of them numbered 16, 17, 21, 22, 26, or 27? These questions are the first questions in a section and they tend to be quite easy—in fact, numbers 16 and 21 are usually a cinch. You might want to redesign your test-taking strategy to make time for these questions—perhaps by not spending so much time on the more difficult questions. Sometimes you can do three or four easy questions in the time it takes to solve one difficult question. This is especially important if you got several of the more difficult questions wrong.

Whatever your pattern of wrong answers, you are the best person to design a plan for improving your performance. Go back and review the strategies for the types of problems that you missed. Review the subject areas in which you did poorly and practice the skills that you need. Experiment with different ways of approaching the test and different ways of using your time. Keep in mind that the GRE CBT, like all standardized tests, has a logical plan behind its construction. By working logically to improve your performance, you will get to know the test better.

ANSWERS TO PRACTICE DRILLS 1–8

Practice Drill 1

1. 1, 2, 3, 4, 5, 6 , 7

2. 5, 15, 25, 35

3. (A) –2   (B) 0   (C) –16   (D) 18   (E) -7   (F) 7
    (G) 12   (H) 6

4. 7, 11, 13, 17, 19, 23, 29, 31, 37, 41, 43, 47

5. $2 \times 7 \times 7$

Practice Drill 2

1. (A) $\frac{11}{24}$ (B) $\frac{19}{35}$ (C) $\frac{3}{5}$

2. (A) $\frac{15}{2}$ (B) $\frac{1}{2}$ (C) $\frac{1}{6}$ (D) $\frac{3}{11}$

3. (A) $\frac{25}{4}$ (B) $\frac{14}{3}$ (C) $\frac{8}{5}$

4. (A) $\frac{12}{5}$ (B) $\frac{33}{56}$ (C) $\frac{65}{12}$

5. (A) $\frac{19}{25}$; 0.76   (B) $\frac{1}{5}$; 0.2   (C) $\frac{3}{2}$; 1.5   (D) $\frac{3}{100}$; 0.03

6. (A) 7.18   (B) 894.89   (C) 1.32   (D) 101.056

7. (A) 0.0438   (B) 19.25   (C) 0.1216

8. (A) 46   (B) 420   (C) 5.4

9. (A) $\frac{7}{100}$ (B) $\frac{12}{100}$ (C) $\frac{8}{10}$ (D) $\frac{331}{1000}$

10. (A) $\dfrac{1}{12}$ (B) $\dfrac{14}{34}$ (C) $\dfrac{99}{100}$

11. (A) 360 (B) 720 (C) 250 (D) 8

12. (A) 165% (B) $\dfrac{7}{10}$ (C) -0.5 (D) 2

Practice Drill 3

1. mean = 8.8; median = 6.5; mode = 6

2. 255

3. (A) $\dfrac{5}{9}$ (B) $\dfrac{7}{8}$ (C) $\dfrac{10}{100}$ or $\dfrac{1}{10}$ (D) $\dfrac{1}{2}$

4. (A) $x = 6$ (B) $x = 45$

5. \$10/hr.

6. 8 in.

7. mean = 845.45; median = 900; mode = 900

Practice Drill 4

1. (A) 27 (B) 625 (C) 64 (D) 169 (E) 225 (F) 64

2. $\sqrt{4}$

3. (A) x^8 (B) $\dfrac{16}{49}$ (C) $\dfrac{1}{8}$ (D) y^{12}

4. $\dfrac{5}{2}$

5. (A) $-\dfrac{1}{9}$ (B) $\dfrac{1}{9}$ (C) -12

Practice Drill 5

1. $x + (y + 7)$

2. $(3n)m$

3. $3a + 3b$

4. $5(ax + 2a + 9)$

5. $(3x + y)(3x - y)$

6. $(2x + 1)(2x + 1)$

7. $(a - 2)(a - 1)$

8. $k^2 + k - 72$

9. $9a^2b^2 + 12ab + 4$

10. $36x^2 - 1$

Practice Drill 6

1. $x = \dfrac{13}{3}$

2. $b = 3$

3. $m = 4$

4. $x = 5$

5. $x = 8; x = -2$

6. $y = 3; y = -3$

7. $x = 10 - \dfrac{5}{2}r$

8. $x = -r$

9. $y = 4; x = 6$

10. $a = 8; b = -52; c = 4$

11. $3x - 8 = 7x + 8$

    $-8 = 4x + 8$

    $-16 = 4x$

    $-4 = x$

12. $x = 4$

13. (A) $x = 0$; $x = -1.5$

    (B) $y = 0$; $y = 3$

    (C) $z = 3$; $z = -1$

    (D) $m = 6$; $m = -0.5$

14. $x = 4$; $y = 2$

Practice Drill 7

1. (A) $80°$ (B) $110°$ (C) $85°$

2. (A) 10   (B) 5   (C) 8

3. 84

4. $\angle 1 = 150°$; $\angle 2 = 30°$

5. $\angle 1 = 10°$; $\angle 2 = 80°$; $\angle 3 = 90°$; $\angle 4 = 10°$

6. $\angle x = 50°$; $\angle ACB = 80°$

Practice Drill 8

1. (A) $65°$ (B) 10   (C) 13

2. 28.26; 18.84; 6.28

3. (A) $(-3, -1)$;   (B) $(2, 2)$;   (C) $(3, 0)$;   (D) $(2, -3)$

4. Possible answer:

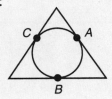

5. V = 64 cubic cm; surface area = 96 square cm

6. $h = l = w = 6$

CHAPTER 3:
Verbal
Review

CHAPTER 3

GRE VERBAL REVIEW

OVERVIEW OF THE VERBAL ABILITY SECTION

The verbal section of the GRE measures what ETS believes are the knowledge and skills needed for graduate study. One such skill is the ability to read scholarly material with a high degree of comprehension. Other subtests are designed to test your ability to reason with words in solving problems. An extensive vocabulary is assumed for this purpose.

TYPES OF QUESTIONS

A typical verbal section will have

7 sentence completion questions

10 verbal analogy questions

6 reading comprehension questions

7 antonym questions

BUILDING A GOOD VOCABULARY IS AN ADVANTAGE

A large vocabulary is a tremendous asset. That's why we've not only given you a vocabulary list of words previously used on the GRE, but also a list of suffixes, prefixes, and roots, some of the words compounded from them, and some tips on how to use the list.

Flash cards are a good way to learn words. From the word list, EACH DAY choose eight to ten (or as many as you can comfortably handle); half should be words whose meaning you vaguely know, and half should be words whose meaning eludes you. On one side of an index card, write the word. Put the definition on the other side and below it write a sentence containing the word. Forming sentences is an important step in vocabulary development. Be sure you use the word correctly and know its part of speech. The part of speech will be especially important on the analogy section, as we will explain later.

Carry these cards with you everywhere. Whenever you have a spare moment, look at a word and try to remember its meaning. Then check yourself by looking at the definition. Once you know a word, replace the card with a new one. This method puts time to use that would otherwise be underutilized or wasted.

Word association is a good technique for memorization. Associate a word with something/someone memorable to you. Perhaps your Aunt Sally is vociferous. Some people find it helpful to associate with something funny or outrageous and thus unforgettable.

Visualization can also be helpful. A juggernaut is an irresistible force that crushes everything before it. It can also mean blind sacrifice. The word is rooted in a religious custom involving the parading of an enormous idol in a large cart. Devout worshippers would prostrate themselves before the cart and were crushed as it rolled by. Visualizing this reminds you of both meanings.

SENTENCE COMPLETION

ETS DIRECTIONS FOR SENTENCE COMPLETION QUESTIONS

DIRECTIONS: Each sentence below has one or two blanks, each blank indicating that something has been omitted. Beneath the sentence are five lettered words or sets of words. Choose the word or set of words for each blank that best fits the meaning of the sentence as a whole.

According to ETS, the purpose of the sentence completion questions is to measure the ability to recognize words or phrases that both logically and stylistically complete the meaning of the sentence. As is the case with so much of the GRE, individual words and their shades of meaning become important in the sentence completions. You are expected to place words in context, stylistically as well as logically.

MAKE THE BEST CHOICE

The word "best" is key here. There will be several choices that fit the blank; you must pick the best one. Because the sentence completion questions are short, each word becomes important.

READ THE SENTENCE AND MENTALLY FILL IN YOUR OWN WORDS

The recommended technique for sentence completion questions is to first read the sentence, filling in the blank(s) with word(s) of your own that make sense. This will help you to focus on what to expect. Then match your own answer with those given.

Throughout the test you should try to eliminate as many of the five possible answers as you can, thus narrowing your choices as much as possible. In the sentence completion questions, you may not know the meaning of some of the choices. After you insert a word of your own in the blank, try to find among the choices a word you think might be a synonym for your word. If you can do so, you will be able to eliminate some words and will improve your odds if you must guess.

For example, you decide that the word needed must mean lateness or delay. Your choices are:

(A) alacrity

(B) promptness

(C) demurrage

(D) acceleration

(E) punctuality

Since "alacrity," "promptness," "acceleration," and "punctuality" do not denote lateness, then the choice must be "demurrage," even if you don't know the meaning of the word. (It's the detention of a boat or railroad car, when being loaded or unloaded, beyond the time agreed on.)

WORK ONE BLANK AT A TIME

Where there are two blanks, insert the first word in blank one. If it doesn't fit, then (A) is not correct. Go on to (B), (C), etc. This technique will help you eliminate several choices. Then, for those choices remaining, fill in both blanks. By eliminating poor choices, you maximize your score if you have to guess on the choices remaining.

BE SURE YOUR CHOICE IS STYLISTICALLY CORRECT

The correct choice must be syntactical, that is, it must use English as it is correctly spoken/written. At a minimum this means that if a noun is called for, the correct answer must be a noun, etc.

Ask yourself whether the missing word will carry on the thought of the sentence or reverse it.

For example: After gardening all day, we were [exhausted]. (Carries on the sentence, completing the meaning as expected.)

For example: In spite of gardening all day, we were quite [energetic]. (Here the expectation is reversed. The clue here is "in spite of.")

As you have just seen, signal or indicator words tell you what kind of answer to expect. These words are also helpful in the reading comprehension passages, but they are especially important here.

On the following page are some commonly used signal words.

KEY WORDS AND PHRASES TO LOOK FOR AND WHAT THEY INDICATE

Contrast or Opposition (These words signal a shift.)

as...as

although

but

despite

however

in spite of

in contrast

nevertheless

notwithstanding

on the other hand

on the contrary

rather than

though

unlike

yet

Support

also

besides

furthermore

in addition

in fact

moreover

Indicating a Result

accordingly

as a result

because

consequently

hence

it can be inferred that

so

this means

therefore

thus

Example

As dedicated as he is to fine art, he does not allow respect to
_____ his sense of fun when writing about it.

(A) inspire   (D) suppress

(B) provoke   (E) satiate

(C) attack

Normally one might expect an art critic to be serious, even pedantic, in writing about art. The phrase **as (dedicated) as...**, however, cues us that a contrast is about to be drawn: Despite the art critic's dedication and respect, he is still able to write about art with a sense of humor. (A), (B), and (E) are all incorrect because they imply that the man's sense of humor is diminished by his respect for fine art. Choice (C), **attack**, seems out of context. Choice (D), **suppress**, completes the thought much better than any of the other words. The man does not allow his respect to suppress his sense of fun.

Example

He was only 5'8"; nevertheless, he was a _____ basketball player.

Even with a word missing we know that this man is a fine player.

EXPECT SENTENCE COMPLETIONS OFTEN TO INVOLVE CONTRAST

A common type of sentence completion involves contrast. When faced with completions having two blanks, if a contrast has been set up, then you can normally expect that the correct pair of word are themselves contrasts or opposites.

Example

Science is often thought of as _____ observation of external reality, concerned only with the attainment of facts; yet scientists are just like other people: they are _____ human beings who exist in a social and personal context.

    (A) reverent...vulnerable   (D) disinterested...passionate

    (B) impartial...intelligent   (E) circumspect...vigorous

    (C) diligent...messy

Yet announces the contrast; therefore, (A) and (B) can be eliminated. (C), (D), and (E) all show contrast, but (C) and (E) are rejected because **messy** and **vigorous** have no bearing on social and personal context; (E) is also rejected because **circumspect** observation of external reality is not as accurate a description of science as unbiased and **disinterested** observation. Therefore, choice (D) is the correct answer.

LOOK FOR KEY WORDS

In order for the GRE to be a true test and not just a guessing game, there must be clues to tip you off to the correct answer. Signal words perform part of this function, but other words are important too. As you read, look for other key words that can assist you in determining meaning. In the sample completions on the next page, we'll point out a few.

SAMPLE SENTENCE COMPLETION QUESTIONS

1.   A careful reading of the text is _____ his argument. On the one hand, scarcely anything can be adduced in support of it, and on the other hand, a great deal can be produced in disproof.

(A) supportive of   (D) neutral toward

(B) unrewarding toward   (E) indicative of

(C) fatal to

The key word here is **support**. Since the passage indicates that there is little to support the argument and much to disprove it, we can eliminate (A). We need an answer which is nonsupportive, so we can also eliminate (B) and (D). (E) simply does not relate to support or disproof of the argument, and therefore is rejected. By elimination we arrive at choice (C), which makes perfect sense. Something *fatal* to an argument is as nonsupportive as you can get.

2. Their mutual _____ seemed clear, but in fact they had a long-standing _____ toward each other.

    (A) admiration...fondness   (D) attraction...animosity

    (B) dislike...hatred   (E) enchantment...affection

    (C) aptitude...antipathy

But indicates a contrast here; we need a pair of opposites. Only (D) meets this need.

3. In recent years, the notion that Columbus discovered America has been caught in the _____ between those who believe this to be an example of white racism and those who _____ the Norsemen as discoverers.

    (A) symposium...question   (D) crossfire...advocate

    (B) discussion...substitute   (E) paradox...prefer

    (C) interplay...support

The key words here are **caught in**, suggesting some sort of fight. Therefore, choices (A), (B), (C), and (E) are rejected, either because they do not convey a dispute or because they do not convey that notion strongly enough. Choice (D) is correct because it suggests a verbal fight and because the term **advocate** is stronger than the other choices, thus furthering the idea of a dispute.

4. The strength of a perceptive biography lies not just in its factual accuracy or in the biographer's prose style, but in his skill in creating the moments that reveal the most _____ psychological truths—the motivations, transformations, and points of conflict—in the life of the subject.

   (A) appealing

   (B) amazing

   (C) profound

   (D) trivial

   (E) fascinating

Since this biography is a perceptive one (i.e., serious), trivial truths cannot be its strength, eliminating choice (D). Choices (A), (B), and (E) can be eliminated: **amazing** suggests the sensational; **appealing** and **fascinating** are not serious enough. Choice (C) is correct. One strength of a serious, perceptive biography would be its uncovering of profound psychological truths.

5. Dryden has no equal in prayers, objurations, politic addresses, and speeches of defiance; he wears the robes that he has borrowed from the orator with a splendid assurance; his accents, although they, too, are borrowed, ring _____. But in poetic narrative his limits are _____.

   (A) musically...interesting

   (B) hollow...substantial

   (C) false...nonexistent

   (D) splendidly...peerless

   (E) true...firmly fixed

But tells us that we are looking for a contrast. **Musically** might be possible for the first blank, but **interesting** does not set up a contrast; eliminate (A). If Dryden is without equal, then his accents will not ring hollow or false; eliminate (B) and (C) on the basis of blank 1. **Splendidly** could work in blank 1, but **peerless** would not set up a contrast in blank 2, so eliminate (D). This leaves choice (E). In a line full of praise, we may be sure that the author believes Dryden's accents ring true, but **firmly fixed** limits sets up a contrast for blank 2, so choice (E) is confirmed.

6. Once again the president reaffirmed his _____ the treaty. Moreover, he indicated that his negotiators were engaged in _____ bargaining.

(A) neutrality toward...serious

(B) opposition to...useful

(C) support of...responsible

(D) conditional support of...diplomatic

(E) antagonism toward...good faith

Moreover indicates that the same thought is continuing here so both terms must be supportive of each other. In choice (A), it is unlikely that neutrality would lead to serious bargaining (and even more unlikely that the president would repeatedly affirm neutrality while simultaneously keeping negotiators on the job). If the president were opposed to the treaty, he would not be involved in useful bargaining, so eliminate (B). If the president were antagonistic toward the treaty, he would not bargain in good faith; eliminate (E). If his support of the treaty was conditional, it is unlikely but possible that diplomatic bargaining would occur. However, he probably would not repeatedly reaffirm conditional support. Choice (C) is best. If the president supported the treaty, then you would expect responsible bargaining.

7. The numerous _____ of the project do not include popularity. The public has traditionally been _____ such projects.

(A) highlights...enamored of   (D) innovations...misled

(B) features...interested in   (E) enticements...wary of

(C) advantages...skeptical of

The use of the word **not** here alerts us that words like **enamored of** and **interested in** are inappropriate for blank 2, thus eliminating (A) and (B). In (D), popularity is not an innovation. In (E), **enticements** could possibly work, and certainly **wary of** is appropriate for blank 2. However, compare this with choice (C). **Advantages** is better than **enticements**, and **skeptical of** fits blank 2 very well.

READING COMPREHENSION

PURPOSE AND CONTENT OF THE READING COMPREHENSION PASSAGES

> **DIRECTIONS:** Each passage in this group is followed by questions based on its content. After reading a passage, choose the best answer to each question. Answer all questions following a passage on the basis of what is stated or implied in that passage.

ETS states that the purpose of the reading comprehension passages is to "measure the ability to read with understanding, insight, and discrimination." Reading comprehension passages test the reader's ability to recognize not only what is explicitly stated, but also to recognize underlying assumptions and the implications of statements in the passage.

Reading comprehension passages are chosen from four different fields: social sciences, humanities, physical sciences, and life sciences. You do not need any specific knowledge or background other than what is presented in the passage in order to answer the questions.

COMMON TYPES OF QUESTIONS

The questions in the reading passages fall into two categories: those where the answer is stated more or less clearly, and those where either the answer is implied or you must reason it out.

Here are some types of reading comprehension questions that ETS frequently uses. As you read your test, keep these categories in mind. Quoted within each category are common ways in which the question is often phrased.

Main Idea

"The title that best expresses the idea of the passage is…."

"The author's primary purpose is…."

"The passage is primarily concerned with…."

You're certain to get at least one question of this type. To answer it, look for the topic sentence. Read the first and last sentences of each paragraph, especially of the introductory and last paragraphs. Think as you read "What's the author's point? What's he/she up to? What's he/she trying to prove?"

If time is running short, you may be able to answer main idea questions without reading the entire passage. Keep this in mind as a last resort, rather than leaving these questions blank.

Answer Explicitly Stated

"According to the selection...."

"Which of the following is stated...."

In this type of question the answer is specifically stated and can be found by skimming the passage.

Implied Answers or Those Requiring Reasoning and Interpretation

The answers to these questions are not explicit. You must draw conclusions based on your interpretation of the passage. Types of implied answers include the following:

Drawing Inferences

"The author implies...."

"It can be inferred that...."

"Apparently the author believes...."

"The author most probably included _____ in the passage in order to...."

Skimming may help to refresh your memory and to clarify your understanding of the passage, but finding the answer will require you to think carefully about the author's intentions.

Applying the Author's Ideas to Other Situations

"Which of the following most probably provides an appropriate analogy for the distinction made in the passage...?"

"The author would be likely to agree with which of the following...?"

"Which of the following statements would most likely begin the paragraph following the last paragraph quoted here...?"

These questions require that you understand the author's line of reasoning and can apply it to other situations.

The Author's Logic, Reasoning, or Persuasive Techniques

"The author resolves the question of _____ by...."

"The argument of the passage best supports which of the following?"

"The author attempts to...."

Here you must use your reasoning to determine the answer.

Tone or Attitude

"The tone of the passage is chiefly...."

"Which of the following best states the author's attitude...?"

Tone or attitude is implied, rather than stated, so you must interpret. Individual words become very important, especially adjectives and adverbs.

Is the author neutral, supportive, enthusiastic, angry, concerned, skeptical, or sarcastic? The tone and words used will vary according to his/her attitude. The phrase "Jones rightly states" suggests approval, while "Jones's frivolous claim" suggests disapproval.

Compare these two descriptions of a man getting on a horse:

He quickly leaped atop his noble stallion.

He painfully clambered onto his faithful nag.

The first conveys an image of bravery and gallantry, while the second conveys a picture of someone worn out by old age or infirmity.

TO PREPARE FOR THE TEST, INCREASE YOUR READING SPEED

When your reading speed picks up, your comprehension normally picks up also. If you read slowly, there is no time like the present to accelerate your speed. You will have even more reading to do in graduate school than you did in college and probably less time to do it. Choose a variety of material—books (including textbooks), magazines (and scholarly journals), newspapers—and practice improving your speed. Concentrate on the basic structure of each sentence: subject, verb, object (who did what to whom). Most other words modify or color the SVO (subject, verb, object) in some way. At the beginning you may even find it helpful to underline the SVO to help you focus on the structure of the sentence and thus on its basic meaning.

Look for the transitional phrases we previously listed for you on page 97. These indicate either shifts in thought or support for the thought.

If you make a mistake in practice tests, go back to the passage and try to find the correct answer. In inferential questions, you won't find a direct answer but should be able to find the clues.

On page 137 there is a list of words that are often confused with each other. Watch for these words on the GRE. For example, a word often used on GRE exams is "discrete," meaning separate and distinct. Do not confuse it with "discreet," meaning judicious in conduct or speech.

A NOTE FOR SLOW READERS

Even if you do not have enough time to read the passage, answer the questions anyway. You have nothing to lose by guessing rather than leaving answers blank, and the odds are that random choice will allow you to answer correctly four or five out of 22 questions. You can improve your odds by eliminating as many of the answer choices as possible. There are certain keywords and concepts that are usually associated with incorrect responses. Learn these keywords and use them effectively when you do not know the answers to reading comprehension questions.

Keep in mind that unlike on paper-and-pencil tests, the GRE CBT exam does not penalize you for guessing. In fact, there is reason to believe that the number of questions you answer overall may have some effect on your score. Therefore, even if you do not have enough time to eliminate answer choices, you should choose an answer to every single question on the exam.

COACHING TIPS FOR GRE READING COMPREHENSION

Read the questions carefully. Make sure you understand what you are being asked before you fill in your answers.

After you have finished the selection and read the questions, re-read the passage. This is the time to search for details.

As you read the passage the second time, analyze the author's ideas. Check for his/her attitude. Be sure to draw a distinction between the facts and the author's interpretation of them. Draw a distinction also between the main idea of the passage and any supporting details.

If there are words in the passage that you don't know, substitute a word which seems to be a synonym, based on the context.

True is Not Always Correct

Don't choose an answer simply because it's true. Be sure it answers the question. A choice may often be perfectly true but may not answer the question.

"Always" is Almost Always Wrong

If an answer contains words like "always" or "never," be very suspicious of it. There are few "no exceptions" absolutes in this world. Mary may love George with all her heart; they may have been married for 50 love-filled years. But surely there have been at least a few moments when she was ready to kick him in the shins.

So, if an answer contains words like **invariably**, **completely**, **without exception** (words without any qualifiers), it is (almost) always the wrong answer.

Take Notes

On scratch paper, note key words and important ideas that you believe are likely to surface in the questions.

Look for transitional phrases (see list on pages 93 and 94). These signposts give you a road map of the author's thought. Take account of them as you read.

A question format that sometimes appears is one in which three or four statements are given, and you must choose from among the following:

(A) I only

(B) III only

(C) I and III only

(D) II and III only

(E) I, II, and III

Questions of this type are perfect for the elimination strategy. If you found that statement I was correct, then the answer must contain I, thus eliminating (B) and (D). If III was definitely incorrect, then you could eliminate any answer containing III, leaving (A) as the correct choice.

TAKE A DEEP BREATH

If you get tired or nervous while doing the GRE, take a couple of deep breaths, and look up and down (to take your eyes away from the computer screen). Remind yourself that you have years and years of schooling behind you, and you're an intelligent person. You will be surprised how much this can help. When you look back, the answer may come to you.

PRACTICE DRILLS

Some years ago there arose what has come to be considered an important distinction regarding the purposes of product and programmatic evaluation. It was noted that evaluation serves two different functions. Formative evaluation collects data about products as they are being developed. It helps the developer to form and modify products in order to meet perceived needs. Occasionally this may result in aborting further development, thus preserving precious resources.

Summative evaluation, on the other hand, determines how worthwhile a fully developed product is, alone or in comparison with other competing products. Rigorous summative evaluations are regularly performed by organizations like *Consumer Reports* magazine or, say, the Insurance Information Institute.

1. The author's main purpose is to

    (A) point out the superiority of summative evaluation over formative.

    (B) point out the essential role of formative evaluation in product development.

    (C) explain the differences between formative and summative evaluations.

    (D) show the need for product and programmatic evaluation.

    (E) show that an important distinction arose 30 years ago.

2. Which of the following is most likely to be true of formative evaluators?

    (A) They are dispassionate observers involved in the development of the product.

    (B) They enter the process only after the product has been developed.

    (C) They are intimately involved in the developmental process.

    (D) They compare the value of the completed product with that of other similar products.

    (E) They are generally nonprofit.

3. Summative evaluation data would be most useful to

    (A) the chief of development for the product involved.

    (B) the chief purchasing officer of a corporation.

    (C) field researchers.

    (D) the chief engineer for the developing company.

    (E) all of the above more or less equally.

EXPLANATIONS

1. **(C)**
    The topic sentence technique will not work perfectly here, but it can help. The first sentence of paragraph one tells us that an important distinction arose; sentence two informs us that evaluation serves two different functions. Thus we are probably being set up for a comparison/contrast. The phrase "on the other hand" in the first sentence of paragraph two continues this concept. It looks as if (C) will be the correct answer, but let's use elimination to confirm it. Nothing that the author says implies that summative evaluations are superior to formative. Eliminate (A). While (E) is true, the main point is not that a distinction arose, but rather what that distinction is. Although both (B) and (D) are shown to be important, neither alone is the main purpose of the passage.

2. **(C)**
    Formative evaluators help to form and modify programs so (B) is eliminated. Nothing is said about nonprofits, so eliminate (E). They may or may not be dispassionate; often those involved in development take a proprietary interest. Eliminate (A). Summative evaluators, not formative, compare the completed product with others. This leaves (C). Anyone who forms and modifies a product is intimately involved in development.

3. **(B)**
    Since a summative evaluation occurs after a product is "fully developed" and can be used for comparison with other products, it would be most useful to someone involved in purchasing an item (B). It may be of some value to each of the other individuals listed, but the purchasing officer would be especially interested.

READING COMPREHENSION PASSAGE

Passive-aggressive personality disorder has as its essential characteristic covert noncompliance to ordinary performance demands made in social and occupational situations. To a greater extent than in other personality disorders, this pattern may be context dependent, appearing only in certain situations.

Aggressive impulses and motives are expressed by passivity. These represent its primary dynamic and may take the form of inaction, inefficiency, procrastination, or obstructionism. It is an interpersonal disorder, the recognition of which depends on the seemingly unjustified frustration and hostility others feel toward such individuals. By the use of verbal expressions indicating compliance or agreement, the passive-aggressive person conceals his actual noncompliance and the secret sadistic satisfaction he derives from the frustration he thereby causes. This dynamic is distinguished from that associated with masochism, in which self-punitive actions are used to control others or to evoke protective responses from them. It is also distinguished from the ambivalence and indecision of obsessive-compulsive persons, who may appear passive and obstructionistic, but are not motivated by a wish to evoke frustration in others.

1. It can be inferred from the passage that a person having passive-aggressive disorder would be most likely to do which of the following?

    (A) Disagree politely with others and act according to his own desires.

    (B) Smile in agreement but delay in fulfilling a request.

    (C) Evoke masochistic reactions in those with whom he deals.

    (D) Provoke aggression from others to satisfy his own masochistic needs.

    (E) Feel ambivalent toward his superiors.

2. According to the selection…

    (A) sexual pleasure is at the root of PA disorder.

    (B) obsessive-compulsive persons do not engage in covert noncompliance.

    (C) the passive-aggressive person's outward expression is in compliance with his inner feelings.

    (D) sadists punish in order to control others.

    (E) passive-aggressive disorder is more likely to appear in some situations than in others.

3. The author implies about passive-aggressive disorder that

    (A) persons with the disorder are nearly always unable to function in normal life.

    (B) the disorder, though common, is often unrecognized.

    (C) persons with PA disorder may present themselves as victims.

    (D) persons with PA disorder feel a great need for nurturing and protection.

(E) persons with the disorder act in solitary communion with them-selves.

4. Based upon the passage, where would passive-aggressive disorders be most likely to be identified in the largest numbers?

(A) In a primitive and loosely structured society

(B) In the higher levels of a hierarchical society such as the military

(C) In a relatively classless society such as a commune

(D) During the Greco-Roman period of history

(E) In the lower levels of a hierarchical society such as the military

EXPLANATIONS

1. **(B)**
Although the question uses the word **inferred**, this is a borderline question whose answer is fairly explicit. Since surface compliance is a characteristic of PA disorder, (A) cannot be true. Those with whom he deals feel hostility and frustration, not masochism. Eliminate (C). The PA person might provoke aggression, but his needs are not masochistic. Eliminate (D). He may feel ambivalent toward his superiors, but the passage gives us no strong clues that this is so. Discard (E). Since agreement and procrastination are characteristics of the PA person, (B) is the best answer.

2. **(E)**
"According to the selection" means we are dealing with a factual question. Skimming can find the answer.

You may feel that anything sadomasochistic has sexual roots, and you may be right. However, we can only go by the passage, not by any outside knowledge we may have. Since nothing sexual is stated or hinted, eliminate (A). Obsessive-compulsive persons do engage in covert non-compliance (but for different reasons). Discard (B). The passage specifi-cally states the dichotomy between the outward appearance of the PA person and his behavior. This eliminates (C). (D) may well be true, but the passage did not state it. This leaves (E). The passage tells us that the disorder is "context dependent, appearing only in certain situations."

3. **(C)**
First, an answer containing an absolute or near absolute (always, nearly always) is nearly always wrong. Eliminate (A) on this basis as well because PA disorder may appear only in certain situations. (B) could have

some truth, but there is nothing to indicate that the problem is common. (In fact, apparently it is not.) (D) is patently false; they act out of sadistic impulses. (E) is also false in that PA is an "interpersonal dynamic." (C) is correct. Recognition of PA depends on the "seemingly unjustified frustration and hostility others feel toward such individuals," that is, on their apparent victimization.

4.   **(E)**
This type of question asks you to understand the author's point and to carry it one step further. This passage is based on psychological/psychiatric research. It is unlikely that such research was done in primitive societies or in earlier time periods. So, eliminate (A) and (D). Since presumably one could not have risen to the higher ranks of the military by being inefficient, an obstructionist, and a procrastinator, scratch (B). It may be possible to find persons with PA in a commune, but since a properly working commune depends on its members working together and having some affection for each other, it seems unlikely the commune could exist for long if many members caused the frustration and hostility characteristic of PA disorder. This leaves (E). It is very possible that some persons in the lower echelons, resentful of superiors who control many aspects of their lives, might salute smartly, say "Yes, sir," and then proceed in an inefficient, procrastinating, or obstructionist manner. This is especially true since PA appears only in certain situations, perhaps only with certain officers.

ANALOGIES

ETS directions for analogies read:

> **DIRECTIONS:** In each of the following questions, a related pair of words or phrases is followed by five lettered pairs of words or phrases. Select the lettered pair that best expresses a relationship similar to that expressed in the original pair.

Analogy questions test your ability to recognize relationships between words or ideas and to know when these relationships are parallel. The analogy subtest is an area where, with practice, you can achieve a very good score.

First, you must find the relationship between the original pair of words. To help you, listed below are some common types of analogies.

The list contains some overlapping and similarities, and the precise names of the categories need not be memorized. It is important, however, that you learn types of relationships to look for.

SOME COMMON TYPES OF ANALOGIES

PART and WHOLE: sole:shoe

WHOLE and PART: hand:fingers

CLASS and MEMBER: fish:salmon

TYPE OF: debate:argument

DEGREE: cool:frigid

OPPOSITES: tall:short

WORKER and TOOL: photographer:camera

WORKER and WORKPLACE: teacher:classroom

CAUSE and EFFECT (RESULT): poison:death

EFFECT and CAUSE: death:poison

ACTION and THAT WHICH PERFORMS IT: fly:plane

PURPOSE (or OBJECT:ACTION): scissors:cut

INDICATION OF: boo:disapproval

SYNONYMS: canine:dog

STUDY OF: linguistics:language

CHARACTERISTIC OF: dexterity:pianist

DEFINITION: hero:courage (by definition, a hero has courage)

LACK-OF-DEFINITION: coward:courage (by definition, a coward lacks courage)

BEFORE YOU TAKE THE TEST, PRACTICE AS MUCH AS YOU CAN

Advice on how to deal with analogy questions is given below. After you have read it, use the practice tests in this book to help you. Practice is particularly valuable with analogies. You can also create your own analogies using the list of common types given above. Creating your own list has the advantage of forcing you to think analogously.

TIPS FOR THE ANALOGY SECTION

Remember the Reasonable and Inevitable or Valid and Necessary Rule

You should keep in mind that there must be a reasonable and necessary connection between two words.

The connection must be VALID; otherwise there would be no point in making the analogy. For example, what reasonable connection could there be between bird:algebra? On the other hand, there is a reasonable connection between fish:salmon since salmon is a type of fish.

The connection must also be NECESSARY or INEVITABLE. There is a necessary connection between photographer:photo since a photographer by definition takes photos. However, the connection between student:photo is only a possible one since a student may or may not take photos.

All GRE analogies will have connections that are reasonable (logical, valid) AND necessary or inevitable. Any choices that fail to meet these criteria should be rejected. If you cannot figure out the connection between the original pair, you can still improve your chances of picking the correct answer by eliminating any choices that do not conform to the above rule.

Make Up a Sentence

Creating a sentence that shows the connection between the two capitalized words is absolutely essential and is the difference between a high or low mark on analogies.

For example, if the first pair of words is APPLAUSE:APPROVAL, your sentence might be: "Applause is an indication of approval (an indication of analogy)." If the first pair is chisel:sculptor, you might say "A chisel is a tool used by a sculptor to perform his work (a tool:worker analogy)."

Be as Precise as Possible

It is important to make your bridge sentence as precise as possible. In the example below, note how a very general sentence can narrow your choices only slightly while a more precise one can lead you to the correct answer.

Example

MINISTER:SERMON::

(A) politician:promises   (D) lecturer:speech

(B) heckler:interruptions   (E) curator:museum

(C) doctor:diagnosis

For example, we could say:

A minister makes/gives sermons.

A politician makes promises.

A heckler makes interruptions.

A doctor makes a diagnosis.

A lecturer makes a speech.

A curator makes a museum ✓ (eliminate).

These sentences only eliminate (E) and aren't a lot of help. But, if we say: "One of the functions of a minister is to teach through sermons" then we eliminate all choices but (D), that is, "One of the functions of a lecturer is to teach through speeches."

The Parts of Speech Must Match

If the capitalized pair are NOUN:NOUN, then the correct answer must also be noun:noun. If the capitalized pair are NOUN:ADJECTIVE, then the correct answer must be noun:adjective, etc. Most analogies involve nouns or adjectives.

You will find this "part of speech" rule most helpful when a word is used in a way that may be unfamiliar to you. Try this one:

Example

RIFLE:RANSACK::

(A) search:destroy   (D) pontificate:discuss

(B) shoot:kill   (E) elucidate:clarify

(C) speak:orate

Since all the choices here are verbs, "rifle" must also be used as a verb. (B) here is probably misleading, then, since it's based on a gun. If you didn't know what the word "rifle" meant when it is used as a verb, then consider what possible type of analogy we have here. (C) and (D) are roughly synonymous while (E) is a true synonym. Possibly, a synonym is needed, so you guess (E). And you're right: "rifle" does mean to ransack.

Be Alert to Multiple Meanings

Even though the part of speech remains the same (unlike our rifle example), a word may have multiple meanings. What about a school (group) of fish, for example? If you are having difficulty figuring out the analogy, perhaps you are using the wrong definition for one of the words.

The Answer Must Be in the Same Order

Make sure that the capitalized words and the pair you choose are in the same order.

COLLAGE:ARTIST   novel:author   composer:sonata

A collage is a work of art created by an artist.

A novel is a work of literary art created by a novelist.

A composer is NOT a work of musical art created by a sonata.

(The reverse is true: a sonata is a work of musical art created by a composer.)

PRACTICE DRILLS

1. SCULPTOR:BLOWTORCH::

   (A) artist:paint

   (B) writer:word processor

   (C) librettist:songwriter

   (D) physician:stethoscope

   (E) conductor:baton

2. LUMBER:ELEPHANT::

   (A) soar:eagle

   (B) scamper:mice

   (C) circumambulate:hippopotamus

   (D) dive:seal

   (E) waddle:duck

3.   BANALITY:TRITE::

    (A) stereotype:racial   (D) aphorism:apt

    (B) genius:intelligent   (E) hackneyed:cutting

    (C) politician:bromide

4.   PLUMP:OBESE::

    (A) lean:emaciated   (D) narrow:elongated

    (B) adipose:turgid   (E) corpulent:swollen

    (C) large:expanded

5.   ABSTEMIOUS:ASCETIC::

    (A) starving:hungry   (D) unrestrained:libertine

    (B) gourmand:gourmet   (E) beneficent:donor

    (C) dogma:iconoclast

6.   LACONIC:PRATE::

    (A) sagacious:think   (D) authoritative:administer

    (B) ascetic:indulge   (E) inquisitive:inquire

    (C) despot:rule

7.   CULPABLE:CENSURE::

    (A) moral:penance   (D) admirable:judgment

    (B) meritorious:reward   (E) affable:praise

    (C) laughable:abuse

EXPLANATIONS

1.   **(B)**
Remember our reasonable/inevitable rule. The SCULPTOR must use the BLOWTORCH as part of his art. Our sentence could be "A sculptor uses a blowtorch in his work." This would eliminate (C)—a LIBRETTIST does not use a SONGWRITER, but it is not too helpful with the rest. How would a SCULPTOR use a BLOWTORCH? To create his art. This would eliminate (D), but would leave (A), (B), and maybe (E). The SCULPTOR uses the BLOWTORCH as a tool, while the artist uses PAINT as a material,

so cross out (A). A WRITER frequently uses a WORD PROCESSOR as a tool to create his art; although a CONDUCTOR uses a BATON as a tool, he does not create art in the same sense as a sculptor does, so (B) is the best choice. Once again, the more precise your bridge sentence, the more helpful it is.

2. **(E)**
If you wonder what reasonable and inevitable connection LUMBER could have with ELEPHANTS, then you'll begin to think that maybe LUMBER doesn't mean wood in this context. When you look at the choices and discover that the first word in each is a verb, then you realize LUMBER, too, must be a verb and that it must involve motion (since all the other choices do). LUMBER means to move clumsily or heavily. This eliminates (A), (B), and (D). If you don't know what CIRCUMAMBULATE means, remember that AMBULATORY means able to move and that circum means "around" (think circumference). A hippo would LUMBER, but since that is not what CIRCUMAMBULATE means, (C) is not the correct answer. This leaves (E).
What if you had no idea of this meaning for LUMBER? Check the other choices. Except for (C), they involve the kind of motion motion characteristic of a bird or other small, light-footed animal. How do elephants walk? Surely not *gracefully*, which gives you some idea of LUMBER's meaning.

3. **(B)**
This is a "definition" analogy. A BANALITY is by definition trite and unoriginal, so our bridge sentence should state this. Although we often see the words paired, a stereotype need not be racial. Politicians may utter many BROMIDES (platitudes), but a politician is not a BROMIDE and, moreover, we need an adjective in blank 2. This leaves (B), (D), and (E). HACKNEYED does not mean to hack, so cutting is not relevant. (It actually means trite, unoriginal, banal.) An APHORISM is a statement of general truth and should be apt. However, a GENIUS is by definition intelligent, so (B) is the best choice.

4. **(A)**
This is a "degree" analogy. OBESE carries plumpness to an extreme. TURGID (swollen) and ADIPOSE (fatty) do not share this relationship. EXPANDED does not necessarily carry large to an extreme, so (B) and (C) are eliminated. (E) can be eliminated on similar grounds. ELONGATED is not excessively narrow. This leaves (A). EMACIATED is lean to the *nth* degree, as in starving.

5. **(D)**
This is a variant of the "degree" analogy. An ASCETIC is one who is

ABSTEMIOUS (abstains) to a very high degree. HUNGRY doesn't mean a high degree of STARVING—eliminate (A). Neither is there a difference of degree between a gourmand (one who enjoys good food) and gourmet (a connoisseur of fine food). An ICONOCLAST challenges DOGMA. No match here either. In (E), a donor is one who is BENEFICENT, but we do not know to what extent. The correct choice is (D). A LIBERTINE is one who is highly unrestrained sexually or morally.

You should be aware here (as in question 4) that the correct choice can be at the opposite end of the spectrum from the original pair. Keep in mind that you are looking for similar relationships, not for synonyms.

6. **(B)**
   This is a "lack of" or "not characteristic of" analogy. A LACONIC person is one of few words and therefore does not PRATE (babble). Does a SAGACIOUS (wise) person not think? Does a DESPOT not rule? An AUTHORITATIVE person not administer? Or an inquisitive person not INQUIRE? Eliminate all but (B). An ASCETIC person does not INDULGE.

7. **(B)**
   A CULPABLE (guilty) person is deserving of CENSURE (condemnation). Is a MORAL person worthy of PENANCE? Is something laughable worthy of abuse? Is something ADMIRABLE worthy of judgment? No. This leaves (B) and (E). Is someone AFFABLE (warm and friendly) deserving of PRAISE? Perhaps. But (B) is a better choice. Something MERITORIOUS merits some sort of a reward even more than someone AFFABLE merits PRAISE.

ANTONYMS

ETS directions for this section read as follows:

DIRECTIONS: Each question below consists of a word printed in capital letters, followed by five lettered words or phrases. Choose the lettered word or phrase that is most nearly opposite in meaning to the word in capital letters. Since some of the questions require you to distinguish fine shades of meaning, be sure to consider all the choices before deciding which one is best.

An antonym is opposite in meaning to a given word. ETS chooses antonyms rather than synonyms because antonym questions require you to reason "from a given concept to its opposite." Words selected for this section are nouns, verbs, or adjectives.

PREPARE BEFORE THE TEST

Antonym choices often require you to make fine distinctions between words so a large vocabulary is a major asset. Vocabulary development is an incremental process; the more time you spend on it, the better the results. A knowledge of word roots, prefixes, and suffixes can make vocabulary improvement more efficient by showing you similarities between word families. See list on page 125. Refresh your memory regarding any foreign language you may know since many words in English have foreign origins. Because a word may be used as a noun in one sentence and as a verb (with a different meaning) in another, you should also learn the parts of speech of each word.

Simply memorizing word lists is of limited usefulness. For a word to be firmly fixed in your memory, you need to use it many times, both orally and in writing. Nothing makes the meaning of a word more clear to you than using it in a sentence.

TIPS FOR THE ANTONYM SECTION

Make Up Your Own Antonym

Make up an antonym of your own for the given word. Then look among the choices for a word with a similar meaning. For example, FRENETIC means frantic or frenzied. An antonym would have to mean calm, easygoing, lethargic.

FRENETIC:

    (A) impervious   (D) taciturn

    (B) frenzied   (E) imperturbable

    (C) hyperactive

Of the choices, FRENZIED and HYPERACTIVE clearly are not correct. TACITURN means "inclined to speak very little"; IMPERVIOUS is "incapable of being influenced." Both are different from FRENETIC, but neither means calm. This leaves IMPERTURBABLE, meaning calm, not easily excited.

Be Sure the Parts of Speech Match

The answer will always be the same part of speech as the capitalized word. The antonym for a noun will always be a noun; the antonym for a verb will always be a verb. Try this example:

QUARTER:

> (A) imbibe   (D) eliminate
>
> (B) house   (E) defund
>
> (C) unite

All the choices given are verbs; therefore, QUARTER must also be used here as a verb. (Yes, HOUSE is a verb as in "to house the homeless.") Since QUARTER means to divide, our choice here would be (C), UNITE. HOUSE could easily have misled us if we were thinking about quartering (housing) soldiers. But, of course, HOUSE would then have to have been a synonym, not an antonym.

Always keep in mind that English words often have multiple meanings even when the part of speech remains the same. Read the example below carefully to see what meaning is needed.

PRIDE:

> (A) one   (D) arrogance
>
> (B) magistrate   (E) self-esteem
>
> (C) immodesty

If this question caused you difficulty, think of a pride of lions (a group). The answer would be (A), ONE.

Look for the Most Nearly Opposite Word

Because not all words have clear opposites (what's the opposite of apple?), you can eliminate from the choices any word that lacks an opposite.

With antonym questions, pick the word that is most nearly opposite to the capitalized word. You may feel that none of the choices are very good, but you can only select from the words given to you. When no answer seems satisfactory, or when several seem possible, you may need a more precise or different definition of the word. ETS has chosen the words carefully; you can be sure that there is an appropriate answer to the question.

Use Word Parts and Foreign Languages to Help You

If you meet an unfamiliar word, look at its parts for clues. Knowing that mal- means bad may help you to figure out maladroit (unskillful). Familiarity with a foreign language can sometimes give you a clue to the meaning of an unfamiliar word. For example, if you know that in Spanish "cantar" means "to sing," you can guess correctly when you meet the English words **canticle** (a song or hymn), or **cantilate** (to chant).

You Know More than You Think You Know

Suppose you were unfamiliar with the word inerrant. You know that "in" means not; "err" refers to wandering (usually from the truth). Inerrant means not wandering from the truth, i.e., free from error.

You needn't be a Latin scholar to know these word parts. You know "err" not only from the word itself, but also from "error." Many words can be deciphered in similar fashion. For example, you know from geometry that "circum" means around so you can figure out **circumambulate** (walking in circles) and **circumlocution** (talking around the point).

Look at the Pattern of the Choices

If you have no idea of the meaning of the word, look at the choices to see if you can find a pattern. If three of the choices seem to indicate dryness, then maybe the given word means wet. This is not foolproof, but may help (in combination with other techniques) if you are totally at a loss.

Use All the Strategies

Success lies in using ALL of the tips we've given you. Each makes a contribution toward finding the correct answer. Used together, they can make the difference between a low score or a high one.

Trust Yourself

After you have followed all of the tips given, have faith in yourself. If you don't know a word, you may at least know what it is NOT. If you're not sure of *salubrious* (promoting health) you probably at least know that you've never heard of it in connection with **dissonant** (inharmonious) or **truculent** (excessively hostile). You can then use the elimination strategy.

PRACTICE DRILLS

1. AMELIORATE:

    (A) decline   (D) arrest

    (B) pause   (E) amputate

    (C) aggravate

2. CLOYING:

(A) bland

(B) flattering

(C) saccharine

(E) acerbic

(D) boring

3. EUPHONY:

(A) eulogy

(D) verbosity

(B) cacophony

(E) brevity

(C) lethargy

4. EPHEMERAL:

(A) constant

(D) brief

(B) perennial

(E) durable

(C) eternal

5. COGENT:

(A) lucid

(D) inerrant

(B) pedagogical

(E) inane

(C) abstruse

6. DEARTH:

(A) sufficiency

(D) parsimony

(B) paucity

(E) cornucopia

(C) voluminous

7. CONTUMACIOUS:

(A) obdurate

(D) malleable

(B) sinuous

(E) spurious

(C) facetious

8. LACONIC:

   (A) terse   (D) open

   (B) taciturn   (E) glib

   (C) loquacious

9. ENCOMIUM:

   (A) aphorism   (D) diatribe

   (B) epitaph   (E) emendation

   (C) euphemism

10. DESICCATE:

   (A) wet   (D) immerse

   (B) humidify   (E) dehydrate

   (C) baptize

EXPLANATIONS

1. **(C)**

   AMELIORATE means to improve or make better. We need a word that makes things worse. PAUSE (B) and ARREST (D) are not what we're looking for. An amputation might make things worse, but it also might be necessary and actually save a life, so eliminate (E). This leaves (A) and (C). DECLINE means to deteriorate and could be appropriate, but (C) is a better choice since AGGRAVATE means to make things worse.

2. **(E)**

   CLOYING means "too sweet or excessively flattering." (B) and (C) are synonyms for cloying. (A) and (D), BLAND and BORING, are not good choices either. Choose (E), ACERBIC, meaning "sour or bitter in taste or manner."

3. **(B)**

   If you had no idea of the meaning of EUPHONY or CACOPHONY, you still might guess that cacophony was your answer, just by the similar endings of the two words. If you also realized that symphony and telephone both have to do with sound, you would guess that "phon" must mean sound. EUPHONY means a pleasing combination of sounds. Its opposite is CACOPHONY, a mixture of harsh and discordant sounds. A EULOGY is a speech of praise, normally for the dead. It cannot be an antonym for EUPHONY, nor can any of the other choices.

4. **(C)**

EPHEMERAL tends to appear on GRE exams. It means very short-lived or transitory so we need a word meaning long-lived. DURABLE meets this criterion and so does PERENNIAL (reappearing each year). CONSTANT has some appeal, but ETERNAL (C) is more of an opposite to ephemeral than any of these and is the correct choice.

5. **(C)**

COGENT means clear and to the point as in a "cogent and convincing argument." LUCID is more of a synonym than an antonym; INERRANT (without error) and PEDAGOGICAL (scholarly and boring) are not antonyms either. INANE (silly and senseless) is a possibility, but ABSTRUSE (hard to understand) is best. Choose (C).

6. **(E)**

DEARTH is "a lack of something." PAUCITY is a synonym and therefore incorrect. PARSIMONY means "excessive frugality" and does not meet our needs. VOLUMINOUS ("large and spacious") is an adjective, and we need a noun. SUFFICIENCY is at the other end of the spectrum from dearth and might seem appropriate, but CORNUCOPIA ("an endless supply") is more nearly opposite in meaning to dearth. Choose (E).

7. **(D)**

Here is a good opportunity to use the strategy of elimination! If CONTUMACIOUS is unfamiliar to you, you may know SINUOUS, FACETIOUS, and SPURIOUS and have never heard of them in connection with contumacious. That leaves OBDURATE (stubborn, unbending) and MALLEABLE (easy to shape or bend). They are opposites of each other so probably one is a synonym of contumacious and the other an antonym. This is a time to guess; the odds are 50–50. If you choose malleable, you'd be correct. Contumacious is "stubbornly rebellious or disobedient."

8. **(C)**

LACONIC means "sparing of words," so TERSE and TACITURN are basically synonyms. Reject (A) and (B). A laconic person is presumably not very open, so we cannot summarily reject OPEN. Similarly we cannot reject GLIB, meaning smooth talking. However, (C), LOQUA-CIOUS (talking excessively), is the best choice.

9. **(D)**

Probably the best strategy here, if you don't know the word, is elimination. Somehow, ENCOMIUM has a "nice" sound to it, as though it's a *com*pliment (perhaps it makes us think of *com*rade, *com*passion, *com*ity). When you are at a loss and no other strategy helps, you must rely on your impressions. If we are right, then "nice" words like EUPHEMISM (a nice way of saying something that's not so nice) and EPITAPH (a statement about a deceased person which epitomizes his or her life) can be eliminated. EMENDATION could sound like a commendation (it isn't) or an amendment or correction (which it is). In neither case would it be the antonym we need. That leaves APHORISM (a terse statement of a general truth) or DIATRIBE (bitter, harsh criticism). Since the dictionary defines encomium as "expression of high praise," diatribe is the antonym we need. Choose (D).

10. **(A)**

All the choices given seem to involve water in some way (DEHYDRATE, of course, means to remove water) so even if you don't know the meaning of DESICCATE, you assume that it has something to do with dryness. If we guess that desiccate means "to dry out thoroughly" (as it does), then WET is more nearly opposite in meaning than HUMIDIFY. IMMERSE probably involves water, but need not. BAPTIZE may involve only a few drops of water or total immersion. The best choice is (A).

BUILD YOUR VOCABULARY USING WORD COMPONENTS

START WITH WHAT YOU ALREADY KNOW

To expand your vocabulary in a systematic way, learn prefixes and suffixes.

Take a word component you are already familiar with and use it to help you learn new words. From words like telephone, saxophone, xylophone, symphony, and phonics, you know that "phon" must mean sound. Building on this you can learn words like "cacophony" and "euphony."

If you know any foreign languages, use them to help you. Many English words are taken from other languages.

USE OUR COMPONENTS LIST

Check the components list on page 125. Each component includes a list of words constructed from it. Familiarize yourself with these. Practice word association by using familiar words to help you remember the meaning of their components. For example, by remembering that a polygon is a many-sided figure, you can move on to "polymorphous" ("having or assuming many forms or shapes"), "polychromatic" ("having many colors"), "polydemic" ("native to many countries"), or "polytonality" (in music "the use of more than one key at the same time").

The flashcard approach we outlined on page 89 can work as well for components as for whole words.

LEARN WORDS IN GROUPS

Take one or two prefixes (or other components) at a time. Learn them and words formed from them. If you have more time, look up more words in the dictionary, and learn them also.

Learn words in groups of synonyms. Take a basic concept, and try to learn as many words as you can that express this concept. If you look up stubborn in a thesaurus, for example, you'll get a list of words including "pertinacious," "contumacious," "obdurate," "indocile," "obstreperous," and "incorrigible." Not all of them may be true synonyms of stubborn, but all share a common core of meaning.

USE ALL OF YOUR SENSES

You learn much better when you use all of your senses; so read, write, say, and hear each word.

MAKE UP A SENTENCE

Write sentences for each word, working in word groups (those with similar components or meanings).

PRACTICE WITH YOUR FRIENDS

Use the words in your everyday vocabulary. Use your friends as a sounding board to help you. Parents and other loved ones are fair game.

KNOW WHEN TO QUIT

You cannot learn every word and every component in the English language. We have listed the most useful or common components and have given you words from previous GRE exams. Learn these as well as you can, then relax.

GRE VOCABULARY WORD COMPONENTS

a-	without	amoral—without morals atheist—one who doesn't believe in God
ab- abs-	away from separation	abhor—to turn away from; loathe abjure—to swear away; renounce aberrant—deviating from the norm
ambi-	both	ambiguous—uncertain in meaning ambivalent—both attracted and repelled simultaneously ambidextrous—equally skillful with each hand
ante-	before	antediluvian—before the flood antebellum—before the war antecede—to go before antecedent—that which went before
anti-	against	antithesis—a contrast of ideas antipathy—strong feeling of dislike
aud-	hear listen	auditory—relating to hearing audient—listening or paying attention
bi-	two	bipedal—having two feet biennial—occurring every two years bimanual—done with two hands
circum-	around	circumnavigate—to fly/sail around circumlocution—talk that is not to the point, roundabout talk circumscribe—to draw a line around; restrict circumspect—prudent; looking around carefully

di-	two	dichromatic—having two colors
	double	dichotomy—separation into two parts
		dilemma—choice between two undesirable alternatives

il-, im-, in-, ir-	not	implacable—not to be appeased
		inarticulate—not able to express oneself
		inclement—not mild (said of weather)
		illicit—not legal
		inchoate—not organized; unformed
		inert—not active
		inept—not competent
		irrevocable—not able to be revoked
		insatiable—not able to be satisfied
		intransigent—not flexible; not able to be swayed, stubborn

luc, lum lun, lus	light	lucent—giving light; shining
		lumen—a unit of light
		luminary—one who shines in a profession
		luminescence—brightness
		luminous—full of light; lustrous
		elucidate—to make clear (bring the light)

mal- male-	bad	maladroit—unskillful
		malevolent—evil
		malapropos—inappropriate
		malfeasance—evil conduct
		malediction—a curse
		malodorous—having a bad odor
		malefactor—an evildoer

mis-	wrong bad hate	misanthrope—hater of mankind
		misogynist—hater of women
		misnomer—the wrong name
		miscreant—an evildoer
		miscast—badly cast

mono-	one	monotone—one unvaried pitch
		monochromatic—having only one color
		monogamy—practice of having only one wife
		monogyny—system permitting only one wife

nat	to be born	natal—relating to birth
nasc	spring forth	innate—inborn
		renascent—reborn
		nascent—being born; developing
omni-	all	omniscient—all knowing
		omnivorous—eating or taking in everything
		omnifarious—of all sorts (varieties)
		omnipotent—all powerful
pan-	all	panacea—a cure for all ills
		pandemic—referring to all peoples
phil-	love	philanderer—man who loves without serious intentions
		philogynist—lover of women
		philologist—student, lover of languages
poly-	many	polymorphic—having many forms
		polyglot—knowing/having many languages
		polygamy—practice of having many wives
		polygon—a many sided figure (geometry)
post-	after	posthumous—after death
	behind	postern—situated in the back
	following	posterity—descendents; those who come after
		posterior—later in time
		postprandial—after the meal
prim-	first	primacy—state of being first in rank
prime-		primal—first, original
		primate—a religious figure who is first in rank
		primogenitor—the earliest ancestor
		primordial—elemental; fundamental
		primogeniture—state of being the first born
pro-	forward	prolix—drawn out; needlessly prolonged
	forth	prolific—fruitful; bringing forth young or fruit
		proliferate—to produce by multiplication of parts
ridi	laughter	ridicule—to mock or laugh at
risi, ri		risible—disposed to laugh
		derision—mocking laughter
		deride—to make fun of

se-	apart away	secede—to separate from seclude—to keep away sequester—to separate from segregate—to separate
sub-	under beneath	subcutaneous—under the skin subterfuge—deception, underhanded evasion subaltern—one below another in rank
un-	not	unalloyed—pure, not mixed unabridged—not shortened
-al	relating to suitable to	theatrical—relating to theater hysterical—relating to hysteria cerebral—relating to the brain nocturnal—relating to night infernal—relating to hell
-ic	or, like	endemic—native to a particular country or people galactic—relating to the galaxy
-ious	full of	pugnacious—full of fight vivacious—full of life rapacious—full of greed malicious—full of evil
-ive	causing	cohesive—making things stick together conjunctive—causing union evocative—causing an image
-tude	state of, condition of	pulchritude—state of possessing beauty rectitude—state of righteousness
-y	full of, state of being	wily—full of tricks wary—watchful

VOCABULARY QUIZ #1

Write the word next to its definition.

ABERRANT   ABSTEMIOUS   COGENT
COMPLIANT   CODA   DISSONANCE
ENERVATE   OBVIATE   OSSIFY
PARADIGM

1. _paradigm_ model; example; pattern   *100%*

2. _abstemious_ sparing in eating or drinking

3. _compliant_ obedient; easily managed

4. _ossify_ change or harden into bone

5. _aberrant_ abnormal or deviant

6. _coda_ the concluding section of a musical or literary composition

7. _cogent_ convincing

8. _obviate_ make unnecessary; to get rid of

9. _dissonance_ discord; lack of musical agreement

10. _enervate_ to weaken

VOCABULARY QUIZ #2

Write the word next to its definition.

ATTENUATE   ASSIDUOUS   BANAL
DESICCATE   DIFFIDENCE   EXTEMPORANEOUS
FACETIOUS   INTRANSIGENCE   LACONIC
PREVARICATE

1. _____ to dry up

2. _____ humorous; jocular

3. _____ diligent

4. _____ trite; commonplace

5. _____ unprepared; off the cuff

6. _____ state of stubborn unwillingness to compromise

7. _____ to lie

8. _____ make thin; weaken

9. _____ shyness

10. _____ terse; using few words

VOCABULARY QUIZ #3

Write the word next to its definition.

ASSUAGE   CACOPHONY   DICHOTOMY
DIFFUSION   DISCRETE   EXTRAPOLATION
GAINSAY   INTRACTABLE   PRISTINE
QUIESCENT

1. _____ primitive; unspoiled; having its original purity

2. _____ branching into two parts; division into two mutually exclusive groups

3. _____ wordiness; spreading in all directions like a gas

4. _____ projection; conjecture; from what is known to infer what is not known

5. _____ unruly; stubborn; obstinate; not docile

6. _____ ease; lessen (pain)

7. _____ separate and distinct

8. _____ at rest; dormant

9. _____ deny

10. _____ harsh noise

VOCABULARY QUIZ #4

Write the word next to its definition.

ASCETIC   BURGEON   DERISION
DISINTERESTED   DISPARATE   EPHEMERAL
EULOGY   GARRULITY   INGENUOUS
MALLEABLE

1. _____ capable of being shaped or formed

2. _____ basically different; unrelated

3. _____ to grow quickly; to sprout

4. _____ talkativeness

5. _____ neutral; impartial

6. _____ ridicule

7. _____ short-lived; fleeting

8. _____ naive; young; unsophisticated

9. _____ austere; practicing self-denial

10. _____ praise; often for the dead

ANSWERS TO QUIZ #1: 1. paradigm 2. abstemious 3. compliant 4. ossify 5. aberrant 6. coda 7. cogent 8. obviate 9. dissonance 10. enervate

ANSWERS TO QUIZ #2: 1. desiccate 2. facetious 3. assiduous 4. banal 5. extemporaneous 6. intransigence 7. prevaricate 8. attenuate 9. diffidence 10. laconic

ANSWERS TO QUIZ #3: 1. pristine 2. dichotomy 3. diffusion 4. extrapolation 5. intractable 6. assuage 7. discrete 8. quiescent 9. gainsay 10. cacophony

ANSWERS TO QUIZ #4: 1. malleable 2. disparate 3. burgeon 4. garrulity 5. disinterested 6. derision 7. ephemeral 8. ingenuous 9. ascetic 10. eulogy

QUIZ #5

Fill in the blanks in the sentences using the words from Practice Drills 1 through 4.

1. The _____ national debt forced the president and Congress finally to take action before the debt grew so large that it overwhelmed us.

2. The school assembly was filled with discord. The fire alarm rang, one band played "Dixie" while another played "The Battle Hymn of the Republic." Dozens of children screamed at each other in several languages while teachers shouted at them to be quiet. It was a moment of pure _____ at P.S. 90.

3. The dispute between the next-door neighbors became so bitter that others on the block urged them to take their disagreement to a _____ arbiter, a third party with no axe to grind, who might help them solve their problem.

4. She's the star of TV's top-rated sitcom, has appeared on the big screen in a string of three box-office smashes, and just inked a $20 million recording contract to boot. Yet she keeps a level head about it all, knowing that fame is _____.

5. His _____ seemed endless. He just talked and talked and talked and talked and talked and....

6. In the hot, dry desert air, the cut flowers eventually became completely _____. Their fragile beauty was perfectly preserved.

7. She was a Gemini, and there was a real _____ between the two sides of her personality. One side was fun loving and sweet tempered; the other was very hard working and somewhat tense.

8. Jack tried to estimate the height of the house by making an _____ from the height of the garage, which he knew was 15 feet high.

9. He was very _____ in preparing the report. He worked nights and weekends for weeks, checking and double-checking everything.

10. He had a very _____ manner. He constantly kidded around, and it was hard to get him to be serious.

11. At the banquet she was suddenly called upon to make an _____ speech. She was so surprised by the request that all she could say was, "Thanks for everything."

12. The child was so _____ that the teacher could do nothing with him. He was very stubborn and would not cooperate in any way.

13. Her _____ was so great that she never went to parties because she was afraid to meet new people.

14. Steven had a tendency to _____ . Even though his father was a shoe salesman, Steve told his classmates stories about his royal ancestry and weekends spent at luxurious country estates.

15. Looking at the littered beach and garbage-filled water, Joe longed for the _____ beach before the settlers arrived to spoil it.

ANSWERS TO QUIZ #5: 1. burgeoning 2. cacophony 3. disinterested 4. ephemeral 5. garrulity 6. desiccated 7. dichotomy 8. extrapolation 9. assiduous 10. facetious 11. extemporaneous 12. intractable 13. diffidence 14. prevaricate 15. pristine

OFTEN-CONFUSED WORDS

Uninterested—Disinterested

UNINTERESTED—not caring; apathetic; having no interest in.

He was uninterested in politics.

DISINTERESTED—neutral; impartial.

A disinterested person may be very interested in something, but he's unbiased.

A judge should be disinterested, but he should be interested in how properly the case is handled.

Note: Disinterested can also mean "uninterested." Check the context carefully to see which meaning is being used.

Discreet—Discrete

DISCREET—showing good judgment in our conduct; being prudent in our behavior.

We confided our secret in Mary because we knew she'd be discreet.

DISCRETE—separate and distinct.

This,.................., is a discrete line of dots, each separate and distinct.

Incredulous—Incredible

INCREDULOUS—skeptical, not believing.

When she told me that Martians had landed in Bensonhurst, I was incredulous.

INCREDIBLE—too extraordinary to be believed (but it can be true).

We heard an incredible tale of heroism in the jungle.

Ingenious—Ingenuous

INGENIOUS—very smart or brilliant.

His ingenious idea made it possible to double production at no additional cost.

INGENUOUS—having a frank and open nature.

An ingenuous person tends to be naive and trusting.

Apposite—Opposite

APPOSITE—apt, pertinent, appropriate.

As we watched the news of gang warfare, Nancy's remark that youth is wasted on the young seemed very apposite.

OPPOSITE—set over against, facing.

We were on opposite sides of the fence.

Illusive—Allusive

ILLUSIVE—from *illusion*; it means unreal, deceiving.

It was as illusive as a mirage.

ALLUSIVE—from *allude* (to refer to in an indirect way, to hint or suggest) and means containing an allusion or reference (often literary) to something else.

His speech, filled with hints of political corruption and scandal, was highly allusive of a bygone era.

Complacent—Complaisant

COMPLACENT—self-satisfied.

He was so complacent and content with the situation that he was sure he'd win without effort.

COMPLAISANT—eager to please, obliging.

He had such a complaisant nature that he'd give you the shirt off his back.

HIGH-FREQUENCY GRE VOCABULARY WORDS

aberrant	adj.	abnormal; straying from the normal or usual path
abstemious	adj.	sparing in use of food or drinks
acerbic	adj.	sour or bitter in taste or manner
alacrity	n.	cheerful promptness or speed
allude	v.	to refer indirectly to something
allusion	n.	an indirect reference (often literary); a hint
altruism	n.	unselfish devotion to the welfare of others rather than self
amalgam	n.	a mixture or combination (often of metals)
amalgamate	v.	to mix, merge, combine
ameliorate	v.	to improve or make better
anachronism	n.	something out of place in time (e.g., an airplane in 1492)

anomaly	n.	an oddity, inconsistency; a deviation from the norm
antipathy	n.	a natural dislike or repugnance
apposite	adj.	suitable; apt; relevant
arcane	adj.	obscure; secret; mysterious
archetype	n.	the first model from which others are copied; prototype
arduous	adj.	laborious, difficult; strenuous
arid	adj.	extremely dry, parched; barren, unimaginative
articulate	adj.	clear, distinct; expressed with clarity; skillful with words
articulate	v.	to utter clearly and distinctly
ascetic	n.	one who leads a simple life of self-denial
ascetic	adj.	rigorously abstinent
aseptic	adj.	germ free
aspersion	n.	slanderous statement; a damaging or derogatory criticism
assiduous	adj.	carefully attentive; industrious
assuage	v.	to relieve; ease; make less severe
astringent	n.	a substance that contracts bodily tissues
astringent	adj.	causing contraction; tightening; stern, austere
atrophy	v.	to waste away, as from lack of use; to wither
attenuate	v.	to make thin or slender; to weaken or dilute
autocracy	n.	an absolute monarchy; government where one person holds power
autocrat	n.	an absolute ruler
baleful	adj.	harmful, malign, detrimental
banal	adj.	trite; without freshness or originality

beneficent	adj.	conferring benefits; kindly; doing good
bilateral	adj.	pertaining to or affecting both sides or two sides; having two sides
bombast	n.	pompous speech; pretentious words
burgeon	v.	to grow or develop quickly
cacophony	n.	a harsh, inharmonious collection of sounds; dissonance
cant	n.	insincere or hypocritical statements of high ideals; the jargon of a particular group or occupation
caprice	n.	a sudden, unpredictable, or whimsical change
catharsis	n.	a purging or relieving of the body or soul
chicanery	n.	trickery or deception
churlishness	n.	crude or surly behavior; behavior of a peasant
circumlocution	n.	a roundabout or indirect way of speaking; not to the point
cloture	n.	a parliamentary procedure to end debate and begin to vote
cloying	adj.	too sugary; too sentimental or flattering
coda	n.	in music, a concluding passage
codify	v.	to organize laws or rules into a systematic collection (code)
cogent	adj.	to the point; clear; convincing in its clarity and presentation
cogitate	v.	to think hard; ponder, meditate
cognitive	adj.	possessing the power to think or meditate; meditative; capable of perception
cognizant	adj.	aware of; perceptive
coherent	adj.	sticking together; connected; logical; consistent

cohesion	n.	the act of sticking together
comeliness	n.	beauty; attractiveness in appearance or behavior
commodious	adj.	spacious and convenient; roomy
complaisance	n.	the quality of being agreeable or eager to please
compliant	adj.	complying; obeying; yielding
connotative	adj.	containing associated meanings in addition to the primary one
constrain	v.	to force, compel; to restrain
contentious	adj.	quarrelsome
contiguous	adj.	touching; or adjoining and close, but not touching
contravene	v.	to act contrary to; to oppose or contradict
conundrum	n.	a puzzle or riddle
converge	v.	to move toward one point (opposite: diverge)
coterie	n.	a clique; a group who meet frequently, usually socially
crass	adj.	stupid, unrefined; gross
debacle	n.	disaster; collapse; a rout
debilitate	v.	to enfeeble; to wear out
decorous	adj.	suitable; proper; seemly
deleterious	adj.	harmful; hurtful; noxious
denigrate	v.	to defame, to blacken or sully; to belittle
deprecate	v.	to express disapproval of; to protest against
deride	v.	to laugh at with contempt; to mock
derision	n.	the act of mocking; ridicule, mockery
diatribe	n.	a bitter or abusive speech
dichotomy	n.	a division into two parts

diffident	adj.	timid; lacking self-confidence
diffuse	adj.	spread out; verbose (wordy); not focused
discourse	v.	to converse; to communicate in orderly fashion
discrete	adj.	separate; individually distinct; composed of distinct parts
disingenuous	adj.	not frank or candid; deceivingly simple (opposite: ingenuous)
disinterested	adj.	neutral; unbiased (alternate meaning: uninterested)
disparate	adj.	unequal, dissimilar; different
disputatious	adj.	argumentative; inclined to disputes
dissemble	v.	to pretend; to feign; to conceal by pretense
dissonance	n.	musical discord; a mingling of inharmonious sounds; nonmusically, disagreement, lack of harmony
dissonant	adj.	not in harmony; in disagreement
ebullience	n.	an overflowing of high spirits; effervescence
ellipsis	n.	omission of words that would make the meaning clear
elucidate	v.	to make clear; to explain
emollient	adj.	softening or soothing to the skin; having power to soften or relax living tissues
encomium	n.	high praise
endemic	adj.	native to a particular area or people
enervate	v.	to weaken; to deprive of nerve or strength
engender	v.	to bring about; beget; to bring forth
ephemeral	adj.	very short-lived; lasting only a short time
eulogy	n.	words of praise, especially for the dead
evanescent	adj.	vanishing quickly; dissipating like a vapor
exigent	adj.	requiring immediate action; urgent, pressing

extemporize	v.	to improvise; to make it up as you go along
extrapolate	v.	to estimate the value of something beyond the scale; to infer what is unknown from something known
facetious	adj.	joking in an awkward or improper manner
feign	v.	pretend
gainsay	v.	to speak against; to contradict; to deny
garrulous	adj.	extremely talkative or wordy
iconoclast	n.	one who smashes revered images; an attacker of cherished beliefs
impassive	adj.	showing no emotion
imperturbable	adj.	calm; not easily excited
impervious	adj.	impenetrable; not allowing anything to pass through; unaffected
implacable	adj.	unwilling to be pacified or appeased
impugn	v.	to attack with words; to question the truthfulness or integrity
inchoate	adj.	not yet fully formed; rudimentary
incisive	adj.	getting to the heart of things; to the point
incredulous	adj.	skeptical
indigenous	adj.	native to a region; inborn or innate
inept	adj.	incompetent; clumsy
inert	adj.	not reacting chemically; inactive
ingenuous	adj.	noble; honorable; candid; also, naive
inherent	adj.	part of the essential character; intrinsic
insipid	adj.	uninteresting, boring, flat, dull
intractable	adj.	stubborn, obstinate; not easily taught or disciplined
intransigent	adj.	uncompromising
intrepid	adj.	fearless, bold

irascible	adj.	prone to anger
laconic	adj.	sparing of words; terse, pithy
loquacious	adj.	very talkative; garrulous
luminous	adj.	emitting light; shining; also enlightened or intelligent
macerate	v.	to soften by steeping in liquid (including stomach juices)
maculate	adj.	spotted, blotched; hence defiled, impure (opposite: immaculate)
maculate	v.	to stain, spot, defile
magnanimity	n.	a quality of nobleness of mind, disdaining meanness or revenge
malevolent	adj.	wishing evil (opposite: benevolent)
malign	v.	to speak evil of
malign	adj.	having an evil disposition toward others (opposite: benign)
malleable	adj.	easy to shape or bend
misanthrope	n.	a hater of mankind
obdurate	adj.	stubborn
obsequious	adj.	servilely attentive; fawning
obviate	v.	to make unnecessary
ossify	v.	to turn to bone; to harden
palpable	adj.	touchable; clear, obvious
panegyric	n.	high praise
paradigm	n.	model, prototype; pattern
paradox	n.	a tenet seemingly contradictory or false, but actually true
parsimonious	adj.	very frugal; unwilling to spend
pedantic	adj.	emphasizing minutiae or form in scholarship or teaching
penurious	adj.	stingy, miserly

perfunctory	adj.	done in a routine, mechanical way, without interest
petulant	adj.	peevish; cranky; rude
placate	v.	to appease or pacify
plethora	n.	a superabundance
prevaricate	v.	to speak equivocally or evasively, i.e., to lie
pristine	adj.	primitive, pure, uncorrupted
propensity	n.	an inclination; a natural tendency toward; a liking for
putrefaction	n.	a smelly mass that is the decomposition of organic matter
putrefy	v.	to decompose; to rot
quiescence	n.	state of being at rest or without motion
rancor	n.	strong ill will; enmity
recalcitrant	adj.	stubbornly rebellious
recondite	adj.	hard to understand; concealed; characterized by profound scholarship
redundant	adj.	superfluous; exceeding what is needed
sagacious	adj.	wise
salubrious	adj.	promoting good health
sinuous	adj.	full of curves; twisting and turning
specious	adj.	plausible, but deceptive; apparently, but not actually, true
spurious	adj.	not genuine, false; bogus
squalid	adj.	filthy; wretched (from squalor)
subjugate	v.	to dominate or enslave
sycophant	n.	a flatterer of important people
taciturn	adj.	inclined to silence; speaking little; dour, stern
tenuous	adj.	thin, slim, delicate; weak

tortuous	adj.	full of twists and turns; not straightforward; possibly deceitful
tractable	adj.	easily managed (opposite: intractable)
truculent	adj.	fierce, savage, cruel
ubiquitous	adj.	omnipresent; present everywhere
vacuous	adj.	dull, stupid; empty-headed
viscous	adj.	thick and sticky (said of fluids)
welter	n.	a confused mass; turmoil

Graduate Record Examination

CHAPTER 4:
Analytical
Writing
Review

CHAPTER 4

ANALYTICAL WRITING REVIEW

OVERVIEW OF THE ANALYTICAL WRITING SECTION

In June 2001, the GRE Board decided to change the format of the GRE General Test. Instead of a section that tests your logic reasoning ability, there is now the Analytical Writing section. This measure will reveal new and different information about you. It tests two skills essential for graduate work: critical thinking and coherent writing. Instead of selecting a multiple-choice answer, you have the opportunity to develop your own response. Your performance on this section of the test can highlight academic strengths that cannot be captured in the other two sections of the GRE. Moreover, you should recognize that it's there because graduate schools make no bones about the centrality of this skill to success in their programs.

This section has two parts:

1) **"Present Your Perspective on an Issue":** A 45-minute task that states an opinion on a general issue and asks you to address the issue from any perspective, provided that you present relevant examples and reasons to explain and support your views.

2) **"Analyze an Argument":** A 30-minute task that requires you to critique an argument by discussing how well reasoned you find it. Instead of agreeing or disagreeing with it, examine if the argument is sound or not.

PREPARING FOR THE WRITING ASSIGNMENT

Writing under pressure can be frustrating, but if you study this review, practice and polish your essay skills, and have a realistic sense of what to expect, you can turn problems into possibilities. The following review will show you how to plan and write a logical, coherent, and interesting essay.

A Six-Point Plan for Success

There's a lot you can do to make the Analytical Writing section easier long before you check your travel route to the test center. Here are six specific strategies to get you in gear:

1. Don't get caught in a blind alley: the pool of computer prompts is completely knowable beforehand. All of the more than 100 topics that have been developed for each writing task are readily available in lists published by ETS and the Graduate Record Examinations Board. You can also find them online. For the "Issue" section, you will be able to pick one out of two essay topics randomly selected by the computer. The "Argument" section does not offer a choice; the computer will select just one random topic to which you will be required to respond.

2. Decide beforehand whether you will type or hand-write your essay. If you want to type your essay, focus on your typing skills. You should aim for a reasonable combination of speed and accuracy so you won't need extra time correcting typos. There won't be spell or grammar checks available on the computers at the test center.

3. You should spend five to 10 minutes to collect and outline your thoughts rather than trying to plan while you write. Lack of thought and development are among the most frequent problems according to test administrators. Pre-planning your essay will help you stay focused.

4. Don't overload your essays with too many ideas, and be sure to develop each concept thoroughly and clearly.

5. Don't let good ideas be undermined by poor transitions. For example, you might want to present your argument and then examine anotherpoint of view. Transitions like "conversely" and "on the other hand" will lend a smoothness and coherence to your prose. Likewise, if you're pointing to a result or effect, transitions like "consequently" or "thus" will help you state your case. Use them with care and precision, and you'll boost your score.

6. Set aside five minutes at the end to copy-edit and proofread your work. Avoiding misspellings and incorrect pronouns or antecedents will help the reader concentrate on the content of your work.

Pre-Writing/Planning

Before you actually begin to write, there are certain preliminary steps you need to take. A few minutes spent planning pays off—your final essay will be more focused, better developed, and clearer. For a 30-minute essay, you should spend five to ten minutes on the pre-writing process.

Understand the Question

Read the essay question carefully and ask yourself the following questions:

- What is the meaning of the topic statement?

- Is the question asking me to persuade the reader of the validity of a certain opinion?

- Am I being asked to agree or disagree with the statement? If so, what will be my thesis (main idea)?

- What kinds of examples can I use to support my thesis? Explore personal experiences, historical evidence, current events, and literary subjects.

Consider Your Audience

Essays would be pointless without an audience. Why write an essay if no one wants or needs to read it? Why add evidence, organize your ideas, or correct bad grammar? The reason to do any of these things is because someone out there needs to understand what you mean or say.

What does the audience need to know to believe you or to come over to your position? Imagine someone you know listening to you declare your position or opinion and then saying, "Oh, yeah? Prove it!" This is your audience—write to them. Ask yourself the following questions so that you will not be confronted with a person who says, "Prove it!"

- What evidence do I need to prove my idea to this skeptic?

- What would he or she disagree with me about?

- What does he or she share with me as common knowledge? What do I need to tell the reader?

WRITING YOUR ESSAY

Once you have considered your position on the topic and thought of several examples to support it, you are ready to begin writing.

Organizing Your Essay

Decide how many paragraphs you will write. In a 30-minute exercise, you will probably have time for no more than four or five paragraphs. With a 45-minute time frame, one would reasonably be expected to produce no more than six or seven paragraphs. In such a format, the first paragraph will be the introduction, the next two or three (or four) will develop your thesis with specific examples, and the final paragraph(s) should constitute a strong conclusion.

The Introduction

The focus of your introduction should be the thesis statement. This statement allows your reader to understand the point and direction of your essay. The statement identifies the central idea of your essay and should clearly state your attitude about the subject. It will also dictate the basic content and organization of your essay. If you do not state your thesis clearly, your essay will suffer.

The thesis is the heart of the essay. Without it, readers won't know what your major message or central idea is in the essay.

The thesis must be something that can be argued or needs to be proven, not just an accepted fact. For example, "Animals are used every day in cosmetic and medical testing," is a fact—it needs no proof. But if the writer says, "Using animals for cosmetic and medical testing is cruel and should be stopped," we have a point that must be supported and defended by the writer.

The thesis can be placed in any paragraph of the essay, but in a short essay, especially one written for evaluative exam purposes, the thesis is most effective when placed in the last sentence of the opening paragraph.

Consider the following sample question:

ESSAY TOPIC:

"That government is best which governs least."

ASSIGNMENT: Do you agree or disagree with this statement? Choose a specific example from current events, personal experience, or your reading to support your position.

After reading the topic statement, decide if you agree or disagree. If you agree with this statement, your thesis statement could be the following:

"Government has the right to protect individuals from interference but no right to extend its powers and activities beyond this function."

This statement clearly states the writer's opinion in a direct manner. It also serves as a blueprint for the essay. The remainder of the introduction should give two or three brief examples that support your thesis.

Supporting Paragraphs

The next two or three paragraphs of your essay will elaborate on the supporting examples you gave in your introduction. Each paragraph should discuss only one idea. Like the introduction, each paragraph should be coherently organized, with a topic sentence and supporting details.

The topic sentence is to each paragraph what the thesis statement is to the essay as a whole. It tells the reader what you plan to discuss in that paragraph. It has a specific subject and is neither too broad nor too narrow. It also establishes the author's attitude and gives the reader a sense of the direction in which the writer is going. An effective topic sentence also arouses the reader's interest.

Although it may occur in the middle or at the end of the paragraph, the topic sentence usually appears at the beginning of the paragraph. Placing it at the beginning is advantageous because it helps you stay focused on the main idea.

The remainder of each paragraph should support the topic sentence with examples and illustrations. Each sentence should progress logically from the previous one and be centrally connected to your topic sentence. Do not include any extraneous material that does not serve to develop your thesis.

Conclusion

Your conclusion should briefly restate your thesis and explain how you have shown it to be true. Since you want to end your essay on a strong note, your conclusion should be concise and effective.

Do not introduce any new topics that you cannot support. If you were watching a movie that suddenly shifted plot and characters at the end, you would be disappointed or even angry. Similarly, conclusions must not drift away from the major focus and message of the essay. Make sure your conclusion is clearly on the topic and represents your perspective without any confusion about what you really mean and believe. The reader will respect you for staying true to your intentions.

The conclusion is your last chance to grab and impress the reader. You can even use humor, if appropriate, but a dramatic close will remind the reader you are serious, even passionate, about what you believe.

EFFECTIVE USE OF LANGUAGE

Clear organization, while vitally important, is not the only factor the graders of your essay consider. You must also demonstrate that you can express your ideas clearly, using correct grammar, diction, usage, spelling, and punctuation. For rules on grammar, usage, and mechanics, consult *The Elements of Style*, Third Edition (Strunk, William Jr. and White, E.B. Boston: Allyn and Bacon. 1979.), and *REA's Handbook of English Grammar, Style, and Writing* (Staff of Research & Education Association, Piscataway, N.J.: Research & Education Association. 2001.).

Point-of-View

Depending on the audience, essays may be written from one of three points of view:

1. *Subjective/Personal* Point of View:

    "I think . . ."

    "I believe cars are more trouble than they are worth."

    "I feel . . ."

2. *Second Person* Point of View ("You" instead of "I" or "We"):

    "If *you* own a car, *you* will soon find out that it is more trouble than it is worth."

3. *Third Person* Point of View (focuses on the idea, not what "I" think of it):

    "*Cars* are more trouble than *they* are worth."

It is very important to maintain a consistent point of view throughout your essay. If you begin writing in the first-person ("I"), do not shift to the second- or third-person in the middle of the essay. Such inconsistency is confusing to your reader and will be penalized by the graders of your essay.

Tone

A writer's tone results from his or her attitude toward the subject and the reader. If the essay question requires you to take a strong stand, the tone of your essay should reflect this.

Your tone should also be appropriate for the subject matter. A serious topic demands a serious tone. For a more light-hearted topic, you may wish to inject some humor into your essay.

Whatever tone you choose, be consistent. Do not make any abrupt shifts in tone in the middle of your essay.

Transitions

Transitions are like the links of a bracelet, holding the beads or major points of your essay together. They help the reader logically follow the flow of your ideas and help you connect major and minor ideas. Transitions are used either at the beginning of a paragraph, or to show the connections among ideas within a single paragraph. Without transitions, you will jar readers and distract them from your ideas.

Here are some typical transitional words and phrases:

Linking similar ideas

again	for example	likewise
also	for instance	moreover

Linking dissimilar/contradictory ideas

although	however	on the other hand
and yet	in spite of	otherwise

Indicating cause, purpose, or result

as	for	so
as a result	for this reason	then

Indicating time or position

above	before	meanwhile
across	beyond	next

Indicating an example or summary

as a result	in any event	in other words
as I have said	in brief	in short

WRITING SKILLS REVIEW

The requirements for informal spoken English are much more relaxed than the rigid rules for "standard written English." While slang, colloquialisms, and other informal expressions are acceptable and sometimes very appropriate in casual speech, they are inappropriate in academic and business writing. More often than not, writers, especially student writers, do not make a distinction between the two: they use the same words, grammar, and sentence structure from their everyday speech in their college papers, albeit unsuccessfully.

SENTENCE STRUCTURE

Parallelism

Parallel structure is used to express matching ideas. It refers to the grammatical balance of a series of any of the following:

Phrases:

The squirrel ran *along the fence*, *up the tree*, and *into his burrow* with a mouthful of acorns.

Adjectives:

The job market is flooded with *very talented*, *highly motivated*, and *well-educated* young people.

Nouns:

You will need a *notebook*, *pencil*, and *dictionary* for the test.

Clauses:

The children were told to decide *which toy they would keep* and *which toy they would give away*.

Verbs:

The farmer *plowed*, *planted*, and *harvested* his corn in record time.

Verbals:

Reading, *writing*, and *calculating* are fundamental skills that all of us should possess.

Correlative conjunctions:

Either you will do your homework *or* you will fail.

Repetition of structural signals:

(such as articles, auxiliaries, prepositions, and conjunctions)

> INCORRECT: I have quit my job, enrolled in school, and am looking for a reliable babysitter.

> CORRECT: I *have quit* my job, *have enrolled* in school, and *am looking* for a reliable babysitter.

Note: Repetition of prepositions is considered formal and is not necessary.

> You can travel *by car, by plane, or by train*; it's all up to you.

OR

> You can travel *by car, plane, or train*; it's all up to you.

When a sentence contains items in a series, check for both punctuation and sentence balance. When you check for punctuation, make sure the commas are used correctly. When you check for parallelism, make sure that the conjunctions connect similar grammatical constructions, such as all adjectives or all clauses.

Misplaced and Dangling Modifiers

A misplaced modifier is one that is in the wrong place in the sentence. Misplaced modifiers come in all forms—words, phrases, and clauses. Sentences containing misplaced modifiers are often very comical: *Mom made me eat the spinach instead of my brother*. Misplaced modifiers, like the one in this sentence, are usually too far away from the word or words they modify. This sentence should read: *Mom made me, instead of my brother, eat the spinach.*

Modifiers like *only*, *nearly*, and *almost* should be placed next to the word they modify and not in front of some other word, especially a verb, that they are not intended to modify.

A modifier is misplaced if it appears to modify the wrong part of the sentence or if we cannot be certain what part of the sentence the writer intended it to modify. To correct a misplaced modifier, move the modifier next to the word it describes.

INCORRECT: She served hamburgers to the men on paper plates.

CORRECT: She served hamburgers on paper plates to the men.

Split infinitives also result in misplaced modifiers. Infinitives consist of the marker *to* plus the plain form of the verb. The two parts of the infinitive make up a grammatical unit that should not be split. Splitting an infinitive is placing an adverb between the *to* and the verb.

INCORRECT: The weather service expects temperatures to not rise.

CORRECT: The weather service expects temperatures not to rise.

Sometimes a split infinitive may be natural and preferable, though it may still bother some readers.

EX: Several U.S. industries expect *to* more than *triple* their use of robots within the next decade.

A squinting modifier is one that may refer to either a preceding or a following word, leaving the reader uncertain about what it is intended to modify. Correct a squinting modifier by moving it next to the word it is intended to modify.

INCORRECT: Snipers who fired on the soldiers often escaped capture.

CORRECT: Snipers who often fired on the soldiers escaped capture.

A dangling modifier is a modifier or verb in search of a subject: the modifying phrase (usually an *-ing* word group, an *-ed* or *-en* word group, or a *to + a verb* word group—participle phrase or infinitive phrase respectively) either appears to modify the wrong word or has nothing to modify. It is literally dangling at the beginning or the end of a sentence. The sentences often look and sound correct: *To be a student government officer, your grades must be above average*. (However, the verbal modifier has nothing to describe. Who is *to be a student government officer*? Your grades?) Questions of this type require you to determine whether a modifier has a headword or whether it is dangling at the beginning or the end of the sentence.

To correct a dangling modifier, reword the sentence by either: 1) changing the modifying phrase to a clause with a subject, or 2) changing the subject of the sentence to the word that should be modified. The following are examples of a dangling gerund, a dangling infinitive, and a dangling participle:

INCORRECT: Shortly after leaving home, the accident occurred.

Who is <u>leaving home</u>, the accident?

CORRECT: Shortly after we left home, the accident occurred.

Fragments

A fragment is an incomplete construction which may or may not have a subject and a verb. Specifically, a fragment is a group of words pretending to be a sentence. Not all fragments appear as separate sentences, however. Often, fragments are separated by semicolons.

INCORRECT: Traffic was stalled for ten miles on the freeway. Because repairs were being made on potholes.

CORRECT: Traffic was stalled for ten miles on the freeway because repairs were being made on potholes.

Run-on/Fused Sentences

A run-on/fused sentence is not necessarily a long sentence or a sentence that the reader considers too long; in fact, a run-on may be two short sentences: *Dry ice does not melt it evaporates.* A run-on results when the writer fuses or runs together two separate sentences without any correct mark of punctuation separating them.

INCORRECT: Knowing how to use a dictionary is no problem each dictionary has a section in the front of the book telling how to use it.

CORRECT: Knowing how to use a dictionary is no problem. Each dictionary has a section in the front of the book telling how to use it.

Even if one or both of the fused sentences contains internal punctuation, the sentence is still a run-on.

INCORRECT: Bob bought dress shoes, a suit, and a nice shirt he needed them for his sister's wedding.

CORRECT: Bob bought dress shoes, a suit, and a nice shirt. He needed them for his sister's wedding.

Comma Splices

A comma splice is the unjustifiable use of only a comma to combine what really is two separate sentences.

INCORRECT: One common error in writing is incorrect spelling, the other is the occasional use of faulty diction.

CORRECT: One common error in writing is incorrect spelling; the other is the occasional use of faulty diction.

Both run-on sentences and comma splices may be corrected in one of the following ways:

RUN-ON: Neal won the award he had the highest score.

COMMA SPLICE: Neal won the award, he had the highest score.

Separate the sentences with a period:

Neal won the award. He had the highest score.

Separate the sentences with a comma and a coordinating conjunction (*and*, *but*, *or*, *nor*, *for*, *yet*, *so*):

Neal won the award, for he had the highest score.

Subordination, Coordination, and Predication

Suppose, for the sake of clarity, you wanted to combine the information in these two sentences to create one statement:

I studied a foreign language. I found English quite easy.

How you decide to combine this information should be determined by the relationship you'd like to show between the two facts. *I studied a foreign language, and I found English quite easy* seems rather illogical. The **coordination** of the two ideas (connecting them with the coordinating conjunction *and* is ineffective. Using **subordination** instead (connecting the sentences with a subordinating conjunction) clearly shows the degree of relative importance between the expressed ideas:

After I studied a foreign language, I found English quite easy.

When using a conjunction, be sure that the sentence parts you are joining are in agreement.

INCORRECT: She loved him dearly but not his dog.

CORRECT: She loved him dearly but she did not love his dog.

A common mistake that is made is to forget that each member of the pair must be followed by the same kind of construction.

> INCORRECT: They complimented them both for their bravery and they thanked them for their kindness.

> CORRECT: They both complimented them for their bravery and thanked them for their kindness.

While refers to time and should not be used as a substitute for *although, and,* or *but*.

> INCORRECT: While I'm usually interested in Fellini movies, I'd rather not go tonight.

> CORRECT: Although I'm usually interested in Fellini movies, I'd rather not go tonight.

Where refers to time and should not be used as a substitute for *that*.

> INCORRECT: We read in the paper where they are making great strides in DNA research.

> CORRECT: We read in the paper that they are making great strides in DNA research.

VERBS

Verb Forms

This section covers the principal parts of some irregular verbs including troublesome verbs like *lie* and *lay*. The use of regular verbs like *look* and *receive* poses no real problem to most writers since the past and past participle forms end in *-ed*; it is the irregular forms which pose the most serious problems—for example, *seen, written,* and *begun*.

Verb Tenses

Tense sequence indicates a logical time sequence.

Use present tense

in statements of universal truth:

> I learned that the sun *is* 150 million km from the Earth.

In statements about the contents of literature and other published works:

> In this book, Sandy *becomes* a nun and *writes* a book on psychology.

Use past tense

in statements concerning writing or publication of a book:

He *wrote* his first book in 1949, and it *was published* in 1952.

Use present perfect tense

for an action that began in the past but continues into the future:

I *have lived* here all my life.

Use past perfect tense

for an earlier action that is mentioned in a later action:

Cindy ate the apple that she *had picked*.

(First she picked it, then she ate it.)

Use future perfect tense

for an action that will have been completed at a specific future time:

By May, I *shall have graduated*.

Use a present participle

for action that occurs at the same time as the verb:

Speeding down the interstate, I saw a cop's flashing lights.

Use a perfect participle

for action that occurred before the main verb:

Having read the directions, I started the test.

Use the subjunctive mood

to express a wish or state a condition contrary to fact:

If it were not raining, we could have a picnic.

in *that* clauses after verbs like *request, recommend, suggest, ask, require*, and *insist*; and after such expressions as *it is important* and *it is necessary*:

It is necessary that all papers *be* submitted on time.

Subject-Verb Agreement

Agreement is the grammatical correspondence between the subject and the verb of a sentence: *I do; we do; they do; he, she, it does*.

Every English verb has five forms, two of which are the bare form (plural) and the *-s* form (singular). Simply put, singular verb forms end in *-s;* plural forms do not.

Study these rules governing subject-verb agreement:

A verb must agree with its subject, not with any additive phrase in the sentence such as a prepositional or verbal phrase. Ignore such phrases.

> Your *copy* of the rules *is* on the desk.

> Ms. Craig's *record* of community service and outstanding teaching *qualifies* her for a promotion.

In an inverted sentence beginning with a prepositional phrase, the verb still agrees with its subject.

> At the end of the summer *come* the best *sales*.

> Under the house *are* some old Mason *jars*.

Prepositional phrases beginning with compound prepositions such as *along with, together with, in addition to,* and *as well as* should be ignored, for they do not affect subject-verb agreement.

> *Gladys Knight*, as well as the Pips, *is* riding the midnight train to Georgia.

A verb must agree with its subject, not its subject complement.

> *Taxes are* a problem.

> A *problem is* taxes.

When a sentence begins with an expletive such as *there, here,* or *it,* the verb agrees with the subject, not the expletive.

> Surely, there *are* several *alumni* who would be interested in forming a group.

> There *are* 50 *students* in my English class.

> There *is* a horrifying *study* on child abuse in *Psychology Today*.

Indefinite pronouns such as *each, either, one, everyone, everybody,* and *everything* are singular.

> *Somebody* in Detroit *loves* me.

> *Does either* [one] of you have a pencil?

Neither of my brothers *has* a car.

Indefinite pronouns such as *several, few, both,* and *many* are plural.

Both of my sorority sisters *have* decided to live off campus.

Few seek the enlightenment of transcendental meditation.

Indefinite pronouns such as *all, some, most,* and *none* may be singular or plural depending on their referents.

Some of the food *is* cold.

Some of the vegetables *are* cold.

I can think of some retorts, but *none seem* appropriate.

None of the children *is* as sweet as Sally.

Fractions such as *one-half* and *one-third* may be singular or plural depending on the referent.

Half of the mail *has* been delivered.

Half of the letters *have* been read.

Subjects joined by *and* take a plural verb unless the subjects are regarded as one item or unit.

Jim and *Tammy were* televangelists.

Simon and Garfunkel is my favorite group.

In cases when the subjects are joined by *or, nor, either . . . or,* or *neither . . . nor,* the verb must agree with the subject closer to it.

Either the teacher or the *students are* responsible.

Neither the students nor the *teacher is* responsible.

Relative pronouns, such as *who, which,* or *that,* which refer to plural antecedents require plural verbs. However, when the relative pronoun refers to a singular subject, the pronoun takes a singular verb.

She is one of the girls *who cheer* on Friday nights.

She is the only cheerleader *who has* a broken leg.

Subjects preceded by *every, each,* and *many a* are singular.

Every man, woman, and child *was* given a life preserver.

Each undergraduate *is* required to pass a proficiency exam.

Many a tear *has* to fall before one matures.

A collective noun, such as *audience, faculty, jury,* etc., requires a singular verb when the group is regarded as a whole, and a plural verb when the members of the group are regarded as individuals.

> The *jury has* made its decision.

> The *faculty are* preparing their grade rosters.

Subjects preceded by *the number of* or *the percentage of* are singular, while subjects preceded by *a number of* or *a percentage of* are plural.

> *The number of* vacationers in Florida *increases* every year.

> *A number of* vacationers *are* young couples.

Titles of books, companies, name brands, and groups are singular or plural depending on their meaning.

> *Great Expectations is* my favorite novel.

> The *Rolling Stones are* performing in the Super Dome.

Certain nouns of Latin and Greek origin have unusual singular and plural forms.

Singular	Plural
criterion	criteria
alumnus	alumni
datum	data
medium	media

> The *data are* available for inspection.

> The only *criterion* for membership *is* a high GPA.

Some nouns such as *deer*, *shrimp*, and *sheep* have the same spellings for both their singular and plural forms. In these cases, the meaning of the sentence will determine whether they are singular or plural.

> *Deer are* beautiful animals.

> The spotted *deer is* licking the sugar cube.

Some nouns like *scissors*, *jeans*, and *wages* have plural forms but no singular counterparts. These nouns almost always take plural verbs.

> The *scissors are* on the table.

> My new *jeans fit* me like a glove.

Words used as examples, not as grammatical parts of the sentence, require singular verbs.

> *Can't is* the contraction for "cannot."

Cats is the plural form of "cat."

Mathematical expressions of subtraction and division require singular verbs, while expressions of addition and multiplication take either singular or plural verbs.

Ten *divided* by two *equals* five.

Five *times* two *equals* ten.

OR   Five *times* two *equal* ten.

Nouns expressing time, distance, weight, and measurement are singular when they refer to a unit and plural when they refer to separate items.

Fifty yards is a short distance.

Ten years have passed since I finished college.

Expressions of quantity are usually plural.

Nine out of ten dentists *recommend* that their patients floss.

Some nouns ending in *-ics,* such as *economics* and *ethics*, take singular verbs when they refer to principles or a field of study; however, when they refer to individual practices, they usually take plural verbs.

Ethics is being taught in the spring.

His unusual business *ethics are* what got him into trouble.

Some nouns like *measles*, *news*, and *calculus* appear to be plural but are actually singular in number. These nouns require singular verbs.

Measles is a very contagious disease.

Calculus requires great skill in algebra.

A verbal noun (infinitive or gerund) serving as a subject is treated as singular, even if the object of the verbal phrase is plural.

Hiding your mistakes *does* not make them go away.

To run five miles *is* my goal.

A noun phrase or clause acting as the subject of a sentence requires a singular verb.

What I need is to be loved.

Whether there is any connection between them is unknown.

Clauses beginning with *what* may be singular or plural depending on the meaning, that is, whether *what* means "the thing" or "the things."

What I want for Christmas is a new motorcycle.

What matters are Clinton's ideas.

A plural subject followed by a singular appositive requires a plural verb; similarly, a singular subject followed by a plural appositive requires a singular verb.

When the girls throw a party, *they* each bring a *gift*.

The *board*, all ten members, *is* meeting today.

PRONOUNS

Pronoun Case

Pronoun case questions test your knowledge of the use of nominative and objective case pronouns:

Nominative Case	Objective Case
I	me
he	him
she	her
we	us
they	them
who	whom

This review section answers the most frequently asked grammar questions: when to use *I* and when to use *me*; when to use *who* and when to use *whom*. Some writers avoid *whom* altogether, and instead of distinguishing between *I* and *me*, many writers incorrectly use *myself*.

Use the nominative case (subject pronouns)

for the subject of a sentence:

We students studied until early morning for the final.

Alan and *I* "burned the midnight oil," too.

for pronouns in apposition to the subject:

Only two students, Alex and *I*, were asked to report on the meeting.

for the predicate nominative/subject complement:

The actors nominated for the award were *she* and *I*.

for the subject of an elliptical clause:

Molly is more experienced than *he*.

for the subject of a subordinate clause:

> Robert is the driver *who* reported the accident.

for the complement of an infinitive with no expressed subject:

> I would not want to be *he*.

Use the objective case (object pronouns)

for the direct object of a sentence:

> Mary invited *us* to her party.

for the object of a preposition:

> The books that were torn belonged to *her*.

> Just between you and *me*, I'm bored.

for the indirect object of a sentence:

> Walter gave a dozen red roses to *her*.

for the appositive of a direct object:

> The committee elected two delegates, Barbara and *me*.

for the object of an infinitive:

> The young boy wanted to help *us* paint the fence.

for the object of a gerund:

> Enlisting *him* was surprisingly easy.

for the object of a past participle:

> Having called the other students and *us*, the secretary went home for the day.

for a pronoun that precedes an infinitive (the subject of an infinitive):

> The supervisor told *him* to work late.

for the complement of an infinitive with an expressed subject:

> The fans thought the best player to be *him*.

for the object of an elliptical clause:

> Bill tackled Joe harder than *me*.

for the object of a verb in apposition:

> Charles invited two extra people, Carmen and *me*, to the party.

When a conjunction connects two pronouns or a pronoun and a noun, remove the "and" and the other pronoun or noun to determine what the correct pronoun form should be:

Mom gave ~~Tom and~~ myself a piece of cake.

Mom gave ~~Tom and~~ I a piece of cake

Mom gave ~~Tom and~~ me a piece of cake.

Removal of these words reveals what the correct pronoun should be:

Mom gave *me* a piece of cake.

The only pronouns that are acceptable after *between* and other prepositions are: *me, her, him, them,* and *whom.* When deciding between *who* and *whom,* try substituting *he* for *who* and *him* for *whom;* then follow these easy transformation steps:

1   Isolate the *who* clause or the *whom* clause:

whom we can trust

2.   Invert the word order, if necessary. Place the words in the clause in the natural order of an English sentence, subject followed by the verb:

we can trust whom

3.   Read the final form with the *he* or *him* inserted:

We can trust ~~whom~~ him.

When a pronoun follows a comparative conjunction like *than* or *as,* complete the elliptical construction to help you determine which pronoun is correct.

She has more credit hours than me [do].

She has more credit hours than I [do].

Pronoun-Antecedent Agreement

These kinds of questions test your knowledge of using an appropriate pronoun to agree with its antecedent in number (singular or plural form) and gender (masculine, feminine, or neuter). An antecedent is a noun or pronoun to which another noun or pronoun refers.

Here are the two basic rules for pronoun reference-antecedent agreement:

1.   Every pronoun must have a conspicuous antecedent.

2.   Every pronoun must agree with its antecedent in number, gender, and person.

When an antecedent is one of dual gender like *student*, *singer*, *artist*, *person*, *citizen*, etc., use *his* or *her*. Some careful writers change the antecedent to a plural noun to avoid using the sexist, singular masculine pronoun *his*:

> INCORRECT: Everyone hopes that he will win the lottery.

> CORRECT: Most people hope that they will win the lottery.

Ordinarily, the relative pronoun *who* is used to refer to people, *which* to refer to things and places, *where* to refer to places, and *that* to refer to places or things. The distinction between *that* and *which* is a grammatical one.

Many writers prefer to use *that* to refer to collective nouns.

> The family *that* plays together, stays together.

Many writers, especially students, are not sure when to use the reflexive case pronoun and when to use the possessive case pronoun. The rules governing the usage of the reflexive case and the possessive case are quite simple.

Use the possessive case

before a noun in a sentence:

> *Our* friend moved during the semester break.

> *My* dog has fleas, but *her* dog doesn't.

before a gerund in a sentence:

> *Her* running helps to relieve stress.

> *His* driving terrified her.

as a noun in a sentence:

> *Mine* was the last test graded that day.

to indicate possession:

> Karen never allows anyone else to drive *her* car.

> Brad thought the book was *his,* but it was someone else's.

Use the reflexive case

as a direct object to rename the subject:

> I kicked *myself.*

as an indirect object to rename the subject:

> Henry bought *himself* a tie.

as an object of a prepositional phrase:

> Tom and Lillie baked the pie for *themselves*.

as a predicate pronoun:

> She hasn't been *herself* lately.

Do not use the reflexive in place of the nominative pronoun:

> INCORRECT: Both Randy and *myself* plan to go.
>
> CORRECT: Both Randy and *I* plan to go.

Notice that reflexive pronouns are not set off by commas:

> INCORRECT: Mary, *herself*, gave him the diploma.
>
> CORRECT: Mary *herself* gave him the diploma.

Pronoun Reference

Pronoun reference questions require you to determine whether the antecedent is conspicuously written in the sentence or whether it is remote, implied, ambiguous, or vague, none of which results in clear writing. Make sure that every italicized pronoun has a conspicuous antecedent and that one pronoun substitutes only for another noun or pronoun, not for an idea or a sentence.

ADJECTIVES AND ADVERBS

Correct Usage

Adjectives are words that modify nouns or pronouns by defining, describing, limiting, or qualifying those nouns or pronouns.

Adverbs are words that modify verbs, adjectives, or other adverbs. They express such ideas as time, place, manner, cause, and degree. Use adjectives as subject complements with linking verbs; use adverbs with action verbs.

The old man's speech was *eloquent*.	ADJECTIVE
Mr. Brown speaks *eloquently*.	ADVERB
Please be *careful*.	ADJECTIVE
Please drive *carefully*.	ADVERB

Good or well

Good is an adjective; its use as an adverb is colloquial and nonstandard.

INCORRECT: He plays *good*.

CORRECT: He looks *good* for an octogenarian.

The quiche tastes very *good*.

Well may be either an adverb or an adjective. As an adjective, *well* means "in good health."

CORRECT: He plays *well*.   ADVERB

My mother is not *well*.   ADJECTIVE

Bad or badly

Bad is an adjective used after sense verbs such as *look*, *smell*, *taste*, *feel*, or *sound*, or after linking verbs (*is, am, are, was, were*).

INCORRECT: I feel *badly* about the delay.

CORRECT: I feel *bad* about the delay.

Badly is an adverb used after all other verbs.

INCORRECT: It doesn't hurt very *bad*.

CORRECT: It doesn't hurt very *badly*.

PUNCTUATION

Commas

Commas should be placed according to standard rules of punctuation for purpose, clarity, and effect. The proper use of commas is explained in the following rules and examples:

In a series:

When more than one adjective describes a noun, use a comma to separate and emphasize each adjective. The comma takes the place of the word *and* in the series.

the long, dark passageway

another confusing, sleepless night

Some adjective-noun combinations are thought of as one word. In these cases, the adjective in front of the adjective-noun combination needs no comma. If you inserted *and* between the adjective-noun combination, it would not make sense.

> a stately oak tree
>
> an exceptional wine glass
>
> my worst report card
>
> a china dinner plate

The comma is also used to separate words, phrases, and whole ideas (clauses); it still takes the place of *and* when used this way.

> an apple, a pear, a fig, and a banana
>
> a lovely lady, an elegant dress, and many admirers
>
> She lowered the shade, closed the curtain, turned off the light, and went to bed.

With a long introductory phrase:

Usually if a phrase of more than five or six words or a dependent clause precedes the subject at the beginning of a sentence, a comma is used to set it off.

> After last night's fiasco at the disco, she couldn't bear the thought of looking at him again.
>
> Whenever I try to talk about politics, my wife leaves the room.
>
> Provided you have said nothing, they will never guess who you are.

It is not necessary to use a comma with a short sentence.

> In January she will go to Switzerland.
>
> After I rest I'll feel better.
>
> During the day no one is home.

If an introductory phrase includes a verb form that is being used as another part of speech (a *verbal*), it must be followed by a comma.

> INCORRECT: When eating Mary never looked up from her plate.
>
> CORRECT: When eating, Mary never looked up from her plate.

> INCORRECT: Having decided to leave Mary James wrote her a letter.
>
> CORRECT: Having decided to leave Mary, James wrote her a letter.

To separate sentences with two main ideas:

To understand this use of the comma, you need to be able to recognize compound sentences. When a sentence contains more than two subjects and verbs (clauses), and the two clauses are joined by a conjunction (*and, but, or, nor, for, yet*), use a comma before the conjunction to show that another clause is coming.

> I thought I knew the poem by heart, but he showed me three lines I had forgotten.
>
> Are we really interested in helping the children, or are we more concerned with protecting our good names?
>
> He is supposed to leave tomorrow, but he is not ready to go.
>
> Jim knows you are disappointed, and he has known it for a long time.

If the two parts of the sentence are short and closely related, it is not necessary to use a comma.

> He threw the ball and the dog ran after it.
>
> Jane played the piano and Michael danced.

Be careful not to confuse a sentence that has a compound verb and a single subject with a compound sentence. If the subject is the same for both verbs, there is no need for a comma.

> INCORRECT: Charles sent some flowers, and wrote a long letter explaining why he had not been able to attend.
>
> CORRECT: Charles sent some flowers and wrote a long letter explaining why he had not been able to attend.

In general, words and phrases that stop the flow of the sentence or are unnecessary for the main idea are set off by commas.

Abbreviations after names:

> Martha Harris, Ph.D., will be the speaker tonight.

Interjections (an exclamation without added grammatical connection):

> Oh, I'm so glad to see you.
>
> I tried so hard, alas, to do it.
>
> Hey, let me out of here.

Direct address:

Roy, won't you open the door for the dog?

I can't understand, Mother, what you are trying to say.

May I ask, Mr. President, why you called us together?

Hey, lady, watch out for that car!

Tag questions:

I'm really hungry, aren't you?

Jerry looks like his father, doesn't he?

Geographical names and addresses:

The concert will be held in Chicago, Illinois, on August 12.

The letter was addressed to Mrs. Marion Heartwell, 1881 Pine Lane, Palo Alto, California 95824.

(Note: No comma is needed before the ZIP code because it is already clearly set off from the state name.)

Transitional words and phrases:

On the other hand, I hope he gets better.

In addition, the phone rang constantly this afternoon.

I'm, nevertheless, going to the beach on Sunday.

You'll find, therefore, that no one is more loyal than I am.

Parenthetical words and phrases:

You will become, I believe, a great statesman.

We know, of course, that this is the only thing to do.

Unusual word order:

The dress, new and crisp, hung in the closet.

With nonrestrictive elements:

Parts of a sentence that modify other parts are sometimes essential to the meaning of the sentence and sometimes not. When a modifying word or group of words is not vital to the meaning of the sentence, it is set off by commas. Since it does not restrict the meaning of the words it modifies, it is called "nonrestrictive." Modifiers that are essential to the meaning of the sentence are called "restrictive" and are not set off by commas.

ESSENTIAL: The girl *who wrote the story* is my sister.

NONESSENTIAL: My sister, *the girl who wrote the story*, has always loved to write.

ESSENTIAL: John Milton's famous poem *Paradise Lost* tells a remarkable story.

NONESSENTIAL: Dante's greatest work, *The Divine Comedy,* marked the beginning of the Renaissance.

To set off direct quotations:

Most direct quotes or quoted materials are set off from the rest of the sentence by commas.

"Please read your part more loudly," the director insisted.

"I won't know what to do," said Michael, "if you leave me."

Note: Commas always go inside the closing quotation mark, even if the comma is not part of the material being quoted.

Be careful not to set off indirect quotes or quotes that are used as subjects or complements.

"To be or not to be" is the famous beginning of a soliloquy in Shakespeare's *Hamlet*. (subject)

She said she would never come back. (indirect quote)

To set off contrasting elements:

Her intelligence, not her beauty, got her the job.

Your plan will take you a little further from, rather than closer to, your destination.

It was a reasonable, though not appealing, idea.

He wanted glory, but found happiness instead.

In dates:

Both forms of the date are acceptable.

She will arrive on April 6, 1998.

He left on 5 December 1980.

Usually, when a subordinate clause is at the end of a sentence, no comma is necessary preceding the clause. However, when a subordinate clause introduces a sentence, a comma should be used after the clause. Some common subordinating conjunctions are:

after	as if
although	because
as	before
even though	till
if	unless
inasmuch as	until
since	when
so that	whenever
though	while

Semicolons

Questions testing semicolon usage require you to be able to distinguish between the semicolon and the comma, and the semicolon and the colon. This review section covers the basic uses of the semicolon: to separate independent clauses not joined by a coordinating conjunction, to separate independent clauses separated by a conjunctive adverb, and to separate items in a series with internal commas. It is important to be consistent; if you use a semicolon between *any* of the items in the series, you must use semicolons to separate *all* of the items in the series.

Usually, a comma follows the conjunctive adverb. Note also that a period can be used to separate two sentences joined by a conjunctive adverb. Some common conjunctive adverbs are:

accordingly	nevertheless
besides	next
consequently	nonetheless
finally	now
furthermore	on the other hand
however	otherwise
indeed	perhaps
in fact	still
moreover	therefore

Then is also used as a conjunctive adverb, but it is not usually followed by a comma.

Use the semicolon

to separate independent clauses not joined by a coordinating conjunction:

> I understand how to use commas; the semicolon I have not yet mastered.

to separate two independent clauses connected by a conjunctive adverb:

> He took great care with his work; *therefore*, he was very successful.

to combine two independent clauses connected by a coordinating conjunction if either or both of the clauses contain other internal punctuation:

> Success in college, some maintain, requires intelligence, industry, and perseverance; *but* others, fewer in number, assert that only personality is important.

to separate items in a series when each item has internal punctuation:

> I bought an old, dilapidated chair; an antique table which was in beautiful condition; and a new, ugly, blue and white rug.

> Call our customer service line for assistance: Arizona, 1-800-555-6020; New Mexico, 1-800-555-5050; California, 1-800-555-3140; or Nevada, 1-800-555-3214.

Do not use the semicolon

to separate a dependent and an independent clause:

> INCORRECT: You should not make such statements; even though they are correct.

> CORRECT: You should not make such statements even though they are correct.

to separate an appositive phrase or clause from a sentence:

> INCORRECT: His immediate aim in life is centered around two things; becoming an engineer and learning to fly an airplane.

> CORRECT: His immediate aim in life is centered around two things: becoming an engineer and learning to fly an airplane.

to precede an explanation or summary of the first clause:

Note: Although the sentence below is punctuated correctly, the use of the semicolon provides a miscue, suggesting that the second clause is merely an extension, not an explanation, of the first clause. The colon provides a better clue.

> WEAK: The first week of camping was wonderful; we lived in cabins instead of tents.

> BETTER: The first week of camping was wonderful: we lived in cabins instead of tents.

to substitute for a comma:

> INCORRECT: My roommate also likes sports; particularly football, basketball, and baseball.

> CORRECT: My roommate also likes sports, particularly football, basketball, and baseball.

to set off other types of phrases or clauses from a sentence:

> INCORRECT: Being of a cynical mind; I should ask for a recount of the ballots.

> CORRECT: Being of a cynical mind, I should ask for a recount of the ballots.

> INCORRECT: The next meeting of the club has been postponed two weeks; inasmuch as both the president and vice-president are out of town.

> CORRECT: The next meeting of the club has been postponed two weeks, inasmuch as both the president and vice-president are out of town.

Note: The semicolon is not a terminal mark of punctuation; therefore, it should not be followed by a capital letter unless the first word in the second clause ordinarily requires capitalization (as in the case of a formal statement, a quotation, or an excerpt from dialogue).

Colons

While it is true that a colon is used to precede a list, one must also make sure that a complete sentence precedes the colon. The colon signals the reader that a list, explanation, or restatement of the preceding will follow. It is like an arrow, indicating that something is to follow. The difference between the colon and the semicolon and between the colon and the period is that the colon is an introductory mark, not a terminal mark. Look at the following examples:

> The Constitution provides for a separation of powers among the three branches of government.

government. The period signals a new sentence.

government; The semicolon signals an interrelated sentence.

government, The comma signals a coordinating conjunction followed by another independent clause.

government: The colon signals a list.

The Constitution provides for a separation of powers among the three branches of *government:* executive, legislative, and judicial.

Ensuring that a complete sentence precedes a colon means following these rules:

Use the colon to introduce a list (one item may constitute a list):

I hate this one course: English.

Three plays by William Shakespeare will be presented in repertory this summer at the University of Michigan: *Hamlet, Macbeth,* and *Othello.*

To introduce a list preceded by *as follows* or *the following*:

The reasons she cited for her success are as follows: integrity, honesty, industry, and a pleasant disposition.

To separate two independent clauses, when the second clause is a restatement or explanation of the first:

All of my high school teachers said one thing in particular: college is going to be difficult.

To introduce a word or word group which is a restatement, explanation, or summary of the first sentence:

These two things he loved: tofu and chick peas.

To introduce a formal appositive:

I am positive there is one appeal which you can't overlook: money.

To separate the introductory words from a quotation which follows, if the quotation is formal, long, or contained in its own paragraph:

The actor then stated: "I would rather be able to adequately play the part of Hamlet than to perform a miraculous operation, deliver a great lecture, or build a magnificent skyscraper."

The colon should be used only after statements that are grammatically complete.

Do *not* use a colon after a verb:

INCORRECT: My favorite holidays are: Christmas, New Year's, and Halloween.

CORRECT: My favorite holidays are* Christmas, New Year's, and Halloween.

Do *not* use a colon after a preposition:

INCORRECT: I enjoy different ethnic foods such as: Greek, Chinese, and Italian.

CORRECT: I enjoy different ethnic foods such as Greek, Chinese, and Italian.

Do *not* use a colon interchangeably with a dash:

INCORRECT: Mathematics, German, English: These gave me the greatest difficulty of all my studies.

CORRECT: Mathematics, German, English—these gave me the greatest difficulty of all my studies.

Information preceding the colon should be a complete sentence regardless of the explanatory information following the clause.

Do *not* use the colon before the words *for example, namely, that is,* or *for instance* even though these words may be introducing a list.

INCORRECT: We agreed to it: namely, to give him a surprise party.

CORRECT: There are a number of well-known American women writers: Nikki Giovanni, Phillis Wheatley, Emily Dickinson, and Maya Angelou.

Colon usage questions test your knowledge of the colon preceding a list, restatement, or explanation. These questions also require you to be able to distinguish between the colon and the period, the colon and the comma, and the colon and the semicolon.

---

* To illustrate or enumerate a number of items, insert "as follows" or "the following" here, and use a colon to introduce the list. These phrases complete the introducing clause.

GRE

Graduate Record Examination

Practice
Test 1

Section 1

TIME: 45 Minutes
Choose 1 of 2 Essays†

ESSAY QUESTION ONE

> **DIRECTIONS:** Present your perspective on the issue below by using relevant reasons and/or examples to support your views. Remember, there is no one "correct" response to the essay topic. Before starting, read the essay topic and its question(s).

Many non-smokers feel that secondhand smoke is hazardous to their health; recent medical research supports their allegations. Smokers feel that they have a right to enjoy this pastime, and that it would be a violation of their constitutional rights to deny them this privilege. The first group wants smoking made illegal, while the second group feels that they are being treated unfairly.

With whom do you agree, the smokers or the non-smokers? Using your own experience, reading, and observations, fully explain your reasoning.

STOP

Do not go on until you are instructed to do so. Use any remaining time to check your work on this portion of the test.

† On the actual test, you will have a choice between two essay topics. You have to write only one essay. To give you the most practice possible we have supplied sample essays for both questions in order to show you the differences between essays that receive a perfect score and those that score less.

TIME: 45 Minutes
Choose 1 of 2 Essays†

ESSAY QUESTION TWO

DIRECTIONS: Present your perspective on the issue below by using relevant reasons and/or examples to support your views. Remember, there is no one "correct" response to the essay topic. Before starting, read the essay topic and its question(s).

A process of trial and error is crucial to the expansion of human knowledge and progress. The emphasis in stories of discovery is almost always on the error, for it is through false starts that real progress is made.

Do you agree with this statement? Why or why not?

STOP

Do not go on until you are instructed to do so. Use any remaining time to check your work on this portion of the test.

---

† On the actual test, you will have a choice between two essay topics. You have to write only one essay. To give you the most practice possible we have supplied sample essays for both questions in order to show you the differences between essays that receive a perfect score and those that score less.

Section 2

TIME: 30 Minutes
1 Essay

DIRECTIONS: Critique the following argument by considering its logical soundness.

A new dog collar is now available with a new special feature—an underground electrical barrier which works with a receiver on your dog's collar. It beeps your dog when he nears the boundary and gives him a small electrical correction if he tries to cross it. It keeps your dog safe and out of trouble without having to resort to expensive fences, run ropes or chains that could injure your pet.

Discuss how logical and/or convincing you find this argument. Be sure to analyze the reasoning and the use of any evidence in the argument. Include suggestions that would make the argument more acceptable and persuasive, and that would allow you to evaluate its conclusion more readily.

STOP

If time remains, you may go back and check your work.

Section 3

TIME: 30 Minutes
30 Questions

NUMBERS: All numbers are real numbers.

FIGURES: Position of points, angles, regions, etc., are assumed to be in the order shown and angle measures are assumed to be positive.

LINES: Assume that lines shown as straight are indeed straight.

DIRECTIONS: Each of the following given set of quantities is placed into either Column A or B. Compare the two quantities to decide whether

(A)   the quantity in Column A is greater;

(B)   the quantity in Column B is greater;

(C)   the two quantities are equal;

(D)   the relationship cannot be determined from the information given.

NOTE: Do not choose (E) since there are only four choices.

COMMON INFORMATION: Information which relates to one or both given quantities is centered in the two columns. A symbol which appears in both columns will indicate the same item in Column A and Column B.

EXAMPLES:

	Column A	Column B
1.	5×4	$5 + 4$

Explanation: The correct answer is (A), since $5 \times 4 = 20$, and $5 + 4 = 9$.

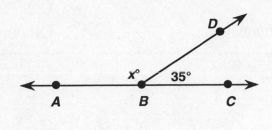

2. $180 - x$ 35

Explanation: The correct answer is (C). Since $\angle$ ABC is a straight angle, its measurement is 180°.

Column A	Column B

$x = 5, y = -3$

1. $(x + y)^2$ $(x - y)^2$

2. $\dfrac{2}{3} + \dfrac{3}{2}$ $\dfrac{5}{2}$

$x > 0, y > 0$

3. $x^2 + y^2$ $(x + y)^2$

The average (arithmetic mean) of
40, 20, 30, 24, 27, and 15 is $\overline{x}$.

4. $\overline{x}$ 26

Column A	Column B

$$4w = 6x = 12y$$

not enough info

5. w y

6. $\dfrac{13}{16}$ $\dfrac{31}{40}$

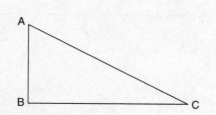

$AB = 8$
$BC = 15$
$AC = 17$

7. $\angle ABC$ $90°$

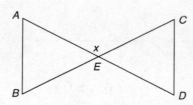

8. $2(\angle x)$ $\angle A + \angle B + \angle C + \angle D$

$w : x = y : z$, x and z are not zero

9. $w + x$ $y + z$

Column A	**Column B**

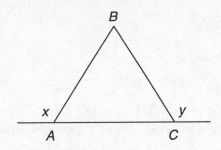

$BA = BC$

10. x y

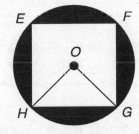

Square *EFGH* is inscribed in circle O. $GO \perp OH$. Area of triangle *GOH* = 12.5.

11. Area of shaded part of figure 9π

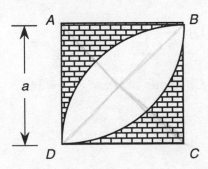

ABCD is a square. The unshaded area represents the intersection of two quadrants. ($\pi = 3.14$)

12.   Shaded area   Unshaded area

Column A	**Column B**

$$m > n > 1$$

13. w^n $\qquad\qquad\qquad\qquad\qquad\qquad$ w^m

Jim buys a dozen oranges and ten apples for $2.20. Jane buys a half dozen oranges and four pears for $1.20. John buys a half dozen pears and three apples for $1.20.

14. Cost of one apple $\qquad\qquad\qquad$ Cost of two pears
and one pear

Given $2a = b$

15. Area of a square, side $= a$ $\qquad$ Area of an isosceles right
triangle with leg $= b$

> **DIRECTIONS:** For the following questions, select the best answer choice to the given question.

16. What part of three-fourths is one-tenth?

   (A) $\dfrac{1}{8}$ $\qquad\qquad\qquad\qquad$ (D) $\dfrac{3}{40}$

   (B) $\dfrac{15}{2}$ $\qquad\qquad\qquad\qquad$ (E) None of these

   (C) $\dfrac{2}{15}$

17. Find the value of x in $2x + 12 = 3x + 9$.

   (A) 1 $\qquad\qquad\qquad\qquad$ (D) 4

   (B) 2 $\qquad\qquad\qquad\qquad$ (E) 5

   (C) 3

18. Peter has five rulers of 30 cm each and three of 20 cm each. What is the average length of Peter's rulers?

    (A) 25   (D) 26.25

    (B) 27   (E) 27.25

    (C) 23

19. Two pounds of pears and one pound of peaches cost $1.40. Three pounds of pears and two pounds of peaches cost $2.40. How much is the combined cost of one pound of pears and one pound of peaches?

    (A) $2.00   (D) $.80

    (B) $1.50   (E) $1.00

    (C) $1.60

20. The sum of three consecutive odd integers is always divisible by (I) 2, (II) 3, (III) 5, or (IV) 6.

    (A) I only   (D) I and III only

    (B) II only   (E) IV only

    (C) III only

Questions 21–25 refer to the charts on the following pages.

United States, Area and Population

	area *		population	
	sq mi	sq km	1970 census	1980 census
Division				
East North Central	244,366	632,905	40,253,000	41,668,000
	248,283	643,050		
States				
Illinois	55,877	144,721	11,114,000	11,418,000
	56,400	146,075		
Indiana	36,189	93,729	5,194,000	5,490,000
	36,291	93,993		
Michigan	56,818	147,158	8,875,000	9,258,000
	58,216	150,779		
Ohio	41,018	106,236	10,652,000	10,797,000
	41,222	106,764		
Wisconsin	54,464	141,061	4,418,000	4,705,000
	56,154	145,438		
East South Central	179,427	464,714	12,804,000	14,663,000
	181,964	471,285†		
States				
Alabama	50,851	131,703	3,444,000	3,890,000
	52,609	133,667		
Kentucky	39,851	103,214	3,219,000	3,661,000
	40,395	104,623		
Mississippi	47,358	122,657	2,217,000	2,521,000
	47,716	123,584		
Tennessee	41,367	107,140	3,924,000	4,591,000
	42,244	109,411		
Middle Atlantic	100,426	260,102†	37,199,000	36,788,000
	102,745	266,108†		
States				
New Jersey	7,532	19,508	7,168,000	7,364,000
	7,836	20,295		
New York	47,869	123,980	18,237,000	17,557,000
	49,576	128,401		
Pennsylvania	45,025	116,614	11,794,000	11,867,000
	45,333	117,412		
Mountain	856,633	2,218,669†	8,281,000	11,369,000
	863,887	2,237,457†		
States				
Arizona	113,563	294,127	1,771,000	2,718,000
	113,909	295,023		
Colorado	103,794	268,825	2,207,000	2,889,000
	104,247	269,998		
Idaho	82,677	214,132	713,000	944,000
	83,557	216,412		
Montana	145,603	377,110	694,000	787,000
	147,138	381,086		
Nevada	109,889	284,611	489,000	799,000
	110,540	286,297		
New Mexico	121,445	314,541	1,016,000	1,300,000
	121,666	315,113		
Utah	82,381	213,366	1,059,000	1,461,000
	84,916	219,931		
Wyoming	97,281	251,957	332,000	471,000
	97,914	253,596		
New England	62,992	163,149†	11,842,000	12,349,000
	66,608	172,514†		
States				
Connecticut	4,870	12,613	3,032,000	3,108,000
	5,009	12,973		
Maine	30,933	80,116	992,000	1,125,000
	33,215	86,026		
Massachusetts	7,833	20,287	5,689,000	5,737,000
	8,257	21,386		
New Hampshire	9,033	23,395	738,000	921,000
	9,304	24,097		
Rhode Island	1,049	2,717	947,000	947,000
	1,214	3,144		
Vermont	9,274	24,020	444,000	511,000
	9,609	24,887		

Courtesy Britannica Book of the Year, Encyclopædia Britannica, Inc., 1982.

	area *		population	
	sq mi	sq km	1970 census	1980 census
Divisions				
Pacific	892,266	2,310,958	26,522,000	31,797,000
	916,728	2,374,315		
States				
Alaska	566,432	1,467,052	300,000	400,000
	586,412	1,518,800		
California	156,537	405,429	19,953,000	23,669,000
	158,693	411,013		
Hawaii	6,425	16,641	769,000	965,000
	6,450	16,705		
Oregon	96,209	249,180	2,091,000	2,633,000
	96,981	251,180		
Washington	66,663	172,656	3,409,000	4,130,000
	68,192	176,616		
South Atlantic	267,352	692,438†	30,671,000	36,942,000
	278,776	772,026		
States				
Delaware	1,982	5,133	548,000	595,000
	2,057	5,328		
District of Columbia††	61	158	757,000	638,000
	67	174		
Florida	54,136	140,212	6,789,000	9,740,000
	58,560	151,670		
Georgia	58,197	150,730	4,590,000	5,464,000
	58,876	152,488		
Maryland	9,891	25,618	3,922,000	4,216,000
	10,577	27,394		
North Carolina	48,880	126,599	5,082,000	5,874,000
	52,586	136,197		
South Carolina	30,280	78,425	2,591,000	3,119,000
	31,055	80,432		
Virginia	39,841	103,188	4,648,000	5,346,000
	40,817	105,716		
West Virginia	24,084	62,377	1,744,000	1,950,000
	24,181	62,628		
West North Central	508,192	1,316,211	16,320,000	17,183,000
	517,247	1,339,664		
States				
Iowa	56,043	145,151	2,824,000	2,913,000
	56,290	145,790		
Kansas	82,056	212,524	2,247,000	2,363,000
	82,264	213,063		
Minnesota	78,289	205,358	3,805,000	4,077,000
	84,068	217,735		
Missouri	69,046	178,828	4,677,000	4,917,000
	69,686	180,486		
Nebraska	76,522	198,191	1,483,000	1,570,000
	77,227	200,017		
North Dakota	69,280	179,434	618,000	653,000
	70,665	183,022		
South Dakota	75,956	196,725	666,000	690,000
	77,047	199,551		
West South Central	429,284	1,111,840†	19,320,000	23,743,000
	438,884	1,136,704		
States				
Arkansas	52,175	135,133	1,923,000	2,286,000
	53,104	137,539		
Louisiana	45,155	116,951	3,641,000	4,204,000
	48,523	125,674		
Oklahoma	68,984	178,668	2,559,000	3,025,000
	69,919	181,089		
Texas	262,970	681,089	11,197,000	14,228,000
	267,338	692,402		
Total United States	3,540,938	9,170,987	203,212,000 §	226,505,000 §
	3,615,122	9,163,123†		

* Where two figures are given, the first is the land area, the second the total area.
† Converted area figures do not add to total given because of rounding.
†† District of Columbia is a federal district.
§ Figures do not add to total given because of rounding.
Source: Official government figures.

21. What is the land area in kilometers of the Pacific division?

    (A) 892,266   (D) 2,374,315

    (B) 916,728   (E) 26,522,000

    (C) 2,310,958

22. What are the divisions with the smallest and the largest land areas?

    (A) New England – Pacific

    (B) Mountain – New England

    (C) Pacific – Pacific

    (D) West North Central – New England

    (E) Mountain – Middle Atlantic

23. What percent of the land area represents the Pacific and East North Central divisions?

    (A) 22.1   (D) 25.2

    (B) 32.1   (E) 6.9

    (C) 42.1

24. What is the average increase of population from 1970–1980 per state in the New England region?

    (A) 84,500   (D) 386,000

    (B) 101,400   (E) 441,000

    (C) 126,750

25. If in the period 1980–1990 the rate of population increase is the same as in the 1970–1980 period, what will the approximate population of the East North Central Division be in 1990?

    (A) 43,083,000   (D) 43,000,000

    (B) 40,251,160   (E) 43,134,710

    (C) 44,653,060

26. One number is 2 more than 3 times another. Their sum is 22. Find the numbers.

    (A) 8, 14

    (B) 2, 20

    (C) 5, 17

    (D) 4, 18

    (E) 10, 12

27. The length of a rectangle is $6L$ and the width is $4W$. What is the perimeter?

    (A) $12L + 8W$

    (B) $12L^2 + 8W^2$

    (C) $6L + 4W$

    (D) $20LW$

    (E) $24LW$

28. If the length of a rectangle is increased by 30% and the width is decreased by 20%, then the area is increased by

    (A) 10%.

    (B) 5%.

    (C) 4%.

    (D) 20%.

    (E) 25%.

29. If n is the first of three consecutive odd numbers, which of the following represents the sum of the three numbers?

    (A) $n + 2$

    (B) $n + 4$

    (C) $n + 6$

    (D) $3n + 6$

    (E) $6(3n)$

30. In the following figure, line l is parallel to line m. If the area of $\triangle ABC$ is 40 cm^2, what is the area of triangle $\triangle ABD$?

Same base +
Same height

SAME !
area

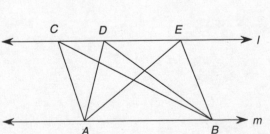

199

(A) Less than 40 cm^2

(B) More than 40 cm^2

(C) The length of segment $\overline{AD}$ times 40 cm

(D) Exactly 40 cm^2

(E) Cannot be determined from the information given.

STOP

If time still remains, you may go back and check your work.
When the time allotted is up, you may go on to the next section.

Section 4

TIME: 30 Minutes
38 Questions

DIRECTIONS: Each of the given sentences has blank spaces which indicate words omitted. Choose the best combination of words which fit into the meaning and structure within the context of the sentence.

1. The frightened mother _____ her young daughter for darting in front of the car.

    (A) implored

    (D) admonished

    (B) extorted

    (E) abolished

    (C) exhorted

2. The family left the country to _____ to Utopia and escape _____ because of religious beliefs.

    (A) emigrate...prosecution

    (D) wander...arraignment

    (B) peregrinate...extortion

    (E) roam...censure

    (C) immigrate...persecution

3. She responded so quickly with a _____ that it was evident the remark had been _____ until the proper time to use it.

    (A) repartee...dormant

    (D) humor...camouflaged

    (B) wit...latent

    (E) sortie...disguised

    (C) satire...hibernating

4. After reading the letter, she _____ that the manager was attempting to _____ a contract with her.

    (A) implied...abrogate

    (B) inferred...negotiate

(C) imposed…nullify   (D) surmised…breech

(E) included…annihilate

5. The defense attorney was satisfied with the acquittal, but the prosecutor felt the judge's decision was _____ .

(A) ambiguous   (D) auspicious

(B) astute   (E) arbitrary

(C) arduous

6. Perhaps the most famous speech in all of Shakespeare's plays is Hamlet's _____ .

(A) colloquy   (D) quandary

(B) palindrome   (E) obloquy

(C) soliloquy

7. During the Middle Ages, many people were inspired to lead more religious lives by the _____ of St. Francis of Assisi.

(A) abnegation   (D) vacillation

(B) turpitude   (E) dichotomy

(C) calumny

DIRECTIONS: In the following questions, a related pair of words is followed by five more pairs of words. Select the pair that best expresses the same relationship as that expressed in the original pair.

---

8. MANDATORY:OPTIONAL::

(A) pious:indignant   (D) chaste:celibate

(B) competent:inept   (E) crass:boorish

(C) opaque:ornate

9. PUNISHMENT:FINE::

(A) hyacinth:flower   (B) orange:peel

(C)   circulation:heart   (D)   puzzle:jigsaw

(E)   sandals:shoes

10.   BANDAGE:WOUND::

(A)   collar:dog   (D)   diaper:baby   *E*

(B)   stamp:envelope   (E)   cast:fracture

(C)   gloves:hands

11.   ESPOUSE:THEORY::

(A)   proponent:opponent   (D)   heretic:blasphemy

(B)   create:innovate   (E)   gourmand:gluttony   *C*

(C)   advocate:hypothesis

12.   TRACTABLE:BIDDABLE::

(A)   torpid:lethargic   (D)   colloquial:formal   *A*

(B)   viscous:liquid   (E)   eccentric:aesthetic

(C)   truculent:contrite

13.   DEIGN:CONDESCEND::

(A)   berate:commend   (D)   imbue:desiccate   *C*

(B)   corroborate:repudiate   (E)   vaunt:wither

(C)   digress:stray

14.   FRAILTY:VICE::

(A)   felony:misdemeanor   (D)   secreted:veiled

(B)   aggravation:rage   (E)   cloister:monastery   *B*

(C)   trite:popular

15.   ANALOGOUS:PARALLEL::

(A)   acidulous:saccharine   (D)   pundit:tyro

(B)   sinuous:tortuous   (E)   mundane:celestial   *B*

(C)   incongruous:homogeneous

16. FINE:AMERCEMENT::

   (A) loss:gain

   (D) lottery:deposit

   (B) forfeiture:reward

   (E) contraband:confiscate

   (C) penalty:mulct

DIRECTIONS: Each passage is followed by questions based on its content. After reading a passage, choose the best answer to each question. Answer all questions based on what is stated or implied in that passage.

Established firmly in popular culture is the notion that each of the two hemispheres of the brain has specialized functions. The left hemisphere, insist proponents of this theory, controls language and logic; the right hemisphere, espousers contend, is the more creative and intuitive half. Many proponents try to classify a person as "right-brained" or "left-brained," suggesting that the two hemispheres do not work together in the same person and, thus, can be considered independent. Because of the supposed independent functions of the two hemispheres and because of their difference in specializations, an activity might engage one part of the brain while the other part is not used at all, they believe. "Right-brained" individuals are the creative, intuitive persons (artists, for instance) of society; "left-brained" persons are the verbal, language-oriented, logical individuals of civilization.

Opponents of the split-brain theory dispute the premise that the hemispheres operate independently simply because of specialized functions; they state that the very fact that the two hemispheres differ in purpose indicates that they must integrate activities and therefore result in processes which are different from and even greater than the processes of either hemisphere. These split-brain theory opponents base their arguments on the fact that when surgery is performed to disconnect the two sides, each can still function well (but not perfectly). They also argue that when a person writes an original story, the left hemisphere works to produce a logical work, but the right hemisphere helps with creativity. The third argument is based on the fact that if a patient has right hemisphere damage, major logical disorders are manifested; in fact, more logical disorders appear than if the left hemisphere suffers damage. The opponents to split-brain theory state that it is impossible to educate one side of the brain without educating the other. They state that there is no evidence that one can be purely right-brained or left-brained.

Educators, then, who seek to modify the curriculum and methods to accommodate the split-brain theory must justify their demands. The burden of proof rests with these innovators who seek to restructure education as it currently exists.

17. To the assertion that the split-brain theory is accurate, the author would probably respond with which of the following?

    (A) Unqualified disagreement   (D) Strong disparagement

    (B) Unquestioning approval   (E) Implied uncertainty

    (C) Complete indifference

18. Which of the following titles best describes the content of the passage?

    (A) A Reassertion of the Validity of the Split-Brain Theory

    (B) A Renunciation of the Split-Brain Theory

    (C) Split Opinions on the Split-Brain Theory

    (D) Modifying the Curriculum to Accommodate the Split-Brain Theory

    (E) A New Theory: The Split-Brain Theory

19. The author uses the term "integrate activities" to mean

    (A) share synaptic connections.

    (B) work together.

    (C) coordinate functions.

    (D) break down tasks into left- and right-brain segments.

    (E) pass information from one hemisphere to the other.

20. According to the information given in the passage, which of the following statements are true?

    I.   The left hemisphere of the brain controls language and logic.

    II. The two hemispheres of the brain control different functions.

III. Evidence exists that suggests that some logical functions are controlled by the right hemisphere.

(A) I only   (D) III only

(B) II only   (E) II and III only

(C) I and II only

21. The most compelling argument that the opponents of the split-brain theory present for their beliefs, according to the author, is which of the following?

(A) When surgery is performed to disconnect the two sides of the brain, both sides continue to operate well — but not perfectly.

(B) When a patient has right hemisphere damage, no logical disorders are manifested.

(C) Because of the independent functions of the two hemispheres, an activity might engage one hemisphere of the brain and not another.

(D) The hemispheres operate independently because of specialized functions.

(E) It is impossible to educate one side of the brain without educating the other.

22. According to the passage, the most significant distinction between proponents and opponents of the split-brain theory is which of the following?

(A) Their beliefs about teaching methods and the curriculum

(B) Proponents state that the two hemispheres differ in purpose and, therefore, must integrate activities.

(C) Opponents state that the hemispheres differ in function and, therefore, cannot integrate activities.

(D) Their beliefs about the functions of the hemispheres of the brain

(E) Their beliefs that the brain is divided into hemispheres

23. Which of the following statements is most compatible with the principles of the split-brain theory?

(A) The fact that the two hemispheres differ in purpose indicates that they must integrate activities.

(B) "Right-brained" individuals are the creative, intuitive persons of society; "left-brained" persons are the verbal, language-oriented, logical individuals of civilization.

(C) It is impossible to educate one side of the brain without educating the other.

(D) More logical disorders appear if the right hemisphere is damaged than if the left hemisphere is damaged.

(E) When surgery is performed to disconnect the two sides of the brain, each can function well.

24. To an assertion that education curriculum and methods should be altered to accommodate proponents of the split-brain theory, the author would most likely respond with which of the following?

(A) This is a definite need in our schools today.

(B) Educators have already made these important modifications.

(C) Justification for these alterations must be provided by proponents of the split-brain theory.

(D) It is impossible to educate one side of the brain without educating the other.

(E) Such alterations might be necessary since "right-brained" persons are the verbal, language-oriented, logical individuals.

Being born female and black were two handicaps Gwendolyn Brooks states that she faced from her birth, in 1917, in Kansas. Brooks was determined to succeed. Despite the lack of encouragement she received from her teachers and others, she was determined to write, and found the first publisher for one of her poems when she was 11.

In 1945 she marketed and sold her first book; national recognition ensued. She applied for and received grants and fellowships from such organizations as the American Academy of Arts and Letters and the Guggenheim Foundation. Later she received the Pulitzer Prize for Poetry; she was the first black woman to receive such an honor.

Brooks was an integrationist in the 1940s and an advocate of black consciousness in the 1960s. Her writing styles show that she is not bound by rules; her works are not devoid of the truth, even about sensitive subjects like the black experience, life in the ghetto, and city life.

Brooks' reaction to fame is atypical. She continues to work—and work hard. She writes, travels, and helps many who are interested in writing. Especially important to her is increasing her knowledge of her black heritage and encouraging other people to do the same. She encourages dedication to the art to would-be writers.

25. Which of the following phrases best describes the passage?

    (A) A discussion of the importance of Gwendolyn Brooks' writings

    (B) An essay on the achievements of Gwendolyn Brooks

    (C) An essay on Gwendolyn Brooks as a black female role model

    (D) A biographical sketch on Gwendolyn Brooks

    (E) A discussion of the handicaps faced by black women writers

26. The passage implies that Brooks received less credit than she deserved primarily because of which of the following?

    (A) She tried to publish too early in her career.

    (B) She was aided by funds received through grants.

    (C) She was a frequent victim of both racial and gender discrimination.

    (D) Her work was too complex to be of widespread interest to others.

    (E) She had no interest in the accolades of her colleagues.

27. According to the passage, Gwendolyn Brooks

    (A) marketed her first book when she was 11 years old.

    (B) achieved national recognition when she received the Pulitzer Prize.

    (C) advocated black consciousness in the 1940s.

    (D) received little encouragement from her teachers.

    (E) avoided "black" topics in her writing.

DIRECTIONS: Each of the following questions provides a given word in capitalized letters followed by five word choices. Choose the best word which is most <u>opposite</u> in meaning to the given word.

28. LUDICROUS:

    (A) mundane

    (B) semaphore

    (C) illogical

    (D) reasonable ✓

    (E) fallacious

29. JEOPARDY:

    (A) danger

    (B) safety

    (C) perjury

    (D) conundrum

    (E) levity ✓

30. AWRY:

    (A) earthy

    (B) crooked

    (C) pied

    (D) dubious

    (E) straight ✓

31. INSIDIOUS:

    (A) precipitant

    (B) incendiary

    (C) decadent

    (D) conducive D

    (E) imprudent

32. CAPRICIOUS:

    (A) impecunious

    (B) juxtaposition

    (C) scrupulous

    (D) copious ✓

    (E) superfluous

33. COMPLACENT:

    (A) compliant

    (B) decorous

    (C) passive

    (D) contentious

    (E) sumptuous ✓

34. DOCILE:

    (A) unruly   (D) uncouth

    (B) raucous   (E) strident

    (C) demure

35. POSTULATE:

    (A) mollify   (D) corroborate

    (B) conjecture   (E) refurbish

    (C) prognosticate

36. CONCORD: *agreement*

    (A) succor   (D) vigilant

    (B) enmity *hatred, ill-will* (E) ennobling

    (C) gripper

37. MALEFACTION: *evil deed*

    (A) affinity   (D) idiosyncratic

    (B) subsidy *gift, form of aid*   (E) cognate

    (C) profligation

38. ZEPHYR:

    (A) tycoon   (D) taciturn

    (B) typhoon   (E) constellation

    (C) coracle

STOP

If time still remains, you may go back and check your work.
When the time allotted is up, you may go on to the next section.

Section 5

TIME: 30 Minutes
30 Questions

NUMBERS: All numbers are real numbers.

FIGURES: Position of points, angles, regions, etc., are assumed to be in the order shown and angle measures are assumed to be positive.

LINES: Assume that lines shown as straight are indeed straight.

DIRECTIONS: Each of the following given set of quantities is placed into either Column A or B. Compare the two quantities to decide whether

(A)   the quantity in Column A is greater;

(B)   the quantity in Column B is greater;

(C)   the two quantities are equal;

(D)   the relationship cannot be determined from the information given.

NOTE: Do not choose (E) since there are only four choices.

COMMON INFORMATION: Information which relates to one or both given quantities is centered in the two columns. A symbol which appears in both columns will indicate the same item in Column A and Column B.

EXAMPLES:

	Column A	Column B
1.	5×4	$5 + 4$

Explanation: The correct answer is (A), since $5 \times 4 = 20$, and $5 + 4 = 9$.

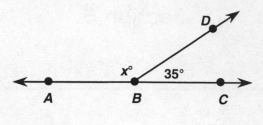

2. $\qquad$ 180 – *x* $\qquad\qquad\qquad$ 35

Explanation: The correct answer is (C). Since ∠ ABC is a straight angle, its measurement is 180°.

Column A	**Column B**
1. Number of minutes in 2½ hours $\quad$ *90*	Number of hours in 6¼ days

$$w : x = y : z$$
$$x \neq 0, \quad z \neq 0$$

2. $\qquad$ $wz - xy$	0

3. $\qquad$ 35% of 7	0.7 of 35

$$\frac{1}{y} < 0$$

4. $\qquad\qquad$ *y*	1

5. $\quad$ $^4\ \dfrac{2}{3}-\dfrac{1}{2}\ \ ^{\frac{3}{6}}\ \ \frac{1}{6}$ $_{6}$	$^{12}_{15}\ \dfrac{4}{5}-\dfrac{2}{3}\ ^{\mathsf{p}}_{15}\quad ^{\frac{2}{5}}_{5}$

$$^{2.5}\quad x + y = 6 \quad ^{3.5}$$
$$3x - y = 4 \qquad 4x = 10$$

6. $\quad$ $^{-1.5}\ x - y\quad ^{7.5}\ \ ^{3.5}$	0

7. $\quad$ $(1 - \sqrt{2})(1 - \sqrt{2})$	$(1 - \sqrt{2})(1 + \sqrt{2})$

212

	Column A	**Column B**

8. Distance between
A(3, 4) and B(−1, 1)

Distance between
C(4, −2) and D(−2, −2)   *B* *6*

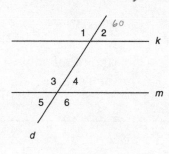

$k \parallel m$
$\angle 2 = 60°$

9. $\angle 5$ *60*   60°   *C*

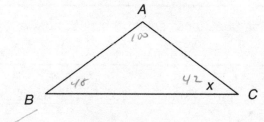

$\angle A = 100°$
$\angle B = 48°$

10.   Side *AB*   Side *BC*   *A*

11. Product of the roots of
$x^2 + 3x - 4$

Product of the roots of
$x^2 + 4x + 4$ *B*

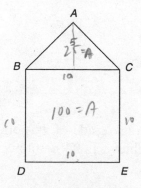

Area of triangle plus
area of square = 125
and perimeter of
square is 40.

12. Twice the length
of line segment *BD*

The shortest distance
from point *A* to line segment *DE*   *A*

213

	Column A	**Column B**

$$\frac{a+2}{a+1} = \frac{a-4}{a-3}$$

A 13. Value of a — 1

A 14. The sum of all angles of a polygon whose sides are all equal — The sum of all angles of a square

$$x < y < z$$

A 15. $|x^2 - y^2|$ — $x^2 - z^2$

DIRECTIONS: For the following questions, select the best answer choice to the given question.

16. A runner takes nine seconds to run a distance of 132 feet. What is the runner's speed in miles per hour?

(A) 9 (B) 10 (C) 11 (D) 12 (E) 13

17. 35 is 7% of what quantity?

(A) 2.45 (B) 5 (C) 245 (D) 50 (E) 500

18. After taking four tests, Joan has an average grade of 79 points. What grade must she get on her fifth test to achieve an 83 point average?

(A) 83 (B) 86 (C) 87 (D) 95 (E) 99

214

3.14
3.14 × 36
1 F 8 4
9 4 2 0
113.04

$\pi \cdot \not{s}^2 = \frac{1}{2} b \cdot h$

19. If a triangle of base 6 units has the same area as a circle of radius 6 units, what is the altitude of the triangle?

A

(A) π   (D) 12π

(B) 3π   (E) 36π

(C) 6π

3.14 · 36

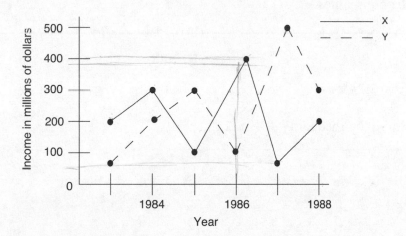

20. A given cube has a surface area of 96 square feet. What is the volume of the cube in cubic feet?

C

(A) 16 $\frac{6A}{6} = \frac{96}{6}$ (D) 96

(B) 36   (E) 216

(C) 64   4·4·4

$113.04 = \frac{1}{2} b \cdot h$

37.6
3)113.04
9
23
21
20

Questions 21–25 refer to the graph below.

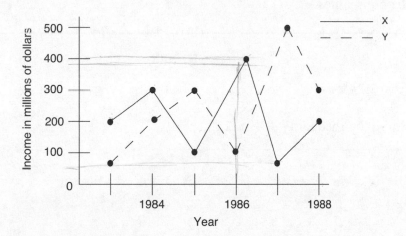

21. What was the average income (in millions) of Company X during the years 1983 to 1986?

(A) 150   (D) 300   D

(B) 200   (E) 400

(C) 250

22. What was the largest difference in earnings (in millions) between the two companies in a given year?

(A) 300   (D) 450   D

(B) 350   (E) 500

(C) 400

23. What was the median income (in millions) of Company X from 1983 through 1988?

    (A) 100   (D) 400

    (B) 200   (E) Can't be determined

    (C) 300

24. What was the largest percent of increase in earnings of Company Y?

    (A) 50%   (D) 300%

    (B) 100%   (E) 400%

    (C) 200%

25. What was the largest percent of decrease in earnings for either one of the companies?

    (A) 50%   (D) 75%

    (B) 100%   (E) 400%

    (C) 200%

26. Solve the inequality $7 - 3x \leq 19$.

    (A) $x = 4$ (D) $x \leq -4$

    (B) $x = -4$ (E) $x \geq 4$

    (C) $x \geq -4$

27. A truck contains 150 small packages, some weighing 1 kg each and some weighing 2 kg each. How many packages weighing 2 kg each are in the truck if the total weight of all the packages is 264 kg?

    (A) 36   (D) 124

    (B) 52   (E) 114

    (C) 88

28. A wheel with a diameter of 3 feet makes a revolution every 2 minutes. How many feet will the wheel travel in 30 minutes?

    (A) 3π (D) 30π

    (B) 6π (E) 15π

    (C) 45π

29. A waitress's income consists of her salary and tips. Her salary is $150 a week. During one week that included a holiday, her tips were $\frac{5}{4}$ of her salary. What fraction of her income for the week came from tips?

(A) $\frac{5}{8}$

(D) $\frac{1}{2}$

(B) $\frac{5}{4}$

(E) $\frac{5}{9}$

(C) $\frac{4}{9}$

30. Each of the integers h, m, and n is divisible by 3. Which of the following integers is <u>always</u> divisible by 9?

I. hm

II. $h + m$

III. $h + m + n$

(A) I only

(D) II and III only

(B) II only

(E) I, II, and III

(C) III only

STOP

If time still remains, you may go back and check your work.
When the time allotted is up, you may go on to the next section.

Section 6

TIME: 30 Minutes
38 Questions

DIRECTIONS: Each of the given sentences has blank spaces which indicate words omitted. Choose the best combination of words which fit into the meaning and structure within the context of the sentence.

---

1. The unmitigated truth is that the author of the essays was _____ in his writing; their publication _____ the teacher's chances for a promotion.

    (A) abusive...enhanced

    (B) laconic...obliterated

    (C) obtuse...obviated

    (D) profound...diminished

    (E) prolific...necessitated.

2. The sales associate tried to _____ trade by distributing business cards.

    (A) elicit

    (B) solicit

    (C) illicit

    (D) elliptic

    (E) conciliate

3. Many doctors now believe that a pregnant woman's _____ for odd foods supplements some lack in her regular diet.

    (A) quirk

    (B) profusion

    (C) pittance

    (D) penchant

    (E) stipend

4. The chairman complained that the committee was wasting too much time on _____ issues, instead of concentrating on the _____ one.

(A) peripheral...essential   (D) superficial...whimsical

(B) scurrilous...tedious   (E) munificent...desultory

(C) trenchant...superfluous

5. The acquisition of exact knowledge is apt to be _____, but it is essential to every kind of excellence.

   (A) wearisome   (D) amorphous   *D*

   (B) equable   (E) eccentric

   (C) erratic

6. The biophysicist's lecture on molecular dynamics was too _____ for many of the students in the audience.

   (A) erudite   (D) inchoate   *C*

   (B) eclectic   (E) amorphous

   (C) abstruse

7. All her attempts to _____ the situation not only failed, but actually seemed to exacerbate the problem.

   (A) excoriate   (D) exculpate   *C*

   (B) disseminate   (E) objurgate

   (C) ameliorate

DIRECTIONS: In the following questions, a related pair of words is followed by five more pairs of words. Select the pair that best expresses the same relationship as that expressed in the original pair.

---

8. GIGGLE:GUFFAW::   *B*

   (A) glove:gauntlet   (D) reprove:berate

   (B) fashion:vogue   (E) wheedle:whine

   (C) sob:weep

9. BENEFICIAL:BALEFUL::

   (A) amiable:anonymous   (B) economical:thrifty

(C) docile:compliant   (D) benign:malice

(E) favorable:ominous

10. ILLUSION:CHARLATAN::

(A) trees:branches   (D) recipe:cook

(B) elements:chemistry   (E) aria:soprano

(C) disease:medicine

11. FUMBLE:FINESSE::

(A) frugal:fluent   (D) impugn:extol

(B) deceive:beguile   (E) abhor:appease

(C) facilitate:expedite

12. PUPA:MOTH::

(A) parapet:wall   (D) tadpole:frog

(B) pommel:saddle   (E) adolescent:adult

(C) stamen:flower

13. VACILLATE:DECISION::

(A) equivocate:commitment   (D) resolve:conclusion

(B) fluctuate:procrastinate (E) ameliorate:resolution

(C) conspire:collusion

14. COALESCE:DISPERSE::

(A) umbrage:offense   (D) elucidate:prevaricate

(B) imprecate:consecrate   (E) debilitate:mitigate

(C) incarcerate:remonstrate

15. CONTUMACIOUS:MUTINEER::

(A) deleterious:renascence   (D) pedagogic:neophyte

(B) ephemeral:biennial   (E) irascible:connoisseur

(C) obsequious:zealot

16. FUSTIAN:BOMBASTIC::

(A) facetious:sardonic

(D) igneous:pecuniary

(B) sanguine:saturnine

(E) nugatory:inordinate

(C) loquacious:garrulous

DIRECTIONS: Each passage is followed by questions based on its content. After reading a passage, choose the best answer to each question. Answer all questions based on what is stated or implied in that passage.

Dr. Harrison Faigel of Brandex University has announced to standardized test-takers across the country the results of his experiment to improve the SAT scores of 30 high school students. Faigel was convinced that student nervousness had affected their scores; to reduce the anxiety of these students who had already been tested, he gave 22 of them a beta blocker before the re-administration of the test. Their scores improved an average of more than 100 points. The other eight (who did not receive the beta blockers) improved only an average of 11 points. Second-time test-takers nationwide improved only an average of 28 points.

Beta blockers are prescription drugs which have been around for 25 years. These medications, which interfere with the effects of adrenaline, have been used for heart conditions and for minor stress such as stage fright—and now for test anxiety. These drugs seem to help test-takers who have low test scores because of test fright, not those who do not "know" the material. Since side effects from these beta blockers do exist, however, some physicians are not ready to prescribe routinely these medications to all test-takers.

17. The author of this article can be best described as which of the following?

(A) Pessimistic

(D) Resigned

(B) Unconcerned

(E) Optimistic

(C) Indifferent

18. The passage suggests which of the following?

    (A) Many researchers will be dissatisfied with Faigel's study be-
        cause he did not use a control group.

    (B) Second-time test-takers nationwide do fine without help; it is the
        first-time test-takers who experience anxiety and a lower score.

    (C) Even without study, preparation, and knowledge of the test ma-
        terial, one can experience help by taking the beta blockers be-
        fore taking a test.

    (D) Adrenaline apparently increases minor stress which may result
        in lower test scores for already nervous students.

    (E) Adrenaline has long been used for heart conditions and for mi-
        nor stress such as stage fright—and now for test anxiety.

19. The passage implies that students' attitudes toward test scores can
    best be described as which of the following?

    (A) Casual disinterest   (D) Pessimism

    (B) Resignation   (E) Concern

    (C) Antagonism

20. The author mentions speculating on the average standardized test
    scores. Which of the following logically ensues?

    (A) Retaking the SAT normally results in a significant increase on the
        scores because of the student's familiarity with the test format.

    (B) The re-administration of tests will be decreased in the future
        since second-time test-takers routinely increase their average
        scores significantly.

    (C) The beta blockers, if used routinely by nervous second-time test-
        takers, may result in an increase in the average standardized test
        scores for the nation.

    (D) Only competitive students will attempt to utilize beta blockers;
        average test scores, therefore, will not be significantly affected.

    (E) Competitive students will try to avail themselves of adrenalin;
        the average scores on standardized tests for the nation will be
        increased.

21. Which of the following best summarizes the author's main point?

    (A) The study by Faigel indicates to the general public that help for general nervousness is at hand through the use of beta blockers.

    (B) Adrenaline increased the performance of 22 second-time test-takers of the SAT.

    (C) Beta blockers seem to improve the average scores of second-time test-takers of the SAT more than 100 points.

    (D) Beta blockers should not be used since they may cause side effects.

    (E) Nervousness does not seem to affect the test scores of students if they "know" the material in the first place.

22. Recognizing that nervousness may affect test scores and developing a plan to reduce the nervousness and to compare the test results is an example of Faigel using which of the following?

    (A) Analysis   (D) Interpretation

    (B) Synthesis   (E) Application

    (C) Deduction

Amyotrophic lateral sclerosis (ALS) is a debilitating disorder which attacks the body's nervous system and renders muscles useless. The disease, which has no known cause or cure, is that which took the life of Lou Gehrig, a member of baseball's Hall of Fame. Even more perplexing is that three former San Francisco 49ers have also died from ALS, which is usually a rare disease. There exists no corroboration for speculations as to whether painkillers, steroids, or even the fertilizers used on playing fields triggered the disease. A solution to the enigma of ALS does not seem imminent.

23. The author's attitude toward ALS is best described as which of the following?

    (A) Amusement   (D) Approval

    (B) Indignation   (E) Resignation

    (C) Indifference

24. Which of the following statements is a correct example of deductive reasoning?

    (A) At least four of the victims of the rare ALS have been athletes; the disease seems to affect active persons more often.

    (B) Four sports figures have died from ALS.

    (C) Since ALS is usually a rare disease, and three victims were from the same football team, some factor in the team's environment may increase the chances of developing the disease.

    (D) Three football players and one baseball player have died from ALS; the next victim will probably be a ballplayer also.

    (E) All four of the most well-known victims of ALS have been males; the disease seems to affect only men.

25. Which of the following words would be the best substitute for the word "corroboration"?

    (A) Support   (D) Analogy

    (B) Evidence   (E) Confirmation

    (C) Reason

26. The topic sentence is which of the following?

    (A) A solution to the enigma of ALS does not seem imminent.

    (B) The disease, which has no known cause or cure, is that which took the life of Lou Gehrig, a member of baseball's Hall of Fame.

    (C) Even more perplexing is that three former San Francisco 49ers have also died from ALS, which is usually a rare disease.

    (D) Amyotrophic lateral sclerosis (ALS) is a debilitating disorder which attacks the body's nervous system and renders muscles useless.

    (E) There exists no corroboration for speculations as to whether painkillers, steroids, or even the fertilizers used on playing fields triggered the disease.

27. Which of the following questions does the passage answer?

    (A) What are the causes of amyotrophic lateral sclerosis?

(B) Who was Lou Gehrig?

(C) What is the cure for amyotrophic lateral sclerosis?

(D) What is amyotrophic lateral sclerosis?

(E) What is the connection between ALS and professional athletes?

DIRECTIONS: Each of the following questions provides a given word in capitalized letters followed by five word choices. Choose the best word which is most <u>opposite</u> in meaning to the given word.

---

28. ODYSSEY: *long series of wanderings*

    (A) journey

    (B) errand *short trip*

    (C) wandering

    (D) voyage

    (E) cruise   *B*

29. ADULTERATE:

    (A) intermix

    (B) hybridize

    (C) interface

    (D) miscegenate

    (E) homogenize   ✓

30. RESPLENDENT:

    (A) wan

    (B) stolid

    (C) shoddy

    (D) trite   ✓

    (E) palatial

31. ALTRUISTIC:

    (A) dogmatic

    (B) abstemious

    (C) fortuitous

    (D) hedonistic   *D*

    (E) apocalyptic

32. VIRILE: manly
    (A) effeminate
    (B) bestial
    (C) equivocal
    (D) choleric
    (E) lecherous

33. BEMOAN: lament
    (A) laugh
    (B) exult rejoice
    (C) commiserate
    (D) acclaim announce
    (E) eulogize

34. MELANCHOLY: sad, depression
    (A) sociability
    (B) serenity
    (C) complacency
    (D) impulsiveness
    (E) exhilaration

35. CLANDESTINE:
    (A) surreptitious
    (B) furtive
    (C) egregious flagrant
    (D) candid
    (E) lurid

36. PROPITIOUS: graciously inclined
    (A) conspicuous
    (B) auspicious
    (C) evanescent
    (D) militant
    (E) aggregative

37. MALAPROPOS: not appropriate
    (A) congruous
    (B) specious
    (C) ponderous
    (D) benign
    (E) propensity

38. UNCOUTH: crude

    (A) melancholy   (D) boorish   E

    (B) ameliorating make mild (E) urbane   polite, civil

    (C) funereal mournful

STOP

If time still remains, you may go back and check your work.
When the time allotted is up, you may go on to the next section.

TEST 1

ANSWER KEY

Sections 1 and 2 — Analytical Writing

Please review the sample essays in the Detailed Explanations.

Section 3 — Quantitative Ability

1. (B)	9. (D)	17. (C)	25. (E)
2. (B)	10. (C)	18. (D)	26. (C)
3. (B)	11. (A)	19. (E)	27. (A)
4. (C)	12. (B)	20. (B)	28. (C)
5. (D)	13. (D)	21. (C)	29. (D)
6. (A)	14. (B)	22. (A)	30. (D)
7. (C)	15. (B)	23. (B)	
8. (C)	16. (C)	24. (A)	

Section 4 — Verbal Ability

1. (D)	11. (C)	21. (A)	31. (D)
2. (C)	12. (A)	22. (D)	32. (C)
3. (A)	13. (C)	23. (B)	33. (D)
4. (B)	14. (B)	24. (C)	34. (A)
5. (E)	15. (B)	25. (D)	35. (D)
6. (C)	16. (C)	26. (C)	36. (B)
7. (A)	17. (E)	27. (D)	37. (B)
8. (B)	18. (C)	28. (D)	38. (B)
9. (D)	19. (C)	29. (B)	
10. (E)	20. (E)	30. (E)	

Section 5 — Quantitative Ability

1.	(C)	9.	(C)	17.	(E)	25.	(D)
2.	(C)	10.	(B)	18.	(E)	26.	(C)
3.	(B)	11.	(B)	19.	(D)	27.	(E)
4.	(B)	12.	(A)	20.	(C)	28.	(C)
5.	(A)	13.	(C)	21.	(C)	29.	(E)
6.	(B)	14.	(D)	22.	(D)	30.	(A)
7.	(A)	15.	(D)	23.	(B)		
8.	(B)	16.	(B)	24.	(E)		

Section 6 — Verbal Ability

1.	(C)	11.	(D)	21.	(C)	31.	(D)
2.	(B)	12.	(D)	22.	(B)	32.	(A)
3.	(D)	13.	(A)	23.	(E)	33.	(B)
4.	(A)	14.	(B)	24.	(C)	34.	(E)
5.	(A)	15.	(B)	25.	(E)	35.	(D)
6.	(C)	16.	(C)	26.	(D)	36.	(D)
7.	(C)	17.	(E)	27.	(D)	37.	(A)
8.	(D)	18.	(D)	28.	(B)	38.	(E)
9.	(E)	19.	(E)	29.	(E)		
10.	(E)	20.	(C)	30.	(C)		

DETAILED EXPLANATIONS OF ANSWERS

Section 1–Analytical Writing

PERSPECTIVES ON AN ISSUE ESSAY TOPIC—ESSAY ONE

Sample Essay Response Scoring 6

Having known a heavy smoker, I can understand how difficult it is to break this habit. The chronic smoker continually asserts the enjoyment that he or she derives from smoking, but smokers often ignore the harmful effects that result for themselves and others around them. I realize that smoking is a powerful addiction, but why should others need to suffer the consequences of another's medical problem? I agree that smoking should be made illegal.

thoughtful opening

strong thesis

I have witnessed children wheeze after their parents smoked in the same room with them for several hours. I myself have often choked in a smoke-filled room, even though I was not the smoker. The odor of a cigarette smoker's clothes precedes him or her into every place that he or she goes. It becomes uncomfortable to visit a friend's home when it has the peculiar odor of old smoke; this makes it difficult for me to breathe freely.

the use of personal experience adds force to the argument

Until cigarettes are classified as the dangerous, addictive drug that they are, smokers will not seek the help they need. They must realize they are harming not only themselves, but the health of those with whom they come into daily contact (car pools, apartment houses, restaurants, etc.) We have come a long way from viewing smoking as romantic, but now it seems that only smokers are blind to the dangers of this habit. Smokers are "in denial." It is the responsibility of the nonsmokers to show this to them by making smoking illegal and offering smokers the health they deserve.

smooth transition

short & therefore strong sentence

As for the help that smoking addicts need, we should concentrate on nicotine addiction in the same manner that we treat other drug addictions. There are always the personal, private clinics, but these are not affordable to everyone. City and state run

well-executed transition between ideas

clinics can service the rest of the smoking population. Perhaps government agencies could accept Medicare and Medicaid to offset the expense. Anti-smoking patches, psychotherapy, support groups, and even cigarette surrogates such as chewing gum could be offered free of charge.

If smoking were to be declared illegal because of its endangerment to everyone's health, then we could not abandon addicted people to their own devices. This would simply lead to an illegal, dangerous "smokers' market," similar to today's drug market. It is our responsibility to make certain that this does not happen; the addicted smoker forced into this position might be your mother, father, brother, sister, or even your child.

good variation in sentence structure

smooth flow of arguments

If I were a smoker, I think that I would feel desperate and lie to myself that I was not harming anyone. No amount of reading newspaper articles about the rise in lung cancer deaths would convince me this is unhealthy to myself and those around me. It would be like reading the Surgeon General's warning on the side of a cigarette box; I would know that something was there, but I would never fully understand its significance. It is a kind of unawareness that lets smokers practice their addiction near little children, invalids, and animals who have no say in the matter. I firmly agree that smoking should be made illegal, but we must provide for those former smokers who are suddenly left empty-handed and addicted.

nicely recapitulates the previous assertions; ability to be sympathetic w/ smokers adds force to argument

Analysis of Sample Essay Response Scoring 6

This paper earns a rating of 6 because it deals with the complexities of the issue: the health hazards of secondhand smoke, the smoker's unawareness of the damage that he or she is causing, the possible position of an addicted smoker if smoking were made illegal, and ways to rejuvenate the addicted smoker. The examples using children, animals, and family members persuasively appeal to the reader's emotions. The suggestion of smokers' clinics is well developed and insightful. The essay is clearly organized, separating the smokers' issues from those of the nonsmoker. The language, including diction and syntactic variety, is clear and controlled. The technical forms of sentence structure, grammar, spelling, and punctuation are satisfactory throughout the essay.

PERSPECTIVES ON AN ISSUE ESSAY TOPIC—ESSAY TWO

Sample Essay Response Scoring 3

Mistakes are just what the name says, mistakes. So to say that a mistake can lead to progress seems to me like just about the dumbest possible thing anyone could say. How can mistakes lead to progress? Mistakes set us back, they don't help us to move forward. This seems pretty obvious to me. Whoever invented the telephone, for instance, did so because he learned how to make something work, not because he made a bunch of mistakes.

too informal, almost to the point of being flip

too informal

Progress comes from smart people having good ideas that work without mistakes. When the space shuttle blew up many years ago, that was not progress, it was a mistake. And we didn't learn from it. We had sent people into space before, and it worked. And we have done so since. So when Challenger blew up, it was because of a mistake, and it did not help to create any positive progress for humankind. I remember I was in school when that happened. It was awful. It was the first real national tragedy I can remember. And it was a sad day especially because a school teacher was on board.

there is no thesis

try not to start a sentence with "and"; avoid repetitive wording

this does not address the essay question

Analysis of Sample Essay Response Scoring 3

The overall language of this essay is too informal. The essayist simply dismisses the essay question without making an argument for or against it. This is supported by the fact that the essay has no thesis. In addition, there is no attempt to understand or assess the subtleties of the topic. In the last paragraph, the essayist is talking about a personal experience without providing a reason for it to be there. The statement that progress is made by smart people having good and flawless ideas is never supported by any example or observation. Also, the essay should have at least one more paragraph. Control of sentence structure, grammar, usage, and mechanics is sufficient.

Section 2–Analytical Writing

ANALYSIS OF AN ARGUMENT ESSAY TOPIC

Sample Essay Response Scoring 6

This argument is logical on the surface, because an electrical "correction" would stop a dog (or any species, for that matter) from continuing the same action which caused the "correction." Repeated doses of "correction" would eventually convince the dog to change direction. It is also feasible that an electrical barrier could be connected to a receiver on the dog's collar. However, there is a flaw in the argument's overall logic. Because "correction" means shock, one must wonder why a pet owner would subject his or her dog to continuous electrical shocks. How logical can it be to keep your dog "safe" by subjecting him to electrical shocks, which are not necessarily safe.

very effective transition

Sustained doses of electrical shock can jar the molecules in your body. Electric shock therapy is used in cases of mentally ill people in an attempt to reorganize their thinking. Who is to say that the same will not happen to dogs? I would like to see sufficient proof that the dog was not being harmed before I would even consider looking at such a product. I am convinced the product will perform as expected, but at what cost to the poor dog?

persuasive argument

effective appeal to emotion

I would also like to see several veterinarians' evaluations of this product. How much current is supplied in that electrical "correction"? How will this affect the dog? In what ways? Upon what research are the answers to these questions based? That raises another issue. If veterinarians take an oath to protect animals, how can they conduct this research at all? I cannot be convinced until I see the results of veterinarians' research that proves this product will not harm dogs. Yet they should not conduct research which may harm dogs. The problem is circular.

good transition between ideas

questions make the weakness of the initial argument visible

this shows the complexity of the subject

I also feel the company that produces this product should be able to provide some verifiable research that explains how the product works. Some significant information that might be provided includes the following: 1) the specific electrical current for each "correction"; 2) how often a "correction" can be administered before it permanently damages the animal; 3) the person who decides on the guidelines for each of the numbers provided as well as his or her qualifications.

good
transition
⟶ ⟨Furthermore,⟩ I would like to read some testimonials from long-term users of this product; I would also like their telephone numbers, so that I might call them and personally verify that there was no ill effect on the dog.

What I find the most illogical and unconvincing aspect of this argument is the use of the word "safe" in conjunction with "electrical corrections." While the scientific reasoning makes sense, this segment of the argument is a paradox; it seems to invalidate the straightforward scientific explanation with a lot of shading, some of it apparently designed to mislead the reader.

cogent
summary
of earlier
raised
objections
- this is a
strong
conclusion

Analysis of Sample Essay Scoring 6

This essay earns a rating of 6: It clearly opposes the argument that this product should be used instead of chains, ropes, or fences to keep dogs within a certain boundary. A counter-argument is raised that makes the product appear unsafe. The essay's ideas are developed cogently, organized logically, and connected by smooth transitions. This can be seen in the paper's persuasive reliance on emotional and moral criteria that answer the coldly scientific argument for the use of this product. While there are minor flaws, the writer demonstrates superior control over language, including diction, syntactic variety, and the conventions of standard written English.

Section 3–Quantitative Ability

1.   **(B)**
   To compare $(x + y)^2$ with $(x - y)^2$, set $x = 5$ and $y = -3$ in each expression and calculate. We get

$$(x + y)^2 = [5 + (-3)]^2 = (5 - 3)^2 = 2^2 = 4 \text{ and}$$
$$(x - y)^2 = [5 - (-3)]^2 = (5 + 3)^2 = 8^2 = 64.$$

Since $64 > 4$ we can conclude that $(x - y)^2$ in Column B is larger than $(x + y)^2$ in Column A for $x = 5$ and $y = -3$.

   If response (A) is chosen then perhaps an error was made in the computation after substituting the values for x and y, respectively. Or, it was assumed that $(x + y)$ is always greater than $(x - y)$ and thus

$$(x + y)^2 \text{ is greater than } (x - y)^2.$$

Response (C) implies that $(x + y)^2 = (x - y)^2$ for $x = 5$ and $y = -3$ which is not possible. Finally, response (D) as a choice is incorrect.

2.   **(B)**

   Simplify Column A: $\dfrac{2}{3} + \dfrac{3}{2} = \dfrac{4}{6} + \dfrac{9}{6} = \dfrac{13}{6}$

Find a common denominator for the fraction in Column B: $\dfrac{5}{2} = \dfrac{15}{6}$

Therefore, Column B is larger than Column A.

3.   **(B)**
   To compare the expression $x^2 + y^2$ in Column A with $(x + y)^2$, one should first assume that these expressions are equal. Then

$$x^2 + y^2 = (x + y)^2 \text{ implies } x^2 + y^2 = x^2 + 2xy + y^2. \quad (1)$$

If x and y are both positive, their squares are also positive. So, a one-to-one comparison of the expression in Column B with the expression in Column A indicates that Column B is larger since it has an extra term, $2xy$, which is positive. Hence, response (B) is correct.

Response (C) is not possible. To see this add $-x^2$ and $-y^2$, respectively, on both sides of (1). So, one obtains

$$x^2 + y^2 - x^2 = x^2 + 2xy + y^2 - x^2$$
$$y^2 = 2xy + y^2$$
$$y^2 - y^2 = 2xy + y^2 - y^2$$
$$0 = 2xy$$

Note that $2xy = 0$ means that either $x = 0$, $y = 0$, or $x = y = 0$. So, the assertion of equality between the two statements leads to a contradiction since the original assumption is that both x and y are positive.

4.   **(C)**

The average (arithmetic mean), $\bar{x}$, of a set of numbers is defined as the sum of all the numbers in the set divided by the number of numbers, n. That is,

$$\bar{x} = \frac{\text{sum of all numbers}}{n}$$

In this problem, calculating the average, $\bar{x}$, of the given numbers, we get

$$\bar{x} = \frac{40 + 20 + 30 + 24 + 27 + 15}{6}$$

$$= \frac{156}{6} = 26$$

So the two quantities in Columns A and B are equal.

5.   **(D)**

To determine the outcome consider the following:

If $4w = 6x = 12y$, then $\frac{4w}{4} = \frac{12y}{4}$ or $w = 3y$. Thus, in general for positive numbers the value of w is always three times as large as the value of y. So response (A) would be correct. But, if one substitutes 0 for w, then w and y have the same value 0. So, the quantities are equal and response (C) is correct. Finally, if the values of w and y are both negative, then response (B) is correct. (For example, if $w = -12$, then $y = -4$ which is larger than w.) Thus, there is not enough information given to make a comparison.

6.   **(A)**

Perhaps the easiest way to approach the comparison of the two quantities is to first find the least common multiple for the denominators, 16 and 40, which is 80. Then, write equivalent fractions using the LCD. The results are

$$\frac{13}{16} \times \frac{5}{5} = \frac{65}{80} \quad \text{and} \quad \frac{31}{40} \times \frac{2}{2} = \frac{62}{80}.$$

Since the numerator, 65, in the equivalent fraction in Column A is greater than the one in Column B, the fraction in Column A is greater.

7. **(C)**

To understand this problem first assume that $\triangle ABC$ is a right triangle. With this assumption the Pythagorean Theorem applies as follows:

$$(AC)^2 = (AB)^2 + (BC)^2.$$

Since the length of the sides of the triangle are given $(AC = 17, AB = 8, BC = 15)$, substitute in the formula and observe whether the result is an equality.

$$(17)^2 = (8)^2 + (15)^2$$
$$289 = 64 + 225$$
$$289 = 289$$

Because the result is an equality, the assumption that the triangle is a right triangle is correct. So, the angle opposite the longest side ($\angle ABC$) must be a right angle. The quantities in the two columns are equal.

8. **(C)**

To explain this answer one needs to first know that the exterior angle of a triangle equals the sum of the measure of both remote interior angles of the triangle. The exterior angle of $\triangle CDE$ is $\angle x$ and the remote interior angles are C and D. So, the sum of angles C and D equals $\angle x$. Similarly, the exterior angle of $\triangle ABE$ is angle x and the remote interior angles are A and B. So, the sum of angles A and B equals $\angle x$. Hence, by substitution, one gets that the quantities in the two columns are equal as follows:

$$\angle x + \angle x = (\angle A + \angle B) + (\angle C + \angle D) \text{ or}$$
$$2(\angle x) = \angle A + \angle B + \angle C + \angle D.$$

9. **(D)**

Note that $w : x = {}^w\!/_x$, and $y : z = {}^y\!/_z$. Thus, ${}^w\!/_x = {}^y\!/_z$ is a proportion. Simplify the proportion by recalling that the product of the extremes equals the product of the means. The result is $wz = xy$. Since the values of w, x, y, and z are both positive and negative real numbers, there is not enough information that will allow comparison of the quantities $w + x$ and $y = z$.

10. **(C)**

Since $\overline{BA}$ equals $\overline{BC}$, $\triangle ABC$ is isosceles. Thus, according to a well-known theorem, the angles BAC and BCA are equal. Since angles x and y

are supplementary angles to *BAC* and *BCA,* respectively, it is clear that

$$\angle x + \angle BAC = 180° \text{ and } \angle y + \angle BCA = 180°.$$

But, since $\angle BAC = \angle BCA$ one can conclude that $\angle x = \angle y$. So, the quantities in the columns are equal.

11. **(A)**

The quantity in Column A is determined by a series of steps. First, observe that radii *OG* and *OH* are equal legs of right triangle *GOH*. Since the area of the right triangle is 12.5, one can easily obtain the length of each leg of the triangle as follows:

$$\text{Area of } GOH = \left(\frac{1}{2}\right)(\text{leg})(\text{leg}) = \left(\frac{1}{2}\right)(\text{leg})^2 = 12.5$$

$$(\text{leg})^2 = 25 \Rightarrow \text{leg} = 5$$

Next, find the area of the square by using the Pythagorean Theorem to obtain the length of side *GH,* the hypotenuse of the right triangle, as follows:

$$(GH)^2 = (\text{leg})^2 + (\text{leg})^2 \Rightarrow (GH)^2 = 50$$

$$\text{or } GH = \sqrt{50} = 5\sqrt{2}$$

Then, the area of the square is $(GH)^2 = 50$.

Now, find the area of the circle as follows: Area $= \pi r^2 = (5)^2\pi = 25\pi$.

Finally, the area of the shaded part of the figure is approximately as follows:

Shaded area $= 25\pi - 50$
$\qquad\qquad = 25(3.14) - 50$
$\qquad\qquad = 78.5 - 50$
$\qquad\qquad = 28.5$

Comparing this value with the value in Column B, $9\pi = 9(3.14) = 28.26$, indicates that the quantity in Column A is larger.

12. **(B)**
First, evaluate the shaded area with the following procedure: This half-shaded area can be expressed by

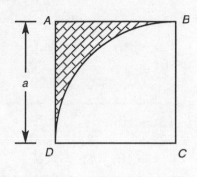

Half-shaded area

$$= (\text{Square area} - \text{Quadrant area})$$

$$= a^2 - \frac{\pi a^2}{4} = a^2\left(1 - \frac{\pi}{4}\right)$$

because the quadrant represents one-fourth of the area of a circle with the radius a. Therefore, the shaded area in the problem will be

$$\text{Shaded area} = 2a^2\left(1 - \frac{\pi}{4}\right) = .43a^2.$$

The unshaded area can be expressed by

$$\text{Unshaded area} = (\text{Square area} - \text{Shaded area})$$

$$= a^2 - 2a^2\left(a - \frac{\pi}{4}\right)$$

$$= a^2\left(\frac{\pi}{2} - 1\right) = .57a^2$$

Therefore, the unshaded area > the shaded area.

13. **(D)**
Since nothing is given about the value of w, the value could be negative or positive. If the w is negative, the value of w^n and w^m can be negative or positive values. If w equals 0 or 1, Column A and B will be equal. If w is positive, then Column B will be greater than Column A.

14. **(B)**
Set up three equations from the information given.

Let x = cost of one orange
Let y = cost of one apple
Let z = cost of one pear

First, solve for the cost of the pear.

$$12x + 10y = 2.20 \quad (1)$$
$$6x + 4z = 1.20 \quad (2)$$
$$ 3y + 6z = 1.20 \quad (3)$$

$$12x + 10y = 2.20 \quad (1)$$
$$12x + 8z = 2.40 \quad \text{Subtract equation (2) multiplied by 2}$$
$$ 10y - 8z = -.20 \quad (4)$$

$$30y + 60z = 12 \quad \text{Equation (3) multiplied by 10}$$
$$30y - 24z = -.6 \quad \text{Subtract equation (4) multiplied by 3}$$
$$84z = 12.6$$
$$z = .15 \quad \text{Cost of one pear}$$

$$10y - 8(.15) = -.20 \quad \text{Find the cost of one apple}$$
$$10y - 1.20 = -.20$$
$$10y = 1.00$$
$$y = .10 \quad \text{Cost of one apple}$$

Column A = .10 + .15 = .25
Column B = 2(.15) = .30

15. **(B)**

The area of the square $= a^2$

The area of the right triangle in terms of $a = \dfrac{(2a)^2}{2} = \dfrac{4a^2}{2} = 2a^2$.

Therefore, Column B is greater than Column A.

16. **(C)**

First, observe that three-fourths is $\frac{3}{4}$ and one tenth is $\frac{1}{10}$. Let x be the unknown part which must be found. Then, one can write from the statement of the problem that the x part of three-fourths is given by

$$\frac{3}{4}x$$

The equation for the problem is given by $\dfrac{3}{4}x = \dfrac{1}{10}$. Multiplying both sides of the equation by the reciprocal of $\dfrac{3}{4}$ one obtains the following:

$$\left(\dfrac{4}{3}\right)\dfrac{3}{4}x = \left(\dfrac{4}{3}\right)\dfrac{1}{10} \text{ or } x = \dfrac{4}{30} \text{ or } x = \dfrac{2}{15}$$

which is choice (C).

Response (D) is obtained by incorrectly finding the product of $\frac{3}{4}$ and $\frac{1}{10}$ to be the unknown part. Response (B) is obtained by dividing $\frac{3}{4}$ by $\frac{1}{10}$.

17. **(C)**
Simplify
$$2x + 12 = 3x + 9.$$
$$12 - 9 = 3x - 2x$$
$$3 - x$$

18. **(D)**

$$\text{Average} = \dfrac{5 \times 30 + 3 \times 20}{8}$$

$$\text{Average} = \dfrac{150 + 60}{8} = \dfrac{210}{8} = 26.25$$

19. **(E)**
Let X = cost of one pound of pears
Let Y = cost of one pound of peaches
$$2X + Y = 1.4 \quad (1)$$
$$3X + 2Y = 2.4 \quad (2)$$

$$4X + 2Y = 2.8 \quad \text{(3) Multiply equation (1) by 2}$$
$$\underline{3X + 2Y = 2.4} \quad \text{(4) Subtract (2) from (3)}$$

$$X = .4 \quad \text{Substitute } X = .4 \text{ in (1)}$$
$$Y = .6$$

Therefore, $X + Y = 1.00$

20. **(B)**
One can represent the three consecutive odd numbers as follows: $2x + 1$, $2x + 3$, and $2x + 5$, respectively. The sum of these numbers is

$$(2x + 1) + (2x + 3) + (2x + 5) = 6x + 9.$$

Clearly 2, 5, and 6 do not divide $6x + 9$ exactly (without a remainder). Hence, answer choices (A), (C), (D), and (E) are incorrect. So, answer choice (B) is correct, that is, the value 3 does divide the sum $6x + 9$ as follows:

$$\frac{(6x+9)}{3} = \frac{3(2x+3)}{3} = 2x+3,$$

the quotient.

21. **(C)**
For area there are two columns, one in sq. mi. and the second in sq. km. In the latter appear two numbers for the Pacific division.

$$2,310,958$$
$$2,374,315$$

The first one is for land area and the second one for total area.

22. **(A)**
The largest division is the Pacific – (2,310,958 km^2 or 892,226 mi^2). The New England division has the smallest area – (163,149 km^2 or 69,992 mi^2).

23. **(B)**
Land area (U.S.)= 9,170,987 km^2
Pacific $\quad\quad$ = 2,310,958 km^2
East N. Central = 632,905 km^2

$$\text{percentage} = \frac{2,310,958 + 632,905}{9,170,987} \times 100\% = 32.1\%$$

24. **(A)**
To find the increase in population from 1970-1980 in the New England area, subtract the population of 1970 from the population of 1980.

$$1980 - 12,349,000$$
$$1970 - 11,842,000$$

Increase in the population of the New England area = 12,349,000 – 11,842,000 = 507,000.
To find the average increase in population of a state in the New England area, divide the increase in population from 1970-1980 by 6, the number of states in the region.

The average increase of a state in the New England area =

$$\frac{507,000}{6} = 84,500.$$

25. **(E)**

First, calculate the rate in the period 1970-80 for the East North Central Division.

$$\frac{\text{Population 1980}}{\text{Population 1970}} = \frac{41,668,000}{40,253,000} = 1.0352.$$

The rate of increase is .0352 or 3.52%.

$$
\begin{aligned}
\text{Population 1990} &= \text{Population 1980} + (0.352 \times \text{Pop. 1980}) \\
&= 41,668,000 + (.0352 \times 41,668,000) \\
&= 43,134,710
\end{aligned}
$$

26. **(C)**

Based on the information given in the first sentence of the problem one needs to first represent the unknown numbers. So let x be a number. Then, the other number is given by $3x + 2$, which is two more than 3 times the first number. So the two numbers are x and $3x + 2$.

Next, form an equation by adding the two numbers and setting the sum equal to 22 and then solve the equation for the two numbers.

$$
\begin{aligned}
x + 3x + 2 &= 22 \\
4x + 2 &= 22 \\
4x &= 20 \\
x &= 5, \text{ one of the numbers.}
\end{aligned}
$$

The other number is given by

$$3x + 2 = 3(5) + 2 = 15 + 2 = 17, \text{ the other number.}$$

Hence, answer choice (C) is correct. The other answer choices fail to satisfy the equation $x + 3x + 2 = 22$.

27. **(A)**

In order to find the perimeter of the rectangle, it is important first to understand the definition, that is, perimeter equals the sum of the dimension of the rectangle. Hence, for the given rectangle,

$$
\begin{aligned}
\text{Perimeter} &= 6L + 4W + 6L + 4W \text{ (Add like terms)} \\
&= 12L + 8W
\end{aligned}
$$

Answer choice (E), $24LW$, is incorrect because it represents the area of the rectangle, which is the product of the length and width. Answer choice

(C), $6L + 4W$, is incorrect because it represents only one-half of the perimeter of the rectangle. Answer choice (D), $20LW$, is incorrect because this response is obtained by simply adding the coefficients of L and W which is an incorrect application of algebra. Finally, answer choice (B), $12L^2 + 8W^2$, is incorrect because it is obtained by using the definition of the perimeter of a rectangle incorrectly as follows: perimeter $= 2L(6L) + 2W(4W)$.

28. **(C)**

Let x be the length of the rectangle. Then, a 30% increase in the length of the rectangle is given by $x + .3x$. Let y be the width of the rectangle. Then, a 20% decrease in the width of the rectangle is given by $y - .2y$. The original area is given by $A = xy$ and the new area is given by:

$$\begin{aligned} A &= (x + .3x)\,(y - .2y) \\ &= xy - .2xy + .3xy - 0.06xy \\ &= xy + 0.04xy \\ &= 1.04xy \end{aligned}$$

So, the new area is 104% of the original area which is a 104% − 100% = 4% increase, which is answer choice (C). The other answer choices are found by either using the perimeter formula or incorrectly finding the increase and decrease in the length and width, respectively.

29. **(D)**

With n being the first odd number, it follows that $n + 2$ and $n + 4$ are the next two odd numbers. This eliminates answer choices (A) and (B) on the basis that each one of them represents only one of the two consecutive odd numbers that follow n. Since the sum of the three consecutive odd numbers is $n + (n + 2) + (n + 4) = 3n + 6$, it follows that neither of answer choices (C) and (E) is correct, which leaves answer choice (D) as correct.

30. **(D)**

The area of a triangle is equal to the product of the length of its base (any one of its sides) and the length of its altitude (the perpendicular segment drawn from the opposite vertex to the base of the triangle or to the line containing the base of the triangle).

For each of the triangles, the segment $\overline{AB}$ can be used as the base. The altitude of ΔABC is the perpendicular distance from C to line m. The altitude of ΔABD is the perpendicular distance from D to line m. Since C and D both lie on line l and and lines l and m are parallel, then the altitudes of the triangles must be equal. Thus the area of ΔABD is 40cm^3.

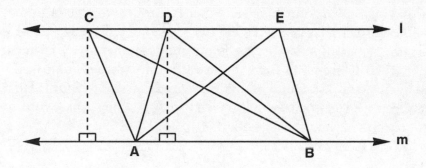

Section 4–Verbal Ability

1. **(D)**
    IMPLORED (A) is a verb meaning begged; it does not fit well into the content of the sentence and is not the right answer. EXTORTED means having drawn something (like money) from someone by force; (B) is not the correct answer. EXHORTED means urged by words of good advice or cautioned; since urging is not the issue here, (C) is incorrect. ADMONISHED seems to fit best since it means warned, reproved, cautioned against specific faults. (D) is the correct answer. ABOLISHED (E) means destroyed or to have put an end to something; this word is too strong for the sentence.

2. **(C)**
    EMIGRATE is usually accompanied by the preposition *from;* this word does not fit. Neither is it likely that there would be a PROSECUTION (a legal suit against) simply because of beliefs, not actions. (A) is not the best answer. PEREGRINATE means to travel, but EXTORTION (drawing something from someone by force) does not fit logically in the sentence. (B) is incorrect. One IMMIGRATES to another place; PERSECUTION (torment, abuse) might be typical for one's beliefs. These are logical choices; (C) is correct. Since WANDER implies no set destination, this choice does not fit well. Coupled with the word ARRAIGNMENT (the act of bringing before a court), (D) is clearly not a suitable choice. ROAM implies no set destination, this choice does not fit well. CENSURE indicates blame or criticism, but is not acceptable coupled with ROAM. Choice (E) is incorrect.

3. **(A)**
    A REPARTEE is a clever, witty retort; DORMANT suggests inactivity of that which is present. A person who bides her time before giving a statement would hold that retort or REPARTEE DORMANT. (A) is the best answer. WIT suggests the power to evoke laughter by remarks showing quick perception; it is not usually preceded by the article *a*. Only one statement is suggested by the sentence. LATENT stresses concealment. (B) is not the best answer. SATIRE is wit used for the purpose of exposing vice. HIBERNATING is the passing of winter in a lethargic state. These two words of choice (C) are not the best choices for the sentence. HUMOR is an ability to see the absurd and the comical in life's situations; it suggests a series of incidents rather than just one retort. CAMOU-

FLAGED implies that which is disguised. The sentence suggests not a disguising of the witty statement but rather a concealment of it until the proper moment. (D) is not the best answer. A SORTIE is a mission or an attack. It does not fit the sentence at all. DISGUISED could fit the sentence, but not when paired with SORTIE. (E) is not the best answer.

4. **(B)**

IMPLIED is a transitive verb; it must have an object. There is no direct object here so IMPLIED does not fit well. ABROGATE is to annul, to abolish. Because IMPLIED does not fit well, (A) should not be selected. INFERRED is an intransitive verb in this sentence; it means to draw conclusions from data given. It fits well in this sentence. NEGOTIATE (procure) fits well in this sentence also. (B) is the correct answer. IMPOSED is to pass off or to obtrude. The word does not fit the meaning of the sentence well at all. NULLIFY (to make or render of no value) fits the sentence but not when coupled with IMPOSED. (C) is not the best choice. SURMISED is to imagine or to guess on slight charges. BREECH is to cover with breeches; a person who selected (D) probably confused BREECH with BREACH (to cancel). INCLUDED means contained; a person who chose (E) probably read the word as concluded, rather than INCLUDED. ANNIHILATE means to make void.

5. **(E)**

The prosecutor was not satisfied with the judge's decision. That means that the correct adjective must be negative, to express this dissatisfaction. AMBIGUOUS (vague), ASTUTE (shrewd), ARDUOUS (laborious, difficult), and AUSPICIOUS (favorable) do not carry a negative connotation. Choices (A), (B), (C), and (D) are all inappropriate adjectives to complete the sentence. Only ARBITRARY (based on one's preference, not on reason) is the logical adjective to complete the sentence. (E) is the correct choice.

6. **(C)**

The missing word must be some form of speech, so PALINDROME (B), a sentence that reads the same forward and backward, and QUANDARY (D), a state of doubt or perplexity, cannot be correct. COLLOQUY (A) is a dialogue, requiring two or more speakers; the sentence refers only to Hamlet, implying that there are no other speakers in the speech referred to. (A) is not the correct choice. SOLILOQUY (C) means a monologue that usually presents the character's inner reflections to the audience and is treated as if unheard by the other actors. Because the sentence refers to a speech and to only a single character, (C) is the correct answer. OBLO-

QUY (E) means to speak abusively or offensively. It is not an appropriate choice.

7. **(A)**

   People were inspired by the ABNEGATION, or self-denial, of St. Francis. (A) is the correct choice. TURPITUDE, which means depravity, is the opposite of the word sought. (B) is not an appropriate choice. CALUMNY (C) refers to false charges or misrepresentation; it is not the correct choice. VACILLATION (D) means indecision; it is not an appropriate word to complete the sentence. DICHOTOMY (E) means a division into two, often contradictory, groups.

8. **(B)**

   MANDATORY (required) and OPTIONAL are antonyms. COMPETENT and INEPT are also antonyms; the correct answer is (B). PIOUS:INDIGNANT (A) and OPAQUE:ORNATE (C) are unrelated pairs. CHASTE:CELIBATE (D) and CRASS:BOORISH (E) are synonymous pairs.

9. **(D)**

   A FINE is a form of PUNISHMENT, and JIGSAW is a form of PUZZLE; therefore, the correct answer is (D). Choices (A), HYACINTH:FLOWER, and (E), SANDALS:SHOES, reflect a specific:general relationship. ORANGE:PEEL reflects a whole:part relationship, so (B) is a wrong choice. HEART is the mechanism that provides CIRCULATION, so (C) is not the correct choice.

10. **(E)**

    The key pair and all of the choice pairs give a first term that is something that is put on the second term. However, a BANDAGE is put on a WOUND to promote healing. Only choice (E) reflects this aspect of the key pair. A CAST is put on a FRACTURE to promote healing.

11. **(C)**

    To ESPOUSE a THEORY is to support and promote it. To ADVOCATE a HYPOTHESIS is to support and promote it; the correct answer is (C). PROPONENT and OPPONENT are opposites; (A) is not the correct answer. CREATE and INNOVATE have synonymous meanings; (B) is not the correct choice. HERETIC:BLASPHEMY and GOURMAND:GLUTTONY both link a noun with an action associated with that noun. (D) and (E) are not correct answers.

12. **(A)**

TRACTABLE and BIDDABLE are synonyms meaning obedient. TORPID and LETHARGIC are synonyms meaning lazy; (A) is the correct answer. VISCOUS:LIQUID and COLLOQUIAL:FORMAL have antonymous relationships; therefore, (B) and (D) are incorrect. TRUCULENT, meaning argumentative, and CONTRITE, or sorry, are unrelated; (C) is not the correct answer. ECCENTRIC (peculiar) and AESTHETIC (tasteful) are also unrelated, so (E) is not the correct answer.

13. **(C)**

DEIGN:CONDESCEND have a synonymous relationship. BERATE (to belittle) and COMMEND (to praise) are antonyms, as are CORROBORATE (to support) and REPUDIATE (to deny). (A) and (B) are incorrect. DIGRESS and STRAY are synonyms; the correct answer is (C). IMBUE (permeate) and DESICCATE (dry out) are not related; (D) is not correct. VAUNT (boast) is unrelated to WITHER (shrivel); (E) is not the answer.

14. **(B)**

A FRAILTY is an imperfection. The term VICE is used to denote a "serious" imperfection. The difference is a matter of degree, with FRAILTY being milder. A FELONY is more serious than a MISDEMEANOR. The analogy is, however, inverted from the example; thus, (A) should not be selected. AGGRAVATION is irritation, annoyance; RAGE is AGGRAVATION ratcheted up to a very high degree. The degree of RAGE is greater than that of AGGRAVATION. Their relationship is that of FRAILTY:VICE. (B) is the correct answer. TRITE is overworked, overused. POPULAR is common. The degree of the two is different, but the analogy is different from that of FRAILTY:VICE. (C) is not the correct answer. SECRETED is more carefully hidden than VEILED; again, the order is inverted from the example. (D) is incorrect. A CLOISTER implies seclusion from the world. A MONASTERY is a CLOISTER for monks. The relationship between CLOISTER and MONASTERY in choice (E) is not the one sought here.

15. **(B)**

ANALOGOUS (similar) and PARALLEL (closely similar) are synonyms. ACIDULOUS (sour) and SACCHARINE (sickeningly sweet) are not synonyms so (A) is incorrect. SINUOUS and TORTUOUS both mean curving, winding. The two are synonymous and, thus, (B) is the best answer. INCONGRUOUS means dissimilar; it is an antonym to HOMOGENEOUS, which suggests similarity. (C) is wrong. A PUNDIT is an expert, while a TYRO is a novice. Since the two are antonyms, (D) is not, therefore, the correct answer. MUNDANE is common, everyday; CELES-

TIAL refers to heavenly. Because MUNDANE is opposite from CELES-
TIAL, (E) should not be selected.

16. **(C)**
   FINE and AMERCEMENT are synonymous for a penalty. LOSS and
GAIN are opposites. FORFEITURE is a fine; REWARD is the opposite.
(B) is incorrect since the pair does not have the same relationship as
FINE:AMERCEMENT. PENALTY and MULCT are synonymous words.
(C) is the correct answer. A LOTTERY is an affair of chance. DEPOSIT
as a noun means that which is entrusted to the care of another, a pledge.
The relationship between the pair is not the synonymous relationship
sought. (D) is incorrect. CONTRABAND is illegal or prohibited com-
merce; it can also refer to goods or merchandise the importation or expor-
tation of which is forbidden. CONFISCATE is a verb meaning to seize or
appropriate; as an adjective it means appropriated or forfeited. The
relationship is not that sought. (E) should not be selected.

17. **(E)**
   There is no evidence that the author disagrees so vehemently with the
split-brain theory as to respond with UNQUALIFIED DISAGREEMENT.
(A) is not the best answer. UNQUESTIONING APPROVAL is not the
attitude of the author; rather she seems willing to listen to both sides,
though she seems more inclined to disagree with the theory. (B) is not the
best answer. The very fact that the author wrote the articles negates the
idea that COMPLETE INDIFFERENCE is the best answer; (C) is not the
best choice. Although the author seems to disagree with the split-brain
theory, STRONG DISPARAGEMENT is not the best answer; (D) should
not be chosen. IMPLIED UNCERTAINTY seems to be the best of the
choices. (E) is the best answer.

18. **(C)**
   (A) is incorrect since the split-brain theory is not reasserted by the
author in the article. Since the split-brain theory is not renunciated by the
author, (B) is not the correct choice. (C) is the best answer since it implies
what the article does—present both sides of the theory. Since modifying
the curriculum is only one part of the article, (D) is incorrect. Since the
split-brain theory is not new, (E) is inaccurate.

19. **(C)**
   The author is saying that, according to the opponents of the split-
brain theory, both hemispheres work on tasks that proponents try to label
"left-" or "right-brained," and that the cooperation between hemispheres

yields a better result than if only one hemisphere had functioned. In this context, to "integrate activities" means to "coordinate functions" to produce the better result. This meaning includes working together (B), separating the task into functions for each hemisphere (D), and sharing needed information between hemispheres (E). There is no reference in the passage to synapses or synaptic connections, so (A) is an inappropriate choice.

20. **(E)**

The passage states that proponents of the split-brain theory insist that "[t]he left hemisphere...controls language and logic." However, opponents of the theory do not think this is correct, so Statement I is false. Both proponents and opponents of the theory agree that the different hemispheres control different functions; that is not a point of contention. Therefore, Statement II is true. The passage states that the third argument presented by opponents of the split-brain theory is the fact that patients who sustain damage to the right hemisphere often show major logical disorders. This suggests that the right hemisphere controls at least some logical functions; therefore, Statement III is true. Choice (E), II and III only, is correct.

21. **(A)**

(A) is the correct answer. (B) is not the correct answer since damage to the right (as well as the left) side of the brain may result in logical disorders. (C) is not the right answer since it has not been proven to the satisfaction of everyone that one hemisphere may be engaged to the exclusion of the other. The article suggests that the two sides work cooperatively. (D) is, therefore, incorrect. The writer suggests that education involves both (not just one) side of the brain. (E) is incorrect.

22. **(D)**

Proponents and opponents do disagree about methods and curriculum but that is not a fundamental difference; (A) is incorrect. (B) is false; proponents do agree that the purposes of the hemispheres do differ but that the integration of activities is not urged, or even thought possible, by many. Opponents do not always state that the two hemispheres differ significantly in function nor do they always believe that integration of the activities is impossible; (C) is incorrect. The beliefs about the functions of the two hemispheres of the brain are the fundamental differences between proponents and opponents of the split-brain theory; (D) is the correct answer. Both groups agree that the brain is divided into hemispheres; this is not the DISTINCTION between the two groups. (E) is not the correct answer.

23. **(B)**

(A) is a statement that OPPONENTS, not PROPONENTS, of the split-brain theory might espouse; (A) is incorrect. (B) is the correct answer. (C) is incorrect; this is a belief of the OPPONENTS of the split-brain theory. (D) is not the correct choice; this finding is one OPPONENTS of the split-brain theory often make known. Statement (E) is one OPPONENTS of the theory use.

24. **(C)**

The author would disagree with (A). (B) is certainly incorrect; the modifications have neither already been made nor are they on the agenda of most educators. (C) is the correct answer. (D) is incorrect; the author's open-minded point of view is not illustrated by this statement. The reader should immediately see (E) as erroneous since it reverses the hemisphere associated by proponents of the theory with language and logic.

25. **(D)**

The passage does include a discussion of the importance of Brooks' writing (A), mentioning the awards she's won and her use of black topics; a list of her achievements (B); a discussion of her importance as a role model (C), referring to her helping young writers and encouraging blacks to learn about their heritage; and does discuss the handicaps of being black and female (E). All of these phrases, however, are too specific to describe the passage well, because the passage encompasses all of these themes. The best phrase to describe the passage is (D), a biographical sketch on Gwendolyn Brooks.

26. **(C)**

Brooks was a published writer by eleven; (A) is incorrect. Grants did not lessen, but heighten, her prestige. (B) is incorrect. (C) is the correct answer. After her first book was sold, she received nationwide recognition; (D) is wrong. Brooks takes an interest in others; (E) is incorrect.

27. **(D)**

All of the statements are false except (D). It was Brooks' first poem that was published when she was eleven; her first book was not marketed until 1945. Choice (A) is false. Brooks received national recognition after her first book was published, before she won the Pulitzer Prize; choice (B) is false. Brooks was an integrationist in the 1940s and advocated black consciousness in the 1960s; choice (C) is false. Brooks did write about the black experience; so choice (E) is false. Brooks did receive little encouragement from her teachers (D), and succeeded despite this lack (line 3).

28. **(D)**
    LUDICROUS means illogical, senseless or absurd. MUNDANE means earthly; it does not relate to LUDICROUS. (A) is not the correct answer. A SEMAPHORE is an apparatus for signaling. (B) does not relate to LUDICROUS. ILLOGICAL is a synonym for LUDICROUS; (C) is not the best choice. REASONABLE is the opposite of LUDICROUS; (D) is the correct answer. FALLACIOUS (E) means logically unsound; it is a synonym for the key word and not the right choice.

29. **(B)**
    DANGER (A) is synonymous with JEOPARDY. SAFETY is the opposite of JEOPARDY, so the correct answer is (B). PERJURY means false swearing. CONUNDRUM is a puzzle. LEVITY means frivolity. (C), (D), and (E) are incorrect choices.

30. **(E)**
    AWRY means askew or bent. EARTHY means unrefined or natural; (A) is not the right answer. CROOKED is a synonym for AWRY; (B) is not correct. PIED means spotted; (C) is incorrect. DUBIOUS means doubtful; (D) is not correct. STRAIGHT (E) is the opposite of AWRY, and the right answer.

31. **(D)**
    INSIDIOUS means wily, sly. PRECIPITANT (A) means rushing ahead. It is not an antonym for INSIDIOUS. INCENDIARY means tending to excite or inflame. (B) should not be selected as the antonym. DECADENT is deteriorating, declining. It is not the opposite of INSIDIOUS; (C) is not the correct answer. CONDUCIVE means helpful. (D) is the opposite of INSIDIOUS. IMPRUDENT means lacking in caution, indiscreet. (E) is not the opposite of INSIDIOUS.

32. **(C)**
    CAPRICIOUS means fanciful, inconstant, apt to change suddenly. IMPECUNIOUS means poor, habitually without money. (A) does not bear an antonymous relationship to CAPRICIOUS. JUXTAPOSITION means place side by side as for the purpose of comparing. (B) is not the correct answer. SCRUPULOUS (C) means to be careful, exact; it can also mean faithful, steadfast — the opposite of CAPRICIOUS. COPIOUS means plentiful, abundant. (D) is not the opposite of CAPRICIOUS. SUPERFLUOUS means excessive, more than enough. (E) is not the antonym sought.

33. **(D)**

CONTENTIOUS, meaning quarrelsome, is the opposite of COMPLACENT, which means contented or smug. The correct choice is (D). COMPLIANT (A) means obedient. DECOROUS (B) means having good taste. PASSIVE (C) is submissive. SUMPTUOUS (E) means luxurious.

34. **(A)**

The antonym of DOCILE (manageable) is UNRULY (disobedient), so the correct choice is (A). RAUCOUS (B) and STRIDENT (E) are synonyms for harsh. DEMURE (C) means coy, and UNCOUTH (D) is crude.

35. **(D)**

To POSTULATE is to merely guess or to hypothesize. MOLLIFY is to appease, to calm. (A) is not the antonym of POSTULATE. CONJECTURE is to guess based on insufficient evidence. (B) is synonymous and not an antonym. PROGNOSTICATE (C) is to guess. It is synonymous with POSTULATE. CORROBORATE is to establish, to confirm. It is the opposite of guessing; (D) is the correct answer. REFURBISH is to brighten or to freshen up. (E) is not directly related to the key word and is not the answer sought.

36. **(B)**

CONCORD is a state of agreement, harmony. SUCCOR is aid, help. (A) is not an antonym for CONCORD and should not be chosen. ENMITY is ill will or hatred; it is the opposite of CONCORD. (B) is the correct answer. A GRIPPER is one who holds a camera or other apparatus. (C) bears no relation to CONCORD and should not be selected as the correct choice. VIGILANT means alertly watchful. It is not directly related to CONCORD. (D) is an inappropriate choice. ENNOBLING means elevating, raising. (E) is not the opposite of the key word and should not be selected.

37. **(B)**

A MALEFACTION is an evil deed, an offense. AFFINITY means an attraction, a likeness. (A) is not the opposite for MALEFACTION. A SUBSIDY is a gift, a form of aid; a SUBSIDY would be the opposite of MALEFACTION (an evil deed). (B) is the correct answer. PROFLIGATION means the act of wasting. It is not the opposite of MALEFACTION. (C) should not be chosen as the correct answer. IDIOSYNCRATIC (D) means peculiar, eccentric. (D) is not an antonym for MALEFACTION. COGNATE means of a similar nature. Since the term is not directly related to MALEFACTION, (E) should not be chosen.

38. **(B)**

A ZEPHYR is a gentle wind. A TYCOON is a wealthy, powerful individual. (A) is incorrect. A TYPHOON is a violent cyclonic storm, just the opposite of a ZEPHYR; (B) is the correct choice. A CORACLE (C) is a small boat and not the answer sought. TACITURN is an adjective meaning quiet, soft-spoken. (D) is not the correct choice. A CONSTELLATION is a pattern of stars. (E) is not the antonym sought.

Section 5–Quantitative Ability

1. **(C)**

    Column A $2\dfrac{1}{2}$ hours $= \dfrac{60 \text{ minutes}}{1 \text{ hour}} \times \dfrac{5}{2}$ hours $= 150$

    Column B $6\dfrac{1}{4}$ days $= \dfrac{24 \text{ hours}}{1 \text{ day}} \times \dfrac{25}{4}$ days $= 150$

2. **(C)**
    Note that $w : x = {}^{w}\!/_{x}$ and $y : z = {}^{y}\!/_{z}$. Thus, ${}^{w}\!/_{x} = {}^{y}\!/_{z}$. Adding the opposite of ${}^{y}\!/_{z}$ to both sides of the equation, we get

    $$\frac{w}{x} + \left(-\frac{y}{z}\right) = \frac{y}{z} + \left(-\frac{y}{z}\right)$$

    $$\frac{w}{x} - \frac{y}{z} = 0$$

Multiplying through by xz, the LCD, we have

$$(xz)\left(\frac{w}{x}\right) - (xz)\left(\frac{y}{z}\right) = (xz)(0)$$

$$wz - xy = 0$$

Hence, the quantities in both columns are equal.

3. **(B)**
    Column A   35% of 7 $= .35 \times 7 = 2.45$
    Column B   0.7 of 35 $= .7 \times 35 = 24.5$

Therefore, Column B is greater than Column A.

4. **(B)**
    The only way for $^{1}\!/_{y}$ to be negative is for y to be negative since the numerator is a positive 1. For example, if $y = 2$, then $\frac{1}{2}$ is not less than 0. So, y is always < 0. Therefore, 1 in Column B is the larger quantity.

5. **(A)**

Column A
$$\frac{2}{3}-\frac{1}{2}=\frac{4}{6}-\frac{3}{6}=\frac{1}{6}$$

Column B
$$\frac{4}{5}-\frac{2}{3}=\frac{12}{15}-\frac{10}{15}=\frac{2}{15}$$

Find a common denominator and compare the fractions.

Column A $= \dfrac{5}{30}$ Column B $= \dfrac{4}{30}$.

Therefore, Column A is greater than Column B.

6. **(B)**
The given equations form a system which can be easily solved by the climination method. By elimination one simply adds the two equations together in order to easily eliminate the y variable and solve for the x variable as follows:

$$x+y=6$$
$$\underline{3x-y=4}$$
$$4x=10 \quad \text{(sum of the equations)}$$

$$\frac{4x}{4}=\frac{10}{4} \text{ or } x=\frac{10}{4}=\frac{5}{2}$$

The next step is to substitute the value of x in $x + y = 6$ and solve for the variable y. The result is

$$\frac{5}{2}+y=6$$
$$\frac{5}{2}+y+\left(-\frac{5}{2}\right)=6+\left(-\frac{5}{2}\right)$$
$$y+0=\frac{12}{2}+\left(-\frac{5}{2}\right)$$
$$y=\frac{7}{2}$$

Finally, note that $x - y = \frac{5}{2} - \frac{7}{2} = -1$. Hence, the quantity in Column B is greater than the quantity in Column A.

7. **(A)**

In Column A expand the indicated product by using the foil method or some other method. Thus, the product of

$$(1-\sqrt{2})(1-\sqrt{2}) = 1 - \sqrt{2} - \sqrt{2} + (\sqrt{2})(\sqrt{2})$$
$$= 1 - 2\sqrt{2} + \sqrt{4}$$
$$= 1 - 2\sqrt{2} + 2$$
$$= 3 - 2\sqrt{2}$$

which is positive.

Similarly, in Column B one expands the indicated product to get

$$(1-\sqrt{2})(1+\sqrt{2}) = 1 - \sqrt{2} + \sqrt{2} - (\sqrt{2})(\sqrt{2})$$
$$= 1 - \sqrt{4}$$
$$= 1 - 2$$
$$= -1$$

Thus, the quantity in Column A is larger.

8. **(B)**

To determine the comparison one needs to know the formula for finding the distance between two points in the plane. The distance between $A(3, 4)$ and $B(-1, 1)$ is found by using the following formula where the subscript 1 refers to coordinates in point A and subscript 2 refers to coordinates in point B.

$$\sqrt{(x_2 - x_1)^2 + (y_2 - y_1)^2} = \sqrt{(-1-3)^2 + (1-4)^2}$$
$$= \sqrt{16+9}$$
$$= \sqrt{25} = 5$$

The distance between $C(4, -2)$ and $D(-2, -2)$ is found using the same formula as follows where the subscript 1 refers to coordinates in point C and subscript 2 refers to coordinates in point D.

$$\sqrt{(-2-4)^2 + [-2-(-2)]^2} = \sqrt{(-6)^2 + (0)^2}$$
$$= \sqrt{36} = 6$$

Hence, the distance from C to D is greater than the distance from A to B.

9. **(C)**

By definition $\angle 4$ and $\angle 5$ are vertical angles and by a theorem vertical angles are equal. Since line segments k and m are parallel, by a theorem the corresponding angles are equal. What are the corresponding angles? They are $\angle 1$, $\angle 3$, and $\angle 5$ on the left side of the diagonal d and $\angle 2$, $\angle 4$, and $\angle 6$ on the right side of the diagonal. It is given that $\angle 2 = 60°$. Since $\angle 4 = \angle 2$, then $\angle 4$ equals 60°. Finally, since $\angle 4$ and $\angle 5$ are equal vertical angles, then $\angle 5$ equals 60°. So the quantities in both columns are equal.

10. **(B)**

Recall that $\triangle ABC$, as well as any triangle, contains 180°. Thus, the measure of $\angle x$ must be the smallest since $\angle A$ is 100° and $\angle B$ is 48°. That is,

$$100 + 48 + x = 180°$$
$$148 + x = 180$$
$$148 + x - 148 = 180 - 148$$
$$x = 32°$$

Now since $\angle A$ (100°) is the largest in $\triangle ABC$, then it is a well-known theorem that the side (BC) which is opposite this angle is the largest side. Thus, it follows that side BC in Column B is greater than side AB in Column A.

11. **(B)**

Factor each equation.

$$x^2 + 3x - 4 = (x - 1)(x + 4)$$

Column A

$$x = 1, -4$$
$$\text{Product} = -4$$
$$x^2 + 4x + 4 = (x + 2)^2$$

Column B

$$x = -2, -2$$
$$\text{Product} = 4$$

Therefore, Column B is greater than Column A.

12. **(A)**

Observe that each side of the square must be 10 since its perimeter is 40. So the information in Column A yields the value 2(10) = 20 units, twice the length of line segment BD.

In Column B the length of the shortest distance from point A to line segment DE is given by the length of a side of the square plus the height of the triangle. The distance from DE to the base of the triangle is 10 units.

The length of the base of the triangle is also 10 units. In order to find the height of the triangle, the area must be known first. The area of the combined figures is given to be 125 square units. But, the

$$\text{area of the square} = e^2 = (10)^2 = 100 \text{ square units.}$$

Thus, the area of the triangle is 25 square units since the total area of the figures is 125 square units.

The formula for the area of the triangle is $A = (\frac{1}{2})bh$. Thus, the height of the triangle is given by

$$h = \frac{2A}{b} = \frac{2(25)}{10} = \frac{50}{10} = 5 \text{ units.}$$

So, the value of the quantity in Column B is $10 + 5 = 15$ units. Hence, the quantity in Column A is larger.

13. **(C)**

$$\frac{a+2}{a+1} = \frac{a-4}{a-3}$$
$$(a+2)(a-3) = (a-4)(a+1)$$
$$a^2 - a - 6 = a^2 - 3a - 4$$
$$a^2 - a - a^2 + 3a = -4 + 6$$
$$2a = 2$$
$$a = 1$$

Therefore, the two quantities are equal.

14. **(D)**

Observe that in order to attempt to compare the two statements there is a need to analyze each. The statement in Column B indicates that a representation of the sum of the angles of a square must be made. Since each of the four angles of a square is a right angle, then one can write the sum of the angles as follows:

$$4(90°) = 360°.$$

On the other hand, the statement in Column B indicates that a representation of the sum of all the angles of a polygon whose sides are equal must be made. The sum of all the angles of any polygon with equal sides will increase with the increasing number of sides of the polygon. Thus, it is not possible to compare the results from the two columns.

15. **(D)**

Try some values into the equations.

If $x = 0$, $y = 1$, and $z = 2$, then Column A = 1 and Column B = -4.

If $x = -2$, $y = -1$, and $z = 0$, then Column A = 3 and Column B = 4.

Therefore, more information is needed to solve the equation.

16. **(B)**

First one must determine the equivalent of 132 ft./9 sec. in terms of miles/hour in order to solve the problem. Recall that 1 hour = 60 min. = 3,600 sec. and 1 mile = 5,280 ft. Thus, one can set up the following proportion:

$$\frac{132\,\text{ft}}{9\,\text{sec}} = \frac{x\,\text{ft}}{1\,\text{hr}} = \frac{x\,\text{ft}}{3,600\,\text{sec}}$$

and solve for x. The result is

$$\frac{9x\,\text{ft}}{\text{sec}} = \frac{132(3,600)\,\text{ft}}{\text{sec}}$$

$$x = \frac{475,200}{9} = 52,800 \text{ ft or 10 miles.}$$

Hence, the speed is 10 miles per hour.

17. **(E)**

Let x = number

$.07x = 35$

$$\frac{.07x}{.07} = \frac{35}{.07}$$

$x = 500$

Therefore, the correct choice is (E).

18. **(E)**

Let x = the score of Joan's last test

$$83 = \frac{4(79) + x}{5}$$

$$83(5) = 316 + x$$

$$415 - 316 = x$$

$$99 = x$$

19. **(D)**

To find the altitude of the triangle one must recall that the area of a triangle is given by

$$A = \left(\frac{1}{2}\right)bh,$$

where b denotes the base and h denotes the altitude. Also, one must recall that the area of a circle is given by

$$A = \pi r^2,$$

where r denotes the radius of the circle.

Since $b = 6$ units then $(\frac{1}{2})(6)h = 3h = A$, the area of the triangle. In addition, since $r = 6$ units, then $A = \pi r^2 = \pi(6)^2 = 36\pi$, the area of the circle. But the area is the same for both figures. Thus,

$$3h = 36\pi$$
$$h = 12\pi$$

is the altitude of the triangle.

20. **(C)**

One needs to first recall that a cube has six equal sized faces. Thus, the area of each face is found by dividing 6 into 96 to obtain 16 square feet. Since each face contains 16 square feet, then one can conclude that each edge of a face is 4 feet long. So, the volume of the cube, given by the formula,

$$V = (\text{length of edge})^3$$

is found to be

$$V = (4 \text{ feet})^3 = 64 \text{ cubic feet.}$$

21. **(C)**

The average income for X Company is obtained by finding the sum of the income over the years 1983 and 1986 and dividing by 4,

$$\frac{(200 + 300 + 100 + 400)}{4} = 250$$

22. **(D)**

By observation one needs only to find the largest spread between corresponding plotted points on the two lines representing the companies. Thus, the largest difference occurred in 1987 where the difference was 450 million (500 − 50).

23. **(B)**

The median is the middle annual earnings for X Company arranged in ascending order. Over the indicated years, the annual earnings in millions are 200, 300, 100, 400, 100, 200, respectively. Arranging these values in ascending order and taking the average of the two in the middle gives the value of 200 million for the median.

24. **(E)**

From the graph notice that the largest increase in earnings of Y Company occurred between 1986 and 1987. The amount of the increase was 400 million. Recall that in order to find the percent of increase use the following formula:

$$\text{Percent increase} = \frac{\text{Amount of increase}}{\text{Original amount}} \times 100$$

$$= \frac{400}{100} \times 100 = 400\%$$

The other answer choices are incorrect as a result of either misapplying the formula or not observing the largest increase in earnings of Y Company.

25. **(D)**

Of the two companies, Company X had the largest decrease in earnings which occurred between 1986 and 1987. The amount of the decrease was 300 million. Recall that in order to find the percent of decrease one uses the following formula:

$$\text{Percent decrease} = \frac{\text{Amount of decrease}}{\text{Original amount}} \times 100$$

$$= \frac{300}{400} \times 100 = 75\%$$

The other answer choices are incorrect as a result of misapplying the formula for the percent of decrease or not observing the largest decrease for X Company on the graph.

26. **(C)**

Simplify

$7 - 3x \leq 19$	
$-3x \leq 19 - 7$	Add -7 to both sides.
$x \geq 12 \div (-3)$	Divide both sides by (-3). The sense of the inequality changes when multiplied or divided by a negative number.
$x \geq -4$	

27. **(E)**

One way to attack this problem is to solve it algebraically.

Let x represent the number of packages weighing 2 kg each. Then $(150 - x)$ represents the number of packages weighing 1 kg each.

Therefore,

$$2x + 1(150 - x) = 264$$
$$2x + 150 - x = 264$$
$$x = 264 - 150$$
$$x = 114$$

Thus, there are 114 packages weighing 2 kg each on the truck.

Another way to solve this problem is to test each of the answer choices. Note that if, for example, the number of packages weighing 2 kg each is 36 (answer choice (A)), then the number of packages weighing 1 kg each will be $(150 - 36) = 114$. Testing the answer choices yields:

(A) $(36)(2) + (150 - 36)(1) = 72 + 114 = 186$ (wrong)
(B) $(52)(2) + (150 - 52)(1) = 104 + 98 = 202$ (wrong)
(C) $(88)(2) + (150-88)(1) = 176 + 62 = 238$ (wrong)
(D) $(124)(2) + (150-124)(1) = 248 + 26 = 274$ (wrong)
(E) $(114)(2) + (150 - 114)(1) = 228 + 36 = 264$ (correct)

28. **(C)**

The wheel will travel in 1 revolution (2 minutes) $C = \pi d = \pi(3) = 3\pi$ feet. In 30 minutes it will travel $\frac{30}{2} = 15$ revolutions. Thus, the wheel will travel $15(3\pi) = 45\pi$ feet in 30 minutes.

29. **(E)**

Note that tips for the week were $\left(\frac{5}{4}\right)(150)$. Thus, the total income was as follows:

$$(1)\ (150) + \left(\frac{5}{4}\right)(150) = \left(\frac{4}{4}\right)(150) + \left(\frac{5}{4}\right)(150)$$

$$= \left(\frac{9}{4}\right)(150)$$

Therefore, tips made up $\dfrac{\left(\frac{5}{4}\right)(150)}{\left(\frac{9}{4}\right)(150)} = \dfrac{\frac{5}{4}}{\frac{9}{4}} = \dfrac{5}{9}$ of her income.

Notice that one could figure out the total income in order to arrive at the solution; however, this would be a waste of time.

30. **(A)**

Since h, m, and n are divisible by 3, first represent each as follows: $h = 3i$, $m = 3j$, and $n = 3k$, where i, j, and k are integers. Now consider the hm as follows:

$$hm = 3i(3j) = 9ij.$$

But clearly, $hm/_9 = 9ij/_9 = ij$. So, hm is divisible by 9.

Using the same technique or by a simple example, it is clear that II and III are not possible. Hence, the other answer choices are not possible.

Section 6–Verbal Ability

1. **(C)**
   (A) is incorrect; ABUSIVE means treating badly or harshly. The term does not fit the sentence very well; ABUSIVE writing probably would not ENHANCE one's chance for a promotion. (B) is not an appropriate choice. Since LACONIC means brief and to the point, this type of writing does not seem grounds to OBLITERATE (wipe out) a teacher's chances for promotion. (C) is the correct answer. OBTUSE means blunt, stupid, not sharp. (For instance, an obtuse angle is not sharp, like an acute angle; it is larger than a right angle.) Such writing might OBVIATE (eliminate) one's chances of a promotion. (D) is incorrect; since PROFOUND means not superficial, and clearly marked by intellectual depth, it does not stand to reason that such writing would DIMINISH (or make less) one's chances for a promotion. The best answer is not (E). The publication of PROLIFIC (many) writings alone does not make necessary (NECESSITATE) the promotion of a teacher.

2. **(B)**
   (A) is not the best choice. ELICIT means to draw out in a skillful way something that is being hidden or held back. Giving business cards is not unique. The best answer is (B). SOLICIT means to ask earnestly, to try to get. Since ILLICIT (C) means illegal, it is an incorrect choice. ELLIPTIC (D) means shaped like an ellipse (with ovals at both ends). CONCILIATE (E) is to win over, to soothe. The word is an inappropriate choice.

3. **(D)**
   A QUIRK is a peculiar behavior trait; a pregnant woman's desire for odd foods is a temporary condition, not a behavior trait; (A) is incorrect. Choice (B), PROFUSION (abundance), is inappropriate. A PITTANCE is a small amount of money; (C) is not the correct choice. A STIPEND is a monetary payment; therefore, (E) is also incorrect. (D) is the appropriate choice; a PENCHANT is a desire or craving.

4. **(A)**
   Of the choices, (A) makes the most sense. A chairman would be likely to complain that time was being wasted on PERIPHERAL (auxiliary or side) issues, instead of on the ESSENTIAL (central or main) one. SCURRILOUS means coarse or indecent language; TEDIOUS means boring. (B) is not an appropriate choice. TRENCHANT, meaning distinct or

clear-cut, and SUPERFLUOUS, meaning unnecessary, would be appropriate choices if their order was reversed, but as it is, (C) is incorrect. SUPERFICIAL, or surface, is an appropriate adjective for the first blank, but WHIMSICAL (fanciful) is not appropriate for the second; (D) is not the correct answer. MUNIFICENT (lavish) and DESULTORY (without order) are not logical adjectives for this sentence. Choice (E) is incorrect.

5. **(A)**
AMORPHOUS, ECCENTRIC, and ERRATIC are all synonyms meaning inconsistent, sporadic. EQUABLE suggests a uniform methodical occurrence. WEARISOME is the correct choice, indicated by the key words "exact," "and," "but," and "essential."

6. **(C)**
ABSTRUSE (C), meaning difficult to comprehend, is the most appropriate choice. A lecture on molecular dynamics would be inherently ERUDITE, or learned; (A) is not the correct choice. The lecture focused on a single topic, so it was not ECLECTIC (varied, diverse). (B) is not the correct answer. INCHOATE (unformed) and AMORPHOUS (having no determined form) are unrelated to the sentence topic, so (D) and (E) are incorrect answers.

7. **(C)**
The clues to this sentence are "not only failed" and "exacerbate." These words imply that the correct choice must be the antonym of EXACERBATE (to worsen). EXCORIATE (to abrade), DISSEMINATE (to spread), EXCULPATE (to clear from fault), and OBJURGATE (to chide vehemently) are all inappropriate choices. AMELIORATE (to improve, to make better) is the necessary antonym; the correct answer is (C).

8. **(D)**
The relationship between GIGGLE and GUFFAW is one of degree. GLOVE:GAUNTLET, FASHION:VOGUE, and SOB:WEEP all exhibit synonymous relationships. Therefore, (A), (B), and (C) are incorrect. (E) WHEEDLE (to entice by flattery) and WHINE (to use a plaintive tone of voice) might both be considered methods of manipulation, but they are not different degrees of the same thing. REPROVE (to kindly correct a fault) and BERATE (to scold vigorously) are different degrees of remonstrating. The correct answer is (D).

9. **(E)**

AMIABLE (friendly) and ANONYMOUS (unknown) are unrelated, as are BENIGN (gentle, mild) and MALICE (desire to cause pain); (A) and (D) are incorrect answers. ECONOMICAL:THRIFTY and DOCILE: COMPLIANT are synonymous relationships. FAVORABLE and OMINOUS are antonyms, as are BENEFICIAL (conferring benefits) and BALEFUL (evil or harmful). The correct answer is (E).

10. **(E)**

A CHARLATAN performs an ILLUSION; a SOPRANO performs an ARIA; therefore, (E) is the correct choice. BRANCHES do not perform TREES; CHEMISTRY does not perform ELEMENTS; MEDICINE treats DISEASE; and a COOK follows a RECIPE. (A), (B), (C), and (D) are incorrect.

11. **(D)**

FUMBLE (to handle something clumsily) and FINESSE (to handle skillfully) are antonyms. FRUGAL (thrifty) and FLUENT (facile in speech) are unrelated. ABHOR (to loathe) and APPEASE (to pacify) are also unrelated. (A) and (E) are not correct choices. DECEIVE and BEGUILE are synonyms, as are FACILITATE and EXPEDITE, meaning to accelerate the process. (B) and (C) do not share the relationship sought. Only IMPUGN (to attack another's character) and EXTOL (to praise highly) share the antonymous relationship; therefore, the correct choice is (D).

12. **(D)**

A PUPA is an immature form of a MOTH, which has to undergo a period of metamorphosis (striking physical change) to become an adult moth. A TADPOLE is an immature form of FROG that also must change significantly to become an adult frog. (D) is the correct choice. PARAPET:WALL are synonyms, so (A) is incorrect. POMMEL: SADDLE and STAMEN:FLOWER exhibit a part:whole relationship; (B) and (C) are incorrect. Choice (E) is inappropriate. An ADOLESCENT is the immature form of many animals, but no striking physical changes occur before it becomes an ADULT.

13. **(A)**

VACILLATE is a verb meaning to waver. DECISION is a noun meaning the act of committing or deciding. A verb and noun which are opposite in meaning are needed from the choices given. EQUIVOCATE is a verb meaning to hedge. COMMITMENT is a noun meaning the act of declaring. The analogy in (A) is the same as for VACILLATE: DECISION. FLUCTUATE is a verb meaning to be changing continually. PROCRASTINATE is a verb meaning to postpone. (B) is not the appropriate answer. CONSPIRE is a verb meaning to act or plan together secretly; COLLUSION is a noun meaning the act of secretly planning together. The relationship of choice (C) is not the same as that between VACILLATE:DECISION. RESOLVE is a verb meaning to come to a decision; CONCLUSION is a noun meaning the close of an argument, debate, or reasoning. (D) is not the correct answer. AMELIORATE means to improve, to make better; RESOLUTION is a noun meaning the act of deciding or determining something. The analogy between AMELIO-RATE:RESOLUTION (E) and between VACILLATE:DECISION is not the same.

14. **(B)**
   COALESCE (to come together) and DISPERSE (to spread out) are antonyms. The only antonymous choice is (B): IMPRECATE (to curse) and CONSECRATE (to bless). UMBRAGE:OFFENSE (A) are synonyms. INCARCERATE (to jail) and REMONSTRATE (to reprove); ELUCI-DATE (to make clear) and PREVARICATE (to lie); and DEBILITATE (to weaken) and MITIGATE (to mollify) are all unrelated terms. (C), (D), and (E) are incorrect.

15. **(B)**
   CONTUMACIOUS means stubbornly disobedient; a MUTINEER is one who resists lawful authority. Being contumacious is an innate quality of a mutineer. Only (B) reflects the same relationship. A BIENNIAL is a flowering plant that only lives for two years; EPHEMERAL means short-lived. Being EPHEMERAL is an innate quality of a BIENNIAL. Choices (A), (C), (D), and (E) do not reflect this relationship. RENASCENCE (rebirth or rising again) is not inherently DELETERIOUS (harmful). A ZEALOT (fanatic) is anything but OBSEQUIOUS (subservient). A NEO-PHYTE (beginner) is not likely to be PEDAGOGIC (befitting a teacher). CONNOISSEUR means expert, IRASCIBLE means irritable; connoisseurs are no more likely to be irascible than anyone else.

16. **(C)**
   FUSTIAN and BOMBASTIC are synonyms meaning pretentious speech or writing. LOQUACIOUS and GARRULOUS are synonyms meaning talkative; therefore, (C) is the correct answer. (A) and (D) are unrelated terms. FACETIOUS means joking and SARDONIC means bitterly ironic. IGNEOUS means having the nature of fire, and PECUNIARY

means relating to money. (B) and (E) are antonymous terms. SANGUINE means optimistic and SATURNINE means gloomy. NUGATORY is insignificant and INORDINATE is excessive.

17. **(E)**
The author of this article is not pessimistic (A) in tone; rather the author seems encouraged by the results of Faigel's study. The author does not have an unconcerned attitude toward the study by Faigel. The very fact that the article was written shows some concern on the part of the author. (B) is not an appropriate answer to the question. Indifferent (C) is not the tone of the writing. The writer is careful to point out the difference in scores between second-time test-takers who had been administered the beta blockers and second-time test-takers who had not been administered the drugs. The author of this article is not resigned. The author states that the drugs "seem to help test-takers"; on the other hand, the writer cautions that side effects do exist. (D) is not correct. The author of the article can best be described as optimistic (E). Again, the writer states that beta blockers "seem to help test-takers who have low scores because of test fright."

18. **(D)**
A control group of eight students was used in Faigel's study. (A) is false. Second-time test-takers increase only 28 points nationally. (B) is false and not the best answer. The article states that the beta blockers cannot help those who do not "know" the material. (C) is false and should not be selected. Adrenaline does increase minor stress and may result in lower test scores; (D) is the best answer. Beta blockers, not adrenaline, have long been used for heart conditions and for minor stress; therefore, (E) is false and not the best answer.

19. **(E)**
Casual disinterest (A) does not seem to aptly describe students who become nervous when taking the SAT. Resignation (B) is not the best descriptive adjective for students who continue to take the SAT to try to improve their test scores. Antagonism is not the attitude suggested by the article. No mention is made of students' possessing an antagonistic attitude or of their trying to eradicate standardized testing; (C) is not the best answer. Pessimism (D) is not the attitude mentioned in the article or suggested by students who continue to retake a standardized test to improve their grades. Concern best describes the attitudes of students who take (and retake) the SAT to try to increase their score and even experience nervousness during the test-taking. (E) seems to be the answer implied (though not stated) by the article.

20. **(C)**

Second-time test-takers nationwide improve only an average of 28 points—not a significant increase. Statisticians would attribute this insignificant increase to the fact that the test is a *reliable* test; students seem to achieve the same test scores each time it is administered unless they do something different in-between test administrations. (A), therefore, is false and an incorrect answer. The author of the passage makes no speculation on limiting the number of administrations of the SAT. (B) is false and should not be chosen. If beta blockers are used, the article suggests that scores of nervous second-time test-takers may be raised. This, in turn, will raise the national average. (C) is correct and the best choice. Raising test scores of even one group of students will affect the national average. (D), therefore, is false and should not be chosen as the correct answer. Adrenalin has not been shown to increase test scores. (E) should be avoided as the correct answer. It is beta blockers that seem to reduce nervousness and increase test scores.

21. **(C)**

The study by Faigel focuses on SAT test-takers. Faigel does not attempt to make any predictions on how the beta blockers might affect the general public should they take them for nervousness; to the contrary, Faigel cautions that beta blockers do have certain side effects. (A) is not the best answer. It was not adrenalin but beta blockers which increased the performance of second-time test-takers of the SAT. (B) is an incorrect answer and should not be selected. Since beta blockers do seem to improve the average scores of second-time test-takers (particularly nervous second-time takers) of the SAT, (C) is a true, appropriate answer. Faigel recognizes that beta blockers do have side effects, but he in no way implies that they should never be used. (D), therefore, is an incorrect answer and should not be chosen. Nervousness *does* seem to affect the test scores of students who "know" the material. Faigel's study suggests by administering beta blockers to help control this nervousness, students can raise their test scores. (E) is not the best answer to this question.

22. **(B)**

ANALYSIS involves separating or breaking down into parts. Faigel's work primarily involved developing a plan (SYNTHESIZING), rather than a separating (ANALYSIS). (A) is not the best answer. Synthesis involves putting together, combining to form a whole. Developing a plan to reduce the nervousness and developing a plan to compare the test results is certainly a synthesizing. (B) is correct and should be chosen. DEDUCTION (C) involves reasoning from the general to the particular. DEDUCTION does not apply to developing a plan to reduce nervousness and to compare test results. INTERPRETATION is used when one gives an explanation; developing a plan does not necessarily involve INTERPRETATION. (D) is not the correct answer. APPLICATION means the act of using a particular case or for a particular purpose; Faigel synthesized, rather than applied, when he developed his research plan. (E) is inappropriate.

23. **(E)**
AMUSEMENT is certainly not the author's tone in this passage. (A) should not be chosen. INDIGNATION (B) is not the author's tone. The author has no source upon which to vent indignation in this passage. The very fact that the author bothered to write the passage negates the idea that the author shows INDIFFERENCE. (C) should not be selected as the best answer. APPROVAL is not the best choice for the author's attitude. There is little that a well-meaning author could approve in this passage. (D) is not an appropriate choice. RESIGNATION (E) is the best choice for the author's attitude. The author is not resigned to never having a cure for ALS; however, the author admits that there may be a waiting period for this cure.

24. **(C)**
Deductive reasoning moves from the general to the particular. Choice (A) leads from the particular (victims of ALS who are athletes) to the general (active persons are more often affected by ALS); therefore, (A) is not the correct answer. Alternative (B) is not a deduction; it is simply a restatement of a fact presented in the passage. Choices (D) and (E) offer faulty reasoning. The fact that the four victims discussed in the passage were all athletes and were all male does not give enough evidence to predict that the next victim will be an athlete (D) or a male (E). One cannot predict that the next victim will follow a pattern based on so small a subset of the total number of ALS victims. Only choice (C) is an example of deductive reasoning. It moves from the general (ALS is rare and the victims were on the same team) to the specific (the team may be exposed to an element which causes ALS).

25. **(E)**
CONFIRMATION is synonymous with CORROBORATION; both mean supported by evidence. SUPPORT (A) and EVIDENCE (B) alone do not carry the same connotation. Evidence can be interpreted in different ways, and support is not always based on evidence. ANALOGY (D), meaning similarity or correlation, is an inappropriate choice. Using REASON (C) in this sentence would imply that all speculations about possible causes of ALS are pointless, thus changing the meaning of the sentence considerably.

26. **(D)**

The non-imminent solution to ALS is a disturbing fact presented in the passage, but it does not give the topic of the paragraph. (A) should not be selected. Statement (B) gives an important supporting detail from the passage but does not give the topic of the paragraph to the reader. Statement (C) adds additional facts, but it does not give the main subject. (D) informs the reader of the topic of the paragraph. It is the correct choice. Statement (E) is taken from the passage and gives supporting details about the puzzle of ALS; it does not, however, give the topic of the sentence.

27. **(D)**

The passage states that the causes (A) and cure (C) for amyotrophic lateral sclerosis are not known; therefore, the passage cannot answer these questions. Furthermore, the passage only mentions who Lou Gehrig was (B), and it makes it clear there is no known connection between ALS and professional athletes (E). The purpose of the passage is to inform readers about amyotrophic lateral sclerosis (D).

28. **(B)**

An ODYSSEY is a long series of wanderings. Since a JOURNEY (A) is a very long trip, it is synonymous with ODYSSEY and an incorrect answer. An ERRAND (B) is a short trip, the opposite of ODYSSEY, and the correct answer. A WANDERING (C), like an ODYSSEY, is a moving about aimlessly; it is not the opposite of ODYSSEY. A VOYAGE is a long journey by water, much like an ODYSSEY; (D) is not the correct answer. A CRUISE is sailing about from place to place; (E) is very similar to ODYSSEY and should not be selected as the right answer.

29. **(E)**

The correct answer is (E). The opposite of ADULTERATE (corrupt, make impure) is HOMOGENIZE (purify). INTERMIX (A) is to mix together. HYBRIDIZE (B) is to interbreed. To INTERFACE (C) is to connect. MISCEGENATE (D) is to mix races.

30. **(C)**

The antonym for RESPLENDENT (splendid, dazzling) is SHODDY (C) (inferior, badly made). WAN (A) is pale; STOLID (B) means dull; TRITE (D) refers to commonplace; and PALATIAL (E) is large and ornate.

31. **(D)**

ALTRUISTIC means unselfishly putting the needs of others before one's own. DOGMATIC (A) means opinionated; it is not the correct answer. ABSTEMIOUS (B) is not the opposite being sought; it refers to using sparingly. FORTUITOUS (C) means a lucky accident. HEDONIS-TIC (D), meaning seeking pleasure for oneself, is the antonym of AL-TRUISTIC. The last choice, APOCALYPTIC (E), refers to revelation or discovery.

32. **(A)**

The antonym of VIRILE (masculine, manly) is EFFEMINATE (A), which means having feminine qualities. BESTIAL (B) refers to having the qualities of a beast. EQUIVOCAL (C) means doubtful. CHOLERIC (D) is easily angered. LECHEROUS (E) means sexually voracious.

33. **(B)**

To BEMOAN is to lament. The correct antonym is (B) EXULT, which means to rejoice greatly. (A) LAUGH is to express mirth. One can rejoice greatly without laughing; (C) COMMISERATE is to feel or show pity for. This alternative is wrong because it is simply unrelated in meaning; (D) ACCLAIM means to announce with loud approval. One can rejoice greatly without announcing anything in any manner; (E) EULOGIZE a person, for example. No object is needed in order to rejoice greatly.

34. **(E)**

The noun MELANCHOLY is derived from the Greek words for "black" *(melas)* and "bile" *(chole),* and it means "sadness and depression of spirits." Its opposite is (E) EXHILARATION, which means stimulated, lively, gay, and comes from the Latin prefix *ex* (interns) and *hilaris* (glad). (Our word "hilarity" also comes from this Latin root.) Alternatives (A), (B), (C), and (D) are wrong because they fail to include the idea of lively and gay. (A) SOCIABILITY means liking the company of others; (B) SE-RENITY means undisturbed or calm; (C) COMPLACENCY means self-satisfied or smug; and (D) IMPULSIVENESS is acting upon impulse.

35. **(D)**

CANDID (D), meaning open and honest, is the opposite of CLAN-DESTINE, which means hidden or private. The correct answer is (D). SURREPTITIOUS (A) and FURTIVE (B) are synonymous with clandes-tine. EGREGIOUS (C) means flagrant, and LURID (E) means gloomy.

36. **(D)**

PROPITIOUS means favorably disposed, graciously inclined. CON-SPICUOUS (A) means obvious to the eye or mind. The two are not antonyms. AUSPICIOUS is a synonym for PROPITIOUS; both mean favorable, fortunate. (B) is, therefore, not the correct answer. EVANES-CENT (C) means dissipating like vapor, vanishing. It is a word that is not related to PROPITIOUS and should not be selected. MILITANT means warlike, fighting. MILITANT is the opposite of PROPITIOUS, or favorably inclined. (D) is the correct answer. AGGREGATIVE means taken together, collective, tending to aggregate. (E) is not a suitable choice as an antonym of PROPITIOUS.

37. **(A)**

MALAPROPOS means not appropriate. (The prefix MAL- means not.) CONGRUOUS means fit, right, suitable; congruous (congruent) angles, for instance, are of the same size and shape. MALAPROPOS and CONGRUOUS are antonyms; (A) is the correct answer. SPECIOUS stresses a clear suggestion of fraud. It does not bear the opposite relationship to MALAPROPOS sought; (B) should not be selected. PONDER-OUS (C) means heavy, dull, bulky, unyieldy. It is certainly not the antonym sought. Since BENIGN means mild, kind, gentle, it is not an antonym for a word meaning not appropriate. (D) should not be selected. PROPENSITY (E) means a natural inclination or bent. It does not suggest an opposite relationship to MALAPROPOS.

38. **(E)**

UNCOUTH means uncultured, crude, boorish, or clumsy. MELAN-CHOLY is gloomy, depressed. Since an UNCOUTH person can be MEL-ANCHOLY, (A) is not an antonym or opposite. AMELIORATING means making milder. It does not have an opposite relationship to UNCOUTH; (B) is not the correct answer. FUNEREAL is an adjective meaning dismal or mournful; it is not the opposite of UNCOUTH. (C) should not be selected as the correct answer. BOORISH is synonymous with UN-COUTH. (D) is not the correct choice. URBANE (E) means polite or civil; it is opposite from UNCOUTH and is the correct answer.

GRE
Graduate Record Examination

Practice
Test 2

To Our Readers

The following REA practice test contains more questions than the actual GRE General Test in order to provide a score that is roughly comparable to what your score would be on the GRE CBT. It is also important to bear in mind that the GRE CBT moves inexorably forward. Thus, unlike in our printed tests, *there's no turning back once you commit to your response.* Despite format differences, our tests will give you an accurate idea of your strengths and weaknesses, provide guidance for further study, and enable you to master the GRE General.

Section 1

TIME: 45 Minutes
Choose 1 of 2 Essays†

ESSAY QUESTION ONE

DIRECTIONS: Present your perspective on the issue below by using relevant reasons and/or examples to support your views. Remember, there is no one "correct" response to the essay topic. Before starting, read the essay topic and its question(s).

Filmmaking has become an industry. Many millions of dollars are spent making movies in Hollywood each year in the hope that millions of people will spend money to see the movies. Some filmmakers argue that this has caused film to become more of a commercial product than an art.

Do you feel this is true? If so, is this a positive or negative change?

STOP

Do not go on until you are instructed to do so. Use any remaining time to check your work on this portion of the test.

† On the actual test, you will have a choice between two essay topics. You have to write only one essay. To give you the most practice possible we have supplied sample essays for both questions in order to show you the differences between essays that receive a perfect score and those that score less.

TIME: 45 Minutes
Choose 1 of 2 Essays†

ESSAY QUESTION TWO

DIRECTIONS: Present your perspective on the issue below by using relevant reasons and/or examples to support your views. Remember, there is no one "correct" response to the essay topic. Before starting, read the essay topic and its question(s).

One method of teaching, pioneered by Socrates, encourages a more active participation by students, through a series of probing questions and exploratory answers. Education should always have such a method built into it, so that students are encouraged to ask questions and have room to take a critical perspective on information, and the way things are. This will give them a better understanding of what is good and what needs change in the world.

Do you think the suggested educational method should be used in today's schools? Explain your opinion using relevant reasons and examples from your own experience.

STOP

Do not go on until you are instructed to do so. Use any remaining time to check your work on this portion of the test.

---

† On the actual test, you will have a choice between two essay topics. You have to write only one essay. To give you the most practice possible we have supplied sample essays for both questions in order to show you the differences between essays that receive a perfect score and those that score less.

SECTION 2

TIME: 30 Minutes
1 Essay

DIRECTIONS: Critique the following argument by considering its logical soundness.

As a composer, I was beginning to wonder what went on in the head of the average Englishman. For several years I had been trying to get in touch with normal people. One time I was in a small town near Oxford. As an elite artist, I found it difficult to relate to the regular population. There was only one concert house in town. It was owned by foreigners and they performed mostly folk music from their own country, wherever that was— really low brow, common music. I found that a lot of the music that people pay to hear is written by people who aren't even from this country. I don't even know what that means.

What is the main point of this argument? What was the author's purpose in writing it? Is it an effective argument? Why or why not?

STOP

If time remains, you may go back and check your work.

Section 3

TIME: 30 Minutes
38 Questions

DIRECTIONS: Each of the given sentences has blank spaces which indicate words omitted. Choose the best combination of words which fit into the meaning and structure within the context of the sentence.

1. A mentally deficient person who has special talents or gifts is correctly referred to as _____; an extraordinary child is referred to as _____.

    (A) proselyte...a progeny

    (B) tainted...prodigious

    (C) a stapes...a progenitor

    (D) a lithographer...portentous

    (E) an idiot savant...a prodigy

2. The domineering male gorilla usually appears _____ in its mating rituals in the wild.

    (A) subjugated

    (B) vanquished

    (C) subdued

    (D) surmounted

    (E) imperious

3. She never took aspirin for her headaches; classical music was a more effective _____.

    (A) antidote

    (B) anodyne

    (C) accolade

    (D) analogy

    (E) anomaly

4. Many professors find it necessary to warn their students against
   _____ when assigning research papers.

   (A) probity   (D) plagiarism

   (B) clarity   (E) umbrage

   (C) calumny

5. He was chosen as club treasurer because he has always been
   _____ about repaying his debts.

   (A) scrupulous   (D) impervious

   (B) munificent   (E) incorrigible

   (C) prodigious

6. Use of the company limousine is just one of the _____ of being
   executive vice-president.

   (A) tenets   (D) perquisites

   (B) prerequisites   (E) precepts

   (C) prerogatives

7. The overall effect of the plangent music, dim lighting, and subdued
   colors was overwhelmingly _____.

   (A) parsimonious   (D) quotidian

   (B) froward   (E) ignominious

   (C) lachrymose

DIRECTIONS: In the following questions, a related pair of words is
followed by five more pairs of words. Select the pair that best expresses the same relationship as that expressed in the original pair.

---

8. SUNDIAL:SUN::

   (A) electricity:water   (D) sun:stars

   (B) moon:tides   (E) light bulb:electricity

   (C) water:rain

9. SAGA:TALE::

   (A) book:page

   (B) poetry:prose

   (C) lyrics:music

   (D) sonnet:verse

   (E) fiction:nonfiction

10. APPLE:PARE::

   (A) cherry:stone

   (B) peach:pit

   (C) grapefruit:peel

   (D) skin:grape

   (E) pomegranate:seeds

11. ALLUSION:REFERENCE::

   (A) brevity:longevity

   (B) conglomeration:accumulation

   (C) antipathy:apathy

   (D) epitome:ennui

   (E) artifice:sincerity

12. STUPENDOUS:AMAZE::

   (A) monstrous:bewilder

   (B) prodigious:perplex

   (C) tremendous:distraction

   (D) confound:atrocious

   (E) heinous:astound

13. COVEY:QUAIL::

   (A) cub:bear

   (B) pride:lions

   (C) stag:deer

   (D) ewe:sheep

   (E) gaggle:ducks

14. CASCADE:CATACLYSM::

   (A) soporific:hypnotic

   (B) defeat:debacle

   (C) scenario:synopsis

   (D) hyperbole:exaggeration

   (E) epitaph:epithet

15. TAUTOLOGOUS:INCONGRUOUS::

    (A) astute:perspicacious   (D) propinquity:proximity

    (B) melange:effluvium   (E) ignominious:magnanimous

    (C) anamnesis:reminiscence

16. ADVENTITIOUS:INHERENT::

    (A) vitiate:adulterate   (D) vicissitude:mutability

    (B) fatuous:asinine   (E) facile:onerous

    (C) anathema:anastrophe

DIRECTIONS: Each passage is followed by questions based on its content. After reading a passage, choose the best answer to each question. Answer all questions based on what is stated or implied in that passage.

Cacti and other succulent plants originate in areas where water is only occasionally available and are, therefore, conditioned to deal with long periods of drought. They possess structural modifications enabling them to store moisture for use in times of scarcity.

Such adaptations may be similar in both groups. (All cacti are succulents but not all succulents are cacti.) Storage areas include thickened leaves, stems, and corms. Leaves, which transpire precious moisture, may be eliminated altogether (with the stem taking over the process of photosynthesis), or the moisture in the leaves may be protected from evaporation by a leathery surface or covered with wiry or velvety hairs, thick spines, or even with a powdery coating.

The very shape of many succulents provides the same protection; globular and columnar forms offer the least exposed area to the drying effects of sun and wind.

Many times there are "look-alikes" in the two groups. Certain cacti coming from the New World closely resemble counterparts in the Euphorbias of Africa.

How do we then differentiate between cacti and other succulents? It is not always easy. Presence or absence of leaves can be helpful; size and brilliance of flowers are also helpful, but the real test comes by learning to recognize the areole.

The areole is possessed by cacti alone and consists of cushion-like modifications on the body of the cactus from which arise spines, hairs (and the barbed hairs or spines of *Opuntia*), flowers, fruit, and often new growth.

The flowers of cacti are usually more conspicuous and most often appear from areoles near the top of the plant. In other succulents they are inclined to be less showy and more likely to emerge from between the leaves or from the base.

In addition, with a very minor possible exception (a form of *Rhipsalis*), all cacti are native to the Western Hemisphere. It is sometimes hard to believe this because of the vast areas of escaped cacti in many parts of the world today.

The majority of other succulents (excluding *Agave, Echeveria, Sedum, Sempervivum* and a few others) are indigenous to Africa and a few scattered areas in the Eastern Hemisphere.

Both cacti and other succulents are excellent subjects for the outdoor garden, greenhouse, or windowsill. They require a minimum of care, provided that they have a requisite amount of sunlight and that their condition of hardiness is respected.

17. Which of the following is the best title for the passage?

   (A) Succulents and Non-Succulents

   (B) Regions of the World and their Vegetation

   (C) Distinguishing Between Succulents and Cacti

   (D) Subjects for the Outdoor Garden

   (E) Characteristics of Cacti and Other Succulents

18. Which features from the list below best distinguish cacti from other succulents?

   (A) Absence of leaves; presence of areoles; large, brilliant flowers; nativity to the Western Hemisphere.

   (B) Presence or absence of leaves; showy flowers which always appear at the top of the plant; indigenous to Africa and a few scattered areas in the Eastern Hemisphere.

(C) The areole; presence of leaves; flowers which are likely to emerge from between the leaves or from the base.

(D) The flowers of cacti are usually more conspicuous and most often appear near the top of the plant; the areole is possessed by cacti alone.

(E) The majority of other succulents are indigenous to Africa and a few scattered areas in the Eastern Hemisphere.

19. Which of the following statements best describes the attitude of the author toward cacti and succulents?

   (A) Cacti are to be chosen over succulents for the home.

   (B) Either are excellent subjects to study in the wild, but to preserve their beauty they should not be removed to the home.

   (C) Both are excellent subjects for botanists to study.

   (D) Both feature interesting adaptations; the cacti is the preferred.

   (E) Both are excellent subjects for the outdoor garden, greenhouse, or windowsill.

20. According to the information given in the passage, which of the following statements is NOT true?

   (A) Cacti and other succulents have evolved in areas where there is little water available.

   (B) Leathery or hairy surfaces, thick spines, and even powdery coatings have evolved to help retard the transpiration of moisture from the leaves of cacti.

   (C) Because of the vast areas of escaped cacti, it is difficult to believe that almost all cacti are native to the Eastern Hemisphere.

   (D) The globular and columnar forms of cacti offer a smaller exposed area to the sun; therefore, drying is reduced and more moisture is retained.

   (E) Both cacti and other succulents are excellent subjects for the outdoor garden, greenhouse, or windowsill since they require minimal care.

21. It could logically follow that the first line of the next paragraph would begin with which of the following?

(A) The size and brilliance of the flowers of the cacti are interesting subjects for further attention.

(B) Cacti and other succulents are generally able to withstand rapid changes in temperature.

(C) The globular and columnar shapes of cacti have been frequent topics of study for artists — particularly those of the American Midwest.

(D) Disney's "The Living Desert" is a full-length feature which focuses on cacti.

(E) A study of the flowers can tell the researcher much about the original location and structural modifications of the cacti.

22. The most compelling reason for choosing cacti over other succulents for a windowsill would be which of the following?

(A) Cacti require less care than do other succulents.

(B) The shape of the cacti is more appealing than that of the other succulents.

(C) Succulents from the Eastern Hemisphere do not adapt well to the Western Hemisphere.

(D) The flowers of cacti are usually more conspicuous and most often appear between the leaves or at the base.

(E) The flowers of cacti are usually more conspicuous and most often appear from areoles near the top of the plant.

23. According to the passage, which of the following statements are true?

I. The areole distinguishes cacti from other succulents.

II. Cactus flowers are more conspicuous and tend to emerge from between the leaves or near the base.

III. The adaptations to conserve moisture are not very similar in cacti and other succulents.

(A) I only   (D) III only

(B) II only   (E) I and III only

(C) I and II only

24. Which of the following would probably best describe the author's reaction to the many laws being enacted to protect the cacti and to prevent their being removed from desert areas or vandalized?

    (A) Apathy   (D) Distaste

    (B) Confusion   (E) Understanding

    (C) Despair

The Jefferson nickel was executed by Felix Schlag, whose design was chosen from among 390 artists' sketches submitted to the government. This national competition carried with it a prize for $1,000. The Director of the Mint, with the approval of the Secretary of the Treasury, had suggested that Thomas Jefferson's likeness be placed on a U.S. coin as a tribute to his outstanding statesmanship and his record of public service. Schlag's splendid portrayal of our third President appears on the obverse. The reverse has an illustration of Monticello, the magnificent home Jefferson built for himself near Charlottesville, Virginia. The mintmark was on the reverse at the right side of Monticello until 1968. After that date, it was moved to the right of Jefferson's wig, beside the date on the obverse.

Jefferson began building Monticello, his dream house, at the age of 20 and finally finished it 40 years later in the twilight of his life. Monticello, pictured in careful detail on the reverse of the nickel, is not an ordinary kind of house. It is rather a revolutionary house for his day. Jefferson was a gadgeteer — a man of creative and inventive genius who put his ideas to practical use. Monticello has an observatory in which Jefferson studied the stars and planets with a telescope. The clock in the main hall not only tells the hour but the days of the week as well, and the gears that drive the hands pass through the wall to a duplicate clock over the porch outside. The house has dozens of other amazing conveniences that have to be seen to be appreciated.

No matter what his talents, Jefferson is remembered as a defender of the human rights of man. He spoke to the world through his pen, preferring to put his thoughts in writing rather than in public speech. In a time when revolution was commonplace in America, Jefferson was asked to write The Declaration of Independence, the ageless announcement of Colonial freedom. His words inspired people and sent out to the world a call to arms in the precious name of liberty:

We hold these Truths to be self-evident, that all men are created equal, that they are endowed by their Creator with certain unalienable Rights, that among these are Life, Liberty and the Pursuit of Happiness.

25. Which of the following best describes the organization of the information in the passage?

(A) The passage begins with a description of the Jefferson nickel, then discusses Jefferson's contributions to the Treasury system.

(B) The passage begins with a discussion of the work of Felix Schlag on the Jefferson nickel, and continues with a discussion of Jefferson's architectural studies.

(C) The passage begins with a description of the contest for the design of the Jefferson nickel, then continues with a discussion of Jefferson's role as author of The Declaration of Independence.

(D) The passage begins with a description and brief history of the Jefferson nickel, and continues with a sketch of Jefferson's architectural interests and his role as a statesman.

(E) The passage begins with a description and brief history of the Jefferson nickel, and continues with a discussion of Jefferson's political beliefs.

26. Where would the mintmark appear on a 1969 nickel?

(A) On the obverse side to the right of Monticello.

(B) On the reverse side to the right of Monticello.

(C) On the obverse side to the right of Jefferson's wig.

(D) On the reverse side to the right of Jefferson's wig.

(E) Mintmarks do not appear after 1968.

27. Which of the following words would be the best substitute for the word "revolutionary" in line 16?

(A) Creative

(B) Unusual

(C) Expensive

(D) Political

(E) Innovative

> **DIRECTIONS:** Each of the following questions provides a given word in capitalized letters followed by five word choices. Choose the best word which is most <u>opposite</u> in meaning to the given word.

28. AVOCATION:

    (A) respite

    (B) profession

    (C) silent

    (D) hobby

    (E) avulsion

29. ADULTERATED:

    (A) ribald

    (B) defiled

    (C) chaste

    (D) infantile

    (E) vicious

30. AUGMENTATION:

    (A) constriction

    (B) accession

    (C) expansion

    (D) perturbation

    (E) satiation

31. TACITURN:

    (A) reticent

    (B) appeased

    (C) reserved

    (D) inveigled

    (E) effusive

32. HELICAL:

    (A) spiral

    (B) coiled

    (C) curved

    (D) straight

    (E) round

33. ASININE:

    (A) fatuous

    (B) cunning

    (C) idiosyncratic

    (D) eccentric

    (E) antithetic

34. SAGACIOUS:

    (A) shrewd

    (B) astute

    (C) procumbent

    (D) ductile

    (E) incapable

35. NADIR:

    (A) zephyr

    (B) knave

    (C) epitome

    (D) kith

    (E) zenith

36. BEATIFIC:

    (A) animalistic

    (B) melancholy

    (C) urbane

    (D) civilized

    (E) similitude

37. TURGID:

    (A) aggressive

    (B) tumid

    (C) bilious

    (D) palpable

    (E) deflated

38. CANAILLE:

    (A) aggregate

    (B) fulgurant

    (C) fulminant

    (D) bridge

    (E) aristocracy

STOP

If time still remains, you may go back and check your work.
When the time allotted is up, you may go on to the next section.

Section 4

TIME: 30 Minutes
30 Questions

NUMBERS: All numbers are real numbers.

FIGURES: Position of points, angles, regions, etc., are assumed to be in the order shown and angle measures are assumed to be positive.

LINES: Assume that lines shown as straight are indeed straight.

DIRECTIONS: Each of the following given set of quantities is placed into either Column A or B. Compare the two quantities to decide whether

(A) the quantity in Column A is greater;

(B) the quantity in Column B is greater;

(C) the two quantities are equal;

(D) the relationship cannot be determined from the information given.

NOTE: Do not choose (E) since there are only four choices.

COMMON INFORMATION: Information which relates to one or both given quantities is centered in the two columns. A symbol which appears in both columns will indicate the same item in Column A and Column B.

EXAMPLES:

Column A	Column B
1. 5×4	$5 + 4$

Explanation: The correct answer is (A), since $5 \times 4 = 20$, and $5 + 4 = 9$.

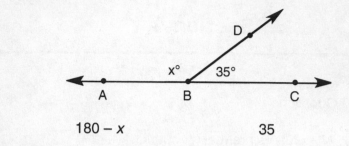

2. $180 - x$ \qquad\qquad 35

Explanation: The correct answer is (C). Since $\angle ABC$ is a straight angle, its measurement is 180°.

Column A	Column B

w, x, y are positive,
$w + x + y = 20$, and $w = x$

	Column A	Column B
1.	x	10
2.	Average of 25, 17, 30, 23, and 15	Average of 13, 35, 11, 25, 9, and 39
3.	0	The largest even integer smaller than 2

$2x + 4y = 12$

	Column A	Column B
4.	x	y

x is a positive integer

	Column A	Column B
5.	$\dfrac{x}{3}$	$.34x$

Column A	**Column B**

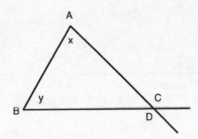

6. $\angle y$ $\angle C - \angle x$

---

7. The values of y in   The values of x in
   $y^2 + 12y + 27 = 0$ $x^2 - 12x + 27 = 0$

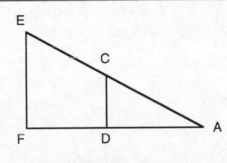

$CD \parallel EF$
$AD = DF$
$CD = 4$
$DF = 3$

8. Side EF 7

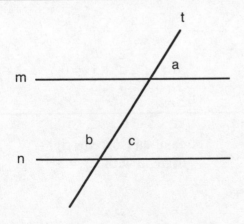

m and n are parallel lines.

9. $\angle b$ $\angle b + \angle c - \angle a$

	Column A	**Column B**

$$0.5x - 0.5y = 3$$

10.	x	y

x is a positive integer.

11.	$\dfrac{5x+7}{x} + \dfrac{8x+10}{4}$	$2x + \dfrac{9x+14}{2x} + 3$

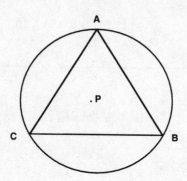

$\triangle ABC$ is inscribed in $\odot P$
$AB = AC$
$m \overset{\frown}{AC} = 145°$

12.	$m \angle C$	$m \overset{\frown}{CB}$

If $v > 0$

13.	If $w^2 - 2wv + v^2 = 0$	If $v^2 + 2xv + x^2 = 0$
	w	x

14.	Area of an equilateral triangle with side $= b$	Area of an isosceles right triangle with leg $= b$

<u>Column A</u>	<u>Column B</u>

Tom can mow the lawn in x hours, Peter can mow the lawn in y hours, and Dan can mow the lawn in z hours. Tom and Dan together are faster than Tom and Peter together.

15. $\qquad$ x $\qquad\qquad\qquad\qquad\qquad\qquad\qquad$ z

---

DIRECTIONS: For the following questions, select the best answer choice to the given question.

16. $\dfrac{x-y}{x+y} - \dfrac{x+y}{x-y} =$

(A) $\dfrac{(4xy)}{\left(x^2 - y^2\right)}$

(B) $\dfrac{(-4xy)}{\left(x^2 - y^2\right)}$

(C) 0

(D) $\dfrac{(-2xy)}{\left(x^2 - y^2\right)}$

(E) -1

17. Find the median for the following set of numbers: 16, 22, 18, 21, 17, 21, 19, and 21.

(A) 21.0

(B) 20.0

(C) 22.0

(D) 19.0

(E) 19.4

18. What is t equal to if $A = P(1 + rt)$?

(A) $A - P - Pr$

(B) $\dfrac{(A + P)}{Pr}$

(C) $\dfrac{A}{P - r}$

(D) $\dfrac{(A - P)}{Pr}$

(E) None of these

19. $4\dfrac{1}{3} - 1\dfrac{5}{6} =$

   (A) $3\dfrac{2}{3}$ (D) $2\dfrac{1}{6}$

   (B) $2\dfrac{1}{2}$ (E) None of these

   (C) $3\dfrac{1}{2}$

20. The number missing in the series, 2, 6, 12, 20, x, 42, 56,

   (A) 36.   (D) 38.

   (B) 24.   (E) 40.

   (C) 30.

Questions 21–25 refer to the graph below.

Cumulative Undergraduate Mathematics Enrollments in the U.S., 1965 – 85
(Thousands of enrollments, fall semester)

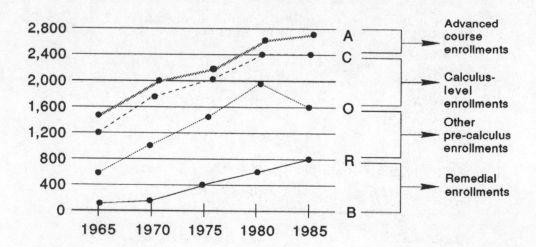

(Note: Area between line segments B and R represents remedial enrollments; between line segments R and O represents other precalculus enrollments; between line segments O and C represents calculus enrollments; and between line segments C and A represents advanced course enrollments.)

21. The total undergraduate mathematics enrollment in the fall of 1975 was about x thousand where x equals about

    (A) 2,800.   (D) 2,200.

    (B) 2,000.   (E) 1,500.

    (C) 2,400.

22. In 1970, the percentage of enrollments in the remedial mathematics category was about

    (A) 21.   (D) 79.

    (B) 10.5.   (E) 89.

    (C) 18.

23. What is the ratio of the calculus-level enrollments 1985:1975?

    (A) 3 : 8   (D) 6 : 5

    (B) 2 : 1   (E) 8 : 3

    (C) 4 : 3

24. Between 1970 and 1985 the number of remedial mathematics enrollments

    (A) increased by about 100%.

    (B) increased by about 150%.

    (C) increased by about 200%.

    (D) increased by about 300%.

    (E) increased by about 350%.

25. What undergraduate enrollment category was fairly constant over the period of the graph?

    (A) Remedial   (D) Advanced course

    (B) Other precalculus   (E) None of the categories

    (C) Calculus level

26. What is the product of $(\sqrt{3} + 6)$ and $(\sqrt{3} - 2)$

    (A) $9 + 4\sqrt{3}$ (B) -9

(C) $-9 + 4\sqrt{3}$ (D) $-9 + 2\sqrt{3}$

(E) 9

27. What is the factorization of $x^2 + ax - 2x - 2a$?

(A) $(x + 2)(x - a)$ (D) $(x - 2)(x - a)$

(B) $(x - 2)(x + a)$ (E) None of these

(C) $(x + 2)(x + a)$

28. Jim is twice as old as Susan. If Jim were 4 years younger and Susan were 3 years older, their ages would differ by 12 years. What is the sum of their ages?

(A) 19   (D) 57

(B) 42   (E) None of these

(C) 56

29. Joe and Jim together have 14 marbles. Jim and Tim together have 10 marbles. Joe and Tim together have 12 marbles. What is the maximum number of marbles that any one of these may have?

(A) 7   (D) 10

(B) 8   (E) 11

(C) 9

30. The range for $|5x - 1| \leq 9$ is

(A) $-\dfrac{8}{5} \leq x \leq 2.$ (D) $-\dfrac{8}{5} \leq x \leq \dfrac{9}{5}.$

(B) $-\dfrac{9}{5} \leq x \leq \dfrac{9}{5}.$ (E) $-\dfrac{8}{5} \geq x$ and $x \geq 2.$

(C) $0 \leq x \leq \dfrac{1}{5}.$

STOP

If time still remains, you may go back and check your work.
When the time allotted is up, you may go on to the next section.

Section 5

TIME: 30 Minutes
38 Questions

DIRECTIONS: Each of the given sentences has blank spaces which indicate words omitted. Choose the best combination of words which fit into the meaning and structure within the context of the sentence.

---

1. The secret agent's taking the one sheet of _____ had an _____ on the lives of many of her companions.

    (A) vellum...edict

    (B) stationary...affect

    (C) stationery...effect

    (D) parchment...obligation

    (E) bond...effigy

2. The weekly program on public radio is the most _____ means of educating the public about pollution.

    (A) proficient

    (B) effusive

    (C) effectual

    (D) capable

    (E) competent

3. The accused appeared _____ since she felt certain the male witness would _____ her alibi.

    (A) sanguine...corroborate

    (B) meddlesome...substantiate

    (C) conjugal...revoke

    (D) garbled...authenticate

    (E) concupiscent...abolish

4. The _____ habits of the wild hawk caused a serious _____ to develop for the chicken farmer.

   (A) marauding...emergency

   (B) parasitic...malady

   (C) saprophytic...insurrection

   (D) predatory...predicament

   (E) meticulous...tête-à-tête

5. Louis Phillipe, so far as was practical, _____ the citizens of foreign states for losses caused by Napoleon.

   (A) repartitioned   (D) subscribed

   (B) apportioned   (E) subsidized

   (C) indemnified

6. Anti-machine groups, such as the 19th century Chartists, flat-Earth societies, and more recently, anti-computer groups, are all examples of _____.

   (A) paranoia   (D) misogynism

   (B) xenophobia   (E) eccentricity

   (C) misoneism

7. The governor was impeached for gross _____, although embezzlement charges were never filed.

   (A) multifariousness   (D) malfeasance

   (B) negligence   (E) recidivism

   (C) malediction

DIRECTIONS: In the following questions, a related pair of words is followed by five more pairs of words. Select the pair that best expresses the same relationship as that expressed in the original pair.

---

8. SOLID:LIQUID::

   (A) oxygen:air   (B) water:steam

(C) dirt:water

(D) grass:wood

(E) fire:air

9. LEAVE:RETURN::

(A) dry:wet

(D) down:up

(B) black:white

(E) left:right

(C) open:close

10. FEALTY:LORD::

(A) patriotism:country

(D) money:creditor

(B) tax:government

(E) belief:religion

(C) fidelity:spouse

11. LINEN:FLAX::

(A) chintz:silk

(D) coal:nylon

(B) madras:linen

(E) chamois:leather

(C) rayon:plastic

12. PUGILISM:FISTS::

(A) lexicographer:animals

(D) archeology:fossils

(B) gynecology:genes

(E) pediatrics:aged

(C) nepotism:relatives

13. DOOR:KEY::

(A) gem:ring

(D) effort:achievement

(B) perfume:aroma

(E) mold:gelatin

(C) enigma:clue

14. EDIFICE:FACADE::

(A) dorsal:ventral

(D) body:skeleton

(B) turtle:shell

(E) counterfeit:fraudulent

(C) anachronism:chronologic

15. DEFICIT:PECULATION::

   (A) attire:dress

   (B) hunger:abstinence

   (C) appear:manifest

   (D) drought:famine

   (E) magistrate:judge

16. UNCTUOUS:BRUSQUE::

   (A) gauche:suave

   (B) abstruse:recondite

   (C) bumptious:deleterious

   (D) lustrous:luminous

   (E) vitriolic:caustic

DIRECTIONS: Each passage is followed by questions based on its content. After reading a passage, choose the best answer to each question. Answer all questions based on what is stated or implied in that passage.

The scientific naming and classification of all organisms is known as taxonomy. Both extant (living) and extinct (no longer existing) organisms are taxonomically classified into specific and carefully defined categories. A single category is called a taxon; multiple categories are taxa.

There have been several classification schemes throughout history. Aristotle devised a system of categorizing plants and animals that was used for almost 2000 years. With the exploration of the New World and the invention of the microscope, more and more organisms were discovered. A universal, comprehensive classification system was needed; one that could be used by all biologists, regardless of language.

The founder of the modern scheme of taxonomy was the Swedish naturalist Carl von Linné (1707-1778). He published his Systema Naturae (Systems of Nature) in 1735; the tenth edition, published in 1758, is still used as the authoritative taxonomical source today. Linné's system is hierarchical. It begins with a large, inclusive taxon called a kingdom, followed by a phylum or a division (for plants), class, order, family, genus, species, and in some cases, subspecies. Each level becomes more specific, until the lowest level describes only one type of organism.

Linné defined two kingdoms, one for plants and one for animals. In 1969, Robert Whittaker developed a new classification system using five kingdoms. This revision reduced, but did not completely eradicate, the confusion faced by biologists attempting to classify organisms, such as fungi, that do not fit into either the plant or animal category.

There is still some debate about the categorization, but a species is generally recognized as a group of organisms that share the same morphological, ecological, and genetic characteristics, and whose members can interbreed and produce fertile offspring.

The current classification system tries to take into account not only how various taxa are related because of shared characteristics, such as all members of Class Aves (birds) have feathers, but also how they are related through evolution.

Linné used Latin, the universal scientific language for centuries, and taxonomy still uses Latin names for all classes of taxa. The complete taxonomical classification of the California grizzly bear, for example, is: Kingdom Animalia, Phylum Chordata, Class Mammalia, Order Carnivora, Family Ursidae, Genus Ursus, Species horribilis.

The genus and specie make up the organism's scientific name, in this case, Ursus horribilis. This is known as the binomial system of nomenclature, also developed by Linné. The genus is always capitalized and underlined, and the specie is always lowercase and either underlined or italicized.

Given any particular species of plant, animal, or other organism that has been discovered and classified, and with sufficient information about its appearance, biochemistry, reproductive habits, and so on, a biologist can determine its taxonomy. When linked with the technology of DNA studies, taxonomy can be a valuable tool to help scientists unlock the evolutionary secrets carried by all organisms.

17. Which of the following is the best title for the passage?

(A) The Contributions of Carl von Linné

(B) Taxonomy and Modern Biological Categorization

(C) How to Categorize Plants and Animals

(D) The Evolution and Categorization of Animals

(E) A Brief History of Taxonomy

18. Based on the information presented in the passage, which of the following statements are true?

    I.   The scientific name for an organism is made up of the genus and specie names.

    II.   There are two kingdoms used to classify all living and extinct organisms.

    III. The taxa family is more specific than the phylum, but less specific than the genus.

    (A) I only   (D) III only

    (B) II only   (E) I and III only

    (C) I and II only

19. The author would be most likely to agree with which of the following statements?

    (A) Taxonomy is necessary to classify different species of organisms, but the current system is too complex and should be simplified.

    (B) Taxonomy is a useful method of classifying different species, but soon new methods will be necessary to distinguish between the new types of organisms being discovered by DNA research.

    (C) The system of taxonomy developed by Linné is the best method devised for categorizing different species, and Whittaker's more recent five kingdom scheme is an unnecessary complication.

    (D) Taxonomy is a useful method of categorizing species, and when combined with new techniques in DNA tracing, it can help scientists trace the evolution of various species.

    (E) Taxonomy has not changed very much since Aristotle devised his system of classification; Linné's biggest contribution to taxonomy was the use of Latin terminology.

20. Which of the following best describes the relationship between the first paragraph and the rest of the passage?

    (A) The first paragraph presents a brief history of taxonomy, and the rest of the passage details how to classify an organism according to the scheme devised by Carl von Linné.

(B) The first paragraph gives a definition of taxonomy, and the rest of the passage is a synopsis of the history of taxonomy, focussing on the contributions made by Carl von Linné and Robert Whittaker.

(C) The first paragraph presents a brief history of the modern system of taxonomy, and the rest of the passage discusses some of the problems inherent in this system.

(D) The first paragraph provides a definition of taxonomy, and the rest of the passage describes the inadequacies of the current method and suggests modifications.

(E) The first paragraph presents a definition of taxonomy, and the rest of the passage includes a brief history of the development of the modern system and an example of how it is used to classify organisms.

21. According to the information given in the passage, what is the binomial system of nomenclature?

(A) The two kingdom system of classifying all organisms developed by Carl von Linné.

(B) The five kingdom system of classifying all organisms developed by Robert Whittaker.

(C) The formation of the scientific name of an organism from the genus and specie names of that organism.

(D) The Aristotelian method of taxonomic classification that was superseded by Linné's method.

(E) The mathematical classification of the Latin terminology used to categorize organisms.

22. All of the following statements about taxonomy are true EXCEPT

(A) A species is usually defined as a group of organisms possessing the same morphological, ecological, and genetic characteristics, whose members can interbreed and produce fertile offspring.

(B) Taxonomy takes evolutionary relationships between organisms into account, as well as the shared characteristics of related taxa.

(C) The hierarchical system developed by Linné moves from the top, specific, level down to the lower, more general, level.

(D) There are many organisms that are neither plant nor animal; these organisms could not be classified under Linné's system, but can be classified using Whittaker's five kingdom system.

(E) Given enough information about any described organism's morphology, biochemistry, reproductive habits, and genetic characteristics, a biologist can determine its taxonomy.

23. According to the passage, taxonomy involves

(A) the scientific naming of all living organisms and their classification into distinct taxa.

(B) the classification of all organisms, extant and extinct, into distinct taxa.

(C) the scientific naming of all organisms, extant and extinct.

(D) the categorization of living organisms into distinct taxa.

(E) the scientific naming of all organisms and their classification into distinct taxa.

24. Paragraph 5 states that a species is a group that shares the same morphological characteristics. The best definition of "morphological characteristics" is

(A) the appearance of the group of organisms.

(B) the reproductive habits of the group of organisms.

(C) the shape of the organisms.

(D) the structure and form of the organisms.

(E) the size and color of the organisms.

Public acceptance of wind energy conversion systems is an important consideration in planning for the widespread application of wind energy. Studies have shown that the environmental impact of such systems is relatively small compared to conventional electric power systems. Wind-powered systems do not require the flooding of large land areas or the alteration of the natural ecology, as do hydroelectric systems. Furthermore, they produce no waste products or thermal or chemical effluents, as fossil-fueled and nuclear-fueled systems do.

Conventional wind turbine systems that generate several megawatts of power require large exposed rotors several hundred feet in diameter, located on high towers. The rotors of such systems, being passive, are practically noiseless. However, special precautions will be necessary to prevent them from causing interference with nearby TV or radio receivers, and some safety measures may be required to prevent damage or injury from possible mishaps in cases where there is danger that the rotors might break or shed ice.

The only other concerns with conventional wind machines are those of aesthetics. Large numbers of units and interconnecting transmission lines will be required in the future if such systems are to have any significant impact on U.S. energy demands. Particular attention is being given, therefore, to the development of attractive designs for the towers, rotors, and nacelles of these conventional systems to avoid "visual pollution."

25. The writer's opinion toward wind energy conversion systems can best be described as which of the following?

    (A) Personal dissatisfaction   (D) Negativism

    (B) Unqualified enthusiasm   (E) Open-mindedness

    (C) Disinterest

26. The article refers to the *nacelles* of the wind energy conversion systems. Which is the best definition of *nacelles*?

    (A) The part of the system which contains the atomic matter used to generate electricity.

    (B) The enclosed part of the system containing generators.

    (C) The part of the system used to reduce the noise, or nacelle, caused by the generation of electricity.

    (D) The nacelles are a part of the high tower on which the rotors are located.

    (E) The nacelles are the blades of the rotors.

27. The limitations of wind energy conversion systems described by the author are which of the following?

    (A) Interference with television and radio receivers, danger from rotors which break or shed ice, and aesthetics.

    (B) Aesthetics, many transmission lines, and noise.

(C) Safety precautions, the large number of units and interconnecting lines required, and large exposed rotors.

(D) The thermal effluents which are a necessary by-product, the noise from the rotors, and the aesthetics.

(E) The visual pollution, the thermal pollution, and the safety precautions mandated.

DIRECTIONS: Each of the following questions provides a given word in capitalized letters followed by five word choices. Choose the best word which is most <u>opposite</u> in meaning to the given word.

---

28. PAUCITY:

    (A) dearth   (D) plethora

    (B) loquacious   (E) lugubrious

    (C) sanative

29. CONSONANCE:

    (A) conscience   (D) contention

    (B) conscious   (E) consign

    (C) coalesce

30. TILT:

    (A) incline   (D) pitch

    (B) align   (E) slant

    (C) list

31. VENIAL:

    (A) hedonic   (D) implacable

    (B) ineffable   (E) heinous

    (C) peccadillo

32. PRODIGAL:

    (A) wandering   (D) frugal

    (B) tarrying   (E) lavish

    (C) spendthrift

33. VIABLE:

    (A) remnant   (D) vestige

    (B) viands   (E) moribund

    (C) subsistence

34. RECUMBENT:

    (A) prone   (D) supine

    (B) obligatory   (E) level

    (C) vertical

35. VOLATILE:

    (A) explosive   (D) deliberate

    (B) impulsive   (E) transitory

    (C) mercurial

36. FACTIOUS:

    (A) bellicose   (D) fractious

    (B) desultory   (E) consonant

    (C) fortuitous

37. PROBITY:

    (A) aesthetics   (D) predilection

    (B) perfidy   (E) complementary

    (C) abeyance

38. FACTITIOUS:

(A) authentic

(B) travesty

(C) pedantic

(D) mordant

(E) rapacious

STOP

If time still remains, you may go back and check your work.
When the time allotted is up, you may go on to the next section.

Section 6

TIME: 30 Minutes

30 Questions

NUMBERS: All numbers are real numbers.

FIGURES: Position of points, angles, regions, etc., are assumed to be in the order shown and angle measures are assumed to be positive.

LINES: Assume that lines shown as straight are indeed straight.

DIRECTIONS: Each of the following given set of quantities is placed into either Column A or B. Compare the two quantities to decide whether

(A)   the quantity in Column A is greater;

(B)   the quantity in Column B is greater;

(C)   the two quantities are equal;

(D)   the relationship cannot be determined from the information given.

NOTE: Do not choose (E) since there are only four choices.

COMMON INFORMATION: Information which relates to one or both given quantities is centered in the two columns. A symbol which appears in both columns will indicate the same item in Column A and Column B.

EXAMPLES:

Column A	Column B
1. 5×4	$5 + 4$

Explanation: The correct answer is (A), since $5 \times 4 = 20$, and $5 + 4 = 9$.

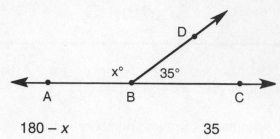

2. $180 - x$ 35

Explanation: The correct answer is (C). Since $\angle ABC$ is a straight angle, its measurement is 180°.

Column A	Column B

x and y are positive integers.

	Column A	Column B
1.	$x^2 + y^2$	$(x + y)^2$

$$x = -2 \qquad y = 4$$

2.	$(x - 1)^2$	$(y - 1)^2$

The lowest common denominator of each group

3.	$\dfrac{2}{3}, \dfrac{5}{12}, \dfrac{7}{8}$	$\dfrac{5}{6}, \dfrac{3}{8}, \dfrac{1}{2}$

4.	30% of 9	0.27

$$2x - 1 = -17$$

5.	x	8

Column A	**Column B**

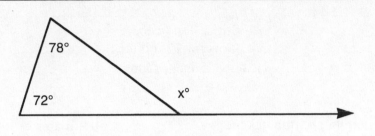

6.	150	x

$$a \neq 0;\; b \neq 0;\; b \neq -1$$

7.	$\dfrac{a}{b}$	$\dfrac{a+1}{b+1}$

$$x = -4;\; y = 2$$

8.	0	$\dfrac{|x| + 2|y|}{5 + x}$

$$x - y \neq 0 \;;\; y \neq 0$$

9.	$\dfrac{x^2 - y^2}{x^3 - x^2 y}$	$\dfrac{x + y}{y}$

Two concentric circles:
Diameter of inner circle is 3.5 units
Diameter of outer circle is 7 units

10.	Circumference of inner circle	½ of circumference of outer circle

315

Column A	**Column B**

A 30-inch-long candle
that burns for 12 minutes
is now 25 inches long

11. The number of minutes the   60 minutes
      whole candle burns

Quadrilateral *ABCD* is a parallelogram; segment $\overline{BE}$
is perpendicular to line $\overline{AD}$; the length of $\overline{BE}$ is 8 cm.

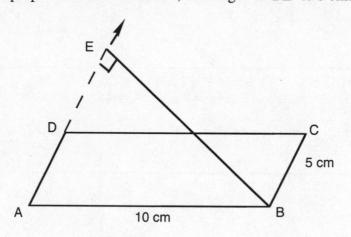

12.   Area of *ABCD*   40 cm²

Gail received a 7% raise last year.
Her salary was $24,000.

13.   Gail's salary now $25,580

14. $8^{2/3}$ $16^{1/2}$

Column A	Column B

$$w : x = y : z$$
$$x \neq 0, z \neq 0$$

15.   0 $wz - xy$

DIRECTIONS: For the following questions, select the best answer choice to the given question.

---

16. $3(a - 1) = 7(a + 2)$. Find a.

    (A) $\dfrac{17}{4}$ (D) $-\dfrac{4}{3}$

    (B) $-\dfrac{17}{4}$ (E) $-\dfrac{3}{4}$

    (C) $-\dfrac{14}{4}$

17. Tom received 89, 94, 86, and 96 on the first four algebra tests. What grade must he receive on his last test to have an average of 92?

    (A) 92   (D) 95

    (B) 94   (E) 96

    (C) 91

18. $(5x - 3)(4x - 6) =$

    (A) $20x^2 - 42x + 18$ (D) $30x^2 - 18$

    (B) $20x^2 - 18$ (E) $18x^2 - 30x - 24$

    (C) $20x^2 - 12x - 18$

19. If the measures of the three angles of a triangle are $(3x + 15)°$, $(5x - 15)°$, and $(2x + 30)°$, what is the measure of each angle?

    (A) 75°   (D) 25°

    (B) 60°   (E) 15°

    (C) 45°

20. $1 + \dfrac{y}{(x-2y)} - \dfrac{y}{(x+2y)} =$

(A) 0

(D) $\dfrac{2x-y}{(x-2y)\,(x+2y)}$

(B) 1

(E) $\dfrac{x^2}{(x-2y)\,(x+2y)}$

(C) $\dfrac{1}{(x-2y)\,(x+2y)}$

Questions 21–25 refer to the following graphs.

The data represents contributions to federal candidates for public office in the late 1970s.

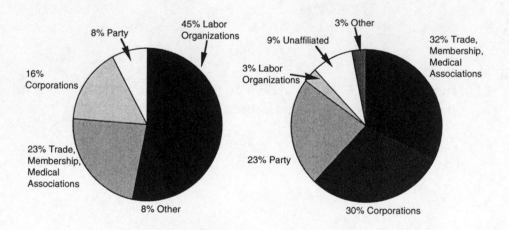

To Democratic Candidates
$21.5 million = 100%

To Republican Candidates
$19.8 million = 100%

21. What is the average percent of contributions to Republican candidates that come from trade, membership, and medical associations?

(A) 23%

(D) 9%

(B) 55%

(E) 45%

(C) 32%

22. What is the average dollar amount (in millions) of support for Democratic candidates that come from the party?

(A) $0.08 million

(D) $5.5 million

(B) $1.72 million

(E) $1.5 million

(C) $2.3 million

23. What is the ratio of the percent contributions of Labor organizations of the Republican candidates to the Democratic candidates?

(A) $1 : 15$

(D) $3 : 8$

(B) $15 : 1$

(E) $9 : 10$

(C) $6 : 100$

24. What is the difference (in millions of dollars) between the average dollar amount of support to Democratic candidates and the average dollar amount of support to Republican candidates that come from labor organizations?

(A) $9.81 million

(D) $8.316 million

(B) $9.675 million

(E) $8.215 million

(C) $9.081 million

25. What is the total dollar amount (in millions) of support for both Democratic and Republican candidates that came from corporations?

(A) $6.608 million

(D) $9.38 million

(B) $12.39 million

(E) $10.049 million

(C) $5.94 million

26. Which of the following equations can be used to find a number x, if the difference between the square of this number and 21 is the same as the product of 4 times the number?

(A) $x - 21 = 4x$

(D) $x + 4x^2 = 21$

(B) $x^2 - 21 = 4x$

(E) $x^2 + 21 = 4x$

(C) $x^2 = 21 - 4x$

27. Emile receives a flat weekly salary of $240 plus 12% commission of the total volume of all sales he makes. What must his dollar volume be in a week if he is to make a total weekly salary of $540?

(A) $2,880   (D) $2,500

(B) $3,600   (E) $2,000

(C) $6,480

28. In the Carco Auto Factory, robots assemble cars. If 3 robots assemble 17 cars in 10 minutes, how many cars can 14 robots assemble in 45 minutes if all robots work at the same rate all the time?

(A) 357   (D) 150

(B) 340   (E) 272

(C) 705

29. If the length of segment $\overline{EB}$; base of triangle *EBC*, is equal to $1/4$ the length of segment $\overline{AB}$ ($\overline{AB}$ is the length of rectangle *ABCD*), and the area of triangle *EBC* is 12 square units, find the area of the shaded region.

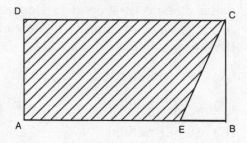

(A) 24 square units   (D) 72 square units

(B) 96 square units   (E) 120 square units

(C) 84 square units

30. A doctor has 40 cc of 2% tincture of iodine. If the iodine is boiled, alcohol is evaporated away and the strength of tincture is raised. How much alcohol must be boiled away in order to raise the strength of the tincture to 8%?

(A) 34 cc   (D) 24 cc

(B) 32 cc   (E) 10 cc

(C) 30 cc

STOP

If time still remains, you may go back and check your work.
When the time allotted is up, you may go on to the next section.

TEST 2

ANSWER KEY

Sections 1 and 2 — Analytical Writing

Please review the sample essays in the Detailed Explanations.

Section 3 — Verbal Ability

1. (E)	11. (B)	21. (B)	31. (E)
2. (E)	12. (E)	22. (E)	32. (D)
3. (B)	13. (B)	23. (A)	33. (B)
4. (D)	14. (B)	24. (E)	34. (E)
5. (A)	15. (E)	25. (D)	35. (E)
6. (D)	16. (E)	26. (C)	36. (B)
7. (C)	17. (E)	27. (E)	37. (E)
8. (E)	18. (D)	28. (B)	38. (E)
9. (D)	19. (E)	29. (C)	
10. (C)	20. (C)	30. (A)	

Section 4 — Quantitative Ability

1. (B)	9. (C)	17. (B)	25. (D)
2. (C)	10. (A)	18. (D)	26. (C)
3. (C)	11. (C)	19. (B)	27. (B)
4. (D)	12. (A)	20. (C)	28. (D)
5. (B)	13. (A)	21. (D)	29. (B)
6. (C)	14. (B)	22. (B)	30. (A)
7. (B)	15. (D)	23. (C)	
8. (A)	16. (B)	24. (D)	

Section 5 — Verbal Ability

1. (C)	11. (E)	21. (C)	31. (E)
2. (C)	12. (C)	22. (C)	32. (D)
3. (A)	13. (C)	23. (E)	33. (E)
4. (D)	14. (B)	24. (D)	34. (C)
5. (C)	15. (B)	25. (E)	35. (D)
6. (C)	16. (A)	26. (B)	36. (E)
7. (D)	17. (B)	27. (A)	37. (B)
8. (B)	18. (E)	28. (D)	38. (A)
9. (C)	19. (D)	29. (D)	
10. (C)	20. (E)	30. (B)	

Section 6 — Quantitative Ability

1. (B)	9. (D)	17. (D)	25. (D)
2. (C)	10. (C)	18. (A)	26. (B)
3. (C)	11. (A)	19. (B)	27. (D)
4. (A)	12. (C)	20. (E)	28. (A)
5. (B)	13. (A)	21. (C)	29. (C)
6. (C)	14. (C)	22. (B)	30. (C)
7. (D)	15. (C)	23. (A)	
8. (B)	16. (B)	24. (C)	

DETAILED EXPLANATIONS OF ANSWERS

Section 1–Analytical Writing

PERSPECTIVES ON AN ISSUE ESSAY TOPIC—ESSAY ONE

Sample Essay Response Scoring 6

Filmmaking in America has become a multimillion dollar industry. Every film produced in Hollywood has a phenomenally large budget. Every aspect of the process is expensive, from the stock upon which the film is printed to the salary of the stars whose presence is necessary to ensure the commercial success of the film. The amount of money spent on films in some ways adds to their appeal. It is part of the glamour which makes the world of stars and directors separate and fascinating. It often seems, however, that this glamour, which is an insubstantial facade, is bought at the price of integrity and artistic value.

solid and coherent elaboration of a position outlined in the question

very precise thesis

This issue raises some very important questions such as whether or not film is an art and whether or not an artist is accountable to his or her audience. I think the answer to the first question is that film is sometimes an art, and that this situation exists when the person or people making the film give thought to both the form and content of their work. A film is made up of many different images and an artistic filmmaker must think of both the composition of each frame and the way in which the frames are edited together. Beyond this, I believe that the artist must give serious consideration to the content of the work. He or she must have some message to relate or some story to tell motivated by a genuine desire to communicate. If the sole creational motivation is to make a profit, a loss of integrity is sure to follow: the filmmaker will be saying what he or she feels people will want to hear, but not what he or she feels inspired to say. A film created under such circumstances lacks integrity, and will not be a work of art.

good line of reasoning that expands the original topic

good variation in sentence structure

effective transition — (This issue leads directly) to the second question, that of whether or not an artist should be accountable to his or her audience. The current situation in the film industry requires that a filmmaker be completely financially dependent on the audience. The fact that Hollywood films are so extravagantly expensive means that a certain audience size must be guaranteed in order for a specific film to be considered a worthwhile project. This system, in which the production and distribution are so closely linked, inevitably requires sacrifices. Frequently, films will be

well-executed transition between ideas — shown to preview audiences during production and the story will be changed to meet audience demand. (Similarly,) since Hollywood is built firmly on a "star system," certain actors or actresses will be chosen for a part not because they are best suited for it, but because they are capable of drawing the biggest crowd at the box office. This is not to suggest that artists create in a vacuum entirely unaware of the response their work will receive. The sense of having a message to relate to a specific audience is powerful and valid. (When the accountability is purely financial and commercial, however, the film is likely to lose its status as a work of art.)

clear and concise concluding sentence

Throughout the history of film there have been people who have believed passionately in film as an art. They have been entranced by the magical quality of flickering lights and shadows, and by the uncanny suitability of the medium for relating stories. These people have always devoted intense thought to the potential of film, delighting in experimenting with new narrative and

this picks up and expands the idea of previous paragraph — technological advances. As film becomes more and more of an expensive industry, and as the glamorous world of film becomes increasingly separated from our daily lives, it becomes more and more difficult to create an "independent" film. In order to create a film based on an artistic vision rather than audience demand, one must seek alternative forms of funding, which are scarce. Even if a filmmaker succeeds in finding the money to produce a film, distribution remains a difficult challenge. Frequently such films are made on a very low budget, and the resulting unusual technical style or story may appeal to only a very small audience, and may only be released in a few smaller theaters or "art houses."

effective reference back to previous line of reasoning — Some Hollywood films are enormously entertaining. Technological advances are constantly being made to enhance the beauty of film images and increase the ability of film to tell a story. It is a sad fact, however, that these skills and techniques are available only to a select group of people working within a closed system. In the ongoing race to compose commercially popular films, the big Hollywood studios will continue to produce sequel after sequel, or stale imitations of the most popular film. Ultimately, this is insulting to the audience, who will grow tired of **strong and** spending money to see films they recognize as all sparkle and no **precise** substance. (In the fervor to please everyone, the filmmakers will **concluding** end up pleasing no one at all.) **statement**

Analysis of Sample Essay Scoring 6

The above essay analyzing an issue is a 6-rated, or outstanding, essay. The essayist takes a strong stance arguing one position on the issue and defends this position in a cohesive, well-organized essay. In discussing many different aspects of the film industry, the author shows a firm grasp of the complexities of the argument. This is further illustrated when he or she suggests that the original question about the commercialization of film gives rise to other questions, such as the nature of film as an art and the role of an artist. These are complicated queries with no clear answers, and the author maintains this sense while engaging in a thorough and clearly written analysis of the issue.

PERSPECTIVES ON AN ISSUE ESSAY TOPIC—ESSAY TWO

Sample Essay Response Scoring 3

Students are in school to learn. (From the teacher.) Discipline *sentence*
  fragment
unnecessary problems are common in this country, not even just in urban *poor*
repetition schools, but even in country schools they have these problems. *sentence*
The lack of discipline leads to poor education. We must work *structure*
together as a society to help maintain the authority of teachers.
This is also   true of skepticism. If students are skeptical, the
teacher will not have control of the class. *poor*
  transition

The school shootings we've all heard so much about are
tragic. These are some of the worst stories we could imagine. *ineffective*
(Why would any student ever go into a school and shoot his class- *question*
mates and teachers?) There is just so much violence in the world, *that*
  does not
and there is not enough faith. Students who have so much rage *relate to*
  the essay
off- need to know that they cannot just act out on it like this. But I am *topic*
topic not saying people shouldn't own guns, because gun ownership is
a fundamental right of all Americans. It is not the guns that kill
the students, but the other students who have the guns.

When students question what they are taught, or don't re-spect their teacher by being skeptical, they are helping to erode our society by making it unstable. Liberals should not be allowed to have any say in education because they want people to ques-tion everything and undermine our values and destroy America. We need good, wholesome teachers and programs designed to teach students to accept authority and to follow the rules.

there is no example to support this point

very vague expression

this statement needs development; it is therefore an ineffective closing sentence

Analysis of Sample Essay Scoring 3

This essay is scored a 3 because it seems to reflect poorly articulated political cliches rather than an argument that is related to the essay topic. The whole essay is poorly organized. It starts with a vague introduction and an undeveloped thesis. The follow-ing transitions between ideas are very weak. There are some po-tentially strong positions in this essay. However, because of the lack of explanations and reasons they are not convincing. The use of undefined terms like "liberals" or "wholesome values" again add to the vagueness of the essay. As a result, it is not clear how the essayist arrives at his closing statement. In addition to this, there are some overly long and fragmented sentences.

Section 2–Analytical Writing

ANALYSIS OF AN ARGUMENT ESSAY TOPIC

Sample Essay Response Scoring 6

The author of this passage is a composer who states that the purpose of his work is to understand the people of England. That does not, however, seem to be the purpose of this particular passage. It is difficult to tell exactly what the main point of this argument is. The author discusses music and its paying audience, but it is unclear what motivates this discussion. This lack of clear focal point is one of several problems which detract from the effectiveness of this argument. Although the passage seems to be written from a genuine emotion, and though it seems that the composer himself feels that he has something important to say, the writing is at best vague, and at worst contradictory, and this results in a generally ineffective argument.

very precise and therefore a strong observation

effective thesis

Since the author takes the time to state a specific agenda, an expectation is raised that the passage will in some way explore this stated topic. Perhaps the initial problem is that the topic is so vague. He mentions that he wants to "...get in touch with the people of England." England is an enormous country comprising millions of people and the phrase "get in touch with" does not clearly describe a pragmatic process for understanding them. The author proceeds to jump from subject to subject, only occasionally touching upon one that might be conceived as understanding Englishmen (and only in regards to music) in a poorly organized and distracting manner.

a substantive stylistic critique

Because the author mentions getting in touch with all of England, we would expect to see evidence of a broad and searching study. However, the author mentions only one place—"a small town." Any findings made here are surely not representative of a majority of English citizens. Furthermore, within this context, he describes only one concert house there, and his reaction to what is performed in this place is from a very personal bias.

good transitions

This biased tone is one of the major flaws of this passage. The author makes no attempt to record neutral observations, but speaks with a judgmental voice. This might be appropriate in an editorial piece, but not in one in which the purpose is to try to

effective transition between statements

understand the thoughts and feelings of an entire population. It is difficult to imagine someone earnestly trying to gauge the public opinion for any other than selfish purposes if he considers himself separated from them because he is part of an artistic "elite." For him to judge the music of others using such words as "low brow" and "common" makes him sound opinionated and arrogant, and reduces his argument's credence considerably.

logic support of this part's first sentence

good transition: it picks up & expands the idea of the previous paragraph

Another aspect of this judgmental tone which is completely out of place is his mention of "foreigners." To disparage the music performed in a concert house owned by "foreigners" is irrelevant and unnecessary, and could cause the reader to believe that the writer is prejudiced and therefore less credible. If his purpose is to evaluate English culture, why does he explore this tangent? He even raises the issue that most of the concert halls where music are performed are owned by people not of his own country, and then inconclusively trails off with "I don't even know what this means."

powerful ideological critique of the biases evident in the initial essay

One gets the sense, in reading this passage, that the author is genuinely searching for something. It is a saving grace that even the judgmental tone and the lack of organization lend this piece a sense of honesty and fervor, as if the author was so caught up in his search that he could not write coolly and clearly. In general, however, the tone tends to be pretentious and lacks focus, and these qualities do not fit well in an effective argument.

the conclusion's tempered tone lends weight to the overall critique

Analysis of Sample Essay Scoring 6

The above essay analyzing an argument is a 6-rated, or outstanding, essay. The argument itself is written by a composer who claims to have a specific purpose, but does not execute that purpose in the writing of the essay. The essayist correctly judges that the writing has no clear focal point, is poorly organized, and arrogantly written. He or she backs up these observations with specific examples and even quotes from the work. The essay is organized in such a way that each negative aspect of the argument is discussed in detail, and each paragraph leads smoothly into the next. The essayist does not dismiss the argument altogether, but shows how it might be written more effectively.

Section 3–Verbal Ability

1. **(E)**
For (A), a PROSELYTE (a new convert) does not fit the first blank. PROGENY (offspring) does not fit blank two well. (A) is not an appropriate choice. TAINTED (infected, spoiled) does not fit blank one. PRODIGIOUS means portentous or wonderful, but coupled with TAINTED, (B) is inappropriate. STAPES is the small stirrup-shaped bone in the inner ear; a PROGENITOR is a forefather. (C) is clearly inappropriate. A LITHOGRAPHER is a person who makes lithographs or prints; LITHOGRAPHER clearly does not fit blank one. PORTENTOUS means ominous, foreboding; it is not appropriate for blank two. (D) is not an appropriate choice. (E) is the best choice, since both terms correctly apply.

2. **(E)**
For (A), SUBJUGATED means conquered. (A) is clearly wrong. VANQUISHED means forced into submission. (B) is inappropriate. SUBDUED or conquered does not fit this sentence; (C) is not right. SURMOUNTED means overcome. (D) should not be selected. IMPERIOUS means domineering, lordly. (E) is correct.

3. **(B)**
An ANTIDOTE is something that counteracts a poison; (A) is not the correct answer. An ANODYNE is something that soothes or alleviates pain. The correct choice is (B). An ACCOLADE is a mark of acknowledgment. (C) is not a correct choice. An ANALOGY is the similarity between two different things. (D) is not correct. An ANOMALY is an irregularity. (E) is not the correct choice.

4. **(D)**
PROBITY, meaning honesty, and CLARITY, meaning clearness, are two qualities professors would urge students to try for, not warn them against. (A) and (B) are inappropriate answers. CALUMNY is the act of making malicious false statements to damage another's reputation. (C) is not an appropriate answer. PLAGIARISM is the act of stealing another's words or thoughts and presenting them as one's own. Many professors do find it necessary to warn their students against this practice. (D) is the correct answer. UMBRAGE means offense. While some students may take offense at being assigned a research paper, professors do not warn against it. (E) is not a correct choice.

5. **(A)**

    SCRUPULOUS means being painstaking and having moral integrity. (A) is the correct choice. MUNIFICENT means very liberal or generous. PRODIGIOUS means extraordinary in amount. (B) and (C) are inappropriate choices. IMPERVIOUS means not capable of being disturbed. (D) is not correct. INCORRIGIBLE means incapable of reform. (E) is not an appropriate answer.

6. **(D)**

    TENETS and PRECEPTS are principles. (A) and (E) are not appropriate answers. PREREQUISITES are things that must be done before something else can be done. (B) is incorrect. PREROGATIVES are exclusive rights or powers. (C) is not the correct answer. PERQUISITES are privileges or profits over and above one's salary. (D) is the correct answer.

7. **(C)**

    The key to this sentence is the word "plangent," which means plaintive or mournful. The correct choice is LACHRYMOSE, which means mournful. PARSIMONIOUS (A) means stingy; it is not correct. FROWARD (B) means contrary or perverse; it is not an appropriate choice. QUOTIDIAN (D) means commonplace or everyday; it is inappropriate. IGNOMINIOUS means dishonorable; (E) is not correct.

8. **(E)**

    A SUNDIAL cannot work without the SUN. ELECTRICITY can work without WATER; there are other means to generate it. (A) is not the right answer. The MOON affects the TIDES, not the other way around. (B) is not correct. WATER can exist without RAIN; the relationship is not the one sought. (C) is not the correct answer. SUN and STARS reflects a member:class relationship. (D) is incorrect. A LIGHT BULB cannot work without ELECTRICITY. The correct answer is (E).

9. **(D)**

    A SAGA is a kind of TALE. The relationship is member:class. A PAGE is part of a BOOK. The relationship is whole:part, so (A) is incorrect. POETRY and PROSE are two different forms of writing. (B) is not the correct answer. LYRICS and MUSIC are both parts of a song. They do not reflect the relationship sought. (C) is not the correct answer. A SONNET is a kind of VERSE. (D) reflects the relationship of member:class and is the correct answer. FICTION and NONFICTION are two different forms of prose writing. (E) is not the correct answer.

10. **(C)**

To PARE an APPLE is to take the skin off it. To STONE a CHERRY and to PIT a PEACH both mean to take the stone or pit out of the middle of the fruit. (A) and (B) are not correct answers. To PEEL a GRAPEFRUIT is to take the skin off it. (C) is the correct answer. SKIN:GRAPE reflects the reverse of the analogy sought. A POMEGRANATE is composed of SEEDS; (E) is not the correct answer.

11. **(B)**

An ALLUSION is a REFERENCE; the relationship is synonymous. BREVITY, meaning shortness, and LONGEVITY, meaning length, are antonyms. (A) is not the correct choice. CONGLOMERATION and ACCUMULATION are synonyms that mean a gathering together. (B) is the correct choice. ANTIPATHY, meaning enmity, and APATHY, meaning indifference, are not synonymous; (C) is not correct. EPITOME means embodiment, and ENNUI means boredom. The words are unrelated and (D) is not the correct answer. ARTIFICE means trick; SINCERITY means honesty. (E) is not synonymous and is not the correct answer.

12. **(E)**

STUPENDOUS means astonishingly impressive. AMAZE is to astonish greatly. MONSTROUS means ugly, fabulous, shocking in wrongness. BEWILDER is to perplex or confuse; it does not imply the surprise seen in AMAZE. Therefore, (A) is not the best answer. PRODIGIOUS means a marvelousness beyond belief. PERPLEX is to puzzle, to confuse. PRODIGIOUS behavior does not necessarily result in perplexity; (B) is not the best answer. TREMENDOUS means having the power to terrify or inspire awe. DISTRACTION implies diversion, perplexity. DISTRACTION does not have the intensity of AMAZE. (C) involves using knowledge of the degree of words; it is not the best answer. CONFOUND implies a temporary mental paralysis. ATROCIOUS implies such savagery as to excite condemnation. The order is not the same as in the example; (D) is incorrect. HEINOUS implies such flagrant conspicuousness that it excites hatred or horror. ASTOUND stresses shock and surprise. Thus, (E) is the best choice.

13. **(B)**

A COVEY is a group of QUAIL. A CUB is a young BEAR. The analogy in (A) is not the same as for COVEY:QUAIL. A group of LIONS is a PRIDE; (B) is correct. A STAG is a male DEER. The analogy is not that of COVEY:QUAIL. (C) should not be chosen. A EWE is a female

SHEEP. Again, the analogy is not that of COVEY:QUAIL. (D) is not the correct answer since the group:individual animal relationship is not there. A GAGGLE is a group of geese, not DUCKS. (E) is not correct.

14. **(B)**

A CASCADE is a small flow of water and a CATACLYSM is a deluge or flood. The relationship is one of degree. A DEFEAT is a loss at a game or battle; a DEBACLE is a humiliating rout. The relationship is one of degree. (B) is the correct answer. SOPORIFIC:HYPNOTIC, SCENARIO:SYNOPSIS, and HYPERBOLE:EXAGGERATION all have synonymous relationships. EPITAPH means a statement in praise, usually after one dies; an EPITHET is an insult. (E) is not the correct answer.

15. **(E)**

TAUTOLOGOUS, meaning redundant, and INCONGRUOUS, meaning contradictory, are antonyms. ASTUTE and PERSPICACIOUS are synonyms; (A) is not the correct answer. MELANGE, meaning a mixture of elements, and EFFLUVIUM, meaning an offensive odor, are unrelated. (B) is not the correct answer. ANAMNESIS and REMINISCENCE are synonyms; (C) is incorrect. PROPINQUITY and PROXIMITY are also synonyms; (D) is not the correct answer. IGNOMINIOUS, meaning dishonorable, and MAGNANIMOUS, meaning having nobility of spirit, are antonyms. The correct answer is (E).

16. **(E)**

ADVENTITIOUS means not innate; INHERENT means innate, or inborn. The terms are antonyms. VITIATE:ADULTERATE, FATUOUS:ASININE, and VICISSITUDE:MUTABILITY all exhibit synonymous relationships; (A), (B), and (D) are incorrect choices. ANATHEMA, which means something accursed, and ANASTROPHE, which means inverting the usual syntactical order for rhetorical effect, are unrelated terms. (D) is not the correct choice. FACILE, meaning easy, and ONEROUS, meaning difficult, are antonyms. (E) is the correct answer.

17. **(E)**

(A) This title is too broad; only cacti and succulents are studied here. (B) This title is not accurate. Regions of the world is not the primary topic of the passage. (C) The passage deals with more than just distinguishing between cacti and succulents. (D) This title is too limiting. (E) is the correct answer.

18. **(D)**

Not all cacti are without leaves so (A) is not the correct answer. Cacti are usually without leaves; cacti are indigenous to the Western Hemisphere. (B) is incorrect. Flowers on a cactus usually emerge from the top, not the base. (C) is incorrect. (D) is the correct answer. (E) is a true statement, but it is not a statement that BEST distinguishes cacti from other succulents.

19. **(E)**

The writer never implies that cacti are to be chosen over other succulents. The wording of the question ("Cacti are to be chosen over succulents...") implies that cacti are not themselves succulents. (A) is not the best answer. The author does not suggest that they are to be left in the wild; the writer actually states that they are excellent subjects for a garden, greenhouse, or windowsill. (B) is incorrect. The author implies that they are excellent subjects for botanists or the home gardener. (C) is incorrect. Both feature interesting adaptations, but the author does not state that one is preferred over the other. (D) is incorrect. (E) is the correct answer.

20. **(C)**

All of the statements are true except (C). Paragraph 8 clearly states that, with a possible minor exception, all cacti are native to the Western, not Eastern, Hemisphere.

21. **(B)**

(A) is not the best answer. After a statement about sunlight and hardiness, it does not logically follow that a section on the flowers would come next. A discussion of the fact that cacti and other succulents are generally able to withstand rapid changes in temperature does logically follow. (B) is a suitable answer. A discussion of artists and their using cacti and other succulents as studies does not seem to flow from the preceding line about hardiness and sunlight. (C) is not an appropriate answer. A reference to a movie does not seem to logically follow after the section on greenhouses, gardens, and hardiness. (D) should not be selected. References to the original location and structural modifications of the cacti do not seem to fit logically at this point. A better place would seem to come earlier in the passage for such an inclusion. (E) is not the best answer.

22. **(E)**

For (A), this statement is not implied by the passage; nothing suggests that cacti require less care. The author does not indicate that the shape of cacti is more appealing than that of other succulents. (B) is incorrect. The author does not indicate that succulents from one hemisphere do not adapt well to the other, or vice versa. (C) is not the best answer. The flowers of cacti do not appear between the leaves or at the base. (D) is incorrect. (E) is the correct answer.

23. **(A)**

Paragraph 6 states that only cacti have areoles. I is a true statement. Paragraph 7 states that cactus flowers are more conspicuous, but they most often appear from areoles near the top of the plant. II is a false statement. The second paragraph states that the adaptations made by both cacti and other succulents "may be similar"; III is a false statement. Since only (I) is true, the correct answer is (A).

24. **(E)**

Considering the author's fondness for cacti and other succulents, he would probably view laws to protect them with UNDERSTANDING (E), not disinterest or APATHY (A), CONFUSION (B), DESPAIR (C), or DISEASE (D).

25. **(D)**

The passage opens with a description of the Jefferson nickel and a brief history of the contest for its design and the changes that have been made to the design over time. The second paragraph discusses Jefferson's interest in architecture and the implementation of his own designs in the building of Monticello. The final paragraph remembers Jefferson as a statesman who defended the rights of man and inspired the American colonists to fight for freedom. (D) summarizes this presentation correctly, and is the right answer. The passage makes no mention of the Treasury system or any contributions Jefferson may have made to it; (A) is not the correct answer. (B), (C), and (E) omit topics discussed in the passage; therefore, they are all incorrect.

26. **(C)**

(C) is the only correct answer. The article states "After that date [1968], it [the mintmark] was moved to the right of Jefferson's wig." Since Jefferson's profile is on the obverse side, (C) is the answer to be chosen. (A) is incorrect since Monticello is on the reverse side. The mintmark is to the right of Jefferson's wig after 1968. Monticello is on the reverse side, but the mintmark is located to the right of Jefferson's wig after 1968. (B) is incorrect. Jefferson is on the obverse (not the reverse) side. (D) is incorrect. (E) is a false statement. Mintmarks appear on all U.S. coins including those minted after 1968. (E) should not be selected.

27. **(E)**
"Revolutionary" in this context means promoting fundamental changes; in other words, Jefferson used new methods and devices in the design of Monticello. CREATIVE implies something different or unusual, but it does not mean basic, fundamental changes. (A) is not the best choice. UNUSUAL does not mean that any fundamental change was made; neither does EXPENSIVE. Both imply critical judgment of the house. (B) and (C) are inappropriate choices. A revolution can be POLITICAL, but a house cannot. (D) is an incorrect choice. Only INNOVATIVE means to introduce a new method or device. (E) is the correct choice.

28. **(B)**
AVOCATION (not to be confused with VOCATION) means hobby. For (A), a RESPITE is a putting off, a postponement, a delay. It is not the opposite of AVOCATION and (A) should not be selected. A PROFESSION is an occupation, a trade. It is the opposite of AVOCATION and (B) is the correct answer. Since SILENT means quiet, (C) is not the best answer. A HOBBY is an interest to which one gives spare time. It is synonymous with AVOCATION and (D) should not be selected. An AVULSION is a forcible separation. (E) is not the correct answer.

29. **(C)**
ADULTERATED means corrupted or impure. RIBALD means irreverent or vulgar; (A) is not the correct answer. DEFILED means contaminated or corrupted. It is a synonym for ADULTERATED, so (B) is not the correct choice. CHASTE means pure. It is the opposite of ADULTERATED; therefore, (C) is the correct answer. INFANTILE means childish; (D) is incorrect. VICIOUS means spiteful or malicious. (E) is incorrect.

30. **(A)**
AUGMENTATION means expansion, enlargement, dilation. CONSTRICTION (A) is the antonym and the correct answer. ACCESSION means an increase, an addition. It is synonymous with AUGMENTATION and (B) should not be selected. EXPANSION means the act of increasing in size. It is synonymous with AUGMENTATION and (C) should not be chosen. PERTURBATION is the state of being disturbed. It is not the

opposite of AUGMENTATION. (D) is not the correct choice. SATIA-TION is the act of satisfying fully, glutting. (E) is not the best choice as the opposite of AUGMENTATION.

31. **(E)**

TACITURN means silent, uncommunicative. In (A), RETICENT means habitually silent. Since it is a synonym for TACITURN, (A) is incorrect. APPEASED means satisfied, made calm, quiet. (B) is wrong. RESERVED means restrained, in control, silent; (C) is synonymous and not the right answer. INVEIGLED means enticed. Since it is not the opposite of TACITURN, (D) should not be selected. EFFUSIVE means overly demonstrative, gushing, unrestrained. It is the antonym and (E) should be selected.

32. **(D)**

A helix is composed of round curves that form a spiral; something that is HELICAL, then, is COILED, SPIRAL, CURVED, and ROUND. (A), (B), (C), and (E) are all incorrect choices. The one choice that is the opposite of HELICAL is STRAIGHT; the correct answer is (D).

33. **(B)**

ASININE means stupid. FATUOUS means foolish. (A) is synonymous with ASININE and should not be chosen. CUNNING is the antonym and (B) is the correct answer. IDIOSYNCRATIC means the following of one's own peculiar temperament. (C) should not be chosen as the best answer. ECCENTRIC means diverges from the usual. (D) is not the best answer. ANTITHETIC means showing clear opposition to; it is not the opposite sought and (E) should not be selected.

34. **(E)**

SAGACIOUS means shrewd. SHREWD is synonymous with SAGACIOUS and (A) should not be selected as the correct answer. ASTUTE means sagacious, shrewd. Since it is a synonym and not an antonym, (B) should not be selected as the correct answer. PROCUMBENT means lying down. (C) is not the antonym sought for SAGACIOUS. DUCTILE is the quality of that which can be drawn out at will. Since it is not an antonym for SAGACIOUS, (D) should not be selected. INCAPABLE means not efficient, not capable, not able. It is the antonym for SAGACIOUS and (E) is the correct answer.

35. **(E)**

The NADIR is the lowest point on a celestial sphere. Its opposite, the highest point, is the ZENITH. (E) is the correct answer. A ZEPHYR (A) is a breeze. A KNAVE (B) is a rascal or rogue. EPITOME (C) means an ideal example. KITH (D) means friends and relatives.

36. **(B)**

BEATIFIC means manifesting bliss, joy. ANIMALISTIC means like an animal. (A) is incorrect. MELANCHOLY means sad. It is the opposite of BEATIFIC and (B) is the correct answer. URBANE means civilized. (C) is an incorrect choice. CIVILIZED means educated, refined. It is not the opposite of BEATIFIC and (D) should not be selected. SIMILITUDE means like a copy. (E) is incorrect.

37. **(E)**

TURGID implies distension, as with air. AGGRESSIVE means having the disposition to dominate. It is not the opposite of TURGID and (A) should not be selected as the correct answer. TUMID, like TURGID, implies having a fullness. It is a synonym for TURGID and (B) is not the antonym sought. BILIOUS means ill-tempered, suffering — as from too much bile. (C) is not the opposite of TURGID. PALPABLE means readily seen, heard, or felt; obvious. Since it is not the opposite of TURGID, (D) should not be selected. DEFLATED is the antonym, or opposite, of TURGID. DEFLATED means reduced the amount of, to let the air out, reduced. (E) is correct.

38. **(E)**

CANAILLE is a mob, a pack, the lowest class of people, the rabble. An AGGREGATE is a mass, a body, a sum total. (A) is not the opposite of CANAILLE. FULGURANT means resembling lightning. (B) is obviously not the opposite of CANAILLE. FULMINANT means attacking suddenly. (C) is not the correct choice. A BRIDGE is a structure built across a river, road, etc. so that people or objects of transportation can get across. (D) is not the right answer. ARISTOCRACY (the upper class) is the opposite of CANAILLE. (E) is correct.

Section 4–Quantitative Ability

1. **(B)**
    Notice that w, x, and y are all positive values and that $w = x$. Now replace w with x in the equation $w + x + y = 20$ and solve for y as follows:

$$w + x + y = 20$$
$$x + x + y = 20$$
$$2x + y = 20$$
$$y = 20 - 2x$$

    Since x and 10 are being compared, assume that x has a value of 10. Then the expression $y = 20 - 2x$ means that $y = 20 - 2x = 20 - 2(10) = 0$. So, $y = 0$ when $x = 10$ leads to a contradiction since y is given to be positive. Thus, x must be smaller in order for y to be positive. Hence, the quantity in Column B is larger.

2. **(C)**
    The average is the sum of the numbers ÷ number of numbers.

Column A: $\dfrac{(25 + 17 + 30 + 23 + 15)}{5} = \dfrac{110}{5} = 22$

Column B: $\dfrac{(13 + 35 + 11 + 25 + 9 + 39)}{6} = \dfrac{132}{6} = 22$

Therefore, the quantities are equal.

3. **(C)**
    Observe that the number 0 is an integer and it is also an even integer because it is divisible by 2. Also, observe that 0 is the largest even integer smaller than 2. Thus, the quantities in both columns are equal.

4. **(D)**
    Try some values of x and y.
    If $x = 0$, then $y = 3$; thus, making Column B greater than Column A.
    If $y = 0$, then $x = 6$; thus, making Column A greater than Column B.
    Therefore, more information is needed to determine the relationship.

5. **(B)**
    Convert Column A or B so they are both either fractions or decimals.

This makes it easier to compare the two expressions.

Column A: $\left(\dfrac{1}{3}\right)x = (.33\overline{3})x$

Column B: $.34x$

Since x is positive, Column B is greater than column A.

6.   **(C)**

Consider the $\triangle ABD$ and the exterior $\angle C$. Recall that one of the basic theorems of geometry indicates the following relation between an exterior angle and certain interior angles of a triangle. That is, the exterior angle of a triangle is equal to the sum of the two nonadjacent interior angles. Note that $\angle x$ and $\angle y$ are nonadjacent interior angles relative to $\angle C$. So, the following holds:

$$\angle x + \angle y = \angle C \text{ and thus, } \angle y = \angle C - \angle x.$$

Hence, the quantities in both columns are equal.

7.   **(B)**

First factor the left-hand side of each equation as follows:

$$y^2 + 12y + 27 = (y + 9)(y + 3) = 0$$
and $\qquad x^2 - 12x + 27 = (x - 9)(x - 3) = 0.$

Notice that the factors are similar except for the signs. However, to compare the values of y in Column A with those of x in Column B, one needs to solve each of the equations as follows:

$(y + 9)(y + 3) = 0$		$(x - 9)(x - 3) = 0$	
$y + 9 = 0$	$y + 3 = 0$	$x - 9 = 0$	$x - 3 = 0$
$y = -9$	$y = -3$	$x = 9$	$x = 3$

Hence, the quantity in Column B will always be greater than the quantity in Column A no matter which value of y or x is chosen.

8.   **(A)**

$\triangle AEF$ and $\triangle ACD$ are similar since sides CD and EF are parallel. Thus, corresponding sides are proportional. So, CD is to EF as AD is to AF or simply $^{CD}/_{EF} = {}^{AD}/_{AF}$. Since $AD = DF = 3$, then $AF = 6$. Thus,

$$\frac{CD}{EF} = \frac{AD}{AF} \text{ or } \frac{4}{EF} = \frac{3}{6} \text{ or } 3EF = 24 \text{ or } EF = 8.$$

So the quantity in Column A is greater than the quantity in Column B.

9.   **(C)**

Since m and n are parallel lines cut by the transversal t, then $\angle a$ and $\angle c$ are corresponding angles. Thus, one can conclude that $\angle a = \angle c$. Because of this equality, the expression in Column B may be simplified by replacing $\angle a$ with $\angle c$ as follows:

$$\angle b + \angle c - \angle a = \angle b + \angle c - (\angle c)$$
$$= \angle b + 0$$
$$= \angle b.$$

Hence, the quantity in Column B is equal to the quantity in Column A.

10.   **(A)**

First simplify the equation by multiplying through by 2 to obtain $x - y = 6$. Then, solve the resulting equation for x to obtain $x = 6 + y$. Hence, x has to be the largest value since it is always 6 units greater than y. So, the quantity in Column A is greater.

11.   **(C)**

To compare the two quantities, first simplify each expression.

$$\text{Simplify Column A} \; = \frac{4(5x+7)}{4x} + \frac{x(8x+10)}{4x}$$

$$= \frac{20x+28+8x^2+10x}{4x}$$

$$= \frac{8x^2+30x+28}{4x}$$

$$= \frac{4x^2+15x+14}{2x}$$

$$\text{Simplify Column B} \; = \frac{2x(2x)}{2x} + \frac{9x+14}{2x} + \frac{2x(3)}{2x}$$

$$= \frac{4x^2+9x+14+6x}{2x}$$

$$= \frac{4x^2+15x+14}{2x}$$

Then find the LCM for the two expressions and compare the numerators.

For Column B $\dfrac{2(4x^2+15x+14)}{2(2x)} = \dfrac{8x^2+30x+28}{4x}$

For Column A $\dfrac{8x^2+30x+28}{4x}$

Therefore, the two quantities are equal.

12. **(A)**

The measure of an inscribed angle is equal to $\frac{1}{2}$ the measure of its arc.

So the $m\angle B = \dfrac{1}{2}mAC$

$= \dfrac{1}{2}(145°)$

$= 72.5°$

Since $AB = AC$, then $m\angle B = m\angle C$.

$m\angle B = m\angle C = 72.5°$

To find $m\widehat{CB}$, use $m\angle A$.

$m\angle A + m\angle B + m\angle C = 180°$. (The interior angles of a triangle = 180°.)

$m\angle A + 72.5° + 72.5° = 180°$

$m\angle A + 145° = 180°$

$m\angle A = 35°$

$= \dfrac{1}{2}m\widehat{CB} = 35°$

$m\widehat{CB} = 35°(2)$

$m\widehat{CB} = 70°$

13. **(A)**

Find the roots of the quadratic equation.

For Column A $w^2 - 2wv + v^2 = (w - v)^2 = 0$
To solve for w
$w - v = 0$
$w = v$

For Column B $v^2 + 2xv + x^2 = (v + x)^2 = 0$

To solve for x

$v + x = 0$

$x = -v$

Since it is given that $v > 0$, Column A will be larger than Column B.

14. **(B)**

To find the area of the equilateral triangle you need the height. Use the Pythagorean theorem.

$$h^2 + \left(\frac{1}{2}b\right)^2 = b^2$$

$$h^2 = b^2 - \left(\frac{b^2}{4}\right)$$

$$= \frac{3b^2}{4}$$

$$h = \frac{\sqrt{3}b}{2}$$

The area is equal to $\frac{1}{2}$ base × height.

$$\text{Area of triangle A} = \left(\frac{1}{2}\right)(b)\left(\frac{\sqrt{3}b}{2}\right)$$

$$= \frac{\sqrt{3}b^2}{4}$$

In the isosceles right triangle the height and base equal b.

$$\text{Area of triangle B} = \left(\frac{1}{2}\right)(b)(b)$$

$$= \frac{b^2}{2}$$

$\frac{1}{2} > \frac{\sqrt{3}}{4}$. Therefore, column B is greater than column A.

15. **(D)**

It may be tempting to make an assumption about the speed of Dan's lawncutting after reading that Peter's speed is slower, but this would be incorrect. It is only safe to assume that Dan's time (z) is faster than Peter's

(y). More information would be needed to answer the question, therefore the correct choice would be (D).

16. **(B)**

$$\frac{(x-y)(x-y)-(x+y)(x+y)}{(x-y)(x+y)}$$

$$\frac{x^2-2xy+y^2-(x^2+2xy+y^2)}{x^2-y^2} = \frac{-4xy}{x^2-y^2}$$

17. **(B)**

The median is the middle value of a set of an odd number of values or the average of the two middle values of a set of an even number of values. Rearrange the set from smallest to largest values:

16, 17, 18, 19, 21, 21, 21, and 22.

$$\frac{(19+21)}{2} = 20.$$

18. **(D)**

In the equation or formula one must first apply the distributive property on the right-hand side as follows:

$$A = P(1 + rt)$$
$$A = P + Prt$$

The next step is to add the opposite of P to both sides of the equation as indicated below.

$$A = P + Prt$$
$$A + (-P) = P + Prt + (-P)$$
$$A - P = Prt$$

Finally, divide both sides of the equation by Pr to obtain the value of t as follows:

$$\frac{(A-P)}{Pr} = \frac{Prt}{Pr}$$
$$\frac{(A-P)}{Pr} = t$$

Hence, the answer choice (D) is correct.

19. **(B)**

$$4\frac{1}{3}-1\frac{5}{6}=4\frac{2}{6}-1\frac{5}{6}$$
$$=\frac{26}{6}-\frac{11}{6}$$
$$=2\frac{3}{6}$$
$$=2\frac{1}{2}$$

20. **(C)**
   The difference between the first two numbers is 4 $(6 - 2)$; the difference between the second and third numbers is 6 $(12 - 6)$ which is two more than the first difference; the difference between the third and fourth numbers is 8 $(20 - 12)$ which is two more than the second difference; the difference between the fourth and fifth numbers is 10 $(x - 20)$. Thus, the value of x is given by $x - 20 = 10$. Solving for x yields $x = 30$. So, the correct answer choice is (C).

21. **(D)**
   Examine the graph and observe that the highest plotted point on the graph directly above 1975 is about 2,200.

22. **(B)**
   Observe that the amount of remedial enrollments in 1970 is 200 thousand. Since the total undergraduate enrollments for 1970 was about 1,900 thousand, one need only form a ratio as follows to find the percent:

$$\frac{200}{1,900}=\frac{2}{19} \text{ or } 10.5\%$$

23. **(C)**
   The calculus-level enrollment of undergraduates equals the area between O and C.

For 1975 $2,000 - 1,400 = 600$
For 1985 $2,400 - 1,600 = 800$

Therefore, the ratio of 1985 : 1975 = 800 : 600 = 8 : 6 = 4 : 3.

24. **(D)**

To find the percent of increase one need only to use the following formula:

$$\text{Percent of increase} = \frac{(\text{amount of increase})}{(\text{original amount})} \times 100$$

Thus,

$$\text{Percent of increase} = \frac{(800 - 200)}{(200)} \times 100$$

$$= \frac{600}{200} \times 100$$

$$= 300\%$$

25. **(D)**

The only category of enrollments in the graph which shows the least amount of variance from year to year is the advanced course enrollments. Notice that the line that represents this category is about the same distance from the calculus-level enrollments for each year in the graph.

26. **(C)**

Observe that to find the product the following multiplications should be done:

$$(\sqrt{3} + 6)(\sqrt{3} - 2) = \sqrt{3}(\sqrt{3} - 2) + 6(\sqrt{3} - 2)$$

$$= 3 - 2\sqrt{3} + 6\sqrt{3} - 12$$

$$= -9 + 4\sqrt{3}$$

27. **(B)**

First, group the expression and then find the monomial factor for each group as follows:

$$(x^2 + ax) + (-2x - 2a) = x(x + a) + (-2)(x + a).$$

Then, the final factorization is formed by using $(x + a)$ and $(x - 2)$. So,

$$x^2 + ax - 2x - 2a = (x - 2)(x + a).$$

Notice that multiplying these two factors together will yield the original algebraic expression. So, (B) is the correct answer choice. The other answer choices are incorrect because when the factors are multiplied together in each case, the results do not yield the original algebraic expression.

28. **(D)**

   The easiest way to determine the result for this problem is to represent the unknown ages, set up an equation, and solve it. Begin by letting x = age of Susan now. Then, $2x$ = the age of Jim now. The next step is to represent Jim's age 4 years ago and Susan's age 3 years from now. Thus, $2x - 4$ = Jim's age 4 years ago. Then, $x + 3$ = Susan's age 3 years from now. Finally an equation can be set up by noting that the age represented by $2x - 4$ differs from the age represented by $x + 2$ by 12 years. So, the equation is given by the following:

$$(2x - 4) - (x + 3) = 12.$$

Solving for x one gets

$$\begin{aligned} 2x - 4 - x - 3 &= 12 \\ x - 7 &= 12 \\ x - 7 + 7 &= 12 + 7 \\ x &= 19, \text{ Susan's age now.} \\ 2x &= 38, \text{ Jim's age now.} \end{aligned}$$

The sum of their ages $(19 + 38)$ is 57.

29. **(B)**

   Let x = Joe's marbles, y = Jim's marbles, and z = Tim's marbles. It is given that

$$\begin{aligned} x + y &= 14 & (1) \\ y + z &= 10 & (2) \\ x + z &= 12 & (3) \end{aligned}$$

Solve equation (2) for y and equation (3) for x. Then substitute their values in equation (1) and solve for z.

$$y + z = 10 \implies y + z - z = 10 - z \implies y = 10 - z$$

and

$$x + z = 12 \implies x + z - z = 12 - z \implies x = 12 - z$$

Thus,

$$\begin{aligned} x + y = 14 \implies (12 - z) + (10 - z) &= 14 \\ -2z + 22 &= 14 \\ -2z + 22 - 22 &= 14 - 22 \\ -2z &= -8 \\ z &= 4, \text{ Tim's marbles.} \end{aligned}$$

Now substitute the value of z in equations (2) and (3), respectively, and solve. The results are

$$y + z = 10 \implies y + 4 - 4 = 10 - 4$$
$$y = 6 \text{ (Jim's marbles)}$$

and

$$y + z = 12 \implies x + 4 - 4 = 12 - 4$$
$$x = 8 \text{ (Joe's marbles)}$$

Joe's marbles, 8, is the maximum number of marbles anyone can have.

30. **(A)**

$|5x - 1| \le 9$ is the same as

$9 \le 5x \quad 1 \le 9$

$1 - 9 \le 5x \le 9 + 1$ Add 1 to each part.

$-8 \le 5x \le 10$

$-\dfrac{8}{5} \le x \le 2$ Divide each part by 5.

Section 5–Verbal Ability

1. **(C)**
    VELLUM (a type of paper) fits the sentence, but EDICT (proclamation) is not appropriate so (A) should not be selected. STATIONARY is an adjective which means not movable; it should not be confused with the writing paper called STATIONERY. AFFECT is a verb; it clearly does not fit the second blank which requires a noun. (B) is incorrect. STATIONERY is a type of writing paper; EFFECT is a noun meaning result. (C) is the correct answer. PARCHMENT (a type of paper) fits the sentence, but OBLIGATION appears out of context. (D) is incorrect. BOND is a type of paper and fits the first blank, but EFFIGY (statue) does not appear suitable for the second. (E) is wrong.

2. **(C)**
    PROFICIENT implies competency above the average. It is most often used in describing people so (A) is incorrect. EFFUSIVE means too emotional; (B) does not fit the sense of the sentence. EFFECTUAL means having the power to produce the exact effect or result. (C) is correct. Both CAPABLE and COMPETENT refer to people, not things. Neither (D) nor (E) are correct.

3. **(A)**
    SANGUINE (hopeful) and CORROBORATE (verify) fit the blanks very well. (A) is the correct answer. MEDDLESOME (interfering in others' affairs) does not fit well in blank one — especially to describe an accused person. When coupled with SUBSTANTIATE (confirm), (B) is clearly not the best answer. CONJUGAL (pertaining to marriage) clearly does not belong in blank one. REVOKE (to repeal) should not be chosen as a correct answer. (C) should not be selected. GARBLED (scrambled, even deliberately mixed up to achieve a result) might best describe a story, an account, a letter — not a person. Since it would be difficult to AUTHENTICATE (verify as true) a garbled "person," (D) is not the best answer. CONCUPISCENT (lustful) and ABOLISH (to do away with) do not fit logically in the sentence. (E) should not be selected.

4. **(D)**
    MARAUDING (going about in search of plunder and booty) and EMERGENCY (a sudden and unforseen crisis, often having the pressure of restrictions) do not fit a sentence about a wild hawk very well. (A) is

not the best choice. PARASITIC (living on others) does not fit the sentence about the hawk very well. Neither does MALADY (a disease, a mental or moral disorder) fit in the second blank. (B) should not be selected. SAPROPHYTIC (living on decaying organic matter) does not apply to a hawk. INSURRECTION (a rising up, a rebellion) does not fit blank two. (C) should not be chosen. PREDATORY (preying upon other animals) and PREDICAMENT (an unpleasant situation) fit the sentence well; (D) is correct. (E) METICULOUS (extremely careful about small details) and TÊTE-À-TÊTE (a private conversation between two people) do not fit the sentence well. (E) is wrong.

5. **(C)**
REPARTITIONED (A) and APPORTIONED (B) are incorrect because they are synonyms meaning "to divide." SUBSCRIBED (D) and SUBSIDIZED (E) are synonyms meaning "to donate," and are therefore incorrect. Only INDEMNIFIED (C) implies reimbursement for loss or damage.

6. **(C)**
PARANOIA is characterized by delusions of persecution or grandeur. (A) is not the correct choice. XENOPHOBIA is the fear and hatred of strangers and foreigners. (B) is not the correct choice. MISONEISM is the fear and hatred of change and innovation. Anti-machine groups, anti-computer groups, and flat-Earthers fear and hate technological and scientific innovations and the changes those innovations entail. (C) is the correct choice. MISOGYNISM is the fear and distrust of women. (D) is not the correct choice. ECCENTRICITY is odd or whimsical behavior. (E) is incorrect.

7. **(D)**
MULTIFARIOUSNESS means diversity; (A) is an inappropriate choice. NEGLIGENCE means failure to exercise due care. The second part of the sentence, "although embezzlement charges were never filed," implies that there was a suspicion of illegal conduct, not just carelessness. (B) is not the correct choice. MALEDICTION means a curse; (C) is not the correct answer. MALFEASANCE means official misconduct. (D) is the correct answer. It is the only choice with the necessary connotation of wrongdoing. RECIDIVISM is the tendency to relapse into criminal behavior. (E) is not the correct answer.

8. **(B)**
A SOLID becomes a LIQUID if exposed to a high enough temperature. OXYGEN is one of the components of AIR. It will not become air,

no matter how much it is heated. (A) is not the correct choice. WATER will become STEAM when heated enough; (B) is the correct answer. DIRT cannot become WATER, GRASS cannot become WOOD, and FIRE cannot become AIR, no matter how they are manipulated. (C), (D), and (E) are incorrect choices.

9. **(C)**

LEAVE:RETURN are opposites, as are all of the answer choices. However, to LEAVE implies that one will RETURN. If something is DRY, there is no implied concept that it will later become WET. If something is BLACK, there is no implication that it will become WHITE. (A) and (B) are incorrect. If something is OPEN, there is an implication that, sooner or later, it may CLOSE. (C) is the correct answer. If something is DOWN, there is no implication that later it will be UP (the South is thought of as "down"—there is no implication that at any time it will be "up"). Something that is LEFT does not usually become RIGHT. (D) and (E) are incorrect.

10. **(C)**

FEALTY is the loyalty one pledges to a LORD through a vow or oath. One feels PATRIOTISM to one's COUNTRY, but one does not take a vow of patriotism. (A) is not the correct answer. One pays TAX to the GOVERNMENT, but the obligation is a legal, not a voluntary, one. (B) is not correct. FIDELITY is the faithfulness one pledges to one's SPOUSE through a marriage vow. (C) is the correct answer. One might owe MONEY to a CREDITOR, but one can incur the debt without taking an oath or vow. (D) is incorrect. One may have a strong BELIEF in RELIGION, but one does not have to take a vow pledging to believe. (E) is incorrect.

11. **(E)**

CHINTZ is made from cotton, not SILK, so (A) is incorrect. MADRAS is made from cotton, not LINEN. (B) is wrong. RAYON is not made from PLASTIC but from cellulose. (C) is incorrect. NYLON is made from COAL, but the order does not duplicate LINEN:FLAX. (D) is incorrect. CHAMOIS is a soft cloth made from LEATHER. (E) is correct.

12. **(C)**

PUGILISM means fighting with the FISTS. FISTS are necessary to PUGILISM. In (A), a LEXICOGRAPHER is one who works with words, one who writes a dictionary. There is no direct relationship between a LEXICOGRAPHER and ANIMALS. (A) is an inappropriate choice. GY-

NECOLOGY is a branch of medical science that deals with the functions and diseases peculiar to women; it is not directly related to GENES. (B) is inappropriate. NEPOTISM is a term relating to RELATIVES; for instance, hiring family to fill positions in a business is called NEPOTISM. (C) is the correct choice. ARCHEOLOGY is a study of the people, customs, and life of ancient times; archeologists may excavate, classify, and study the remains of ancient cities, tools, monuments, or other records that remain. It is paleontology (not archeology) that is a study of FOSSILS. (D) is an incorrect choice. PEDIATRICS is a branch of medicine dealing with children's diseases and the care of babies and children. It is geriatrics which is the science which deals with the study of the AGED and their diseases. (E) is incorrect.

13. **(C)**
    A KEY can be used to unlock a DOOR. This relationship is also evidenced in alternative (C) ENIGMA:CLUE. A CLUE may unlock a riddle. The relationship in (A) GEM:RING is that of use. A GEM may be used in a RING. The relationship in (B) PERFUME:AROMA is that of entity and characteristic. AROMA is characteristic of PERFUME. Alternative (D) EFFORT:ACHIEVEMENT presents the relationship of prerequisite:event. EFFORT is a prerequisite to ACHIEVEMENT. In the final alternative (E), a MOLD may be used to shape GELATIN.

14. **(B)**
    An EDIFICE is a building; a FACADE is the front part of a building or any part that faces a street or other open area. A FACADE, then, is the outer part of an EDIFICE. For (A), DORSAL is on, of, or near the back; VENTRAL is of or having to do with the belly — the opposite of DORSAL. Since this opposite relationship is not the same as that between EDIFICE:FACADE, (A) should not be chosen. Since the SHELL is the outer covering of a TURTLE (just as a FACADE is the outer part of an EDIFICE), (B) is the correct answer. ANACHRONISM is the act of putting some thing, person, or event where it does not belong. CHRONOLOGIC, like chronological, means arranged in the order in which the events happened. The two are opposite in meaning; they do not fit the pattern of EDIFICE:FACADE. (C) is incorrect. A SKELETON is the inner (not the outer) part of the BODY. (D) should not be selected since the two words do not have the same relationship as do EDIFICE: FACADE. COUNTERFEIT and FRAUDULENT are two words which are synonymous. (E) is incorrect.

15. **(B)**

A DEFICIT is the result of PECULATION (the act of embezzling). For (A), ATTIRE is synonymous for DRESS, so (A) is not the correct answer. HUNGER is the result of ABSTINENCE. (B) is the correct answer. APPEAR and MANIFEST are synonymous verbs. The analogy is not that sought. (C) is incorrect. FAMINE is the result of DROUGHT; the order is inverted, however. (D) is incorrect. A MAGISTRATE is very similar to a JUDGE; this is not the analogy sought, however. (E) is incorrect.

16. **(A)**

UNCTUOUS, meaning fawning or ingratiating, and BRUSQUE, meaning rude or abrupt, are antonyms. GAUCHE, which means lacking social grace or awkward, and SUAVE, which means well-mannered or smooth, are also antonyms. (A) is the correct answer. ABSTRUSE and RECONDITE are synonyms for difficult to comprehend. (B) is not the correct choice. BUMPTIOUS, meaning impertinent, and DELETERIOUS, meaning harmful, are unrelated. (C) is not the correct answer. LUS-TROUS and LUMINOUS are synonyms for bright; (D) is not the correct choice. VITRIOLIC and CAUSTIC are synonyms meaning harshly sarcastic, bitter. (E) is incorrect.

17. **(B)**

The passage does discuss the contributions of Carl von Linné to taxonomy (A), but the passage also discusses the categorization of plants and animals (C), and a brief history of taxonomy (E). While the passage mentions that taxonomy takes the evolutionary relationships of various taxa and that taxonomy can be a valuable tool for tracing the evolutionary paths of all organisms, the passage does not discuss the evolution of animals. Therefore, (D) is not an appropriate title. Only (B) is general enough to be an appropriate choice. The passage does give a brief history of taxonomy and discusses the modern categorization of organisms by biologists.

18. **(E)**

Paragraph 8 states that the scientific name of an organism is made up of the genus and specie name (I); this is the binomial system of nomenclature. Paragraph 3 gives the ranking of the hierarchy used for taxonomy. It is evident from this listing that the phylum is the second-highest (most general) tier, and that the genus is the second-lowest (most specific) tier. The family taxa lies in between genus and phylum; III is a true statement. While Linné's system of classification used only two kingdoms, paragraph 4 states that in 1969, Robert Whittaker devised a system based on five kingdoms, to allow for the classification of the organisms that are neither plants nor animals. II is not a true statement. Therefore, (E), I and III only, is the correct answer.

19. **(D)**

The author never describes the current method of taxonomy as complex and never mentions simplification. (A) is not the correct answer. The author does not claim that DNA research has discovered any new organisms, or that new methods of classification will soon be necessary. (B) is not correct. The author states that Whittaker's five kingdom scheme has made it less difficult for biologists to categorize organisms, such as fungi, that do not fit into the two kingdoms used by Linné. (C) is not the correct answer. In the last paragraph of the passage, the author states that utilizing taxonomic methods with DNA research can provide a valuable tool to scientists studying the evolution of all organisms. The author would be most likely to agree with (D). The author points out that there have been several taxonomic schemes throughout history, and that Linné proposed the specific, distinctive method used today. (E) is not the correct choice.

20. **(E)**

The first paragraph does not present a brief history of taxonomy, so answers (A) and (C) cannot be correct. The first paragraph does present a definition of taxonomy, but the remainder of the passage is not a synopsis of the history of taxonomy (B) or a description of the inadequacies of the current taxonomic method (D). The remainder of the passage does include a brief history of taxonomic methods, and does provide an example of the taxonomic classification of the California grizzly bear. (E) is the correct answer.

21. **(C)**

Paragraph 8 clearly defines the binomial system of nomenclature as the practice of using the genus and specie names of an organism to form the scientific name for that organism. Choices (A), (B), (D), and (E) are therefore incorrect. The correct answer is (C).

22. **(C)**

Choices (A), (B), (D), and (E) are all true. Paragraph 3 clearly states that Linné's hierarchy begins with a large, inclusive (general) taxa, and that each subsequent level becomes more specific, until the bottom level describes a single type of organism. Statement (C) is false.

23. **(E)**

Taxonomy is defined in paragraph 1 as the scientific naming and classification of all organisms. The paragraph makes it clear that all organisms, living or extinct, are taxonomically classified into specific taxa. The correct answer is (E). (A) and (D) are not correct because they specify only living organisms. (B) and (C) are incorrect because they omit the scientific naming of organisms.

24. **(D)**
Morphology is the structure and form of an object. Thus, the morphological characteristics of an organism are those pertaining to the structure and form of the organism. (D) is the correct answer. Structure and form include appearance (A), shape (C), and size and color (E), but also include internal characteristics. The reproductive habits of the organism (B) are not morphological characteristics.

25. **(E)**
(A), personal dissatisfaction toward wind energy conversion systems, is not the predominant mood in the passage. The writer gives both the good and the bad points in using such a system. (A) should not be selected. Unqualified enthusiasm is not the writer's feeling toward the wind conversion system; the writer keeps an open mind and informs the reader of the strengths and weaknesses of the wind energy conversion system. (B) is not an acceptable answer. The very fact that the writer takes the time to write the passage negates the possibility that disinterest is the prevailing mood in the article. (C) should not be selected. (D) Negativism is not the tone of the article. Rather, the writer presents an objective view (both good and bad points) of the wind energy conversion system. (E) Open-mindedness is the correct answer since the writer appears completely objective in the treatment and expressed feelings toward the wind energy conversion system.

26. **(B)**
Wind energy conversion systems do not use atomic matter to generate electricity, so (A) is not correct. Paragraph 2, line 4, states that these systems are practically noiseless, so there is no need for a part to reduce the noise. (C) is not the correct answer. The passage makes no mention of a special part of the high tower on which the rotors are located. (D) is not the answer. The blades of the rotors are called blades, not *nacelles*. (E) is incorrect. Paragraph 2 defines a wind turbine system as a system that generates power with rotors on towers. From the last line of the passage, it can be inferred that the nacelles are a part of the system other than the towers or the rotors. The *nacelles* must contain the generators; that is the only part of the system other than the towers or rotors. (B) is the correct answer.

27. **(A)**

Paragraph 2 mentions that precautions will be necessary to prevent wind energy conversion systems from interfering with television and radio reception, and that safety measures must be taken to prevent damage from rotors which break or shed ice. Paragraph 3 discusses the aesthetics of these systems. (A) is the correct answer. (B) is not the correct answer; these energy systems are practically noiseless. (C) is incorrect because the large rotors in and of themselves do not present a safety threat. (D) and (E) are not correct because there are no thermal effluents generated by these systems.

28. **(D)**

PAUCITY means a lack. DEARTH (A) is a scarcity. It is not an antonym for PAUCITY; it is more like a synonym. (A) should not be selected as the correct answer. (B) LOQUACIOUS means talkative. It is an incorrect choice. (C) SANATIVE (an adjective) means curative, healing. It is not a correct answer choice. PLETHORA (D) is a vast amount, a great excess. It is the opposite of PAUCITY and the correct choice. (E) LUGUBRIOUS means mournful. It is not an appropriate choice.

29. **(D)**

CONSONANCE means agreement. In (A), CONSCIENCE is the sense of the moral goodness of one's own conduct. It is not related to CONSONANCE. (B) CONSCIOUS means aware, sensible. It is unrelated to CONSONANCE. (C) COALESCE is synonymous with blend (which suggests a mixing). (D) CONTENTION suggests argument. CONSONANCE suggests harmony, agreement, accordance. CONTENTION is the opposite of CONSONANCE. (D) is the opposite and the correct answer. (E) CONSIGN is to commit, to entrust. It is not related to CONSONANCE and should not be selected.

30. **(B)**

ALIGN, which means to straighten, to line up, is the antonym of TILT, which means to place at an angle. INCLINE (A), LIST (C), PITCH (D), and SLANT (E) are all synonymous with TILT, and are incorrect choices.

31. **(E)**

VENIAL means forgivable. (A) HEDONIC means pertaining to pleasure. It is not antonymous with VENIAL. (B) INEFFABLE means indescribable, difficult to put in words. It should not be selected as the opposite of VENIAL. (B) is incorrect. PECCADILLO (C) means small offense. (C) should not be selected. (D) IMPLACABLE means not of a nature to be placated or appeased easily. (D) is incorrect. HEINOUS means abominable, outrageous. Since it suggests unforgivable behavior, (E) is the correct answer.

32. **(D)**

PRODIGAL is an adjective meaning given to extravagant expenditures. WANDERING (A) (roving, roaming) does not relate to PRODIGAL; (A) should not be selected. TARRYING (staying) does not relate to PRODIGAL; (B) is incorrect. SPENDTHRIFT (squanderer) is synonymous with PRODIGAL so (C) is incorrect. FRUGAL (in the habit of saving) is the opposite of PRODIGAL and so (D) is the correct answer. LAVISH (in the habit of spending with profusion or squandering) is synonymous with PRODIGAL. (E) should not be chosen.

33. **(E)**

The opposite of VIABLE, which means capable of life, is MORIBUND, which means dying, or in the process of dying. The correct answer is (E). REMNANT (A) means a small trace or remaining piece. VIANDS (B) means food or provisions. SUBSISTENCE (C) is existence or the means of existence. VESTIGE (D) means a trace or visible sign of something that is lost.

34. **(C)**

RECUMBENT means lying down. PRONE (A), SUPINE (D), and LEVEL (E) are all synonymous with RECUMBENT. OBLIGATORY means mandatory or required, so (B) is not the correct answer. Only VERTICAL (C), or upright, is the opposite of RECUMBENT. The correct answer is (C).

35. **(D)**

VOLATILE has several meanings, including EXPLOSIVE (A), IMPULSIVE (B), MERCURIAL (C), and TRANSITORY (E). The only choice given that means the opposite of VOLATILE is DELIBERATE, meaning to give thorough consideration to or steady; the correct answer is (D).

36. **(E)**

FACTIOUS means inclined to dispute. BELLICOSE means aggressive. It is not the opposite of FACTIOUS; (A) should not be selected. DESULTORY (B) means without plan. It is not directly related to FACTIOUS and should not be selected as the opposite. FORTUITOUS (C) means accidental. It is not the opposite of FACTIOUS and should not be selected. FRACTIOUS (D) means troublesome. It is similar in meaning to (not opposite from) FACTIOUS. CONSONANT means harmonious. It is the opposite of FACTIOUS. (E) is the correct answer.

37. **(B)**
PROBITY is tried and proven honesty. (A) AESTHETICS is a sense of beauty. It is not the opposite of PROBITY and should not be selected. (B) PERFIDY is faithlessness. It is the opposite of PROBITY and should be selected as the right answer. (C) ABEYANCE is the act of suspending. It is not the opposite of PROBITY and, hence, should not be chosen. Since PREDILECTION is the act of having positive feelings toward something, it should not be selected as the opposite of PROBITY. (D) is incorrect. (E) COMPLEMENTARY is serving to fill out or complete; it can also mean mutually supplying each other's lack. (E) is not the opposite of PROBITY and should not be selected as the correct answer.

38. **(A)**
FACTITIOUS means artificial. AUTHENTIC means genuine, real. It is the opposite of FACTITIOUS and, hence, (A) is the correct answer. TRAVESTY is a caricature. (B) should not be selected as the correct answer. (C) PEDANTIC means in a manner that makes a display of learning. Since it is not the opposite of FACTITIOUS, it should not be selected as the correct answer. (D) MORDANT means biting or stinging. It is not directly related to FACTITIOUS and should not be selected as the correct answer. (E) RAPACIOUS means grasping. Since it is not the opposite of FACTITIOUS, it should not be selected as the correct answer.

Section 6–Quantitative Ability

1. **(B)**

Consider the quantity given in Column B, $(x + y)^2$. Performing the indicated operation yields,

$$(x + y)^2 = (x + y)(x + y)$$
$$= x^2 + 2xy + y^2$$
$$= x^2 + y^2 + 2xy$$

Since both x and y are positive integers it follows that both xy and $2xy$ are positive quantities (positive times positive equals positive). Hence, whatever the value of $x^2 + y^2$ is, the quantity in Column B, $(x + y)^2 = x^2 + y^2 + 2xy$, is greater than the quantity in Column A, $x^2 + y^2$.

2. **(C)**

Column A $\qquad (x - 1)^2 = (-2 - 1)^2 = (-3)^2 = 9$

Column B $\qquad (y - 1)^2 = (4 - 1)^2 = (3)^2 = 9$

Therefore, the amounts are the same.

3. **(C)**

The lowest common denominator looks at the factors of each group.

Column A $\qquad 3 = 3 \times 1$
$$12 = 3 \times 2 \times 2 = 3 \times 2^2$$
$$8 = 2 \times 2 \times 2 = 2^3$$
$$\text{LCD} = 3 \times 2^3 = 24$$

Column B $\qquad 6 = 2 \times 3$
$$8 = 2 \times 2 \times 2 = 2^3$$
$$2 = 2 \times 1$$
$$\text{LCD} = 2^3 \times 3 = 24$$

Therefore, the quantities are equal.

4. **(A)**

Column A $\qquad 30\%$ of $9 = .30 \times 9 = 2.7$

Therefore, Column A is greater than Column B.

5. **(B)**

Column A $\quad 2x - 1 = -17$

$$2x = -17 + 1$$
$$2x = -16$$
$$x = -8$$

Therefore, Column B is greater than Column A.

6. **(C)**

Label the vertices of the given triangle *A*, *B*, *C*, and let $y°$ represent the measure of $\angle ABC$ (the third interior angle of the given triangle) as shown in the figure.

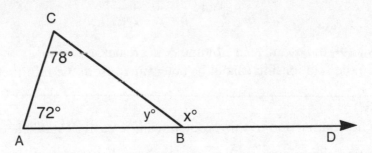

Note that $\angle DBC$ is an exterior angle of $\triangle ABC$. Since the measure of an exterior angle of a triangle is equal to the sum of the measures of the two non-adjacent angles of the triangle, it follows that

$$x = 78 + 72$$
$$= 150.$$

So the quantities in Columns A and B are equal.

Another way to attack this comparison problem is to recall that:

(i)   The sum of the measures of the three interior angles of a triangle is equal to 180°.

(ii) The sum of the measures of two supplementary angles is equal to 180°.

In our problem, $\angle ABC$ and $\angle DBC$ are supplementary angles. Hence, $x + y = 180$.

Now,

$$78 + 72 + y = 180 \text{ [Note (i) above]}$$
$$150 + y = 180$$
$$x + y = 180 \text{ [Note (ii) above]}$$

Hence, $\quad 150 + y = x + y$ which implies $x = 150$.

7. **(D)**

With the exception of the restrictions on a and b given in the center, $a \neq -1$, $b \neq 0$, and $a \neq b$, no information is given about the value of a or b. Hence, the relationship between the two quantities in Columns A and B indeterminate. For example, if $a = 2$, and $b = 3$, then

$$\frac{a}{b} = \frac{2}{3} \text{ and } \frac{a+1}{b+1} = \frac{2+1}{3+1} = \frac{3}{4}.$$

In this case, the quantity in Column B is greater. But if $a = 3$, and $b = 2$, then

$$\frac{a}{b} = \frac{3}{2} \text{ and } \frac{a+1}{b+1} = \frac{3+1}{2+1} = \frac{4}{3}.$$

In this case, the quantity in Column A is greater.
So the relationship cannot be determined from the information given.

8. **(B)**

The comparison in this problem can be easily established by simply evaluating the quantity $\frac{|x| + 2|y|}{5+(-4)}$, given in Column B, when $x = -4$, and $y = 2$. This gives

$$\frac{|x|+2|y|}{5+x} = \frac{|-4| + 2|2|}{5+(-4)} = \frac{4+4}{5-4} = \frac{8}{1} = 8.$$

Recall: the absolute value of a real number, x, is given by

$$|x| = \begin{cases} x & \text{if } x \geq 0 \\ -x & \text{if } x < 0. \end{cases}$$

Thus, $|-4| = -(-4) = 4$, and $|2| = 2$. So the quantity in Column B is greater.

9. **(D)**

In the quantity, $\frac{x^2 - y^2}{x^3 - x^2 y}$, the numerator can be factored as $x^2 - y^2 = (x - y)(x + y)$, and the denominator can be factored as $x^3 - x^2 y = x^2(x - y)$.

Hence,

$$\frac{x^2 - y^2}{x^3 - x^2 y} = \frac{(x-y)(x+y)}{x^2(x-y)}$$

$$= \frac{x+y}{x^2} \quad (\text{since } x - y \neq 0).$$

Since no other information is given about the value of x or y, the relationship is indeterminate. For example, if $x = 2$ and $y = -3$, then

$$\frac{x+y}{x^2} = \frac{2+(-3)}{(2)^2} = \frac{-1}{4} = -\frac{1}{4}, \text{ and}$$

$$\frac{x+y}{y} = \frac{2+(-3)}{-3} = \frac{-1}{-3} = \frac{1}{3}.$$

So the quantity in Column B is greater.
  However, if $x = 1$, and $y = -1$, then

$$\frac{x+y}{x^2} = \frac{1+(-1)}{1} = 0, \text{ and } \frac{x+y}{y} = \frac{1+(-1)}{-1} = 0.$$

So the two quantities in Columns A and B are equal.

10. **(C)**
  Recall that the circumference, C, of a circle is equal to π times the diameter. Thus, for the inner circle one obtains

$$C = \pi d = \pi(3.5) = 3.5\pi.$$

For the outer circle one obtains

$$C = \pi d = \pi(7) = 7\pi.$$

One-half of the circumference of the outer circle is $\left(\frac{1}{2}\right)(7\pi) = 3.5\pi$. Thus, the quantities in Columns A and B are equal.

11. **(A)**
  After the 30-inch long candle burns for 12 minutes, it becomes 25 inches long. This means that 5 inches of the candle have burned out in 12 minutes.
  To find the total time it takes the whole candle to burn, a direct proportion can be used. Let x be the total time the whole candle burns. Then the appropriate proportion is

$$\frac{\text{number of inches burned } y}{\text{number of inches burned } x} = \frac{\text{burning time } y}{\text{burning time } x}$$

In this problem, we have

$$\frac{5}{12} = \frac{30}{x}$$

Solving this proportion for x, we obtain

$$5x = (30)(12)$$
$$5x = 360$$
$$x = \frac{360}{5}$$
$$x = 72$$

Thus, the whole candle burns in 72 minutes. So, the quantity in Column A is greater.

12. **(C)**

The area of a parallelogram is equal to the product of the length of any of its sides and the length of the perpendicular segment drawn from the opposite vertex to that side or the line containing that side.

In this problem, segment $\overline{AD}$ is one of the sides of the parallelogram $ABCD$, and segment $\overline{BE}$ is perpendicular to line $\overline{AE}$ of which segment $\overline{AD}$ is a subset (line $\overline{AE}$ contains side $\overline{AD}$).

Hence, the area of the parallelogram $ABCD$ is equal to (the length of $\overline{AD}$) × (the length of $\overline{BE}$). Thus,

$$\text{Area} = (5 \text{ cm}) \times (8 \text{ cm})$$
$$= 40 \text{ cm}^2.$$

So the two quantities in Columns A and B are equal.

13. **(A)**

Because Gail received a 7% increase over last year's salary ($24,000), it follows that her salary this year is equal to $24,000 + 7% of $24,000. Thus,

$(24,000) (7\%)=$ (1) Calculate 7% of 24,000
$(24,000) (.07)=1680$ (2) Remember that 7% is equal to .07
                                                        Substitute .07 into the equation

$24,000 + 1680 = x$ (3) Because her salary increased, *add* 7% of 24,000 to 24,000

Becasue 25,680 is a larger number than 25,580, the quantity in Column A is greater.

14. **(C)**

Column A
$$8^{\frac{2}{3}} = \sqrt[3]{8^2} = \sqrt[3]{64} = 4$$

Column B
$$16^{\frac{1}{2}} = \sqrt{16} = 4$$

Therefore, the quantities are equal.

15. **(C)**

Given $w : x = y : z$ or $\dfrac{w}{x} = \dfrac{y}{z}$

$$w = \frac{(xy)}{z}$$

Column B $wz - xy$
$$= \left[\frac{(xy)}{z}\right]z - xy$$
$$= xy - xy = 0$$

Therefore, the quantities are equal.

16. **(B)**
$$3(a - 1) = 7(a + 2)$$
$$3a - 3 = 7a + 14$$
$$-3 - 14 = 7a - 3a$$
$$-17 = 4a$$
$$-\frac{17}{4} = a$$

17. **(D)**

    Let x = the grade of Tom's last test

    $$\frac{89 + 94 + 86 + 96 + x}{5} = 92$$

    $$89 + 94 + 86 + 96 + x = 92(5)$$
    $$x = 460 - 365$$
    $$x = 95$$

18. **(A)**

    $$\begin{aligned}
    (5x - 3)(4x - 6) &= 5x(4x - 6) - 3(4x - 6) \\
    &= 20x^2 - 30x - 12x + 18 \\
    &= 20x^2 - 42x + 18
    \end{aligned}$$

19. **(B)**

    This problem can be solved easily by simply using the fact that the sum of the measures of the three interior angles of a triangle is 180°. Thus,

    $$\begin{aligned}
    (3x + 15) + (5x - 15) + (2x + 30) &= 180 \\
    3x + 5x + 2x + 30 &= 180 \\
    10x &= 180 - 30 \\
    10x &= 150 \\
    x &= 15
    \end{aligned}$$

This gives us the measure of the
  first angle $= (3x + 15)° = (3 \times 15 + 15)° = 60°$
  second angle $= (5x - 15)° = (5 \times 15 - 15)° = 60°$
  third angle $= (2x + 30)° = (2 \times 15 + 30)° = 60°$

20. **(E)**

    When adding and/or subtracting rational expressions with unlike denominators, we must express all expressions as fractions with the same denominator, usually called the least common denominator. To find the least common denominator of a set of rational expressions,

    (i)   Factor each denominator completely and express repeated factors as powers.
    (ii) Write each different factor that appears in any denominator.
    (iii) Raise each factor in step (ii) to the highest power it occurs in any denominator.
    (iv) The least common denominator is the product of all factors found in step (iii).

In this problem, denominators in factored form are:

$$1 = 1$$
$$x - 2y = (x - 2y)$$
$$x + 2y = (x + 2y)$$

Hence, all the different factors are 1, $(x - 2y)$, and $(x + 2y)$. This gives us $1(x - 2y)(x + 2y)$ as the least common denominator.

Performing the indicated operations yields:

$$1 + \frac{y}{(x - 2y)} - \frac{y}{x + 2y} =$$

$$= \frac{(x - 2y)(x + 2y)}{(x - 2y)(x + 2y)} + \frac{y(x + 2y)}{(x - 2y)(x + 2y)} - \frac{y(x - 2y)}{(x - 2y)(x + 2y)}$$

$$= \frac{x^2 - 4y^2 + xy + 2y^2 - xy + 2y^2}{(x - 2y)(x + 2y)}$$

$$= \frac{x^2}{(x - 2y)(x + 2y)}$$

21. **(C)**

This question can be answered by reading the chart directly. Data about contributions to Republican candidates is given by the pie chart on below. The chart indicates that 32% of all contributions to Republican candidates came from trade, membership, and medical associations.

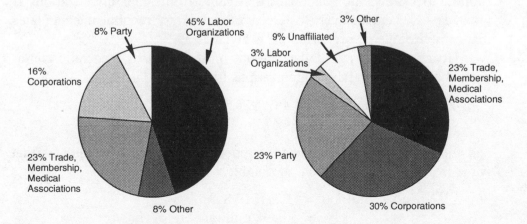

22. **(B)**

Data about contributions to Democratic candidates is given by the pie chart on the previous page. Reading the chart directly, we find out that 8% of all contributions to Democratic candidates came from the party.

To find the dollar amount of support that corresponds to 8%, we need to calculate 8% of the total dollar amount of support to Democratic candidates. That is, we need to calculate 8% of $21.5 million. Hence, the average dollar amount of support to Democratic candidates that came from the party is equal to

$$(0.08) (\$21.5 \text{ million}) = \$1.72 \text{ million}.$$

This eliminates answer choices (A), (C), (D), and (E) and gives answer choice (B) as the correct answer.

23. **(A)**

To find the percent contributions from Labor organizations look at the pie chart and read the amount from the chart.

Republican candidates receive   3%

Democratic candidates receive   45%

Set up the ratio of Republican amount to Democratic amount

$$3 : 45 = 1 : 15.$$

24. **(C)**

From the pie charts on the previous page, the average percent of support to Democratic candidates that came from labor organizations is given as 45%, and the average percent of support to Republican candidates that came from labor organizations is given as 3%.

Hence, the average dollar amount of support to Democratic candidates that came from labor organizations is equal to

$$45\% \text{ of } \$21.5 \text{ million} = (.45) (\$21.5 \text{ million})$$
$$= \$9.675 \text{ million}$$

and the average dollar amount of support to Republican candidates that came from labor organizations is equal to

$$3\% \text{ of } \$19.8 \text{ million} = (.03) (\$19.8 \text{ million})$$
$$= \$0.594 \text{ million}.$$

Thus, the difference, in millions of dollars, between the average dollar amount of support to Democratic candidates and Republican candidates that came from labor organizations is equal to

$$\$9.675 \text{ million} - \$0.594 \text{ million} = \$9.081 \text{ million}.$$

25. **(D)**

Obviously, the total dollar amount of support for both Democratic and Republican candidates that came from corporations is equal to the sum of the dollar amount of support for Democratic candidates and the dollar amount of support for Republican candidates.

From the pie chart, the percent of contributions to Democratic candidates that came from corporations is given as 16%, and the percent of contributions to Republican candidates that came from corporations is given as 30%.

Hence, the dollar amount of support for Democratic candidates that came from corporations is equal to

$$16\% \text{ of } \$21.5 \text{ million} = (0.16)\,(\$21.5 \text{ million})$$
$$= \$3.44 \text{ million}$$

and the dollar amount of support for Republican candidates that came from corporations is equal to

$$30\% \text{ of } \$19.8 \text{ million} = (0.30)\,(\$19.8 \text{ million})$$
$$= \$5.94 \text{ million}.$$

Thus, total dollar amount of support for both Democratic and Republican candidates that came from corporations is equal to

$$\$3.44 \text{ million} + \$5.94 \text{ million} = \$9.38 \text{ million}.$$

26. **(B)**

This problem can be easily solved by simply translating the English statements into algebraic expressions. "The difference between the square of this number, x^2, and 21" can be written as $x^2 - 21$. "Is the same as" means equal (=). "The product of 4 times the number" can be written as $4x$. Thus, the information in this problem can be written as follows:

$$x^2 - 21 = 4x.$$

Answer choice (A) is eliminated because the left-hand side of the equation, $x - 21 = 4x$, gives the difference between the number x and 21 and not the difference between the square of the number x and 21. Answer choice (C) is eliminated because it states that the difference between 21 and 4 times the number x is equal to the square of the number x. In addition, neither of the equations $x + 4x^2 = 21$, and $x^2 + 21 = 4x$ is equivalent to the equation $x^2 - 21 = 4x$, which was obtained by translating the English statements in this problem into algebraic expressions. Thus, answer choices (D) and (E) are also eliminated leaving answer choice (B) as the only correct choice.

27. **(D)**

Since we do not know Emile's dollar volume during the week in question, we can assign this amount the value of x.

Now, Emile's total salary of $540 can be divided into two parts; one part is his flat salary of $240, and the other part is his salary from commissions which amounts to $540 - $240 = $300. This part of his salary is equal to 12% of his dollar volume, x. Thus, 12% of $x = $300. This means

$$(0.12)x = 300$$
$$x = 300/0.12 = \$2,500.$$

Another way to attack this problem is to test each answer choice as follows:

(A) $(0.12)(\$2,800) = \$345.60 \neq \$300$ (wrong)
(B) $(0.12)(\$3,600) = \$432 \neq \$300$ (wrong)
(C) $(0.12)(\$6,400) = \$768 \neq \$300$ (wrong)
(D) $(0.12)(\$2,500) = \$300$ (correct)
(E) $(0.12)(\$2,000) = \$240 \neq \$300$ (wrong)

28. **(A)**

One method for attacking this problem is to let x be the number of cars that 14 robots can assemble in 45 minutes. Because the robots work at the same rate all the time, we can express this rate by using the information that 3 robots can assemble 17 cars in 10 minutes.

Now, if 3 robots can assemble 17 cars in 10 minutes, then 3 robots can assemble $^{17}/_{10}$ cars in 1 minute. Consequently, 1 robot assembles $\frac{1}{3}(^{17}/_{10})$ or $^{17}/_{30}$ of a car in 1 minute.

Similarly, if 14 robots assemble x cars in 45 minutes, then the 14 robots assemble $^{x}/_{45}$ cars in 1 minute. Thus, 1 robot assembles $^{1}/_{14}(^{x}/_{45})$, or $^{x}/_{14(45)}$ of a car in 1 minute. Because the rates are equal, we have the proportion

$$\frac{x}{14(45)} = \frac{17}{30}$$

$$\frac{x}{630} = \frac{17}{30}$$

Solving this proportion for x yields

$$30x = (630)(17)$$
$$= 10,710$$
$$x = \frac{10,710}{30} = 357.$$

29. **(C)**

Let (AB) represent the measure (length) of segment $\overline{AB}$, then the length of rectangle $ABCD$ is equal to (AB) and the length of its width is (BC).

Obviously, the area of shaded region is equal to the area of rectangle $ABCD$ minus the area of triangle EBC.

Recall that the area of a rectangle is equal to the product of the measure of its length and the measure of its width. Thus,

$$\text{Area of rectangle } ABCD = (AB)\,(BC)$$

The area of any triangle is equal to $\frac{1}{2}$ times the measure of its base (any side of the triangle) times the measure of its altitude (the length of the perpendicular segment drawn from the vertex opposite the base to that base or to the line containing the base). That is, the area of a triangle is equal to $\frac{1}{2} bh$.

Thus,

$$\text{Area of triangle } EBC = \frac{1}{2}(EB)\,(BC).$$

But $(EB) = \frac{1}{4}(AB)$, hence,

$$\text{Area of triangle } EBC = \frac{1}{2}\left[\frac{1}{4}(AB)\right](BC)$$
$$= \frac{1}{8}(AB)\,(BC)$$

Since the area of triangle ABC is equal to 12 square units, we have

$$\frac{1}{8}(AB)\,(BC) = 12$$

or

$$(AB)\,(BC) = 96.$$

But, (AB) (BC) is the area of rectangle $ABCD$. Hence, area of rectangle $ABCD = 96$ square units.

Thus, area of shaded region $= 96 - 12 = 84$ square units.

30. **(C)**

Since we have evaporation occurring in this problem, we shall be using subtraction.

Let $x =$ the number of cc of alcohol evaporated. Then $(40 - x) =$ the number of cc in the resulting solution.

A diagram as in the following figure is helpful.

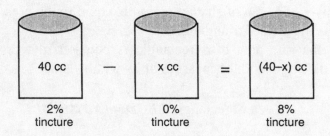

2% of 40 cc $=$ the number of cc of iodine in original solution.
0% of x cc $=$ number of cc of iodine in the alcohol evaporated.
8% of $(40 - x)$ cc $=$ number of cc of iodine in the resulting solution.

Using this relationship,

(Iodine in original solution) – (Iodine in evaporated solution)
$=$ (Iodine in resulting solution).

We get

$$(0.02)(40) - 0(x) = (0.08)(40 - x)$$
$$0.8 - 0 = 3.2 - 0.08x$$
$$0.08x = 3.2 - 0.8$$
$$0.08x = 2.4$$
$$x = \frac{2.4}{.08} = 30$$

Thus, 30 cc of alcohol must be evaporated in order to raise the strength of the tincture to 8%.

GRE

Graduate Record Examination

Practice
Test 3

Section 1

TIME: 45 Minutes
Choose 1 of 2 Essays†

ESSAY QUESTION ONE

> **DIRECTIONS:** Present your perspective on the issue below by using relevant reasons and/or examples to support your views. Remember, there is no one "correct" response to the essay topic. Before starting, read the essay topic and its question(s).

The assumption that the creation of responsible citizens is one of the main purposes of our school system raises complicated questions: what is a responsible citizen, and how can school-based practices be employed in the creation of one? There are many ideas about possible educational reforms which aim to answer these questions. At one extreme are those who demand a return to a more traditional education, who advise a study of more classical, scholarly subjects. At the other extreme are those who feel that any skill a student exhibits, from painting to auto mechanics, should be stressed as strongly as math or English.

Which educational method do you think would be the most effective? Why? What flaws do you find in the other theory? Explain your position using relevant reasons and examples drawn from your own experience, observations, or reading.

STOP

Do not go on until you are instructed to do so. Use any remaining time to check your work on this portion of the test.

† On the actual test, you will have a choice between two essay topics. You have to write only one essay. To give you the most practice possible we have supplied sample essays for both questions in order to show you the differences between essays that receive a perfect score and those that score less.

TIME: 45 Minutes
Choose 1 of 2 Essays†

ESSAY QUESTION TWO

DIRECTIONS: Present your perspective on the issue below by using relevant reasons and/or examples to support your views. Remember, there is no one "correct" response to the essay topic. Before starting, read the essay topic and its question(s).

It is now possible to see the world in great detail through television, movies, and the Internet. Such advances in technology not only make the world "smaller" but also make obsolete the need to travel at all.

Do you think this is true? Explain your position on this subject using relevant examples of your own experiences or observations.

STOP

Do not go on until you are instructed to do so. Use any remaining time to check your work on this portion of the test.

---

† On the actual test, you will have a choice between two essay topics. You have to write only one essay. To give you the most practice possible we have supplied sample essays for both questions in order to show you the differences between essays that receive a perfect score and those that score less.

Section 2

TIME: 30 Minutes
1 Essay

DIRECTIONS: Critique the following argument by considering its logical soundness.

It has long been known that a lifestyle in which the diet consists predominantly of fruits, vegetables, and grains is the most healthy. Studies have shown that eating a lot of meat can contribute to heart disease and high cholesterol. A trip to the grocery store can verify that meat is a more expensive source of protein than tofu, eggs, cheese, nuts, and grains. Most importantly, it has become obvious that raising livestock is the least economically sound food production method available. The land used to raise food for livestock could be much more efficiently used to grow food that could feed the hungry people of the world. It may seem difficult to change the system, but we can certainly change our own lifestyle. How can we not when we see the pleading eyes of starving children staring at us in the pages of a magazine, and we realize that if everyone in the world was a vegetarian, no one would have to go hungry?

What is the main point of this argument? Do you think the author had a specific goal in mind when making this argument? Do you think this argument is effective? What are its strengths and what are its weaknesses?

STOP

If time remains, you may go back and check your work.

Section 3

TIME: 30 Minutes

30 Questions

NUMBERS: All numbers are real numbers.

FIGURES: Position of points, angles, regions, etc., are assumed to be in the order shown and angle measures are assumed to be positive.

LINES: Assume that lines shown as straight are indeed straight.

DIRECTIONS: Each of the following given set of quantities is placed into either Column A or B. Compare the two quantities to decide whether

(A)   the quantity in Column A is greater;

(B)   the quantity in Column B is greater;

(C)   the two quantities are equal;

(D)   the relationship cannot be determined from the information given.

NOTE: Do not choose (E) since there are only four choices.

COMMON INFORMATION: Information which relates to one or both given quantities is centered in the two columns. A symbol which appears in both columns will indicate the same item in Column A and Column B.

EXAMPLES:

Column A	Column B
1. 5×4	$5 + 4$

Explanation: The correct answer is (A), since $5 \times 4 = 20$, and $5 + 4 = 9$.

2.

| $180 - x$ | 35 |

Explanation: The correct answer is (C). Since $\angle ABC$ is a straight angle, its measurement is 180°.

Column A	Column B

$$x > y > z, \quad z > 0$$

1. $\dfrac{1}{xy}$ $\dfrac{1}{yz}$

$$x^2 = y + 2 = 5$$

2. x y

3. The least common multiple of 20, 24, 32   The least common multiple of 2, 15, 32

$$x = 5, y = -3$$

4. $(x + y)^2$ $(x - y)^2$

$$W = 4, X = 3, \text{ and } Y = -2$$

5. $(2WY)^2$ $(2Y)^2 (4W)$

	Column A	**Column B**

$$x = -y$$

6.	x	y

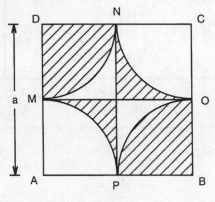

ABCD is a square with side *a. M, N, O,* and *P* are middle points. *MND, MPA, POB,* and *ONC* are four quadrants.

7.	Shaded area	$\dfrac{a^2}{4}$

The length of a ruler is *L*. This value is increased by 10%, and then decreased by 10%.

8.	*L*	Final length

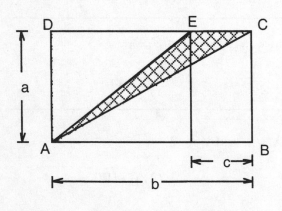

ABCD is a rectangle with *b > a.*

9.	Shaded area	$\dfrac{bc}{2}$

Column A	Column B

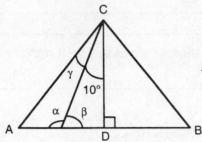

ABC is an equilateral triangle.

10. $\alpha - \beta$ γ

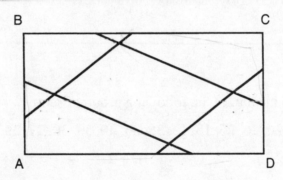

11.   Number of quadrilaterals   8

$$\text{If} \quad R^S = R^2 - S^2, \quad S^R = S^2 - R^2, \quad R \neq S$$

12. $\dfrac{R^S}{S^R}$ $\dfrac{S^R}{R^S}$

13. $\dfrac{1}{5}$ of 0.2% of \$1,000 $\left(\dfrac{1}{5}\right)$% of 0.2 of \$1,000

$$0 < X < 2$$

14. X^2 X^3

$$m > n > 0$$

15. x^m x^n

DIRECTIONS: For the following questions, select the best answer choice to the given question.

---

16. What is the value of the following expression: $\dfrac{1}{1+\dfrac{1}{1+\frac{1}{4}}}$?

    (A) $\dfrac{9}{5}$ (D) 2

    (B) $\dfrac{5}{9}$ (E) 4

    (C) $\dfrac{1}{2}$

17. What is the median of the following group of scores?

    27, 27, 26, 26, 26, 26, 18, 13, 36, 36, 30, 30, 30, 27, 29

    (A) 30   (D) 27

    (B) 26   (E) 36

    (C) 25.4

18. The solution of the equation $4 - 5(2y + 4) = 4$ is

    (A) $-\dfrac{2}{5}$.   (D) -2.

    (B) 8.   (E) none of these.

    (C) 4.

19. If $0 < a < 1$ and $b > 1$, which is the largest value?

    (A) $\dfrac{a}{b}$ (D) $\left(\dfrac{b}{a}\right)^2$

    (B) $\dfrac{b}{a}$ (E) Cannot be determined

    (C) $\left(\dfrac{a}{b}\right)^2$

20. The side of a square increases 10% and the area increases $5.25(\text{ft})^2$. What was the original value of the side of the square?

    (A) 3 ft   (D) 4 ft

    (B) 2 ft   (E) 5 ft

    (C) 1 ft

Questions 21–25 refer to the graph below.

Portion of Doctoral Degrees in the Mathematical Sciences Awarded to U.S. Citizens in 1986

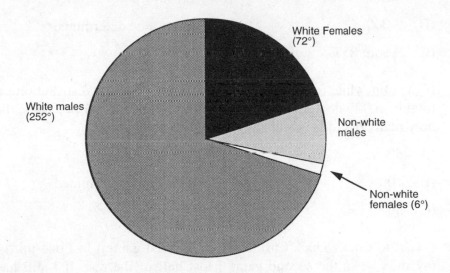

21. What percent of the Ph.D. degrees were awarded in 1986 to non-white males?

    (A) 30   (D) 20

    (B) $8^{1}/_{3}$ (E) None of these

    (C) $4^{1}/_{6}$

22. Given the distribution of doctorates awarded in Mathematical Sciences in the U.S. in 1986, what is the ratio of white males' degrees to those given to males who are not white?

    (A) 1 to 8.4   (D) 42 to 1

    (B) 3.5 to 1   (E) None of these

    (C) 8.4 to 1

23. If 4,000 doctorates were awarded in mathematical sciences, how many were awarded to white female U.S. citizens?

    (A) 800   (D) 1,120

    (B) 2,880   (E) None of these

    (C) 3,200

24. If 600 white females represent 72° of the pie chart depicting the total distribution of doctorates awarded in the Mathematical Sciences in the U.S. in 1986, then how many were awarded to white males?

    (A) 432   (D) 2,100

    (B) 3,000   (E) Cannot be determined

    (C) About 857

25. If the non-white female category represents 6° of the distribution of a total of 6,000 doctorates awarded in the Mathematical Sciences, then how many doctorates were awarded in this category?

    (A) 50   (D) 1,000

    (B) 100   (E) Cannot be determined

    (C) 500

26. I went to Lucky Duck Casino and in the first game I lost one-third of my money; in the second game I lost half of the rest. If I still have $1,000, how much money did I have when I arrived at the casino?

    (A) $1,000   (D) $6,000

    (B) $2,000   (E) $12,000

    (C) $3,000

27. What is the length of side *BC*?

    (A) 3

    (B) 5

    (C) $\sqrt{34}$

    (D) 7

    (E) None of these

A(2,6)   C(5,6)

B(2,1)

28. Given $\dfrac{(\alpha + x) + y}{x + y} = \dfrac{\beta + y}{y}, \dfrac{x}{y} =$

    (A) $\dfrac{\alpha}{\beta}$

    (D) $\dfrac{\alpha}{\beta} - 1$

    (B) $\dfrac{\beta}{\alpha}$

    (E) 1

    (C) $\dfrac{\beta}{\alpha - 1}$

29. Which of the following options is correct for the figure?

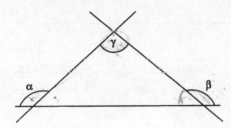

    (A) $\alpha + \beta + \gamma = 180°$

    (B) $\gamma - \alpha + 180° = \beta$

    (C) $\alpha = \beta + \gamma$

    (D) $\gamma = \alpha + \beta$

    (E) $\alpha = 180° - \beta - \gamma$

30. If $3^x > 1$, then x

    (A) $0 < x < 1$

    (D) $x > 0$

    (B) $x \geq 0$

    (E) $x > 1$

    (C) $x \geq 1$

STOP

If time still remains, you may go back and check your work.
When the time allotted is up, you may go on to the next section.

Section 4

TIME: 30 Minutes
38 Questions

DIRECTIONS: Each of the given sentences has blank spaces which indicate words omitted. Choose the best combination of words which fit into the meaning and structure within the context of the sentence.

---

1. Fear persisted, and with it persisted an animosity toward the sister; undoubtedly this was the psychological _____ of the incest taboo.

   (A) antithesis

   (B) impression

   (C) resemblance

   (D) variance

   (E) correlate

2. The sociologist interpreted _____ as being socially shared ideas about what is right and _____ as specific models of behaviors for a surrounding environment.

   (A) culture...laws

   (B) mores...technologies

   (C) class...caste

   (D) sanctions...folkways

   (E) values...norms

3. Soulé is five feet five inches tall and inclines toward stoutness, but his erect bearing and quick movements tend to _____ this.

   (A) emphasize

   (B) conceal

   (C) negate

   (D) camouflage

   (E) disavow

4. A man may be moral without being _____ , but he cannot be _____ without being moral.

(A) devout...pious

(D) pious...religious

(B) altruistic...veracious

(E) iniquitous...contrite

(C) chaste...precise

5. He was eagerly interested and wanted to experiment on himself, although ultimately _____ on account of his age.

    (A) deterred

    (D) dissuaded

    (B) accommodated

    (E) acclimated

    (C) reconciled

6. The enthusiastic teacher described the talented student's clever display as _____.

    (A) ingenuous

    (D) adroit

    (B) incongruous

    (E) prosaic

    (C) indolent

7. The practiced _____ displayed with _____ three pastes which he represented as costly gems to the buyers.

    (A) charlatan...diffidence

    (B) mountebank...self-possession

    (C) empiric...concern

    (D) swindler...aplomb

    (E) imposture...assurance

DIRECTIONS: In the following questions, a related pair of words is followed by five more pairs of words. Select the pair that best expresses the same relationship as that expressed in the original pair.

---

8. CATAPULT:PROJECTILE::

    (A) glacier:ice

    (D) prototype:replica

    (B) precipice:cliff

    (E) perspiration:emit

    (C) transmit:message

9. VITAMIN C:SCURVY::

    (A) sun:skin cancer   (D) rickets:calcium

    (B) niacin:pellagra   (E) plague:rats

    (C) goiter:iodine

10. CONVEY:DUCT::

    (A) transport:transfer   (D) autograph:biography

    (B) pollute:filter   (E) falsify:fabricate

    (C) decipher:key

11. BENEVOLENCE:PHILANTHROPY::

    (A) tolerance:bigotry   (D) amiability:complaisant

    (B) lenity:virulence   (E) penurious:hoard

    (C) haunt:sporadic

12. DESIRE:WANT::

    (A) penchant:partiality   (D) aspire:seek

    (B) supineness:propensity   (E) avidity:greed

    (C) disdain:inattention

13. PHYLUM:CLASSIFICATION::

    (A) cat:feline   (D) medal:honor

    (B) commitment:vow   (E) control:harness

    (C) lie:deceit

14. ARACHNIDS:ARTHROPOD::

    (A) particle:atom   (D) theosophy:monastery

    (B) spear:aperture   (E) cornice:furniture

    (C) rayon:bengaline

15. SERVICE:CHEVRON::

    (A) rank:coronet   (B) decent:libertine

   (C) chaste:virtuous   (D) lascivious:licentious

   (E) ligurgics:atheism

16. SPOONERISM:TRANSPOSITION::

   (A) Alpha:Omega   (D) colon:semicolon

   (B) spree:carousal   (E) rhetorician:profundity

   (C) repudiation:sanction

DIRECTIONS: Each passage is followed by questions based on its content. After reading a passage, choose the best answer to each question. Answer all questions based on what is stated or implied in that passage.

Père Claude Jean Allouez explored Lake Superior from 1665 to 1667. At his little mission station near the western end of the lake, he heard from the Indians of a great river to the west. Père Jacques Marquette determined to investigate. In 1673, accompanied by Louis Jolliet and five others, he left St. Ignace Mission and ascended the Fox River, which flows into Green Bay, crossed over to the Wisconsin River, and followed it to the upper Mississippi. The party then descended the Mississippi to the mouth of the Arkansas. These Frenchmen were not the first Europeans to sight or travel the Mississippi; De Soto and Moscoso had done so a century and a half before.

The report of the exploration was rushed back to Quebec, where, in 1672, Count Frontenac had arrived as Governor of the province. He and his friend, the remarkable La Salle — who earlier may have penetrated the Ohio River Valley — listened with deep interest. Prior to that time, the two men had been involved in projects to open the Western Lake country to French trade.

17. The author's attitude toward Allouez and Marquette is best described as

   (A) admiring and speculative. (D) interested and analytical.

   (B) critical and biased.   (E) inconclusive and tentative.

   (C) objective and positive.

18. Through his exploration, Marquette discovered

    (A) he needed to travel north to reach his southern destination.

    (B) a river he had not expected to find.

    (C) he was not the first Frenchman to travel the river.

    (D) a new route for transporting French settlers to the West.

    (E) French settlements already existed.

19. Frontenac and La Salle had been involved in projects for opening the lake country. The passage implies the projects were related to

    (A) missionary work.

    (B) agriculture.

    (C) fur trading.

    (D) surveying and exploring.

    (E) water transportation.

20. All of the following are either stated or implied in the passage EXCEPT

    (A) Allouez explored the western end of Lake Superior.

    (B) Marquette and his party were the first Frenchmen to travel the Mississippi River.

    (C) La Salle explored the Mississippi River valley.

    (D) Marquette had to follow the Wisconsin River to reach the Mississippi.

    (E) Marquette did not travel past the Arkansas River

Dr. Robert H. Goddard, at one time a physics professor at Clark University, Worcester, Massachusetts, was largely responsible for the sudden interest in rockets back in the twenties. When Dr. Goddard first started his experiments with rockets, no related technical information was available. He started a new science, industry, and field of engineering. Through his scientific experiments, he pointed the way to the development of rockets as we know them today. The Smithsonian Institution agreed to finance his experiments in 1920. From these experiments he wrote a paper titled "A Method of Reaching Extreme Altitudes," in which he outlined a space rocket of the step (multistage) principle, theoretically capable of reaching the moon.

Goddard discovered that with a properly shaped, smooth, tapered nozzle he could increase the ejection velocity eight times with the same weight of fuel. This would not only drive a rocket eight times faster, but sixty-four times farther, according to his theory. Early in his experiments he found that solid-fuel rockets would not give him the high power or the duration of power needed for a dependable supersonic motor capable of extreme altitudes. On 16 March 1926, after many trials, Dr. Goddard successfully fired, for the first time in history, a liquid-fuel rocket into the air. It attained an altitude of 184 feet and a speed of 60 mph. This seems small as compared to present-day speeds and heights of missile flights, but instead of trying to achieve speed or altitude at this time, Dr. Goddard was trying to develop a dependable rocket motor.

Dr. Goddard later was the first to fire a rocket that reached a speed faster than the speed of sound. He was the first to develop a gyroscopic steering apparatus for rockets. He was the first to use vanes in the jet stream for rocket stabilization during the initial phase of a rocket flight. And he was the first to patent the idea of step rockets. After proving on paper and in actual tests that a rocket can travel in a vacuum, he developed the mathematical theory of rocket propulsion and rocket flight, including basic designs for long-range rockets. All of this information was available to our military men before World War II, but evidently its immediate use did not seem applicable. Near the end of World War II we started intense work on rocket-powered guided missiles, using the experiments and developments of Dr. Goddard and the American Rocket Society.

21. Which of the following questions does the passage best answer?

    (A) How did Dr. Goddard become interested in rocket science?

    (B) How did Dr. Goddard develop the new field of rocket science?

    (C) How is a multistage rocket capable of reaching the moon?

    (D) Why is liquid fuel more dependable than solid fuel?

    (E) How did the American Rocket Society get its start?

22. One can assume from the article that

    (A) all factors being equal, the proper shape of the rocket nozzle would increase the ejection velocity and travel distance.

    (B) solid-fuel rockets would give higher power and duration.

    (C) a blunt nozzle would negatively affect speed and distance.

    (D) supersonic motors are needed for extreme altitudes.

    (E) the first successfully fired liquid fueled rocket was for developing a dependable rocket motor.

23. The first step in Dr. Goddard's development of a feasible rocket was

    (A) the mathematical theory of rocket propulsion and rocket flight.

    (B) the development of liquid rocket fuel.

    (C) the development and use of vanes for rocket stabilizing.

    (D) the development of the gyroscope.

    (E) his thesis for multistage rocket design.

24. It can be inferred from the selection that Goddard's mathematical theory and design

    (A) are applicable to other types of rocket-powered vehicles.

    (B) include basic designs for long-range rockets.

    (C) utilize vanes in jet streams for rocket stabilization.

    (D) tested rocket travel in a vacuum.

    (E) produced gyroscopic steering apparatus.

25. How is this passage organized?

    (A) Chronologically

    (B) Pro and con

    (C) Like an argumentative essay

    (D) Comparatively

    (E) Scientifically

26. Dr. Goddard is responsible for

    I.   developing a rocket motor.

    II. developing liquid rocket fuel.

    III. developing rocket-powered guided missiles.

    (A) I only
    (B) I and II only
    (C) III only
    (D) II and III only
    (E) I, II, and III

27. All of the following are true EXCEPT

    (A) Dr. Goddard is the father of the science of rocketry.

    (B) Dr. Goddard demonstrated that a rocket could travel in a vacuum.

    (C) Dr. Goddard founded the American Rocket Society.

    (D) Dr. Goddard developed a rocket that broke the sound barrier.

    (E) Dr. Goddard was a physics professor.

DIRECTIONS: Each of the following questions provides a given word in capitalized letters followed by five word choices. Choose the best word which is most <u>opposite</u> in meaning to the given word.

---

28. PROCLIVITY:

    (A) penchant
    (B) deflection
    (C) dilatory
    (D) diminish
    (E) procedure

29. REMOTE:

    (A) foreign
    (B) proximate
    (C) parallax
    (D) inapposite
    (E) propinquity

30. TREPIDATION:

    (A) apprehension
    (B) sagacity

    (C) perturbation   (D) agitation

    (E) courage

31. ABYSS:

    (A) zenith   (D) interstice

    (B) profundity   (E) depression

    (C) interval

32. CORPULENT:

    (A) portly   (D) anorexic

    (B) vociferate   (E) adverse

    (C) becoming

33. ABJECT:

    (A) caring   (D) objective

    (B) joyful   (E) rational

    (C) empathetic

34. RESERVED:

    (A) chivalrous   (D) cultivated

    (B) affable   (E) well-bred

    (C) ingratiating

35. CALORIC:

    (A) fervor   (D) zero

    (B) modicum   (E) frigidity

    (C) temperature

36. FERAL:

    (A) voracious   (D) exacting

    (B) unconscientious (E) cultivated

    (C) savage

37. UNCTUOUS:

    (A) scrupulous   (D) agitated

    (B) morose   (E) ingratiating

    (C) ravenous

38. INVIDIOUS:

    (A) repugnant   (D) reconcilable

    (B) obscure   (E) perturbed

    (C) ransomed

STOP

If time still remains, you may go back and check your work.
When the time allotted is up, you may go on to the next section.

Section 5

TIME: 30 Minutes
38 Questions

DIRECTIONS: Each of the given sentences has blank spaces which indicate words omitted. Choose the best combination of words which fit into the meaning and structure within the context of the sentence.

1. Not all persons whose lives are _____ remain provincial; some have the intellectual and personal characteristics which enable them to develop a/an _____ orientation to life.

   (A) confined...philanthropic

   (B) limited...progressive

   (C) circumscribed...enterprising

   (D) restricted...cosmopolitan

   (E) restrained...hedonistic

2. Committees are ineffective when they cannot agree upon what to do or just how to go about accomplishing it; this situation is a/an _____ of faulty _____ of committee responsibility.

   (A) factor...acceptance   (D) part...guidelines

   (B) cause...guidelines   (E) example...direction

   (C) result...specifications

3. The cook prepared a particularly rich shellfish purée, or _____, for the honored guests.

   (A) pottage   (D) bouillon

   (B) bisque   (E) soufflé

   (C) broth

4. The work of those government officials who must live in hostile foreign countries is full of perils— _____ for their families and _____ for themselves.

   (A) moderate...hazardous   (D) minimal...dangerous

   (B) hazardous...moderate   (E) dangerous...moderate

   (C) perils...also

5. Increasing specialization on the part of workers results in better communication and higher degrees of achievement of goals in relation to the immediate work group or department, but decreases effectiveness of communication among groups or departments and the focus on institutional goals; this presents managers with the problems of increasing _____ and providing _____ .

   (A) coordination...vision   (D) retraining...articulation

   (B) supervision...mission   (E) relationship...orientation

   (C) support...direction

6. She was a perfect receptionist for the complaint department because with her _____ temperament she was not easily aroused.

   (A) impassive   (D) apathetic

   (B) stoic   (E) stolid

   (C) phlegmatic

7. As an ardent _____ of parental leave benefits, James had few _____ among the women at the meeting.

   (A) opponent...supporters   (D) foe...enemies

   (B) supporter...friends   (E) advocate...backers

   (C) activist...foes

DIRECTIONS: In the following questions, a related pair of words is followed by five more pairs of words. Select the pair that best expresses the same relationship as that expressed in the original pair.

8. TWEETER:WOOFER::

   (A) grade:slope
   (B) high:low
   (C) replicate:duplicate
   (D) tutelage:protection
   (E) isosceles:equal

9. ARC:CIRCUMFERENCE::

   (A) moon:earth
   (B) hour:day
   (C) cabin:mansion
   (D) exercise:rest
   (E) knowledge:wisdom

10. FACADE:BUILDING::

    (A) grill:car
    (B) tongue:shoe
    (C) sheath:knife
    (D) picture:frame
    (E) head:body

11. GRASS:EROSION::

    (A) root:tree
    (B) air:tire
    (C) clouds:rain
    (D) dam:water
    (E) breeze:flag

12. COMPULSORY:REQUIRED::

    (A) committed:avowed
    (B) normal:aberrant
    (C) free:democratic
    (D) voluntary:mandatory
    (E) schooled:learned

13. NERVOUS:POISE::

    (A) angry:sensibility
    (B) frightened:confidence
    (C) empathetic:rationality
    (D) energetic:enthusiasm
    (E) calm:laziness

14. LATENCY:EXPOSITION::

    (A) pleonasm:verbiage   (D) indigested:structured

    (B) indigent:poverty   (E) incoherence:immiscibility

    (C) argonaut:astronaut

15. AGGRANDIZE:AUGMENT::

    (A) declension:ascent   (D) increment:diminution

    (B) abatement:extenuation   (E) vincture:segregation

    (C) adjunct:detruncate

16. INTOXICATION:INEBRIATION::

    (A) gluttony:voracity   (D) plover:sandpiper

    (B) turban:hat   (E) peregrine:falcon

    (C) vim:fatigue

DIRECTIONS: Each passage is followed by questions based on its content. After reading a passage, choose the best answer to each question. Answer all questions based on what is stated or implied in that passage.

The crisis came in the spring of 1775, predictably in Massachusetts. Late on the night of April 18 the Royal Governor, General Thomas Gage, alarmed at the militancy of the rebels, dispatched 600 troops from Boston to seize a major supply depot at Concord. Almost simultaneously the Boston council of safety, aware of Gage's intentions, directed Paul Revere and William Dawes to ride ahead to warn militia units and citizens along the way of the British approach, as well as John Hancock and Samuel Adams, who were staying at nearby Lexington. Forewarned, the two men went into hiding.

About 77 militiamen confronted the redcoats when they plodded into Lexington at dawn. After some tense moments, as the sorely outnumbered colonials were dispersing, blood was shed. More flowed at Concord and much more along the route of the British as they retreated to Boston, harassed most of the way by an aroused citizenry. What had once been merely protest had devolved into open warfare; the War for Independence had begun.

17. In the selection the author was attempting to portray

    (A) the need for more diplomacy by the colonists before the Revolution began.

    (B) the overeaction of the British which started the Revolutionary War.

    (C) the nationalistic attitude of the colonists prior to the Revolutionary War.

    (D) the predictability of the Revolutionary War beginning in Massachusetts.

    (E) the events leading up to the Revolutionary War.

18. The attitude of the author toward British redcoats could best be described as one of

    (A) admiration for their excellent fighting ability.

    (B) disrespect for the redcoats.

    (C) criticism for lack of military discipline.

    (D) scorn for their readiness.

    (E) sympathy because the British lacked the heart to fight.

19. From information given in the selection, which of the following statements is the most correct?

    (A) The colonists were better fighters than the British because they were outnumbered.

    (B) There were colonial spies among the British ranks.

    (C) The colonists were well organized to fight a conflict.

    (D) All the revolutionary spokesmen for the colonists were forced to go underground.

    (E) The time for diplomacy had ended.

Michael Faraday, English physicist and chemist, was born in Newington, Surrey, on September 22, 1791. Faraday was one of ten children of a poverty-stricken blacksmith. He had little formal education. At 14 he was apprenticed to a bookbinder who allowed the boy to read books and attend scientific lectures. During a lecture given by Sir Humphry Davy,

Faraday took notes, which he sent to the scientist. Because of the excellence of these notes, he later became Davy's assistant at the Royal Institution.

From then on Faraday developed rapidly as a scientist and was awarded many honors. In 1825 he became Director of the Royal Institution and was made professor of chemistry for life in 1833. However, he belonged to a religious group, now extinct, which didn't approve of worldly rewards. Because of this he declined knighthood and the presidency of the Royal Society of which he was a member. His religious convictions also made him refuse to prepare poison gas for Britain's use in the Crimean War.

Faraday was one of the greatest experimental geniuses in the physical sciences. In 1822, impressed by the discovery that an electric current produced a magnetic field, he determined that it was possible to make magnetism produce electricity. He later showed that a movable wire carrying an electric current will rotate around a fixed magnet. Faraday had converted electricity and magnetic forces into mechanical energy, and from this experiment came the principle of the electric motor.

Between 1823 and 1825 he devised methods to liquefy gases, produced below-zero temperatures on the Fahrenheit scale in the laboratory for the first time, and he discovered benzene, a compound important for future work in representing molecular structures in organic chemistry.

His next contribution was in the field of electrochemistry. Davy had produced pure metals by passing an electric current through molten compounds of these metals. Faraday named this process electrolysis.

Michael Faraday died in Hampton Court near London on August 25, 1867. He left the world the richest heritage of scientific knowledge since Isaac Newton. His significant discoveries include the principle of electromagnetic induction, the field concept that describes the way objects interact, and the two basic laws of electrolysis.

20. The author's attitude toward Michael Faraday is best described as one of

    (A) admiration.   (D) condescension.

    (B) disrespect.   (E) subjectivity.

    (C) distrust.

21. According to the passage, which of the following was not an accomplishment of Michael Faraday?

    (A) Conversion of electricity and magnetic forces into mechanical energy

    (B) Devised methods to liquefy gases

    (C) Produced pure metals by passing an electric current through molten compounds of these metals

    (D) Discovered benzene

    (E) Made magnetism-produced electricity

22. Which of the following best states the author's main point?

    (A) Anyone can make a contribution to a field of study with enough desire.

    (B) Michael Faraday made his contributions because he had the opportunities presented to him.

    (C) Michael Faraday made his contributions from the contributions of others, namely Sir Humphry Davy.

    (D) It was difficult for Michael Faraday to work in his field because he did not believe in worldly rewards.

    (E) Michael Faraday was a self-educated scientific genius.

23. The author provides information that would answer all but which of the following questions?

    (A) What is the process of electrolysis?

    (B) How did Faraday produce mechanical energy?

    (C) What method was used to liquefy gases?

    (D) How may an electromagnetic field be produced?

    (E) What's the basic principle of the electric motor?

24. According to the article, which of the following terms was coined by Faraday in the course of his work?

    (A) valence   (D) electrolyte

    (B) anode   (E) electrolysis

    (C) electrode

25. The author notes that the scientist's religious convictions were responsible for all of Faraday's actions EXCEPT

    (A) declining knighthood.

    (B) declining the position of Director of the Royal Institution.

    (C) declining the presidency of the Royal Society.

    (D) refusing to prepare poison gas for Britain's use in the Crimean War.

    (E) disapproval of worldly rewards.

26. Which of the following had the greatest impact on the future life of Michael Faraday?

    (A) Birthplace

    (B) Family

    (C) Poverty

    (D) Apprenticeship

    (E) Association with Sir Humphry Davy

27. Which of the following titles would best describe the author's intent in this selection?

    (A) Michael Faraday, His Life and Work

    (B) Michael Faraday and the History of Electrolysis

    (C) Michael Faraday and His Work at the Royal Institute

    (D) Michael Faraday and Sir Humphry Davy

    (E) Michael Faraday and Electromagnetic Induction

DIRECTIONS: Each of the following questions provides a given word in capitalized letters followed by five word choices. Choose the best word which is most <u>opposite</u> in meaning to the given word.

---

28. FORTUITOUS:

    (A) sad   (B) unfruitful

(C) unlucky   (D) disenchanted

(E) miserable

29. ARCHAIC:

(A) exalted   (D) invisible

(B) modern   (E) noble

(C) angelic

30. INSERT:

(A) exude   (D) explore

(B) extend   (E) extinguish

(C) extract

31. LOQUACIOUS:

(A) daring   (D) wealthy

(B) tedious   (E) haughty

(C) silent

32. MYRIAD:

(A) passel   (D) profuse

(B) diverse   (E) individual

(C) legion

33. NEFARIOUS:

(A) insubordinate   (D) nervous

(B) good   (E) stubborn

(C) dangerous

34. AMELIORATE:

(A) clarify   (D) amend

(B) mandate   (E) worsen

(C) insist

35. REQUISITE:

    (A) alternative   (D) abhorrent

    (B) futile   (E) superfluous

    (C) prerequisite

36. PARSIMONIOUS:

    (A) peculiar   (D) patronizing

    (B) passionate   (E) pernicious

    (C) prodigal

37. OBDURATE:

    (A) affable   (D) credulous

    (B) unsavory   (E) penitent

    (C) prevaricating

38. INSIPID:

    (A) obtuse   (D) tasty

    (B) humble   (E) jealous

    (C) maternal

STOP

If time still remains, you may go back and check your work.
When the time allotted is up, you may go on to the next section.

Section 6

TIME: 30 Minutes
30 Questions

NUMBERS: All numbers are real numbers.

FIGURES: Position of points, angles, regions, etc., are assumed to be in the order shown and angle measures are assumed to be positive.

LINES: Assume that lines shown as straight are indeed straight.

DIRECTIONS: Each of the following given set of quantities is placed into either Column A or B. Compare the two quantities to decide whether

(A)   the quantity in Column A is greater;

(B)   the quantity in Column B is greater;

(C)   the two quantities are equal;

(D)   the relationship cannot be determined from the information given.

NOTE: Do not choose (E) since there are only four choices.

COMMON INFORMATION: Information which relates to one or both given quantities is centered in the two columns. A symbol which appears in both columns will indicate the same item in Column A and Column B.

EXAMPLES:

Column A	Column B
1. 5×4	$5 + 4$

Explanation: The correct answer is (A), since $5 \times 4 = 20$, and $5 + 4 = 9$.

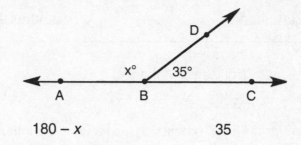

2. $180 - x$ 35

Explanation: The correct answer is (C). Since $\angle ABC$ is a straight angle, its measurement is 180°.

	Column A	**Column B**

$$3^x = 81$$

1. x 3

$$x + 2y > 4$$

2. x y

A group of 5 students reported that they earned the following amounts during summer vacation:
$8,000, $9,000, $2,000, $10,000, $6,000.

3.   Average income   Median income

---

a and b are positive integers; $b \geq 2$

4. $\dfrac{a}{b}$ $\dfrac{a+1}{b-1}$

---

5. $\dfrac{120}{200}$ $\dfrac{4}{5}$

Column A	**Column B**

Jim earns *d* dollars in *h* hours.

6. Jim's earnings in (*h* + 20) hours $\qquad$ $\left(d + \dfrac{20d}{h}\right)$ dollars

---

Given △*BED* with *b* (the measure of $\overline{ED}$)
greater than *e* (the measure of side $\overline{BD}$)

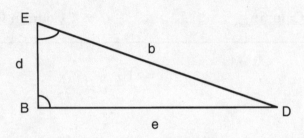

7. Measure of ∠*B* $\qquad$ Measure of ∠*E*

The ratio of boys to girls in Mr. Good's class is 3 : 4
and in Ms. Garcia's class is 4 : 5. The two classes
have the same number of students.

8. Number of boys in $\qquad$ Number of boys in
   Mr. Good's class $\qquad$ Ms. Garcia's class

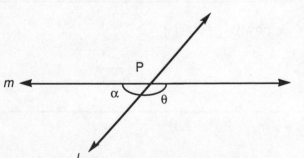

Lines *l* and *m* intersect
at point *P* such that the
measure of ∠θ is 3 times
the measure of
∠α

9. Measure of ∠θ $\qquad$ 135°

<u>Column A</u>	<u>Column B</u>

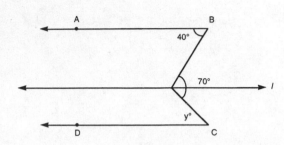

Line l is parallel to ray $\overrightarrow{BA}$ and parallel to ray $\overrightarrow{CD}$.

10.	y	30°

$$\frac{1}{x} = \frac{\sqrt{0.0016}}{5}$$

11.	x	12.5

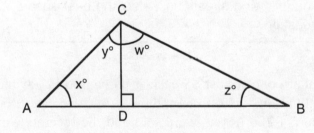

$\overline{CD}$ is perpendicular to $\overline{AB}$.

12.	$x - y$	$w - z$

13.	$\dfrac{x-3}{4} + \dfrac{x+7}{3}$	$\dfrac{7x+19}{7}$

Column A	Column B

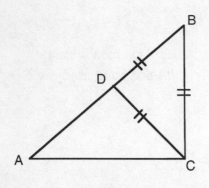

Line segments $\overline{BC} = \overline{CD} = \overline{BD}$
and $\overline{BC} \perp \overline{AC}$

14. $\overline{AC}$	$\overline{CD}$

15. Product of the roots of the equation $x^2 + 3x + 2 = 0$	-1

> **DIRECTIONS:** For the following questions, select the best answer choice to the given question.

16. Tickets for a particular concert cost $5 each if purchased in advance and $7 each if bought at the box office on the day of the concert. For this particular concert, 1,200 tickets were sold and the receipts were $6,700. How many tickets were bought at the box office on the day of the concert?

    (A) 500   (D) 350

    (B) 700   (E) 200

    (C) 600

17. If $2a + 2b = 1$, and $6a - 2b = 5$, which of the following statements is true?

    (A) $3a - b = 5$ (D) $a + b < 3a - b$

    (B) $a + b > 3a - b$ (E) $a + b = -1$

    (C) $a + b = -2$

18. If $6x + 12 = 5$, then the value of $(x + 2)$ is

    (A) $-\frac{19}{6}$.   (D) $3\frac{1}{6}$.

    (B) $-1\frac{1}{6}$.   (E) $1\frac{1}{6}$.

    (C) $\frac{5}{6}$.

19. The most economical price among the following prices is

    (A) 10 oz. for 16¢.   (D) 20 oz. for 34¢.

    (B) 2 oz. for 3¢.   (E) 8 oz. for 13¢.

    (C) 4 oz. for 7¢.

20. For non-zero numbers p, q, r, and s, $p/q = r/s$. Which of the following statements is true?

    (A) $\dfrac{p+q}{p} = \dfrac{r+s}{r}$ (D) $\dfrac{p-q}{q} = \dfrac{s-r}{r}$

    (B) $\dfrac{p}{r} = \dfrac{q}{r}$ (E) $\dfrac{q}{p-q} = \dfrac{r}{s-r}$

    (C) $\dfrac{r}{s} = \dfrac{q}{p}$

Questions 21–25 refer to the chart on the next page. The data represents the sales and advertising for Company B in thousands of dollars (to the nearest ten thousand dollars).

21. From 1979 to 1983 inclusive, the average advertising for Company B is approximately

    (A) $53,000.   (D) $54,000.

    (B) $60,000.   (E) $80,000.

    (C) $80,000.

22. From 1981 to 1988 inclusive, what was the amount of the greatest increase in sales from one year to the next?

    (A) $70,000   (D) $60,000

    (B) $110,000   (E) $40,000

    (C) $140,000

Sales and Advertising for Company B
(In thousands of dollars – to the nearest ten thousand dollars)

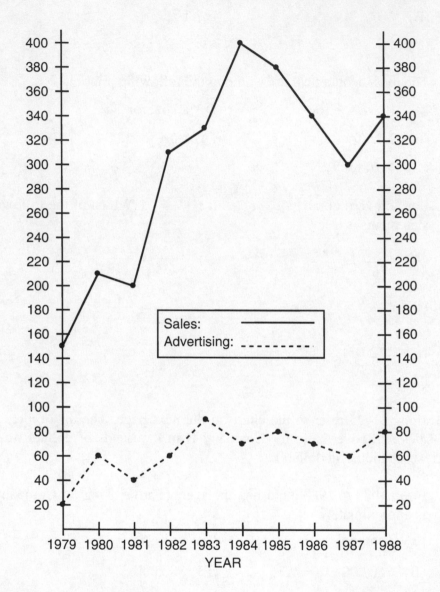

23. In how many of the years shown was advertising equal to or greater than 25% of sales?

(A) 6

(B) 5

(C) 4

(D) 3

(E) 2

24. From 1982 to 1988 inclusive, in which year did sales change by the greatest percent over the previous year?

    (A) 1982   (D) 1986

    (B) 1984   (E) 1988

    (C) 1985

25. From 1979 to 1988 inclusive, in which year did advertising increase while sales decreased over the previous year?

    (A) 1980   (D) 1987

    (B) 1983   (E) 1988

    (C) 1985

26. Line $\overleftrightarrow{AB}$ is the perpendicular bisector of segment $\overline{CP}$ (P is not shown). Then P is the same as which of the following points?

    (A) G

    (B) F

    (C) H

    (D) K

    (E) D

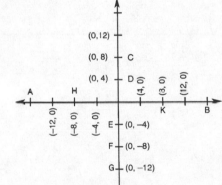

27. In the figure shown, all segments meet at right angles. Find the figure's perimeter in terms of r and s.

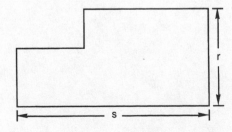

    (A) $r + s$ (D) $r^2 + s^2$

    (B) $2r + s$ (E) $2r + 2s$

    (C) $2s + r$

28. If *n* is an integer, which of the following represents an odd number?

    (A) $2n + 3$ (D) $3n$

    (B) $2n$ (E) $n + 1$

    (C) $2n + 2$

29. A postal truck leaves its station and heads for Chicago, averaging 40 mph. An error in the mailing schedule is spotted and 24 minutes after the truck leaves, a car is sent to overtake the truck. If the car averages 50 mph, how long will it take to catch the postal truck?

    (A) 2.6 hours   (D) 1.5 hours

    (B) 3 hours   (E) 1.6 hours

    (C) 2 hours

30. $\sqrt{75} - 3\sqrt{48} + \sqrt{147} =$

    (A) $3\sqrt{3}$ (D) 3

    (B) $7\sqrt{3}$ (E) $\sqrt{3}$

    (C) 0

STOP

If time still remains, you may go back and check your work.

TEST 3

ANSWER KEY

Sections 1 and 2 — Analytical Writing

Please review the sample essays in the Detailed Explanations.

Section 3 — Quantitative Ability

1. (B)	9. (B)	17. (D)	25. (B)
2. (B)	10. (C)	18. (D)	26. (C)
3. (C)	11. (A)	19. (D)	27. (C)
4. (B)	12. (C)	20. (E)	28. (D)
5. (C)	13. (C)	21. (B)	29. (B)
6. (D)	14. (D)	22. (C)	30. (D)
7. (A)	15. (D)	23. (A)	
8. (A)	16. (B)	24. (D)	

Section 4 — Verbal Ability

1. (E)	11. (E)	21. (B)	31. (A)
2. (E)	12. (E)	22. (C)	32. (D)
3. (D)	13. (D)	23. (E)	33. (B)
4. (D)	14. (C)	24. (A)	34. (B)
5. (D)	15. (A)	25. (A)	35. (E)
6. (D)	16. (B)	26. (B)	36. (E)
7. (D)	17. (C)	27. (C)	37. (D)
8. (C)	18. (A)	28. (B)	38. (D)
9. (B)	19. (C)	29. (B)	
10. (C)	20. (C)	30. (E)	

Section 5 — Verbal Ability

1. (D)	11. (D)	21. (C)	31. (C)
2. (C)	12. (A)	22. (E)	32. (E)
3. (B)	13. (B)	23. (C)	33. (B)
4. (C)	14. (D)	24. (E)	34. (E)
5. (A)	15. (B)	25. (B)	35. (E)
6. (C)	16. (A)	26. (D)	36. (C)
7. (A)	17. (E)	27. (A)	37. (E)
8. (B)	18. (B)	28. (C)	38. (D)
9. (B)	19. (E)	29. (B)	
10. (A)	20. (A)	30. (C)	

Section 6 — Quantitative Ability

1. (A)	9. (C)	17. (D)	25. (C)
2. (D)	10. (C)	18. (C)	26. (B)
3. (B)	11. (A)	19. (B)	27. (E)
4. (B)	12. (D)	20. (A)	28. (A)
5. (B)	13. (D)	21. (D)	29. (E)
6. (C)	14. (A)	22. (B)	30. (C)
7. (A)	15. (A)	23. (E)	
8. (B)	16. (D)	24. (A)	

DETAILED EXPLANATIONS OF ANSWERS

Section 1–Analytical Writing

PERSPECTIVES ON AN ISSUE ESSAY TOPIC—ESSAY ONE

Sample Essay Response Scoring 6

Americans are legally required to spend most of their childhood and young adulthood in school. Ideally, time so spent should be a valuable and enriching experience. When a person receives a high school or college diploma, they hopefully have become a responsible citizen, ready to enter society and give back some of what they have been given through their education. It is indeed difficult to define exactly what constitutes a "responsible citizen," or to decide the best way to create such an individual. However, I think it is important that we allow such a definition to change, and that we realize that our educational methods have to change as well. Ours is a complicated, fast-paced world, and new skills are necessary to survive in this environment. While I think that a broad range of knowledge is helpful and people should be required to learn about subjects they might not personally be motivated to explore, I also believe that all knowledge and skills are valuable, and that it is important to encourage a student in exactly the areas that interest him or her.

One advantage to teaching less traditional subjects is that it becomes increasingly likely that the student is learning because he or she wants to, and not because information is being forced upon them. It seems that all too often, students are seen as little more than computers who can be programmed with knowledge; no thought is given to whether or not that information is of interest or value to them. It seems that something which is learned merely because it may appear on a test is not likely to be remember-

effective sentence variety

shows a solid ability to discuss both positions put forth in the question

well-articulated argument

the use of a metaphor strengthens the argument

415

ed long after that test has been taken. If a study is encouraged to explore a skill or a subject that he or she finds interesting, however, it is probable that he or she will not only remember what was learned about that subject, but will be encouraged to learn more about other related subjects; furthermore, the student will be eager to share what he or she has learned.

strong rationale bolsters the stated position

argument of previous paragraph is here made negative-- this shows complexity of the essay topic

This is not the case with an archaic curriculum which stresses skills and knowledge which are no longer of use to the student. It is unfair to assume that every student will have the same interests in school or the same needs once they leave school. If the canon of knowledge one must learn is prescribed by forces that are perceived to be remote from the students' experience, it is probable that a large number of students will be left feeling neglected or apathetic. Such educational requirements will be viewed as chores and eventually the students' discouragement will ensue.

highly effective use of rhetorical questions

If this is true for students whose family encourages their studies, how much more true must it be for those whose parents are uninterested or even abusive? The conflicts some children face are completely removed from the subjects held to be important in school. If a child is hungry or cold, unloved or abused, how can he or she be expected to connect algebra to the frightening realities of everyday life?

A genuine interest in a subject, when encouraged and nurtured, might give such a student a sense of hope that would help him or her to survive in school and would provide skills which would be useful once he or she graduated. Knowledge, when acquired through personal choice rather than as a chore, is one of the few things in this life that we can hold onto, that no one can take from us, and that we can build on throughout our lives.

persuasive and logically presented example

Knowledge could provide not only a good reason for a student to go to school, but on a deeper level, a good reason for him or her to live. It is further probable that a student with such a positive scholastic experience would graduate with more to offer society, and would be ready to begin a rewarding career and less likely to resort to crime or to be burdened with poverty.

A responsible citizen is one who shows concern for the welfare of the society in which he or she lives and tries to add something valuable to it. A positive scholastic experience which nurtures pre-existing interests and practical applicable skills is the most likely to produce such a person. Of course, many subjects already being taught are important, but it is possible to incorporate a new emphasis in learning without removing the broad scope of knowledge. Schools could become a place to which most people will actively want to go, where they will learn to feel better about themselves and about their place in a community.

effective concluding argument

Analysis of Sample Essay Scoring 6

This essay would rate a score of 6. The writer is asked to choose one side of an issue, and effectively argue why they have chosen that position. In this essay, once the author has chosen one side, he or she clearly sets out several reasons for that choice. The specific question is about education; this essay examines many levels on which education is expected to work, taking into account both those students with supportive parents and those who have difficult home lives. The essay is well-organized and arranges the various reasons it explores in such a way that they lead easily into one another, and they all tie back to the original theme.

PERSPECTIVES ON AN ISSUE ESSAY TOPIC—ESSAY TWO

Sample Essay Response Scoring 3

Through the internet we can now see what it looks like in other places, even more than we could with television. So, it might follow, why from now on would anyone ever need to be a tourist? Tourism may have nothing useful to offer us now that we are a society that gets so much information from the internet.

ineffective transition because the previous sentence is very vague

And yet, there may be more to it than that. For instance. There are limits to what TV and computers can bring us such as how things taste and feel and smell. Maybe they will be able to someday, but right now, you can't tell what a bakery in Paris or a beer garden in Berlin smells like, or how a meal made in India tastes. Those are things you have to be there for.

very unspecific

fragment

poor sentence structure

very abrupt ending; no transition between ideas

Tourism is a way to learn and have fun. It is a way to see the world and stimulate the economy of other nations. I spent my junior year of college studying in Amsterdam, a big city in Holland. While there, I learned to speak conversational Dutch (the language they speak there) and I met many interesting people. Some of the people I met were other American students, but some were also Dutch people that I still correspond with occasionally. This experience has helped me to grow as an individual, and I am thankful for it.

it is unclear how this relates to the essay topic

Analysis of Sample Essay Scoring 3

This essay is scored a 3 because it offers only a limited analysis of the essay topic. The first paragraph is starting to outline a position but it is too brief and choppy to succeed. The essayist fails to connect ideas to the opening statement; examples are never fully developed. The second paragraph ends very abruptly. The reference to the writer's personal experience is an attempt to formulate a position but it goes on for too long and loses its relevance to the argument. Transitions between ideas are weak. The sudden end of the essay leaves it ultimately unclear whether any real argument has been made. Aside from a few long or fragmented sentences the use of language is adequate.

Section 2–Analytical Writing

ANALYSIS OF AN ARGUMENT ESSAY TOPIC

Sample Essay Response Scoring 6

In this argument, the author is compiling a list of reasons why it would be preferable for Americans to adopt a vegetarian diet. She has the definite goal to persuade the reader to undergo a change in lifestyle. In the process of setting forth her argument, she disparages our economic system and our food production system, and it is in this context that she calls upon the individual to change his or her own actions. The argument is extremely effective because it uses unusual lines of reasoning that might be convincing to people who ordinarily believe that they have no interest in vegetarianism. It is subtly persuasive in that it appeals to our emotions while appearing to be purely factual and intellectual.

clear identification of the rhetorical posture adopted in initial essay

well-executed transition between ideas

good example to support argument

Many arguments for vegetarianism tend to make it look like an unusual lifestyle, suitable for only few people. Traditional discussions on the subject might not appeal to a majority of the population, particularly in a country such as America where the raising and eating of meat is seen as a longstanding and valuable institution.

effective analysis of the initial essay

The strength of the argument set forth in this passage is that it does not seem to speak to only a few people interested in an alternative lifestyle, but to everyone in America, with arguments that affect everyone on many levels, whether they are aware of it or not. It does this by discussing institutions upon which every citizen depends, namely the economic and the food production systems, and by showing how the long-term tradition of meat-eating might not be as practical as has been commonly believed.

the use of examples from the initial essay makes this analysis very strong

One effective debating skill that this passage employs is to list a variety of arguments only to state that they are not as important as the main argument. In this way, the author manages to set forth these arguments, which are persuasive in their own right, and in so doing to lend even more cogency to her final point. In this passage, these are issues of health and money, two subjects which appeal to every individual, as nothing is more convincing than to speak to someone's pocketbook or to their very life. These subjects are so important that to follow them up by saying, "Most importantly...." makes what follows seem worthy of very close attention.

good —————
transition

Another extremely effective technique that this passage employs is the subtlety with which it appeals to the emotions. Any argument which does so too directly is likely to cause suspicion. If the author had overtly tried to make the reader feel guilty in an effort to provoke a change in his or her lifestyle, she would instead have caused the reader to feel defensive. Instead, she appears to call upon the reader's common sense, to show how we could all be healthier and richer if we adopted the eating practices she recommends. The one instance in which she does appeal directly to the emotions, and perhaps tries to cause a feeling of guilt, is in the final sentence when she mentions starving children. This is one of the few sections of the argument which does not seem as powerfully reasoned or as persuasive.

very precise
sentences
add weight
to the
content
of this
paragraph

good
transition
to a critique
of some
short-
comings in
the initial
essay

Although this passage is very strong, it might be made even more so with the addition of specific statistics or examples. If the author could have provided exact numbers to show how our food production system causes waste, or examples of a food production system which would be more cost-effective, it might have made the passage more convincing. If, for instance, she had provided a dollar figure for the money spent on meat production as opposed to that necessary to produce plant foods, or shown what that money could buy for the consumer, she might have appealed to a broader and more skeptical audience.

Very
specific
and
therefore
very
effective

It is very difficult to make sweeping changes in the lifestyle of an entire country. This is particularly true if those changes involve something so basic as the production and consumption of food. The author makes her argument persuasive with a combination of vigorous conviction and subtle intellectual reasoning that does justice to the complexity of her task.

highly effective ending: it acknowledges the complexity of the issue, but maintains the admiration for the style of the initial essay

Analysis of Sample Essay Scoring 6

This essay would earn a 6. The original argument is a complicated list of problems with our food production and economic system. Throughout the piece, the essayist correctly reads the main point of the argument—to try and persuade the reader to change his or her lifestyle and consume less meat. The essay proceeds to show how this is effectively set out in the argument, recognizing even subtle methods of persuasion. The organization helps the essayist to examine each element in as much depth as possible in a short space before moving on to the next, and the connections between the paragraphs are smooth and clear.

Section 3–Quantitative Ability

1. **(B)**
     (B) is correct. The value of $xy > yz$ but the comparison is using them in the denominator.

2. **(B)**
     (B) is correct. Solving for $x^2 = 5$ and $y + 2 = 5$, $x = \pm\sqrt{5}$ and $y = 3$. This means that $x < y$.

3. **(C)**
     (C) is correct. The least common multiples are the same for both A and B. The prime factorization of the numbers in Column A are: $20 = 2 \times 2 \times 5$; $24 = 2 \times 2 \times 2 \times 3$; $32 = 2 \times 2 \times 2 \times 2 \times 2$. The unique factors are 2, 3, and 5. The LCM is $2^5 \times 3 \times 5 = 480$. The prime factorization of the numbers in Column B are: $2 = 2^1$; $15 = 3 \times 5$; $32 = 2 \times 2 \times 2 \times 2 \times 2$. The unique factors are 2, 3, and 5. The LCM is $2^5 \times 3 \times 5 = 480$.

4. **(B)**
     (B) is correct. Substitute $x = 5$ and $y = -3$ in each of the expressions to obtain $(x + y)^2 = [5 + (-3)]^2 = (5 - 3)^2 = 2^2 = 4$ for Column A and $(x - y)^2 = [5 - (-3)]^2 = (5 + 3)^2 = 8^2 = 64$ for Column B.

5. **(C)**
     (C) is correct. Substitute $W = 4$ and $Y = -2$ in the expressions. $(2WY)^2 = [2 \times 4 \times (-2)]^2 = (-16)^2 = 256$ for Column A and $(2Y)^2 (4W) = [2 \times (-2)]^2 (4 \times 4) = (-4)^2 (16) = (16)(16) = 256$ for Column B. Therefore, the quantities are equal. $X = 3$ is unnecessary information.

6. **(D)**
     Choices (A), (B), and (C) are incorrect. The relationship of x and y changes depending on the value set on one of the variables. (D) is the correct answer. The relationship of x and y changes depending on the value set on one of the variables.

     Given that $x = -y$
     if $y > 0$, then $x < 0$ and $y > x$
     if $y < 0$, then $x > 0$ and $y < x$
     if $y = 0$, then $x = 0$ and $y = x$.

The relationship cannot be determined from the information given.

7. **(A)**

(A) is correct. Rearranging the shaded area one can see that the shaded area = half the square area or

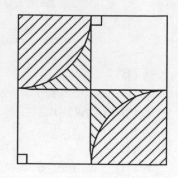

$$\frac{a^2}{4} + \frac{a^2}{4} = \frac{2a^2}{4} = \frac{a^2}{2}$$

$\frac{a^2}{2}$ is bigger than $\frac{a^2}{4}$; therefore, choices (B), (C), and (D) are incorrect.

8. **(A)**

(A) is correct. When the ruler increases by 10%, the length will be

$L + 10\%$ of $L = L + 0.10L = 1.1L$.

When the ruler is decreased by 10%

$1.1L - 10\%$ of $1.1L = 1.1L - (0.10)1.1L = .99L$ (final length).

$L > .99L$ or the original length is greater than the final length. Choices (B) and (C) are incorrect. Check to see if the correct comparisons were used. (D) is incorrect. To do the required calculation no further information is needed.

9. **(B)**

Choice (B) is correct. The shaded area is triangle *AEC*, so the area is

$$\frac{\text{height} \times \text{base}}{2} = \frac{ac}{2}$$

but it is given that $b > a$. Therefore, $\frac{bc}{2} > \frac{ac}{2}$.

10. **(C)**

(C) is correct. Since $\triangle ABC$ is an equilateral triangle, $\angle ACD = 30°$, so,

$$\gamma + 10° = 30°$$
or
$$\gamma = 20°$$

and
$$10° + \beta + 90° = 180°$$
$$\beta = 80°$$
$$\alpha + \beta = 180°$$
$$\alpha = 100°$$
therefore, $\alpha - \beta = 20° = \gamma$.

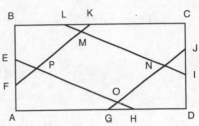

11. **(A)**

(A) is correct. Label the figure using the letters *E, F, G, H, I, J, K, L, M, N, O,* and *P*. The quadrilaterals are: *ABCD, FPHA, GOEA, HOJD, INGD, JNLC, KMIC, LMFB, EPKB,* and *MNOP*. The total number is 10. Choices (B), (C), and (D) are incorrect. Label the figure using the letters *E, F, G, H, I, J, K, L, M, N, O, P* at the vertices not labeled. Find the quadrilateral or four-sided figures.

12. **(C)**

(C) is correct. Given $R^S = R^2 - S^2$ and $S^R = S^2 - R^2$. Then

$$\frac{R^S}{S^R} = \frac{(R^2 - S^2)}{(S^2 - R^2)}$$

$$= \frac{(R - S)(R + S)}{(S - R)(S + R)}$$

$$= \frac{(R - S)}{(S - R)}$$

$$= -1$$

By the similar reduction of terms, $\dfrac{S^R}{R^S} = -1$. Therefore, the values are equal.

13. **(C)**

(C) is correct.

$$\tfrac{1}{5} \text{ of } 0.2\% \text{ of } \$1,000 = .2 \times .002 \times 1,000 = 0.4 \text{ and}$$

$$(\tfrac{1}{5})\% \text{ of } 0.2 \text{ of } \$1,000 = .002 \times .2 \times 1,000 = 0.4$$

Therefore, the quantities are equal.

14. **(D)**

(D) is correct. For any value of $X > 1$, it will be true that $X^2 > X$, and $X^3 > X^2$.

For example, when $X = 2$, $2^2 = 4$, $2^3 = 8$, and $8 > 4$.

Therefore, $X^3 > X^2$ when $1 < X < 2$. But when $X = 1$, $X^3 = X^2 = 1$.

But in the interval $0 < X < 1$, $X^2 < X$ and $X^3 < X^2$.

For example, when $X = 0.1$, $(0.1)^3 = 0.001$, $(0.1)^2 = 0.01$, and $0.001 < 0.01$.

Therefore, $X^3 > X^2$ when $1 < X < 2$,

$$X^3 = X^2 \text{ when } 1 = X,$$

and $X^3 < X^2$ when $0 < X < 1$.

15. **(D)**

Choices (A), (B), and (C) are incorrect. This is true for values of $x > 1$. Try some values of $x < 1$. (D) is correct. If $x = 0$ or 1, $x^m = x^n$.

If $x > 1$, $x^m > x^n$.
If $0 < x < 1$, $x^n > x^m$.

If $x < 0$, the results can be $x^m > x^n$, $x^m < x^n$, or the answer becomes irrational. Therefore, more information would be needed to determine the relationship.

16. **(B)**

Choices (A), (C), (D) and (E) are incorrect. Remember that, to divide, the denominator must be inverted. This must be done at each complex fraction. (B) is correct. To reduce this expression

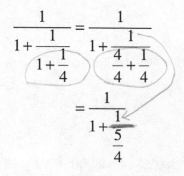

$$\cfrac{1}{1 + \cfrac{1}{1 + \cfrac{1}{4}}} = \cfrac{1}{1 + \cfrac{1}{\frac{4}{4} + \frac{1}{4}}}$$

$$= \cfrac{1}{1 + \cfrac{1}{\frac{5}{4}}}$$

$$= \frac{1}{1+\dfrac{4}{5}} = \frac{1}{\dfrac{5}{5}+\dfrac{4}{5}}$$

$$= \frac{1}{\dfrac{9}{5}}$$

$$= \frac{5}{9}$$

17. **(D)**

Choices (A), (B), and (C) are incorrect. This is not the median. The median is the middle value in a sequence of numbers when the numbers are arranged in ascending or descending order. (D) is correct. The median is the middle value in a sequence of numbers when the numbers are arranged in ascending or descending order. When this is done 27 is the median value.

18. **(D)**

Choices (A), (B), and (C) are incorrect. Try substituting the answer in the original equation. Simplify the equation. Remember that an equation can be multiplied, divided, subtracted, or added by the same number on both sides of the equal sign to help reduce it. (D) is correct.

$$4 - 5(2y + 4) = 4$$

$4 - 10y - 20 = 4$ On the left-hand side of the equation apply the distributive property.

$4 - 20 - 4 = 10y$ Add $10y$ and -4 to both sides of the equation to isolate the terms with y.

$$-20 = 10y$$

$-2 = y$ Divide both sides by 10.

19. **(D)**

Choices (A), (B), (C), and (E) are incorrect. Given that $0 < a < 1$ and $b > 1$, then $a/b < 1$. It is true that this amount is more than $(a/b)^2$, but it is not the largest value. (D) is correct. Given that $0 < a < 1$ and $b > 1$, then $a/b < 1$, $b/a > 1$ so $b/a > a/b$, and $(b/a)^2 > (a/b)^2 \times (b/a)^2 > (b/a)$ since $b/a > 1$. Therefore, $(b/a)^2$ is the largest value. To prove this, substitute in numbers for a and b following the given conditions. If $a = 1/2$ and $b = 2$ are used, the answers obtained are (A) $1/4$, (B) 4, (C) $1/16$, and (D) 16.

20. **(E)**

Choices (A), (B), (C), and (D) are incorrect. Remember that the area of a square is $A = s^2$ and 10% is equivalent to .1 more on the side, so $1.1s$ is the length of the new side. The new area is $(1.1s)^2$. (E) is correct. The original square with side s has an area $A = s^2$. The new square's side = $1.1s$ and $A' = (1.1s)^2 = 1.21s^2 = 1.21A$. Given that the new area is 5.25 (ft)² more

$$\text{or } A' - A = 5.25$$
$$1.21s^2 - s^2 = 5.25$$
$$.21s^2 = 5.25$$
$$s^2 = 25$$
$$s = 5$$

21. **(B)**

(B) is correct. The portion of the pie chart showing non-white males can be found by adding together the other degrees and subtracting the sum from 360° to obtain 30°. To find the percentage, use the ratio of non-white males/the whole or $30°/360° = 8\frac{1}{3}\%$.

22. **(C)**

(A) is incorrect. Be careful in setting up the ratio—that is, white males to non-white males. (B) is incorrect. Ascertain the segment of the pie that is being used for the non-white males. (C) is correct. You need the proportion of non-white males awarded degrees. Add the given degrees in the circle and subtract the sum from 360° and obtain 30°. The ratio is $\frac{252}{30}$ or $\frac{8.4}{1}$ or 8.4 to 1. (D) is incorrect. Make sure that the correct portion is being used for the non-white males. (E) is incorrect. You need to find the proportion of non-white males awarded degrees. Remember, there are 360° in a circle and thus in this pie chart.

23. **(A)**

(A) is correct. To find the number of degrees awarded to white females, first find the percentage of white females or $\frac{72}{360} = 20\%$. Multiply the percentage by the total number of degrees awarded.

$$20\% \text{ of } 4,000 = .20 \times 4,000 = 800.$$

(B) is incorrect. The wrong percentage was used to calculate the number of degrees awarded to white females. Remember that this is a pie chart with 360° in the total chart. (C) is incorrect. The wrong percentage may have been used to find the number of degrees awarded to white females. Remember to use the number of white females divided by the whole number when finding the percentage of white females. (D) is incorrect. Remember to use the number of white females divided by the whole number and that the chart is a pie chart with 360°. (E) is incorrect. Find the percentage of white females and multiply it by the total number of degrees awarded.

24. **(D)**

(A) is incorrect. This value is too small since there are over 3 times more white males awarded degrees compared to white females. Rework the ratio of white females to white males from the pie chart and set up a proportion to find the number of degrees awarded to white males. (B) is incorrect. Be careful setting up the ratio of white females/white males. (C) is incorrect. This value is too small since there are over 3 times more white males awarded degrees compared to white females. Rework the ratio of white females to white males from the pie chart and set up a proportion to find the number of degrees awarded to white males. (D) is correct. Let x = the number of degrees awarded to white males. The ratio from the pie chart of white females to white males is $^{72}/_{252}$ and the ratio of degrees of white females to white males is $^{600}/_{x.}$ Then form a proportion $^{72}/_{252} = {}^{600}/_x$ and solve for x to find the number of degrees awarded to white males.

$$\frac{72}{252} = \frac{600}{x} \text{ or } \frac{72}{x} = 252(600) \text{ or } x = 2,100.$$

(E) is incorrect. With the pie chart there is enough information to solve for the number of white males awarded degrees. Find the ratio of white females to white males and then solve the proportion to find the number of degrees awarded.

25. **(B)**

(A) is incorrect. Recheck the ratio of non-white females/whole population awarded degrees. (B) is correct. The percentage of non-white females can be found by the ratio of 6°/360°. Then multiply the percentage by the total number of degrees awarded to find the number of degrees awarded to non-white females. (6/360) × 6,000 = degrees awarded to non-white females 36,000/360 = 100. (C) is incorrect. Recheck the ratio of non-white females/the whole population awarded degrees. (D) is incorrect. This number is too big since there are only 6°/360°, non-white females/the whole population. Recheck the ratio of non-white females/the whole population. (E) is incorrect. There is enough information with the pie chart to find the ratio of non-white females/the whole population.

26. **(C)**

(A) is incorrect. This answer is too small since this is the same amount that I had at the end and I had lost some in two games. Let $x =$ the amount of money that I arrived with at the casino. Then set up an equation that follows the given problem. Choices (B), (D), and (E) are also incorrect. Read the problem carefully and make sure that the money lost is subtracted from the equation. Let $x =$ the amount of money that I arrived with at the casino. Then set up an equation that follows the given problem. (C) is correct. Let $x =$ the amount of money that I arrived with at the casino. Then set up an equation that follows the given problem. As follows:

$$x - \frac{1}{3}x = \frac{2}{3}x = \text{the amount of money left after the first game.}$$

$$\frac{2}{3}x - \frac{1}{2}\left(\frac{2}{3}x\right) = \frac{1}{3}x = \text{the amount of money left at the end.}$$

$$\$1,000 = \frac{1}{3}x = \text{information given in the problem.}$$

$$x = \$3,000, \text{ the amount of money at the start.}$$

27. **(C)**

(A) This answer is incorrect. The difference between the x-coordinates for points B and C is not the length of BC. Use the Pythagorean theorem to find the length of side BC. (B) is incorrect. The difference between the y-coordinates for points B and C is not the length of BC. Use the Pythagorean theorem to find the length of side BC. (C) is correct. Since the triangle ABC is a right triangle, use the Pythagorean theorem to find the length of side BC. The length of side AC is $5 - 2 = 3$ and the length of side AB is $6 - 1 = 5$. Find the length of BC as follows:

$$(BC)^2 = (AC)^2 + (AB)^2$$
$$(BC)^2 = 3^2 + 5^2$$
$$(BC)^2 = 9 + 25$$
$$BC = \sqrt{34}$$

Alternatively, use the distance formula: $d = \sqrt{(x_1 - x_2)^2 + (y_1 - y_2)^2}$. This will give the same answers. (D) is also incorrect. Simply adding the y-coordinates of points B and C will not give the length of BC. Use the Pythagorean theorem to find the length of side BC. (E) is incorrect. Use the Pythagorean theorem to find the length of side BC.

28. **(D)**

Choices (A), (B), (C), and (E) are incorrect. Rearrange the expressions to isolate x/y. (D) is correct. To find an expression for x/y as a function of $\alpha + \beta$

$$\frac{(\alpha + x) + y}{x + y} = \frac{\beta + y}{y}$$

$$\frac{\alpha + (x + y)}{x + y} = \frac{\beta + y}{y}$$

Rearrange

$$\frac{\alpha}{x + y} + \frac{x + y}{x + y} = \frac{\beta}{y} + \frac{y}{y}$$

$$\frac{\alpha}{x + y} + 1 = \frac{\beta}{y} + 1$$

$$\frac{\alpha}{x + y} = \frac{\beta}{y}$$

$$\frac{\alpha}{\beta} = \frac{x + y}{y}$$

$$\frac{\alpha}{\beta} = \frac{x}{y} + \frac{y}{y}$$

$$\frac{\alpha}{\beta} = \frac{x}{y} + 1$$

$$\frac{x}{y} = \frac{\alpha}{\beta} - 1$$

29. **(B)**

Choices (A), (C), (D), and (E) are incorrect. Remember that the sum of the angles of a triangle = 180° and a straight angle = 180°. (B) is correct. Redraw the figure and put the interior angles in the triangle.

The sum of the interior angles is 180°.

$$(180° - \alpha) + (180° - \beta) + \gamma = 180°$$

Simplify

$$180° + \gamma - \alpha = \beta$$

or

$$\gamma - \alpha + 180° = \beta$$

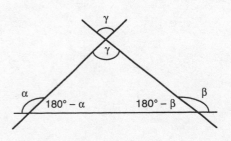

429

30. **(D)**

Choices (A), (B), (C), and (E) are incorrect. While the values are true, it does not account for all acceptable values of x. Try some values of $x > 1$. (D) is correct. Given $3^x > 1$. If $x = 0$, then $3^0 = 1$. Therefore, $x > 0$ to obtain a value > 1.

Section 4–Verbal Ability

1. **(E)**
   (A) is incorrect. ANTITHESIS means opposition or contrast. (B) is not appropriate; IMPRESSION means influence. RESEMBLANCE (C) means likeness. VARIANCE (D) means difference or disagreement. (E) is correct. CORRELATE refers to two things that intimately complement each other (e.g., salt and pepper).

2. **(E)**
   Answer (A) is not appropriate. CULTURE is more than just ideas about what is right; CULTURE is all the modes of thought, behavior, and production that are handed down from one generation to another. LAWS are norms that have been enacted through the formal process of government; all moral rules of behavior are not laws. These two sociological terms are not appropriate answers; (B) is incorrect. MORES are strongly sanctioned norms that people consider vital; TECHNOLOGIES are 1) things and 2) norms for usual things that are found in society. (C) is not an appropriate answer. CLASS is a social stratum defined primarily by economic criteria like occupation, income, and wealth; CASTE is a social stratum into which people are born and in which they remain for life. (D) is incorrect. SANCTIONS are rewards and punishments for adhering to or violating rules of behavior; FOLKWAYS are rules of behavior which are less strongly sanctioned. Neither term is appropriate in this instance. (E) is the appropriate choice. VALUES are ideas about what is right; NORMS are specific models of behavior for a surrounding environment.

3. **(D)**
   EMPHASIZE (A) means to stress. (B) is incorrect; CONCEAL means to remove from view. NEGATE (C) means to deny. (D) is correct. CAMOUFLAGE means to disguise, which is the best choice, since his stoutness is being somewhat disguised or covered over by his erect bearing and quickness of movement. (E) is incorrect; DISAVOW means to deny.

4. **(D)**
   (A) is not appropriate; DEVOUT means dedicated to religion; PIOUS means self-consciously virtuous. (B) is incorrect. ALTRUISTIC means concerned for the well-being of others; VERACIOUS means truthful. (C) is not the best choice. CHASTE means pure in thought and deed; PRE-

CISE means exact. (D) is correct. PIOUS and RELIGIOUS (conscientiously faithful) are essentially synonymous. (E) is incorrect. INIQUITOUS means wicked, sinful; CONTRITE means apologetic.

5. **(D)**

DETERRED (A) means to have discouraged or inhibited. ACCOMMODATED (B) means reconciled. RECONCILED (C) means brought into agreement. (D) is correct. DISSUADED means advised against. (E) is incorrect; ACCLIMATED means used to or familiar with something.

6. **(D)**

(A) is not the right answer. If you chose this answer, you probably confused the word INGENUOUS (candid, forthright) with INGENIOUS (clever). (B) is incorrect; INCONGRUOUS means not corresponding to what is right and proper. Since INDOLENT (C) means lazy, it is not suitable in this context. (D) is correct. ADROIT means ingenious, an appropriate adjective for the sentence. PROSAIC (E) means dull, tedious, or commonplace.

7. **(D)**

(A) is incorrect. A CHARLATAN is a quack, a pretender of knowledge and ability; this term comes close but does not exactly describe a person who tries to sell goods which are misrepresented. DIFFIDENCE means unusually shy or timid and certainly does not describe a practiced con artist. (B) is not the best answer. MOUNTEBANK is synonymous with CHARLATAN; it means a quack, a pretender of knowledge and ability. The term does not aptly describe a con artist in jewels, although SELF-POSSESSION does fit. (C) is not the best choice. An EMPIRIC is a quack; the term is best suited to a pretender of knowledge or ability. Neither does CONCERN fit the blank well. (D) is correct. A SWINDLER (one who cheats, one who obtains money or property by fraud) fits well, as does APLOMB (self-possession). (E) is not correct. If you selected (E), you probably confused IMPOSTURE (a fraudulent item) with impostor (one who imposes on others for the sake of deception). ASSURANCE does fit, but IMPOSTURE is incorrect.

8. **(C)**

CATAPULT means to throw or to shoot from a weapon. A PROJECTILE is that which has been hurled or shot, as from a sling-shot. (A) is incorrect. A GLACIER is a large mass of ice; ICE is the substance from which the glacier is made. The analogy in (A) is an object:composition relationship — quite different from the analogy existing between CATA-

PULT and PROJECTILE. (B) is not correct. A PRECIPICE is a CLIFF; the two are synonyms — (B) is not the type of analogy illustrated by the question. (C) is the correct response. TRANSMIT means to send; a MESSAGE is words sent from one person to another. The analogy between TRANSMIT (to send) and MESSAGE (words sent) is the same as that between CATAPULT and PROJECTILE. (D) is incorrect. A PROTOTYPE is an original; a REPLICA is a copy. The two are opposites, or antonyms; therefore, (D) would not be a suitable choice in this instance. (E) is incorrect; although the same relationship is present between EMIT (give out) and PERSPIRATION (that which is given out) as between CATAPULT and PROJECTILE, the order is different.

9. **(B)**
A lack of VITAMIN C causes SCURVY; taking VITAMIN C helps cure SCURVY. (A) is incorrect. The SUN causes SKIN CANCER; care in the SUN can help prevent SKIN CANCER. The analogy is not the same. (B) is the correct answer since NIACIN can prevent PELLAGRA. (C) is incorrect; IODINE in the diet can prevent GOITER. The order is not the same as for VITAMIN C:SCURVY. (D) is incorrect. The order for RICKETS:CALCIUM is different than for VITAMIN C:SCURVY. (E) is incorrect. The PLAGUE is carried by fleas on infected RATS; the analogy is not the same as for VITAMIN C:SCURVY.

10. **(C)**
CONVEY is a verb which means to carry or transfer; DUCT is a noun which means a tube or canal for carrying. To CONVEY, or carry something, one might use a DUCT. (A) is incorrect. TRANSPORT means to carry across. TRANSFER means to bear across. These two words do not have the same relationship as the verb and noun above. (B) is incorrect. POLLUTE means to make dirty; a FILTER, on the other hand, can be used to remove dirt. (B) is not analogous to CONVEY and DUCT. (C) is correct. To DECIPHER or solve a code, one might use a KEY, which might be an explanation or a book of answers. The relationship between DECIPHER and KEY (C) is the same as that between CONVEY and DUCT. (D) is incorrect. An AUTOGRAPH is a writing written by one's self; a BIOGRAPHY is a writing about someone's life. These terms do not bear the same analogy as CONVEY and DUCT. (E) is incorrect. FALSIFY is a verb meaning to lie or make false; FABRICATE is also a verb meaning to forge or devise falsely. These two verbs are not analogous to the verb and noun CONVEY and DUCT.

11. **(E)**

BENEVOLENCE refers to the "will" to do good; while PHILAN-THROPY indicates the act of giving, specifically money, on a large scale, thereby creating a cause-and-effect relationship. (A) is incorrect; TOLER-ANCE would not have created a cause:effect relationship with BIGOTRY. LENITY and VIRULENCE (B) are near antonyms in definition, with LENITY referring to indulgence while VIRULENCE describes extreme bitterness. (C) is incorrect; SPORADIC means to occur occasionally, while HAUNT suggests appearing continually. AMIABILITY and COM-PLAISANT (D) both refer to being generally agreeable. (E) is correct. PENURIOUS suggests extreme frugality resulting in HOARDING, a cause-and-effect relationship.

12. **(E)**

(A) is incorrect. PENCHANT and PARTIALITY are nearly synony-mous, both meaning to incline to an attachment to something. (B) is not the correct choice. PROPENSITY is an antonym of SUPINENESS, with PRO-PENSITY referring to an irresistible attachment to a thing; while SUPINE-NESS suggests the opposite, "apathetic passivity." (C) is incorrect. DIS-DAIN suggests looking upon something with scorn. INATTENTION im-plies a lack of concentration. ASPIRE and SEEK (D) are synonymous, both implying the searching for and laboring to attain. (E) is the correct answer. DESIRE is defined as a longing or craving which is a more intense form of WANT, just as AVIDITY is defined as a consuming GREED. Therefore, DESIRE and AVIDITY denote a maximum degree of WANT and GREED.

13. **(D)**

CAT:FELINE (A) presents an animal and its class. COMMIT-MENT:VOW (B) presents synonyms. LIE:DECEIT (C) presents an ex-ample of the second term through the first term. (D) is correct. This is an analogy of purpose. The purpose served by PHYLUM is that of CLASSI-FICATION. The purpose of a MEDAL is to HONOR the recipient. (E) is incorrect. CONTROL:HARNESS is a relationship function—the function of a harness is to control.

14. **(C)**

PARTICLE and ATOM (A) have a part-to-whole relationship. SPEAR and APERTURE (B) are synonymous. (C) is correct. RAYON and BEN-GALINE have a member:class relationship. THEOSOPHY and MONAS-TERY (D) have a relationship of purpose. (E) is incorrect. CORNICE is an architectural embellishment and is not related to FURNITURE.

15. **(A)**

(A) is correct because RANK:CORONET contains a cause-and-effect relationship, as do the lead words, SERVICE and CHEVRON. DECENT: LIBERTINE (B) refer to attitude and lifestyle, as do the synonymous pairs CHASTE:VIRTUOUS (C) and LASCIVIOUS:LICENTIOUS (D). Choice (E) is incorrect; LITURGIC refers to the study of worship, while its antonym ATHEISM means the denial of the existence of God.

16. **(B)**

(A) is incorrect. ALPHA:OMEGA, (beginning:end), are opposites. (B) is correct. SPREE and CAROUSAL are synonymous, as are SPOO-NERISM and TRANSPOSITION, in which the initial sounds of two or more words are rearranged. (C) is incorrect. REPUDIATION means rejection and is the opposite of SANCTION, which means condone. (D) is incorrect. COLON and SEMICOLON are two punctuation marks; they don't have a synonymous relationship like the example words. (E) is incorrect. A RHETORICIAN is an orator; PROFUNDITY means intellectual depth. The two words are not necessarily related, and they aren't synonyms, as are the example words.

17. **(C)**

The author does not speculate (A), or analyze (D), and the author is neither critical nor biased (B). There is nothing tentative (E) about the facts stated in the passage. The best description of the author's attitude is (C), objective and positive.

18. **(A)**

(A) is the correct choice; the key contextual words are "ascended" and "descended." (B) is incorrect; sentence two states the opposite: "he heard from the Indians of a great river to the west." (C) is incorrect; this is stated in the last sentence of paragraph one. (D) is incorrect; it is an inferred statement. (E) is incorrect, since no reference was made to French settlements.

19. **(C)**

The passage neither states nor implies that the projects were related to missionary work (A), agriculture (B), surveying and exploring (D), or water transportation (E). The correct answer is (C); the last sentence of the passage mentions "French trade," and the French trade with the Indians was based on fur trading.

20. **(C)**

(A) is incorrect. The passage states that Allouez explored Lake Superior and lived near its western end. (B) is not correct. While Marquette's party were not the first Europeans to travel the Mississippi River, they were the first Frenchmen to do so. (C) is correct. The passage states that LaSalle explored the Ohio River Valley, not the Mississippi River Valley. (D) is incorrect. The passage states that Marquette did have to follow the Wisconsin River to reach the Mississippi River. (E) is not correct. The passage states that Marquette's party travelled down the Mississippi River to the mouth of the Arkansas River.

21. **(B)**

The passage does not directly answer the questions "How did Dr. Goddard become interested in rocket science?" (A), "How is a multistage rocket capable of reaching the moon?" (C), "Why is liquid fuel more dependable than solid fuel?" (D), or "How did the American Rocket Society get its start?" (E). The passage best answers the question "How did Dr. Goddard develop the new field of rocket science?" (B)

22. **(C)**

The fact that, all factors being equal, the proper shape of the rocket nozzle would increase the ejection velocity and travel distance, is stated outright in the passage, so (A) is not something to be "assumed." Choice (B), solid fuel rockets would give higher power and duration, is a contradiction of information given in the third sentence of paragraph two. The correct answer is (C). The first sentence of the second paragraph implies that a blunt nozzle would negatively affect speed and distance. The second paragraph states that supersonic motors must be "dependable," so (D) is not an appropriate choice. The passage neither states nor implies that the first successfully fired liquid fueled rocket was for developing a dependable rocket motor, so therefore (E) is not the correct choice.

23. **(E)**

The first step in Dr. Goddard's development of a feasible rocket was his thesis for multistage rocket design (E), not the mathematical theory of rocket propulsion and rocket flight (A), the development of liquid rocket fuel (B), the development and use of vanes for rocket stabilization (C), or the development of the gyroscope (D).

24. **(A)**

One can infer from the statement "proving on paper and in actual test that a rocket can travel in a vacuum" that Goddard's mathematical theory and design are applicable to other types of rocket-powered vehicles (A). The passage explicitly states, rather than implies, that Goddard's mathematical theory and design include basic designs for long-range rockets (B), utilizes vanes in jet streams for rocket stabilization (C), tested rocket travel in a vacuum (D), and produced gyroscopic steering apparatus (E).

25. **(A)**

(A) is correct. The essay shows the development of the rocket over time. There are no pros or cons (B) presented. The essay is not argumentative (C) nor is it a comparative essay (D). (E) is incorrect. The essay is organized chronologically, not scientifically.

26. **(B)**

Dr. Goddard is responsible for developing a rocket motor (I) and for developing liquid rocket fuel (II), but he did not develop rocket-powered guided missles (III). Therefore, the correct answer is (B), I and II only.

27. **(C)**

Dr. Goddard is the father of the science of rocketry (A), he demonstrated that a rocket could travel in a vacuum (B), he developed a rocket that broke the sound barrier (D), and he was a physics professor (E). The only untrue statement is (C); Dr. Goddard did not found the American Rocket Society.

28. **(B)**

PROCLIVITY and PENCHANT (A) are synonyms. (B) is correct. PROCLIVITY means a strong inclination, DEFLECTION is an attempt to avoid. DILATORY (C) means delay-causing. DIMINISH (D) means to lessen. PROCEDURE (E) is a particular way of doing something and is not related to the example word.

29. **(B)**

FOREIGN (A) suggests being situated outside a place and is synonymous with REMOTE. PROXIMATE (B) means nearness in space and is the correct answer. PARALLAX (C) indicates an apparent difference in the direction of an object as seen from two perspectives. INAPPOSITE (D) refers to being not relevant. PROPINQUITY (E) denotes a closeness in a relationship.

30. **(E)**

(A) is incorrect. TREPIDATION and APPREHENSION are synonymous, meaning "fear." SAGACITY (B) means the mental capacity to discern character. PERTURBATION (C) refers to the degree of apprehension. AGITATION (D) implies an emotional state accompanied by irregular movement. (E) is correct. COURAGE is defined as mental and moral strength, as opposed to TREPIDATION.

31. **(A)**
(A) is correct. ZENITH is the highest point, making it opposite to ABYSS, the lowest point. PROFUNDITY (B) means intellectual depth. An INTERVAL (C) is a space of time between two events. An INTERSTICE (D) is a space of time between two events. A DEPRESSION (E) is a low point, a point below average, making it too similar in meaning to ABYSS, the lowest point.

32. **(D)**
CORPULENT means solid, dense, fleshy, or fat. PORTLY (A) means stout, obese, or fat. This synonym should not be selected. VOCIFERATE means to cry out loudly. It bears no relationship to CORPULENT; (B) is incorrect. BECOMING can be used as an adjective meaning befitting or suitable. Since it is not the opposite of CORPULENT, (C) should not be selected as the correct answer. ANOREXIC (D) means suppressing appetite for food and, hence, thin; it is the opposite of CORPULENT and the correct choice. ADVERSE means acting against. Corpulence can have an adverse effect on health, but it is not the antonym of ADVERSE; (E) is not the correct choice.

33. **(B)**
ABJECT means miserable; CARING (A) is not related. (B) is correct. ABJECT is an adjective which means miserable or wretched. Its opposite in the list given is JOYFUL. EMPATHETIC (C) means emotionally sensitive. OBJECTIVE (D) means without bias or prejudice. RATIONAL (E) means sensible, or based on reasoning, as a rational response.

34. **(B)**
(A) is incorrect. CHIVALROUS means gallant or courteous. RESERVED means undemonstrative, self-restrained, or distant. Its opposite in the list given is AFFABLE (B), which means friendly or sociable. INGRATIATING (C) means bringing oneself into another's favor. CULTIVATED (D) means developed, as in a developed mind. WELL-BRED (E) means showing good breeding, courteous, or considerate.

35. **(E)**
(A) is incorrect. FERVOR is a degree of warmth. MODICUM (B) is a small portion. TEMPERATURE (C) is a measure of hot or cold. ZERO

(D) is the point at which the temperature scale begins. (E) is correct. FRIGIDITY refers to coldness; CALORIC refers to heat.

36. **(E)**

The adjective FERAL means wild or untamed. VORACIOUS means excessively eager, immoderate, gluttonous, ravenous. It certainly is not the opposite of FERAL and (A) should not be chosen. UNCONSCIENTIOUS means not influenced by (a strict regard to) the dictates of conscience. It is seemingly unrelated to FERAL. (B) is wrong. SAVAGE means uncivilized, uncultivated, ferocious. It is not the opposite of FERAL; (C) is an incorrect answer. EXACTING means severe in making demands; it does not bear an opposite relationship to FERAL. (D) is a poor choice. (E) CULTIVATED means improved, or refined. It is the opposite of FERAL; (E) is the correct answer.

37. **(D)**

UNCTUOUS means smug, characterized by a pretense, especially in trying to persuade or influence others. SCRUPULOUS (A) means careful, exacting. It is not the opposite of UNCTUOUS. MOROSE means gloomy. (B) is not an antonym for UNCTUOUS and should not be selected. RAVENOUS means eager. Since it is not the opposite of UNCTUOUS, (C) is not a suitable choice. AGITATED involves a loss of calmness; there are nervous and emotional signs of emotional excitement. This is quite the opposite of the smug exterior of an unctuous person. (D) is the correct answer. INGRATIATING suggests an attempt to win favor; often the INGRATIATING person uses a servile approach to win favor. A smooth exterior, like that implied with UNCTUOUS, makes the two similar — not opposite. (E) is not the right answer.

38. **(D)**

INVIDIOUS means likely to give offense, tending to excite ill will. REPUGNANT means distasteful, repellent, hostile; it is more similar than opposite to INVIDIOUS. (A) should not be selected. OBSCURE means not clearly understood. The word does not have the opposite relationship sought; (B) should not be selected. RANSOMED means redeemed, delivered. It is not an antonym for INVIDIOUS. RECONCILABLE means capable of being brought into harmony; it is quite the opposite of INVIDIOUS, which means likely to give offense. (D) is, therefore, the correct answer. PERTURBED (E) means agitated, disturbed, troubled profoundly; it is not the opposite of INVIDIOUS and should not be selected.

Section 5—Verbal Ability

1. **(D)**
   Any of the initial terms would be appropriate. In this instance, the semicolon is equivalent to "but," so you need to determine which term is most nearly the opposite of *provincial*. COSMOPOLITAN (free from local, provincial, or national ideas or prejudices) is the only word that is opposite in meaning to provincial. (D) is correct. PHILANTHROPIC (A), PROGRESSIVE (B), ENTERPRISING (C), and HEDONISTIC (E) are inappropriate choices.

2. **(C)**
   The situation described is more than just a FACTOR (A), a PART (D), or an EXAMPLE (E). The situation described is the predictable RESULT (C) of not specifically identifying a goal or task and the procedure for attaining and completing it.

3. **(B)**
   (A) is incorrect. Because POTTAGE (or POTAGE) is a thick stew-like soup made of either vegetables alone or meat and vegetables, this answer is not appropriate. (B) is correct; BISQUE is a particularly rich purée, often made of shellfish. (C) is incorrect. BROTH is the liquid in which any meat or vegetable has been boiled. (D) is incorrect. BOUILLON is concentrated and clarified broth of beef or vegetables. (E) is not the correct answer. A SOUFFLÉ is a dish puffed by cooking; a "rich shellfish purée" would not be puffed.

4. **(C)**
   The sentence does not imply that workers and families face different levels of danger; therefore, MODERATE...HAZARDOUS (A), HAZARDOUS...MODERATE (B), MINIMAL...DANGEROUS (D), and DANGEROUS...MODERATE (E) are incorrect. Both officials and their families faced perilous situations; therefore, PERILS...ALSO (C) is the correct answer.

5. **(A)**
   (A) is the correct choice. Facilitating communication among work groups within an organization is specifically a coordination problem; it is not a problem of supervision (B), support (C), retraining (D), or relationship (E).

6. **(C)**

(A) is not the correct answer. IMPASSIVE implies showing or feeling no emotion or sensation. Showing *no* emotion would not be an asset when working with the public. (B) is not the correct answer since indifference would not be an asset to an employee. A STOIC is indifferent to pain or pleasure. (C) is the best answer. PHLEGMATIC implies a temperament or constitution hard to arouse. (D) is incorrect. APATHETIC means lacking normal feeling or interest; indifferent; listless. A person lacking normal feeling or interest would not be an asset for a business. (E) is incorrect; it is not appropriate. STOLID means dull — not the best attribute for a complaint department.

7. **(A)**

(A) is correct. The women would not be likely to support someone who opposes parental leave benefits. (B) is incorrect. A SUPPORTER of parental leave benefits would have many friends among women. (C) is not the correct choice. It's impossible to be an "ACTIVIST *of*"; James would have to be an "ACTIVIST *for*." (D) and (E) are inappropriate choices. A FOE of parental leave benefits would have *many* ENEMIES among women. An ADVOCATE of parental leave benefits would find *many* BACKERS among women.

8. **(B)**

(A) is incorrect. GRADE:SLOPE is a synonymous relationship. (B) is correct. HIGH and LOW are opposites, as are TWEETER (a small loudspeaker for reproducing high frequency sounds) and WOOFER (a large loudspeaker for reproducing low frequency sounds). (C) is incorrect. REPLICATE:DUPLICATE is a synonymous relationship. (D) is incorrect. TUTELAGE:PROTECTION is a synonymous relationship. (E) is incorrect. ISOSCELES:EQUAL is a synonymous relationship.

9. **(B)**

(B) is correct. An ARC is a part, or segment, of a circle's CIRCUMFERENCE. An HOUR is a part of a DAY. MOON:EARTH (A), CABIN:MANSION (C), EXERCISE:REST (D), and KNOWLEDGE: WISDOM (E) do not reflect the part-to-whole relationship.

10. **(A)**

A FACADE is the front or main face of a BUILDING. The corresponding analogy is (A) GRILL:CAR. A GRILL is the front or main face of a CAR. In relation to the other alternatives, a TONGUE is on the top of a SHOE, a SHEATH is around a KNIFE, a PICTURE is in a FRAME, and a HEAD is on top of the BODY.

11. **(D)**

The relationship in this analogy is one of effect. GRASS retards or stops EROSION. The corresponding alternative is (D). A DAM retards or stops WATER. Alternatives (A), (B), (C), and (E) are inaccurate because ROOTS do not retard or stop a TREE, AIR does not retard a TIRE, CLOUDS do not retard RAIN, and BREEZES do not stop a FLAG.

12. **(A)**

(A) is correct. COMMITTED and AVOWED are synonyms. (B) is incorrect. NORMAL and ABERRANT are antonyms. (C) is incorrect. FREE and DEMOCRATIC are a cause-and-effect relationship. (D) is incorrect. VOLUNTARY and MANDATORY are antonyms. (E) is incorrect. SCHOOLED and LEARNED are cause-and-effect relationship.

13. **(B)**

(A) ANGRY:SENSIBILITY is not right because SENSIBILITY (the capacity for physical sensation) can be present simultaneously with ANGER. (B) is correct. To be NERVOUS is to lack POISE. This relationship also exists between FRIGHTENED:CONFIDENCE. To be FRIGHTENED is to lack CONFIDENCE. (C) EMPATHETIC:RATIONALITY is incorrect because a person can be RATIONAL and also be EMPATHETIC. (D) ENERGETIC:ENTHUSIASM is incorrect because an ENERGETIC person does have ENTHUSIASM. (E) CALM:LAZINESS is incorrect because a CALM person may or may not lack LAZINESS.

14. **(D)**

(A) is incorrect. LATENCY:EXPOSITION are antonymous; PLEONASM:VERBIAGE are synonyms that refer to redundancy. (B) is incorrect. INDIGENT and POVERTY are synonyms that refer to being without money. ARGONAUTS and ASTRONAUTS (C) are both navigators of sorts. (D) is correct. INDIGESTED and STRUCTURED are antonyms. INCOHERENCE and IMMISCIBILITY (E) are synonyms that refer to lack of cohesiveness.

15. **(B)**

(A) is incorrect. DECLENSION and ASCENT are antonyms, unlike the example words, which are synonyms. (B) is correct. AGGRANDIZE means to make (appear) greater; AUGMENT means to add to. ABATE-

MENT and EXTENUATION both mean a forgiveness. ADJUNCT and DETRUNCATE (C) are antonyms. INCREMENT and DIMINUTION (D) are antonyms. VINCTURE and SEGREGATION (E) are antonyms.

16. **(A)**

(A) is correct. Both the example and GLUTTONY:VORACITY share similar meanings. (B) is incorrect. TURBAN and HAT have a member:class relationship. (C) is incorrect. VIM means energy and is the opposite of FATIGUE. (D) is incorrect. A PLOVER is a type of SANDPIPER. (E) is incorrect. A PEREGRINE is a kind of FALCON.

17. **(E)**

(E) is correct. The author was attempting to portray the events leading up to the Revolutionary War. In the final sentence, after some detail, the author states "...the War for Independence had begun." There was no attempt at diplomacy by the Colonists (A). Answer (B) is incorrect. General Thomas Gage probably did overreact, but that was not the theme of the selection. Even though nationalism had united most colonists (C), the author does not mention this point. (D) is incorrect. The author does state this premise in the first sentence, but does not enlarge the theme.

18. **(B)**

The correct answer is (B). A disrespect for the redcoats can be inferred from the information the author presents about the manner in which the soldiers entered Lexington, the numbers of redcoats, and the redcoats' retreat back to Boston. The passage neither stated nor implied that the author admired the redcoats' fighting ability (A), scorned their readiness (D), sympathized with their lack of heart (E), or criticized their lack of military discipline (C).

19. **(E)**

(E) is correct. War could not be averted, and the time of mere protest had ended. In relation to (A), there is no statement in the selection that the colonists were better fighters, even though this could be inferred since they were outnumbered and eventually drove the British back to Boston. (B) is wrong because even though the colonists knew of General Gage's intentions almost instantaneously, the author makes no statement about spies. (C) is also incorrect. There was a supply depot at Concord but the author does not comment on the preparation of the colonists and a communications network. (D) is incorrect because there were many colonial spokesmen for the revolution and the author speaks of only two in the area at the time.

20. **(A)**

The author begins the article with Faraday's accomplishments in spite of a lack of formal education. The implication here is regard and admiration for this person. In relation to alternatives (B) and (C), the author implies neither disrespect nor distrust. In relation to alternative (E), the selection is written in objective terms without any intellectual or emotional identification with the subject. In relation to alternative (D), the author does not minimize Faraday's accomplishments or imply that any of Faraday's actions was inferior to those of others.

21. **(C)**

(C) was not an accomplishment of Faraday's; this process was first accomplished by Sir Humphry Davy. Conversion of electricity and magnetic forces into mechanical energy (A), the devision of methods of liquefy gases (B), the discovery of benzene (D), and the making of magnesium-produced electricity were accomplished by Faraday.

22. **(E)**

The author's main point is that Faraday was a self-educated genius (E). The author makes a point of discussing his contributions, as well as Faraday's lack of formal education, and the educational opportunities made available to him during his apprenticeship with the bookbinder.

23. **(C)**

(C) is correct. The author does not explain that gas is liquefied by lowering the temperature. The passage provides information about the process of electrolysis (A), how Faraday produced mechanical energy (B), how an electromagnetic field may be produced (D), and the basic principle for the electric motor (E).

24. **(E)**

(A) is incorrect. VALENCE is not discussed in the passage. (B) is incorrect. ANODE is not discussed in the passage, although Faraday did coin the term. ELECTRODE (C) is not discussed in the passage, although Faraday did coin the term. ELECTROLYTE (D) is not discussed in the passage, although Faraday did coin the term. (E) is correct. The passage ends by mentioning Faraday's coinage of ELECTROLYSIS.

25. **(B)**

(B) is correct. Becoming Director of the Royal Institution was a step along Faraday's professional career path. The actions identified in (A), (C), and (E) each involve his disbelief in and declining of worldly rewards as part of his belief system; and alternative (D) presents a clear moral choice again based upon his personal convictions.

26. **(D)**

(D) is correct. It was the apprenticeship to the bookbinder that allowed him the opportunity to read and to attend scientific lectures that eventually developed his association with Sir Humphry Davy. (A) is incorrect; his birthplace evidently played little part. (B) and (C) are also incorrect. Being one of ten children and experiencing poverty may have meant that apprenticing family members was forthcoming, but these were not the events that made an impact. (E) is incorrect; the association between the two men came after the interest in science had begun.

27. **(A)**

(A) is correct. The selection is a brief history of the life and work of the scientist Michael Faraday. (B) is incorrect; electrolysis is only one part of the selection. (C) is incorrect; it can be assumed that most of the work specifically was done at the Royal Institution, but this was not stated. (D) is incorrect. Sir Humphry Davy's relationship with Faraday is not the focus of the passage. (E) is incorrect; electromagnetic induction was described but was never referred to by name except in paragraph one.

28. **(C)**

SAD (A) is an emotional state of being. UNFRUITFUL (B) means unproductive. (C) is correct. FORTUITOUS means lucky; the opposite is UNLUCKY. DISENCHANTED (D) is an emotional state of being. MISERABLE (E) is an emotional state of being.

29. **(B)**

EXALTED (A) is an adjective meaning noble or elevated. The adjective ARCHAIC comes from the Greek word for ancient. Its opposite in the list given is MODERN (B). ANGELIC (C) refers to a beautiful, good, angel-like person. (D) INVISIBLE means unable to be seen or imperceptible. (E) NOBLE means famous or renowned.

30. **(C)**

EXUDE (A) means to ooze or to radiate. (B) EXTEND means to stretch forth. To INSERT means to put or fit into something else. Its opposite is EXTRACT (C), meaning to draw out, as to extract a tooth. (D) EXPLORE means to examine carefully. EXTINGUISH (E) means to put out or destroy, as one might put out a fire.

31. **(C)**
    DARING (A) means fearless, bold. TEDIOUS (B) means long and dull, tiresome. LOQUACIOUS means very talkative. Its opposite is SILENT (C). WEALTHY (D) means rich. (E) is incorrect. HAUGHTY means showing great pride in oneself and contempt for others, arrogant.

32. **(E)**
    PASSEL (A) means a group, especially a fairly large group. DIVERSE (B) means different or varied. LEGION (C) means a large number, a multitude. PROFUSE (D) means giving or given freely and abundantly. MYRIAD carries the meaning of a great number of persons or things. Its opposite here is INDIVIDUAL (E), meaning existing as a separate thing or being, or relating to a single person or thing.

33. **(B)**
    INSUBORDINATE (A) means disrespectful. (B) is correct. The adjective NEFARIOUS means wicked. Its opposite in the list given is GOOD. DANGEROUS (C) means having potential to harm. NERVOUS (D) means jumpy. STUBBORN (E) is an unrelated personal characteristic.

34. **(E)**
    CLARIFY (A) means to make clear. MANDATE (B) means to order. INSIST (C) means to take a stand and maintain it. AMEND (D) means to improve. (E) is correct. AMELIORATE conveys the idea to make or become better, to improve. Its opposite in the list given is WORSEN.

35. **(E)**
    ALTERNATIVE (A) is one of several possible choices. FUTILE (B) means useless; as in a futile attempt. PREREQUISITE (C) is something required beforehand as a necessary condition, for instance, a French I class would be a prerequisite for a French II class. ABHORRENT (D) carries the meaning detestable, as an abhorrent action. REQUISITE is an adjective meaning necessary or required. Its opposite is SUPERFLUOUS (E), meaning unnecessary or excessive.

36. **(C)**
    PECULIAR (A) means deviating from the customary. PASSIONATE (B) means fired with intense feeling. PARSIMONIOUS means excessively frugal. A parsimonious person is often referred to as a miserly person, a stingy person, or a tightfisted person. Its opposite is PRODIGAL (C). A prodigal person is one who is excessively extravagant in relation to

money. PATRONIZING (D) means treating in an indulgent manner. PERNICIOUS (E) means extremely destructive or harmful.

37. **(E)**
OBDURATE means hardened in feeling, unyielding. AFFABLE (A) means gracious, courteous, sociable, amiable. It is dissimilar from OBDU-RATE but not the exact opposite. UNSAVORY means morally offensive. (B) is not an antonym for OBDURATE. PREVARICATING means telling falsehoods. (C) is not directly related to OBDURATE and should not be selected as the antonym. CREDULOUS means believable. (D) is not the opposite sought. PENITENT means sorry for sins or faults. It is the opposite of OBDURATE. (E) is the antonym sought.

38. **(D)**
INSIPID (A) means not tasty. OBTUSE means blunt. HUMBLE (B) means unpretentious or moderate. MATERNAL (C) means like a mother. (D) is correct. TASTY is the opposite of INSIPID. JEALOUS (E) means resentfully envious.

Section 6—Quantitative Ability

1. **(A)**
    (A) is correct. Solve for x. Note that 81 can be factored into its prime factors as

    $81 = 3 \times 3 \times 3 \times 3$ or $3^x = 3^4$. Therefore, $x = 4$.

    Choices (B), (C), and (D) are incorrect. Check the answer by placing the value of Column B into the given equation, 3^x.

2. **(D)**
    (D) is correct. Since no information about the value of x or y is given, no relationship between the two quantities can be determined. For example, if $x = 0$, then $y > 2$. If $y = 0$, then $x > 4$.

3. **(B)**
    Choices (A), (C), (D), and (E) are incorrect. The median of a set of numbers arranged in an increasing or decreasing order is the middle value of a set of odd number values or the average of the two middle numbers if the number of numbers is even. The arithmetic average is the sum of the values divided by the number of variables. (B) is correct. The median of a set of numbers arranged in an increasing or decreasing order is the middle value of a set of odd number values or the average of the two middle numbers if the number of numbers is even. The arithmetic average is the sum of the values divided by the number of variables. In this problem the average income = the sum ÷ 5.

    $$\frac{(\$8,000 + \$9,000 + \$2,000 + \$10,000 + \$6,000)}{5} = \frac{\$35,000}{5} = \$7,000$$

    Rearrange the numbers in decreasing order:

    $10,000 $9,000 $8,000 $6,000 $2,000.

    Therefore, the median is $8,000. The median > the average.

4. **(B)**
    (B) is correct. To compare the two rational expressions requires rewriting them with a common denominator.

    In this problem the least common denominator of b and $(b - 1)$ is $b(b - 1)$. Rewriting both expressions with the same denominator

$$\frac{a}{b} = \frac{a(b-1)}{b(b-1)} = \frac{ab-a}{b(b-1)}$$

and

$$\frac{a+1}{b-1} = \frac{b(a+1)}{b(b-1)} = \frac{ab+b}{b(b-1)}$$

Compare $ab - a$ to $ab + b$ or $-a$ to b. It is given that both are positive integers and $b \geq 2$. Since the value of a is subtracted from the expression in Column A and a value of $b \geq 2$ is added to the expression in Column B, the quantity in Column B is larger than the quantity in Column A. Another solution is simply to substitute in a value for B. If $B = 2$, Column A is $a/2$ and Column B is $a + 1$.

5. **(B)**
   Choices (A), (C), and (D) are incorrect. Reduce the fraction in Column A to its simplest terms. Then compare it to the fraction in Column B. Make sure they both have the same denominator. (B) is correct. Reduce the fraction in Column A to its simplest terms to yield:

$$\frac{120}{200} = \frac{2\times2\times2\times3\times5}{2\times2\times2\times5\times5} = \frac{3}{5}$$

Since the reduced fraction in Column A has the same denominator as the fraction in Column B, the fraction can be compared directly. $3/5 < 4/5$.

6. **(C)**
   Choices (A), (B), and (D) are incorrect. Find the rate or dollars/hour to find the dollars earned in $(h + 20)$ hours. Hours cannot be compared to dollars. (C) is correct. To compare the two quantities the rate or dollars/hour is needed to find how much is earned in $(h + 20)$ hours.

$$\text{The rate} = \frac{d}{h} \text{ and the amount earned} = \left(\frac{d}{h}\right) \times (h+20)$$

$$= \frac{dh}{h} + \frac{20d}{h}$$

$$= d + \frac{20d}{h} \text{ dollars.}$$

Therefore, the quantities in Column A and Column B are equal.

7. **(A)**

(A) is correct. In any triangle, if the sides of the triangle are not congruent, then the larger angle lies opposite the longer side. Let $m \angle x$ denote the measure of angle x. Given $b > e$, then the $m \angle B >$ the $m \angle E$. Choices (B), (C), and (D) are incorrect. Remember that in any triangle, if the sides of the triangle are not congruent, then the larger angle lies opposite the longer side.

8. **(B)**

Choices (A), (C), and (D) are incorrect. Change the ratio of boys to girls to the number of boys in the class. Compare the number of boys in each class by obtaining the common denominator and looking at the value in the numerator. (B) is correct. Let x be the number of students in each of the two classes. It is given that the ratio of boys to girls in Mr. Good's class is 3 : 4. This means 3 out of every 7 students in Mr. Good's class are boys or $3x/7$ boys. Similarly, the ratio of boys to girls in Ms. Garcia's class is 4 : 5. This means 4 out of every 9 students in Ms. Garcia's class are boys or $4x/9$ boys.

To compare $3x/7$ to $4x/9$ find the least common denominator. The LCM is 63.

$$\frac{3x}{7} = \frac{9(3x)}{63} = \frac{27x}{63} \qquad \frac{4x}{9} = \frac{7(4x)}{63} = \frac{28x}{63}$$

$27x/63 < 28x/63$. Therefore, the quantity in Column B is larger than that in Column A.

9. **(C)**

(C) is correct. Let $m \angle \alpha$ denote the measure of angle α. Since lines l and m are intersecting at point P, angles α and θ are supplementary angles, or their sum equals $180°$. $m \angle \alpha + m \angle \theta = 180°$.

Given $m \angle \theta$ is 3 times the $m \angle \alpha$ or $m \angle \theta = 3m \angle \alpha$.

$$
\begin{aligned}
m \angle \alpha + m \angle \theta &= 180° \\
m \angle \alpha + 3m \angle \alpha &= 180° \\
4m \angle \alpha &= 180° \\
m \angle \alpha &= 45° \\
m \angle \theta &= 3m \angle \alpha \\
&= 3(45°) \\
&= 135°
\end{aligned}
$$

Therefore, the two quantities are equal. Choices (A), (B), and (D) are incorrect. There is enough information given to find the measure of the angle in Column A. Remember that the sum of supplementary angles equals 180°.

10. **(C)**

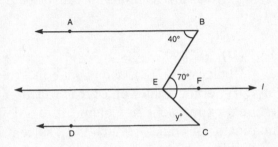

Choices (A), (B), and (D) are incorrect. Remember that alternate interior angles are equal. Recheck which angles were used to find the measure of $\angle y$. (C) is correct. Let $m \angle a$ represent the measure of angle a; and E and F be points on line l as shown in the figure. Since line l is parallel to ray $\overrightarrow{BA}$ and line BE is a transversal, angles BEF and ABE are alternate interior angles. This means that $m \angle BEF = m \angle ABE = 40°$.

Given that $m \angle BEF + m \angle FEC = 70°$, then
$$40° + m \angle FEC = 70°$$
$$m \angle FEC = 30°$$

It is given that line l is parallel to ray $\overrightarrow{CD}$ and line $\overleftrightarrow{EC}$ is a transversal. Therefore, $\angle FEC$ and $\angle ECD$ are alternate interior angles. This means $m \angle ECD = 30° = y$. Therefore, the angle in Column A = the angle in Column B.

11. **(A)**

(A) is correct. $^1/_x = \sqrt{0.0016}/5$ could be treated like a proportion. The product of the extremes equals the product of the means. To obtain

$$\sqrt{0.0016}x = 5(1)$$
$$0.04x = 5$$
$$x = 125$$

Therefore, $x > 12.5$ in Column B. Choices (B), (C), and (D) are incorrect. Recheck the square root of 0.0016 and the value calculated for x.

12. **(D)**

(D) is correct. From the information given, $\angle CD$ is perpendicular to $\angle AB$. This means $\angle CDB$ and $\angle CDA$ are right angles and triangles $\triangle CBD$ and $\triangle CDA$ are right triangles. Since the sum of the measures of the three interior angles of a triangle is 180°, and the measure of a right angle is 90°,

$$x + y = 90° \text{ and } w + z = 90°.$$

This does not give any information about the value of $x - y$ or the value of $w - z$. Thus, the relationship cannot be determined from the information given.

13. **(D)**

Choices (A), (B), and (C) are incorrect. This is true for some values of x. Try some values of x greater than $-^{19}\!/_7$. (D) is correct. First, add the rational expressions in Column A. To do this find the least common denominator of 4 and 3, which is 12 since it is the smallest number divisible by both 4 and 3.

$$\frac{3(x-3)}{3(4)} + \frac{4(x+7)}{4(3)}$$

$$= \frac{3x-9}{12} + \frac{4x+28}{12}$$

$$= \frac{3x-9+4x+28}{12}$$

$$= \frac{7x+19}{12}$$

So the rational expression in Column A is $(7x + 19)/12$ and in Column B is $(7x + 19)/7$. Compare the values for positive and negative values of x. If $(7x + 19)$ is a positive value, then Column B will be larger, but if $(7x + 19)$ is a negative value, then Column A will be larger. Therefore, there is not enough information given to solve the problem.

14. **(A)**

(A) is correct. Given that $BC = CD = BD$, triangle BCD is equilateral, and each of the three angles is equal to 60°. Since it is also given that $BC \perp AC$, it can be deduced from the figure that:

$$m \angle BCD + m \angle ACD = 60° + m \angle ACD = 90° \text{ or } m \angle ACD = 30°.$$

The $m \angle ADC$ can be found since it is a supplementary angle with $\angle BDC$.

$$m \angle ADC + m \angle BDC = m \angle ADC + 60° = 180° \text{ or } m \angle ADC = 120°.$$

The $m \angle DAC$ can be found by adding the angles in triangle $ADC = 180°$.

$$m \angle DAC + m \angle ADC + m \angle ACD = 180°.$$

$$m \angle DAC + 120° + 30° = 180° \text{ or } m \angle DAC = 30°.$$

Thus, segment AC is greater than segment CD, since segment AC is opposite a larger angle (120°) than segment CD (angle of 30°). Therefore, Column A > Column B. Choices (B), (C), and (D) are incorrect. Use the given information to find the angles of triangle DAC. Remember that the segment opposite the larger angle is larger than the segment opposite the smaller angle.

15. **(A)**
    (A) is correct. Find the roots of the quadratic equation in Column A.

$x^2 + 3x + 2 = 0$ may be factored as

$$(x + 2)(x + 1) = 0$$
$$x + 1 = 0$$
$$x = -1$$

Solve for the roots

$$x + 2 = 0$$
$$x = -2$$

The roots are –2 and –1. The product of the roots = (–2) (–1) = 2, which is larger than the quantity in Column B. Choices (B), (C), and (D) are incorrect. It is true that one root is less than the quantity in Column B. Find the product of the roots in Column A.

16. **(D)**
    Choices (A), (B), (C), and (E) are incorrect. Create an algebraic formula to find the number of tickets bought at the box office. Recheck the solution with the given information. (D) is correct. Let x be the number of tickets bought at the box office. Then the number of tickets purchased in advance equals $(1,200 - x)$. Set up the formula with the rest of the information as follows:

$$5(1,200 - x) + 7x = 6,700$$
$$6,000 - 5x + 7x = 6,700$$
$$2x = 6,700 - 6,000$$
$$2x = 700$$
$$x = 350$$

17. **(D)**
    Choices (A), (B), (C) and (E) are incorrect. Rewrite the equations and compare to the statements given. Be careful when simplifying. (D) is

correct. One method to solve this problem is to rewrite the equations and compare the results.

$$2a + 2b = 1 \qquad \text{and} \qquad 6a - 2b = 5$$
$$2(a + b) = 1 \qquad\qquad\qquad 2(3a - b) = 5$$
$$(a + b) = \frac{1}{2} \qquad\qquad\qquad (3a - b) = \frac{5}{2}$$

Therefore $(a + b) < (3a - b)$ since $\frac{1}{2} < \frac{5}{2}$.

Another method to solve this problem is to solve for a and b:

$$2a + 2b = 1$$
$$+6a - 2b = 5$$
$$8a + 0b = 6$$
$$8a = 6$$
$$a = \frac{6}{8} = \frac{3}{4}$$
$$2\left(\frac{3}{4}\right) + 2b = 1$$
$$2b = 1 - 1\frac{1}{2}$$
$$2b = -\frac{1}{2}$$
$$b = -\frac{1}{4}$$

These numbers can then be substituted into the equation given.

18. **(C)**

(C) is correct. One way to solve the problem is to find the value of x, then substitute it into $(x + 2)$. Another way is to factor the equation as

$$6x + 12 = 5$$
$$6(x + 2) = 5$$
$$(x + 2) = \frac{5}{6}. \quad \text{This gives the answer directly.}$$

Choices (A), (B), and (D) are incorrect. Solve for x and find the value of $(x + 2)$. (E) is incorrect. Solve for x and find the value of $(x + 2)$.

19. **(B)**

Choices (A), (D), and (E) are incorrect. Find the price per ounce for the given prices. Compare the prices. (B) is correct. Divide each price by the number of ounces in each price to obtain the following prices per ounce for the given prices:

$$\frac{16}{10} \quad \frac{3}{2} \quad \frac{7}{4} \quad \frac{34}{20} \quad \frac{13}{8}$$

Then find the least common denominator, 40, to be able to compare the prices.

$$\frac{64}{40} \quad \frac{60}{40} \quad \frac{70}{40} \quad \frac{68}{40} \quad \frac{65}{40}$$

Since the smallest fraction is $^{60}/_{40}$, it follows that the most economical price among the given prices is 2 oz. for 3¢.

20. **(A)**

(A) is correct. Equivalent proportions have equal cross-multiplication products. The cross-multiplication products for the original proportion, $^p/_q = ^r/_s$, For this proportion:

$$\frac{p+q}{p} = \frac{r+s}{r}$$

then
$$(p + q)r = p(r + s)$$
$$pr + qr = pr + ps$$
$$qr = ps$$

Therefore, this proportion is equivalent to the original one.

21. **(D)**

(A) is incorrect. This is the average for 1980 to 1982. (B) is incorrect. This answer is the mode, or the most frequently occurring amount in the observations. The average, or arithmetic mean, is equal to the sum of all observations divided by the number of observations. (C) is incorrect. This is the average of 1979 and 1983, not the years inclusive. (D) is correct. The average, or arithmetic mean, is equal to the sum of all observations divided by the number of observations. In this problem the observations are the amount of advertising for the years 1979 through 1983:

$$20,000 + 60,000 + 40,000 + 60,000 + 90,000 = 270,000$$

The number of observations is equal to 5.

Therefore, the average $= \dfrac{270,000}{5} = 54,000.$

(E) is incorrect. The average, or arithmetic mean, is equal to the sum of all observations divided by the number of observations.

22. **(B)**

(A) is incorrect. This is the increase in 1984 but it is not the largest increase. Make a chart of the years that show increases in sales over the previous year and find the greatest increase. (B) is correct. Make a chart of the years that show increases in sales over the previous year and find the greatest increase. Note that the graph shows an increase in sales during each of the years 1982, 1983, 1984, and 1988 as follows:

Year	Increase in sales over the previous year (in dollars)
1982	$310,000 - 200,000 = 110,000$
1983	$330,000 - 310,000 = 20,000$
1984	$400,000 - 330,000 = 70,000$
1988	$340,000 - 300,000 = 40,000$

The amount of greatest increase in sales from one year to the next was $110,000. (C) is incorrect. The question did not ask for the total increase from 1981 to 1988. Make a chart of the years that shows increases in sales over the previous year and find the greatest increase. (D) is incorrect. The increase is for 1980 and it was not included in the years to check. Make a chart of the years that shows increases in sales over the previous year and find the greatest increase. (E) is incorrect. This increase is for 1988 but is not the largest from 1981 to 1988 inclusive. Make a chart of the years that shows increases in sales over the previous year and find the greatest increase.

23. **(E)**

(E) is correct. By calculating 25% of the amount of sales for each year, and then comparing the result with the amount of advertising for that year, this question can be answered. Dividing the amount of sales for each year by 4 is equivalent to taking 25% of the amount of sales.

From the graph, the following chart can be obtained:

Year	Sales (in dollars) divided by 4	Advertising (in dollars)
1979	37.5	20
1980	52.5	60
1981	50.0	40
1982	77.5	60
1983	82.5	90
1984	100.0	70
1985	95.0	80
1986	85.0	70
1987	75.0	60
1988	85.0	80

The table indicates that in only two years was advertising equal to or greater than 25% of sales.

24. **(A)**

(A) is correct. To calculate the percent change of sales for each year over the previous year use the formula:

$$\text{percent change} = \frac{\text{change in sales}}{\text{sales of previous year}}$$

$$= \frac{\text{sales of this year} - \text{sales of previous year}}{\text{sales of previous year}}$$

The percent change for (A) 1982

$$= \frac{310,000 - 200,000}{200,000} = \frac{110,000}{200,000} = \frac{11}{20} = 55\%.$$

Similarly 1984 is 21%, 1985 is –5%, 1986 is –11%, and 1987 is 13%. Therefore, the largest amount of change was in 1982.

25. **(C)**

Choices (A), (B), (D), and (E) are incorrect. It is true that advertising increased over the previous year, but the sales increased, which was not what the question asked for. Carefully read what is required for advertising and sales to do over the previous year. (C) is correct. Making a table shows what happened in the years listed as possible choices.

	Change	
Year	Sales	Advertising
1980	Increase	Increase
1983	Increase	Increase
1985	Decrease	Increase
1987	Decrease	Decrease
1988	Increase	Increase

The table shows that only in 1985 did advertising increase while sales decreased.

26. **(B)**

Choices (A), (C), (D), and (E) are incorrect. Name line $\overleftrightarrow{AB}$ the x-axis and line $\overleftrightarrow{CG}$ the y-axis and use the midpoint formula to find the perpendicular bisector. The point will be on $\overleftrightarrow{CG}$, but G is not the midpoint. (B) is correct. By naming line $\overleftrightarrow{AB}$ the x-axis and line $\overleftrightarrow{CG}$ the y-axis obtain the coordinate plane, or the xy-plane. Using the midpoint formula is one way to find the perpendicular bisector.

$$\text{Midpoint formula, } MP = \left[\frac{(x_1 + x_2)}{2}, \frac{(y_1 + y_2)}{2} \right]$$

Know that the midpoint will be the origin, (0, 0), and (x_1, y_1) is point C, (0, 8).

Find (x_2, y_2).

For x_2, $0 = \dfrac{(0 + x_2)}{2}$ For y_2, $0 = \dfrac{(8 + y_2)}{2}$

$0 = 0 + x_2$ $0 = 8 + y_2$

$0 = x_2$ $-8 = y_2$

Therefore, the point P is (0, −8) or F.

27. **(E)**

(E) is correct. Label the vertices of the given figure A, B, C, D, E, F, and the segment $\overline{DE}$ to meet $\overline{AB}$ at G, and let mAB denote the length of segment $\overline{AB}$. Since all the segments in the figure meet at right angles, quadrilaterals AGEF and GBCD are rectangles.

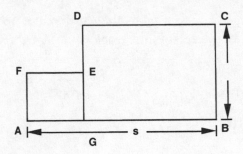

$$m\overline{DE} + m\overline{EG} = m\overline{CB} = r$$

$m\overline{EG} = m\overline{AF}$ since $AGEF$ is a rectangle. Then $m\overline{AF} + m\overline{ED} = r$.

Also, $m\overline{DC} = m\overline{GB}$ since $GBCD$ is a rectangle, and $m\overline{FE} = m\overline{AG}$ since $AGEF$ is a rectangle.

$$m\overline{DC} + m\overline{EF} = m\overline{GB} + m\overline{AG} = m\overline{AB} = s$$

The perimeter of a closed polygon is equal to the sum of the measure of its segments. The perimeter of the given figure is equal to

$$m\overline{AB} + m\overline{BC} + m\overline{CD} + m\overline{DE} + m\overline{EF} + m\overline{AF}$$
$$= m\overline{AB} + m\overline{BC} + m\overline{DC} + m\overline{EF} + \left(m\overline{ED} + m\overline{AF}\right)$$
$$= s + r + s + r$$
$$= 2s + 2r$$

28. **(A)**

   (A) is correct. n can be an odd number or an even number. $2n$ is an even number and $2n + 3$ is odd because even + odd = odd. (B) is incorrect. n can be an odd number or an even number. $2n$ is always an even number. (C) is incorrect. n can be an odd number or an even number. $2n$ is an even number and $2n + 2$ is even because even + even = even. (D) is incorrect. n can be an odd number or an even number. When n is odd, $3n$ is odd (odd × odd = odd). But this is not true if n is an even number, since $3n$ is even (odd × even = even). (E) is incorrect. n can be an odd number or an even number. When n is even, $n + 1$ will be odd. But this is not true if n is an odd number, since $n + 1$ is even.

29. **(E)**

   Choices (A), (B), (C), and (D) are incorrect. Use Distance = Rate × Time and set up an algebraic equation to solve for the time. Let t be the time, in hours, it takes the car to catch up with the postal truck. Then the time of travel of the truck should be $(t + {}^{24}\!/_{60})$ hours. (E) is correct. Use Distance = Rate × Time and set up an algebraic equation to solve for the time. Let t be the time, in hours, it takes the car to catch up with the postal truck. Then the time of travel of the truck should be $(t + {}^{24}\!/_{60})$ hours.

Using the distance formula:

Truck: $d_t = 40(t + 0.4)$

$= 40t + 16$

Car: $d_c = 50t$

But the distance traveled by the truck and car will be the same, so

$$d_t = d_c$$
$$40t + 16 = 50t$$
$$16 = 10t$$
$$t = 1.6$$

Thus, it takes the car 1.6 hours to catch up with the postal truck.

30. **(C)**

Choices (A), (B), (D), and (E) are incorrect. Try to factor the numbers that are under the square root sign and perform the indicated operations. (C) is correct. Factor the numbers that are under the square root sign to be able to perform the indicated operations.

$$\sqrt{75} - 3\sqrt{48} + \sqrt{147} = \sqrt{(25)(3)} - 3\sqrt{(16)(3)} + \sqrt{(49)(3)}$$
$$= 5\sqrt{3} - 3(4)\sqrt{3} + 7\sqrt{3}$$
$$= 5\sqrt{3} - 12\sqrt{3} + 7\sqrt{3}$$
$$= (5 - 12 + 7)\sqrt{3}$$
$$= (0)\sqrt{3}$$
$$= 0$$

GRE
Graduate Record Examination

Practice
Test 4

Section 1

TIME: 45 Minutes
Choose 1 of 2 Essays†

ESSAY QUESTION ONE

DIRECTIONS: Present your perspective on the issue below by using relevant reasons and/or examples to support your views. Remember, there is no one "correct" response to the essay topic. Before starting, read the essay topic and its question(s).

Many parents and educators believe that a 180-day school year is not enough. Statistics showing the educational backsliding of many students from June to September and crime reports claiming increased teen activity during summer months are used to support this idea. Local administrators often oppose the wall-to-wall calendar on the basis of current funding inadequacies, while teachers cite their disciplinary problems with vacation-starved students.

Which captures your interest, the projected benefits of year-round public education or the reasons against it? Defend your position, citing relevant reasons and/or examples taken from your own experience, reading, or personal observations.

STOP

Do not go on until you are instructed to do so. Use any remaining time to check your work on this portion of the test.

---

† On the actual test, you will have a choice between two essay topics. You have to write only one essay. To give you the most practice possible we have supplied sample essays for both questions in order to show you the differences between essays that receive a perfect score and those that score less.

TIME: 45 Minutes
Choose 1 of 2 Essays†

ESSAY QUESTION TWO

DIRECTIONS: Present your perspective on the issue below by using relevant reasons and/or examples to support your views. Remember, there is no one "correct" response to the essay topic. Before starting, read the essay topic and its question(s).

The study of the past reveals that the problems of humankind are universal. That is, people in different eras have consistently experienced the same hardships, difficulties, and sources of contention.

Do you agree with this statement? Explain your position using your own experience, observations, and ideas.

STOP

Do not go on until you are instructed to do so. Use any remaining time to check your work on this portion of the test.

---

† **On the actual test, you will have a choice between two essay topics. You have to write only one essay. To give you the most practice possible we have supplied sample essays for both questions in order to show you the differences between essays that receive a perfect score and those that score less.**

Section 2

TIME: 30 Minutes
1 Essay

DIRECTIONS: Critique the following argument by considering its logical soundness.

While the prohibition of liquor failed in America in the 1920s, now may be the time to license the consumption of alcohol. Our culture's advocacy of drinking causes many to leave unexamined the role of alcohol in their lives. Alcohol is a major factor in our national health care crisis, and statistics show that liquor is the leading accomplice to violent crimes. The consumption license could be revoked after alcohol-related crimes and accidents. Its written examination would require drinkers to become educated about alcohol's devastating effects on the human body and our society as a whole.

Discuss the degree to which you find this argument logically persuasive. In presenting your perspective, be certain to analyze the argument's use of evidence and line of reasoning. Also discuss what, if anything, would make the argument more solid and convincing or would assist you to better judge its conclusion.

STOP

If time remains, you may go back and check your work.

Section 3

TIME: 30 Minutes
          38 Questions

DIRECTIONS: Each of the given sentences has blank spaces which indicate words omitted. Choose the best combination of words which fit into the meaning and structure within the context of the sentence.

1. The sustenance was given so _____ that it did not _____ the patient with new life and vigor.

    (A) infrequently...imbue   (D) sporadically...inoculate

    (B) uncommonly...infuse   (E) rarely...leaven

    (C) scarcely...suffuse

2. Ages of fierceness have suppressed what is naturally kindly in the _____ of ordinary men and women.

    (A) condition   (D) disposition

    (B) character   (E) evolution

    (C) phenomenon

3. His lonely bachelor life consisted of _____ living and caring for his property.

    (A) parsimonious   (D) paltry

    (B) exorbitant   (E) prudent

    (C) prodigal

4. The taxi driver saved the woman from a burning car, proving himself a(n) _____ example of the human race.

   (A) singular   (D) subjugated

   (B) amoral   (E) officious

   (C) malfeasant

5. The effect of the internal strain and instability on his system was, over time, _____.

   (A) invidious   (D) abhorrent

   (B) compatible   (E) congenial

   (C) alluring

6. The rational mind of a(n) _____ and _____ person is by nature guided by his own theories and believes "What must be, will be."

   (A) irresolute...authoritarian   (D) capricious...dogmatic

   (B) determined...dogmatic   (E) recidivist...vacillating

   (C) doctrinaire...authoritarian

7. To remain at _____ with his wife seemed to him almost a disaster.

   (A) disparity   (D) misogamy

   (B) transcendency   (E) variance

   (C) concord

DIRECTIONS: In the following questions, a related pair of words is followed by five more pairs of words. Select the pair that best expresses the same relationship as that expressed in the original pair.

---

8. ESCHATOLOGY:FINALITY::

   (A) estuary:inlet   (D) geometry:lines

   (B) escrow:document   (E) empiricism:observations

   (C) health:exercise

9. AFFABLE:FRIENDLY::

   (A) fun:smile
   (B) amicable:congenial
   (C) hilarious:delight
   (D) speak:conversation
   (E) outspoken:taciturn

10. BANDAGE:GAUZE::

   (A) labyrinth:confusion
   (B) cement:gravel
   (C) meter:prosody
   (D) timbre:sound
   (E) metal:gold

11. COURAGE:GALLANTRY::

   (A) cowardice:timidity
   (B) poltroonery:fortitude
   (C) chivalry:pusillanimity
   (D) anxiety:solicitude
   (E) agitation:perturbation

12. PRIDE:HAUGHTINESS::

   (A) arrogance:submission
   (B) abasement:crestless
   (C) affability:supercilious
   (D) vainglory:pomposity
   (E) diplomatic:inconsonant

13. CALORIE:HEAT::

   (A) sand:cement
   (B) succumb:yield
   (C) metronome:music
   (D) calipers:diameter
   (E) retaliation:forgiveness

14. STARS:CONSTELLATION::

   (A) sky:planets
   (B) vitamins:food
   (C) television:telephone
   (D) continent:nations
   (E) air:oxygen

15. HALCYON:MARTIAL::

   (A) peaceful:warlike
   (B) evil:tyranny

(C) wash:dirty

(D) auspicious:fanciful

(E) poor:pittance

16. ALLUDE:HINT::

   (A) shy:conspicuous

   (D) self-conscious:assertive

   (B) boisterous:obstreperous

   (E) infer:deduce

   (C) intelligent:sagacious

DIRECTIONS: Each passage is followed by questions based on its content. After reading a passage, choose the best answer to each question. Answer all questions based on what is stated or implied in that passage.

The major debilitating symptoms of Alzheimer's disease include serious forgetfulness — particularly about recent events — and confusion. At first, the individual experiences only minor and almost imperceptible symptoms that are often attributed to emotional upsets or other physical illnesses. Gradually, however, the person becomes more forgetful and this may be reported by anxious relatives. The person may neglect to turn off the oven, may misplace things, may recheck to see if a task was done, may take longer to complete a chore that was previously routine, or may repeat already answered questions. As the disease progresses, memory loss and such changes in personality, mood, and behavior as confusion, irritability, restlessness, and agitation, are likely to appear. Judgment, concentration, orientation, writing, reading, speech, motor behavior, and naming of objects may also be affected. Even when a loving and caring family is available to give support, the victim of Alzheimer's disease is most likely to spend his or her last days in a nursing home or long-term care institution. At this time, there is no cure.

17. The author's purpose for writing this passage is

   (A) to demonstrate how forgetfulness is the first stage of Alzheimer's disease.

   (B) to illustrate how the family of an Alzheimer's patient is affected.

   (C) to document the typical progression of Alzheimer's disease.

(D) to warn that emotional upsets can lead to the development of Alzheimer's disease.

(E) to prove the importance of finding a cure for Alzheimer's disease.

18. This passage implies that victims of Alzheimer's disease will probably

    (A) have only sporadic memories of childhood events.

    (B) retain their cognitive functions.

    (C) lose their cognitive functions without incurring personality and behavioral changes.

    (D) spend their last days at home with their families.

    (E) retain the ability to perform those skills learned prior to the onset of the disease.

19. Serious forgetfulness is described as being debilitating due to

    (A) the length of time needed to complete a task.

    (B) a loss of judgment and concentration.

    (C) the loss of sensory functions.

    (D) the extreme amount of care needed for the patient.

    (E) the inability to read and write.

20. The passage supplies information for verifying which of the following assumptions?

    (A) The Alzheimer's patient has a specific illness at the onset of the disease.

    (B) Skill mastery is retained after cognitive functioning is diminished.

    (C) Personality changes may be a major symptom of the disease.

    (D) Senility and Alzheimer's disease are synonymous.

    (E) Long-term care is necessary for all patients.

A submarine was first used as an offensive weapon during the American Revolutionary War. The *Turtle*, a one-man submersible designed by an American inventor named David Bushnell and hand operated by a screw propeller, attempted to sink a British man-of-war in New York Harbor. The plan was to attach a charge of gunpowder to the ship's bottom with screws and explode it with a time fuse. After repeated failures to force the screws through the copper sheathing of the hull of HMS *Eagle*, the submarine gave up and withdrew, exploding its powder a short distance from the *Eagle*. Although the attack was unsuccessful, it caused the British to move their blockading ships from the harbor to the outer bay.

On 17 February 1864, a Confederate craft, a hand-propelled submersible, carrying a crew of eight men, sank a Federal corvette that was blockading Charleston Harbor. The hit was accomplished by a torpedo suspended ahead of the Confederate Hunley as she rammed the Union frigate *Housatonic*, and is the first recorded instance of a submarine sinking a warship.

The submarine first became a major component in naval warfare during World War I, when Germany demonstrated its full potentialities. Wholesale sinking of Allied shipping by the German U-boats almost swung the war in favor of the Central Powers. Then, as now, the submarine's greatest advantage was that it could operate beneath the ocean surface where detection was difficult. Sinking a submarine was comparatively easy, once it was found — but finding it before it could attack was another matter.

During the closing months of World War I, the Allied Submarine Devices Investigation Committee was formed to obtain from science and technology more effective underwater detection equipment. The committee developed a reasonably accurate device for locating a submerged submarine. This device was a trainable hydrophone, which was attached to the bottom of the ASW ship, and used to detect screw noises and other sounds that came from a submarine. Although the committee disbanded after World War I, the British made improvements on the locating device during the interval between then and World War II, and named it ASDIC after the committee.

American scientists further improved on the device, calling it sonar, a name derived from the underlined initials of the words sound navigation and ranging.

At the end of World War II, the United States improved the snorkel (a device for bringing air to the crew and engines when operating submerged on diesels) and developed the Guppy (short for greater underwater propulsion power), a conversion of the fleet-type submarine of World War II fame. The superstructure was changed by reducing the surface area, streamlining every protruding object, and enclosing the periscope shears in a streamlined metal fairing. Performance increased greatly with improved electronic equipment, additional battery capacity, and the addition of the snorkel.

21. This passage is organized to best show

    (A) the invention of the submarine.

    (B) how engineers realized the importance of streamlined submarine design.

    (C) the evolution of the submarine.

    (D) events leading to the development of the snorkel.

    (E) how the submarine was used in WWII.

22. According to the passage, the submarine's success was due in part to its ability to

    (A) strike and escape undetected.

    (B) move swifter than other vessels.

    (C) remain underwater for longer periods of time.

    (D) submerge to great depths while being hunted.

    (E) run silently.

23. The passage implies that one of the most pressing modifications needed for the submarine was to

    (A) streamline its shape.

    (B) enlarge the submarine for accommodating more torpedoes and men.

    (C) reduce the noise caused by the submarine.

    (D) modify for staying submerged longer.

    (E) add a snorkel.

24. The passage states that in the first submarine offensive the submarine

    (A) encountered and sank German U-boats.

    (B) sank a ship belonging to its own nation.

    (C) torpedoed a British man-of-war.

    (D) sank nothing and exploded its powder away from its target.

    (E) was detected and was itself destroyed.

25. It is implied that

    (A) ASDIC was formed to obtain technology for underwater detection.

    (B) ASDIC developed an accurate device for locating submarines.

    (C) the hydrophone was attached to the bottom of the ship.

    (D) the technology of the hydrophone is being used currently.

    (E) ASDIC was formed to develop technology to defend U.S. shipping.

26. All of the following are true EXCEPT

    (A) The first underwater vehicle was designed for only one person.

    (B) Submarines were hand propelled until the German U-boats of WWII.

    (C) In WWI, the Allied Submarine Devices Investigation Committee sought to obtain a means for locating submersed vehicles.

    (D) SONAR was developed by British and American scientists.

    (E) A Guppy is a modification of a WWII fleet submarine.

27. From the passage, one can infer that

    (A) David Bushnell was indirectly responsible for the sinking of a Federal corvette in Charleston Harbor.

    (B) David Bushnell invented the *Turtle*.

    (C) the *Turtle* was a one-man submarine.

    (D) the *Turtle* sank the *Eagle* on February 19, 1864.

    (E) the design of the *Turtle* was a response to science fiction.

DIRECTIONS: Each of the following questions provides a given word in capitalized letters followed by five word choices. Choose the best word which is most <u>opposite</u> in meaning to the given word.

---

28. FATIGUE:

    (A) exhaustion   (D) enervate

    (B) vestment   (E) refection

    (C) prostration

29. PREVALENCE:

    (A) permeate
    (B) currency
    (C) advantage
    (D) subordinate
    (E) penetrate

30. DISPERSION:

    (A) edit
    (B) radiation
    (C) diffusion
    (D) compilation
    (E) educe

31. NONEXISTENCE:

    (A) absolute
    (B) nullity
    (C) abeyance
    (D) void
    (E) amorphism

32. APPEND:

    (A) curtail
    (B) sever
    (C) accessorize
    (D) adjust
    (E) adhere

33. HARMONY:

    (A) euphony
    (B) anomaly
    (C) subordinate
    (D) gradation
    (E) collateral

34. PRECEDENCE:

    (A) preliminaries
    (B) preference
    (C) consequence
    (D) antecedent
    (E) prefix

35. PUNCTILIOUS:

    (A) somber
    (B) genial

(C) particular   (D) negligent

(E) antagonistic

36. CONTRAST:

   (A) oppose   (D) adapt

   (B) foil   (E) coalesce

   (C) refute

37. RESOLUTION:

   (A) analysis   (D) catalysis

   (B) disloyalty   (E) synthesis

   (C) obdurateness

38. ABSTRUSE:

   (A) perspicacious   (D) insidious

   (B) meretricious   (E) incongruous

   (C) lugubrious

STOP

If time still remains, you may go back and check your work.
When the time allotted is up, you may go on to the next section.

Section 4

Column A	Column B
1. $\quad 5 \times 4$	$5 + 4$

Explanation: The correct answer is (A), since $5 \times 4 = 20$, and $5 + 4 = 9$.

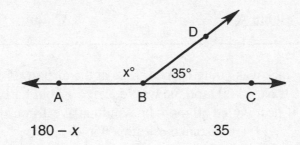

| 2. | $180 - x$ | 35 |

Explanation: The correct answer is (C). Since $\angle ABC$ is a straight angle, its measurement is 180°.

| **Column A** | **Column B** |

$a, b,$ and c are integers

| 1. | ac | bc |

$2x + y = 6; x - y = 4$

| 2. | 2 | y |

For all real numbers $a, b,$ and $c,$
$$a \times b = a + b - ab$$

| 3. | -20 | $(-4) \times 5$ |

| 4. | $x - y/6$ | $\dfrac{x-y}{6}$ |

A car travels 400 miles on 20 gallons of gasoline.

| 5. | Number of gallons of gasoline consumed on a trip of 900 miles | 40 |

| **Column A** | **Column B** |

Jack was going to meet Jane at the airport. If
he traveled 60 mph, he would arrive 1 hour early;
and if he traveled 30 mph, he would arrive 1 hour late.
(Distance = Rate × Time)

6.　　Distance to the airport　　　　　　　120 miles

Lines *l* and *m* meet when extended to the right.

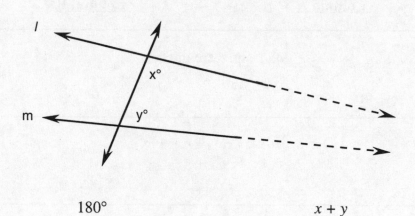

7.　　　　　180°　　　　　　　　　　　　*x* + *y*

The total price of 2 shirts and 2 ties is $80.

8.　　The price of one shirt　　　　　The price of one tie

$m\overline{AB}$ represents the measure of segment $\overline{AB}$;

$$m\overline{AY} > m\overline{XZ}$$

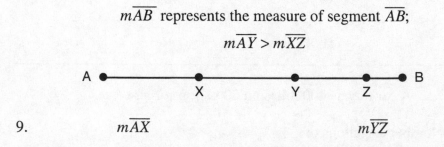

9.　　　　$m\overline{AX}$　　　　　　　　　　$m\overline{YZ}$

Column A	Column B

l, *m*, and *n* are lines.

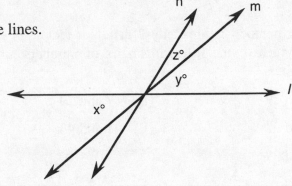

10. $x + z$ $y + z$

Given a cube with length of a side equal to *d* units

11.   Surface area of cube   Volume of cube

$$3x + y + z = 15$$

12. x 5

$$x > 0$$

13. $5.1x$ $\sqrt{25.1x^2}$

14. $\sqrt{9} + \sqrt{7}$ $\sqrt{16}$

Given an equilateral triangle
whose perimeter is 30 units

15.   Area of triangle $30\sqrt{3}$

> **DIRECTIONS:** For the following questions, select the best answer choice to the given question.

16. A counting number with exactly 2 different factors is called a prime number. Which of the following pairs of numbers are consecutive prime numbers?

    (A) 27 and 29   (D) 37 and 29

    (B) 31 and 33   (E) 41 and 43

    (C) 35 and 37

17. If n and k are even integers, which of the following is an even integer?

    (A) $n + k + 1$ (D) $(n - 3)(k + 1)$

    (B) $(n - 1)(k + 1)$ (E) $2(n + k) + 1$

    (C) $2(n + k + 1)$

18. If $V = \pi b^2 \left(r - \dfrac{b}{3} \right)$, then r is equal to

    (A) $\dfrac{V}{\pi b^2} + \dfrac{b}{3}.$ (D) $V + \dfrac{b}{3}.$

    (B) $\dfrac{V}{\pi b^2} + \dfrac{b}{3\pi}.$ (E) $V + \dfrac{\pi b}{3}.$

    (C) $\dfrac{V}{\pi b^2} + 3b.$

19. A used car dealer reduced the price of all the cars on his lot by $300. If a car was originally priced at $1,195, what percent (to the nearest tenth) is the markdown of the sale price?

    (A) 29.3%   (D) 25.1%

    (B) 8.4%   (E) 33.5%

    (C) 37.7%

20. If lines l, m, and n intersect at point p, express $x + y$ in terms of a.

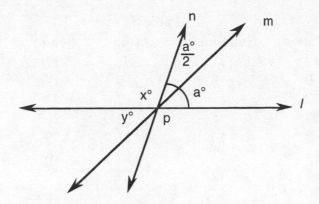

(A) $180 - \dfrac{a}{2}$

(D) $a - 180$

(B) $\dfrac{a}{2} - 180$

(E) $180 - a$

(C) $90 - \dfrac{a}{2}$

Questions 21–25 refer to the following tables.

Table 1 represents the amount of money (to the nearest dollar) spent by 50 state university students in the school's bookstore during the month of August 1988 on textbooks. Table 1 is broken down by students' class rank, and Table 2 represents the amount of money spent by the same 50 students in the school's bookstore during August 1988 on items other than textbooks.

Table 1

	Freshman	Sophomore	Junior	Senior	Graduate
	$180	$158	$179	$166	$116
	195	191	194	189	153
	168	202	210	190	98
	184	173	203	157	121
	205	187	183	203	92
	208	212	177	171	118
	184	197	192	180	126
	178	181	169	164	114
	163	166	198	188	119
	196	180	204	170	96
Total	$1,861	$1,847	$1,909	$1,778	$1,153

Table 2

Freshman	Sophomore	Junior	Senior	Graduate
$12	$15	$13	$27	$14
9	13	15	19	10
12	14	17	23	7
14	15	24	23	26
12	13	21	25	14
14	11	19	16	10
5	12	15	32	16
10	14	17	26	17
13	17	20	23	19
13	16	19	27	19
Total $114	$140	$180	$241	$152

21. Among all the students' class ranks, which class shows the greatest relative variation in the amount of money spent in the school's bookstore on items other than textbooks?

    (A) Graduate   (D) Sophomore

    (B) Senior   (E) Freshman

    (C) Junior

22. What is the ratio of the average amount a junior spends on textbooks to the average amount a junior spends on items other than textbooks?

    (A) .09 : 1   (D) 10.6 : 1

    (B) 7.4 : 1   (E) 13.2 : 1

    (C) .14 : 1

23. Approximately, what is the difference between the average amount of money spent in the school's bookstore in August by a senior class student and the average amount of money spent by a graduate class student?

    (A) $63   (D) $78

    (B) $89   (E) $68

    (C) $71

24. If the freshman class had 3,000 students in it during August, which of the following is the best approximation for the total amount of money spent by the entire freshman class in the school's bookstore in August?

    (A) $567,300
    (B) $596,100
    (C) $572,700
    (D) $605,700
    (E) $592,500

25. If state university enrollment in August 1988 totaled 10,000 students, and the freshman class had 3,000 students in it, approximately what is the percent of the amount of money spent by the freshman class in the school's bookstore in August on items other than textbooks of the total amount of money spent by the entire student body on items other than textbooks?

    (A) 14%
    (B) 21%
    (C) 30%
    (D) 33%
    (E) 39%

26. Which of the following equations can be used to find a woman's present age, if she is now 6 times as old as her son, and next year, her age will be equal to the square of her son's age?

    (A) $6w + 1 = w^2 + 1$
    (B) $6(w + 1) = w^2 + 1$
    (C) $6(w + 1) = (w + 1)^2$
    (D) $6w + 1 = (w + 1)^2$
    (E) $w + 6 = (w + 1)^2$

27. The measure of an inscribed angle is equal to one-half the measure of its inscribed arc. In the figure shown, $\triangle ABC$ is inscribed in circle O, and $\overleftrightarrow{BD}$ is tangent to the circle at point B. If the measure of $\angle CBD$ is 70°, what is the measure of $\angle BAC$?

    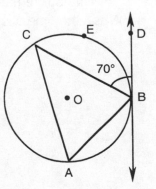

    (A) 110°
    (B) 70°
    (C) 140°
    (D) 35°
    (E) 40°

28. If R, S, and Q can wallpaper a house in 8 hours and R and S can do it in 12 hours, how long will it take Q alone to wallpaper the house?

    (A) 12 hours

    (B) 24 hours

    (C) 8 hours

    (D) 20 hours

    (E) 28 hours

29. The quotient of $\dfrac{\left(x^2 - 5x + 3\right)}{(x+2)}$ is

    (A) $x - 7 + \dfrac{17}{(x+2)}.$

    (B) $\dfrac{x-3+9}{(x+2)}.$

    (C) $\dfrac{x-7-11}{(x+2)}.$

    (D) $\dfrac{x-3-3}{(x+2)}.$

    (E) $\dfrac{x+3-3}{(x+2)}.$

30. An old picture has dimensions 33 inches by 24 inches. What one length must be cut from each dimension so that the ratio of the shorter side to the longer side is 2 : 3?

    (A) 2 inches

    (B) 6 inches

    (C) 9 inches

    (D) $10^1/_2$ inches

    (E) 3 inches

STOP

If time still remains, you may go back and check your work.
When the time allotted is up, you may go on to the next section.

Section 5

TIME: 30 Minutes
30 Questions

NUMBERS: All numbers are real numbers.

FIGURES: Position of points, angles, regions, etc., are assumed to be in the order shown and angle measures are assumed to be positive.

LINES: Assume that lines shown as straight are indeed straight.

DIRECTIONS: Each of the following given set of quantities is placed into either Column A or B. Compare the two quantities to decide whether

(A)   the quantity in Column A is greater;

(B)   the quantity in Column B is greater;

(C)   the two quantities are equal;

(D)   the relationship cannot be determined from the information given.

NOTE: Do not choose (E) since there are only four choices.

COMMON INFORMATION: Information which relates to one or both given quantities is centered in the two columns. A symbol which appears in both columns will indicate the same item in Column A and Column B.

EXAMPLES:

Column A	Column B
1. 5×4	$5 + 4$

Explanation: The correct answer is (A), since $5 \times 4 = 20$, and $5 + 4 = 9$.

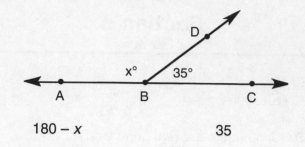

2. $180 - x$ 35

Explanation: The correct answer is (C). Since $\angle ABC$ is a straight angle, its measurement is 180°.

Column A	**Column B**

$$f(x,y) = \frac{2x+y}{y^2}$$

1. $f(1, 1)$ $f(1, 2)$

One boy sleeps 14 hours per day (1 month = 30 days).

2.   Number of hours that the   Number of hours that the
     boy sleeps in 3 weeks.   boy doesn't sleep in a month.

60% of $x + 2$ is 36.

3. x 60

x is an integer such that
$$-1 \le 2x + 1 < 2$$

4.   0 x

5.   The average of 18, 20,   The average of 17, 19, 21,
     22, 24, 26   23, 25, 27

<u>**Column A**</u>	<u>**Column B**</u>

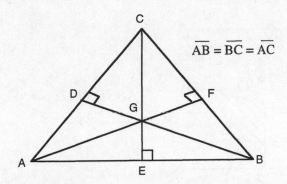

$$\overline{AB} = \overline{BC} = \overline{AC}$$

6.   Number of triangles   15

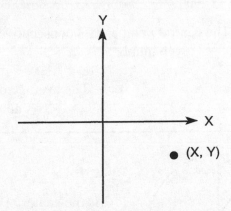

(*X, Y*) is a point in the fourth quadrant.

7.   *X*   2*Y*

ABCD is a rectangle.

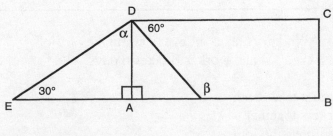

8. $\alpha + \beta$ 180°

| <u>**Column A**</u> | <u>**Column B**</u> |

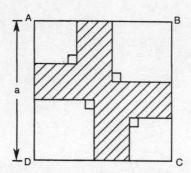

ABCD is a square.

9.   Perimeter of shaded area $4a$

The central number of 3 consecutive
even numbers is $2x + 2$.

10. $2x$ The average of the three even
numbers

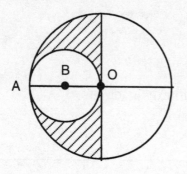

O is the center of the circle,
$BO = BA$, OA = Radius (r).

11. $\pi r^2/4$ Shaded area

Worker A takes 4 days to complete one job,
and worker B takes 6 days.

12.   Time it takes both   2.5 days
workers together to
complete the job

<u>Column A</u>	<u>Column B</u>

$$m > n$$

13.	m^2	n^2

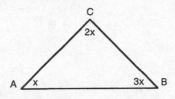

14.	$3x$	$90°$

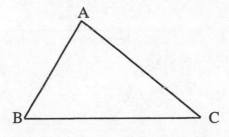

$$m\angle A > m\angle B \quad \text{and} \quad \angle C = 60°$$

15.	Side AB	Side BC

DIRECTIONS: For the following questions, select the best answer choice to the given question.

16. If $a \times b = 6a - 2bx$, $a = 9$, and $b = 6$, then $x =$

(A) 2.

(B) 0.

(C) 1.

(D) 4.

(E) 3.

17. In a class of 40 students, 30 speak French and 20 speak German. What is the lowest possible number of students who speak both languages?

    (A) 5   (D) 10

    (B) 20   (E) 30

    (C) 15

18. The value of B in the equation $a = \left(\dfrac{h}{2}\right)(B + b)$ is

    (A) $\dfrac{(2a - b)}{h}$.   (D) $\dfrac{2a}{h} - b$.

    (B) $\dfrac{2h}{a - b}$.   (E) none of these.

    (C) $2a - b$.

19. In the figure, ABC is an equilateral triangle. What is the value of α if AT is the bisector of $\angle BAC$?

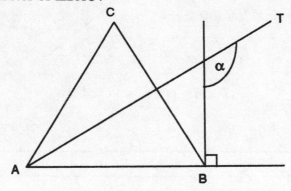

    (A) 60°   (D) 45°

    (B) 90°   (E) 135°

    (C) 120°

20. What is the reciprocal of $1 : {}^{8}/_{3}$?

    (A) $\dfrac{8}{3}$ (D) $1\dfrac{3}{8}$

    (B) $\dfrac{3}{8}$ (E) $1 + \dfrac{8}{3}$

    (C) $1\dfrac{8}{3}$

Questions 21–25 refer to the following graphs.

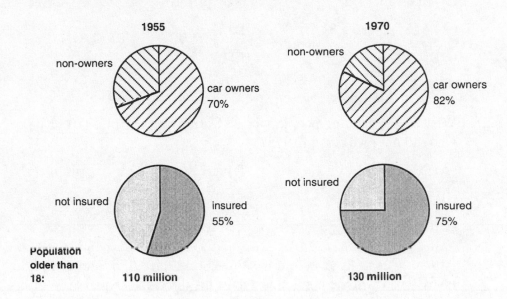

1955

non-owners

car owners
70%

1970

non-owners

car owners
82%

not insured

insured
55%

not insured

insured
75%

Population
older than
18:                      110 million   130 million

In doing the analysis, consider everyone who is older than 18 as a car owner
or a non-car owner.

21. The number of people with car insurance in 1970 was approximately

    (A) 42 million.   (D) 98 million.

    (B) 80 million.   (E) 130 million.

    (C) 107 million.

22. What was the increase in the number of car owners with insurance
from 1955 to 1970?

    (A) 20 million   (D) 37 million

    (B) 37.65 million   (E) 29.6 million

    (C) 30 million

23. What was the percent increase of the number of car owners from
1955 to 1970 (approximately)?

    (A) 38.4%   (D) 18.2%

    (B) 27.8%   (E) 88.3%

    (C) 17.1%

24. What is the ratio of cars without insurance in 1970 to cars without insurance in 1955?

   (A) .55   (D) 1.30

   (B) 1.89   (E) 1.18

   (C) .77

25. What is the ratio of people who did not own cars in 1970 to those who did not own cars in 1955?

   (A) 1.41   (D) .22

   (B) 0.71   (E) 0.60

   (C) .43

26. A man who is 40 years old has three sons, ages 6, 3, and 1. In how many years will the combined age of his three sons equal 80% of his age?

   (A) 5   (D) 20

   (B) 10   (E) 25

   (C) 15

27. Which of the following statements are true, if

$$x + y + z = 10$$

$$y \geq 5$$

$$4 \geq z \geq 3$$

   I. $x < z$

   II. $x > y$

   III. $x + z \leq y$

   (A) I only   (D) I and III only

   (B) II only   (E) I, II, and III

   (C) III only

28. $\left[\dfrac{.0003 \times 9 \times 10^{-1}}{18 \times 10^{-4}} \right]^{-1} =$

    (A) $\dfrac{20}{3}$

    (D) $\dfrac{2}{3}$

    (B) $\dfrac{3}{20}$

    (E) $\dfrac{19}{3}$

    (C) $\dfrac{3}{2}$

29. The perimeter of a square inscribed in the circumference of radius R is

    (A) $4R$.

    (D) $4R\sqrt{2}$.

    (B) $8R$.

    (E) $8R\sqrt{2}$.

    (C) $2R\sqrt{2}$.

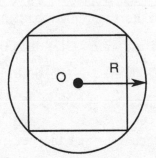

30. $\sqrt{x\sqrt{x\sqrt{x}}} =$

    (A) $x^{7/8}$

    (D) $x^{3/4}$

    (B) $x^{7/4}$

    (E) $x^{15/8}$

    (C) $x^{15/16}$

STOP

If time still remains, you may go back and check your work.
When the time allotted is up, you may go on to the next section.

Section 6

TIME: 30 Minutes
38 Questions

DIRECTIONS: Each of the given sentences has blank spaces which indicate words omitted. Choose the best combination of words which fit into the meaning and structure within the context of the sentence.

---

1. A storm of _____ swept over the country when _____ at the highest levels of the government became common knowledge.

    (A) indignation...corruption   (D) uncertainty...graft

    (B) protest...cooperation   (E) indifference...actions

    (C) praise...dedication

2. The hive is constructed so that the bee may work all around each frame and so that the _____, when full, may be _____ without disturbing the other frames.

    (A) bee...handled   (D) vessel...destroyed

    (B) latter...removed   (E) queen...carried off

    (C) hive...taken

3. You should not praise a man for being incorrupt if he has never had _____, because in such a case his incorruptibility may be merely a lack of _____.

    (A) wealth...desire   (D) power...opportunity

    (B) fame...temptation   (E) status...necessity

    (C) prestige...purpose

4. The chairman rapped _____ for order; but owing to the extreme _____ of the audience, he soon gave up the attempt.

(A) twice...ennui
(D) timidly...chaos

(B) vigorously...enthusiasm
(E) lightly...disharmony

(C) quickly...interest

5. Zoologists would use the word _____ to describe a cow and the word _____ to describe a hog.

(A) herbivorous...omnivorous
(D) vegetarian...carnivorous

(B) omnipotent...scavenger
(E) autotrophic...heterotrophic

(C) saprophyte...parasite

6. It is not the personal qualities of an individual which permit independence and self-sufficiency _____ the myriad of public services which undergird modern life that permit the _____ of independence and self-sufficiency.

(A) just...existence
(D) but...illusion

(B) indeed...reality
(E) besides...self-delusion

(C) only...presence

7. The issue of further development in the community had caused much _____ among the residents, who were concerned that it would permanently change the village's way of life.

(A) acrimony
(D) prurience

(B) parsimony
(E) complacence

(C) capriciousness

DIRECTIONS: In the following questions, a related pair of words is followed by five more pairs of words. Select the pair that best expresses the same relationship as that expressed in the original pair.

---

8. SOCIABILITY:SOCIOPATH::

(A) delusion:schizophrenic
(D) illusion:psychotic

(B) sensitivity:psychic
(E) calm:neurotic

(C) space:claustrophobic

9.   SAND:DUNE::

   (A) tree:forest   (D) clamor:tumult

   (B) rock:boulder   (E) twig:log

   (C) shower:deluge

10. VARIABLE:EQUATION::

   (A) oxygen:water   (D) clay:sculpture

   (B) paramecia:amoeba   (E) furnace:heat

   (C) analysis:summary

11. DECODE:UNDERSTAND::

   (A) detonate:explode   (D) skill:practice

   (B) study:research   (E) sow:reap

   (C) destroy:build

12. CIRCULATORY:HEART::

   (A) excretory:sweat   (D) digestive:kidney

   (B) neurological:skeleton (E) reproductive:testes

   (C) lungs:respiratory

13. QUART:LITER::

   (A) yard:acre   (D) liter:gallon

   (B) yard:meter   (E) mile:kilogram

   (C) ounce:kilowatt

14. QUILL:FOUNTAIN PEN::

   (A) rural:urban   (D) solo:quartet

   (B) young:old   (E) mangle:iron

   (C) truce:peace

15. EXPURGATE:CENSOR::

   (A) expunge:wash   (B) repudiate:reject

(C) frenetic:french

(D) phrenetic:phoneme

(E) wrought:excited

16. RIB:UMBRELLA::

(A) leg:table

(D) hinge:door

(B) stud:wall

(E) knob:drawer

(C) shelf:closet

DIRECTIONS: Each passage is followed by questions based on its content. After reading a passage, choose the best answer to each question. Answer all questions based on what is stated or implied in that passage.

Our heritage is richer because of the men and women of France who came to this continent and explored and settled the wilderness. The breadth of their achievements and the depth of the heritage they bequeathed to the United States transcends their small numbers. A substantial part of this heritage was mixed into the mainstream of America through 6,000 unhappy Acadians, who were expelled in 1755 from Acadia (Nova Scotia) by the British, its new rulers under the terms of the Treaty of Utrecht. The Acadians at first scattered throughout the British colonies, from Maine to Georgia, but most of them finally settled in Louisiana. Henry Wadsworth Longfellow's poem *Evangeline*, an epic about the Acadian odyssey, is the most widely known tribute to the French heritage in the United States.

Other persecuted Huguenots, also seeking refuge and religious freedom, contributed another equally important segment of our French heritage. They settled in clusters from Rhode Island to South Carolina, especially in Charleston, and enriched the cultural patterns evolving in the colonies. Therefore, much of the flavor of France in the United States today stems not from areas that once were French colonies but from French settlers in the British colonies.

17. The author gives primary emphasis to

(A) racial persecution by the British.

(B) those French who settled in Louisiana.

(C) those French who settled in the wilderness.

(D) an epic of the French odyssey.

(E) French heritage in America.

18. It can be inferred that the Acadians were

(A) British.   (D) unhappy.

(B) persecuted.   (E) reclusive.

(C) gypsies.

19. The author viewed the coming of the French to America as

(A) auspicious.   (D) unlikely.

(B) unfortunate.   (E) foreboding.

(C) inevitable.

Pennsylvania was the most successful of the proprietary colonies. Admiral Sir William Penn was a wealthy and respected friend of Charles II. His son, William, was an associate of George Fox, founder of the Society of Friends—a despised Quaker. When the senior Penn died, in 1670, his Quaker son inherited not only the friendship of the Crown but also an outstanding unpaid debt of some magnitude owed to his father by the King. As settlement, in 1681 he received a grant of land in America, called "Pennsylvania," which he decided to use as a refuge for his persecuted coreligionists. It was a princely domain, extending along the Delaware River from the 40th to the 43rd parallel. As Proprietor, Penn was both ruler and landlord. The restrictions on the grant were essentially the same as those imposed on the second Lord Baltimore: colonial laws had to be in harmony with those of England and had to be assented to by a representative assembly.

Penn lost little time in advertising his grant and the terms on which he offered settlement. He promised religious freedom and virtually total self-government. More than 1,000 colonists arrived the first year, most of whom were Mennonites and Quakers. Penn himself arrived in 1682 at New Castle and spent the winter at Upland, a Swedish settlement on the Delaware that the English had taken over; he renamed it Chester. He founded a capital city a few miles upstream and named it Philadelphia — the City of Brotherly Love. Well situated and well planned, it grew rapidly. Within two years, it had more than 600 houses, many of them handsome brick residences surrounded by lawns and gardens.

Shiploads of Quakers poured into the colony. By the summer of 1683, more than 3,000 settlers had arrived. Welsh, Germans, Scotch-Irish, Mennonites, Quakers, Jews, and Baptists mingled in a New World utopia. Not even the great Puritan migration had populated a colony so fast. Pennsylvania soon rivaled Massachusetts, New York, and Virginia. In part its prosperity was attributable to its splendid location and fertile soils, but even more to the proprietor's felicitous administration. In a series of laws — the Great Law and the First and Second Frames of Government — Penn created one of the most humane and progressive governments then in existence. It was characterized by broad principles of religious toleration, a well-organized bicameral legislature, and forward-looking penal code.

Another reason for the colony's growth was that, unlike the other colonies, it was not troubled by the Indians. Penn had bought their lands and made a series of peace treaties that were scrupulously fair and rigidly adhered to. For more than half a century, Indians and whites lived in Pennsylvania in peace. Quaker farmers, who were never armed, could leave their children with neighboring "savages" when they went into town for a visit.

By any measure, Penn's "Holy Experiment" was a magnificent success. Penn proved that a state could function smoothly on Quaker principles, without oaths, arms, or priests, and that these principles encouraged individual morality and freedom of conscience. Furthermore, ever a good businessman, he made a personal fortune while treating his subjects with unbending fairness and honesty.

20. Which of the following statements would the author most likely agree with?

    (A) The King of England imposed severe restrictions on Penn's land grant.

    (B) Penn was an opportunistic businessman.

    (C) The Indians of Pennsylvania were savages.

    (D) Penn was too friendly with the King of England.

    (E) Indians didn't bother the settlers because they were permitted to practice their own religion.

21. The author mentions the "Holy Experiment" as an example of

    (A) English-Colonial collaboration.

    (B) an early bicameral.

    (C) a treaty with Indians.

    (D) religious toleration.

    (E) a reason for establishing a proprietary colony.

22. Which of the following was NOT true of Pennsylvania's colony?

    (A) Rapid settlement

    (B) Refuge for religious non-conformists

    (C) Tolerant state religion

    (D) Proprietary government

    (E) Laws in harmony with those of England

23. It can be inferred from the selection that

    (A) all other colonies would have grown more rapidly if they had been organized in a manner similar to Pennsylvania.

    (B) all colonies should have been in harmony with the laws of England and had a representative assembly.

    (C) those colonies that were awards for service from the crown were better-administered.

    (D) the Pennsylvania Colony was the first colony to experience a tolerance for a number of nationalities and varied religious groups.

    (E) life with the Indians would have been much easier in other colonies if land had been purchased and treaties adhered to.

24. The "Great Law" and the "First and Second Frames of Government"

    (A) established Penn's political reputation.

    (B) created treaties with the Indians.

    (C) became the basis of a progressive republic form of government.

    (D) placed restrictions on immigration.

    (E) had to be overturned when they became inefficient.

25. After the summer of 1683 the Pennsylvania colony could be referred to as

    (A) a "melting-pot" colony.

    (B) a Quaker colony.

    (C) the largest American colony.

    (D) a Colonial Republic.

    (E) the first "democratic" colony.

26. According to the selection, as religious freedom was guaranteed, all of the following religious sects were mentioned as settlers in Pennsylvania except

    (A) Catholics.   (D) Mennonites.

    (B) Jews.   (E) Quakers.

    (C) Baptists.

27. The author uses which of the following writing techniques?

    (A) Syllogistic form

    (B) Development of an analogy

    (C) Literary allusion

    (D) Direct quotation

    (E) Supporting facts

DIRECTIONS: Each of the following questions provides a given word in capitalized letters followed by five word choices. Choose the best word which is most <u>opposite</u> in meaning to the given word.

---

28. ADDICT:

    (A) cease   (D) alienate

    (B) deprive   (E) estrange

    (C) wean

29. UNDERMINE:

    (A) reinforce   (D) consolidate

    (B) reestablish   (E) corroborate

    (C) restore

30. RELIGIOUS:

    (A) malevolent   (D) impious

    (B) secular   (E) unrighteous

    (C) evil

31. CORROBORATE:

    (A) abrogate   (D) disprove

    (B) disclaim   (E) doubt

    (C) contradict

32. UNIFORM:

    (A) asymmetrical   (D) disassembled

    (B) confusion   (E) various

    (C) chaos

33. RUDE:

    (A) urbane   (D) friendly

    (B) debonair   (E) confident

    (C) pleasant

34. UNINTELLIGIBLE:

    (A) explicable   (D) rational

    (B) solvable   (E) apparent

    (C) recognizable

35. ABRIDGMENT:

    (A) epitome   (B) concision

(C) laconic   (D) compendium

(E) redundant

36. REPUDIATE:

   (A) adore   (D) admire

   (B) agree   (E) adopt

   (C) advocate

37. GLUTTONOUS:

   (A) voracious   (D) abstemious

   (B) fastidious   (E) austere

   (C) ascetic

38. CAPRICIOUS:

   (A) stuffy   (D) sagacious

   (B) steadfast   (E) sybaritic

   (C) scurrilous

STOP

If time still remains, you may go back and check your work.
When the time allotted is up, you may go on to the next section.

TEST 4

ANSWER KEY

Sections 1 and 2 — Analytical Writing

Please review the sample essays in the Detailed Explanations.

Section 3 — Verbal Ability

1. (A)	11. (A)	21. (C)	31. (A)
2. (D)	12. (D)	22. (A)	32. (B)
3. (A)	13. (D)	23. (C)	33. (B)
4. (A)	14. (B)	24. (D)	34. (C)
5. (A)	15. (A)	25. (D)	35. (D)
6. (C)	16. (E)	26. (B)	36. (E)
7. (E)	17. (C)	27. (A)	37. (E)
8. (E)	18. (A)	28. (E)	38. (A)
9. (B)	19. (C)	29. (D)	
10. (E)	20. (C)	30. (D)	

Section 4 — Quantitative Ability

1. (D)	9. (A)	17. (C)	25. (B)
2. (A)	10. (C)	18. (A)	26. (D)
3. (B)	11. (D)	19. (E)	27. (B)
4. (D)	12. (D)	20. (A)	28. (B)
5. (A)	13. (A)	21. (A)	29. (A)
6. (C)	14. (A)	22. (D)	30. (B)
7. (A)	15. (B)	23. (C)	
8. (D)	16. (E)	24. (E)	

Section 5 — Quantitative Ability

1. (A)	9. (C)	17. (D)	25. (B)
2. (B)	10. (B)	18. (D)	26. (B)
3. (B)	11. (C)	19. (C)	27. (D)
4. (D)	12. (B)	20. (A)	28. (A)
5. (C)	13. (D)	21. (B)	29. (D)
6. (A)	14. (C)	22. (B)	30. (A)
7. (A)	15. (B)	23. (A)	
8. (C)	16. (B)	24. (C)	

Section 6 — Verbal Ability

1. (A)	11. (E)	21. (D)	31. (C)
2. (B)	12. (E)	22. (C)	32. (E)
3. (D)	13. (B)	23. (E)	33. (A)
4. (B)	14. (C)	24. (C)	34. (E)
5. (A)	15. (B)	25. (A)	35. (E)
6. (D)	16. (B)	26. (A)	36. (E)
7. (A)	17. (E)	27. (E)	37. (D)
8. (E)	18. (B)	28. (C)	38. (B)
9. (A)	19. (A)	29. (A)	
10. (A)	20. (B)	30. (B)	

DETAILED EXPLANATIONS OF ANSWERS

Section 1–Analytical Writing

PERSPECTIVES ON AN ISSUE ESSAY TOPIC—ESSAY ONE

Sample Essay Response Scoring 6

As a carry-over from an agricultural based society, the "summers off" school calendar seems currently arbitrary and ripe to be eliminated. However, this calendar, by virtue of its constancy, has spawned various major and minor economies and social systems. Just as "no man is an island," the school calendar cannot be considered properly without noting the way in which it affects other aspects of society.

clearly states the essay's topic

good rhetorical maneuvers

precise & well-set up thesis

In an era self-conscious of "quality time" spent between and among family members, the classic family vacation is not to be shrugged off. Vacations in all industries and businesses are crowded into gaps in the school calendar, obviously favoring the summer months which allow each mom and dad their turn. This social convention affords quality time without requiring children to miss school. Without children's synchronized vacation, a significant portion of classroom time would be spent in repetition for the benefit of returning children—an inevitability which would undermine the purposes of the year-round calendar. Even if summer vacation were reduced to one month, many industries would groan over the effort to function efficiently with such a great percentage of their workers scrambling for time off within the same month.

nice variation in the sentence structure

smooth transition between supporting arguments

Other economic issues related to family vacations are seasonal home rentals and food services at popular vacation areas. Often entire towns depend upon tourists' beach badges and the rental money that justifies high property taxes. Many of those who tread water in tourists' service industries like restaurants and hotels have difficulty in the current calendar. These industries need a reliable season in order to properly adjust the size of their staffs to meet the demands made by patrons.

deals well with the complexity of the issue

Not every family is part of the tourist equation, though, because some cannot afford the traditional family vacation. However, — **good transition** — these families may depend upon their older children's opportunity to find work during these boom months, as waiters, temporary vacation relief in non-skilled factory positions, and amusement park attendants. In the absence of a "summers off" calendar, such families would be deprived of this needed income. Similarly, economic status would divide student peers based on who took the most time off for vacation. Poorer students whose parents have limited vacation time would feel punished that they are in school more than their peers. This would create a negative image of school for these youngsters. In today's calendar, "How I spent my summer vacation" inevitably varies along socioeconomic lines, but the number of days is an undeniable equalizer.

another excellent transition

Another factor which must be considered is that some forms of education can only occur outside of the school year. While it is a stigma in itself, summer school provides many students the needed opportunity to catch up and to avoid the greater stigma of repeating an entire school year. Other forms of education are less academic in nature. Many consider a summer job to be a valuable — **very good argument to support the main idea** — supplement to the year's book work. Similarly, summer camps provide unique experiences in relation to exploring nature, developing physical skills, being away from home, and interacting with peers in a situation of cohabitation.

With today's school budgets, the feasibility of the year-round school calendar is obviously doubtful. When one considers the economic and sociological problems that it would create, its advantages are also called into question. The simple fact is that the — **solid and effective reference back to previously made points** — "summers off" calendar employs people in various direct and indirect ways. In addition, it provides opportunities for learning experiences beyond the range of the classroom, including such simplicities as intra-family interaction.

Analysis of Sample Essay Scoring 6

This response would rate a 6: it displays a command of the English language, is well organized, selects a firm position, and argues it persuasively and insightfully. The essay introduces its two lines of argument, social and economic, and has a smooth transition between them in the body. The observations that families require the summer season for quality time and for older children's monetary contributions are both probing and convincing. It was important that the essay pointed out the economic effect on all industries, not merely the tourist-oriented, seasonal and location-specific ones. Another significant point made by the essay was that not all learning occurs in the classroom.

PERSPECTIVES ON AN ISSUE ESSAY TOPIC—ESSAY TWO

Sample Essay Response Scoring 4

Many students do not like taking history classes. They find them boring, or ask why it is important to know about things that happened a long time ago. Especially younger students might find it difficult to see how studying the past can be of use or value to them. And this is very common. Students all across America complain that the subject of history is just not for them, and at times it might seem like we just have to say—are they right? Or is there some way we can make the study of history seem relevant?

awkward sentence structure

there should be an assertive thesis instead of a vague question

To say that the study of history is most relevant because it teaches us that people in different time periods are all the same, as the statement above implies, is potentially a very grave mistake. The study of history seems to me more about seeing the continuity and the breaks between different eras. It is important to understand that while some aspects of human behavior might be constant, there is also such a thing as historical specificity— some cultures in some times and places are simply distinct from others. We might say that like cavemen we are hungry, we procreate, we are aggressive toward each other, and find all sorts of other similarities as well in addition to these I have just named. But this does not mean that our 21st century society is indistinct from cavemen. To imply, then, that things are always the same is stupid.

these statements should be in the first paragraph & lead up to a thesis

too vague

redundant

this makes the essay sound very unsophisticated

Even looking at time periods that are closer together, we can see the same pattern of both similarities and dissimilarities. Like how today we drive cars. And in the 1800's they did not. So even if in both the 1800's and today, in very macro terms, the different societies have much in common, there is probably much more that is different—different values, different priorities, different ways of understanding the world. Even different things were illegal then.

these sentences are fragmented

It is important to study history to understand how society changes, while retaining some basic similarities, perhaps even ones that can be traced back to the dawn of civilization. But we must always remember that history is about change. <u>It is not static</u> <u>and constant.</u> *short sentences add force to a statement*

Analysis of Sample Essay Scoring 4

This essay would score a 4. It shows a good deal of logical flow from one idea to the next and is well organized. However, because of the questions posed in the opening paragraph the beginning of the essay is weak. Also, there is no thesis. The essayist's position does not become clear until the middle of the second paragraph. Some statements need further elaboration; the essayist states that different things were illegal in the 1800's but he does not give an example. Long or fragmented sentences lead to a lack of clarity. The overall tone of the essay is too informal, the use of words like "stupid" should be avoided entirely. The conclusion is strong but it lacks a connection back to the argument.

Section 2–Analytical Writing

ANALYSIS OF AN ARGUMENT ESSAY TOPIC

Sample Essay Response Scoring 6

The proposal of an alcohol consumption license is a plan to force education on adults, but for most drugs (even illegal ones) education is simply offered, and made known to be available. While the proposal attempts to distance itself from Prohibition, it too would make alcohol a "controlled substance." The status of limited control is meant to give a certain leverage, actually creating the ability to force the education.

concise, accurate wording of topic

The author suggests that the gap between drinking and non-drinking is this education. He argues that the privileged status of alcohol places it in a cultural blind spot. Whether or not this is true is distinct from whether the government has the right to impose an educational agenda on adults. An adult has the same right to remain ignorant of any subject he or she chooses as he or she has the right to pursue an education. Tobacco users have no desire to be force-fed cancer statistics, just as egg lovers cannot be bothered to learn their cholesterol count.

good transition to a critique of the initial essay

The strongest points made by the author were his references to health care and violent crime. These issues bring drinking beyond the realm of individual concern to a position where a person's choice to drink can affect others physically and financially. However, by referring to alcohol as an "accomplice" to crime, the author characterized alcohol as an independent agent willfully assisting violence. This statement weakens the argument by overextending alcohol's role in violent crime. While the presence of the health care and crime issues justify an effort to educate the public about the consequences of alcohol consumption, it does not justify the proposed enforcement of education.

here, the initial essay's merits are tied into a critique

By making reference to a "written examination" the proposal takes a significant turn. The consumption license is not a counterpart to a liquor license, but a parallel to a driver's license. It is a license to operate an inebriated biological machine. This implied metaphor is a major weakness in the argument. Driver's tests do not require one to operate a vehicle with defective steering, inadequate headlights, and a blaring radio—nor does it allow a quiet radio. Driving is a complicated system of situations and corre-

precise; effective use of language

sophisticated discussion of initial essay

sponding rules, and thus requires tests. Drinking alcohol simply impairs one's judgment while one is in society's system of situations and corresponding rules, which each of us has studied firsthand throughout our lives.

short, blunt sentence conveys emphasis

To be an effective argument, this proposal needs to demonstrate that drinking creates an entirely new set of circumstances compared to sobriety. It does not. Drinking simply impairs judgment—within familiar circumstances it alters one's perspective. The goal of the written examination is obviously to teach people frightening information that would influence them not to drink. The goal of a driver's test is to teach people to drive.

Analysis of Sample Essay Scoring 6

This response would rate a 6: it effectively analyzes and critiques the main points of the argument in strong, persuasive English. The author identified the argument's attempt to liken its proposed license to a driver's license and he proceeded to discredit this alleged parallel. The author does not challenge the proposal's evidence, but points out the intended means of delivery, described as by "force." The response contains varying sentence lengths which alternate and effectively accentuate certain points.

Section 3–Verbal Ability

1. **(A)**

(A) is the correct answer. INFREQUENTLY (at wide intervals) fits the sentence. IMBUE means to permeate. (B) is not the best choice. IN-FUSE requires that which gives new life and vigor to be the object; it clearly does not fit here since *patient* is the direct object. (C) is not the correct answer. SUFFUSE is a spreading through, as of color. (D) is incorrect; SPORADICALLY implies irregularity; INOCULATE means imbruing a person with something that acts like a disease germ. (E) is not the best choice; LEAVEN means to transform a mass, like yeast in dough.

2. **(D)**

(A) is not the best choice; CONDITION is a prerequisite which must be satisfied. (B) is incorrect; PHENOMENON refers to appearances. (C) is inappropriate; CHARACTER is an accumulation of qualities which distinguish an individual at any one time. (D) is correct. DISPOSITION is the correct choice because it is the predominating habit of one's mind developed over time. The word "ages" implies recurring action over a period of time. (E) is incorrect; EVOLUTION is the slow change from one state to another.

3. **(A)**

PARSIMONIOUS (A) means frugal or stingy. EXORBITANT (B) implies expensive living which is contradicted by the phrase "lonely bachelor life ... caring for his property ... adding to it." (C) is incorrect. PRODIGAL refers to wasteful living. PALTRY (D) suggests that life is unimportant. (E) is incorrect; PRUDENT denotes economical living.

4. **(A)**

(A) is correct. SINGULAR here means exceptional. AMORAL (B) means without morals. A MALFEASANT (C) is usually a public official who commits a wrong. (D) SUBJUGATED means conquered. (E) OFFI-CIOUS means dutiful or informal.

5. **(A)**

(A) is correct. INVIDIOUS means of a kind to cause harm or resentment. COMPATIBLE (B) means complementary. (C) ALLURING means attractive. ABHORRENT (D) means hateful. CONGENIAL (E) means friendly and easy to be with.

6. **(C)**

(A) is not the best answer. IRRESOLUTE means uncertain. (B) is inappropriate. DOGMATIC means arrogant. (C) is correct. DOCTRINAIRE means dictatorial; an AUTHORITARIAN is one who believes in blind submission to authority. (D) should not be chosen; CAPRICIOUS means impulsive, without reason. (E) is incorrect. RECIDIVIST means habitual (as in criminal); VACILLATING means uncertain.

7. **(E)**

DISPARITY (A) means distinctness. (B) TRANSCENDENCY refers to exceeding limitations. (C) CONCORD suggests agreement. (D) MISOGAMY implies celibacy. (E) is correct. VARIANCE is that state which precedes action. "To remain" implies the speaker is at a stationary point with a possibility to turn back.

8. **(E)**

ESCHATOLOGY is a doctrine concerning final matters, i.e., death. An ESTUARY (A) is a type of an INLET. An ESCROW is a type of DOCUMENT (B) which is put into the hands of a third party until demands are fulfilled. Good HEALTH requires EXERCISE (C). Geometry is the study of points, LINES (D), angles, and shapes. EMPIRICISM (E), is any doctrine which is based solely on experience or observations and does not rely upon any theory. Empiricism is based upon OBSERVATIONS. (E) is the correct answer.

9. **(B)**

FUN and SMILE (A) are cause and effect. FUN provides amusement or enjoyment producing the SMILE. FRIENDLY and AFFABLE are synonymous as AMICABLE and CONGENIAL (B) are synonymous. HILARIOUS and DELIGHT (C) are cause and effect, with HILARIOUS being an exhilaration of the spirit which is expressed in emotion called DELIGHT. SPEAK and CONVERSION (D) are a part:whole relationship. SPEAK means to utter, as CONVERSATION is an oral exchange. TACITURN and OUTSPOKEN (E) are antonyms, TACITURN meaning inclined not to talk, while OUTSPOKEN means inclined to speak.

10. **(E)**

This analogy is one of category and example. GAUZE is an example of a BANDAGE material. The answer (E) METAL:GOLD also expresses this same relationship. Gold is an example of a metal. LABYRINTH: CONFUSION (A) is a cause-and-effect analogy. CEMENT:GRAVEL (B) is a whole-to-part analogy. METER:PROSODY (C) is a part-to-whole analogy. TIMBRE:SOUND (B) is also a part-to-whole analogy. Timbre is a quality of sound.

11. **(A)**

(A) is correct. TIMIDITY is encompassed in COWARDICE even as GALLANTRY is encompassed in COURAGE. Both are an act of the will, resulting in action. POLTROONERY and FORTITUDE (B) are antonyms, with POLTROONERY referring to cowardice and FORTITUDE suggesting strength of mind to bear pain with courage. PUSILLANIMITY and CHIVALRY (C) are antonyms. PUSILLANIMITY refers to cowardice and CHIVALRY to martial valor, marked with honor. ANXIETY and SOLICITUDE (D) are synonyms referring to a state of mind resulting in uneasiness. AGITATION and PERTURBATION (E) are synonymous, referring to a troubled mind.

12. **(D)**

ARROGANCE and SUBMISSION (A) are antonyms with ARROGANCE meaning a feeling of superiority and SUBMISSION referring to a feeling of humility. ABASEMENT and CRESTLESS (B) are antonyms of action versus inaction. CRESTLESS refers to one of low birth and ABASEMENT suggests the lowering of another in rank or esteem. AFFABILITY and SUPERCILIOUS (C) are antonyms of exhibited action. AFFABILITY infers graciousness while SUPERCILIOUS implies crudeness. (D) is correct. PRIDE and HAUGHTINESS are synonyms referring to an attitude of superiority as is VAINGLORY and POMPOSITY. DIPLOMATIC and INCONSONANT (E) are antonyms. DIPLOMATIC indicates a good natured disposition while INCONSONANT suggests an unsympathetic, unfeeling personality.

13. **(D)**

(D) is correct. A CALORIE measures HEAT, and CALIPERS measure DIAMETER. SAND is an ingredient of CEMENT (A); SUCCUMB and YIELD (B) are synonyms; a METRONOME provides a consistent beat for MUSIC (C); and RETALIATION is an opposite of FORGIVENESS (E).

14. **(B)**

(B) is the best response. STARS are constituents of a CONSTELLATION, thus establishing a part-to-whole relationship. Likewise, VITAMINS and FOOD have a part-to-whole relationship. While PLANETS are found in the SKY (A), they are not specific constituents of it. TELEVISION and TELEPHONE (C) have no such relationship between them. A CONTINENT *can* be constituted by NATIONS (D), but this is not always the case, and, morever, it would be a whole-to-part relationship, the reverse of what we're seeking. AIR and OXYGEN (E) are, again, in a whole-to-part relationship.

15. **(A)**

(A) is correct. HALCYON and MARTIAL are antonyms. HALCYON is an adjective meaning peaceful or calm. MARTIAL is an adjective meaning warlike. PEACEFUL and WARLIKE (A) are also antonyms. EVIL and TYRANNY (B) are synonyms. WASH:DIRTY (C) is an action:cause relationship. Something that is FANCIFUL is whimsical or imaginary. AUSPICIOUS means successful or favorable. There is no discernible relationship between AUSPICIOUS and FANCIFUL (D). PITTANCE (E), meaning a very small amount (usually money), is often a characteristic of the POOR.

16. **(E)**

SHY and CONSPICUOUS (A) are antonyms of actions. SHY suggests being easily frightened, disposed to avoid a person or thing. CONSPICUOUS denotes the desire to attract attention. OBSTREPEROUS and BOISTEROUS (B) are synonyms implying loud action. INTELLIGENT and SAGACIOUS (C) are synonyms implying the ability to know. SELF-CONSCIOUS and ASSERTIVE (D) are antonyms. (E) is correct. INFER and DEDUCE are synonymous like ALLUDE and HINT.

17. **(C)**

(A) is incorrect. Forgetfulness is often the first manifestation of the disease, but it is not considered the first stage. (B) is incorrect. This is not the main point of the passage. (C) is correct; the author's purpose for writing this passage is to document the typical progression of Alzheimer's disease. (D) is incorrect. It is not yet known for certain how and why Alzheimer's occurs. (E) is incorrect. Finding a cure for this disease is not mentioned or alluded to in the passage.

18. **(A)**

(A) is correct. The passage does imply that victims of Alzheimer's disease lose most of their memories of childhood events. The passage does not imply that victims retain their cognitive functions (B). The passage implies that victims of Alzheimer's do incur personality and behavioral changes (C). The passage states that victims of the disease are likely to spend their last days in a long-term care facility (D). The passage does not imply that patients retain the abilities they had before the onset of the disease (E).

19. **(C)**

The passage describes serious forgetfulness as debilitating due to the loss of sensory functions (C). While the passage does describe the length of time needed to complete a task (A), the loss of judgement and concentration

(B), the extreme amount of care needed (D), and the inability to read and write (E), these are not described as aspects of serious forgetfulness.

20. **(C)**

(C) is correct. The passage states that personality change is likely as the disease progresses. The passage does not verify that the Alzheimer's patient has a specific illness at the outset of the disease (A), that skill mastery is maintained after cognitive functioning is diminished (B), that senility and Alzheimer's disease are synonymous (D), or that long-term care is necessary for all patients (E).

21. **(C)**

The passage is organized chronologically to show the development of the submarine (C). The passage is not organized to best show the invention of the submarine (A), how engineers realized the importance of streamlined submarine design (B), the events leading to the development of the snorkel (D), or how the submarine was used in WWII (E).

22. **(A)**

(A) is correct. The third paragraph states "…the submarine's greatest advantage was that it could operate beneath the ocean surface where detection was difficult." The passage does not state that the submarine's success was due in part to its ability to move swifter than other vessels (B), remain underwater for longer periods of time (C), submerge to great depths while being hunted (D), or to run silently (E).

23. **(C)**

The passage does not imply that one of the most pressing modifications needed for the submarine was to streamline its shape (A), enlarge it to accommodate more torpedoes and men (B), to stay submerged longer (D), or to add a snorkel (E). Paragraph four states that a hydrophone was "used to detect screw noises and other sounds." Therefore, the correct answer is (C).

24. **(D)**

The fourth sentence of the first paragraph states that in the first submarine offensive the submarine sank nothing and exploded its powder away from its target (D). The passage does not state that in the first submarine offensive the submarine sank German U-boats (A), sank a ship of its own nation (B), torpedoed a British man-of-war (C), or was detected and destroyed (E).

25. **(D)**

The passage implies that the technology of the hydrophone is being used currently (D). It does not imply that ASDIC was formed to obtain technology for underwater detection (A) or to develop technology to defend U.S. shipping (E), or that ASDIC developed an accurate device for locating submarines (B). The passage states, not implies, that the hydrophone was attached to the bottom of the ship (C).

26. **(B)**

The correct answer is (B); it is not true that submarines were hand propelled until the German U-boats of WWII. It is true that the first underwater vehicle was designed for only one person (A); that in WWI, the Allied Submarine Devices Investigation Committee sought to obtain a means for locating submerged vehicles (C); that SONAR was developed by British and American scientists (D); and that a Guppy is a modification of a WWII fleet submarine (E).

27. **(A)**

(A) is correct. Since the submersible designed by David Bushnell sank the Federal corvette, Bushnell could be considered "indirectly responsible" for the sinking. (B) is incorrect. This is stated outright; look for something implied. (C) is incorrect. This is stated outright; look for something implied. (D) is incorrect. The *Turtle* was unsuccessful in attempting to sink the *Eagle*. (E) is incorrect. This is neither stated nor implied in the passage.

28. **(E)**

EXHAUSTION (A) is a synonym of FATIGUE. (B) is incorrect. VESTMENT is an article of clothing. (C) is incorrect. PROSTRATION is a synonym. ENERVATE (D) means lacking vigor. (E) is correct. REFECTION means refreshment, restoration.

29. **(D)**

PERMEATE (A) is a verb; PREVALENCE is not. (B) is incorrect. CURRENCY means general acceptance (synonym). ADVANTAGE (C) is a superior position. (D) is correct. PREVALENCE means dominance; SUBORDINATE means lesser in importance. PENETRATE (E) is a verb; PREVALENCE is not.

30. **(D)**

(A) is incorrect. EDIT means to refine or shorten. RADIATION (B) is the process of emitting (dispersing) energy. DIFFUSION (C) means to scatter; it is synonymous with DISPERSION. (D) is correct. COMPILATION means to bring together; DISPERSION means to scatter. EDUCE (E) means to draw out.

31. **(A)**

(A) is correct. ABSOLUTE denotes the essence of existence, which is the opposite of NONEXISTENT. A NULLITY (B) is nonexistent or valueless. ABEYANCE (C) means a temporary inactivity. A VOID (D) refers to having no value or existence. AMORPHISM (E) is something without shape, but not without existence.

32. **(B)**

CURTAIL (A) means to make less of. (B) is correct. SEVER means to cut off; APPEND means to add on. (C) ACCESSORIZE means to decorate. ADJUST (D) means to resolve, settle. ADHERE (E) means to stick to.

33. **(B)**

EUPHONY (A) also refers to pleasing music or words. (B) is correct. ANOMALY means deviation from the norm, something not harmonious. SUBORDINATE (C) means lower in position. GRADATION (D) means successive steps or degrees. COLLATERAL (E) means supporting, accompanying.

34. **(C)**

PRELIMINARIES (A) is close in meaning to PRECEDENCE, preceding in time or importance. PREFERENCE (B) is close in meaning to PRECEDENCE. (C) is correct. CONSEQUENCE is something of secondary result. ANTECEDENT (D) is close in meaning to PRECEDENCE. PREFIX (E) is close in meaning to PRECEDENCE.

35. **(D)**

PUNCTILIOUS means very exact, very careful. SOMBER (A) means melancholy, grave, depressing. It does not have an opposite meaning from PUNCTILIOUS. GENIAL means kindly, cheerful, cheering, of or pertaining to marriage. (B) is clearly not related to PUNCTILIOUS. PARTICULAR is a synonym for PUNCTILIOUS since it means concerned with or attentive to details. (C) is not the right answer. NEGLI-

GENT (careless, inattentive, indifferent) is the opposite (synonym) of PUNCTILIOUS (careful, exacting). (D) is, therefore, the correct answer. ANTAGONISTIC (E) means hostile. It is not the opposite of PUNCTILIOUS and should not be selected as the correct answer.

36. **(E)**
OPPOSE (A) means to resist. (B) is not the right answer. FOIL means to enhance by CONTRAST. (C) is not correct. REFUTE means to prove wrong. ADAPT (D) means to make fit. This is close, but it's not the best answer. (E) is correct. COALESCE means to join together.

37. **(E)**
ANALYSIS (A) means separation of the whole into parts. (B) is not correct. DISLOYALTY means lack of loyalty. OBDURATENESS (C) means stubbornness, inflexibility. (D) is not the best answer; CATALYSIS is a chemical reaction. (E) is correct. SYNTHESIS refers to bringing together; RESOLUTION is a noun meaning a reduction into smaller parts.

38. **(A)**
ABSTRUSE means difficult to understand. (A) is correct. PERSPICACIOUS means plain to the understanding. It is the opposite of ABSTRUSE. MERETRICIOUS (B) means in a cheap, showy way. It is not the antonym for ABSTRUSE. LUGUBRIOUS (C) means looking or sounding profoundly sad. It is not the opposite of ABSTRUSE. (D) is incorrect. INSIDIOUS means alluring but dangerous. (E) is incorrect. INCONGRUOUS means incompatible.

Section 4—Quantitative Ability

1. **(D)**

Choices (A), (B), and (C) are incorrect. For some values of a, b, and c this could be true. Try some values of a, b, and c both negative and positive. (D) is correct. No specific information about a, b, and c is given except that they are integers. Therefore, the relationship between the two quantities in Column A and Column B cannot be determined. For example, if $a = 2$, $b = 3$, and $c = 4$, then $ac = 8$ and $bc = 12$. Therefore, Column B is greater than Column A. But if $a = 2$, $b = 3$, and $c = -4$, then $ac = -8$ and $bc = -12$. Therefore, Column A is greater than Column B.

2. **(A)**

(A) is correct. To solve this system of linear equations one can start by solving the equation $x - y = 4$ for x in terms of y. Thus
$$x = 4 + y.$$
Substitute this value for x in the equation $2x + y = 6$ and solve for y.

$$2(4 + y) + y = 6$$
$$8 + 2y + y = 6$$
$$3y = 6 - 8$$
$$3y = -2$$
$$y = -\frac{2}{3}.$$

Therefore, Column A is greater than Column B. Choices (B), (C), and (D) are incorrect. For each answer selection, to solve the system of linear equations, one can start by solving the equation $x - y = 4$ for x in terms of y, then solve y in the equation $2x + y = 6$.

3. **(B)**

(B) is correct. Simplify Column B by multiplication. $a = -4$ and $b = 5$.

$$(-4) \times (5) = (-4) + 5 - (-4)(5)$$
$$= -4 + 5 - (-20)$$
$$= 1 + 20$$
$$= 21$$

Therefore, Column B is greater than Column A.

4. **(D)**

(D) is correct. In Column A, since there are no parentheses setting off the quantity x–y, order of operations requires that division is performed before subtraction. Thus, depending on the numbers used for x and y, Column A may be greater than, less than, or equal to Column B. The relationship cannot be determined.

5. **(A)**

(A) is correct. A proportion from the given information to find the number of gallons consumed on a trip of 900 miles is one method of solving the problem.

Let g = the number of gallons consumed on a trip of 900 miles.

$$20 \text{ gallons} : 400 \text{ gallons} = g : 900 \text{ miles}$$

$$\text{or } \frac{20}{400} = \frac{g}{900}$$

$$\frac{(20 \times 900)}{400} = g$$

$$45 \text{ gallons} = g$$

Another method is to determine how many miles the car gets per gallon, thus:

$$\frac{400 \text{ miles}}{20 \text{ gallons}} = \frac{20 \text{ miles}}{\text{gallon}}.$$

On a trip of 900 miles,

$$\frac{900 \text{ miles}}{20 \text{ miles} / \text{gallon}} = 45 \text{ gallons will be used.}$$

6. **(C)**

(C) is correct. Use the (Distance = Rate × Time) to set up equations about information that is known. $d = rt$ or $t = d / r$. For example, traveling at a rate of 60 mph, the time of travel is equal to $d/60$. But Jack arrived an hour early or 1 hour less than t.

$$\frac{d}{60} = t - 1 \text{ or } \frac{d}{60} + 1 = t.$$

By similar reasoning for the 30 mph trip one obtains:

$$\frac{d}{30} = t + 1 \text{ (arrived an hour late) or } \frac{d}{30} - 1 = t.$$

Since the correct time of travel is a constant, one can combine the following equation:

$$\frac{d}{60} + 1 = \frac{d}{30} - 1$$

$$1 + 1 = \frac{d}{30} - \frac{d}{60}$$

$$2 = \left(\frac{2}{2}\right) \times \left(\frac{2}{30}\right) - \frac{d}{60}$$

$$= \frac{2d - d}{60}$$

$$2(60) = d$$

$$120 = d$$

Choices (A), (B), and (D) are incorrect. Use the (Distance = Rate × Time) to set up equations about information that is known. $d = rt$ or $t = {}^d/_r$. For example, traveling at a rate of 60 mph, the time of travel is equal to ${}^d/_{60}$. But Jack arrived an hour early or 1 hour less than t. ${}^d/_{60} = t - 1$. Similar equations can be derived for the 30 mph trip. Solve for the distance.

7. **(A)**

(A) is correct. Extend lines l and m to where they would meet. The resultant figure would be a triangle. Let z be the angle at the point where lines l and m would meet. Since the interior angles of a triangle equal 180°, the following equation can be obtained:

$$x + y + z = 180°$$
$$x + y = 180° - z$$
$$z > 0°, \text{ therefore } (x + y) < 180°.$$

Choices (B), (C), and (D) are incorrect. Extend lines l and m to where they would meet and analyze the angles of the resultant figure.

8. **(D)**

(D) is correct. First you should set up an algebraic equation with the given information.

Let s = the price of one shirt in dollars and t = the price of one tie in dollars.

Given: $2s + 2t = 80$ or $s + t = 40$.

The information given allows for the writing of one equation with two variables. As no other information is given, the prices of ties and shirts cannot be determined.

9. **(A)**

(A) is correct. The line segments can be added together to obtain:

$$m\overline{AY} = m\overline{AX} + m\overline{XY} \quad \text{and} \quad m\overline{XZ} = m\overline{XY} + m\overline{YZ}.$$

Given $m\overline{AY} > m\overline{XZ}$,

$$m\overline{AX} + m\overline{XY} > m\overline{XY} + m\overline{YZ}.$$

Subtracting $m\overline{XY}$ from both sides of the inequality

$$m\overline{AX} + m\overline{XY} - m\overline{XY} > m\overline{XY} + m\overline{YZ} - m\overline{XY}.$$

Therefore, $m\overline{AX} > m\overline{YZ}$. So the quantity in Column A is greater.

Choices (B), (C), and (D) are incorrect. The line segments can be added together to obtain:

$$m\overline{AY} = m\overline{AX} + m\overline{XY} \quad \text{and} \quad m\overline{XZ} = m\overline{XY} + m\overline{YZ}.$$

10. **(C)**

Choices (A), (B), and (D) are incorrect. Remember that vertical angles formed by two intersecting lines are equal. (C) is correct. Since vertical angles formed by two intersecting lines are equal, $x = y$. Adding the same angle, z, to x and y the quantities remain equal. $x + z = y + z$.

11. **(D)**

Choices (A), (B), and (C) are incorrect. Use the formulas for the surface area of a cube and for the volume of a cube to compare different values of d. It is true for $d < 6$. Try some values of $d \geq 6$. (D) is correct. Use the formulas for the surface area of a cube and for the volume of a cube to compare different values of d. The surface area of a cube is the sum of the areas of the 6 faces of the cube. The area of each face $d(d) = d^2$. The surface area of the cube = $6d^2$. The volume of a cube = d^3. Since d has no particular value try any.

If $d > 6$, then $dd^2 > 6d^2$ or $d^3 > 6d^2$.
If $d = 6$, then $dd^2 = 6d^2$ or $6^3 = 6(6)^2$.
If $d < 6$, then $dd^2 < 6d^2$ or $d^3 < 6d^2$.

Therefore, the relationship between Column A and Column B cannot be determined.

12. **(D)**

(D) is correct. Solve the given statement for x.

$$3x + y + z = 15$$

$$3x = 15 - y - z$$

$$x = \frac{15 - y - z}{3}$$

$$x = 5 - \frac{(y + z)}{3}$$

Since no information about y and z is given, no relationship between Column A and Column B can be determined.

13. **(A)**

(A) is correct. To compare the two expressions square the expression in Column A. (Taking the square root of the expression in Column B would be very difficult.)

$\sqrt{(5.1x)^2} = \sqrt{26.01x^2}$ From this one could obtain $[(5.1x)^2]^{1/2} = (26.01x^2)^{1/2}$.

$\sqrt{25.1x^2} < \sqrt{26.01x^2}$ or Column A > Column B.

Choices (B), (C), and (D) are incorrect. To compare the two expressions either square the expression in Column A or find the square root of the expression in Column B.

14. **(A)**

(A) is correct. Take the square roots or approximate square roots of the expressions to compare the two quantities.

Column A: $\sqrt{9} = 3$ and $\sqrt{7} > 2$, then $\sqrt{9} + \sqrt{7} > 5$.

Column B: $\sqrt{16} = 4$.

Therefore, Column A is greater than Column B.

Choices (B), (C), and (D) are incorrect. Take the square roots or approximate square roots of the expressions to compare the two quantities.

15. **(B)**

Choices (A), (C), and (D) are incorrect. Use the formula to find the area of an equilateral triangle or use the Pythagorean theorem to find the altitude and the formula to find the area of a triangle. (B) is correct. Use the formula to find the area of an equilateral triangle or use the Pythagorean theorem to find the altitude and the formula to find the area of a triangle.

The area of an equilateral triangle $A = (\frac{1}{2})b \times h$ where h = altitude and b = height.

The altitude can be found by:

$$l^2 + \left(\frac{1}{2}s\right)^2 = s^2 \text{ where } s = 10$$

$$l^2 + (5)^2 = (10)^2$$

$$l^2 + 25 = 100$$

$$l^2 = 75 \text{ or } l = 75 = 5\sqrt{3}$$

The area of a triangle

$$= \frac{(bh)}{2} = \frac{\left[(10)(5\sqrt{3})\right]}{2}$$

$$= \frac{(50\sqrt{3})}{2}$$

$$= 25\sqrt{3}$$

This quantity is less than $30\sqrt{3}$ – Column B.

16. **(E)**

(E) is correct. Find the prime factors for each number in the pair. Remember that a prime number is a number that does not have any factors besides itself and 1. Both 41 and 43 are divisible only by 1 and themselves. This is the only pair that is a consecutive prime pair.

17. **(C)**

(C) is correct. Remember that an even number + an odd number = an odd number, an even number + an even number = an even number, and an odd number + an odd number = an even number. Multiplication: even × even = even, even × odd = even, and odd × odd = odd.

$$2(n + k + 1) = \text{even}(\text{even} + \text{even} + \text{odd}) = \text{even}(\text{odd}) = \text{even}$$

18. **(A)**

(A) is correct. Solve the equation for r.

$$V = \pi b^2 \left(r - \frac{b}{3} \right)$$

$$\frac{V}{\pi b^2} = \left(r - \frac{b}{3} \right) \text{ or } r = \left(\frac{V}{\pi b^2} \right) + \frac{b}{3}$$

Choices (B), (C), (D), and (E) are incorrect. Solve the equation for r. Be careful with the terms when simplifying the equation.

19. **(E)**

Choices (A), (B), (C), and (D) are incorrect. Find the sale price, then find the percent of the markdown on the sale price. (E) is correct. Find the sale price.

$$\$1,195 - \$300 = \$895.$$

The percent of the markdown on the sale price:

$$\frac{\text{markdown}}{\text{sale price}} \times 100\% \qquad \frac{300}{895} \times 100\% = 33.5\%$$

20. **(A)**

(A) is correct. Remember that a straight angle equals 180°. Since m is a line it follows that:

$$x + y + \frac{a}{2} = 180°. \text{ Therefore, } x + y = 180° - \frac{a}{2}.$$

Choices (B), (C), (D), and (E) are incorrect. Remember that a straight angle equals 180°.

21. **(A)**

(A) is correct. The range is the difference between the least number and the greatest number. Use the information from Table 2 to compare the ranges.

Amount of money spent on items other than textbooks

Class rank	Greatest amount	Least amount	Range
Freshman	$14	$ 5	$ 9
Sophomore	17	11	6
Junior	24	13	11
Senior	32	16	16
Graduate	26	7	19

Therefore, the graduate students have the greatest range in the amount of money spent in the school's bookstore on items other than textbooks. Choices (B), (C), (D), and (E) are incorrect. The range is the difference between the least number and the greatest number. Use the information from Table 2 to compare the ranges.

22. **(D)**

(D) is correct. Find the average amount a junior would spend on textbooks and on items other than textbooks. Set up the ratio of amount spent on textbooks : amount spent on items other than textbooks. The average equals total amount/number of items. The table has the total for 10 students.

Average amount spent on textbooks $= \dfrac{1,909}{10} = 190.9$

Average amount spent on items other than textbooks $= \dfrac{180}{10} = 18$

The ratio is 190.9 : 18. This reduces to 10.6 : 1.

23. **(C)**

(A) is incorrect. This is the average difference of the amount of money spent on textbooks. The total amount spent in the bookstore is equal to the sum of money spent on textbooks plus other items. (B) is incorrect. This is the difference in the items other than textbooks. The total amount spent in the bookstore is equal to the sum of money spent on textbooks plus other items. Remember to take the average for a senior student and a graduate student. (C) is correct. The total amount spent in the bookstore is equal to the sum of money spent on textbooks plus other items. The average must be found for the senior class and the graduate class.

Senior class student average $= \dfrac{1,778 + 241}{10} = \dfrac{2,019}{10} = 201.9 \approx 202$

Graduate class student average $= \dfrac{1{,}153+152}{10} = \dfrac{1{,}305}{10} = 130.5 \approx 131$

The difference between the average amount of money spent in the school's bookstore in August by a senior student and the average amount of money spent by a graduate student is equal to $202 - $131 = $71. (D) is incorrect. This is the difference between a graduate student and a junior. (E) is incorrect. This is the difference between a sophomore student and a graduate student.

24. **(E)**
(A) is incorrect. This is the total amount the freshman class spent on textbooks, not on both textbooks and items other than textbooks. (B) is incorrect. This is the total amount the sophomore class, not the freshman class, would spend if there were 3,000 students. (C) is incorrect. This is the amount the junior class would spend on textbooks if there were 3,000 students, not the total amount that the freshman class would spend. (D) is incorrect. This is the total amount the sophomore class, not the freshman class, would spend if there were 3,000 students. (E) is correct. Find the total amount spent on textbooks and on items other than textbooks by freshmen. Find the average per student and then solve for 3,000 freshmen.

Total amount spent by freshmen = $1,861 + $114 = $1,975.

The average spent by freshmen $= \dfrac{\$1{,}975}{10} = \$197.50$.

Total for 3,000 students = $197.50 × 3,000 = $592,500.

25. **(B)**
Choices (A), (C), (D), and (E) are incorrect. This is the percent of the amount of money spent by the 10 freshmen on items other than textbooks of the 50 students represented in the tables. You need to approximate the total amount of money spent in the bookstore on items other than textbooks by the entire student body, 10,000 students, and by the freshman class, 3,000 students. Finally, the percentage is obtained by dividing the amount spent by the freshmen by the total amount spent. (B) is correct. You need to approximate the total amount of money spent in the bookstore on items other than textbooks by the entire student body, 10,000 students, and by the freshman class, 3,000 students. Finally, the percentage is obtained by dividing the amount spent by the freshmen by the total amount spent.

Calculate the total amount of money spent by the entire student body on items other than textbooks. The average of the total amount of money spent by any student in the school can be approximated by taking the average of the total amount spent by any one of the group of 50 students.

$$\frac{\text{sum of all amounts spent by the 50 students}}{50} = \frac{114 + 140 + 180 + 241 + 152}{50}$$

$$= \frac{827}{50} \approx \$16.54.$$

The total amount spent by the student body is

$$(10,000)(\$16.54) = \$165,400.$$

Calculate the total amount of money spent by the freshman class on items other than textbooks. The average of the amount of money spent by any freshman is the total spent by the 10 freshmen divided by 10.

$$\frac{\$114}{10} = \$11.40$$

Since there are 3,000 freshmen, the total amount for the freshman class equals

$$(3,000)(\$11.40) = \$34,200.$$

The required percent =

$$\frac{34,200}{165,400} \times 100 = 21\%.$$

26. **(D)**
    Choices (A), (B), (C), and (E) are incorrect. Let w be the son's age. The son's age next year will be $w + 1$. With the other given information you can find an equivalent formula to find the mother's age. (D) is correct. Let w be the son's age. Then the mother's age is $6w$. The son's age next year will be $w + 1$ and the mother's age will be $6w + 1$. It is also given that the mother's age will be the square of her son's age. Thus, $6w + 1 = (w + 1)^2$.

27. **(B)**
    (B) is correct. An angle formed by a tangent and a chord is equal in degrees to one-half its intercepted arc. Also, an incribed angle is equal to one-half its intercepted arc. Let $m \angle A$ = the measure of angle A, $m\, (\overset{\frown}{ABC})$ = the measure of $\overset{\frown}{ABC}$. Since $\angle DBC$ is formed by a tangent to circle O, $\overset{\leftrightarrow}{BD}$, and a chord, $\overline{CD}$, intersecting at the point of tangency, B, then

$$m\angle CBD = \frac{1}{2}m(\overset{\frown}{BEC})$$

$$70° = \frac{1}{2}m(\overset{\frown}{BEC})$$

$$m(\overset{\frown}{BEC}) = (70°)(2)$$

$$m(\overset{\frown}{BEC}) = 140°$$

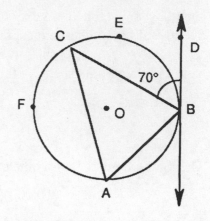

Since $\angle BAC$ is an inscribed angle in

the $\overset{\frown}{BAC}$, and since $\overset{\frown}{BEC}$ is intercepted

by $\angle BAC$, *then*

$$m\angle BAC = \frac{1}{2}m(\overset{\frown}{BEC})$$

$$= \frac{1}{2}(140°)$$

$$= 70°$$

Choices (A), (C), (D), and (E) are incorrect. An angle formed by a tangent and a chord is equal in degrees to one-half its intercepted arc.

28. **(B)**

(A) is incorrect. Solve by setting up the work problem. Let x equal the number of hours it will take Q to wallpaper alone. (B) is correct. Let x equal the number of hours it will take Q to wallpaper alone. Then Q can wallpaper $1/x$ of the house in 1 hour. Given that R, S, and Q can wallpaper the house in 8 hours or $1/8$ of the house in 1 hour, and R and S can wallpaper the house in 12 hours or $1/12$ of the house in 1 hour. Then,

$$\frac{1}{x} + \frac{1}{12} = \frac{1}{8}$$

$$\frac{12 + x}{12x} = \frac{1}{8}$$

$$8(12 + x) = 12x$$

$$96 + 8x = 12x$$

$$96 = 12x - 8x$$

$$96 = 4x$$

$$24 = x$$

29. **(A)**

(A) is correct. To find the quotient and the remainder one can use either the long division procedure or the synthetic division procedure.

$$\frac{(x^2 - 5x + 3)}{(x + 2)}$$

$$
\begin{array}{r}
x - 7 \\
x + 2 \overline{\smash{\big)}\, x^2 - 5x + 3} \\
\underline{x^2 + 2x} \\
-7x + 3 \\
\underline{-7x - 14} \\
+ 17
\end{array}
$$

$$x - 7 + \frac{17}{(x + 2)}.$$

Choices (B), (C), (D), and (E) are incorrect. To find the quotient and the remainder one can use either the long division procedure or the synthetic division procedure.

30. **(B)**

(B) is correct. Let x = the amount to cut off from each dimension so that the ratio of the shorter side to the longer side is $^2/_3$. Cutting off x from each dimension will give $(24 - x)$ inches and $(33 - x)$ inches.

Since the ratio of the shorter side to the longer side is $^2/_3$, then

$$\frac{(24 - x)}{(33 - x)} = \frac{2}{3}.$$

Solve for x.

$$
\begin{aligned}
3(24 - x) &= 2(33 - x) \\
72 - 3x &= 66 - 2x \\
x &= 6.
\end{aligned}
$$

Choices (A), (C), (D), and (E) are incorrect. Let x = the amount to cut off from each dimension so that the ratio of the shorter side to the longer side is $^2/_3$.

Section 5—Quantitative Ability

1. **(A)**

(A) is correct. Substituting the values of x and y into the $f(x, y)$,

$$f(1, 1) = \frac{[(2 \times 1) + 1]}{1^2} = \frac{[2 + 1]}{1} = \frac{3}{1} = 3 \text{ and}$$

$$f(1, 2) = \frac{[(2 \times 1) + 2]}{2^2} = \frac{[2 + 2]}{4} = \frac{4}{4} = 1.$$

Therefore, $f(1, 1) > f(1, 2)$. Choices (B), (C), and (D) are incorrect. The y value in Column B may be larger, but you have to put the values into the given $f(x, y)$.

2. **(B)**

(B) is correct. First, calculate the number of hours that the boy sleeps in 3 weeks.

$$\frac{14 \text{ hours}}{\text{day}} \times \frac{7 \text{ days}}{\text{week}} \times 3 \text{ weeks} = 294 \text{ hours.}$$

Then calculate the hours that the boy does not sleep in a month.

$$\frac{10 \text{ hours}}{\text{day}} \times \frac{30 \text{ days}}{\text{month}} \times 1 \text{ month} = 300 \text{ hours.}$$

3. **(B)**

Choices (A), (C), and (D) are incorrect. Remember that 60% of a quantity is the same as .60 multiplied by the quantity. (B) is correct. Solve for x.

$$.60(x + 2) = 36$$
$$.6x + 1.2 = 36$$
$$.6x = 34.8$$
$$x = 58$$

4. **(D)**

(A) is incorrect. Simplify the inequality to determine the value of x. Remember that 0 is an integer. (B) is incorrect. Simplify the inequality to determine the value of x. (C) is incorrect. Simplify the inequality to determine the value of x. Remember that integers can be negative or positive.

(D) is correct. Simplify the inequality to determine the value of x.

$$-1 \leq 2x + 1 < 2$$
$$-1 + (-1) \leq 2x + 1 + (-1) < 2 + (-1)$$
$$-2 \leq 2x < 1$$

$$\frac{-2}{2} \leq \frac{2x}{2} \leq \frac{1}{2}$$

$$-1 \leq x < \frac{1}{2}$$

The value of x may be either -1 or 0 since x must be an integer. Column B can be either less than or equal to Column A.

5. **(C)**

Choices (A), (B), and (D) are incorrect. The average is the sum of the variables divided by the number of variables. Note that the number of variables in Column A is 5 and in Column B is 6. (C) is correct. The average is the sum of the variables divided by the number of variables.

Column A: $\dfrac{(18 + 20 + 22 + 24 + 26)}{5} = \dfrac{(110)}{5} = 22$

Column B: $\dfrac{(17 + 19 + 21 + 23 + 25 + 27)}{6} = \dfrac{(132)}{6} = 22$

Therefore the quantities are equal.

6. **(A)**

(A) is correct. The triangles are:

ABC	Equilateral	(1)
AGC, CGB, AGB	Isosceles	(3)
AFC, AFB, AGD, GDC, CBD, CEA		
AGE, GEB, BDA, BDC, GFB, GFC	Scalene	(12)

The total number of triangles is 16. Therefore, Column A is larger than Column B.

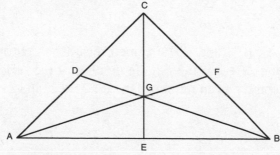

Choices (B), (C), and (D) are incorrect. Label all possible vertices for a triangle on the figure. Remember that a triangle is any three-sided polygon.

7. **(A)**

(A) is correct. Since (X, Y) is a point in the fourth quadrant,

X will always be a positive value and

Y will always be a negative value, then

$$X > Y \text{ and also } X > 2Y.$$

Choices (B), (C), and (D) are incorrect. The absolute value of $2Y$ may be greater than X, but the point is in the fourth quadrant.

8. **(C)**

Choices (A), (B), and (D) are incorrect. To find α and β remember that the interior angles in a triangle equal 180° and those in a quadrilateral equal 360°. (C) is correct. Label the figure with letter M at the vertex of β. Since $ABCD$ is a rectangle, $\angle DAB$ is 90° and $\angle EAD$ is 90°.

In triangle EAD

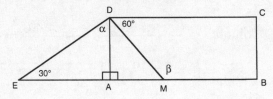

$$90° + 30° + \alpha = 180°$$
$$\alpha = 60°$$

In quadrilateral $DMBC$

$$60° + \beta + 90° + 90° = 360°$$
$$\beta = 120°$$

Therefore, $\alpha + \beta = 180°$.

9. **(C)**

Choices (A), (B), and (D) are incorrect. The perimeter is equal to the sum of the lengths of all segments. Remember that opposite sides of a parallelogram are equal. (C) is correct. Since opposite sides of a parallelogram are equal, the perimeter of the shaded area is equal to the perimeter of the square $ABCD$. The perimeter is equal to $4a$.

10. **(B)**

Choices (A), (C), and (D) are incorrect. Consecutive even numbers increase by 2 and $2x + 2$ is the middle number of the series. (B) is correct. The three consecutive even numbers are $2x$, $2x + 2$, and $2x + 4$.

$$\text{Average} = \frac{[2x + (2x+2) + (2x+4)]}{3}$$

$$\text{Average} = \frac{(6x+6)}{3}$$

$$= 2x + 2$$

$$2x + 2 > 2x$$

11. **(C)**

Choices (A), (B), and (D) are incorrect. The shaded area is the area of the half-circle minus the area of the small circle. The area of a circle is πr^2. (C) is correct. To compare both alternatives, calculate the shaded area.

Shaded area = half of circle (radius r) − circle (radius $\frac{r}{2}$)

$$\text{Shaded area} = \frac{(\pi r^2)}{2} - \pi\left(\frac{r}{2}\right)^2$$

$$= \frac{(\pi r^2)}{2} - \frac{(\pi r^2)}{4} = \frac{(\pi r^2)}{4}$$

Therefore, the two quantities are equal.

12. **(B)**

Choices (A), (C) and (D) are incorrect. Let x = days required to complete the job if A and B work together and solve the work problem.

$$\frac{1}{4} + \frac{1}{6} = \frac{1}{x} \text{ or } \frac{5}{12} = \frac{1}{x} \qquad x = \frac{12}{5} = 2.4 \text{ days}$$

13. **(D)**

Choices (A), (B), and (C) are incorrect. It is true for $m > 0$ and $n > 0$. Try values of m and n that are less than zero. (D) is correct. Given that $m > n$, then

if m > 0 and $n > 0$,
then $m^2 > n^2$,
if $m = |n|$
then $m^2 = n^2$,
if $m < 0$ and $n < 0$,
then $m^2 < n^2$.

The answer cannot be determined from the information given.

14. **(C)**
    Choices (A), (B), and (C) are incorrect. The sum of the interior angles of a triangle equals 180°, and the quantity in Column A equals $3X$. (C) is correct. The sum of the interior angles of a triangle equals 180°.

$$X + 2X + 3X = 180°$$
$$6X = 180°$$
$$X = 30°$$

Therefore, $3X = 90°$. Column A equals Column B.

15. **(B)**
    Choices (A), (C), and (D) are incorrect. The angles in a triangle equal 180°. The sides opposite a larger angle are greater than the sides opposite a smaller angle. (B) is correct. Since the measure of $\angle C$ is 60°, then the sum of $\angle A$ and $\angle B$ equal 120°. Since it is given that $\angle A > \angle B$, then $\angle A$ is > 60°. BC lies opposite $\angle A$ which is larger than 60°. Therefore, side BC is larger than side AB which lies opposite $\angle C$ which equals 60°.

16. **(B)**
    Choices (A), (C), (D), and (E) are incorrect. Insert the values of a and b into the expression to solve for x. The value of $a = 9$ and the value of $b = 6$. (B) is correct. If $a \times b = 6a - 2bx$ then

$$9 \times 6 = (6 \times 9) - [2 \times 6 \times (x)] = 54 - 12x$$
and $$9 \times 6 = 54$$
so $$54 - 12x = 54$$
$$54 - 54 - 12x = 54 - 54 = 0$$
$$x = 0$$

17. **(D)**
    Choices (A), (B), (C), and (E) are incorrect. Set up an algebraic problem with $x =$ the students who speak both French and German. Total class = students who speak only French + students who speak only German + students who speak both French and German. (D) is correct. Set up an algebraic problem with $x =$ the students who speak both French and German.

Therefore, the number of students who speak only French = $30 - x$

and the number of students who speak only German = $20 - x$

Total class = students who speak only French + students who speak only German + students who speak both French and German.

$$40 = (30 - x) + (20 - x) + x$$
$$40 = 50 - x$$
$$10 = x$$

18. **(D)**

Choices (A), (B), (C), and (E) are incorrect. Simplify the equation and solve for *B*. Be careful keeping terms within parentheses.(D) is correct. Simplify the equation and solve for *B*.

$$a = \left(\frac{h}{2}\right)(B + b)$$

$$\frac{2a}{h} = B + b \quad \text{Multiply both sides by } \left(\frac{2}{h}\right).$$

$$\frac{2a}{h} - b = B \quad \text{Solve for } B.$$

19. **(C)**

Choices (A), (B), (D), and (E) are incorrect. Remember that the bisector of an angle is one-half the angle and an equilateral triangle has three equal angles. (C) is correct. Put into the figure the values of the angles that are given from the information.

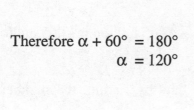

Therefore $\alpha + 60° = 180°$
$\alpha = 120°$

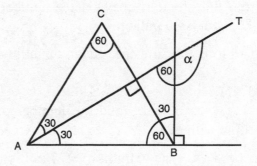

20. **(A)**

(A) is correct. First, the number is

$$1 : \frac{1}{\frac{8}{3}} = 1 \times \frac{3}{8} = \frac{3}{8}$$

The reciprocal of ⅜ is ⅛. (B) and (E) are incorrect. Find the number, then find the reciprocal.

21. **(B)**

Choices (A), (C), (D), and (E) are incorrect. This is the number of people with car insurance in 1955. Find the number of people with cars and then find the number of people with car insurance in 1970. (B) is correct. The number of people owning cars in 1970 equals

$$\frac{82}{100} \text{ (130 million)} = 106.6 \text{ million.}$$

Of these, 75% had insurance:

$$.75(106.6 \text{ million}) \approx 80 \text{ million.}$$

22. **(B)**

Choices (A), (C), (D), and (E) are incorrect. This amount is the difference in population from 1955 to 1970. Find the number of people with cars and then find the number of people with car insurance in 1955 and 1970. (B) is correct. The number of people with cars in 1955 equals

$$.70 \text{ (110 million)} = 77 \text{ million.}$$

The number of people with car insurance is

$$.55 \text{ (77 million)} = 42.35 \text{ million.}$$

From the previous question the number of people with car insurance in 1970 equals 80 million.

Therefore, the difference equals 80 million – 42.35 million = 37.65 million.

23. **(A)**

(A) is correct. Find the number of cars by finding the number of people with cars.

In 1955   .7 (110 million) = 77 million cars.

In 1970   .82 (130 million) = 106.6 million cars.

$$\text{Percent increase} = \left[\frac{(\text{number of cars in 1970 - number of cars in 1955})}{\text{cars in 1955}} \right] \times 100$$

$$= \left[\frac{(106.6 - 77)}{77} \right] x100 = 38.4\%.$$

Choices (B), (C), (D), and (E) are incorrect. The percent increase is equal to

$$\left[\frac{(\text{new amount - old amount})}{\text{old amount}} \right] \times 100.$$

24. **(C)**
Choices (A), (B), (D), and (E) are incorrect. This is the ratio of the percent of the uninsured in 1970 to the percent of the uninsured in 1955. The needed ratio is the ratio of cars without insurance in 1970 to cars without insurance in 1955. (C) is correct.

Cars without insurance in 1970 = .25 × .82 × 130 = 26.65 million.

Cars without insurance in 1955 = .45 × .70 × 110 = 34.65 million.

So the required ratio $= \dfrac{26.65}{34.65} = .77$.

25. **(B)**
Choices (A), (C), (D), and (E) are incorrect. This is the ratio of people without cars in 1955 to people without cars in 1970. The ratio needed is the ratio of people without cars in 1970 to people without cars in 1955. (B) is correct.

People without cars in 1970 = Total people in 1970
– People with cars in 1970.

130 million – 106.6 million = 23.4 million.

People without cars in 1955 = Total people in 1955
– People with cars in 1955.

110 million – 77 million = 33 million.

$$\frac{\text{people without cars in 1970}}{\text{people without cars in 1955}} = \frac{23.4 \text{ million}}{33 \text{ million}} = .71.$$

26. **(B)**
Choices (A), (C), (D), and (E) are incorrect. Let n = the number of years until the combined age of the sons equals 80% of the father's age. Remember to add n to each age. (B) is correct. Let n = the number of years until the combined age of the sons equals 80% of the father's age.

Their ages will be

    father = 40 + n
    son #1 = 6 + n
    son #2 = 3 + n
    son #3 = 1 + n.

Therefore,

$$(6 + n) + (3 + n) + (1 + n) = .80(40 + n)$$
$$10 + 3n = 32 + .8n$$
$$2.2n = 22$$
$$n = 10$$

27. **(D)**

Choices (A), (B), (C), and (E) are incorrect. Statement I is true but it is not the only true statement. Rearrange the given expression to analyze $x + z = 10 - y$. (D) is correct. Rearrange the given expression to find x.

$$x = 10 - y - z$$

If the smallest values for y and z are used, the largest value of x will be obtained.

$$x = 10 - 5 - 3 = 2$$

Therefore, $x < z$ and $x < y$.

Now rearrange the expression to analyze the third statement.

$$x + z = 10 - y$$

If $y = 5$ (the smallest value of y), then $x + z = 5$.

But if $y > 5$, then $x + z < 5$.

Therefore $x + z \leq y$. This means that only I and III are true.

28. **(A)**

(A) is correct. The expression can be simplified by factoring to

$$\left[\frac{.0003 \times 9 \times 10^{-1}}{18 \times 10^{-4}} \right]^{-1} = \left[\frac{3 \times 10^{-4} \times 9 \times 10^{-1}}{18 \times 10^{-4}} \right]^{-1}$$

Simplify

$$\left[\frac{3 \times 10^{-1}}{2} \right]^{-1} = \left[\frac{2}{3 \times 10^{-1}} \right]^{1}$$

or

$$\frac{2 \times 10}{3} = \frac{20}{3}$$

(B) is incorrect. Remember to do the required operations in the brackets. (C) is incorrect. Carefully multiply or factor the decimal and remember to do the required operations in the brackets. (D) is incorrect. Carefully multiply or factor the decimal. (E) is incorrect. Carefully multiply or factor the decimal.

29. **(D)**

(A) is incorrect. The length of the side of the inscribed square is not equal to *R*. *R* is the length of half of the diagonal. Use the Pythagorean theorem to find the length of the side. (B) is incorrect. The length of the side of the inscribed square is not equal to 2*R* but is the diagonal. Use the Pythagorean theorem to find the length of the side. (C) is incorrect.

$$\frac{R\sqrt{2}}{2}$$

is not the length of the side of the inscribed square. Use the Pythagorean theorem to find the length of the side. (D) is correct. Use the Pythagorean theorem to find the length of the side. The diagonal of the inscribed square is equal to 2*R*.

$$s^2 + s^2 = (2R)^2$$
$$2s^2 = 4R^2$$
$$s^2 = 2R^2$$
$$s = \sqrt{2}R$$

The perimeter of a square is equal to $4s = 4R\sqrt{2}$.

(E) is incorrect. $2R\sqrt{2}$ is not the length of the side of the inscribed square. Use the Pythagorean theorem to find the length of the side.

30. **(A)**

(A) is correct. To simplify reduce the square roots to fractional exponents.

$$\sqrt{x\sqrt{x\sqrt{x}}} = \sqrt{x\sqrt{x(x)^{1/2}}} = \sqrt{x\sqrt{x^{3/2}}}$$
$$= \sqrt{x(x)^{3/4}} = \sqrt{x^{7/4}}$$
$$= x^{7/8}$$

Choices (B), (C), (D), ad (E) are incorrect. To simplify reduce the square roots to fractional exponents. Remember that $a^p a^q = a^{(p+q)}$ and $(a^p)^q = a^{pq}$.

Section 6–Verbal Ability

1. **(A)**

(A) is correct. A "storm of INDIGNATION" arises when CORRUPTION is known. (B) is incorrect because people do not PROTEST COOPERATION. (C) is incorrect; it does not fit the context of the sentence. (D) is incorrect; it does not fit the context of the sentence. (E) is incorrect. "A storm of INDIFFERENCE" is a contradictory phrase.

2. **(B)**

(A) is incorrect because it is not the BEE which is HANDLED without disturbing the "other bees." (B) is correct. The LATTER refers to the frame. The frame is REMOVED without disturbing the other frames. (C) is incorrect because it is not the HIVE which is TAKEN without disturbing the "other hives." (D) is wrong because it is not the VESSEL which is DESTROYED without disturbing the "other vessels." (E) is incorrect; the choice does not make sense.

3. **(D)**

(D) is correct. We most closely associate POWER with the OPPORTUNITY for corruption. WEALTH (A) is also associated, but a wealthy person does not usually DESIRE to be corrupt. FAME (B), PRESTIGE (C), and STATUS (E) do not carry the connotation of corruption which POWER (D) does.

4. **(B)**

(B) is the correct alternative. An enthusiastic audience, by virtue of the clapping or other noise they produce could make even a vigorous rapping for order a futile attempt on the part of the chairman. (A) is wrong because boredom or weariness on the part of an audience would not make it impossible to get their attention. A bored and weary audience is not a loud, noisy group. (C) is incorrect because the phrase "he soon gave up the attempt" implies that the chairman was unsuccessful in getting the attention of the audience. In (C) the audience is "interested." His quick rapping would be successful. (D) is wrong because a chairman cannot be timid when calling for order. (E) is also incorrect because a chairman would not rap lightly when calling for order.

5. **(A)**

HERBIVOROUS animals, like the cow, subsist on grass and other plants; OMNIVOROUS animals, like the hog, eat any sort of food; (A) is correct. (B) is incorrect. A SCAVENGER eats refuse; OMNIPOTENT means having infinite power. (C) is incorrect; a SAPROPHYTE lives on decaying vegetation; a PARASITE takes what it requires from invading and destroying living plant and animal tissue. Neither term is applicable to the cow or hog. (D) is incorrect. A VEGETARIAN eats no meat (and sometimes no animal products) because of health reasons or principles opposing the killing of animals; CARNIVOROUS animals are flesh-eating. Cows do not consciously make the choice to be plant-eaters; hogs eat more than just meat. (E) is not the best answer. AUTOTROPHIC means self-feeding like green plants; HETEROTROPHIC means fed by others.

6. **(D)**

The key to this problem lies in noticing the negative which appears early in the sentence: "…not…(but)…" is the usual and logical pattern of usage. Here, "…not personal qualities but public services…" is the accurate statement. None of the other terms which appears first in the alternative pairs permits the meaning to stay intact by offering a contrast. Since it is the public services which undergird our lives rather than personal qualities, per se, which enable independence, the feeling of personal independence and self-sufficiency is really more illusion than fact.

7. **(A)**

(A) is correct. ACRIMONY means bitter feelings. PARSIMONY (B) refers to thriftiness. CAPRICIOUSNESS (C) means unpredictability. PRURIENCE (D) is the quality of being characterized by unseemly desires. None of these appropriately describes the residents reaction to the issue. (E) is incorrect. COMPLACENCE demonstrates an unconcern—and the residents are certainly concerned.

8. **(E)**

(A) is incorrect. The first term in the analogy identifies a term NOT possessed by the kind of person identified by the second term. A SCHIZOPHRENIC may have DELUSIONs. (B), (C), and (D) are incorrect. A PSYCHIC does profess to have SENSITIVITY, a CLAUSTROPHOBIC's fears center on SPACE, and a PSYCHOTIC may have ILLUSIONs. (E) is correct. A NEUROTIC is NOT characterized by CALM.

9. **(A)**

(A) is correct. The key relationship here is multiplicity. Many grains of SAND may form a DUNE. The answer is (A) because many TREES may form a FOREST. (B) is wrong because many ROCKS do not form a BOULDER. (C) is incorrect because SHOWER:DELUGE presents a relationship of intensity. A light rain or SHOWER, when intensified, becomes a DELUGE. (D) is incorrect because CLAMOR and TUMULT are interchangeable terms. (E) is wrong because many TWIGS do not form a LOG.

10. **(A)**

(A) is correct. The analogy here is that of simple to complex. In math, a VARIABLE is less complex than an EQUATION. The correct answer is (A) OXYGEN:WATER. OXYGEN is a simpler element than WATER, which contains both hydrogen and oxygen. (B) is incorrect. PARAMECIA and AMOEBA are both simple one-celled life forms. (C) is incorrect. In ANALYSIS:SUMMARY, the first term identifies a more complex process than the second term. Here the relationship is complex to simple. (D) is incorrect. CLAY:SCULPTURE presents an analogy of use: CLAY is used to make a SCULPTURE. (E) is incorrect. FURNACE:HEAT is an analogy of function; a FURNACE produces HEAT.

11. **(E)**

(A) is incorrect; DETONATE is synonymous with EXPLODE. (B) is incorrect; it is an analogy of whole-to-part. STUDY may include a RESEARCH component. (C) is wrong because the analogy here is that of opposition. To DESTROY is the opposite of to BUILD. (D) is wrong because the second term does not identify the purpose of the first term. (E) is correct. This is an analogy of purpose. One DECODES in order to UNDERSTAND. One SOWS in order to REAP, or harvest.

12. **(E)**

The HEART is a part of the CIRCULATORY system. The part comes before the whole in this analogy. (A) is incorrect. The EXCRETORY system of the body secretes SWEAT, but the analogy is not whole to part. (B) is incorrect; the NEUROLOGICAL system involves the nervous system. The SKELETON is a part of the skeletal system. (C) is incorrect. The LUNGS are a part of the RESPIRATORY system, but the order is not the same as for CIRCULATORY:HEART. (D) is incorrect; a KIDNEY is not a part of the DIGESTIVE system. (E) is the correct answer, since the TESTES are a part of the male REPRODUCTIVE system.

13. **(B)**

QUART is the English measure of volume; LITER is the metric volume measure. (A) is incorrect. YARD is the English measure of length; ACRE is an English, not a metric, measurement. (B) is correct. YARD is the English measure of length; METER is the metric measure. (C) is incorrect. OUNCE is an English measure of mass (weight). KILO-WATT is a unit of work. The relationship between the two is not that of measuring the same unit. (D) is incorrect. LITER is the metric unit of volume; GALLON is the English unit. The two are inverted, however, from that of the example. (E) is incorrect. MILE is an English measure of length. KILOGRAM is a metric measurement of mass (weight). The relationship is English to metric, but the thing measured is different. (E) is incorrect.

14. **(C)**

(C) is correct. A QUILL is a precursor of the FOUNTAIN PEN. In the correct alternative, (C), a TRUCE is a precursor of PEACE. (A) is incorrect. The relationship RURAL:URBAN is one of opposites. (B) is incorrect. The relationship YOUNG:OLD is one of progression. A young person, in time, progresses in age and becomes old. A quill does not progress in time to become a fountain pen. (D) is incorrect. The relationship in SOLO:QUARTET is a numerical one, specifically a one-to-four relationship. (E) is incorrect. Both a MANGLE and an IRON serve the same purpose, but a MANGLE is specifically designed to IRON certain kinds of items.

15. **(B)**

(A) is incorrect. EXPURGATE and CENSOR are synonyms. EX-PUNGE means to erase; it is not a synonym of WASH. (B) is correct. EXPURGATE and CENSOR are synonyms, as are REJECT and REPU-DIATE. (C) is incorrect. FRENETIC and FRENCH are not related. (D) is incorrect. PHRENETIC and PHONEME are not related. (E) is incorrect. WROUGHT means brought about; it is not a synonym of EXCITED.

16. **(B)**

The RIBS of an UMBRELLA are a kind of frame and help give it its shape. (B) is correct. STUDS help give a WALL its shape. LEG:TABLE (A), SHELF:CLOSET (C), HINGE:DOOR (D), and KNOB:DRAWER (E) are all part-to-whole relationships.

17. **(E)**

(A) is incorrect. Even though the British forced the French out of Nova Scotia, they were allowed to settle in the American colonies. (B) is not correct because the author mentions these two different groups of

Frenchmen. (C) is wrong because the author mentions these two different groups of Frenchmen. (D) is not correct as the odyssey spoken of by the author was Longfellow's *Evangeline*. (E) is correct; the author discusses the French heritage in America through the entire article.

18. **(B)**

(A) is incorrect, as the Acadians were French. (B) is correct. The Acadians were run out of Nova Scotia. The author also discusses "Other persecuted Huguenots." (C) is incorrect because the Acadians were stable and dispersed themselves in the society of the American colonies and settled in Louisiana. (D) is not correct because nothing can be inferred about happiness. (E) is wrong because the Acadians "enriched the cultural patterns evolving in the colonies," and this does not suggest that the Acadians were reclusive.

19. **(A)**

(A) is the correct answer as the author's views are favorable or auspicious toward America's French heritage. Unfortunate (B) would be a negative reaction and an incorrect response. Inevitable (C) may be inferred by the reader since the French were relocated and settled in the colonies, but cannot be inferred from the author's viewpoint as expressed. Unlikely (D) cannot be inferred from the selection. Foreboding (E) is incorrect because it refers to negative things.

20. **(B)**

(A) is incorrect. The stipulations seemed to be reasonable to Penn. (B) is correct. Penn "lost no time in advertising," he was a "felicitous" administrator, and "made a personal fortune." (C) is not correct. The people of the time probably regarded Indians as savages, but that is not the author's opinion. (D) is wrong. Nothing in the passage indicates Penn was especially favored by the King. (E) is incorrect. The passage states that Indians maintained friendly relations with the settlers because Penn kept his word.

21. **(D)**

(D) is correct. In the final paragraph the author states that the "Holy Experiment" encouraged individuals' morality and freedom of conscience. (A) is incorrect. Even though English-Colonial collaboration, a bicameral legislation, and a treaty with the Indians were important factors in the development of the Pennsylvania colony, they were considered as part of the "Holy Experiment." (B) is not correct. Even though English-Colonial collaboration, a bicameral legislation, and a treaty with the Indians were important factors in the development of the Pennsylvania colony, they were considered as part of the "Holy Experiment." (C) is not the right answer. Even though English-Colonial collaboration, a bicameral legislation, and a treaty with the Indians were important factors in the development of the Pennsylvania colony, they were considered as part of the "Holy Experiment." (E) is incorrect because other proprietary colonies were not founded on the same premise.

22. **(C)**

(C) is correct. The colony did not have a state religion; it was open to all religions and nationalities. Rapid settlement (A), refuge for religious non-conformists (B), a proprietary government (D), and laws in harmony with those of England (E) are all accurate descriptions of Pennsylvania's colony.

23. **(E)**

(E) is correct. In paragraph four the passage states that "unlike the other colonies, it was not troubled by the Indians. Penn had bought their lands and made a series of peace treaties that were scrupulously fair and rigidly adhered to." There is no support in the passage for (A), (B), (C), or (D).

24. **(C)**

(A) is incorrect. In terms of today Penn would be considered a politician; in his terms he was a humanitarian. (B) is incorrect because although there were treaties with the Indians, this was only one of several factors which contributed to the government's being a progressive one. (C) is correct. Religious toleration, bicameral legislature, and forward-looking penal code all added to a progressive (i.e., republic) form of government. (D) is incorrect because there were no restrictions on immigration. (E) is incorrect because the "Great Law" and the "First and Second Frames of Government" were never overturned.

25. **(A)**

(A) is correct. Even though the author never calls Pennsylvania a melting pot, because of the guarantee of freedoms, several nationalities as well as several religious sects settled in the colony, making it a "melting-pot" society. Pennsylvania could not be referred to as a solely Quaker colony (B), the largest American colony (C), a Colonial Republic (D), or the first "democratic" colony (E).

26. **(A)**

(A) is correct. The passage does not mention Catholic settlers. It does mention Jews (B), Baptists (C), Mennonites (D), and Quakers (E).

27. **(E)**

(A) is incorrect; syllogism is the presentation of a major and a minor premise, and a conclusion drawn from the two premises. (B) is incorrect. An analogy is the "inference that certain resemblances imply further similarity." (C) is an incorrect answer. A literary allusion is to compare a point with some concept or period in literature. (D) is not correct. The author made no attempt to quote other authors. (E) is the correct answer. He uses facts to show growth. The colony was awarded in 1681 and by the summer of 1683 there were 3,000 settlers.

28. **(C)**

(A) is incorrect. CEASE means to stop. (B) is not correct. DEPRIVE means to deny. (C) is correct. ADDICT means to surrender to a habit. WEAN means to withdraw from a habit. (D) is wrong. ALIENATE means to make unfriendly something that was once friendly. (E) is inappropriate. ESTRANGE means to alienate.

29. **(A)**

(A) is correct. To UNDERMINE is to weaken or injure, especially by subtle or insidious means. Its opposite is REINFORCE, meaning to strengthen, support, or buttress. (B) is incorrect. To REESTABLISH means to rebuild. (C) is incorrect. To RESTORE is to return to a former state. (D) is incorrect. To CONSOLIDATE is to combine several things into one, thereby achieving greater strength. UNDERMINE and REINFORCE can apply to a single structure. (E) is incorrect. To CORROBORATE is to support by confirming rather than by buttressing.

30. **(B)**

(A) is incorrect. A MALEVOLENT person wishes harm or evil to others. (B) is correct. The opposite of RELIGIOUS is SECULAR, or worldly. EVIL (C) is the antonym for good. (D) IMPIOUS means irreverent. UNRIGHTEOUS (E) is the antonym for righteous.

31. **(C)**

(A) ABROGATE is to abolish or annul. (B) is incorrect. DISCLAIM is to give up any claim. (C) is correct. To CORROBORATE is to confirm or to support. The opposite of confirm or strengthen is CONTRADICT, literally, to speak against something, to be contrary to something. DISPROVE (D) is to prove something false. (E) DOUBT is to tend to disbelieve.

32. **(E)**
    (A) is wrong because ASYMMETRICAL refers to lack of balance in size, shape, or position. CONFUSION (B) refers to a state of disorder. (C) CHAOS refers to a state of disorder. (D) is wrong because DISASSEMBLED means separated into component parts. (E) is correct. A UNIFORM thing does not vary from others, in form, rate, or degree. It is like all others of the same class. Its opposite is VARIOUS, which means differing one from another; of several kinds.

33. **(A)**
    (A) is correct. RUDE is an adjective meaning crude, rough, or unrefined. Its opposite is URBANE, polite in a smooth, polished manner. DEBONAIR (B) means genial. PLEASANT (C) means agreeable. (D) is incorrect. The opposite of FRIENDLY is unfriendly, and while an unfriendly person may be rude, unfriendliness is not a prerequisite for rudeness. Friendly people can be crude as well. (E) is not correct. The opposite of CONFIDENT is uncertain or unsure of oneself. A rude person may be very confident and sure of himself.

34. **(E)**
    EXPLICABLE (A) means able to be explained. (B) is incorrect. SOLVABLE means able to be solved. (C) is not correct. RECOGNIZABLE means discernible. This is close, but it's not the best choice. (D) is incorrect. RATIONAL means based on reason. (E) is correct. UNINTELLIGIBLE means unclear, not able to be understood. APPARENT means evident, obvious, readily seen.

35. **(E)**
    EPITOME, CONCISION, LACONIC, and COMPENDIUM are similar in meaning to ABRIDGMENT. REDUNDANT (E) has the opposite meaning of "in excess of."

36. **(E)**
    (A) is incorrect. ADORE means to love greatly. AGREE (B) means to be in accord with. ADVOCATE (C) means to speak in favor of. (D) is not correct. ADMIRE means to esteem highly. (E) is correct. REPUDIATE means to separate from, to disown or disavow. ADOPT means to accept as one's own.

37. **(D)**

(A) is incorrect. A person with a VORACIOUS appetite craves large amounts of food. (B) is wrong; a FASTIDIOUS person is one who is not easily pleased. (C) is not correct; an ASCETIC is one who is self-denying. (D) is correct. A GLUTTONOUS individual is one who eats to excess, while an ABSTEMIOUS person is one who is moderate or temperate in eating or drinking. An AUSTERE (E) person is one who is stern, harsh, or morally strict.

38. **(B)**

CAPRICIOUS is an adjective meaning erratic, subject to sudden impulsive changes. Its opposite is (B) STEADFAST, meaning fixed, or constant. The alternatives all identify personal qualities unrelated to the term CAPRICIOUS or the term STEADFAST. (A) STUFFY means dull. (C) SCURRILOUS means abusive or offensive. (D) SAGACIOUS means shrewd or astute, and (E) SYBARITIC means sensualistic or hedonistic (given to pleasure).

GRE

Graduate Record Examination

Practice
Test 5

Section 1

TIME: 45 Minutes
Choose 1 of 2 Essays†

ESSAY QUESTION ONE

> **DIRECTIONS:** Present your perspective on the issue below by using relevant reasons and/or examples to support your views. Remember, there is no one "correct" response to the essay topic. Before starting, read the essay topic and its question(s).

Many people maintain that women are not as likely to be successful in the world of business as men are.

Do you think this is true? Why or why not?

STOP

Do not go on until you are instructed to do so. Use any remaining time to check your work on this portion of the test.

† On the actual test, you will have a choice between two essay topics. You have to write only one essay. To give you the most practice possible we have supplied sample essays for both questions in order to show you the differences between essays that receive a perfect score and those that score less.

TIME: 45 Minutes
Choose 1 of 2 Essays†

ESSAY QUESTION TWO

DIRECTIONS: Present your perspective on the issue below by using relevant reasons and/or examples to support your views. Remember, there is no one "correct" response to the essay topic. Before starting, read the essay topic and its question(s).

One of the most critical issues facing a democracy is how public money is spent. Elected officials have as one of their primary tasks the proper use of tax revenues. In a diverse society, it is often difficult to have a standard view on how to allocate funds. It seems reasonable to assert, however, that as long as there are needy people, public money should not be spent on cultivating cultural or artistic ventures.

Do you agree with this statement? Why or why not? Explain your position with relevant reasons and examples.

STOP

Do not go on until you are instructed to do so. Use any remaining time to check your work on this portion of the test.

---

† On the actual test, you will have a choice between two essay topics. You have to write only one essay. To give you the most practice possible we have supplied sample essays for both questions in order to show you the differences between essays that receive a perfect score and those that score less.

Section 2

TIME: 30 Minutes
1 Essay

DIRECTIONS: Critique the following argument by considering its logical soundness.

"The turn of the century brought about a sudden shift in values in America. Industrialization and urbanization caused a movement from small towns to big cities, from personal to impersonal, from the individual to the crowd. Morally, there was a shift from values directed and governed from within to more of a concern with appearances. The growth of consumer culture was accompanied by a growth in advertising, and it suddenly became necessary for the individual to sell him or herself as a product."

What is the main point of this argument? Is this argument convincing? Why or why not? Can you tell how the author felt about the subject in the passage? Are the changes discussed in a positive or negative light? What would make this argument more convincing?

STOP

If time remains, you may go back and check your work.

Section 3

TIME: 30 Minutes
38 Questions

DIRECTIONS: Each of the given sentences has blank spaces which indicate words omitted. Choose the best combination of words which fit into the meaning and structure within the context of the sentence.

1. Educators may be divided into two general groups based on their thinking in relation to prerequisites: the first group would set them high in order that time and money not be _____ expended; the second would set them low in order that those who might be able to benefit not be _____ .

    (A) pointlessly...tempted

    (B) wastefully...charged

    (C) carelessly...failed

    (D) unnecessarily...enrolled

    (E) needlessly...denied

2. The computer is a(n) _____ tool, for if one neglects to save a file, it cannot be recalled.

    (A) ominous

    (B) complicated

    (C) essential

    (D) difficult

    (E) unforgiving

3. Living out the _____ consequences of choices made, he realized the meager nature of his existence: his life was not to be so _____ as he had once assumed it would be.

    (A) surprising...intricate

    (B) unexpected...exciting

    (C) inevitable...full

    (D) boring...predictable

    (E) happy...unusual

4. Those in power continue to enrich themselves at public expense and this with clear conscience, because they live by a legal rather than a moral ethic: An action is _____ provided there is no law specifically _____ it.

    (A) good...prohibiting

    (B) wrong...enforcing

    (C) ethical...stopping

    (D) unethical...legalizing

    (E) sound...allowing

5. The botanist explained that the plant which is _____ lives more than two years, while the plant which is _____ may store food and grow one year and may reproduce and die in another season.

    (A) binary...annual

    (B) perennial...biennial

    (C) semi-annual...centennial

    (D) evergreen...deciduous

    (E) decennial...triennial

6. Anthropology's _____ rhetoric sometimes presents piecemeal cultural observations as a cohesive analysis of the entire cultural structure.

    (A) synodic

    (B) chthonic

    (C) synchronic

    (D) chimeric

    (E) synecdochic

7. The gift shop's plethora of garish native clothing and indigenous crafts was meant to be impressive, but the actual effect was _____ .

    (A) iniquitous

    (B) meretricious

    (C) opprobrious

    (D) vivacious

    (E) mendacious

DIRECTIONS: In the following questions, a related pair of words is followed by five more pairs of words. Select the pair that best expresses the same relationship as that expressed in the original pair.

---

8. IGNORANT:KNOWLEDGE::

    (A) fast:hunger   (D) despair:hope

    (B) old:antique   (E) good:better

    (C) syllable:word

9. INDICATIVE:MOOD::

    (A) present:past   (D) declarative:imperative

    (B) pronoun:preposition   (E) future:tense

    (C) sentence:clause

10. GAUNTLET:HAND::

    (A) cannon:ball   (D) lance:shield

    (B) sword:hand   (E) armor:body

    (C) body:shield

11. SYMPHONY:FUGUE::

    (A) book:novel   (D) novel:short story

    (B) diary:entry   (E) prologue:appendix

    (C) essay:topic sentence

12. DETRIMENTAL:ADVANTAGEOUS::

    (A) amiable:capricious   (D) sapid:insipid

    (B) doubt:qualm   (E) banal:trivial

    (C) staid:stoic

13. MARINATE:BEEF::

    (A) visit:friend   (D) swim:lap

    (B) paste:wallpaper   (E) eat:cake

    (C) study:book

14. SYCOPHANT:SINCERITY::

    (A) pedant:detail   (B) skeptic:certitude

(C) gambler:luck   (D) mercenary:money

(E) fugitive:flight

15. ANTAGONIST:ADVERSARY::

     (A) opponent:ally   (D) rival:emulator

     (B) competitor:auxiliary   (E) foe:accomplice

     (C) enemy:confederate

16. LEGERDEMAIN:MAGICIAN::

     (A) eyesight:gunslinger   (D) oven:baker

     (B) lecture:professor   (E) peacoat:sailor

     (C) chaps:cowboy

DIRECTIONS: Each passage is followed by questions based on its content. After reading a passage, choose the best answer to each question. Answer all questions based on what is stated or implied in that passage.

The atmosphere is the medium in which air pollutants are emitted and transported from the source to the receptor. Although this sounds simple on the surface, it is perhaps the most complex and least understood facet of air pollution. Many variables influence the character of a given chemical species from the time it leaves the source until it reaches the receptor. A few examples will suffice to illustrate the complexity of the situation.

First, consider emission. Pollutants can be emitted from a point source such as a power plant, a line source such as a highway, or an area source such as a city or large industrial complex. The emission point may be close to the ground (e.g., the tailpipe of a car) or over a thousand feet in height (e.g., high stacks of a power plant). Thus, elevation alone has a tremendous influence on how rapidly the pollutant will be dispersed and diluted before it reaches a receptor. The relative size of the pollution source is an obvious variable. Time of emission is important because meteorological conditions vary throughout the day. The atmosphere is more stable at night, and less dilution occurs then. During the day, sunlight plays an important part in transforming the chemical species of pollutants.

Second, consider the transport phenomenon. Many attempts have been made to characterize the vertical and horizontal dispersion of pollution from point and line sources. Many mathematical equations and models have been developed. Each has deficiencies because of the variability of sources, source strength, topography, and other factors. From the receptor standpoint, this is the important phase because, if the pollutants are not adequately dispersed and diluted, atmospheric insults will occur.

There are many factors to consider and it should be kept in mind that a nearby source does not necessarily imply that damage will result.

17. Which of the following best states the author's main point?

    (A) The atmosphere is the medium in which air pollutants are emitted and transported.

    (B) Scientists have a high degree of accuracy when calculating the pollutant dispersion.

    (C) A nearby pollutant source may be an indication that change will result.

    (D) There are many alternatives that influence the character of pollutants.

    (E) Both highway emission and large complex emission are the largest sources of atmospheric pollutants.

18. The author discussed several variables that affect the transporting of pollutants. Which of the following is NOT a variable mentioned by the author?

    (A) Relative size of the pollution source

    (B) Daytime

    (C) Elevation

    (D) Atmosphere

    (E) Nighttime

19. The author mentions "vertical and horizontal dispersion of pollution from point and line sources" because

    (A) there must be a horizontal movement as well as a vertical movement before there can be atmospheric and vegetation damage.

(B) there are deficiencies in the mathematical formulas because of the variabilities of sources, source strength, topography, and other factors.

(C) if the pollutants are not adequately dispersed and diluted, atmospheric insults will occur.

(D) although it may sound simple on the surface, it is perhaps the most complex and least understood facet of air pollution.

(E) there are many factors to consider and vertical and horizontal dispersion are the most important.

The two-man crosscut saw was evidently known by the Romans though little used by them. It was not until the middle of the fifteenth century that the crosscut saw came into fairly common use in Europe. Records exist of the crosscut being used for cutting logs in the United States between 1635 and 1681. About 1880, Pennsylvania lumbermen began felling trees with the crosscut. Before that time all trees had been ax-felled and crosscut into lengths.

Until the fifteenth century, the two-man crosscut saw was of a plain tooth pattern. The M tooth pattern seems to have been developed and used in south Germany in the 1400s. Even as late as 1900, most of the European crosscuts still used the plain tooth pattern with a few exceptions of M tooth being used. Not until fairly recently was the saw with a raker or "drag" developed.

In the case of plain, M, and Great American tooth patterns, each tooth both cuts the wood and clears out the shavings. In the case of the champion, lance, and perforated lance tooth, however, cutter teeth cut the wood fibers and the rakers remove the scored wood from the cut.

By the time crosscut use was at its peak, a large number of tooth patterns had been developed, each presumably suited to a particular set of conditions.

Saws can be divided into two types: two-man and one-man. Generally speaking, a one-man saw is shorter, but its defining characteristic is that it is asymmetric. Both one- and two-man crosscuts can be used by either one or two persons.

At one time, one-man crosscuts were made in lengths from 3 to 6 feet. Two-man saws were made in lengths from 4 to 12 feet for the Pacific

Northwest, and 16 feet for the California redwoods. If a longer saw was needed, two shorter saws were sometimes brazed together.

There are two basic saw patterns for the two-man saw: the felling pattern for felling trees and the bucking pattern for cutting up trees once they are on the ground. Each has characteristics suited to its use.

The felling saw has a concave back and is relatively light and flexible. It is light so less effort is needed to move it back and forth when felling a tree. It is flexible to conform to the arc a sawyer's arms take when sawing, and it is narrow tooth-to-back, enabling the sawyer to place a wedge in the cut behind the saw sooner than with a wide saw.

The bucking saw has a straight back; it is much thicker tooth-to-back than the felling saw, so it is heavier and stiffer. A bucking saw traditionally is run by one person, so it is a fairly stiff saw to help prevent buckling on the push stroke. The more weight put on a saw, the faster it will cut, so the weight of a bucking saw is an asset.

20. After reading the selection, the title that best fits is

   (A) The Crosscut Saw and the American Development.

   (B) The Crosscut Saw and the Development of the Lumber Industry.

   (C) The Crosscut Saw, A European Gift.

   (D) The Crosscut Saw, A European Development.

   (E) The Crosscut Saw.

21. The author refers to asymmetric in order to

   (A) inform the reader that both the one-man and two-man crosscut saws can be used by either one or two persons.

   (B) reveal that there are different lengths of crosscut saws.

   (C) introduce the two saw patterns for the two-man saw.

   (D) define the basic characteristic of the shorter one-man crosscut saw.

   (E) describe the large tooth, small tooth formation.

22. The author mentions plain, champion, and lance as examples of

   (A) tooth formation in crosscut saws.

(B) types of crosscut saws.

(C) generations of crosscut saws.

(D) crosscut saw improvements developed in Germany.

(E) crosscut saw improvements developed in America.

23. From the comments about the Romans and the crosscut saw, it can be concluded

(A) the felling saw was used more widely by the Romans because of the additional slavepower needed to run it.

(B) the Romans spread its use throughout Europe.

(C) the Romans introduced the perforated lance tooth.

(D) the Romans made little use of the saw.

(E) at the end of the Roman Empire, a number of tooth patterns had been developed.

24. From the author's description of the bucking saw, it can be inferred that the saw

(A) has the lance tooth pattern.

(B) is from four to twelve feet long.

(C) was introduced to America from Germany.

(D) was perfected on the European continent.

(E) is traditionally a two-man saw.

25. According to the author, there are two basic patterns for the two-man saw. One saw has a concave back and is light and flexible

(A) to conform to the arc a sawyer's arms make when sawing.

(B) and is traditionally operated by one person which makes it easier to saw through large trees.

(C) and the more weight put on the saw the faster it will cut.

(D) since the large number of teeth cleans the cut of shavings.

(E) with a champion tooth pattern.

26. The crosscut saw has several tooth patterns, but the "M" tooth pattern was introduced first in

    (A) Rome.   (D) Germany.

    (B) the United States.   (E) France.

    (C) England.

27. According to the selection, all of the following are true of the crosscut saw EXCEPT

    (A) it was not until the late nineteenth century that the crosscut saw was used to fell trees.

    (B) the "M" tooth pattern was developed in Europe in the fifteenth century.

    (C) generally the longer crosscut saws, those of 16 feet, were developed for thick forests in the Pacific Northwest.

    (D) the two basic two-man crosscut patterns are the felling saw and the bucking saw.

    (E) the Great American tooth pattern is designed so each tooth both cuts the wood and clears out the shavings.

DIRECTIONS: Each of the following questions provides a given word in capitalized letters followed by five word choices. Choose the best word which is most <u>opposite</u> in meaning to the given word.

---

28. REPULSIVE:

    (A) elegant   (D) pleasant

    (B) beauteous   (E) amicable

    (C) alluring

29. CALAMITY:

    (A) favor   (D) benefit

    (B) advantage   (E) boon

    (C) value

30. AUDACIOUS:

    (A) complaisant   (D) impudent

    (B) fastidious   (E) insolent

    (C) impertinent

31. CALCULATING:

    (A) rash   (D) quixotic

    (B) daring   (E) wild

    (C) risky

32. INFAMOUS:

    (A) idolized   (D) illustrious

    (B) ignominious   (E) gracious

    (C) unknown

33. GERMANE:

    (A) trenchant   (D) fatuous

    (B) fecund   (E) partisan

    (C) pertinent

34. ALLEVIATE:

    (A) intensify   (D) aggravate

    (B) interfere   (E) obviate

    (C) irritate

35. CONSUMMATE:

    (A) perfect   (D) crude

    (B) hungry   (E) complete

    (C) unsuccessful

36. DISSEMBLE:

    (A) betray   (B) put together

(C) resemble   (D) agree

(E) resolve

37. STENTORIAN:

   (A) styptical   (D) vociferous

   (B) egregious   (E) subdued

   (C) invidious

38. IMPOLITIC:

   (A) tactless   (D) civil

   (B) recalcitrance   (E) political

   (C) poltroonery

STOP

If time still remains, you may go back and check your work.
When the time allotted is up, you may go on to the next section.

Section 4

	Column A	Column B
1.	5×4	$5 + 4$

Explanation: The correct answer is (A), since $5 \times 4 = 20$, and $5 + 4 = 9$.

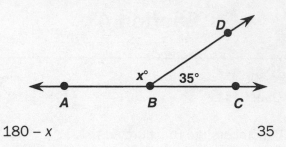

2.   180 – x   35

Explanation: The correct answer is (C). Since angle *ABC* is a straight angle, its measurement is 180°.

<u>**Column A**</u>   <u>**Column B**</u>

1.   The difference between b
         $a + b$ and $a - b$

$$n = p^2, p > 1$$

2. n p

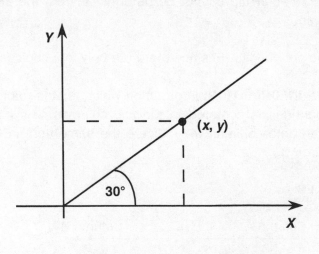

3. x y

<u>**Column A**</u>	<u>**Column B**</u>

If $a \times b = 2ab - 1$ and $b \times a = 2a - 1$
$a, b > 1$

4.	$\dfrac{a \times b}{b \times a}$	$\dfrac{b \times a}{a \times b}$

5.	The mode of 10, 9, 10, 21, 10, 10, 14	The mean of 14, 10, 9, 10, 17

$MN \parallel CA$

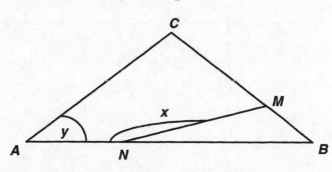

6.	$x + y$	$180°$

$x < 0$
$y < 0$

7.	$x - y$	0

$a + 1;\ a + 4;\ a + 3;\ a + 6;\ a + 5;\ 10$

8.	a	2

Column A	Column B

Area of a right triangle ABC = 60.5 square units
segment AC = segment CB

9.   Length of AC 11 units

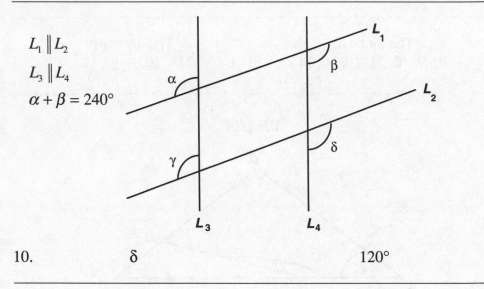

$L_1 \parallel L_2$
$L_3 \parallel L_4$
$\alpha + \beta = 240°$

10.   δ   120°

$ABCD$ and $A'B'C'D'$ are squares of side a.

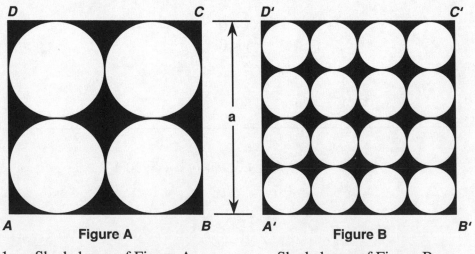

Figure A   **Figure B**

11.   Shaded area of Figure A   Shaded area of Figure B

Column A	**Column B**

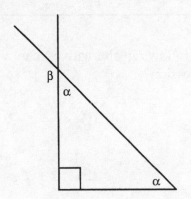

12. | β | 3α |

Worker A completed a job in 10 days, worker B in 8 days, and worker C in 5 days.

13. Time that it takes workers A and B together | Time that it takes worker C

$$\underbrace{3+3+3+\ldots}_{m \text{ times}} > \underbrace{4+4+4+4+\ldots}_{p \text{ times}}$$

14. | $\dfrac{m}{p}$ | 2 |

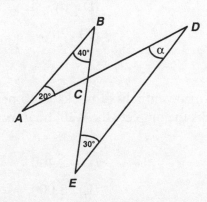

15. | α | $30°$ |

DIRECTIONS: For the following questions, select the best answer choice to the given question.

16. In which of the following alternatives can we simplify *a* without changing the expression?

(A) $\dfrac{x/a}{a/x}$

(D) $\dfrac{x^a}{2^a}$

(B) $\dfrac{x+a}{x-a}$

(E) $ax + a$

(C) $\dfrac{ax-a}{a}$

17. In a group of 30 people the average height is 6 feet and 2 inches. Therefore, we can assume that

I. everyone is 6 feet and 2 inches.

II. most of the people are 6 feet and 2 inches.

III. not all could be taller than 6 feet and 2 inches.

(A) I only

(D) I and II only

(B) II only

(E) I, II, and III

(C) III only

18. If $a/x - b/y = c$ and $xy = 1/c$, then $bx =$

(A) $1 - ay$.

(D) $ay - 1$.

(B) ay.

(E) $2ay$.

(C) $ay + 1$.

19. One wall being made entirely of bricks is 40 percent built. If we need 1,200 more bricks to complete the wall, how many bricks will the wall have?

(A) 1,500

(D) 2,400

(B) 1,800

(E) 3,000

(C) 2,000

20. If $x : y = 1 : 2$ and $y : z = 2 : 3$, then

    I. $x : y : z = 1 : 2 : 3$

    II. $x : z = 2 : 6$

    III. $x/y : y/z = 3 : 4$

    (A) I only   (D) I and II only

    (B) II only   (E) I, II, and III

    (C) III only

Questions 21–25.

Adapted from *Scholastic Update*, 5/5/89. Vol. 121, N. 17.

	China	Soviet Union
Area (sq. mi)	3.7 million	8.7 million
Population	1.1 billion	289 million
Percentage Under 15	39% (1960)	31% (1960)
	25% (1990)	25% (1990)
Percent Who Live in Cities	19% (1960)	49% (1960)
	21% (1990)	68% (1990)
Life Expectancy	60 (1970)	70 (1970)
	69 (1990)	72 (1990)
Infant Mortality	81 (1970)	26 (1970)
(deaths per 1,000 births)	32 (1990)	22 (1990)
Birth Rate	37 (1970)	18 (1970)
(births per 1,000 pop.)	18 (1990)	18 (1990)
Citizens per Doctor	1,757	267
Students (Ages 9–15) per teacher	42	25
Literacy	70%	99%
Gross National Product (GNP)	$315 billion	$2 trillion
Percent of GNP to Military	7%	11.5%
Exports to U.S.	$9.3 billion	$470 million
Imports from U.S.	$5.03 billion	$1.5 billion

21. How many people are more than 15 years old in China (1990)?

    (A) 825 million   (D) 671 million

    (B) 8.25 billion   (E) 216.75 million

    (C) .0825 billion

22. What is the approximate annual per capita income in China?

   (A) $2,864   (D) $3,000

   (B) $286.4   (E) $315

   (C) $300

23. How many people under age 15 lived in China's cities in 1990?

   (A) 49,130,000   (D) 231,000,000

   (B) 57,750,000   (E) 275,000,000

   (C) 81,510,000

24. What is the approximate ratio of doctors between the Soviet Union and China, respectively?

   (A) .578   (D) 6.58

   (B) 1.729   (E) .263

   (C) .152

25. How many newborns died in the Soviet Union in 1990?

   (A) 11,444   (D) Cannot be determined.

   (B) 114,000   (E) 114,444

   (C) 1,144,444

26. What percent of 260 is 13?

   (A) .05%   (D) .5%

   (B) 5%   (E) 20%

   (C) 50%

27. $\dfrac{1-\frac{1}{1-x}}{1-\frac{1}{1-\frac{1}{x}}} =$

   (A) x (D) $-x$

   (B) $\dfrac{1}{x}$ (E) 1

   (C) $\dfrac{-1}{x}$

28. In a college bookstore where all books are the same price, $a + b$ books are selling for $1,000. Myron buys 12 books and for each one has a discount of $1. How much does Myron need to pay?

(A) $[(a + b) - 1] \times 12$

(D) $[a + b] \times 12$

(B) $[(a + b)/1,000 - 1] \times 12$

(E) $(a + b)$

(C) $[(1,000/(a + b)) - 1] \times 12$

29. Which of the following numbers is the smallest?

(A) $-.666$

(D) $\dfrac{-660}{1,000}$

(B) $-.66$

(E) $-.\overline{6}$

(C) $-.6$

30. What is the value of x?

(A) $20°$ (D) $90°$

(B) $40°$ (E) $30°$

(C) $60°$

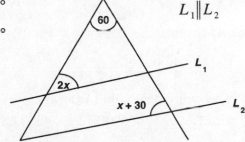

STOP

If time still remains, you may go back and check your work.
When the time allotted is up, you may go on to the next section.

Section 5

TIME: 30 Minutes
        38 Questions

DIRECTIONS: Each of the given sentences has blank spaces which indicate words omitted. Choose the best combination of words which fit into the meaning and structure within the context of the sentence.

---

1. The direct, _____ influence of Protestantism has been to isolate and individualize man.

    (A) sensible

    (B) immediate

    (C) licentious

    (D) capitulated

    (E) obeisant

2. The words <u>tear</u> (fluid from the eye) and <u>tear</u> (to rip) are examples of _____ ; the words <u>pear</u> and <u>pair</u> are examples of _____ .

    (A) homographs...homophones

    (B) homonyms...homophones

    (C) homographs...heteronyms

    (D) heteronyms...homographs

    (E) homophones...homonyms

3. Sophia thought that, after such a sin, the least Amy could do was to show _____ .

    (A) callosity

    (B) obduracy

    (C) contrition

    (D) trepidation

    (E) phlegmacy

4. Considering its severity, treatment of the _____ of the depression was begun; however, the physicians proposed to treat all aspects of the disease.

   (A) stages

   (B) appearance

   (C) symptoms

   (D) phases

   (E) etiology

5. "Fate went its way uncompromisingly to the end." This is the _____ of this interesting, dignified apology of one of Austria's Elder Statesmen.

   (A) leitmotiv

   (B) portraiture

   (C) roulade

   (D) theme

   (E) subject

6. Tempers were _____ and _____ in the fiery furnace of domestic tribulation.

   (A) pliant...malleable

   (B) spectacular...visible

   (C) tenacious...evanescent

   (D) aphonic...tumultuous

   (E) fulminating...mellifluous

7. We cannot explain away this deliberate act as due to the _____ of age, or accept the other excuses with which his admirers have sought to _____ it.

   (A) ineptitude...rationalize

   (B) perspicacity...vindicate

   (C) sagacity...syllogize

   (D) psychosis...exculpate

   (E) ignorance...palliate

DIRECTIONS: In the following questions, a related pair of words is followed by five more pairs of words. Select the pair that best expresses the same relationship as that expressed in the original pair.

---

8. GAZPACHO:SOUP::

   (A) wine:dinner

   (B) yeast:bread

(C) paella:fish   (D) bratwurst:sausage

(E) sauce:spaghetti

9. SUN:SOLAR SYSTEM::

(A) moon:earth   (D) molecule:atom

(B) island:archipelago   (E) verses:poem

(C) galaxy:star

10. SOUFFLE:EGGS::

(A) coconut:macaroon   (D) mousse:cream

(B) pear:nectar   (E) tomato:fruit

(C) pigs:truffle

11. THEORY:SPECULATION::

(A) deposition:refutation   (D) supposition:surmise

(B) hypothesis:absolute   (E) feasibility:inconceivableness

(C) diagnosis:obtuseness

12. CUBISM:ART::

(A) plant life:biology   (D) plagiarist:mercature

(B) jocundity:amusement   (E) sequestration:urbanity

(C) Wall Street:Stock Exchange

13. APOTHEOSIZE:CANONIZE::

(A) deprecation:servility   (D) sinecure:aberration

(B) smorgasbord:paltry   (E) specious:complaisant

(C) permeate:pervade

14. PARSIMONIOUS:NIGGARDLY::

(A) mendicant:benefactor   (D) miserly:stingy

(B) avarice:generosity   (E) penurious:squandering

(C) convoluted:complicated

15. MERIDIAN:PARALLEL::

   (A) east:west

   (B) north:south

   (C) longitude:latitude

   (D) map:globe

   (E) compass:direction

16. PORIFERAN:SPONGE::

   (A) gulf:chasm

   (B) pillory:ridicule

   (C) eulogy:panegyric

   (D) congratulations:felicitations

   (E) stalwart:staunch

DIRECTIONS: Each passage is followed by questions based on its content. After reading a passage, choose the best answer to each question. Answer all questions based on what is stated or implied in that passage.

The torpedo is a self-propelled underwater weapon having either a high-explosive or a nuclear warhead. Conventional warheads are loaded with up to 1,000 pounds of HBX explosive.

Underwater explosion of the torpedo warhead increases its destructive effect. When a projectile explodes, a part of its force is absorbed by the surrounding air. Upon explosion of the torpedo warhead, the water transfers almost the full force of the explosion to the hull of the target ship.

Fleet-type and Guppy submarines are fitted with 10 tubes, 6 in the bow and 4 in the stern. Spare torpedoes are carried in ready racks near the tubes. On war patrol, a submarine of this type usually puts to sea with a load of 28 torpedoes aboard.

Torpedoes are propelled by gas turbines or electric motors. Turbine types have maximum speeds of 30 to 45 knots, with a maximum effective range of as much as $7\frac{1}{2}$ miles. Electric torpedoes usually have less speed and range than turbine types, but from the submariners point of view, they have the advantage of leaving no visible wake.

17. Which of the following is the best title for the passage?

    (A) The Dynamics of Underwater Explosions

    (B) The Efficacy of Conventional vs. Nuclear Warheads

    (C) Standard Submarine Equipment and Armament

    (D) How Torpedoes Work

    (E) Torpedo Functions and Deployment

18. The passage infers that gas turbined torpedoes are less preferred because

    (A) a visible wake is left behind.

    (B) their speed and range exceed that of the electric torpedo.

    (C) they are of less weight.

    (D) no sound is created upon firing.

    (E) destruction of the target is less than that caused by the electric torpedo.

19. The passage compares conventional warheads to nuclear warheads by stating that

    (A) nuclear warheads are guided by electric turbines while conventional warheads are guided by gas turbines.

    (B) nuclear warheads have less weight than conventional warheads.

    (C) conventional warheads are less likely than nuclear warheads to destroy the smaller target.

    (D) the explosive force of both conventional and nuclear warheads is in part absorbed by air if exploded above the water.

    (E) nuclear warheads have a greater degree of accuracy when aimed at an underwater target than does the conventional warhead.

20. The passage suggests that although the torpedo is self-propelled, the function of the turbine is to

    (A) give direction to the torpedo.

    (B) provide additional power and speed.

    (C) deliver the explosive without sound.

(D) maintain a balanced weight and force for the Guppy.

(E) inflict greater damage on a moving target.

Juan Ponce de Léon was the first Spaniard to touch the shores of the present United States. As Columbus had not remotely realized the extent of his momentous discovery, so de Léon never dreamed that his "island" of Florida was a peninsular extension of the vast North American continent. After coming to the New World with Columbus in 1493, he had led the occupation of Puerto Rico in 1508 and governed it from 1509 to 1512. In 1509, he started a colony at Caparra, later abandoned in favor of San Juan. He was one of the first of the *adelantados*—men who "advanced" the Spanish Empire by conquest, subjugation of the Indians, and establishment of quasi-military government.

In 1513, the aging King Ferdinand awarded de Léon a patent to conquer and govern the Bimini Islands, in the Bahamas, of which the Spaniards had heard but not yet seen. According to a persistent legend, there de Léon would find the marvelous spring whose waters would restore lost youth and vigor. So many wonders had the Spaniards already encountered in the Western Hemisphere that only a cynic would have doubted the existence of such a spring.

In March 1513, de Léon sailed off confidently from Puerto Rico for the Bahamas. Landing briefly at San Salvador, Bahamas, he wound through uncharted islands until he sighted an extensive coastline. He had no reason to suspect that it was anything more than an island, but he followed the coast for a day without rounding its end or finding a suitable landing place. He named the "island" *La Florida*, probably because of the season—*Pascua Florida*, or the Easter festival of flowers. The name came to be applied by the Spanish to the entire present Southeastern United States and beyond.

Then, near the 30th parallel, not far from the site of St. Augustine, de Léon landed at the mouth of the St. Johns River. Determined to be the first to circumnavigate the "island," he turned south, traced the coast around the tip of the peninsula, passed through the treacherous waters of the Florida Keys, and moved up the western coast, perhaps reaching Tampa Bay. After seven weeks, he gave up hope of circling the northern tip of his "island"; it was incredibly large—bigger even than Cuba—and he may have suspected that he had discovered the long sought mainland. If so, it all belonged to his King, for he had earlier planted the Spanish flag and claimed Florida and all lands contiguous to it for Ferdinand.

Of gold and restorative waters, de Léon had seen nothing; of hostile Indians, predecessors of the Seminoles, he had seen too much. Returning to Puerto Rico in September 1513, he reprovisioned and then spent the next six weeks back in the Bahamas fruitlessly searching for the fountain of youth. Before the year was out, he sailed for Spain empty-handed. Ferdinand rewarded him, however, with new patents to the "islands" of Bimini and Florida, but he was to bear the expense of conquest.

Not until 1521 was de Léon able to return to take possession of his grant. By that time, his search for the fountain of youth took on a more immediate importance—for he was 61 years of age. At large cost he equipped two ships, enlisted 200 men, and set out to found a permanent base from which an exhaustive search could be conducted for the fabled fountain. Not only did he fail to find the fountain, but he also lost his life. Almost as soon as he landed on the western shore of Florida, probably near Tampa Bay, Indians attacked, killed scores of men, and mortally wounded de Léon himself. The expedition hastily retreated to Cuba, where the "valiant Lion," as his epitaph was to read, died.

21. Which of the following best describes the relationship between the first paragraph and the rest of the passage?

   (A) The first paragraph discusses the early years of Ponce de Léon's career, and the rest of the passage describes the later years.

   (B) The first paragraph describes how Ponce de Léon heard of the fountain of youth, and the rest of the passage details his search for it.

   (C) The first paragraph discusses Ponce de Léon's motives for becoming an *adelantado*, and the rest of the passage describes his career as an explorer.

   (D) The first paragraph describes how Ponce de Léon discovered Florida, and the rest of the passage tells how he tried to discover the fountain of youth there.

   (E) The first paragraph describes Ponce de Léon's first voyage with Columbus, and the rest of the passage details his attempts to circumnavigate Florida.

22. Although Ponce de Léon was an explorer, the passage suggests that his main goal was to

   (A) conquer and govern the Bimini Islands.

   (B) locate the fountain of youth.

   (C) circumnavigate Florida.

   (D) claim his royally awarded patents.

   (E) subdue the Seminole Indians.

23. Ponce de Léon was classified as an *adelantado* because he

   (A) was a great explorer.

   (B) was the first Spaniard to see the shores of the United States.

   (C) was awarded patents by the king for the Bahamas and Florida.

   (D) conquered and ruled by military force.

   (E) claimed Florida for the king of Spain.

24. According to the information given in the passage, which of the following statements is/are true?

   I.   Ponce de Léon received royal funding for the conquest of Florida.

   II. Belief in the existence of a "fountain of youth" was widespread among the Spanish explorers.

   III. Ponce de Léon claimed Florida for Spain, and was rewarded with a royal patent to Florida and Bimini.

   (A) I only   (D) III only

   (B) II only   (E) II and III only

   (C) I and II only

25. All of the following are true EXCEPT

   (A) Ponce de Léon was motivated by a desire to discover the fountain of youth.

   (B) The King of Spain rewarded Ponce de Léon with a patent to govern Florida and Bimini.

(C) legend held that the fountain of youth was in Florida.

(D) hostile natives mortally wounded Ponce de Léon.

(E) Ponce de Léon was one of the first *adelantados*.

26. The author's presentation can best be described as

(A) a discussion of the Spanish attempts to discover the fountain of youth.

(B) a list of the conquests of Ponce de Léon.

(C) an outline of the Spanish discovery of Florida.

(D) an essay on the career of Juan Ponce de Léon.

(E) a discussion of the Spanish treatment of New World natives.

27. Ponce de Léon advanced the Spanish Empire by conquests, subjugation of the original inhabitants, and military rule. The passage suggests

(A) Ponce de Léon was an explorer, soldier, and government administrator.

(B) his expeditions were followed by military forces.

(C) his expeditions were comprised only of soldiers.

(D) each explored location served as the point of departure for the next expedition.

(E) Ponce de Léon was subject to no man although he claimed all discovered lands for his king.

DIRECTIONS: Each of the following questions provides a given word in capitalized letters followed by five word choices. Choose the best word which is most <u>opposite</u> in meaning to the given word.

---

28. SUBLIMINAL:

(A) conscious   (D) turpitude

(B) subversive   (E) explicit

(C) termagant

29. FLAVOR:

    (A) insipid
    (B) sentient
    (C) tactility
    (D) nares
    (E) taste

30. TRANSCENDENT:

    (A) average
    (B) superlunar
    (C) suspension
    (D) vermiculated
    (E) sterling

31. FACTIOUS:

    (A) convoluted
    (B) cooperative
    (C) curved
    (D) cunning
    (E) cowardly

32. SKEW:

    (A) slant
    (B) contraposition
    (C) convolution
    (D) oblique
    (E) parallel

33. ACRIDITY:

    (A) pungency
    (B) insipid
    (C) acerbity
    (D) mordancy
    (E) savoriness

34. SPECTACLE:

    (A) phenomenon
    (B) perspective
    (C) ostentation
    (D) precarious
    (E) eclipse

35. VELOCITY:

    (A) extricate
    (B) towage

(C) languor

(D) kinematics

(E) circuitous

36. RAUCOUS:

(A) stridulation

(D) vociferation

(B) percussion

(E) ejaculation

(C) susurrus

37. SCINTILLATION:

(A) gleam

(D) tenebrific

(B) lucidity

(E) obscuration

(C) nimbus

38. OCCLUSION:

(A) conduction

(D) preclusion

(B) impediment

(E) perforation

(C) quiescence

STOP

If time still remains, you may go back and check your work.
When the time allotted is up, you may go on to the next section.

Section 6

Column A	Column B
1. 5×4	$5 + 4$

Explanation: The correct answer is (A), since $5 \times 4 = 20$, and $5 + 4 = 9$.

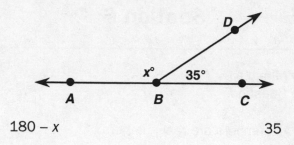

2. $180 - x$ 35

Explanation: The correct answer is (C). Since angle *ABC* is a straight angle, its measurement is 180°.

Column A	**Column B**

1. $\left(\dfrac{5}{9}\right)^2$ $\left(\dfrac{9}{5}\right)^{-2}$

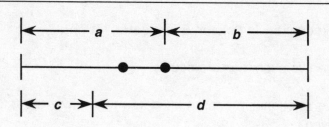

2. $a + d$ $b + c$

$$1 - 2x > x - 5$$

3. x 2

4.   Average of   Average of
      25, 17, 30, 23, and 15   13, 35, 11, 25, 9, and 39

5. $(8 - 3 \times 4)^2$ $[(8 - 3) \times 4]^2$

	Column A	**Column B**
6.	5% of 45 is x	45 is 5% of x
7.	Area of a circle: diameter 16	Area of a rectangle: length 64, width π

x is not equal to 0.

8.	$\dfrac{1}{x}$	x

$2, 5, 11, x, 47, 95, \dots$

9.	x	$\dfrac{(11+47)}{2}$

$x > 1$

10.	$\dfrac{1}{\dfrac{1}{x(x)}}$	$\dfrac{\dfrac{1}{x(x-1)}}{\dfrac{x}{x-1}}$
11.	The area of a circle with radius x	The circumference of a circle with radius x

$x > y$

12.	$|x|$	$|y|$

$x > 0, y > 0$

13.	$\sqrt{\dfrac{y}{2}}\sqrt{\dfrac{2y}{x}}$	$\dfrac{y\sqrt{x}}{x}$

Column A	Column B

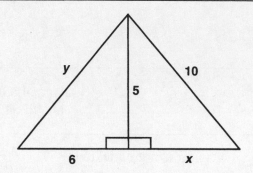

14. x y

15. $\dfrac{2x - \frac{y-5}{6}}{\frac{y-5}{3} - 4x}$ -0.5

DIRECTIONS: For the following questions, select the best answer choice to the given question.

---

16. Which of the following has the smallest value?

    (A) $\dfrac{1}{0.2}$ (D) $\dfrac{0.2}{0.1}$

    (B) $\dfrac{0.1}{2}$ (E) $\dfrac{2}{0.1}$

    (C) $\dfrac{0.2}{1}$

17. What is the smallest positive number that leaves a remainder of 2 when the number is divided by 3, 4, or 5?

    (A) 22   (D) 122

    (B) 42   (E) 182

    (C) 62

18. Suppose the average of two numbers is *WX*. If the first number is *X*, what is the other number?

   (A) $WX - X$

   (B) $2WX - W$

   (C) W

   (D) $WX - 2X$

   (E) $2WX - X$

19. A square is inscribed in a circle of area 18π. What is the length of a side of the square?

   (A) 6

   (B) 3

   (C) $3\sqrt{2}$

   (D) $6\sqrt{2}$

   (E) Cannot be determined.

20. If $\triangle ABC$ has $\angle A = 35°$ and $\angle B = 85°$, then the measure of $\angle x$ in degrees is

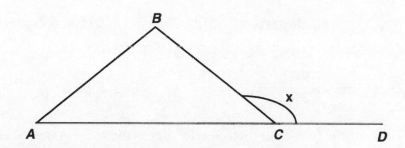

   (A) 85.

   (B) 90.

   (C) 100.

   (D) 120.

   (E) 180.

Questions 21–22 refer to the following table.

Table of Weight Distribution of a 70,000-Gram Man
(Weights of some organs given)

Organ	Wt in Grams	Organ	Wt in Grams
Skeleton	10,000	Muscles	30,000
Blood	5,000	Intestinal tract	2,000
Liver	1,700	Lungs	1,000
Brain	1,500		

21. Which expression represents the total body weight if the weight of the skeleton is represented by S grams?

    (A) $7S$

    (B) $70,000S$

    (C) $60S$

    (D) $S + 6$

    (E) Cannot be determined.

22. If 40 percent of the weight of the blood is made up of cells, what percent (to the nearest tenth) of the total body weight is made up of blood cells?

    (A) 7.1

    (B) 3.6

    (C) 1.4

    (D) 2.8

    (E) 9.9

Question 23 refers to the following table:

	% Cholesterol	% Fat	% Carbohydrates
Food A	10	20	30
Food B	20	15	10
Food C	20	10	40

23. Which of the following diets would supply the most grams of cholesterol?

    (A) 500 grams of A

    (B) 250 grams of B

    (C) 150 grams of A and 200 grams of B

    (D) 200 grams of B and 200 grams of C

    (E) 350 grams of C

Questions 24–25 refer to the following table:

Payroll Summary of Company X

Position Title	Number in Position	Total Amount Paid to Employees in the Position
Vice President/Manager	5	$ 250,000
Team Leader/Coordinator	25	1,000,000
Assembly Line Worker	500	12,500,000
Total	530	$ 13,750,000

24. What percent (to the nearest tenth) makes up the wages paid to the vice presidents/managers?

    (A) 18.2   (D) 9.4

    (B) 1.9   (E) 2.8

    (C) 1.8

25. What is the ratio of the wages earned by a team leader/coordinator to the wages earned by an assembly line worker?

    (A) 8 : 5   (D) 1 : 20

    (B) 5 : 8   (E) 1 : 12

    (C) 25 : 500

26. Three times the first of three consecutive odd integers is three more than twice the third. What is the second of the three consecutive odd integers?

    (A) 7   (D) 13

    (B) 9   (E) 15

    (C) 11

27. A fraction has a value of $\frac{2}{5}$. If the numerator is decreased by 2 and the denominator increased by 1, then the resulting fraction is $\frac{1}{4}$. What is the value of the numerator of the original fraction?

(A) 2   (D) 5

(B) 3   (E) 6

(C) 4

28. Jay and his brother Ray own a janitorial service. Jay can do a cleaning job alone in 5 hours and Ray can do the same job in 4 hours. How long will it take them to do the cleaning job together?

(A) 5 hours   (D) $2\frac{2}{9}$ hours

(B) 1 hour   (E) $4\frac{1}{2}$ hours

(C) 4 hours

29. A box contains 6 red marbles and 4 blue marbles. What is the probability that if 2 marbles are simultaneously drawn from the box, both will be red?

(A) $\frac{2}{3}$ (D) $\frac{1}{5}$

(B) $\frac{1}{3}$ (E) $\frac{2}{5}$

(C) $\frac{1}{2}$

30. If the angles of a $\triangle ABC$ are in the ratio of 3 : 5 : 7, then the triangle is

(A) acute.   (D) obtuse.

(B) right.   (E) equilateral.

(C) isosceles.

STOP

If time still remains, you may go back and check your work.
When the time allotted is up, you may go on to the next section.

TEST 5

ANSWER KEY

Sections 1 and 2 — Analytical Writing

Please review the sample essays in the Detailed Explanations.

Section 3 — Verbal Ability

1. (E)	11. (D)	21. (D)	31. (A)
2. (E)	12. (D)	22. (A)	32. (D)
3. (C)	13. (B)	23. (D)	33. (D)
4. (A)	14. (B)	24. (B)	34. (D)
5. (B)	15. (D)	25. (A)	35. (D)
6. (E)	16. (B)	26. (D)	36. (A)
7. (B)	17. (A)	27. (C)	37. (E)
8. (D)	18. (D)	28. (C)	38. (D)
9. (E)	19. (C)	29. (E)	
10. (E)	20. (E)	30. (A)	

Section 4 — Quantitative Ability

1. (D)	9. (C)	17. (C)	25. (E)
2. (A)	10. (C)	18. (D)	26. (B)
3. (A)	11. (C)	19. (C)	27. (D)
4. (A)	12. (C)	20. (E)	28. (C)
5. (B)	13. (B)	21. (A)	29. (E)
6. (C)	14. (D)	22. (B)	30. (E)
7. (D)	15. (C)	23. (B)	
8. (C)	16. (C)	24. (B)	

Section 5 — Verbal Ability

1. (A)	11. (D)	21. (A)	31. (B)
2. (A)	12. (A)	22. (B)	32. (E)
3. (C)	13. (C)	23. (D)	33. (E)
4. (E)	14. (D)	24. (E)	34. (E)
5. (A)	15. (C)	25. (C)	35. (C)
6. (A)	16. (C)	26. (D)	36. (C)
7. (E)	17. (E)	27. (D)	37. (D)
8. (D)	18. (A)	28. (A)	38. (E)
9. (B)	19. (D)	29. (A)	
10. (D)	20. (B)	30. (A)	

Section 6 — Quantitative Ability

1. (C)	9. (B)	17. (C)	25. (A)
2. (A)	10. (A)	18. (E)	26. (D)
3. (B)	11. (D)	19. (A)	27. (E)
4. (C)	12. (D)	20. (D)	28. (D)
5. (B)	13. (C)	21. (A)	29. (B)
6. (B)	14. (A)	22. (D)	30. (A)
7. (C)	15. (C)	23. (D)	
8. (D)	16. (B)	24. (C)	

DETAILED EXPLANATIONS OF ANSWERS

Section 1–Analytical Writing

PERSPECTIVES ON AN ISSUE ESSAY TOPIC—ESSAY ONE

Sample Essay Response Scoring 6

In America, the world of business is largely a public sphere. It was created at a time when men ruled the public world but women were expected to maintain the private. Therefore, for many years, it was rare for women to operate in this realm. After the second world war, however, the distinction between men's and women's roles became less sharply defined. At this point women had to learn to function by the rules of the public sphere as they entered the realm of business. Although it may have been difficult at first to learn these rules, or to gain acceptance from their male colleagues, there is absolutely no reason that women should be less successful than men in the world of business.

very good & precise example to set up a thesis

clear direct thesis

To maintain that there are "natural" differences in the personalities of men and women is dangerous. The debate between nature and nurture is a complicated one. It is nearly impossible to determine if personality traits are governed by chemical/biological urges or socially constructed rules. One thing that is certain, however, is that the rules that govern business are not natural. They are imposed from the outside and are completely artificial. Since this is the case, it should be possible for anyone to learn them given the proper exposure.

very precise vocabulary

Some people may argue that women have certain character traits that make them less suited for work in the field of business, and that remains true regardless of whether or not these traits are present from birth or learned throughout life. For instance, some might say that women are not capable of being competitive and aggressive, and that it is irrelevant if this is caused by a hormone deficiency or by a difference in upbringing. In either case, history has proven this supposition to be wrong. Throughout

well-executed transition between ideas

here, a good example supports the point made in this paragraph

time, the records have offered visions of women who were strong and powerful, who conquered and ruled nations and changed the course of history. Certainly there are some women who are not aggressive, but this is true of men as well. There are a large number of men who are not ruled by cutthroat, aggressive instincts. Thus it is true that certain people are not as likely to succeed in business, but it is not fair to apply this to women alone.

good transition

(Another argument) frequently posited by those who believe women are less likely to be successful in the world of business is that women must carry, deliver, and raise babies. If a woman decides to have a baby, it will take many months out of her life during which time she will be completely unable to work. Once she's had the baby, it will require her constant attention. Even when it is grown to become a toddler or a child, it is still likely to make frequent and unpredictable demands on her time.

points are well-connected

Although all of this may be true, it should not stand in the way of women being successful in business. (First of all,) it is not a given that all women will choose to have children. Childbearing is not necessarily an innate urge that all women must respond to. Many women live full and fulfilled lives and never have children at all. (Secondly,) even if a woman should choose to have children, this need not necessarily interfere with her career. Pregnant women are still capable people, despite myths of their vulnerability. (Furthermore,) with constant advances in computers and fax machines, it is frequently possible for women to bring home much of their work. Ideally, having a baby will require as much time from the father as from the mother, yet nobody would suggest this as an excuse to keep men out of business.

solid conclusion that refers back to points made in the essay

There is no natural reason for women to be any less successful in business than men. If, for some reason, they are less accepted by their colleagues, taken less seriously, or paid smaller salaries for the same quality of work, the problem is with the system, and not with the businesswomen themselves. If the problem is with the system, then it can be changed, and perhaps eventually no one will question the validity of women as professional people.

Analysis of Sample Essay Scoring 6

The above essay is at the level of a 6 because of its effective, well-articulated approach to analyzing an issue. From the initial paragraph, the author explores the root of the issue, establishing a historical background for the world of business. In this opening statement, he or she chooses one side of the issue which is then maintained and effectively argued throughout the essay. Although the question is brief, it raises some complex gender issues, and the essayist recognizes this and proceeds to examine these issues in as much depth as time allows. The organization of the essay is effective; each paragraph identifies a possible argument opposing the essayist's position. The paragraphs also give evidence and examples to disprove the arguments. The essay is written in simple, clear language, which helps to make the subtleties of the issue more easily understood and the position of the essayist more powerful.

PERSPECTIVES ON AN ISSUE ESSAY TOPIC—ESSAY TWO

Sample Essay Response Scoring 4

this sentence is too long; the idea behind it gets lost

The statement above is perhaps a valid one, but one that lacks fuller consideration of what funding the arts might really mean for a society in terms of costs and more importantly for what I am going to say here, potential benefits. I feel that using public resources for the arts can have a very positive impact by allowing very creative and expressive people to improve the way we see and think about the world.

good set-up to larger argument, but it should be followed up in the next paragraph

too vague

It is true that it seems a bad idea to give money to support arts projects if that money could help people who are hungry or jobless. But as countless studies have shown, merely giving money to people in need does not correct the problems that made them needy in the first place. Rather, it merely helps them at that moment, but does not help them to stay fed or solvent permanently. Public money needs to be spent smarter.

ambiguous pronoun use

Artists make the world a better place, and, also, a more humane place. They make the world seem more beautiful and life seem more worthwhile. In a world with many problems, art can help people feel better about the world.

poor transition

Art can also be a force of education. Drama, film, television, books, paintings, and music, can teach prople to appreciate themselves and others more fully, and perhaps then can serve to help bring people out of poverty. Like maybe a play can help someone who is a drug addict stop doing that and become more productive citizen.

this example needs elaboration

The arts are an integral part of daily living, they brighten up everyone's day. So while it is certainly true that public funds should not go to artists at the expense of the needy, there are doubtless creative ways to support the arts and thereby also help the needy.

tone is too formal

very strong concluding sentence

Analysis of Sample Essay Scoring 4

This essay receives a score of 4 because it adequately deals with the given issue. It is well structured and there are no contradictory elements. However, transitions between ideas are weak and this interferes with the flow of the argument. At times, there is a lack of evidence and examples so that the essay seems rather vague. The statement that public money should be spent in a better way is very strong. Yet, there is no suggestion how this might be done. Some of the sentences are too long. Especially in the opening paragraph the essayist should try to be as precise and clear as possible. The overall control of sentence structure, spelling, and grammar is satisfactory.

Section 2–Analytical Writing

ANALYSIS OF AN ARGUMENT ESSAY TOPIC

Sample Essay Response Scoring 6

The main point of this argument is to describe a turbulent moment in American history and to show how societal changes affected and reflected the nature of individual people. It shows how a society, over a period of time, <u>acts like a piece of woven material</u> in which one strand added or taken away can change the complexion of the whole. Specifically, the focus of the argument is on individual values, and how industrialization and urbanization created a new culture which was both a cause and a result of a new emphasis on appearances and salesmanship. This argument is effective in that it establishes a broad picture of a complex situation in a very short passage.

this simile shows an effective use of language

concise & accurate formulation of the initial essay's topic

The greatest strength of this passage is that it manages to connect many different levels of a variegated circumstance in such a way that they seem simple to understand. Broad historical movements such as industrialization and urbanization are very complicated in their own right. They have a great impact on every aspect of a country, from the more removed political and economic domains right down to the most personal, such as diet choices or leisure time entertainment. In this argument, the author manages to choose one specific area in which change occurred and show in a logical sequence how historical events can cause changes in individuals.

good expansion on the points made in the initial argument

The author of the passage goes beyond this to show not only how and why the change in values occurred, but also to show that once the value were different, they began to cause changes as well. This is a further example of how successfully the author crystallizes an involved and difficult situation. It is difficult to say which changes first, a society or what it holds valuable. These things are connected in a cycle of cause and effect in which it becomes impossible to separate the action from the actor. The author of the passage relays the vagaries and complexities of this relationship without making it seem impossibly confusing.

great use of language & sentence structure

<u>(Perhaps, however,)</u> this ability to clearly and unequivocally state a case leads to oversimplification. <u>It is one of the weak-</u>

good transition

smooth transition into a critique

nesses of the argument that it takes for granted a certain acceptance of the part of the reader and does not fully explore the
intricate subtleties of the topic it describes. Words such as
"value" and "culture" constantly undergo a process of re-evaluation.
It is especially necessary in a historical piece to establish a definition for terms such as those found within the context of the
historical period under discussion. In this way, the reader would
not only have a clearer idea of the climate within which the argument was being made, but would also appreciate the fact that the
author had addressed the potential complexities of the situation
before he or she decided on a certain interpretation.

very precise wording & therefore a strong critique

Another addition which might make this argument more convincing would be the use of specific examples. If we were given a
concrete notion of what makes a culture "consumer," an actual
example of contemporary advertisements, or a sense of precisely
what had been valued as opposed to what was increasingly becoming valued, it might make the argument seem less vague and
therefore more effective.

effective transition

If the author does have a specific position on the topic, it is
not overtly stated. If any judgment is implied, it is one of slight
disapproval, but we glean this only from possible negative conno-
tations of certain words and phrases. The most notable of these
is the image of an individual selling him or herself, which is
difficult to conceive in a positive light. Perhaps this seeming lack
of bias is helpful in making the argument more convincing, because it is usually easier to trust the scholarly judgment of someone who is not distracted by a personal agenda.

precise analysis of tone

We witness the strength of this argument because the author
sets forth a position in such a way that it appears to be a simple
statement of information. The passage deals with complex issues
in such a way that they seem simple. It further presents a specific
and a singular reading of a historical event as if it were the only
possible one. Although these qualities may not produce as thorough a coverage or as unbiased a reading as possible, they are
the essential elements of a good argument.

solid conclusion

Analysis of Sample Essay Scoring 6

The above essay analyzing an argument is very well done; it
would rate a 6. In the first paragraph it effectively recognizes that
the main point of the argument is the effect of a historical movement on individual people. It proceeds to show why the argument
is convincingly written, citing first how the author expresses a

large amount of material in a short space, and secondly how the author crystallizes confusing issues. It then suggests a possible flaw with the argument: it might oversimplify the situation. The next paragraph shows how this problem might be eliminated by the use of concrete examples. The penultimate paragraph explores a more general analysis of whether or not the author of the argument had a specific position on the topic, and this return to the general leads smoothly into the conclusion which ties back to the original paragraph, binding the piece together without restating what has already been said. All of the ideas in the piece are fully developed, carefully organized, and exhibit an understanding of the argument's most important elements.

Section 3–Verbal Ability

1. **(E)**
    The first terms given for each pair are synonyms with each other. Each fits the meaning of the sentence. The key, then, to this problem will be with the second term. The last clause, including the second blank, can be assumed to carry an idea which contrasts with the idea expressed before it. The sentence as a whole identifies two opposing views. The opposing ideas are: (1) set prerequisites high so student and teacher time is not wasted on students who will not be successful; and (2) set prerequisites low so all those who can possibly benefit will have a chance. The answer is (E) NEEDLESSLY...DENIED. TEMPTED (A), CHARGED (B), FAILED (C), and ENROLLED (D) are wrong because they do not carry through the opposing thought.

2. **(E)**
    The second half of this sentence cites an example to support the assertion made in the first part of the sentence. The computer is UNFORGIVING because if one neglects to save a program, that program is lost. It cannot be recalled. The other alternatives, (A) OMINOUS (threatening), (B) COMPLICATED, (C) ESSENTIAL, and (D) DIFFICULT, do not express the idea of no reprieve for a mistake made as does (E) UNFORGIVING.

3. **(C)**
    The correct answer is INEVITABLE...FULL (C). The consequences of choices made may be SURPRISING (A), UNEXPECTED (B), BORING (D), or HAPPY (E), but they are always inevitable. This is the reason that (C) INEVITABLE is the only acceptable first term given. In relation to the second term, the missing word must be one which contrasts with "meager," meaning "poor, not full or rich." (C) FULL is the only one of the second terms given which does contrast with "meager."

4. **(A)**
    Alternative (B) WRONG...ENFORCING is wrong because law does not enforce wrong actions; ETHICAL...STOPPING (C) is incorrect because law does not stop behaviors, law merely prohibits certain behaviors; UNETHICAL...LEGALIZING (D) is inappropriate because law does not legalize unethical behavior; SOUND...ALLOWING (E) is not correct because laws do not allow or disallow sound actions; they prohibit certain

actions. Law does not PROHIBIT actions that are GOOD; therefore, the answer is (A).

5. **(B)**

BINARY means made of two parts; it does not fit the sentence. ANNUAL is not the correct term for a plant which lives two years. (A) is not the correct answer. Since PERENNIAL means a plant which lives more than two years and since a BIENNIAL plant continues for two years and then perishes, (B) is the correct answer. (C) SEMI-ANNUAL means two times per year; a CENTENNIAL celebration marks 100 years, (C) is clearly incorrect. An EVERGREEN is green the year round; a DECIDU-OUS tree casts its leaves. Choice (D) does not relate directly to the context. DECENNIAL means continuing for ten years; TRIENNIAL means continuing for three years. (E) should not be selected.

6. **(E)**

The key to this sentence is that something "piecemeal" is presented as "entire." A synecdoche is a figure of speech that substitutes the part for the whole, or the whole for the part. SYNECDOCHIC (E) rhetoric presents partial (piecemeal) observations as a whole (entire) analytical structure. CHTHONIC (infernal) and CHIMERIC (imaginary) both imply a judgment of the rhetoric, not a description of it; thus, (B) and (D) are inappropriate choices. SYNODIC (A) refers to the conjunction of celestial bodies, and SYNCHRONIC (C) refers to events happening within a limited time period.

7. **(B)**

A gift shop's display cannot be INIQUITOUS (wicked), OPPRO-BRIOUS (reproachful), or MENDACIOUS (deceitful). (A), (C), and (E) are incorrect choices. A display also cannot be VIVACIOUS (lively), which also lacks the negative connotation suggested by "garish" and "meant to be impressive." A display can be MERETRICIOUS (B), or gaudily attractive but of little worth.

8. **(D)**

To be IGNORANT is to lack KNOWLEDGE. This relationship is also present in alternative DESPAIR:HOPE (D). To DESPAIR is to lack HOPE. The relationship in alternative (A) FAST:HUNGER is one of cause and effect. OLD:ANTIQUE (B) is an analogy of degree. An item must be considered very OLD to be ANTIQUE. SYLLABLE:WORD (C) presents a part-to-whole analogy. GOOD:BETTER (E) is an analogy of degree.

9. **(E)**
This analogy is a part-to-whole analogy. The INDICATIVE mood is a subset of the concept MOOD. PRESENT and PAST (A) are both tenses and in this regard they share equal status. Neither is a subset of the other, as is the case with the analogy given. PRONOUNS and PREPOSITIONS (B) are the names given to two different parts of speech. They are both parts of a whole that could be called "parts of speech." (C) is a whole-to-part analogy. A SENTENCE may contain a CLAUSE. In the analogy given, the part is listed before the whole. Alternative (D) gives two of the four kinds of sentences. Each is in this regard a "part." There is no "whole" mentioned. (E) is the correct answer because it is a part-to-whole analogy. The FUTURE is one of six parts or subsets within TENSE. The others are present, past, present perfect, past perfect, and future perfect.

10. **(E)**
A GAUNTLET is a protective device for the HAND. A CANNON is not a protective device for the BALL. (A) is not the correct answer. A SWORD is not a protective device for the HAND. (B) is an incorrect answer. A SHIELD does protect the BODY, but it is an inverted analogy. (C) is incorrect. A SHIELD is a protection against a LANCE; this is not the analogy sought. (D) is incorrect. ARMOR does protect the BODY. (E) is the correct answer.

11. **(D)**
A SYMPHONY and a FUGUE identify two different genres (types or kinds) of music. NOVEL:SHORT STORY (D) identifies two genres or kinds of literature, and is the correct answer. Alternatives (A), (B), and (C) are inaccurate because the second term in each is a subset of the first term. A NOVEL is a type of BOOK, an ENTRY is found in a DIARY, and a TOPIC SENTENCE is found in an ESSAY. (E) is inaccurate because PROLOGUE and APPENDIX are both parts of a book.

12. **(D)**
DETRIMENTAL (hindering) and ADVANTAGEOUS (helpful) are antonyms. SAPID (pleasant to taste) and INSIPID (bland or lacking in taste) reflect this antonymous relationship, so (D) is the correct choice. (B) and (E) are synonymous. AMIABLE (friendly) and CAPRICIOUS (arbitrary) (A), and STAID (grave, sober) and STOIC (impassive) (C) are character traits. They do not reflect the antonymous relationship of the key pair.

13. **(B)**
One MARINATES a piece of BEEF in preparation for cooking and

eating it. (B) is the correct answer; one PASTES WALLPAPER in preparation for hanging it. The element of preparation is lacking in the incorrect alternatives. One simply VISITS a FRIEND (A), STUDIES a BOOK (C), SWIMS a LAP (D), or EATS a CAKE (E).

14. **(B)**

A SYCOPHANT (one who seeks favor by flattering people of wealth or fame) lacks SINCERITY. The correct answer is SKEPTIC: CERTITUDE (B). A SKEPTIC (one who doubts) lacks CERTITUDE. A PEDANT is concerned with DETAIL (A); a GAMBLER relies on LUCK (B); a MERCENARY acts in order to make MONEY (D); and a FUGITIVE is in FLIGHT (E).

15. **(D)**

An ANTAGONIST is an opponent; an ADVERSARY is also an opponent or foe. The two are synonymous. An ALLY is a helper or auxiliary, the opposite of OPPONENT. Choice (A) is not correct. An AUXILIARY is a helper or ally, the opposite of COMPETITOR. Choice (B) should not be chosen. A CONFEDERATE (friend) is the opposite of ENEMY. Choice (C) is incorrect. An EMULATOR is a competitor; it is synonymous with RIVAL. (D) is the right answer. An ACCOMPLICE is an associate in crime; a FOE is a rival; (E) is incorrect.

16. **(B)**

LEGERDEMAIN (sleight of hand) is the stock-in-trade of the MAGICIAN. A LECTURE (B) is the stock-in-trade of a PROFESSOR. A GUNSLINGER needs good EYESIGHT (A), but EYESIGHT is not a GUNSLINGER's stock-in-trade. A COWBOY wears CHAPS (C), a BAKER uses an OVEN (D), and a SAILOR wears a PEACOAT (E).

17. **(A)**

(A) is the correct answer. The author's main point is that the atmosphere is the medium in which air pollutants are emitted and transported. (B) is incorrect, as the formula developed by scientists have deficiencies, as pointed out by the author in paragraph three. (C) is incorrect. The author makes a statement to the contrary in the last sentence of the selection. (D) is incorrect. The word alternative is misused. (E) is incorrect. The author does not point out the largest sources of air pollutants.

18. **(D)**

(D) is not a variable. The author only mentions the atmosphere as it is affected by the time of day. (A), (B), (C), and (E) are variables. The author states, "the relative size of the pollution source is an obvious variable"; "during the day, sunlight plays an important part in transforming the chemical species of pollutants;" speaks of the "tremendous influence" of elevation; and explains the night is more stable, and less dilution occurs.

19. **(C)**

(C) is the correct choice. The author makes the point in the last sentence of paragraph three that if pollutants are not adequately dispersed and diluted, insults will occur. The author does not state that there must be horizontal as well as vertical movement before atmospheric and vegetation damage occur (A) or that vertical and horizontal dispersion are the most important factors to consider (E). The author only mentions that there are deficiencies in the mathematical formulas because of the many variables (B) to indicate the difficulty of accurate calculations. The author mentions that although it may sound simple on the surface, it is perhaps the most complex and least understood facet of air pollution (D) when discussing the atmosphere as the medium in which air pollutants are emitted and transported, now when discussing horizontal and vertical dispersion.

20. **(E)**

(E) is the correct answer. The author, even though briefly, has written a history of the crosscut saw. (A), (C), and (D) are incorrect. The nations are only named to help build the history of the development of the cross-cut saw. (B) is incorrect. The lumber industry is only mentioned by the author to help build the history of the saw.

21. **(D)**

The author does state that both one- and two-man saws can be used by either one or two persons (A) and that there are different lengths of crosscut saws (B). The author also does discuss the two saw patterns for the two-man saw (C) and the large tooth, small tooth formation (E). However, the reference to asymmetric defines the basic characteristic of the one-man crosscut saw (D) in paragraph four.

22. **(A)**

(A) is the correct answer. The plain tooth pattern is the original. The champion and lance patterns are cutter teeth, which not only cut the wood, but also remove the scored wood from the cut. (B) and (C) are incorrect. The types of crosscut saws (B) are one-man and two-man saws. Of the generation saws (C), the felling saw and the bucking saw are the only ones mentioned. (D) and (E) are incorrect. The author does not mention where the improvements were made.

23. **(D)**

(D) is the correct answer because the author states in the first line that the Romans made little use of the crosscut saw. One cannot conclude from the passage that the Romans used the felling saw more widely (A), that the Romans spread the use of the crosscut saw throughout Europe (B), that the Romans introduced the perforated lance tooth (C), or that a number of tooth patterns had been developed by the end of the Roman Empire (E).

24. **(B)**

(B) is the correct answer. In paragraph six the author states that the two-man saws were made in lengths from four to twelve feet. When describing the bucking saw in the final paragraph, the author describes it as traditionally being run by one person, making (E) incorrect. Nothing in the passage could allow the reader to infer that the bucking saw (A) has only a lance tooth pattern, (C) was introduced from Germany, or (D) was perfected on the European continent.

25. **(A)**

(A) is the correct answer. The author makes this point in the eighth paragraph. (B) is incorrect. In the author's explanation of the use of the felling saw, there is no mention of it being a one-man or two-man saw. (C) is incorrect. This is a characteristic of the heavier bucking saw. (D) and (E) are incorrect. The author makes no comment as to the number of teeth or the tooth pattern.

26. **(D)**

(D) is the correct answer. The author mentions in paragraph two of the selection that the "M" tooth pattern was introduced in Germany. (A), (B), (C), and (E) are incorrect.

27. **(C)**

All are characteristics of the crosscut saw except (C). The 16-foot crosscut saw was developed for the large redwoods in California, not for the thick forests of the Pacific Northwest.

28. **(C)**

The adjective REPULSIVE means disgusting or causing strong dislike or aversion. Its opposite is (C) ALLURING, meaning attractive or tempting. The other alternatives are wrong because they do not include the idea of attract. (A) ELEGANT means richness or grace of manner or dress; (B) BEAUTEOUS means having beauty; (D) PLEASANT means agreeable; and (E) AMICABLE means friendly.

29. **(E)**

A CALAMITY is a great misfortune or disaster. Its opposite is a welcome benefit or blessing, a BOON (E). Both words share the quality of intensity, great misfortune and great benefit. Alternatives (A), (B), (C), and (D) do not have this element of intensity. (D) BENEFIT refers to anything contributing to improvement, great or small; (B) ADVANTAGE focuses on the idea of superiority rather than great benefit; (C) VALUE means have worth *per se*; and (A) FAVOR refers to any kind of obliging act.

30. **(A)**

AUDACIOUS means recklessly bold. (A) COMPLAISANT (disposed to comply) is the antonym for AUDACIOUS. The correct answer is (A). (B) FASTIDIOUS means being difficult to please, delicate to a fault. The word is not the opposite of AUDACIOUS so (B) should not be selected. (C) IMPERTINENT is the exceeding of the bounds of propriety. It is more synonymous than antonymous with AUDACIOUS. (C) should not be selected. (D) IMPUDENT is being bold, blunt, pert; rather than being an antonym for AUDACIOUS, the word is a synonym. (D) should not be chosen as the correct answer. (E) INSOLENT is being insulting and overbearing. It is definitely not the opposite of AUDACIOUS and should not be chosen as the correct answer.

31. **(A)**

The antonym for CALCULATING (shrewd or cunning) is (A) RASH (too hasty in acting or speaking; reckless). Alternative (B) DARING is wrong because it has to do with the courage or bravery a person has rather than hastiness or lack of planning; (C) RISKY is wrong because it has to do with exposure to harm, not with hastiness in action; (D) QUIXOTIC is wrong because it means idealistically romantic and has more to do with purpose of action taken rather than kind (hastiness); (E) WILD is wrong because it means lacking social or moral restraint. A rash action may be reckless but is not necessarily dissolute, or bad.

32. **(D)**

The antonym for INFAMOUS (notorious; having a bad reputation) is (D) ILLUSTRIOUS (distinguished; outstanding; famous). (A) IDOLIZED is wrong because it means to admire excessively. An infamous person and an honorable person might both be idolized by different persons. (B) IGNOMINIOUS means literally without name, without reputation, shamed, or disgraced. This word is close in meaning to infamous. (C) UNKNOWN is wrong because not to be known or not to have a reputation at all is not the opposite of having a negative reputation. (E) GRACIOUS is wrong because it means having charm or courtesy, and an infamous person may just as well have these characteristics as not.

33. **(D)**

TRENCHANT (distinct, clear-cut), FECUND (fruitful), and PARTISAN (biased) are unrelated to GERMANE; therefore, (A), (B), and (E) are inappropriate choices. PERTINENT (relevant) is synonymous to GERMANE, so (C) is incorrect. FATUOUS (silly, trivial) is the opposite of GERMANE. The correct response is (D).

34. **(D)**

ALLEVIATE means to lessen or relieve pain and to decrease. Its opposite is (D) AGGRAVATE which means to make worse. Alternative (A) INTENSIFY means to make stronger; (B) INTERFERE means to meddle; (C) IRRITATE means to provoke to anger or annoy; and (E) OBVIATE means to make unnecessary, or to do away with or prevent by effective measures.

35. **(D)**

CONSUMMATE means complete or perfect. Its opposite is (D) CRUDE meaning unfinished; in a raw or natural condition. Alternatives (A) PERFECT and (E) COMPLETE are wrong because they are synonyms for the word CONSUMMATE. Alternative (B) HUNGRY is unrelated to consummate in meaning, as is (C) UNSUCCESSFUL.

36. **(A)**

DISSEMBLE is a verb meaning to conceal (the truth, one's feelings, etc.) under a false appearance. Its opposite is BETRAY, meaning to fail to uphold, to expose treacherously. DISSEMBLE and BETRAY both occur with an element of false appearance or treachery. (B) PUT TOGETHER (assemble) has as its opposite the word disassemble. Alternative (C) RESEMBLE means to be like or similar to. The opposite of (D) AGREE is to disagree or to not be in accord with. (E) RESOLVE means to analyze or solve a problem.

37. **(E)**

STENTORIAN means loud. (A) STYPTICAL means producing a contraction of a blood vessel; astringent; binding. It is not the opposite of STENTORIAN and should not be selected as the correct answer. (B) EGREGIOUS means extraordinarily bad; flagrant. It is not related to STENTORIAN. (B) should not be selected as the correct answer. (C) INVIDIOUS is used to describe a character such that it cannot be used without causing ill will. Since (C) is not related to STENTORIAN, it should not be selected as the right choice. (D) VOCIFEROUS means making a loud outcry. Since it is not antonymous with STENTORIAN, (D) should not be selected. (E) SUBDUED means quiet. It is the opposite of STENTORIAN and is the correct answer.

38. **(D)**

Choice (D) is correct. IMPOLITIC means not polite. To be CIVIL (D) is to be courteous, or polite. TACTLESS (A) implies a lack of savoir faire. Choice (B), RECALCITRANCE, means to be in defiance of authority, or in resistance. POLTOONERY (C) is a synonym for cowardice. POLITICAL (E) means of or relating to government.

Section 4–Quantitative Ability

1. **(D)**
    The difference between $a + b$ and $a - b$ is:

    $$a + b - (a - b) = a + b - a + b$$
    $$= 2b$$
    $$\text{if} \quad b > 0 \quad \text{then} \quad 2b > b$$
    $$\text{if} \quad b = 0 \quad \text{then} \quad 2b = b$$
    $$\text{if} \quad b < 0 \quad \text{then} \quad 2b < b,$$

hence, the answer cannot be determined.

2. **(A)**
    Since $n = p^2$, where $p > 1$, it is always such that $p^2 > p$. Therefore, $n > p$.

3. **(A)**
    Redraw the graph and put in another line $x = y$. Comparing both points (x_0, y_0) and (x_0, y_1) we can see that

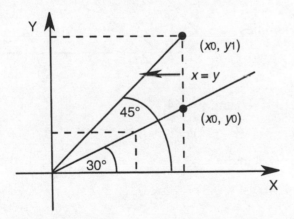

$$x_0 = y_1$$
$$y_1 > y_0$$
$$\text{so, } x_0 > y_0.$$

4. **(A)**
    Given $a \times b = 2ab - b$ and $b \times a = 2a - 1$,

    $$\frac{a \times b}{b \times a} = \frac{2ab - b}{2a - 1} = \frac{b(2a - 1)}{(2a - 1)} = b$$

    and

    $$\frac{b \times a}{a \times b} = \frac{2a - 1}{2ab - b} = \frac{2a - 1}{b(2a - 1)} = \frac{1}{b}.$$

Because

$$b > 1, \; b > \frac{1}{b}.$$

5. **(B)**

Column A

The mode is the most frequently occurring value in a set of figures.
The mode = 10.

Column B

The mean is the sum of the figures divided by the number of values.

$$\text{The mean } = \frac{(14 + 10 + 9 + 10 + 17)}{5}$$

$$= \frac{60}{5} = 12.$$

Therefore, Column B is greater than Column A.

6. **(C)**

Redraw the figure. Because $\overline{MN} \parallel \overline{CA}, \angle MNB = \angle CAB, x + \angle MNB = 180°$. Therefore, $x + y = 180°$. Therefore, the two quantities are equal.

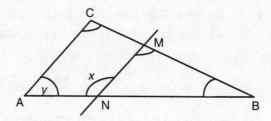

7. **(D)**

As a first example, let $x = -3$ and $y = -4$.

$$x - y = -3 - (-4) = 1 > 0.$$

As a second example, let $x = -4$ and $y = -3$.

$$x - y = -4 - (-3) = -1 < 0.$$

8. **(C)**

We can rewrite the succession as

$$x, \; x + 3, \; x + 2, \; x + 5, \; x + 4, \; 10$$

where $x = a + 1$.

If we take the differences these are

$$3, -1, 3, -1, \ldots$$

Therefore,
$$10 - (x + 4) = 3$$
$$- (x + 4) = -7$$
$$x = 3$$

Putting x into the equation, we get $3 = a + 1$, or $a = 2$.

9. **(C)**

The formula for the area of a triangle is $A = (\frac{1}{2})$ (Base) (Height). So

for triangle ABC the lengths of the base and height are given to be equal, that is, segment AC = segment CB. Thus, let the variable $x = AC = CB$ and substitute in the area formula to get the following:

$$\text{Area} = \left(\frac{1}{2}\right)(x)\,(x) = 60.5 \text{ square units}$$

Now solve for x,

$$\left(\frac{1}{2}\right)x^2 = 60.5 \text{ square units}$$

$$x^2 = 121 \text{ square units}$$

$$x = 11 \text{ units}$$

Hence, the quantities in the two columns are equal.

10. **(C)**

Given that $L_1 \parallel L_2$, $\alpha = \gamma$. Given that $L_3 \parallel L_4$, $\beta = \delta$. But $\alpha = \beta$, so, $\alpha = \beta = \gamma = \delta$. From $\alpha + \beta = 240°$, we have $\alpha = \beta = \gamma = \delta = 120°$.

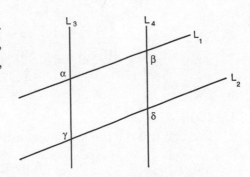

11. **(C)**

In Figure A each circle has a radius of $a/4$. The shaded area =

Area of the square – Area of the four circles

In Figure A: Shaded area $= a^2 - 4\left[\pi\left(\dfrac{a}{4}\right)^2\right]$

$$= a^2 - \frac{4\pi a^2}{16} = a^2 - \frac{\pi a^2}{4} = a^2\left(1 - \frac{\pi}{4}\right)$$

In Figure B each circle has a radius of $\dfrac{a}{8}$.

$$\text{Shaded area} = a^2 - 16\left[\pi\left(\frac{a}{8}\right)^2\right]$$

$$= a^2 - \frac{16\pi a^2}{64} = a^2 - \frac{\pi a^2}{4} = a^2\left(1 - \frac{\pi}{4}\right)$$

The shaded areas are equal.

12. **(C)**

Redraw the figure. We have

$$\alpha + \alpha + 90° = 180°$$
$$2\alpha = 90°$$
$$\alpha = 45°$$

and
$$\alpha + \beta = 180°$$
$$\beta = 180° - 45°$$
$$\beta = 135°$$

Also, $3a = 45 \times 3 = 135°$.

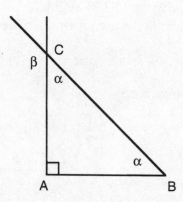

13. **(B)**

Let x = time that it takes A and B together to complete the job. Then,

$$\frac{1}{10} + \frac{1}{8} = \frac{1}{x} = \frac{9}{40} = \frac{1}{x} = x = \frac{40}{9} = 4.\overline{4}$$
$$4.\overline{4} < 5$$

14. **(D)**

We can rewrite the statement as

$$3m > 4p,$$

therefore,

$$\frac{m}{p} > \frac{4}{3},$$

but not necessarily bigger than 2.

15. **(C)**

Redraw the figure. In the triangle ABC

$$20° + 40° + x° = 180°$$
$$x = 120°$$

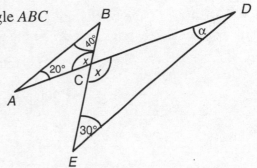

In the triangle ECD

$$30° + x + \alpha = 180°$$
$$30° + 120 + \alpha = 180°$$
$$\alpha = 30°$$

16. **(C)**

We can simplify a in alternative (C) as shown below.

$$\frac{ax - a}{a} = \frac{a(x-1)}{a} = x - 1$$

In all of the other choices, simplification of a changes the expression.

17. **(C)**

The average of the heights can be 6 feet and 2 inches when no one is this height. Therefore, only statement III is correct.

18. **(D)**

We need to find the expression for bx as a function of y, where

$$\frac{a}{x} - \frac{b}{y} = c \text{ and } xy = \frac{1}{c}$$

Using the first expression $\dfrac{a}{x} - \dfrac{b}{y} = c$, we get

$$\frac{ay - bx}{xy} = c = ay - bx = cxy$$

Substituting the second expression in the right side, we have

$$ay - bx = c\left(\frac{1}{c}\right)$$
$$= ay - bx = 1$$
$$= bx = ay - 1$$

19. **(C)**

If 40% of the bricks are already put in the wall and we need 1,200 more, then 1,200 bricks = 60% of the total bricks. Letting

$$x = \text{total bricks},$$

$$1,200 = \frac{60x}{100}$$

$$x = \frac{12,000}{6}$$

$$x = 2,000$$

20. **(E)**

If $x : y = 1 : 2$
and $y : z = 2 : 3$
then $x : y : z = 1 : 2 : 3$
and $x : z = 1 : 3$
or $x : z = 2 : 6$.
Given $x : y = 1 : 2$,

$$\frac{x}{y} = \frac{1}{2}$$

and $y : z = 2 : 3$,

$$\frac{y}{z} = \frac{2}{3}.$$

Therefore $\dfrac{x}{y} : \dfrac{y}{z} = \dfrac{1}{2} : \dfrac{2}{3}$,

$$: \frac{y}{z} = \frac{1}{2} \times \frac{3}{2}$$

$$: \frac{y}{z} = \frac{3}{4}.$$

Therefore, propositions I, II, and III are true.

21. **(A)**

In 1990 the percentage under the age of 15 in China will be 25%; therefore, 75% will be older than 15. Then

$$\frac{75}{100}(1.1 \text{ billion}) = .825 \text{ billion}$$

or 825 million

22. **(B)**

The annual per capita income is:

$$\frac{\text{Gross National Product (GNP)}}{\text{Population}}$$

In this case

$$\frac{\$315 \text{ billion}}{1.1 \text{ billion (citizens)}} = 286.4 \left(\frac{\$}{\text{citizen}}\right)$$

23. **(B)**

To find the number of people under 15 who live in cities in China in 1990, you need to know:

Population = 1.1 billion
Percentage under 15 = 25%
Percentage that live in cities = 21%
Number that live in cities under 15 = $1.1 \times 10^9 \times .25 \times .21$
$$= 57,750,000$$

24. **(B)**

First, calculate the number of doctors in each country.
Soviet Union:

$$\frac{289 \text{ million (citizens)}}{267 \text{ (citizens/doctor)}} = 1.082397 \times 10^6 \text{ doctors}$$

China:

$$\frac{1.1 \text{ billion (citizens)}}{1,757 \text{ (citizens/doctor)}} = 626,067 \text{ doctors}$$

$$\frac{\text{No. of Drs., USSR}}{\text{No. of Drs., China}} = \frac{1.082397 \times 10^6}{626,067} \approx 1.729$$

25. **(E)**

To solve the problem we need to know

a) Population
b) Birth Rate, and
c) Infant Mortality

$$\text{Newborn in 1990} = \text{Birth Rate} \times \text{number of citizens}$$

$$= \frac{18}{1,000} \times 289,000,000$$

$$= 5.202 \times 10^6$$

$$\text{Newborn that will die} = \text{Infant Mortality Rate} \times$$
$$\text{Newborn in 1990}$$

$$= \frac{22}{1,000} \times 5.202 \times 10^6$$

$$= 1.14444 \times 10^5 = 114,444$$

26. **(B)**

In order to find what percent of 260 is 13, one needs only to form the following equation:

$$x\%(260) = 13$$

$$\frac{x(260)}{100} = 13$$

$$260x = 13(100)$$

$$x = \frac{1,300}{260} = 5\%$$

27. **(D)**

$$\frac{1 - \frac{1}{1-x}}{1 - \frac{1}{1 - \frac{1}{x}}} = \frac{1 - \frac{1}{1-x}}{1 - \frac{x}{x-1}} = \frac{(1-x)(1 - \frac{1}{1-x})}{(1-x)(1 - \frac{x}{x-1})} = \frac{1 - x - 1}{1 - x + x} = -x$$

28. **(C)**

$a + b$ books = \$1,000.
Let 1 book = x.

$$x = \frac{1,000}{a + b} \left(\frac{\$}{\text{book}} \right)$$

Myron bought each one for \$1 less. He paid

$$\frac{1,000}{a + b} - 1 \left(\frac{\$}{\text{book}} \right)$$

Therefore, for 12 he paid

$$\left(\frac{1,000}{a+b} - 1\right) \times 12.$$

29. **(E)**

    If we express all the numbers as decimals, we have

    (A)   −.6660

    (B)   −.6600

    (C)   −.6000

    (D)   −.6600

    (E)   −.$\overline{6666}$...

The smallest one is (E).

30. **(E)**

    Redraw the figure as below since $L_1 \| L_2$.

    $2x + x + 30° + 60° = 180°$

    $3x + 90° = 180°$

    $3x = 90°$

    $x = 30°$

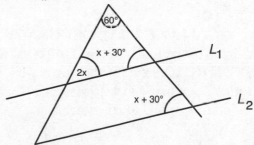

Section 5–Verbal Ability

1. **(A)**
    IMMEDIATE (B) refers to brevity of time which is inferentially contradicted. CAPITULATED (D) and OBEISANT (E) refer to submission. "Individualized man" contradicts this concept. LICENTIOUS (C) suggests a lack of restraint. SENSIBLE (A) is the correct choice, implying the obvious through its effects. The contextual clues are "isolates" and "individualized" which are the effects in a cause:effect relationship.

2. **(A)**
    HOMOGRAPHS and HETERONYMS both are words that are spelled the same but have different pronunciations and meanings. HOMO-PHONES are words that sound alike but are different in meaning and spelling. HOMONYMS are words that are spelled and pronounced the same but have different meanings. (A) is the best answer.

3. **(C)**
    CALLOSITY (A), OBDURACY (B), and PHLEGMACY (E) reflect a lack of feelings. TREPIDATION (D) reveals excitement due to fear. CONTRITION (C) is the correct choice; "sin" is the contextual clue. It reflects a sorrow that arises out of love of God and a realization one has failed to respond to His grace.

4. **(E)**
    ETIOLOGY (E), meaning the causes of a disease, is correct. AP-PEARANCE (B) and SYMPTOMS (C) both refer to the effects of the depression; it is the causes of the disease that are treated, not the effects, so both (B) and (C) are inappropriate choices. STAGES (A) and PHASES (D) are synonymous, referring to the course of the disease over time. Again, it is the causes of the disease that are treated, not the course of the disease, so (A) and (D) are not correct answers.

5. **(A)**
    PORTRAITURE (B) and ROULADE (C) refer to music. THEME (D) and SUBJECT (E) refer to literature. Only LEITMOTIV (A) refers to a repeated phrase associated with a particular person or mood.

6. **(A)**
    (B) combines visibility with appearance. Emotions are not seen, only the behavior resulting from those emotions. (C) combines cohesion with

disappear. They are not relevant. (D) combines silence with tumult. They are not relevant. (E) combines violence with music. They also are not relevant. (A) is the correct choice. PLIANT and MALLEABLE are synonyms meaning flexible.

7. **(E)**

A "deliberate act" would not have been caused by INEPTITUDE (A), which is the quality or state of being unable to do something. PERSPICACITY (B), a keen mental understanding, would not need excuses to VINDICATE it. SAGACITY (C) denotes wisdom and would not need to be explained away. PSYCHOSIS (D), meaning insanity, does not have anything in particular to do with the aging process. IGNORANCE (E) could be due to youth and PALLIATE, to mitigate or lessen an offense, would complete the sentence best. Therefore, choice (E) is correct.

8. **(D)**

GAZPACHO is a cold SOUP made of various vegetables. The key relationship in this analogy is that the first term is one kind of the entity identified by the second term. The correct answer is (D). BRATWURST is one kind of SAUSAGE. None of the other alternatives fits the *A*-is-one-kind-of-*B* analogy. PAELLA (C) is a dish that has various kinds of FISH in it, but is not a kind of fish.

9. **(B)**

The SUN is a part of the SOLAR SYSTEM, along with the celestial bodies that revolve around it. The MOON is not a part of the EARTH; therefore, (A) is not the best answer. An ISLAND is a part of an ARCHIPELAGO, or group of islands, so (B) is the right answer. A GALAXY is formed from STARS, not vice-versa, so (C) is not correct. Similarly, a MOLECULE is made up of ATOMS; therefore, (D) is incorrect. (E) is a possible answer; however, VERSES is plural in contrast to SUN (singular).

10. **(D)**

A SOUFFLE is usually made from EGGS. COCONUT is often an ingredient in a MACAROON. The order, however, for COCONUT: MACAROON is not the same as for SOUFFLE:EGGS; (A) is not the correct answer. A PEAR does contain NECTAR; a pear, however, is not made from a recipe nor does it contain any added ingredients. (B) is not the right answer. PIGS are trained to find TRUFFLES, an underground fungus. The relationship in (C) obviously is not the same as that between SOUFFLE:EGGS. MOUSSE is a rich pudding-like dessert which contains CREAM. The analogy between MOUSSE:CREAM (D) and SOUFFLE:

EGGS is apparent. A TOMATO is a FRUIT (not a vegetable), but it is not analogous to SOUFFLE:EGGS. (E) is not the correct choice.

11. **(D)**

Although (A), (B), (C), and (E) are all antonymous relationships, they contain nuances of meaning. DEPOSITION:REFUTATION (A) suggests evidence versus contrary evidence. HYPOTHESIS:ABSOLUTE (B) denotes certainty versus uncertainty. DIAGNOSIS:OBTUSENESS (C) is defined as discrimination versus indiscrimination. FEASIBILITY: INCONCEIVABLENESS (E) relates to possible versus impossible. (D) is the correct choice. SUPPOSITION:SURMISE have the same relationship as THEORY and SPECULATION as well as the same meaning.

12. **(A)**

(D) and (E) both are contained in an antonymous relationship. PLAGIARIST:MERCATURE refer to stealing versus buying. SEQUES-TRATION:URBANITY denotes seclusion versus sociality. (C) relates to the whole:part relationship. (B) is a synonymous relationship implying fun. (A) is the correct choice. It is a part:whole relationship. PLANT LIFE is a part of the study of life: BIOLOGY, as CUBISM is a style of ART.

13. **(C)**

APOTHEOSIZE (to glorify or deify) and CANONIZE (to glorify, to exalt, to declare a deceased person a saint) are synonymous. DEPRECA-TION (disapproval, with regret) and SERVILITY (submissiveness) do not have the synonymous relationship sought so (A) should not be selected. SMORGASBORD suggests an abundance of something—especially food. PALTRY indicates a minimum amount. Since the two are antonyms, (B) should not be selected. PERMEATE and PERVADE are synonyms meaning to spread or diffuse itself through. (C) is, therefore, the correct answer. A SINECURE is a job with little work; an ABERRATION is the act of deviating—especially from what is right. (D) is not the best answer. SPE-CIOUS (plausible but false) and COMPLAISANT (amiable) do not have the synonymous relationship sought. (E) is not an appropriate choice.

14. **(D)**

PARSIMONIOUS and NIGGARDLY are synonyms meaning mi-serly or stingy; therefore, MISERLY:STINGY (D) is the correct answer. The relationship being sought is synonymous; AVARICE: GENEROSITY and PENURIOUS:SQUANDERING are antonyms, there-fore (B) and (E) are incorrect. A MENDICANT is a beggar and a BENE-FACTOR is one who gives kindly help; the relationship is not synonymous, and so (A) is not correct. Although CONVOLUTED and COMPLICATED can be used synonymously, something can be COMPLICATED without being CONVOLUTED. A person cannot be NIGGARDLY without being PARSIMONIOUS; thus, (C) does not reflect the same relationship and is not an appropriate choice.

15. **(C)**

The relationship between MERIDIAN and PARALLEL is that between two different types of lines on a map; they are used together to locate a point, compute distance, etc. The two are not just opposite terms; they must be used together for location, computation, etc. EAST and WEST are opposites, as are NORTH and SOUTH, so (A) and (D) are incorrect. LONGITUDE and LATITUDE compare well with MERIDIAN and PARALLEL. Through MERIDIANS one arrives at LONGITUDE; through PARALLELS one arrives at LATITUDE. Both LONGITUDE and LATITUDE are used for locations as are MERIDIANS and PARALLELS. (C) is the best answer. A MAP is a drawing representing the earth's surface; a GLOBE is a sphere with a map of the world on it. The two are not necessarily used together. They do not have the same analogy as do MERIDIAN:PARALLEL. (D) is not the best answer. A COMPASS is used to find DIRECTION. The analogy is not the same as is MERIDIAN:PARALLEL. (E) is not the best answer.

16. **(C)**

PORIFERAN is a type of SPONGE, so the relationship being sought is subset:set. Only (C) reflects this type of relationship. A EULOGY is a speech given in praise of the dead, and a PANEGYRIC is a speech given in praise; therefore, a EULOGY is a type of PANEGYRIC. (A), (D), and (E) are all synonymous relationships. (B) is a cause-and-effect relationship.

17. **(E)**

Choice (A) implies that the passage will ONLY discuss underwater explosions. Choice (B) suggests that the passage will ONLY discuss the pros and cons of the two types of warheads. (C) would be appropriate only if the passage listed ALL of the standard equipment and weaponry of both fleet-type and Guppy submarines. (D) implies that the passage will be confined to a discussion of the mechanics of torpedoes. Only (E) is general enough to suggest that more than one fact about torpedoes will be discussed.

18. **(A)**

Paragraph four states that the electric torpedo has the advantage of no visible wake, implying gas turbines leave a wake, which is a disadvantage. There is no support for (B), (C), (D), or (E).

19. **(D)**

Choices (A), (B), (C), and (E) all differentiate between conventional and nuclear warheads. However, paragraph two only mentions "a projectile," making no distinctions between the two types. Therefore, choice (D), which makes no differentiation, is the correct answer.

20. **(B)**

Paragraph four states "Electric torpedoes usually have less speed and range than turbine types," inferring that turbines provide additional power and speed (B). Nowhere in the passage is it stated or implied that turbines give the torpedo direction (A), deliver the explosive silently (C), affects the weight and force of the Guppy (D), or inflicts greater damage (E).

21. **(A)**

The first paragraph discusses the early years of Ponce de Léon's career, and the rest of the passage details the later years (A). The first paragraph does NOT describe how Ponce de Léon heard about the fountain of youth (B), or how he discovered Florida (D). While the first paragraph does mention that Ponce de Léon was one of the first *adelantados,* it does not discuss his motives for becoming one, so (C) cannot be the answer. The first paragraph does mention Ponce de Léon's voyage with Columbus (E), but the rest of the passage does more than detail Ponce de Léon's attempt to circumnavigate Florida.

22. **(B)**

(A) is stated in paragraph two. Paragraph four states "determined to be first to circumnavigate the island." The article states de Léon was awarded a patent for the Bahamas and much later received new patents for the Bahamas and Florida; therefore, (D) is incorrect. Paragraph five states that de Léon had seen too much of the hostile Indians. Hence, (E) is incorrect. (B) is the correct answer. Paragraph five refers to de Léon fruitlessly searching for the fountain of youth.

23. **(D)**

(A) is implied, therefore, incorrect. (B), (C), and (E) are true statements relating to de Léon; however, paragraph one states he was an *adelantado* because he "advanced the Spanish Empire by conquest, subjugation of Indians and establishment of quasi-military government." Therefore, (D) is the correct answer.

24. **(E)**

Paragraph two states that the Spanish had already seen so many wonders in the New World that "only a cynic would have doubted the existence" of the fountain of youth (II). In paragraph four, the passage states that Ponce de Léon had "claimed Florida and all lands contiguous to it" for the Spanish crown, and paragraph five states that the king rewarded Ponce de Léon with "new patents" to Florida and Bimini (III). The same paragraph also states that Ponce de Léon had "to bear the expense of conquest" for his new lands, so (I) is false. (E) is the correct choice: (II) and (III) are true.

25. **(C)**

Ponce de Léon was motivated by a desire to discover the fountain of youth (A), and he discovered Florida during his search for the mythical spring. He came to the New World as one of the first *adelantados* (E), and was rewarded for claiming Florida and Bimini for Spain with royal patents to conquer and govern those territories (B). When Ponce de Léon returned to Florida to carry out his patent, he was mortally wounded by Seminoles trying to prevent the Spanish seizure of their land (D). Only (C) is false; paragraph two states that the Spanish had heard of the Bahamas, where legend held there was a "marvelous spring whose waters would restore lost youth."

26. **(D)**

The author's presentation discusses more than the fruitless search to locate the fountain of youth, so (A) is not the correct answer. Similarly, the passage is more than just a list of Ponce de Léon's conquests (B) or an outline of the discovery of Florida (C). There is no discussion of the Spanish treatment of the native peoples of the New World, so (E) is not correct. Therefore, the passage can only be described as an essay on Ponce de Léon's career (D).

27. **(D)**

(A) is stated in the description of *adelantado*. (B) is inferred. (C) is a negative statement. (D) is the correct choice. Ponce de Léon governed Puerto Rico, then used it as a point of departure for his expedition to the Bahamas. (E) is incorrect; de Léon was a subject of the Spanish King.

28. **(A)**
   SUBLIMINAL implies an unawareness. CONSCIOUS means wholly conscious, existing, felt. It is the antonym for SUBLIMINAL and (A) should be selected. SUBVERSIVE is that which ruins or overthrows. It is not an antonym for SUBLIMINAL. (B) is incorrect. A TERMAGANT is a quarrelsome woman; it is unrelated to SUBLIMINAL. (C) should not be chosen. TURPITUDE is depravity. Since it is not the antonym for SUBLIMINAL, (D) should not be chosen. EXPLICIT means unfolded or explained, which is not the opposite sought.

29. **(A)**
   (B) refers to sense impressions in general. (C), (D), and (E) suggest the avenues through which sense perception occurs. INSIPID (A) (lacking in taste) is the opposite of FLAVOR (something which affects the taste).

30. **(A)**
   TRANSCENDENT implies an above average standing. AVERAGE is the antonym and, hence, (A) is the right answer. SUPERLUNAR is being above the moon, not of this world. Since it is not the antonym sought, (B) should not be selected. SUSPENSION means the act of holding for a time, hanging. It is not the opposite and, hence, (C) is not an appropriate answer. VERMICULATED means formed with irregular lines or impressions. It is not related to TRANSCENDENT and (D) is not the correct choice. STERLING implies an above average standing; it is synonymous with, not an antonym for, TRANSCENDENT. (E) is not the correct choice.

31. **(B)**
   A faction is a group of dissenters who work in common against the main body or organization. FACTIOUS means "produced by faction." The opposite of FACTIOUS is COOPERATIVE (B). The other alternatives have no relationship to the word FACTIOUS. CONVOLUTED (A) means coiled, or complicated; CURVED (C) refers to a line having no straight part; CUNNING (D) means crafty; and COWARDLY (E) means in the manner of a coward or lacking courage.

32. **(E)**
   SLANT (A) and OBLIQUE (D) are synonymous of SKEW. CONTRAPOSITION (B) refers to inversion. CONVOLUTION (C) refers to being coiled. PARALLEL (E) is defined as "extending in the same direction, not meeting" which is the opposite of SKEW, which means a deviation from a straight line.

33. **(E)**

PUNGENCY (A) is synonymous with ACRIDITY, meaning a bitter taste or odor. ACERBITY (C) and MORDANCY (D) both refer to bitter or harsh words or thoughts. INSIPID (B) suggests blandness. Only SAVORINESS (E), meaning pleasant to taste, is the opposite of ACRIDITY.

34. **(E)**

PHENOMENON (A) refers to the observable fact or event. PERSPECTIVE (B) refers to the ability to view things in their true importance. OSTENTATION (C) suggests an unearned display. PRECARIOUS (D) is defined as doubtful. ECLIPSE (E), to remove from view, is the opposite of SPECTACLE which is defined as "something exhibited to view as unusual or notable."

35. **(C)**

LANGUOR (C), meaning inactivity, is the opposite of VELOCITY, which means speed. EXTRICATE (A), meaning to free or untangle, does not refer to speed and is incorrect. TOWAGE (B), KINEMATICS (D), and CIRCUITOUS (E) all refer to motion, not speed, and are inappropriate answers.

36. **(C)**

STRIDULATION (A), VOCIFERATION (D), and EJACULATION (E) are all types of noise even as RAUCOUS is a type of noise. PERCUSSION (B) is the impact of the noise on the ear. SUSURRUS (C), meaning a whispering sound, is the opposite of RAUCOUS.

37. **(D)**

GLEAM (A) is defined as a small bright light. LUCIDITY (B) refers to the luminosity from that light. NIMBUS (C) suggests the luminous vapor surrounding the light. OBSCURATION (E) denotes an inadequate amount of light. TENEBRIFIC (D) (causing darkness) is the opposite of SCINTILLATION (rapid changes of brightness).

38. **(E)**

(A) and (C) are antonyms. CONDUCTION refers to motion while QUIESCENCE refers to lack of motion. (B) is a synonym of OCCLUSION with both suggesting obstruction. (D) is defined as prevention. (E) PERFORATION (hole made by piercing or boring) is the opposite of OCCLUSION.

Section 6–Quantitative Ability

1. **(C)**
   Note that

   $$\left(\frac{5}{9}\right)^2 = \frac{25}{81} \text{ and } \left(\frac{9}{5}\right)^{-2} = \frac{9^{-2}}{5^{-2}} = \left(\frac{1}{9}\right)^2 \left(\frac{5}{1}\right)^2 = \left(\frac{1}{81}\right)(25) = \frac{25}{81}.$$

   Hence, the quantities in the two columns are equal.

2. **(A)**
   From the diagram in question 2, $a > c$, $d > b$. Adding these two inequalities, one obtains

   $$a + d > b + c.$$

   So the quantity in Column A is greater.

3. **(B)**
   One way to attack this comparison problem is to simply solve the given inequality for the variable x. Thus,

   $$
   \begin{aligned}
   1 - 2x &> x - 5 \\
   1 + 5 &> x + 2x \\
   6 &> 3x \\
   2 &> x
   \end{aligned}
   $$

   So the quantity in Column B is greater.

4. **(C)**
   The average is the sum of the values / number of values.

   Column A $\qquad \dfrac{(25 + 17 + 30 + 23 + 15)}{5} = \dfrac{110}{5} = 22$

   Column B $\qquad \dfrac{(13 + 35 + 11 + 25 + 9 + 39)}{6} = \dfrac{132}{6} = 22$

   Therefore, the quantities are equal.

5. **(B)**
   Operations inside the parentheses are done first. Then using the order of operations, multiplication and division are done before addition and subtraction.

Column A $(8 - 3 \times 4)^2 = (8 - 12)^2 = (-4)^2 = 16$

Column B $(8 - 3 \times 4)^2 = [5 \times 4]^2 = [20]^2 = 400$

6. **(B)**

Observe that 5% of 45 is x may be written as $0.05(45) = x$ or $x = 2.25$. Similarly, 45 is 5% of x may be written as $45 = 0.05x$ or $x = {}^{45}\!/_{0.05} = 900$. Hence, the quantity in Column B is greater.

7. **(C)**

Note that the diameter = twice the radius. So, the radius of the circle in Column A is 8 since the diameter is 16.

Thus,

$$\text{Area of circle} = \pi r^2 = \pi(8)^2 = 64\pi$$

and the

$$\text{Area of rectangle} = \text{length} \times \text{width} = 64\pi.$$

Hence, the quantities in both columns are equal.

8. **(D)**

Note that if $x > 1$ or $-1 < x < 0$, then any number x is greater than $1\!/_x$. But, if $x < -1$ or $0 < x < 1$, then any number x is less than $1\!/_x$. So, one cannot tell which quantity in the columns is greater.

9. **(B)**

An examination of the sequence of numbers shows that the second number, 5, is 2(first number) + 1 = 2(2) + 1; the third number, 11, is 2(second number) + 1 = 2(5) + 1; the fourth number, x, is 2(third number) + 1 = 2(11) + 1 = 22 + 1 = 23; etc. In Column B, the result of $(11 + 47)/2 = 58/2 = 29$. So, the quantity in Column B is greater.

10. **(A)**

One must first simplify each of the complex fractions. Thus,

$$\frac{1}{\frac{1}{x(x)}} = \frac{1}{1} \times \frac{x(x)}{1} = x^2 \quad \text{and} \quad \frac{x(x-1)\frac{1}{x(x-1)}}{x(x-1)\frac{x}{x-1}} = \frac{1}{x^2}$$

Since $x > 1$, then $x^2 > \dfrac{1}{x^2}$. So, the function in Column A is greater than the function in Column B.

11. **(D)**

Recall that the area of the circle is πx^2. Also, recall that the circumference of the circle is $2\pi x$. Because nothing is said about the radius x, it is impossible to determine whether the area of the circle or the circumference is greater. The problem lies in the fact that, if $x > 1$, then x^2 is larger than x. On the other hand, if $x < 1$, then x^2 is smaller than x. In either case, the comparison is affected. So, there is not enough information to make the comparison.

12. **(D)**

Assume that $x > y > 0$. Then, $|x| > |y|$. On the other hand, assume that $0 > x > y$. This means that both x and y are negative. Then, when the absolute value is taken, the direction of the inequality is changed, so $|x| < |y|$. Hence, from the information given in the problem, it is impossible to compare the quantities in the columns.

13. **(C)**

Simplify the expression in Column A as follows:

$$\sqrt{\frac{y}{2}}\sqrt{\frac{2y}{x}} = \sqrt{\frac{2yy}{2x}} = \sqrt{\frac{y^2}{x}} = \frac{y}{\sqrt{x}}.$$

But,

$$\frac{y}{\sqrt{x}} = \frac{y}{\sqrt{x}} \times \frac{\sqrt{x}}{\sqrt{x}} = \frac{y\sqrt{x}}{\sqrt{x^2}} = \frac{y\sqrt{x}}{x}$$

So, the quantity in Column A is equal to the quantity in Column B.

14. **(A)**

Since the triangle on the right is a right triangle, then using the Pythagorean Theorem one can write:

$$x^2 + 5^2 = 10^2$$
$$x^2 = 100 - 25$$
$$x^2 = 75$$
$$x = \sqrt{75}$$

Similarly, since the triangle on the left is a right triangle, the same theorem enables one to write:

$$5^2 + 6^2 = y^2$$
$$25 + 36 = y^2$$
$$61 = y^2$$
$$\sqrt{61} = y$$

So, since $\sqrt{75}$ is greater than $\sqrt{61}$, it is clear that x in Column A is greater.

15. **(C)**

Simplify the expression in Column A. The LCD for the rational expressions in the numerator and denominator is 6. So,

$$\frac{6(2x) - 6\left(\frac{y-5}{6}\right)}{6\left(\frac{y-5}{3}\right) - 6(4x)} = \frac{12x - y + 5}{2y - 10 - 24x}$$

$$= \frac{12x - y + 5}{-2(12x - y + 5)} = \frac{1}{-2} = -0.5.$$

Hence, the quantity in Column A is equal to the quantity in Column B.

16. **(B)**

Note that $\dfrac{.1}{2} = \dfrac{.1 \times 10}{2 \times 10} = \dfrac{1}{20}$ for response (B).

For choice (A), $\dfrac{1}{.2} = \dfrac{1 \times 10}{.2 \times 10} = \dfrac{10}{2} = 5$ which is larger than $\dfrac{1}{20}$.

For choice (C), $\dfrac{.2}{1} = \dfrac{.2 \times 10}{1 \times 10} = \dfrac{2}{10} = \dfrac{1}{5}$ which is larger than $\dfrac{1}{20}$.

For choice (D), $\dfrac{.2}{.1} = \dfrac{.2 \times 10}{.1 \times 10} = \dfrac{2}{1} = 2$ which is larger than $\dfrac{1}{20}$.

For choice (E), $\dfrac{2}{.1} = \dfrac{2 \times 10}{.1 \times 10} = \dfrac{20}{1} = 20$ which is larger than $\dfrac{1}{20}$.

17. **(C)**

First find the least common multiple (LCM) of 3, 4, and 5 which is simply $3 \times 4 \times 5 = 60$. Since 3 divides 60, 4 divides 60, and 5 divides 60, then one needs only to add 2 to 60 in order to guarantee that the remainder in each case will be 2 when 3, 4, and 5, respectively, are divided into 62.

18. **(E)**

Since X is the first number, then let y represent the second number in the average of two numbers. Thus, from what is given in the problem, one can write:

$$\frac{X + y}{2} = WX,$$

the average. Solving for y gives the other number. Hence,

$$X + y = 2WX$$
$$y = 2WX - X,$$

the second number.

19. **(A)**

The formula for the area of a circle is $A = \pi r^2$. Since the area of the circle is 18π, then it is true that

$$\pi r^2 = 18\pi \quad \text{or} \quad r^2 = 18 \quad \text{or} \quad r = \sqrt{18} = 3\sqrt{2}.$$

Then, the diameter of the circle is $2r = 2(3\sqrt{2}) = 6\sqrt{2}$. The diameter of the circle bisects the inscribed square into two equal triangles which are $45° - 45° - 90°$ triangles. Since the diameter of the circle is also the hypotenuse of each of the triangles, $6\sqrt{2}$, and the sides x of each are equal, one can write the following using the Pythagorean Theorem:

$$x^2 + x^2 = (6\sqrt{2})^2$$
$$2x^2 = 36(2)$$
$$x^2 = 36$$
$$x = 6,$$

the length of a side of the square.

So, the correct answer choice is (A). The other answer choices are obtained by failing to find the correct diameter of the circle or failing to use the Pythagorean Theorem correctly.

20. **(D)**

The measure of the exterior angle x of triangle ABC is equal to the sum of the measures of the two remote interior angles, A and B, respectively. Thus,

$$\text{angle } x = 35° + 85° = 120°.$$

Another approach is to remember that the sum of the angles in triangle ABC is $35 + 85 + \text{angle } C = 180°$. Hence, angle $C = 60°$. Then, since angle C and angle x are supplementary angles, it follows that angle x must be $120°$ since angle C is $60°$.

21. **(A)**

To find the solution one needs to set up a proportion. Thus, let x denote the total body weight in grams and S denote the weight of the skeleton. Then, the following proportion can be formed.

$$\frac{\text{weight of skeleton}}{\text{total body weight}} = \frac{10,000 \text{ grams}}{70,000 \text{ grams}} = \frac{S}{x}$$

Thus,

$$\frac{1}{7} = \frac{S}{x} \Rightarrow x = 7S,$$

which is response (A).

22. (D)

Since 40% of the weight of blood is made up of cells, then the weight of the cells is 0.4 times 5,000 grams, or 2,000 grams. So, to find the percent of the total body weight that is made up of blood cells, form the following ratio and change the result to a percent.

$$\frac{2,000}{70,000} = \frac{1}{35} = 0.028 = 2.8\%$$

23. (D)

This question requires that all answers be compared. Choice (A) gives $500 \times 0.10 = 50$ grams of cholesterol. Choice (B) gives $250 \times 0.20 = 50$ grams. Answer choice (C) gives $(150 \times 0.10) + (200 \times 0.20) = 15 + 40 = 55$ grams of cholesterol. Answer choice (D) yields $(200 \times 0.20) + (200 \times 0.20) = 80$ grams of cholesterol, and (E) gives $350 \times 0.20 = 70$ grams of cholesterol. Thus, choice (D) gives the most cholesterol.

24. (C)

Since the total amount of the payroll for the company is $13,750,000 and the wages paid to vice presidents/managers amount to $250,000, then the percent of wages paid to this position group is found as follows:

$$\frac{250,000}{13,750,000} = \frac{250}{13,750} = \frac{1}{55} = .018 = 1.8\%$$

25. (A)

To find the ratio of the wages earned by a team leader to the wages earned by an assembly worker, the average wages of each must be found.

$$\text{Average wages for a team leader} = \frac{1,000,000}{25} = 40,000$$

$$\text{Average wages for an assembly worker} = \frac{12,500,000}{500} = 25,000$$

The ratio can be written as $\dfrac{40,000}{25,000} = \dfrac{40}{25} = \dfrac{8}{5}$ or as 8 : 5.

26. **(D)**

Let x = the first odd integer, $x + 2$ = the second consecutive odd integer, and $x + 4$ = the third consecutive odd integer. Then, the following equation can be written based on what is given in the problem. Solve the equation.

$$3x = 2(x + 4) + 3$$
$$3x = 2x + 8 + 3$$
$$3x - 2x = 11$$
$$x = 11,$$

the first odd integer.

So, the second consecutive odd integer is $x + 2 = 11 + 2 = 13$.

27. **(E)**

If a fraction has a value of $\frac{2}{5}$, one can write an equivalent fraction for $\frac{2}{5}$ as $\frac{2x}{5x}$. Thus, the original numerator may be represented by $2x$ and the original denominator by $5x$. So, in accordance with the problem, one can write:

$$\frac{2x - 2}{5x + 1} = \frac{1}{4}$$

or by cross multiplying: $8x - 8 = 5x + 1$. Now solving the last equation yields the value of x in the representation, $2x$, of the original numerator of the fraction. Thus,

$$8x - 8 = 5x + 1$$
$$8x - 5x = 1 + 8$$
$$3x = 9$$
$$x = 3$$

So, the original value of the numerator is $2x = 2(3) = 6$.

28. **(D)**

The traditional way to solve this problem is to set up and solve an equation. Consider what part of the job could be done in 1 hour by each person. Thus, Jay could do $\frac{1}{5}$ of the job in 1 hour and Ray could do $\frac{1}{4}$ of the job in the same amount of time. What is unknown is the part of the job they could do together in 1 hour, which can be represented by $\frac{1}{x}$. The x represents the amount of time the brothers can do the job together.

The sum of the amount of the job each brother can do in 1 hour equals the amount of the job they can do together in 1 hour. Hence, the equation is given by:

$$\frac{1}{5} + \frac{1}{4} = \frac{1}{x}$$

Solving for *x* you calculate as follows:

$$\frac{1}{5}\times\frac{4}{4}+\frac{1}{4}\times\frac{5}{5}=\frac{1}{x}$$

Side Notes

1) Find the LCD.

$$\frac{4}{20}+\frac{5}{20}=\frac{1}{x}$$

2) Add like fractions on left side of equation.

$$\frac{9}{20}=\frac{1}{x}$$

3) Cross multiply.

$$9x=20$$

4) Divide by 9 on both sides of the equation.

$$\frac{9x}{9}=\frac{20}{9}$$

$$x=\frac{20}{9}\ \text{or}\ 2\frac{2}{9}\ \text{hours}.$$

To understand why answer choices (A), (C), and (E) are incorrect one should consider another approach to the solution of the problem. The approach is referred to as a "logical" or "reasonable" method. It is logical to believe that since Ray can complete the job in 4 hours by himself, he should finish the job in less than 4 hours with the help of his brother. Hence, answer choice (A) cannot be correct. Finally, answer choice (B), 1 hour, is also incorrect. To see this one needs to assume for a moment that Jay could also do the cleaning job in 4 hours rather than the required 5 hours. Then together the brothers should be able to complete the job in one-half of the time or just 2 hours. Thus, it is logical that answer choice (B) does not represent enough time for both to do the job using the assumption.

29. **(B)**

First find the number of different ways of drawing two marbles from the box. Use the permutation formula as follows:

$$P(10,2)=\frac{10!}{(10-2)!}=\frac{10!}{8!}=\frac{10(9)(8!)}{8!}=10(9)=90\ \text{ways}.$$

Then find the number of different ways of drawing two red marbles from the box. Use the permutation formula as follows:

$$P(6,2)=\frac{6!}{(6-2)!}=\frac{6!}{4!}=\frac{6(5)(4!)}{4!}=6(5)=30\ \text{ways}.$$

Finally, to get the probability, form a ratio of $P(6, 2)$ to $P(10, 2)$. One gets the following:

The probability of drawing two red marbles from the box = $^{30}\!/_{90} = \frac{1}{3}$.

30. **(A)**
Note that the ratio $(3 : 5 : 7)$ of the angles in the triangle ABC can be represented as three distinct angles, $3x$, $5x$, and $7x$. Since the total number of degrees in a triangle is $180°$, one can write and solve the equation.

$$3x + 5x + 7x = 180$$
$$15x = 180$$
$$x = 12$$

Thus, the measures of the angles in triangle ABC are:

$$3x = 3(12) = 36°, 5x = 5(12) = 60°, \text{ and } 7x = 7(12) = 84°,$$

respectively. Since each of the three angles is less than $90°$, then triangle ABC is an acute triangle.

Practice
Test 6

Section 1

TIME: 45 Minutes
Choose 1 of 2 Essays†

ESSAY QUESTION ONE

DIRECTIONS: Present your perspective on the issue below by using relevant reasons and/or examples to support your views. Remember, there is no one "correct" response to the essay topic. Before starting, read the essay topic and its question(s).

Some publishers complain that the reduced rate at which public libraries buy new books unduly sours the market, and that copyright laws should require libraries to give suitable compensation based on circulation. These publishers fail to acknowledge the role public libraries play in creating avid readers and therefore the book-buying market.

Which captures your interest, the complaint that libraries sour publishers' markets or the reply given? Defend your position, citing relevant reasons and/or examples taken from your own experience, reading, or personal observations.

STOP

Do not go on until you are instructed to do so. Use any remaining time to check your work on this portion of the test.

† On the actual test, you will have a choice between two essay topics. You have to write only one essay. To give you the most practice possible we have supplied sample essays for both questions in order to show you the differences between essays that receive a perfect score and those that score less.

TIME: 45 Minutes
Choose 1 of 2 Essays†

ESSAY QUESTION TWO

DIRECTIONS: Present your perspective on the issue below by using relevant reasons and/or examples to support your views. Remember, there is no one "correct" response to the essay topic. Before starting, read the essay topic and its question(s).

The increasing availability of visual modes of communication have rendered the printed word obsolete. In the near future, learning will proceed from sources like television and books will become increasingly rare and archaic.

Do you agree that books will soon lose their importance as a source of knowledge? Provide examples of your own observations, reading, and experience to explain your position.

STOP

Do not go on until you are instructed to do so. Use any remaining time to check your work on this portion of the test.

---

† On the actual test, you will have a choice between two essay topics. You have to write only one essay. To give you the most practice possible we have supplied sample essays for both questions in order to show you the differences between essays that receive a perfect score and those that score less.

Section 2

TIME: 30 Minutes
1 Essay

> **DIRECTIONS:** Critique the following argument by considering its logical soundness.

Newspaper recycling is a wasteful exercise that should be abandoned. Recollected paper is so abundant that less than ten percent is ever put to a second use, and few dealers can survive the over-supplied market. America's recycling campaign has not prevented newspapers from filling our nation's garbage dumps—it has only made them more neatly stacked, at a cost which most towns must pass on to their citizens.

Discuss the degree to which you find this argument logically persuasive. In presenting your perspective, be certain to analyze the argument's use of evidence and line of reasoning. Also discuss what, if anything, would make the argument more solid and convincing, or would assist you to better judge its conclusion.

STOP

If time remains, you may go back and check your work.

Section 3

TIME: 30 Minutes
30 Questions

NUMBERS: All numbers are real numbers.

FIGURES: Position of points, angles, regions, etc., are assumed to be in the order shown and angle measures are assumed to be positive.

LINES: Assume that lines shown as straight are indeed straight.

DIRECTIONS: Each of the following given set of quantities is placed into either Column A or B. Compare the two quantities to decide whether

(A)   the quantity in Column A is greater;

(B)   the quantity in Column B is greater;

(C)   the two quantities are equal;

(D)   the relationship cannot be determined from the information given.

NOTE: Do not choose (E) since there are only four choices.

COMMON INFORMATION: Information which relates to one or both given quantities is centered in the two columns. A symbol which appears in both columns will indicate the same item in Column A and Column B.

EXAMPLES:

Column A	Column B
1. 5×4	$5 + 4$

Explanation: The correct answer is (A), since $5 \times 4 = 20$, and $5 + 4 = 9$.

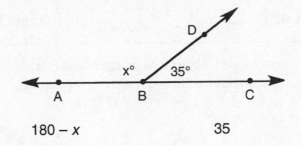

2. $180 - x$ 35

Explanation: The correct answer is (C). Since $\angle ABC$ is a straight angle, its measurement is 180°.

<u>Column A</u>	<u>Column B</u>

$$x - y \neq 0$$

1. $x + y$ $\dfrac{x^2 - y^2}{x - y}$

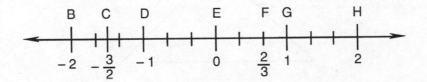

2. $\dfrac{2}{3}$ The coordinate of the midpoint of segment $\overline{DH}$

3.   5.4048 $0.105 + 0.5 - 3.1029 + 8$

A farmer calculates that out of every 100 seeds of corn he plants, he harvests 48 ears of corn. In a year, his harvest was 72,000 ears of corn.

4.   Number of seeds planted   85,000

<u>Column A</u>	<u>Column B</u>

C represents a Celsius temperature and F represents the equivalent in Fahrenheit temperature.
$$C = \frac{5}{9}(F - 32).$$

5.	65°F	20°C

A class's average (arithmetic mean) on a reading test was 27.5 out of 40. The 19 girls in the class scored a total of 532 points.

6.	Total points scored by the 11 boys in the class	287

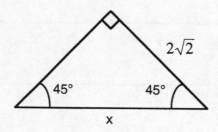

7.	x	4

If 288 is added to a certain number n, the result will be equal to three times the amount by which the number exceeds 12.

8.	n	276

a is a real number and $0 < a < 1$.

9.	a	a^2

Column A	**Column B**

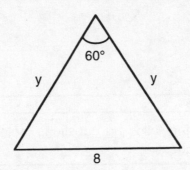

10. $3y$ 24

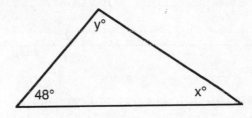

11. x y

$$a < b$$

12. a^2 b^2

13.   An integer < -1 Its reciprocal

An automatic coin counter at a bank indicates that
$65 in dimes and quarters was processed.
There were 389 coins.

14.   Number of quarters   215

Column A	**Column B**

15. $1 + \dfrac{1}{t}$ $\qquad\qquad\qquad\qquad$ $\dfrac{\dfrac{1}{t}}{\dfrac{1}{t+1}}$

DIRECTIONS: For the following questions, select the best answer choice to the given question.

16. If $x - (4x - 8) + 9 + (6x - 8) = 9 - x + 24$, then $x =$

(A) 4.

(B) 2.

(C) 8.

(D) 6.

(E) 10.

17. If x and y are two different real numbers and $xz = yz$, then what is the value of z?

(A) $x - y$

(B) 1

(C) $\dfrac{x}{y}$

(D) $\dfrac{y}{x}$

(E) 0

18. If it takes s sacks of grain to feed c chickens, how many sacks of grain are needed to feed k chickens?

(A) $\dfrac{ck}{s}$

(B) $\dfrac{k}{cs}$

(C) $\dfrac{cs}{k}$

(D) $\dfrac{c}{sk}$

(E) $\dfrac{sk}{c}$

19. The following ratio

$$40 \text{ seconds} : 1\tfrac{1}{2} \text{ minutes} : \tfrac{1}{6} \text{ hour}$$

can be expressed in lowest terms as

(A) 4 : 9 : 60   (D) $^2/_3 : 1^1/_2 : 10$

(B) 4 : 9 : 6   (E) 60 : 9 : 4

(C) 40 : 90 : 60

20. Tilda's car gets 34 miles per gallon of gasoline and Naomi's car gets 8 miles per gallon. When traveling from Washington, D.C. to Philadelphia, they both used a whole number of gallons of gasoline. How far is it from Philadelphia to Washington, D.C.?

(A) 21 miles   (D) 136 miles

(B) 32 miles   (E) 170 miles

(C) 68 miles

Questions 21–25 refer to the following graph.

The data represent the number of bushels (to the nearest 5 bushels) of wheat and corn produced by RQS farm from 1975 to 1985.

Number of bushels (to the nearest 5 bushels) of wheat and corn produced by farm RQS from 1975 – 1985

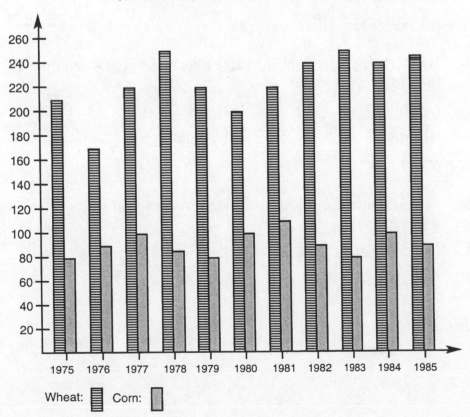

21. In which year was the least number of bushels of wheat produced?

    (A) 1976   (D) 1982

    (B) 1978   (E) 1984

    (C) 1980

22. In which year did the greatest decline in corn production occur?

    (A) 1978   (D) 1983

    (B) 1980   (E) 1985

    (C) 1982

23. During which year or years did the corn production decrease while the wheat production increased?

    (A) 1978 only

    (B) 1978 and 1985 only

    (C) 1982 and 1985 only

    (D) 1982, 1983, and 1985 only

    (E) 1978, 1982, 1983, and 1985

24. What was the percentage increase of the wheat production from 1975 to 1978?

    (A) 0%   (D) 16%

    (B) 4.8%   (E) 19%

    (C) 14.2%

25. During which year was the combined production of wheat and corn at a maximum?

    (A) 1978   (D) 1984

    (B) 1981   (E) 1985

    (C) 1983

26. In the five-pointed star shown, what is the sum of the measures of angles *A, B, C, D,* and *E*?

    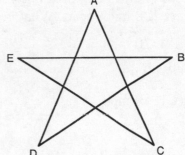

    (A) 108°

    (B) 72°

    (C) 36°

    (D) 150°

    (E) 180°

27. If $a/b < 0$ and $c/d > 0$, which of the following statements is true?

    (A) $\dfrac{a}{b} \times \dfrac{c}{d} < 0$

    (D) $\dfrac{a}{b} + \dfrac{c}{d} > 0$

    (B) $\dfrac{a}{b} \times \dfrac{c}{d} > 0$

    (E) $\dfrac{a}{b} = \dfrac{c}{d}$

    (C) $\dfrac{a}{b} + \dfrac{c}{d} < 0$

28. Which of the following equations can be used to find a number *n*, such that if you multiply it by 3 and take 2 away, the result is 5 times as great as if you divide the number by 3 and add 2?

    (A) $3n - 2 = 5 + \left(\dfrac{n}{3} + 2\right)$

    (D) $5(3n - 2) = \dfrac{n}{3} + 2$

    (B) $3n - 2 = 5\left(\dfrac{n}{3} + 2\right)$

    (E) $5n - 2 = \dfrac{n}{3} + 2$

    (C) $3n - 2 = \dfrac{5n}{3} + 2$

29. If *m* and *n* are consecutive integers, and $m < n$, which one of the following statements is always true?

    (A) $n - m$ is even.

    (D) $n^2 - m^2$ is odd.

    (B) *m* must be odd.

    (E) *n* must be even.

    (C) $m^2 + n^2$ is even.

30. Pete and Lynn travel on bicycles from the same place, in opposite directions, Pete traveling 4 mph faster than Lynn. After 5 hours, they are 120 miles apart. What is Lynn's rate of travel?

(A) 20 mph   (D) 12 mph

(B) 9 mph   (E) 14 mph

(C) 10 mph

STOP

If time still remains, you may go back and check your work.
When the time allotted is up, you may go on to the next section.

Section 4

TIME: 30 Minutes
        38 Questions

DIRECTIONS: Each of the given sentences has blank spaces which indicate words omitted. Choose the best combination of words which fit into the meaning and structure within the context of the sentence.

---

1. In preparing a recommendation for his student, the professor _____ his statements in order to express his reservations.

   (A) lengthened   (D) formed

   (B) qualified   (E) constructed

   (C) wrote

2. _____ is a key variable in relation to achievement; talent, support, effort, and practice are all important, but the fact remains: those who _____ to succeed go the furthest.

   (A) Potential...need   (D) Training...struggle

   (B) Desire...want   (E) Education...hope

   (C) Heredity...train

3. A teacher must learn to be _____ to all students, but unduly _____ with none.

   (A) civil...rude   (D) accepting...pleased

   (B) objective...hostile (E) interesting...attentive

   (C) friendly...familiar

4. The reason that restaurants have their waitresses and others introduce themselves by their first names is that the _____ of familiarity

may _____ the customer's inclination to be critical of the service rendered or the meal received.

(A) appearance...reduce   (D) growth...limit

(B) affliction...retard   (E) pleasure...deny

(C) reality...prohibit

5. He knew that all available evidence indicated the invalidity of the theory in question; nevertheless, he personally _____ it.

(A) researched   (D) repudiated

(B) supported   (E) explored

(C) investigated

6. What ever might be in her head, it was neither love, nor romance, nor any of the emotions usually _____ to the young.

(A) sejunctioned   (D) rescinded

(B) segregated   (E) scissioned

(C) ascribed

7. The poet who wrote "Gather ye rosebuds while ye may" was lamenting the _____ of youth.

(A) efflorescence   (D) coalescence

(B) acquiescence   (E) effervescence

(C) evanescence

DIRECTIONS: In the following questions, a related pair of words is followed by five more pairs of words. Select the pair that best expresses the same relationship as that expressed in the original pair.

---

8. COCOON:BUTTERFLY::

(A) apple:pie   (D) adolescent:adult

(B) blossom:fruit   (E) wood:house

(C) awareness:understanding

9. MINUTE:HOUR::

   (A) meter:kilometer   (D) student:class

   (B) alto:choir   (E) boxcar:train

   (C) state:federation

10. AVERSION:FONDNESS::

   (A) equivalent:commensurate   (D) execrable:foul

   (B) tantamount:equal   (E) odious:laudable

   (C) farrier:blacksmith

11. OXIDATION:RUST::

   (A) burning:napalm   (D) ignorance:education

   (B) hunger:starvation   (E) poverty:alcoholism

   (C) investment:dividends

12. RAIN:PRECIPITATION::

   (A) copper:metal   (D) wind:abrasion

   (B) ice:glacier   (E) heat:evaporation

   (C) oil:shale

13. HARD-HEARTED:EMPATHY::

   (A) ambivalent:decisiveness   (D) creative:dogmatism

   (B) assertive:independence   (E) vengeful:friendship

   (C) competitive:adversary

14. RETINUE:FOLLOWER::

   (A) animal:menagerie   (D) detritus:debris

   (B) state:federation   (E) tune:medley

   (C) word:vocabulary

15. NEBULOUS:PELLUCID::

   (A) luminous:incandescent   (B) cacophonic:harmonic

(C) meticulous:precise (D) ingenuous:innocuous

(E) fallacious:deceptive

16. ANGER:RAGE::

(A) stubborn:recalcitrant (D) lucid:perspicuous

(B) quarrelsome:pugnacious (E) failure:fiasco

(C) irritable:irascible

DIRECTIONS: Each passage is followed by questions based on its content. After reading a passage, choose the best answer to each question. Answer all questions based on what is stated or implied in that passage.

We believe that our Earth is about 4.6 billion years old. At present we are forced to look to other bodies in the solar system for hints as to what the early history of the Earth was like. Studies of our Moon, Mercury, Mars, and the large satellites of Jupiter and Saturn have provided ample evidence that all of these objects were bombarded by bodies with a wide variety of sizes shortly after they had formed. This same bombardment must have affected the Earth as well. The lunar record indicates that the rate of impacts decreased to its present low level about 4 billion years ago. On the Earth, subsequent erosion and crustal motions have obliterated the craters that must have formed during this epoch. Since it is generally believed that life on Earth began during this period, the bombardment must have been part of the environment within which this event occurred.

17. Which of the following best states the author's main point?

(A) The Earth is an old body having its beginning about 4.6 billion years ago.

(B) During its early history, the Earth was bombarded by bodies.

(C) Mercury, Mars, Jupiter, and Saturn were in place before Earth.

(D) It is because of the Earth's atmosphere that it shows no after-effects of the bombardment.

(E) The Earth's moon actually protected the Earth from much body bombardment.

18. Bombardment of the Earth at one time by various-sized bodies is

    (A) indicated by subsequent erosion patterns.

    (B) documented fact.

    (C) proven by the lunar record.

    (D) a necessary environmental factor for the formation of life forms.

    (E) inferred from what happened on certain other planetary bodies.

19. Which of the following bodies was not studied to give evidence that the Earth was bombarded in its conceptual history?

    (A) Mars   (D) Jupiter

    (B) Mercury   (E) Satellites of Saturn

    (C) Earth's moon

Life in colonial times was harsh, and the refinements of the mother country were ordinarily lacking. The colonists, however, soon began to mold their English culture into the fresh environment of a new land. The influence of religion permeated the entire way of life. In most Southern colonies, the Anglican church was the legally established church. In New England, the Puritans were dominant; and in Pennsylvania, the Quakers. Especially in the New England colonies, the local or village church was the hub of community life; the authorities strictly enforced the Sabbath and sometimes banished nonbelievers and dissenters.

Unfortunately, the same sort of religious intolerance, bigotry, and superstition associated with the age of the Reformation in Europe also prevailed in some of the colonies, though on a lesser scale. In the last half of the seventeenth century, during sporadic outbreaks of religious fanaticism and hysteria, Massachusetts and Connecticut authorities tried and hanged several women as "witches." Early in the seventeenth century, some other witchcraft persecution occurred in Virginia, North Carolina, and Rhode Island. As the decades passed, however, religious toleration developed in the colonies.

Because of the strong religious influence in the colonies, especially in New England, religious instruction and Bible reading played an important part in education. In Massachusetts, for example, the law of 1645 required each community with 50 households to establish an elementary school.

Two years later the same colony passed the "Deluder Satan" law which required each town of 100 families to maintain a grammar school for the purpose of providing religious, as well as general, instruction. In the Southern colonies, only a few privately endowed free schools existed. Private tutors instructed the sons of well-to-do planters, who completed their educations in English universities. Young males in poor families throughout the colonies were ordinarily apprenticed for vocational education.

By 1700, two colleges had been founded: Harvard, established by the Massachusetts Legislature in 1636; and William and Mary, in Virginia, which originated in 1693 under a royal charter. Other cultural activities before 1700 were limited. The few literary products of the colonists, mostly historical narratives, journals, sermons, and some poetry, were printed in England. The *Bay Psalm Book* (1640) was the first book printed in the colonies. Artists and composers were few, and their output was of a relatively simple character.

20. The passage would most likely be found in

    (A) an essay about colonial religion, in a church bulletin.

    (B) an essay in a news magazine, on the religious history of the United States.

    (C) an article on witchcraft, in a popular magazine.

    (D) a novel set in eighteenth century New England.

    (E) an essay on religion and education in a historical journal.

21. The author mentions the *Bay Psalm Book* because it was

    (A) required reading in the Massachusetts grammar school.

    (B) the basis upon which women were tried for witchcraft.

    (C) the first book printed in the colonies.

    (D) the basis for the Anglican church in America.

    (E) outlawed in Massachusetts as blasphemous.

22. The impetus for free, public-supported schools came from

    (A) the New England colonies.

    (B) Pennsylvania.

(C) Massachusetts.

(D) the Southern colonies.

(E) private tutors.

23. Which of the following is NOT a true evaluation of life in the early colonies?

(A) There was religious toleration from Massachusetts to Virginia.

(B) Life was harsh.

(C) The comforts found in England were lacking.

(D) Local literary works were limited to historical narratives, journals, sermons, and some poetry.

(E) Artists and composers were few.

24. According to the author, those students taking advantage of the apprenticeship programs came from

(A) New York.   (D) Virginia.

(B) the aristocracy.   (E) poor families.

(C) plantations.

25. It can be inferred from the article that private tutors were educators among the aristocracy in

(A) Pennsylvania.   (D) New York.

(B) the Middle colonies. (E) the Southern colonies.

(C) the New England colonies.

26. According to the selection, which of the following was NOT a result of religious bigotry?

(A) There was an outbreak of religious fanaticism and hysteria.

(B) The Puritan colony had the best record for religious tolerance.

(C) Massachusetts and Connecticut hanged women as witches.

(D) Witchcraft persecution took place in a few other states.

(E) The seventeenth and eighteenth centuries were the two worst eras for religious intolerance.

27. Which of the following cannot be construed from the selection about Harvard University?

    (A) It originated under a royal charter.

    (B) It was the first college in America.

    (C) It was one of two colleges operating by 1700.

    (D) It was created by the Massachusetts Legislature.

    (E) It was founded in 1636.

DIRECTIONS: Each of the following questions provides a given word in capitalized letters followed by five word choices. Choose the best word which is most <u>opposite</u> in meaning to the given word.

---

28. PREVENT:

    (A) invite   (D) demand

    (B) permit   (E) urge

    (C) encourage

29. RESERVED:

    (A) affable   (D) unexpected

    (B) saved   (E) reticent

    (C) given

30. ILLUSORY:

    (A) evident   (D) obvious

    (B) meaningful   (E) factual

    (C) soluble

31. OSCILLATE:

    (A) moor   (D) vacillate

    (B) stabilize   (E) undulate

    (C) balance

32. EULOGISTIC:
    - (A) officious
    - (B) censorious
    - (C) depressed
    - (D) incomprehensible
    - (E) obstinate

33. SCRUPULOUS:
    - (A) meticulous
    - (B) painstaking
    - (C) careless
    - (D) honest
    - (E) forgetful

34. CENSURE:
    - (A) court
    - (B) accept
    - (C) flatter
    - (D) adulate
    - (E) commend

35. ALLEGIANCE:
    - (A) disapprobation
    - (B) treachery
    - (C) incompatibility
    - (D) dissension
    - (E) disputation

36. LUGUBRIOUS:
    - (A) joyous
    - (B) energetic
    - (C) rapid
    - (D) facile
    - (E) healthy

37. BELLICOSE:
    - (A) pulchritudinous
    - (B) obdurate
    - (C) anorexic
    - (D) seraphic
    - (E) pacific

38. BANEFUL:

    (A) respected   (D) beneficial

    (B) beautiful   (E) honorable

    (C) reckless

STOP

If time still remains, you may go back and check your work.
When the time allotted is up, you may go on to the next section.

Section 5

TIME: 30 Minutes
            30 Questions

NUMBERS: All numbers are real numbers.

FIGURES: Position of points, angles, regions, etc., are assumed to be in the order shown and angle measures are assumed to be positive.

LINES: Assume that lines shown as straight are indeed straight.

DIRECTIONS: Each of the following given set of quantities is placed into either Column A or B. Compare the two quantities to decide whether

(A)   the quantity in Column A is greater;

(B)   the quantity in Column B is greater;

(C)   the two quantities are equal;

(D)   the relationship cannot be determined from the information given.

NOTE: Do not choose (E) since there are only four choices.

COMMON INFORMATION: Information which relates to one or both given quantities is centered in the two columns. A symbol which appears in both columns will indicate the same item in Column A and Column B.

EXAMPLES:

Column A	Column B
1. 5×4	$5 + 4$

Explanation: The correct answer is (A), since $5 \times 4 = 20$, and $5 + 4 = 9$.

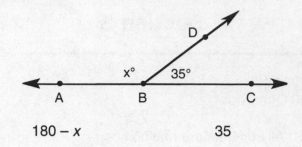

2. $180 - x$ 35

Explanation: The correct answer is (C). Since $\angle ABC$ is a straight angle, its measurement is 180°.

	<u>Column A</u>	<u>Column B</u>

1. The average of 5 consecutive numbers where x is the central number

    The average of 3 consecutive numbers where x is the central number

---

$$n > 2$$

2.   Half of n squared $\dfrac{n}{2}$

$$b < 0, \ y \neq a$$

3. $\dfrac{ab - by}{y - a}$ b

If we define $(a, b) = a + 3b$
and $(2, 3) = (3, x)$

4.   2 x

$$y = x - 2$$

5. $y + 3$ $x - 1$

Column A	Column B

The cost of 1 ft × 1 ft of fabric is $4.

6. Cost of 2 ft × 2 ft piece of fabric | 10

---

7. 30% of 40 | 40% of 30

In a Boeing 747 with 320 seats, 73 women are traveling and 20% of the seats are empty.

8. Men that are traveling | 185

A is bigger than *P*, and *B* is not less than *P*.

9. *A* | *B*

The sum of three consecutive even numbers is 42.

10. First number | 11

$m < 0$, $n < 0$, and $m > n$

11. $\dfrac{m}{n}$ | $\dfrac{n}{m}$

$p > 0$, $q > 0$, and $p \neq q$

12. $p + q$ | $\dfrac{p^2 - q^2}{q - p}$

Column A	**Column B**

13.

$$\cfrac{1}{4-\cfrac{1+\cfrac{1}{2}}{1-\cfrac{1}{2}}}$$

2

---

x, y, and z are non-zero integers and $x > y > z$.

14.

$\dfrac{x}{y}$

$\dfrac{z}{y}$

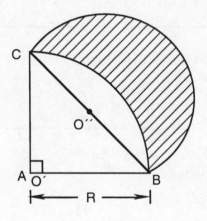

O' is the center of quadrant
O'' is the center of semicircle

15.   Shaded area R^2

DIRECTIONS: For the following questions, select the best answer choice to the given question.

16. Reduce the following expression, $a > b > 0$

$$\left[(\sqrt{(a+b)})^2 - \sqrt{(a-b)^2}\right]$$

(A) $2a$ (D) a

(B) $2(a-b)$ (E) b

(C) $2b$

17. $\dfrac{x+y}{y} = a; \quad \dfrac{y}{x} =$

(A) 1   (D) $a-1$

(B) a (E) $\dfrac{1}{(a-1)}$

(C) $\dfrac{1}{a}$

18. I filled ⅔ of my swimming pool with 1,800 ft³ of water. What is the total capacity of my swimming pool?

(A) 2,400 ft³   (D) 3,600 ft³

(B) 2,700 ft³   (E) 3,200 ft³

(C) 3,000 ft³

19. $\left[\left(\dfrac{x}{y}\right)^{-1} - \left(\dfrac{y}{x}\right)^{-1} \right]^{-1} =$

(A) xy (D) $y^2 - x^2$

(B) $\dfrac{1}{xy}$ (E) $\dfrac{xy}{\left(y^2 - x^2\right)}$

(C) $x^2 - y^2$

20. One year ago Pat was three times his sister's age. Next year he will be only twice her age. How old will Pat be in five more years?

(A) 8   (D) 13

(B) 12   (E) 15

(C) 11

Questions 21–25 refer to the following table:

Birth Rates and Death Rates per 1,000 Population and Infant Mortality per 1,000 Live Births in Selected Countries, 1957

Country	Birth rate	Death rate	Infant mortality	Country	Birth rate	Death rate	Infant mortality
North America				Norway	18.2	8.6	21
Alaska	35.1	5.9	39	Poland	27.5	9.5	77
Canada	28.3	8.2	31	Portugal	23.7	11.4	89
Costa Rica	39.2	10.1	92	Rumania	24.2	9.9	81
Dominican Republic	40.9	8.6	74	Spain	21.7	10.0	48
El Salvador	48.9	13.8	87	Sweden	14.6	9.9	17
Guatemala	49.4	20.6	89	Switzerland	17.7	10.0	23
Honduras	43.1	10.4	55	United Kingdom	16.5	11.5	24
Mexico	46.9	12.9	69	England and Wales	16.1	11.5	23
Panama	40.4	9.4	56	Scotland	19.0	11.9	29
Puerto Rico	32.4	7.0	51	Northern Ireland	21.5	10.9	29
Trinidad and Tobago	36.7	9.3	55	Yugoslavia	23.5	10.5	101
United States	25.3	9.6	26				
				Asia			
South America				Ceylon	36.5	10.1	67
Argentina	23.8	8.2	58	Hong Kong	37.9	7.5	56
Chile	35.4	11.9	112	India	24.2	11.8	100
Ecuador	45.5	15.2	113	Iran	37.8	8.3	–
Peru	36.6	9.0	94	Israel	27.9	6.5	33
Uruguay	11.4	7.0	73	Japan	17.2	8.3	39
Venezuela	46.7	9.9	67	Jordan	39.7	8.6	74
				Malaya	45.5	11.3	78
Europe				Singapore	42.9	7.3	43
Austria	16.8	12.7	44	Syria	24.3	5.6	54
Belgium	16.9	12.4	35	Formosa (Taiwan)	41.4	8.5	34
Bulgaria	19.5	9.4	72				
Czechoslovakia	18.9	10.0	31	**Africa**			
Denmark	16.7	9.3	23	Union of South Africa			
Finland	20.1	9.4	28	(Europeans)	25.6	8.8	31
France	18.5	12.0	29	Mauritius	43.1	13.0	66
Germany (western)	17.0	11.3	36				
Greece	19.2	7.6	44	**Oceania**			
Hungary	17.0	10.6	59	Australia	22.9	8.8	21
Ireland	21.2	11.9	33	Hawaii	20.2	5.8	24
Italy	18.2	10.0	50	New Zealand (total)	26.2	9.3	24
Luxembourg	15.7	12.1	37	Europeans	24.8	9.3	20
Netherlands	21.2	7.5	17	Maoris	46.3	10.1	58

Courtesy Britannica Book of the Year: 1959, Encyclopædia Britannica, Inc.

21. What country has the lowest infant mortality?

    (A) United States   (D) Netherlands

    (B) Iran   (E) Sweden and Netherlands

    (C) Sweden

22. Assuming the United States had a population of 200 million, how many births were there in 1957?

(A) 5.06×10^6 (D) 5.06×10^4

(B) 5.06×10^5 (E) 5.06×10^3

(C) 5.06×10^7

23. Which geographic area had the greatest range in birth rate?

(A) North America   (D) Africa

(B) South America   (E) Oceania

(C) Asia

24. What is the ratio of the average birth rate to the average death rate in Africa?

(A) .65   (D) 3.15

(B) .82   (E) 3.32

(C) 2.91

25. What is the percentage of infants in the total death rate in the United States?

(A) 68.5%   (D) 26%

(B) .685%   (E) 27.1%

(C) 6.85%

26. Which of the following integers is the square of an integer for every integer x?

(A) $x^2 + x$ (D) $x^2 + 2x - 4$

(B) $x^2 + 1$ (E) $x^2 + 2x + 1$

(C) $x^2 + 2x$

27. A line segment is drawn from the point (3, 5) to the point (9, 13). What are the coordinates of the midpoint of the line segment?

(A) (9, 6)   (D) (6, 8)

(B) (12, 18)   (E) (3, 4)

(C) (6, 9)

28. Twenty percent of U.S. citizens have traveled out of the United States more than two times. Seventy percent have not traveled out of the United States. Therefore,

    I.   10% have traveled one time.

    II.   10% have traveled one or two times.

    III. 80% have traveled less than two times.

    (A) I only   (D) II and III only

    (B) II only   (E) I and III

    (C) III only

29. $\dfrac{(x^2)^{-4}(x^{-2})^3}{(x^{-3})^{-5}} =$

    (A) x^5 (D) x^7

    (B) $\dfrac{1}{x^{14}}$ (E) x^{29}

    (C) $\dfrac{1}{x^{29}}$

30. What is the value(s) of x in the equation $(4x - 3)^2 = 4$?

    (A) $\dfrac{5}{4}$ (D) $\dfrac{1}{2}, \dfrac{5}{2}$

    (B) $\dfrac{1}{4}$ (E) $\dfrac{5}{2}, \dfrac{1}{5}$

    (C) $\dfrac{5}{4}, \dfrac{1}{4}$

STOP

If time still remains, you may go back and check your work.
When the time allotted is up, you may go on to the next section.

Section 6

TIME: 30 Minutes
38 Questions

DIRECTIONS: Each of the given sentences has blank spaces which indicate words omitted. Choose the best combination of words which fit into the meaning and structure within the context of the sentence.

1. The acquisition of exact knowledge is apt to be _____ , but it is essential to every kind of excellence.

   (A) wearisome   (D) amorphous

   (B) equable   (E) eccentric

   (C) erratic

2. His walk to return the stolen goods is likely to be _____ by any event since his feeling of _____ toward the coming punishment is so intense.

   (A) procrastinated...sorrow   (D) precipitated...woe

   (B) hastened...grief   (E) hindered...anguish

   (C) detained...regret

3. There was something _____ about it, and in intangible ways one was made to feel that the worst was about to come.

   (A) ominous   (D) celestial

   (B) tutelary   (E) mythical

   (C) nymphonic

4. Strange things happen on a racetrack, where human _____ and equine hearts fashion bonds beyond the comprehension of the outside world.

(A) aristocrats   (D) avarice

(B) covetousness   (E) derelicts

(C) greed

5. The _____ policy of Walpole was regarded by the people as a national humiliation.

     (A) pliant   (D) malleable

     (B) impartial   (E) histrionic

     (C) pacific

6. Since the calendar year originally contained only 355 days, an extra month was occasionally _____ .

     (A) contingent   (D) superadded

     (B) introduced   (E) intercalated

     (C) incidental

7. The dock reeked, not of ordinary salt air but instead was _____ of seaweed and dead fish.

     (A) malodorous   (D) pungent

     (B) rankling   (E) redolent

     (C) poignant

DIRECTIONS: In the following questions, the given pair of words contains a specific relationship to each other. Select the best pair of the choices which expresses the same relationship as the given.

---

8. SUN:STARS::

     (A) piranha:fish   (D) shrub:tree

     (B) plank:block   (E) emotion:mood

     (C) color:hue

9. ACCRUE:AMASS::

     (A) berate:beget   (B) appease:antagonize

(C) engender:enhance   (D) absolve:acquit

(E) oscillate:ostracize

10. SYNTAX:LANGUAGE::

(A) color:painting   (D) measurement:science

(B) rhetoric:philosophy (E) sound:music

(C) water:rain

11. ANXIETY:STRESS::

(A) aphanite:rock   (D) insult:invective

(B) Apollo:mythology   (E) destruction:inutility

(C) brevity:conciseness

12. VIE:RIVAL::

(A) requiem:death   (D) fugue:composition

(B) lurid:ruddy   (E) compete:emulate

(C) hallmark:unique

13. KEEL:DECK::

(A) glasses:see   (D) index:glossary

(B) sugar:syrup   (E) grass:lawn

(C) rock:geology

14. RECREATION:SWIM::

(A) perspire:run   (D) gyron:airfoil

(B) suffocate:breath   (E) flourish:thrive

(C) gymkhana:driving skill

15. DONNISH:PEDANT::

(A) redolent:ammonia   (D) pedagogic:teacher

(B) jocund:pessimist   (E) esoteric:simpleton

(C) salacious:minister

16. FRACTIONS:DECIMALS::

(A) phonics:word recognition   (D) volumes:library

(B) French:English   (E) harmony:music

(C) health:physical activity

DIRECTIONS: Each passage is followed by questions based on its content. After reading a passage, choose the best answer to each question. Answer all questions based on what is stated or implied in that passage.

A cave is a natural opening in the ground extending beyond the zone of light and large enough to permit the entry of man. Occurring in a wide variety of rock types and caused by widely differing geologic processes, caves range in size from single small rooms to interconnecting passages many miles long. The scientific study of caves is called speleology (from the Greek words *spelaion* for cave and *logos* for study). It is a composite science based on geology, hydrology, biology, and archaeology, and thus holds special interest for earth scientists of the U.S. Geological Survey.

Caves have been natural attractions since prehistoric times. Prolific evidence of early man's interest has been discovered in caves scattered throughout the world. Fragments of skeletons of some of the earliest man-like creatures (Australopithecines) have been discovered in cave deposits in South Africa, and the first evidence of primitive Neanderthal man was found in a cave in the Neander Valley of Germany. Cro-Magnon man created his remarkable murals on the walls of caves in southern France and northern Spain where he took refuge more than 10,000 years ago during the chill of the Ice Age.

17. The author's main purpose is

(A) to define the science of speleology.

(B) to define the interests of the U.S. Geological Survey.

(C) to discuss the finding of the earliest human remains.

(D) to discuss various salient facts about caves.

(E) to discuss the locations of the oldest known caves.

18. It can be inferred that the U.S. Geological Survey is primarily interested in caves because of

    (A) the clues they reveal about early man and his environment.

    (B) the evidence needed to learn about primitive Neanderthal man.

    (C) the murals on the walls.

    (D) the interconnected passages.

    (E) the wide variety of rock types.

19. The term *speleology* is defined as

    (A) the study of early man.

    (B) the study of water.

    (C) the study of life.

    (D) the study of caves.

    (E) the study of earth, water, life, and early man.

20. The passage describes evidence of the Neanderthal man's habitat as being in Germany, while evidence of the Cro-Magnon man has been found in France and Spain. The Cro-Magnon man selected Spain and France due to

    (A) a shortage of available food near to the Neanderthal man.

    (B) more temperate weather than found in Germany.

    (C) more nomadic space needed for both the Neanderthal and Cro-Magnon man.

    (D) its proximity to South Africa and his ancestors.

    (E) his preference of the plains to the mountains.

Americans traveling in Europe have for many years been impressed by the large areas around cities that are devoted to small garden plots.

To the casual observer these appear to be simply clusters of miniature truck gardens with scattered fruit trees. More discerning travelers are impressed by the obvious care lavished on these plots. Gardens are weed-free, crops are bountiful, fruit trees are carefully pruned, hedges are clipped, huts and tool sheds — if present — are usually neat and well-tended, and every square foot is carefully utilized. Many garden areas have a festive air, with flags flying.

Try as he will, the traveler will find little reference to these garden areas in guidebooks, on guided tours, or in tourist information bureaus. There are few readily available sources of information for the American on the small garden movement in Europe.

Names given to these areas in Europe vary from the general (such as "garden colonies"), to the manner in which they are allocated ("allotment gardens"), or the facilities they include (such as "hut colonies," which refer to the tool sheds or small houses on garden plots in some countries). Often these collections of individual garden plots are referred to as "workers' gardens." Many simply are called "small gardens" or "small-garden areas."

For centuries people have needed to live in cities and towns in order to find jobs — yet have desired the greenery, the cleaner air, and the opportunity to garden that rarely are available except in rural or rural-urban fringe areas.

Living space has always been at a premium in cities and towns; there has been little green space — and even less space for gardens. During the Middle Ages, when cities were walled for protection, there was little open space of any type within the walls, and gardens flourished in front of city gates.

Similar crowded conditions occurred several hundred years later when the industrial revolution forced rapid city growth. Ground space was at a premium, so houses were squeezed together side by side, pushed behind into alleys and inner courtyards, or forced up — into five- and six-story buildings with several apartments on each floor.

Many rooms had no outside light. Ventilation was almost nonexistent. Added to this were other poor health conditions, including a general lack of sanitary facilities, inadequate heating, and meager and unwholesome food — all compounded by the terrible crowding as the workers and their families swarmed into the cities. Lack of air, lack of sunlight, and unsanitary, overcrowded conditions were a way of life for most working people.

One of the measures provided to relieve people living in such unhealthy conditions in England was a law in 1819 that provided for leasing land for small gardens to the poor and unemployed. Later, other countries in Europe promulgated laws regarding provision of small-garden areas for city people.

Gardens for working people, the poor, and the unemployed were provided as a health measure by city governments, philanthropists, and some factory owners. Gardens also became a way to help ensure social stability by providing a link to the countryside that the workers had left, as well as a means of improving the quality of life.

By the mid-1800s the small-garden movement had appeared in most European countries, either as an independent effort to meet the local conditions, or influenced by work in neighboring countries. The movement continued to grow into the early twentieth century and began to be considered as a factor in planning urban areas.

21. The author most likely thinks his audience is

    (A) American tourists traveling to European cities.

    (B) American gardeners interested in European techniques.

    (C) American city-planners searching for reasonable ways to maintain garden space in urban areas.

    (D) students of European history.

    (E) American landscape artists.

22. Small houses found on the garden plots are primarily used

    (A) for weekend lodging.

    (B) for tool storage.

    (C) for harvest collecting.

    (D) for tourist identification of the small gardens.

    (E) for government regulations.

23. The passage implies that during the Middle Ages little open space existed within the walls of a city due to

    (A) vast populations crowded within the walls.

    (B) dwellings crowded together.

    (C) building walls requiring extensive resources.

    (D) the difficulty of defending walled cities.

    (E) the peoples' preference to sleep only within the walls.

24. Information supplied within the passage would answer which of the following questions?

    (A) Legal precedence for small gardens was set in what nation?

    (B) The "party spirit" surrounding gardens is related to what festival?

    (C) How are garden sizes determined?

    (D) How may additional information be acquired concerning small gardens in Europe?

    (E) How did neighboring countries influence the spread of small gardens throughout Europe?

25. According to the information given in the passage, which of the following statements are true?

    I.   England has more small-garden areas than the other European countries.

    II. Garden areas were used to help ensure social stability during the industrial revolution.

    III. The small-garden movement has been a factor in urban planning for centuries.

    (A) I only   (D) III only

    (B) II only   (E) I and III only

    (C) I and II only

26. Which of the following statements would the author be LEAST likely to agree with?

    (A) Throughout history, it has been more important to use land in urban areas for living space than for cultivation.

    (B) American tourists are charmed by the picturesque garden areas around many European cities.

    (C) Gardens provide health and social benefits, including cleaner air and psychological links to the past.

    (D) Philanthropists supported small-garden areas, but factory owners and government officials did not.

(E) Maintaining green areas in and around urban areas should be an important priority for city planners.

27. The passage implies a correlation between cultural stability and small-garden tending which is reflected by

   (A) the care lavished upon the gardens.

   (B) the efficiently utilized gardens.

   (C) a festive air surrounding the gardens.

   (D) a continuation of their cultural heritage.

   (E) the improved welfare of the people.

DIRECTIONS: Each of the following questions provides a given word in capitalized letters followed by five word choices. Choose the best word which is most <u>opposite</u> in meaning to the given word.

---

28. CESSATION:

   (A) perpetuation   (D) methodicalness

   (B) innovation   (E) latent

   (C) abeyance

29. ABRUPT:

   (A) inaffable   (D) perpetuity

   (B) extempore   (E) momentary

   (C) insolence

30. GENERIC:

   (A) general   (D) specific

   (B) analogous   (E) typical

   (C) collective

31. RECURRENT:

   (A) infinite   (B) reiterate

(C) repetition   (D) succinct

(E) terse

32. MUTATION:

   (A) variation   (D) innovation

   (B) deviation   (E) perpetuation

   (C) alteration

33. VERSATILITY:

   (A) inclination   (D) vicissitude

   (B) vacillation   (E) constancy

   (C) fluctuation

34. ITINERANT:

   (A) illegitimate   (D) gaudy

   (B) permanent   (E) felted

   (C) idyllic

35. NEBULOUS:

   (A) conclusive   (D) saturnine

   (B) spurious   (E) ambiguous

   (C) frigate

36. EXIGUITY:

   (A) paucity   (D) capacity

   (B) eccentric   (E) reduction

   (C) decimation

37. ENERVATION:

   (A) strenuous   (D) ardor

   (B) stress   (E) languor

   (C) flaccidity

38. PREPONDERANCE:

   (A) influence

   (B) prevalence

   (C) dominance

   (D) auspice

   (E) impotence

STOP

If time still remains, you may go back and check your work.
When the time allotted is up, you may go on to the next section.

TEST 6

ANSWER KEY

Sections 1 and 2 — Analytical Writing

Please review the sample essays in the Detailed Explanations.

Section 3 — Quantitative Ability

1. (C)	9. (A)	17. (E)	25. (D)
2. (A)	10. (C)	18. (E)	26. (E)
3. (B)	11. (D)	19. (A)	27. (A)
4. (A)	12. (D)	20. (D)	28. (B)
5. (B)	13. (B)	21. (A)	29. (D)
6. (A)	14. (B)	22. (C)	30. (C)
7. (C)	15. (C)	23. (E)	
8. (B)	16. (D)	24. (E)	

Section 4 — Verbal Ability

1. (B)	11. (C)	21. (C)	31. (B)
2. (B)	12. (A)	22. (C)	32. (B)
3. (C)	13. (A)	23. (A)	33. (C)
4. (A)	14. (D)	24. (E)	34. (E)
5. (B)	15. (B)	25. (E)	35. (B)
6. (C)	16. (E)	26. (B)	36. (A)
7. (C)	17. (B)	27. (A)	37. (E)
8. (D)	18. (E)	28. (B)	38. (D)
9. (A)	19. (D)	29. (A)	
10. (E)	20. (E)	30. (E)	

Section 5 — Quantitative Ability

1. (C)	9. (D)	17. (E)	25. (C)
2. (A)	10. (A)	18. (B)	26. (E)
3. (A)	11. (B)	19. (E)	27. (C)
4. (B)	12. (A)	20. (B)	28. (B)
5. (A)	13. (B)	21. (E)	29. (C)
6. (A)	14. (D)	22. (A)	30. (C)
7. (C)	15. (B)	23. (B)	
8. (B)	16. (C)	24. (D)	

Section 6 — Verbal Ability

1. (A)	11. (E)	21. (A)	31. (A)
2. (E)	12. (E)	22. (B)	32. (E)
3. (A)	13. (D)	23. (D)	33. (E)
4. (E)	14. (C)	24. (A)	34. (B)
5. (C)	15. (D)	25. (B)	35. (A)
6. (E)	16. (A)	26. (D)	36. (D)
7. (E)	17. (D)	27. (D)	37. (A)
8. (A)	18. (A)	28. (A)	38. (E)
9. (D)	19. (D)	29. (D)	
10. (B)	20. (B)	30. (D)	

DETAILED EXPLANATIONS
OF ANSWERS

Section 1–Analytical Writing

PERSPECTIVES ON AN ISSUE ESSAY TOPIC—ESSAY ONE

Sample Essay Response Scoring 6

forceful articulation of essayist's position — The role which libraries play in educating individuals and entire communities is far too important to be overlooked during a discussion of money. Libraries waken and nurture a love of reading in so many more people than the number of books the institutions can afford to buy. In their busy process of educating the world, libraries daily accidently spill their patrons into bookstores.

Every community scrambles to give itself a library, and every library scrambles for a slightly bigger budget, and every budget committee scrambles to squeeze in that extra book. That extra book *interesting use of vocabulary* is so important to libraries because it is about something or by someone they have never read before, and they cannot wait to see it awaken a new interest in their communities. All this scrambling should tell you how precarious a library's situation is, especially in smaller towns. Libraries invariably sweat over their underbudgeting. *good elaboration of the point made in this paragraph* — To eliminate their purchasing discount or to effectively do so by charging copyright fees could close many libraries, or reduce them to merely updating encyclopedias and periodicals. This would not only destroy the direct market which is the libraries themselves, but it would also paralyze their most significant functions.

very precise & effective wording — Consider the scholarly use of libraries. These institutions provide a location and atmosphere for research and learning. Without the ability to purchase new books as they become available, libraries would fail the needs of their erudite patrons. Such a purchasing system would single-handedly impede the *smooth transition to a different example* advance of technology, multicultural understanding, artistic insight, and economic relief. In the age of the information highway, raw data travels at the speed of electricity. Studies, reports and theories must also travel from scholar to peer and student as quickly as possible, and not become mired in copyright restrictions.

To be able to compete in tomorrow's instantaneous world, today's students must learn to keep abreast in the current torrent of the printed word.

impressive use of language

In order to fully appreciate the intergenerational impact of threatening the library system, one must consider that libraries turn bored children into little readers. Many families would not be able to afford to keep up with the reading appetite of their children if libraries were not available. This would greatly affect the eldest children who may lack hand-me-down books, and who, in turn, would set a non-reading example for younger siblings. The weighty opinions of psychologists and sociologists and even the doctrines of political correctness have reached into the children's sections of our libraries to mark as "inappropriate" various classics which were written at less informed and less sensitive times. Thus, libraries are more dependent on new books to meet the needs of young readers than any other age group. From meeting these needs we gain a more intelligent and well-adjusted future generation who will not only be lawmakers and teachers, but book-buyers as well.

logically presented example

good transition

good variation in the sentence structure

In short, the library system must be allowed to flourish because it creates the book-buying public. From opening the minds of children to putting scholars in communication with one another, libraries produce a mindset where reading is doing, where reading is how lives are spent. The fact that a literary market exists alongside libraries proves that readers do buy books. They buy the books that are worth keeping, and buy for loved ones books they wish them to own.

ending is well-written & gives overall position a convincing sense of urgency

Analysis of Sample Scoring 6

This response would rate a 6 because it is well organized, contains few writing flaws, demonstrates a strong command of diction and syntactic variety, and is firmly centered over a persuasive position on the issue. The response begins with the idea that reading begins in libraries. After depicting the familiar scenario of library budgets, it threatens the destruction of libraries. The role of libraries in creating readers and a demand for books is creatively explored.

PERSPECTIVES ON AN ISSUE ESSAY TOPIC—ESSAY TWO

Sample Essay Response Scoring 4

too informal

unnecessary insertion

Television, or T.V., is such a big deal nowadays that some people might think all you need to do to know about anything is to

turn on a television. This is, however, not exactly quite right.
Or, to be even more blunt, this is wrong. I think that television is
inadequate for learning as much as people should know about
today's complex world.

redundant
unnecessary repetition
very vague expression

There are some good and enlightening shows on TV. Like PBS.
On some channels, they have shows about history, science,
health, the law, and politics, that could help people who don't like
to, or don't have the time, to read to understand more about
these important things. I once saw a show on TV all about World
War I. The use of TV programs in classrooms might even help grab
the attention of some students who might otherwise be put off by
their teacher, who maybe they find a bit boring but who would find
the TV show more exciting and worthy to watch and listen to.

fragment
unnecessary & distracting
sentence is too long

But there is a limit to what TV can teach us. You can get
more information in a book than in a TV show, especially if the TV
show has to have commercials. TV can suggest some of the really
important points, but it cannot ever give them in-depth treatment
that a subtle or sharp analysis in writing can. And TV is harder to
refer back to than a book. Even if you tape a show, it is harder to
keep rewinding and replaying it every time you want to remember
or study something, than it is to carry around or have handy a
book you can open to find the information you want. Reading is
also a way to help focus concentration and make the most of
mental energy, whereas TV tends to dull the senses.

weak transition
very well-developed argument

Replacing books with TV is simply not a promising way to
improve our minds. There is no reason why they cannot complement each other, so that we can use both as educational—and
pleasurable—resources for information and entertainment. The
Internet, however, might combine both what books and TV have to
offer, and make both obsolete.

strong closing idea
final thought is not connected to previous points and therefore distracting

Analysis of Sample Essay Scoring 4

This essay clearly establishes its thesis and adequately discusses it. The essayist's statement that it is harder to refer back to
a TV than to a book is well developed. The point that TV tends to
dull the senses lacks an example and is not sufficiently supported.
Likewise, the idea that TV and books can complement each other
could have been discussed in more detail. The essay's last sentence introduces an entirely new idea, which shows a lack of
organization. The overall use of language is satisfying although
some sentences are either fragmented or too long. This slows
down the flow of the essay. The transitions between ideas are
adequate.

Section 2–Analytical Writing

ANALYSIS OF AN ARGUMENT ESSAY TOPIC

Sample Essay Response Scoring 6

good sentence variety

The very idea that recycling may be a myth, even if only for one resource, is very captivating. Once suggested, it must be explored. A drive through any town on "newspaper day" certainly leaves one open to the suggestion that an overabundance of recyclable newspaper is possible and even likely. The argument's reference to dealers in these recyclable goods sends one's mind to explore how these markets can work. While bottles and aluminum cans are easy to imagine being melted down and put to use again, limitations suggest themselves in the recycling of paper. Also, many households can go for days without producing an empty can or bottle. How can one effectively sell used paper when seemingly every daily newspaper in America is being turned in for recycling?

serious consideration of initial essay's argument

forceful use of language

Despite these suggestions generated by the argument, a more analytical look at the essay finds ready flaws. The phrase "less than ten percent" is far too vague to be convincing. Ten is a round number and yet the real world is never smooth or perfectly square. A more specific number, even "10.0", is required to convince today's statistic-saturated public. Yet even with a figure of two decimal places this statistic requires a source, and, more importantly, a timeframe to which it applies. This time issue relates to the argument's failure to acknowledge advances in technology which makes use of the recycled paper—a likelihood if this resource is reportedly so cheap.

very precise & therefore effective critique

good transition

The argument ends with a persuasive picture in which newspapers land in our dumps anyway, "neatly stacked" at the cost of the taxpayer. While emotionally influential, this image should be backed by statistics demonstrating a minimal effect of recycling on garbage dump influx. Waste disposal locations are required to keep tonnage records which note sources and characterize content, such as household or industrial. If the claims of the argument are true, the data would be available to show significant deposits of newspapers from "recycling" municipalities. This absence of hard data undermines the strong emotional impact of this claim.

good variation in the sentence structure

very direct & therefore sound critique

The argument's line of reasoning equates the absence of extensive recycling with a need to discontinue paper collection.

687

smooth start of a more theoretical critique —— Such a position fails to realize the significance of "recycling" as a philosophy and an ideal. Establishing the habit of reuse is more than half the battle in learning to insure a cleaner tomorrow, even when that reuse is a fiction. The practice of collecting recyclables is valuable before recycling is possible, because it conditions the public to accept the chore. More importantly, the premature recycling makes the resource readily available, inviting industry to find a use for it.

good transition ——————— To be more successful, the argument should have provided support for its evidence. The claim that only ten percent of paper is actually recycled required more detail and sources which would reinforce its credibility. The lack of pictures and statistics minimized the impact of the allegation that most newspapers still retire to garbage dumps. In support of its line of reasoning, the author should have anticipated and discredited the idea that the recycling may have a value beyond whether or not all or most of the paper ever sees a second use. On the whole, the argument was reasonable but hollow. *very clear and effective concluding sentence*

Analysis of Sample Essay Scoring 6

This analysis would rate a 6 because it organizes its ideas logically and intelligently with smooth transitions, it distinctly identifies and sharply analyzes the crucial points of the argument, and it demonstrates a strong command of the English language with, at worst, minor flaws. This analysis explores the initial effectiveness of the argument to demonstrate its strengths. Afterward, the analysis points out the lack of depth of the main points and their wounding lack of credited source references. Finally, the line of reasoning was creatively and legitimately challenged. This format provided a smooth and well-organized structure for the analysis.

Section 3–Quantitative Ability

1. **(C)**
Consider the quantity $\dfrac{x^2 - y^2}{x - y}$. It can be written as

$$\frac{x^2 - y^2}{x - y} = \frac{(x - y)(x + y)}{(x - y)}.$$

Since $x - y \neq 0$, we can divide both the numerator and the denominator by $(x - y)$. This yields

$$\frac{x^2 - y^2}{x - y} = \frac{(x - y)(x + y)}{(x - y)} = x + y$$

Thus, no matter what the values of x and y are, as long as $x - y \neq 0$, the two quantities in Columns A and B are equal.

2. **(A)**
The distance on a horizontal line from a point P, that corresponds to a real number a, to a point Q that lies on the same line and corresponds to the real number b, is defined as the non-negative difference between a and b.

Let AB denote the distance from the point A to the point B where A and B lie on the same horizontal line. In the above figure, the distance from F to H is given by

$$FH = 2 - \frac{2}{3} = \frac{4}{3}$$

and the distance from F to D is equal to the non-negative difference of -1 and $2/3$, which is equal to

$$-\left(-1 - \frac{2}{3}\right) = -\left(-\frac{5}{3}\right)$$
$$= \frac{5}{3}$$

Thus, if P is the midpoint of segment $\overline{DH}$ that corresponds to the real number x, then the distance from D to P is equal to the distance from P to H. That is,

$$DP = DH$$
$$x - (-1) = 2 - x$$
$$x + 1 = 2 - x$$
$$2x = a$$
$$x = \frac{1}{2}$$

So the quantity in Column A is greater.

Another method of solving this problem is the following:

Using the midpoint formula, $\dfrac{|x_1 - x_2|}{2}$, the midpoint of segment $\overline{DH}$ is

$$\frac{|2 - (-1)|}{2} = \frac{1}{2} \times \frac{2}{3} > \frac{1}{2}.$$

3.   **(B)**
   The easiest and the most direct way to compare the two quantities in Columns A and B is to perform the indicated operations in the quantity given in Column B. This involves addition and subtraction of decimals.
   In general, adding and subtracting decimals is a three-step process:
   (i)   List all the numbers vertically lining up the decimal points.
   (ii)   Add the numbers as if they were whole numbers.
   (iii)   Insert the decimal point in the sum directly below the decimal points in the numbers being added or subtracted.
   In this problem, $0.105 + 0.5 + 8 = 8.605$, since

$$
\begin{array}{r}
0.105 \\
0.500 \\
\underline{8.000} \\
8.605
\end{array}
$$

Hence, $0.105 + 0.5 - 3.1029 + 8 = 8.605 - 3.1029 = 5.5021$ since

$$
\begin{array}{r}
8.6050 \\
\underline{-3.1029} \\
5.5021
\end{array}
$$

So the quantity in Column B is greater.

4. **(A)**

Since the more seeds the farmer plants, the more ears of corn he harvests, it follows that a direct proportion can be used to solve this problem.

$$\frac{\text{Number of seeds planted } x}{\text{Number of seeds planted } y} = \frac{\text{Number of ears of corn harvested } x}{\text{Number of ears of corn harvested } y}$$

In this problem,

$$\frac{100}{y} = \frac{48}{72,000}$$

Cross-multiplication yields,

$$48y = (100)(72,000)$$

$$y = \frac{(100)(72,000)}{48}$$

$$= 150,000$$

So the quantity in Column A is greater.

5. **(B)**

From the centered information, we can convert a Fahrenheit temperature to a Celsius temperature or vice versa by simply using the formula

$$C = \frac{5}{9}(F - 32)$$

In this problem, to compare the quantities in Columns A and B, convert 65°F to a Celsius temperature. Thus,

$$C = \frac{5}{9}(F - 32)$$

$$C = \frac{5}{9}(65 - 32)$$

$$= \frac{5}{9}(33) = 18\frac{1}{3}$$

Thus, 65°F is equivalent to $18\frac{1}{3}$°C; the quantity in Column B is greater.

6.   **(A)**

The average (arithmetic mean), $\bar{x}$, of a set of scores is equal to the sum of all scores divided by the number of all scores, n. Thus,

$$\bar{x} = \frac{\text{sum of all scores}}{n}$$

In this problem, there are 19 girls and 11 boys in the class, so $n = 19 + 11 = 30$. Thus,

$$\bar{x} = \frac{\text{sum of all scores}}{n}$$

$$27.5 = \frac{\text{sum of all scores}}{30}$$

Cross-multiplication yields

$$\text{sum of all scores} = (27.5)(30)$$
$$= 825$$

Note that,

$$\text{sum of all scores} = \text{sum of the scores of all}$$
$$19 \text{ girls} + \text{sum of all scores of 11 boys}$$

Hence, $825 = 532 +$ sum of scores of all 11 boys which yields

$$\text{sum of scores of all 11 boys} = 825 - 532$$
$$= 293$$

So the quantity in Column A is greater.

7.   **(C)**

Label the vertices of the triangle A, B and C, and let $\overline{AB}$ represent the length of side AB

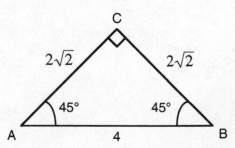

From the centered information, triangle ABC is a right isosceles triangle. Hence, $\overline{CA} = \overline{CB} = 2\sqrt{2}$.

Since ABC is a right triangle, by Pythagorean theorem (if a and b are the lengths of the shorter sides (legs) of a right triangle and c is the length of the longer side (hypotenuse), then $a^2 + b^2 = c^2$) it follows that

$$(\overline{AB})^2 = (\overline{AC})^2 + (\overline{BC})^2$$
$$(\overline{AB})^2 = (2\sqrt{2})^2 + (2\sqrt{2})^2$$
$$= 4(2) + 4(2)$$
$$= 8 + 8$$
$$= 16$$

Taking the square root of both sides of the equation $(AB)^2 = 16$, yields $\overline{AB} = 4$. Therefore, the quantities in both columns are equal.

8. **(B)**

To determine the value of n, one needs to translate the centered information into an algebraic equation with one variable, n, then solve it for n.

Thus,

$$288 + n = 3(n - 12)$$
$$288 + n = 3n - 36$$
$$288 + 36 = 3n - n$$
$$2n = 324$$
$$n = 162$$

Therefore, the quantity in Column B is greater.

9. **(A)**

This comparison problem can be attacked by recalling that when both sides of an inequality are multiplied by the same negative number, the inequality changes direction, and when multiplying both sides by the same positive number, the inequality does not change direction. That is,

if $x < y$ and $c < 0$, then $cx > cy$, and if $x > y$ and $c < 0$, then $cx < cy$. But if $x < y$ and $c > 0$, then $cx < cy$, and if $x > y$ and $c > 0$, then $cx > cy$.

In our problem, since $0 < a < 1$, it follows that

$$a < 1 \quad \text{and} \quad a > 0.$$

Thus, multiplying both sides of the inequality

$$a < 1$$

by the same positive number a ($a > 0$), does not change the direction of the inequality. Hence,

$$a < 1$$
$$a \times a < a \times 1$$
$$a^2 < a \quad \text{or} \quad a > a^2.$$

Thus, the quantity in Column A is greater.

10. **(C)**
Label the vertices of the triangle A, B and C, let $m \angle A$ denote the measure of angle A, and AB denote the length of side AB.

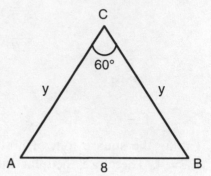

From the central information, $\overline{AC} = y$ and $\overline{BC} = y$, hence, triangle ABC is an isosceles triangle. This means that $m \angle A = m \angle B$.

Because the sum of the measures of the three interior angles of a triangle is equal to $180°$, it follows that

$$m \angle A + m \angle B + m \angle C = 180$$
$$m \angle A + m \angle B + 60 = 180$$
$$m \angle A + m \angle B = 180 - 60$$
$$m \angle A + m \angle B = 120$$

since $m \angle A = m \angle B$, it follows that

$$m \angle A = 60° \text{ and } m \angle B = 60°.$$

Thus, triangle ABC is an equilateral triangle. That is, all of its sides have equal lengths. Hence, $y = 8$ and $3y = 3(8) = 24$. Therefore, the quantities in Columns A and B are equal.

11. **(D)**
Since the sum of the measures of the three interior angles of a triangle is equal to $180°$, it follows from the centered information that

$$x + y + 40 = 180$$
$$x + y = 180 - 40$$
$$x + y = 140$$

Since no information is given about the value of x or y, the relationship between the two quantities given in Columns A and B cannot be determined.

12. **(D)**
Since $a < b$, it follows that one might conclude that a^2 is greater than b^2. This is not the case.

Since no other information is given about the value of x or y, the relationship between the two quantities is indeterminate. For example, if $a = -3$ and $b = -2$, then $a < b$, $a^2 = -(3)^2 = 9$, and $b^2 = (-2)^2 = 4$. In this case, $a^2 > b^2$. But if $a = 3$ and $b = 4$, then $a < b$, $a^2 = (3)^2 = 9$, and $b^2 = (4)^2 = 16$. In this case $a^2 < b^2$.

13. **(B)**

Observe that if an integer is less than −1 then it is negative and its reciprocal is also a negative rational number. However, the reciprocal is larger than −1. For example, consider the integer −2. Its reciprocal is $-\frac{1}{2}$ which is larger. Thus, the quantity in Column B is larger than the quantity in Column A.

14. **(B)**

The easiest and the most direct approach to attack this problem is to express the centered information in an algebraic equation in one variable and solve for the variable. To do so, let q be the number of quarters processed, then the number of dimes processed will be $(389 - q)$.

Since each quarter is 25¢ and each dime is 10¢, it follows that the total amount of money processed is equal to $25q + 10(389 - q)$. Also, the total amount of money processed is \$65. Thus, expressed in an algebraic equation, the centered information states that

$$25q + 10(389 - q) = 6{,}500$$
$$25q + 3{,}890 - 10q = 6{,}500$$
$$15q = 6{,}500 - 3{,}890$$
$$15q = 2{,}610$$
$$q = \frac{2610}{15} = 174$$

Thus, the number of quarters processed was 174, and so the quantity in Column B is greater.

15. **(C)**

One must simplify each of these expressions before a comparison can be made. Thus,

$$1 + \frac{1}{t} = \frac{t}{t} + \frac{1}{t} = \frac{t+1}{t} \text{ and } \frac{\frac{1}{t}}{\frac{1}{t+1}} = \frac{1}{t} \times \frac{t+1}{1} = \frac{t+1}{t}$$

Hence, the quantities in both columns are equal.

16. **(D)**

The most direct way to solve this problem is to perform the indicated operations in the given equation and solve it for x. Thus,

$$x - (4x - 8) + 9 + (6x - 8) = 9 - x + 24$$
$$x - 4x + 8 + 9 + 6x - 8 = 9 - x + 24$$
$$(x + 6x - 4x) + (8 - 8 + 9) = (9 + 24) - x$$
$$(7x - 4x) + 9 = 33 - x$$
$$3x + x = 33 - 9$$
$$4x = 24$$
$$x = 6$$

17. **(E)**

Observe that $xz = yz$ implies that $x = y$ if z is not 0. But x and y are two different real numbers according to the original assumption in the problem. So, the only possible way for the equality to hold is for z to have a value of 0.

18. **(E)**

Obviously, the more (less) chickens we have, the more (less) sacks of grain needed. Thus, this problem can be solved by using a direct proportion as follows:

$$\frac{\text{Number of sacks of feed } x}{\text{Number of chickens } x} = \frac{\text{Number of sacks of feed } y}{\text{Number of chickens } y}$$

Since it takes s sacks of grain to feed c chickens it follows that the correct proportion to use is

$$\frac{s}{c} = \frac{y}{k}$$

where y is the required number of sacks of grain needed to feed k chickens. Solving this proportion for y in terms of s, c, and k yields

$$\frac{s}{c} = \frac{y}{k}$$
$$cy = sk$$
$$y = \frac{sk}{c}$$

19. **(A)**

One of the simplest and most direct methods for attacking this problem is as follows:

1. Express each quantity in the same unit of measure which yields

$$40 \text{ seconds} = 40 \text{ seconds}$$

$$1\frac{1}{2} \text{ minutes} = 90 \text{ seconds}$$

$$\frac{1}{6} \text{ hour} = \frac{1}{6} \times 60 \text{ minutes} = 10 \text{ minutes}$$

$$= 10(60) = 600 \text{ seconds}$$

Thus, the given ratio expressed in the same units of measure is

$$40 \text{ seconds} : 90 \text{ seconds} : 600 \text{ seconds}$$

2. Since a ratio, $a : b$ can be written as a/b, it follows that the ratio

$$40 \text{ seconds} : 90 \text{ seconds}$$

can be written as
$$\frac{40 \text{ seconds}}{90 \text{ seconds}} = \frac{40}{90}$$

Similarly, the ratio

$$90 \text{ seconds} : 600 \text{ seconds}$$

can be written as
$$\frac{90 \text{ seconds}}{600 \text{ seconds}} = \frac{90}{600}$$

Thus, removing the common unit, seconds, from the ratio obtained in step (1) above yields the ratio

$$40 : 90 : 600$$

3. Dividing by the highest common factor of 40, 90, and 600, which is 10, we obtain

$$4 : 9 : 60$$

20. **(D)**

Tilda's car gets 34 miles per gallon of gasoline, and Naomi's car gets eight miles per gallon. Since each of them used a whole number of gallons of gasoline in traveling from Washington, D.C, to Philadelphia, it follows that the distance between the two cities must be a multiple of the two numbers 34 and 8.

The least common multiple of two (or more) whole numbers is the smallest non-zero whole number that is a multiple of both (all) of the numbers.

The least common multiple of 34 and 8 can be found by factoring each of 34 and 8 into their prime factors expressed in exponential form as follows:

$$8 = 2 \times 2 \times 2 = 2^3$$
$$34 = 2 \times 17$$

Then the least common common multiple of 34 and 8 is equal to $2^3 \times 17$ = 136.

Another procedure for finding the least common multiple of two whole numbers is called the intersection-of-sets method. First, find the set of all positive multiples of both numbers, then find the set of all common multiples of both numbers, and, finally, pick the least element in the set.

In this problem, multiples of 8 are

$$8, 16, 24, 32, 40, 48, 56, 64, 72, 80, 88, 96, 104,$$
$$112, 120, 128, 136, 144, 152, 160, 168, \ldots$$

Multiples of 34 are

$$34, 68, 102, 136, 170, \ldots$$

The intersection of the multiples of 8 and 34 is the set

$$\{136, 272, 408, \ldots\}$$

Because 136 is the least common multiple of 34 and 8, the distance from Washington, D.C., to Philadelphia is 136 miles.

Yet another way to attack this problem is to check if any of the answer choices is a common multiple of both 34 and 8. Checking the answer choices given yields

(A) 21 is not a multiple of 34 or 8.

(B) 32 is a multiple of 8, but not of 34.

(C) 68 is a multiple of 34, but not of 8.

(D) 136 is a multiple of both 34 and 8.

(E) 170 is a multiple of 34, but not of 8.

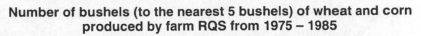

Number of bushels (to the nearest 5 bushels) of wheat and corn produced by farm RQS from 1975 – 1985

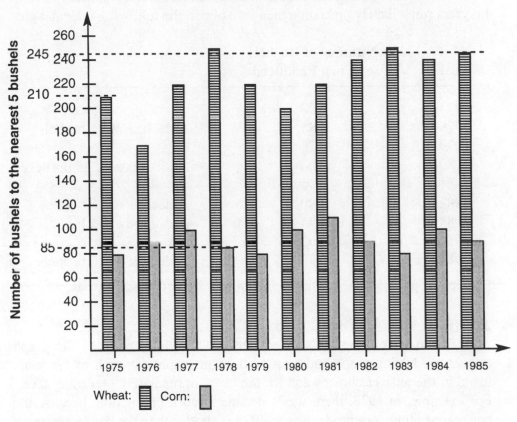

21. **(A)**

This is simply a graph-reading question. To determine the least number of bushels of wheat produced, locate the shortest bar of wheat production for the years 1976, 1978, 1980, 1982, and 1984. The reason for considering these years is because they are listed as possible answers. By inspection of the graph, we find that the shortest bar representing wheat production is the one representing the wheat production for 1976. Thus, the least number of bushels of wheat was produced in 1976.

22. **(C)**

As in problem 21, this is a matter of reading the part of the graph which represents the corn production. One needs only to look for the corn production of each of the years given in the answer choices and the production of the years immediately preceding each of them. For example, to find the number of bushels of corn produced in 1978, we locate the bar of corn production for 1978, then draw a horizontal line from the top of the bar to the vertical axis. The point where this horizontal line meets the vertical axis represents the number of bushels of corn produced in 1978.

The graph shows that 85 bushels of corn were produced in 1978.

Now, reading the graph for the years given as possible answers and for the years immediately preceding them, we obtain the following information:

Year	Number of Bushels of Corn Produced	
1977	100	
1978	85	A decline of 15 bushels
1979	75	
1980	100	An increase of 25 bushels
1981	110	
1982	90	A decline of 20 bushels
1983	75	A decline of 15 bushels
1984	100	
1985	90	A decline of 10 bushels

Thus, the greatest decline in corn production occurred in 1982.

23. **(E)**

This question can be answered by reading both parts of the graph (wheat production graph and corn production graph) for each of the years listed in the answer choices and for the years immediately preceding them. For example, in 1978, there was a decline in corn production, because the bar representing corn production in 1978 is shorter than the bar representing corn production in 1977. Also, in 1978, there was an increase in wheat production because the bar representing wheat production in 1978 is longer than the bar representing wheat production in 1977. By inspecting the given graphs in this fashion, we find out that corn production decreased and wheat production increased in each of the years 1978, 1982, 1983, and 1985.

24. **(E)**

The percent increase is found by the difference in wheat production divided by the initial year's wheat production. The wheat production in 1975 = 210 bushels and the wheat production in 1978 = 250 bushels.

The percent increase

$$= \frac{1978 \text{ wheat production} - 1975 \text{ wheat production} \times 100\%}{1975 \text{ wheat production}}$$

$$= \frac{250 - 210}{210} \times 100\%$$

$$= 19\%$$

25. **(D)**

This question requires reading the graphs, listing the number of bushels of wheat and the number of bushels of corn produced in each of the years listed as possible answers in the answer choices (A) through (E), and then adding the number of bushels of wheat produced each year to the number of bushels of corn produced in the same year. The largest number obtained represents the maximum combined production. Thus, reading the graphs yields the following information:

Year	Number of Bushels of Wheat Produced	Number of Bushels of Corn Produced	Total
1978	250	85	335
1981	220	110	330
1983	250	75	325
1984	240	100	340
1985	245	90	335

Thus, from the above table, the combined production of wheat and corn was at a maximum in 1984.

26. **(E)**

Let $m \angle A$ represent the measure of angle A. Though there are several ways to attack this question, one way is to recall that the sum of the measures of the three interior angles of a triangle is equal to 180°, and the measure of an exterior angle of a triangle is equal to the sum of the measures of the two non-adjacent interior angles of the triangle.

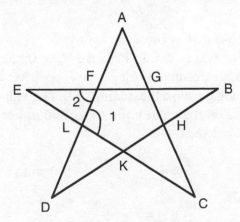

We can now start by considering triangle *ACL*. Of course,

$$m \angle A + m \angle C + m \angle 1 = 180°, \ldots \qquad (1)$$

But $\angle 1$ is an exterior angle to triangle *LEF*, thus,

$$m \angle 1 = m \angle E + m \angle 2.$$

Substituting this in equation (1) yields,

$$m \angle A + m \angle C + m \angle E + m \angle 2 = 180°, \ldots \qquad (2)$$

However, $\angle 2$ is an exterior angle to triangle *FBD*, thus,

$$m \angle 2 = m \angle B + m \angle D.$$

Substituting this result in equation (2) yields,

$$m \angle A + m \angle C + m \angle E + m \angle B + m \angle D = 180°.$$

Thus, the sum of the measures of angles *A, B, C, D*, and *E* is equal to 180°.

27. **(A)**

Recall that for all real numbers p, q, r, and s, if $p/q < 0$, and $r/s > 0$, then

$$\frac{p}{q} \times \frac{r}{s} < 0$$

(negative × positive = negative.)

In this problem, we have $a/b < 0$, and $c/d > 0$, thus,

$$\frac{a}{b} \times \frac{c}{d} < 0.$$

So answer choice (A) is the correct answer.

Answer choice (B) is wrong because $a/b < 0$, and $c/d > 0$ imply that $a/b \times c/d$ cannot be greater than 0 (negative × positive = negative). Answer choice (C) are wrong because the quantity $a/b \times c/d$ can either be positive or negative depending on the values of a, b, c, and d. For example, if $a = -1$, $b = 2$, $c = 4$, and $d = 3$ then

$$\frac{a}{b} = -\frac{1}{2} < 0, \frac{c}{d} = \frac{4}{3} > 0 \text{ and}$$

$$\frac{a}{b} + \frac{c}{d} = -\frac{1}{2} + \frac{4}{3} = \frac{5}{6} > 0.$$

However, if $a = -5$, $b = 2$, $c = 1$, and $d = 2$, then

$$\frac{a}{b} = -\frac{5}{2} < 0, \frac{c}{d} = \frac{1}{2} > 0, \text{ and}$$

$$\frac{a}{b} + \frac{c}{d} = -\frac{5}{2} + \frac{1}{1} = -2 < 0.$$

Answer choice (E) is wrong on the basis that it is impossible to have a real number which is positive and negative at the same time.

28. **(B)**

Translating the given information into algebra yields the equation that can be used to find the required number, n.

$$3n - 2 = 5[(n \div 3) + 2]$$
$$3n - 2 = 5(n/3 + 2)$$

This equation is the same as the equation given in answer choice (B).

29. **(D)**

If m and n are consecutive integers, and $m < n$, it follows that
$$n = m + 1$$

Now, we can check each of the answer choices (A) through (E) as follows:

(A) $n - m = (m + 1) - m = m + 1 - m = 1$, which is odd. Thus, the statement in answer choice (A) is false.

(B) Since no specific information is given about the integer m, m can be an odd integer or an even integer. So, the statement in answer choice (B) is false.

(C) $m^2 + n^2 = m^2 + (m + 1)^2 = m^2 + m^2 + 2m + 1$
$$= 2m^2 + 2m + 1$$
$$= 2(m^2 + m) + 1$$

Since 2 times any integer (even or odd) yields an even integer, it follows that $2(m^2 + m)$ is an even integer, and hence, $2(m^2 + m) + 1$ is an odd integer. Hence, the statement in answer choice (C) is false.

(D) $n^2 - m^2 = (m + 1)^2 - m^2 = m^2 + 2m + 1 - m^2$
$$= 2m + 1$$

Again, since 2 times any integer (even or odd) yields an even integer, it follows that $2m$ is an even integer and $2m + 1$ is always an odd integer. Hence, the statement in answer choice (D) is correct.

(E)   Since *m* and *n* are any pair of two consecutive integers, it follows that *m* can be an even integer or an odd integer. Since $n = m + 1$, it follows that if *m* is odd, then *n* is even and if *m* is even, then *n* is odd. Thus, the statement in answer choice (E) is false.

30. **(C)**

Certainly, the easiest and the most direct way to answer this question is to translate the given information into an algebraic equation in one unknown variable, then solve it for that variable.

In this problem, the distance traveled, the time of travel, and the rate of travel are involved. The relationship between these three quantities is given by

$$\text{Distance} = \text{Rate} \times \text{Time}$$

So, let *r* be Lynn's rate of travel in miles per hour. Then Pete's rate of travel will be $(r + 4)$ miles per hour. After 5 hours of travel, the distance traveled by

Pete is
$$\begin{aligned} d_1 &= \text{Rate} \times \text{Time} \\ &= (r + 4)\, 5 = (5r + 20) \text{ miles} \end{aligned}$$

Lynn is
$$\begin{aligned} d_2 &= \text{Rate} \times \text{Time} \\ &= r(5) = 5r \text{ miles} \end{aligned}$$

Since they are traveling in opposite directions, the total distance, *d*, traveled by both is equal to the sum of the distances traveled by both. A diagram as in the following figure is helpful.

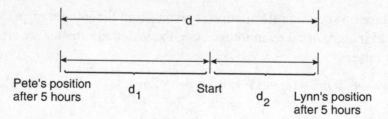

Pete's position after 5 hours d_1 Start d_2 Lynn's position after 5 hours

Now, total distance after 5 hours of travel is

$$\begin{aligned} d &= d_1 + d_2 \\ &= (5r + 20) + 5r \\ &= 5r + 20 + 5r \\ &= 10r + 20 \end{aligned}$$

But, we also know that they are 120 miles apart after 5 hours of travel. Thus,

$$10r + 20 = 120$$
$$10r = 120 - 20$$
$$10r = 100$$
$$r = 10$$

This means Lynn is traveling at the rate of 10 mph.

Section 4–Verbal Ability

1. **(B)**
The professor QUALIFIED (B) (delimited) his statements in order to express his reservations. WROTE (C), FORMED (D), and CONSTRUCTED (E) are not specific enough. LENGTHENED (A) is unrelated logically to the thought.

2. **(B)**
The first blank identifies a key variable in relation to achievement and the second blank reiterates the importance of this same variable. The key phrase here is "...but the fact remains...." The answer is alternative (B), because DESIRE and WANT are synonymous. To want is to desire. The synonymous relationship required by the sentence is not present in the choices given in the other alternatives.

3. **(C)**
The blanks in this sentence require words which refer to the same emotion or quality, with the first being desirable and the second being not desirable (unduly ____). The word "but" precedes a qualifying thought, as well. The correct answer is alternative (C) FRIENDLY...(unduly) FAMILIAR. Alternatives (A), (B), (D), and (E) would be acceptable in the sentence if the word "but" were replaced with an "and," which would not require a contrary thought.

4. **(A)**
The correct answer is (A) APPEARANCE...REDUCE. The persons in question remain strangers to each other but on the surface they share a first-name basis. (B) is wrong because having a waitress give a customer her first name is not an AFFLICTION (cause of suffering) which would RETARD (slow) a person's criticism. (C) is wrong because the familiarity in the situation described is merely apparent, not a REALITY. Alternative (D) is wrong because the time necessary for meaningful familiarity to grow is not present in the situation described. (E) is wrong because no degree of familiarity would completely DENY a customer the ability to criticize.

5. **(B)**
The key to this problem lies in recognizing the fact that the word "nevertheless" precedes information that is contrary to the thought presented in the first part of the sentence. Evidence which indicates invalidity

of a theory is the opposite of SUPPORT. The correct answer is (B) for this reason. Alternatives (A) RESEARCHED, (C) INVESTIGATED, and (E) EXPLORED make sense, but do not express an idea contrary to the thought. Alternative (D) REPUDIATED is wrong because repudiate (to disavow) agrees with the thought presented rather than contradicts it.

6. **(C)**
(A) is incorrect. SEJUNCTIONED refers to separation. (B) is incorrect. SEGREGATED connotes isolation. (C) is correct. ASCRIBED means to give to someone something that is not apparent, but inferred from action. (D) is incorrect. RESCINDED means took back. (E) is incorrect. SCISSIONED means divided.

7. **(C)**
The poet was mourning a quality of youth, so the correct choice must be a property to be regretted. The flowering, or EFFLORESCENCE, of youth is usually celebrated, not regretted. Agreeableness, or ACQUIESCENCE, is not generally held to be a quality of youth, nor is COALESCENCE (unity, coming together). While EFFERVESCENCE, or liveliness, is a quality of youth, it is not a lamented one. Therefore, (A), (B), (D), and (E) are all inappropriate choices. It is the fleetingness, or EVANESCENCE, of youth that the poet is mourning.

8. **(D)**
A COCOON undergoes a metamorphosis which results in a changed form and appearance. This situation also exists in relation to ADOLESCENT:ADULT (D). APPLE:PIE (A) and WOOD:HOUSE (E) both require external actions to effect the change. In relation to BLOSSOM:FRUIT (B), pollination is an external happening without which step the fruit does not appear. AWARENESS:UNDERSTANDING (C) is incorrect because awareness does not always result in understanding.

9. **(A)**
This analogy is one of part to whole, but also includes the idea of progression. A certain number of MINUTES must elapse before an HOUR has passed. Likewise, in METER:KILOMETER (A), a certain number of meters is required to be in place before a kilometer can be said to exist. CHOIR may have any number of ALTOS (B) or even no altos and can still exist. FEDERATION may have any number of STATES (C), and TRAIN may have any number of BOXCARS (E).

10. **(E)**

AVERSION means strong dislike; FONDNESS implies attachment or affection. The two are opposite. EQUIVALENT and COMMENSURATE (A) are synonyms for equal. TANTAMOUNT and EQUAL (B) are synonyms for the same, equivalent. A FARRIER is another name for a BLACKSMITH. The two are the same so (C) is not the best choice. EXECRABLE and FOUL (D) are synonymous terms for very dirty, contemptible. ODIOUS means provoking hatred; LAUDABLE is that which can be looked upon with approval. The two are opposites. (E) is the best answer.

11. **(C)**

The process of OXIDATION causes RUST. This relationship is also found in alternative (C). INVESTMENT causes or results in DIVIDENDS. NAPALM causes BURNING (A); the relationship is the reverse of the one sought. HUNGER is not a cause of STARVATION (B), IGNORANCE does not cause EDUCATION (D), and POVERTY does not cause ALCOHOLISM (E).

12. **(A)**

RAIN is a form of PRECIPITATION. The analogy is one of example:class. The correct answer is COPPER:METAL (A). COPPER is an example of a METAL. The analogy in ICE:GLACIER (B) is wrong because a glacier is made up of ICE, but ICE is not necessarily an example of a GLACIER. In relation to OIL:SHALE (C), OIL is found in SHALE, but is not an example of SHALE. WIND:ABRASION (D) has the relationship of cause:effect. WIND is a cause of ABRASION. This relationship also exists in HEAT:EVAPORATION (E), as HEAT is a cause of EVAPORATION.

13. **(A)**

A person who is HARD-HEARTED lacks EMPATHY. The same relationship is evident in alternative (A) AMBIVALENT:DECISIVENESS, as a person who is AMBIVALENT lacks DECISIVENESS. This relationship does not exist in ASSERTIVE:INDEPENDENCE (B), COMPETITIVE:ADVERSARY (C), CREATIVE:DOGMATISM (D), or VENGEFUL:FRIENDSHIP (E).

14. **(D)**

A RETINUE is a group of FOLLOWERS. The corresponding analogy is found in DETRITUS:DEBRIS (D), since an accumulation of DEBRIS is referred to as DETRITUS. The first term in the analogies refers to a collection of those things or items referred to by the second term. In each of the remaining alternatives, the reference to the whole follows instead of precedes reference to the part.

15. **(B)**

NEBULOUS (cloudy, obscure) and PELLUCID (transparent) are antonyms; only CACOPHONIC and HARMONIC reflect this antonymous relationship. LUMINOUS and INCANDESCENT (A), METICULOUS and PRECISE (C), and FALLACIOUS and DECEPTIVE (E) are all synonymous pairs. INGENUOUS (innate ability) and INNOCUOUS (harmless) are unrelated terms, so (D) is not an appropriate choice.

16. **(E)**

RAGE is a heightened form of ANGER. In the correct alternative, which is (E), a FIASCO is a heightened form of FAILURE. A FIASCO is a complete, ridiculous failure. The other alternatives each present synonymous pairs of words. Although the second term in each pair may appear more serious, in meaning it is the same.

17. **(B)**

The entire selection is an attempt to show that the Earth was bombarded during its early history. (A) is incorrect. The author speculates it began 4.6 billion years ago but this is not the main point. (C) is incorrect. The author does not claim these bodies were in place prior to Earth. (D) is incorrect. The author only discusses the possibility. (E) is incorrect. The Moon reveals a bombardment, but the author does not imply this.

18. **(E)**

The author implies this when he states, "This same bombardment must have affected the Earth as well." (A) and (B) are incorrect since it was not a stated fact. (C) is incorrect. The author has attempted to use this observation to show the Earth could not have been missed. (D) is incorrect. The author notes that it was during this period that life began.

19. **(D)**

The author mentions that Mars (A), Mercury (B), the Earth's moon (C), and the satellites of Saturn (E) were studied to give evidence that the Earth was bombarded in its conceptual history. While the author also mentions the *satellites* of Jupiter, he does not mention Jupiter (D).

20. **(E)**

The tone of the passage is formal and impartial, presenting factual information without presenting opinions about the material. There is no attempt to link any of the religions mentioned to any present religion, so it is unlikely that the passage is from an essay in a church bulletin. (A) is not the correct answer. The author's style is more formal than the style of magazine articles, so (B) and (C) are not appropriate choices. Because the material in the passage is factual, not fictional, and there is no attempt to link the material to any specific characters, the passage is not from a novel, and (D) is an incorrect choice. A formal and impartial passage discussing the history of religion and education in colonial America is most likely to be found in a historical journal. The correct answer is (E).

21. **(C)**

The author states in the final paragraph of the selection that the *Bay Psalm Book* was the first book printed in the colonies (C). (A), (B), (D), and (E) are incorrect.

22. **(C)**

In 1645 and again in 1647, the Massachusetts Legislature passed laws requiring communities to support education first for elementary school and then for grammar school. (A), (B), (D), and (E) are incorrect.

23. **(A)**

There was religious "intolerance" as the author describes in paragraph two. (B) and (C) are incorrect. Both are mentioned in the second paragraph. (D) and (E) are incorrect and stated in the last paragraph.

24. **(E)**

The author indicates in the last sentence of paragraph three that the students taking advantage of the apprenticeship programs came from poor families (E).

25. **(E)**

In paragraph three, line eight, the author notes, "Private tutors instructed the sons of well-to-do planters,..." This sentence follows a sentence that discusses the Southern colonies.

26. **(B)**

The author does not mention this in the article. It can be clearly inferred from the selection that the Puritans were not tolerant. (A), (C), and (D) are mentioned in paragraph two. (E) can be clearly inferred from paragraph two.

27. **(A)**

The final paragraph states that William and Mary was created by royal charter and Harvard was established by the Massachusetts Legislature in 1636.

28. **(B)**

To PREVENT is to stop someone from doing something or to keep something from happening. The antonym in this case is PERMIT (B), which means to allow to be done, to consent to. Alternatives are INVITE (A) (to ask to come somewhere or do something); ENCOURAGE (C) (to give support to); DEMAND (D) (to require); and URGE (E) (to advocate). They are unrelated to the meaning needed.

29. **(A)**

RESERVED means self-restrained or reticent. Its opposite is (A) AFFABLE, meaning friendly. SAVED (B) is a synonym for reserved when it means kept in reserve or set apart. RETICENT (E) (quiet) is also a synonym for reserved. GIVEN (C) (accustomed to be habit) and UNEXPECTED (D) (unforeseen) are unrelated to the meaning of affable.

30. **(E)**

ILLUSORY means an unreal or misleading appearance or image. Its opposite is FACTUAL (E), meaning of or containing facts; real, actual. EVIDENT (A) is wrong because both an illusory image and a factual image could be evident, that is, easy to see or perceive. MEANINGFUL (B) (what is meant or intended to be significant) could also apply to both illusory and factual events. SOLUBLE (C) (able to be solved) is unrelated in meaning to illusory. OBVIOUS (D) (easy to understand) is wrong because it may apply to both illusory (misleading) and factual occurrences.

31. **(B)**

To OSCILLATE is to swing to and fro. The opposite of oscillation is stabilization. To STABILIZE (B) is to keep from changing; to make steady. MOOR (A) is wrong because it means to tie down; BALANCE (C) is wrong because it means to bring into proportion or harmony. VACILLATE and UNDULATE (E) are both wrong because these words are synonyms for the term given, oscillate.

32. **(B)**

A EULOGISTIC speech is one in which a person or thing is praised highly. The antonym of eulogistic is CENSORIOUS (B), meaning harshly critical. The alternatives are incorrect because they do not express the idea of a critical response. OFFICIOUS (A) (offering unwanted advice or services); DEPRESSED (C) (sad, dejected); INCOMPREHENSIBLE (D) (not understandable); and OBSTINATE (E) (determined to have one's way) do not include the idea of critical attitudes or actions.

33. **(C)**

A SCRUPULOUS person is one who is careful of details, or precise in the manner he goes about work. The antonym is CARELESS (C) (not paying enough heed; neglectful). Alternatives (A), (B), and (D) are wrong because they are similar in meaning to the term given. Alternative (E) is simply unrelated to the meaning needed.

34. **(E)**

To CENSURE is to condemn as wrong. COMMEND (E) is the correct antonym. To commend is to recommend or to praise. COURT (A) is wrong because it means to pay attention to so as to get something; FLATTER (C) and ADULATE (D) both have an element of insincerity; to flatter is to praise insincerely, and to adulate is to favor upon. ACCEPT (B) lacks the intensity of commend or praise; it simply means to approve.

35. **(B)**

ALLEGIANCE is loyalty or devotion. Its opposite is TREACHERY (B), which is betrayal of trust or disloyalty. The alternatives are wrong because they include in their meanings ideas which are only a part of disloyalty. DISAPPROBATION (A) means disapproval; INCOMPATIBILITY (C) means an ability to reconcile two points of view; DISSENSION (D) and DISPUTATION (E) carry meanings of dissenting, disagreeing, or quarreling.

36. **(A)**

LUGUBRIOUS means very sad or mournful. The opposite in the list given is JOYOUS (A). The incorrect alternatives are ENERGETIC (B) (having energy; vigorous); RAPID (C) (moving or occurring with speed); FACILE (D) (done easily); and HEALTHY (E) (having good health). None of the alternatives has the meaning of joyous.

37. **(E)**

BELLICOSE means quarrelsome or warlike. Its opposite is PA-CIFIC, which comes from the Latin word for peace, which is *pax*. In English, pacific means peaceful, calm, or tranquil. PULCHRITUDINOUS (A) means beautiful, OBDURATE (B) means hard-headed or stubborn; ANOREXIC (C) means having an obsession with loss; a loss of desire to eat; and SERAPHIC (D) means angelic. None of these words carries a meaning related to peacefulness.

38. **(D)**

BANEFUL means harmful or ruinous. Its opposite is BENEFICIAL (D), which means favorable, producing benefits, or advantageous. RE-SPECTED (A) (held in esteem, honor, or regard); BEAUTIFUL (B) (having beauty); RECKLESS (C) (heedless, rash); and HONORABLE (E) (worthy of honor) are unrelated to the meaning needed.

Section 5–Quantitative Ability

1. **(C)**

Let five consecutive numbers where x is the central number be: $x - 2, x - 1, x, x + 1, x + 2$. Then

$$\text{Average} = \frac{x - 2 + x - 1 + x + x + 1 + x + 2}{5} = x$$

In the second case, let three consecutive numbers be: $x - 1, x, x + 1$. Then

$$\text{Average} = \frac{x - 1 + x + x + 1}{3} = x$$

So, both averages are equal.

2. **(A)**

Half of n square $= \dfrac{n^2}{2}$ if $n > 2$ then $\dfrac{n}{2} > 1$, therefore $\dfrac{n^2}{2} > \dfrac{n}{2}$.

3. **(A)**

$$\frac{ab - by}{y - a} = \frac{b(a - y)}{(y - a)} = \frac{b(a - y)}{-(a - y)} = -b$$

given $b < 0$; $-b > b$.

4. **(B)**

Given that

$$(a, b) = a + 3b$$
$$(2, 3) = 2 + 3 \times 3 = 11$$
$$(3, x) = 3 + 3x$$

and

$$(2, 3) = (3, x)$$
$$11 = 3 + 3x$$
$$x = \frac{8}{3} > 2$$

5. **(A)**

$$y = x - 2$$

Add 3 to both sides:

$$y + 3 = x + 1$$

For any value of x, we always have $x + 1 > x - 1$, thus,

$$y + 3 > x - 1.$$

6. **(A)**
   1 foot^2 of fabric costs $4. 2 feet by 2 feet or 4 square feet will cost $16, and $16 > 10$.

7. **(C)**

   $$30\% \text{ of } 40 = \frac{30}{100} \times 40 = 12.$$

   $$40\% \text{ of } 40 = \frac{40}{100} \times 30 = 12.$$

8. **(B)**
   Men = x;   Women = 73.

   $$\text{Empty seats} = \frac{20}{100}\,(320) = 64$$

   Women + Men + Empty seats = 320

   $$73 + x + 64 = 320$$
   $$x = 183 < 185$$

9. **(D)**
   The statement says

   $$A > P$$
   $$B \geq P$$

   Therefore, it can be $A > B$, $A = B$, $A < B$.

10. **(A)**
    We can define an even number as $2x$, and the following numbers will be $2x + 2$ and $2x + 4$. Therefore,

    $$2x + 2x + 2 + 2x + 4 = 42$$
    $$6x + 6 = 42$$
    $$6x = 36$$
    $$x = 6$$

Remember that the first number was $2x$, which is 12 if $x = 6$.

11. **(B)**

Since $m < 0$, $n < 0$, and $n/_m > 0$. Also, $m > n$ gives us $m/_n < 1$, $n/_m > 1$ (remember m, $n < 0$) therefore $n/_m > m/_n$. To confirm this, substitute -1 for m and -2 for n. Thus, $m/_n = \frac{1}{2}$ and $n/_m = 2$.

12. **(A)**

$$\frac{p^2 - q^2}{q - p} = \frac{(p-q)(p+q)}{-(p-q)} = -(p+q)$$

and $p + q > -(p + q)$ since $p + q > 0$.

13. **(B)**

$$\frac{1}{4 - \dfrac{1+\frac{1}{2}}{1-\frac{1}{2}}} = \frac{1}{4 - \dfrac{\frac{3}{2}}{\frac{1}{2}}} = \frac{1}{4-3} = 1.$$

14. **(D)**

Since x, y and z are integers, it follows that x, y and z could be positive or negative. If y is negative, then z is negative, and x could be positive or it could be negative. In either case, we get $x/_y < z/_y$. For example, if $y = -3$, $z = -6$, and $x = 6$, then,

$$x > y > z;\quad \frac{x}{y} = \frac{6}{-3} = -2;\quad \frac{z}{y} = -\left(\frac{6}{3}\right) = 2;$$

and $x/_y < z/_y$. Also, if $y = -6$, $z = -12$, and $x = -3$, then

$$x > y > z;\quad \frac{x}{y} = \frac{1}{2};\quad \frac{z}{y} = -\left(\frac{12}{6}\right) = 2;$$

and again $x/_y < z/_y$.

However, if y is positive, then x is positive, and z could be positive or negative. In either case, $x/_y < z/_y$. For example, if $y = 10$, $x = 20$, and $z = 5$, then

$$x > y > z;\quad \frac{x}{y} = \frac{20}{10} = 2;\quad \frac{z}{y} = \frac{5}{10} = \frac{1}{2};\quad \text{and } \frac{x}{y} > \frac{z}{y}.$$

Thus, since no specific information is given about x, y and z, the relationship between the two quantities given in Columns A and B is indeterminate.

15. **(B)**

Redraw the figure. Assigning M, N, and R the respective areas, then area $= R^2/2$. By using the Pythagorean theorem

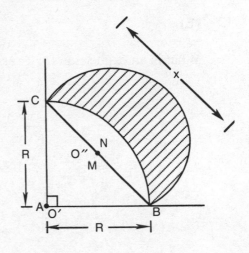

$$R^2 + R^2 = x^2$$

$$R\sqrt{2} = x$$

$$\text{Area } M = \frac{R^2}{2}.$$

Area $N =$ Area Quadrant $-$ Area M

$$= \frac{\pi R^2}{4} - \frac{R^2}{2} = R^2\left(\frac{\pi}{4} - \frac{1}{2}\right)$$

Shaded Area $=$ Area P $=$ Semicircle Area $-$ Area N

$$= \frac{\pi\left(\dfrac{R\sqrt{2}}{2}\right)^2}{2} - R^2\left(\frac{\pi}{4} - \frac{1}{2}\right)$$

$$\text{Area } P = \frac{\pi R^2}{4} - \frac{\pi R^2}{4} + \frac{R^2}{2}$$

$$\text{Area } P = \frac{R^2}{2}$$

16. **(C)**

So, $\left(\sqrt{a+b}\right)^2 = a+b$, $\sqrt{(a-b)^2} = a-b$ since $a > b$.

$$\left[\left(\sqrt{a+b}\right)^2 - \sqrt{(a-b)^2}\right] = [(a+b) - (a-b)]$$

$$= [a+b-a+b]$$

$$= 2b$$

17. **(E)**

What is an expression for $\dfrac{y}{x}$ as a function of a if $\dfrac{x+y}{y} = a$?

$$\frac{x=y}{y} = a$$

$$\frac{x}{y} + \frac{y}{y} = a$$

$$\frac{x}{y} + 1 = a$$

$$\frac{x}{y} = a - 1$$

$$\frac{y}{x} = \frac{1}{a-1}$$

18. **(B)**

Let x be the total capacity of the swimming pool, then $\dfrac{2}{3}x = 1,800$.

$$x = \frac{1,800 \times 3}{2} = 2,700 \text{ ft}^3$$

The correct answer is (B).

19. **(E)** $\left[\left(\dfrac{x}{y}\right)^{-1} - \left(\dfrac{y}{x}\right)^{-1}\right]^{-1} = \left[\left(\dfrac{y}{x}\right)^{1} - \left(\dfrac{x}{y}\right)^{1}\right]^{-1}$

$$= \left[\frac{y}{x} - \frac{x}{y}\right]^{-1} = \left[\frac{y^2 - x^2}{xy}\right]^{-1}$$

$$= \left[\frac{xy}{y^2 - x^2}\right] = \frac{xy}{y^2 - x^2}$$

20. **(B)**

	Past	Present	Future
Pat	$x - 1$	x	$x + 1$
Sister	$y - 1$	y	$y + 1$

One year ago…

$$x - 1 = 3(y - 1)$$

Next year…

$$x + 1 = 2(y + 1)$$
$$x = 7$$
$$y = 3$$

Pat will be 12 years old in five more years.

21. **(E)**

Looking at the table, the countries that have the lowest infant mortality are Sweden and The Netherlands, each one with 17. Note that Iran is not 0.

22. **(A)**

We had 25.3 births per 1,000 citizens, therefore

$$200 \text{ million (citizens)} \times \frac{25.3 \text{ births}}{1,000 \text{ citizens}} = 5.06 \times 10^6 \text{ (Births)}$$

23. **(B)**

The range is the difference between the largest and smallest rate. From the table, South America had the greatest range.

Ecuador = 45.5 and Uruguay = 11.4

The range is 45.5 – 11.4 = 34.1.

24. **(D)**

The average birth rate in Africa = $\dfrac{(25.6 + 43.1)}{2} = 34.35$.

The average death rate in Africa = $\dfrac{(8.8 + 13.0)}{2} = 10.9$.

The ratio of average birth rate/average death rate = $\dfrac{34.35}{10.9} = 3.15$.

25. **(C)**

In the U.S. we had 9.6 deaths per 1,000 citizens and an infant mortality rate of 26 per 1,000 births and also 25.3 births per 1,000 citizens. Therefore,

$$\text{Total death} = \frac{9.6}{1,000} \text{ citizens}$$

$$\text{Infant death} = \frac{26 \text{ deaths}}{1,000 \text{ births}} \times \frac{25.3 \text{ births}}{1,000 \text{ citizens}}$$

$$\text{Infant death} = \frac{.658}{1,000} \text{ citizens.}$$

Let x be the desired percentage, then

$$x = \frac{0.658}{9.6} \times 100\%$$
$$= 6.85\%$$

26. (E)

If $x = 1$ then response (B) is 2, response (A) is 2, response (C) is 3, and response (D) is -1. Thus, response (E) is the only response possible. Consider response (E). Notice that by factoring the expression one gets

$$x^2 + 2x + 1 = (x + 1)(x + 1) = (x + 1)^2$$

which is the square of an integer for every integer x.

27. (C)

In order to find the midpoint of the line segment between two points one must know the formula. It is given by an ordered pair (x, y) where x is formed by the average of the x-coordinates and y is formed by the average of the y-coordinates of the two points. Thus, the midpoint is

$$x = \frac{3+9}{2} = \frac{12}{2} = 6 \text{ and } y = \frac{5+13}{2} = \frac{18}{2} = 9$$

or the ordered pair (6, 9).

28. (B)

Twenty percent have traveled more than two times. Seventy percent have never traveled. Therefore, 10 percent have traveled one or two times.

29. (C)

First expand $(x^2)^{-4}$ to obtain x^{-8} since the rule is $(x^m)^n = x^{mn}$. Similarly, expand $(x^{-2})^3$ to obtain x^{-6} and $(x^{-3})^{-5}$ to obtain x^{+15}. Hence, the original expression may be written as

$$\frac{(x^{-8})(x^{-6})}{x^{15}} \qquad (1)$$

By using another of the rules for handling exponents, which states that $x^m x^n = x^{m+n}$, one can determine the results of expression (1) as follows:

$$\frac{(x^{-8})(x^{-6})}{x^{15}} = \frac{x^{-14}}{x^{15}}.$$ (2)

Finally, from expression (2) move the numerator, which has a negative exponent, into the denominator by changing the sign of the exponent and then multiply by the existing denominator to obtain the results as follows:

$$\frac{x^{-14}}{x^{15}} = \frac{1}{(x^{15})(x^{14})} = \frac{1}{x^{29}}$$

Hence, answer choice (C) is correct.

30. **(C)**

Take the square root of both sides of the equation to form two first equations and solve each for x as follows:

$$\sqrt{(4x-3)^2} = \sqrt{4} \qquad \text{and} \qquad \sqrt{(4x-3)^2} = -\sqrt{4}$$
$$4x - 3 = 2 \qquad\qquad\qquad 4x - 3 = -2$$
$$4x = 2 + 3 \qquad\qquad\qquad 4x = -2 + 3$$
$$x = \frac{5}{4} \qquad\qquad\qquad\qquad x = \frac{1}{4}$$

Hence, the values of x are $5/4$ and $1/4$, respectively, which is answer choice (C). Notice also that answer choices (A) and (B) each satisfy the original equation, but two values of x are required since the equation is quadratic.

Section 6—Verbal Ability

1. **(A)**
AMORPHOUS (D), ECCENTRIC (E), and ERRATIC (C) are all synonyms meaning inconsistent, sporadic. EQUABLE (B) suggests a uniform methodical occurrence. WEARISOME (A) is the correct choice, indicated by the key words "exact," "and," "but," and "essential."

2. **(E)**
In (A), SORROW is mental suffering and does not fit well in the sentence. It is unlikely that a walk toward punishment would HASTEN the pace. (B) is incorrect. REGRET toward punishment that has not as yet been administered to an individual does not seem appropriate. (C) is incorrect. PRECIPITATED means hastened; (D) does not fit the sentence sense. (E) is the correct choice. ANGUISH implies agony, mental pain toward an event. HINDERED means stalled, retained.

3. **(A)**
TUTELARY (B), MYTHICAL (E), CELESTIAL (D), and NYMPHONIC (C) are synonymous with shades of meaning referring to heavenly beings related to pagan gods. "Worst" is the key word suggesting the perception of an event as evil. OMINOUS (A) is the correct choice, being defined as foreshadowing of evil.

4. **(E)**
"Strange" eliminates ARISTOCRATS (A) which would have been a bond between equals. AVARICE (D), GREED (C), and COVETOUSNESS (B) are behaviors, therefore unable to form a bond. DERELICTS (E) is the correct choice, suggesting bonds being developed between opposites.

5. **(C)**
PLIANT (A) and MALLEABLE (D) are synonymous and reflect the ability to bend or be flexible. HISTRIONIC (E) refers to the dramatic. IMPARTIAL (B) suggests an equality among all. Flexibility, dramatic, and impartiality are positive characteristics of a policy. Only PACIFIC (C) could be perceived as weak.

6. **(E)**
CONTINGENT (A) and INCIDENTAL (C) refer to chance and superfluous. INTRODUCED (B) suggests to bring forth for the first time; while

SUPERADDED (D) implies to add to something already complete. The passage implies the necessity of repeating the addition of an extra month, therefore eliminating CONTINGENT, INCIDENTAL, SUPERADDED, and INTRODUCED. The correct choice is INTERCALATED (E) meaning to insert among existing elements.

7. **(E)**
PUNGENT (D), POIGNANT (C), and RANKLING (B) refer to a sharp, irritating sensation; while MALODOROUS (A) suggests an offensive odor. The key word, "reek," indicates a strong, disagreeable odor that is typically emitted by seaweed and dead fish. Therefore, REDOLENT (E), meaning "diffusing a strong odor," is the correct choice.

8. **(A)**
SUN:STARS and PIRANHA:FISH are both member:class relationships, so (A) is the correct choice. PLANK:BLOCK, COLOR:HUE, and EMOTION:MOOD all reflect synonymous relationships, so (B), (C), and (E) are incorrect answers. SHRUB:TREE has a member:member relationship; therefore, (D) is incorrect.

9. **(D)**
ACCRUE and AMASS are synonyms meaning to collect or accumulate. ABSOLVE and ACQUIT are synonyms meaning to forgive; (D) is the correct answer. None of the other alternatives are synonyms. BERATE means to scold and BEGET (A) means to produce. APPEASE (to placate) and ANTAGONIZE (B) (to incur hostility) are antonyms. ENGENDER means to create and ENHANCE (C) means to improve. OSCILLATE is defined as to fluctuate and OSTRACIZE (E) is to cast out.

10. **(B)**
SYNTAX:LANGUAGE reflects a part:whole relationship, and so do all of the answer choices. However, SYNTAX is not just a part of LANGUAGE, it is the part that defines the structure of the language. COLOR does not define the structure of a PAINTING (A); WATER does not define the structure of RAIN (C); MEASUREMENT does not define the structure of SCIENCE (D); and SOUND does not define the structure of MUSIC (E). RHETORIC, meaning the argument used, does define the structure of PHILOSOPHY; different rhetoric will produce different philosophies. Therefore, (B) is the correct answer.

11. **(E)**

ANXIETY and STRESS have a cause-and-effect relationship just as DESTRUCTION is a cause and the effect is found in INUTILITY (E). APHANITE and ROCK (A) as well as APOLLO and MYTHOLOGY (B) have a member:class relationship. BREVITY and CONCISENESS (C) have a synonymous relationship. INSULT and INVECTIVE (D) contain a part-to-whole relationship.

12. **(E)**

REQUIEM and DEATH (A) are a relationship of purpose. LURID and RUDDY (B) belong to an antonymous relationship. HALLMARK and UNIQUE (C) are synonymous, as are FUGUE and COMPOSITION (D). COMPETE and EMULATE (E) are synonymous with VIE and RIVAL. COMPETE, EMULATE, VIE, and RIVAL are all synonyms for endeavor to equal or excel.

13. **(D)**

GLASSES and SEE (A) are a cause-and-effect relationship. SUGAR: SYRUP (B) are a member:member relationship. ROCK and GEOLOGY (C), and GRASS and LAWN (E) are part-to-whole relationships. INDEX and GLOSSARY (D) are parts of a book, as KEEL and DECK are parts of a boat. It is a part-to-part relationship.

14. **(C)**

PERSPIRE and RUN (A) have a cause-and-effect relationship. SUF-FOCATE and BREATH (B) are antonymous in relationship. GYRON and AIRFOIL (D) are synonymous in their relationship as are FLOURISH and THRIVE (E). (C) is the correct choice. GYMKHANA has a whole-to-part relationship with DRIVING SKILL as SWIM is a part of the whole of recreation.

15. **(D)**

PEDAGOGIC is an adjective correctly describing a TEACHER (D), just as DONNISH is an adjective correctly describing a PEDANT. REDO-LENT does not describe AMMONIA (A), a PESSIMIST is not JOCUND (B), a MINISTER cannot be described as SALACIOUS (C), and a SIMPLETON is not ESOTERIC (E).

16. **(A)**

PHONICS and WORD RECOGNITION (A) have a part-to-part rela-tionship. FRENCH and ENGLISH (B) have a whole-to-whole relation-ship. VOLUMES and LIBRARY (D) have a part-to-whole relationship.

HEALTH and PHYSICAL ACTIVITY (C) also have a part-to-whole relationship. HARMONY and MUSIC (E) have a part-to-whole relationship. FRACTIONS and DECIMALS are part of the unidentified subject of mathematics as PHONICS and WORD RECOGNITION are a part of the unidentified subject of reading.

17. **(D)**
The author does define speleology (A) and states that caves are of special interest to the U.S. Geological Survey (B). The author also discusses the discovery of the fossil remains of early man (C) in some of the oldest caves known to man (E). However, the author mentions all of these topics within a general discussion of caves and interesting facts about them. Therefore, (D) is the correct answer.

18. **(A)**
(A) is the correct choice. It can be inferred from the sentence which defines *speleology* as "…a composite science based on geology, hydrology, biology, and archeology…" that the U.S. Geological Survey is interested in caves because of the clues they reveal about early man and his environment (A). The murals on the walls (C), the interconnected passages (D), and the wide variety of rock types (E) are all aspects of cave study, but they are only partial reasons for study. The evidence needed to learn about Neanderthal man (B) is what the U.S. Geological Survey hopes to find through the study of caves; it is not the reason for the study.

19. **(D)**
Speleology is defined in sentence three of paragraph one as the study of caves (D). It cannot be defined as the study of early man (A), water (B), life (C), or earth, water, life, and early man (E).

20. **(B)**
(B) is the correct choice, inferred from the last sentence of paragraph two. "… he took refuge more than 10,000 years ago during the chill of the Ice Age." The key contextual clues are "refuge" and "chill of the Ice Age," suggesting that Germany was too cold for Cro-Magnon man. (A), (C), (D), and (E) are not satisfactory reasons for finding Cro-Magnon man in Spain and France.

21. **(A)**
The first paragraph states that "Americans traveling to Europe have…been impressed by the large areas around cities…devoted to small garden plots." The third paragraph claims that "Try as he will, the traveler

will find little reference to these garden areas..." The remainder of the passage is devoted to providing information about these garden areas, in general terms. The correct answer is (A). The passage does not provide any techniques or technical or historical information to interest gardeners (B), city-planners (C), history students (D), or landscape artists (E).

22. **(B)**

Paragraph 4 supports choice (B) by the following phrase: "'hut colonies' which refer to the toolsheds or small houses on garden plots in some countries." There is no such support for (A), (C), (D), or (E).

23. **(D)**

Paragraph 6 implies that walled cities were only large enough to protect the people, due to the difficulty of defending them; therefore, the gardens were outside because there was little open space inside the walled city. There is no support for (A), (B), (C), or (E).

24. **(A)**

Choice (A) can be answered by information given in paragraph 9: "in England was a law in 1819 that provided for leasing land...." The passage does not provide the answers to the questions "How are garden sizes determined?" (C), "How may additional information be acquired concerning small gardens in Europe?" (D), or "How did neighboring countries influence that spread of small gardens throughout Europe?" (E). The passage does not link the gardens to any particular festival (B).

25. **(B)**

The passage does not provide any information to support the idea that there are more small-garden areas in England than anywhere else. Therefore, (I) is false. Paragraph ten states that "Gardens also became a way to ensure social stability..." Since the passage informs the reader that the first law providing garden areas was passed during the industrial revolution in 1819 (paragraph nine), (II) is true. The last sentence of the passage states that the small-garden "movement continued to grow into the early twentieth century and began to be considered as a factor in planning urban areas." This indicates that the movement was not a factor before the early twentieth century, so (III) is false. Answer (B), (II) only, is correct.

26. **(D)**

The author would be least likely to agree with (D). In paragraph ten, the author states that city governments (and therefore government officials), philanthropists, and some factory owners all provided garden areas for the urban lower classes. All of the other statements can be inferred from the information given in the passage.

27. **(D)**

Paragraph 10 states "to help ensure social stability by providing a link to the countryside that the workers had left,..." This implies that the workers' cultural heritage would be found in the countryside (D). The passage does not state or imply that any correlation between cultural stability and small garden tending is reflected by the care lavished on the gardens (A), the efficiently utilized gardens (B), the festive air surrounding the gardens (C), or the improved welfare of the people (E).

28. **(A)**

LATENT (E) and ABEYANCE (C) both imply temporary inactivity. INNOVATION (B) and METHODICALNESS (D) are antonyms. INNOVATION suggests change, METHODICALNESS refers to habitually proceeding with no change but in a predetermined manner. PERPETUATION (A) is the opposite of CESSATION. PERPETUATION denotes to continue forever; CESSATION is defined as to stop.

29. **(D)**

INAFFABLE (A) and INSOLENCE (C) refer to attitude. EXTEMPORE (B) and MOMENTARY (E) are synonyms referring to "instantly." ABRUPT, sudden termination, is the opposite of PERPETUITY (D), meaning everlasting.

30. **(D)**

GENERAL (A), ANALOGOUS (B), COLLECTIVE (C), and TYPICAL (E), are all synonyms of GENERIC, with SPECIFIC (D) being the antonym, meaning belonging to one class as distinguished from all others, as opposed to the meaning of GENERIC: symbolic of whole or majority. It is distinctiveness versus conformity.

31. **(A)**

REITERATE (B) and RECURRENT are synonymous, referring to the repeating of something. SUCCINCT (D) and TERSE (E) express the quality of what has been said. REPETITION (C) has the more general meaning of performing again by either the same or different agents. Only INFINITE (A) is the opposite of RECURRENT; endless versus intermittent.

32. **(E)**

INNOVATION (D) suggests making a change which may be either temporary or permanent, while ALTERATION (C) refers to making something different without changing it into something else. VARIATION (A) denotes having many forms and types but not the changing of those forms or types. DEVIATION (B) implies turning aside from a standard. Only PERPETUATION (E), meaning continuing endlessly, is the opposite of MUTATION, which is defined as a permanent change.

33. **(E)**

INCLINATION (A) and FLUCTUATION (C) both imply uncertain movement, while VACILLATION (B) suggests to waver in the mind. VICISSITUDE (D) implies the result of change while CONSTANCY (E), meaning unchanging, is the opposite of VERSATILITY, which means to change readily.

34. **(B)**

ITINERANT is an adjective describing one who travels from place to place. ILLEGITIMATE (A) means that which is illegal or gotten illegally; it is not related to ITINERANT. PERMANENT means fixed, non-moving. (B) is clearly the antonym for ITINERANT. IDYLLIC (C) means picturesque, simple, pleasing. It is possible that the life of an ITINERANT might be IDYLLIC, but there does not necessarily have to be a relation between IDYLLIC and ITINERANT. GAUDY (D) means showy, cheaply brilliant; it is an antonym for IDYLLIC, but it does not have an opposite relation to ITINERANT and should not be selected as the correct answer. FELTED (E) means matted; hence, it is not the correct choice since it it not an antonym for the key word ITINERANT.

35. **(A)**

NEBULOUS means unclear, vague, and indefinite. Since CONCLUSIVE (A) means leaving no room for doubt, it is the opposite of NEBULOUS and the right answer. SPURIOUS (B) means false, not genuine, counterfeit, illegitimate. A FRIGATE (C) is a ship and, therefore, not the right answer. SATURNINE (D) means heavy, dull, gloomy. It is not the opposite of NEBULOUS. AMBIGUOUS means doubtful or uncertain. (E) is not an antonym for NEBULOUS.

36. **(D)**

DECIMATION (C) and REDUCTION (E) are synonyms, both inferring the act of diminishing in number. PAUCITY (A) and EXIGUITY are also synonyms describing a scarceness in number. ECCENTRIC (B) has no reference to quantity but only alludes to deviating from an established pattern. CAPACITY (D) is the opposite of EXIGUITY, since CAPACITY infers a completeness in number.

37. **(A)**

STRESS (B) and ARDOR (D) both imply extreme effort. LAN-GUOR (E), ENERVATION, and FLACCIDITY (C) are synonymous and imply a lack of effort. Only STRENUOUS (A), defined as vigorous, active, is the opposite of ENERVATION.

38. **(E)**

INFLUENCE (A) describes an act of the will by producing an effect without apparent force. PREVALENCE (B) and DOMINANCE (C) are synonyms, while AUSPICE (D) refers to protection. IMPOTENCE (E) (powerless) is the opposite of PREPONDERANCE which means a superiority of power.

GRE
Graduate Record Examination

Answer
Sheets

GRE General – Test 1
ANSWER SHEET
(Essay answer sheets are in the back of the book.)

SECTION 3	SECTION 4
1. Ⓐ Ⓑ Ⓒ Ⓓ Ⓔ	1. Ⓐ Ⓑ Ⓒ Ⓓ Ⓔ
2. Ⓐ Ⓑ Ⓒ Ⓓ Ⓔ	2. Ⓐ Ⓑ Ⓒ Ⓓ Ⓔ
3. Ⓐ Ⓑ Ⓒ Ⓓ Ⓔ	3. Ⓐ Ⓑ Ⓒ Ⓓ Ⓔ
4. Ⓐ Ⓑ Ⓒ Ⓓ Ⓔ	4. Ⓐ Ⓑ Ⓒ Ⓓ Ⓔ
5. Ⓐ Ⓑ Ⓒ Ⓓ Ⓔ	5. Ⓐ Ⓑ Ⓒ Ⓓ Ⓔ
6. Ⓐ Ⓑ Ⓒ Ⓓ Ⓔ	6. Ⓐ Ⓑ Ⓒ Ⓓ Ⓔ
7. Ⓐ Ⓑ Ⓒ Ⓓ Ⓔ	7. Ⓐ Ⓑ Ⓒ Ⓓ Ⓔ
8. Ⓐ Ⓑ Ⓒ Ⓓ Ⓔ	8. Ⓐ Ⓑ Ⓒ Ⓓ Ⓔ
9. Ⓐ Ⓑ Ⓒ Ⓓ Ⓔ	9. Ⓐ Ⓑ Ⓒ Ⓓ Ⓔ
10. Ⓐ Ⓑ Ⓒ Ⓓ Ⓔ	10. Ⓐ Ⓑ Ⓒ Ⓓ Ⓔ
11. Ⓐ Ⓑ Ⓒ Ⓓ Ⓔ	11. Ⓐ Ⓑ Ⓒ Ⓓ Ⓔ
12. Ⓐ Ⓑ Ⓒ Ⓓ Ⓔ	12. Ⓐ Ⓑ Ⓒ Ⓓ Ⓔ
13. Ⓐ Ⓑ Ⓒ Ⓓ Ⓔ	13. Ⓐ Ⓑ Ⓒ Ⓓ Ⓔ
14. Ⓐ Ⓑ Ⓒ Ⓓ Ⓔ	14. Ⓐ Ⓑ Ⓒ Ⓓ Ⓔ
15. Ⓐ Ⓑ Ⓒ Ⓓ Ⓔ	15. Ⓐ Ⓑ Ⓒ Ⓓ Ⓔ
16. Ⓐ Ⓑ Ⓒ Ⓓ Ⓔ	16. Ⓐ Ⓑ Ⓒ Ⓓ Ⓔ
17. Ⓐ Ⓑ Ⓒ Ⓓ Ⓔ	17. Ⓐ Ⓑ Ⓒ Ⓓ Ⓔ
18. Ⓐ Ⓑ Ⓒ Ⓓ Ⓔ	18. Ⓐ Ⓑ Ⓒ Ⓓ Ⓔ
19. Ⓐ Ⓑ Ⓒ Ⓓ Ⓔ	19. Ⓐ Ⓑ Ⓒ Ⓓ Ⓔ
20. Ⓐ Ⓑ Ⓒ Ⓓ Ⓔ	20. Ⓐ Ⓑ Ⓒ Ⓓ Ⓔ
21. Ⓐ Ⓑ Ⓒ Ⓓ Ⓔ	21. Ⓐ Ⓑ Ⓒ Ⓓ Ⓔ
22. Ⓐ Ⓑ Ⓒ Ⓓ Ⓔ	22. Ⓐ Ⓑ Ⓒ Ⓓ Ⓔ
23. Ⓐ Ⓑ Ⓒ Ⓓ Ⓔ	23. Ⓐ Ⓑ Ⓒ Ⓓ Ⓔ
24. Ⓐ Ⓑ Ⓒ Ⓓ Ⓔ	24. Ⓐ Ⓑ Ⓒ Ⓓ Ⓔ
25. Ⓐ Ⓑ Ⓒ Ⓓ Ⓔ	25. Ⓐ Ⓑ Ⓒ Ⓓ Ⓔ
26. Ⓐ Ⓑ Ⓒ Ⓓ Ⓔ	26. Ⓐ Ⓑ Ⓒ Ⓓ Ⓔ
27. Ⓐ Ⓑ Ⓒ Ⓓ Ⓔ	27. Ⓐ Ⓑ Ⓒ Ⓓ Ⓔ
28. Ⓐ Ⓑ Ⓒ Ⓓ Ⓔ	28. Ⓐ Ⓑ Ⓒ Ⓓ Ⓔ
29. Ⓐ Ⓑ Ⓒ Ⓓ Ⓔ	29. Ⓐ Ⓑ Ⓒ Ⓓ Ⓔ
30. Ⓐ Ⓑ Ⓒ Ⓓ Ⓔ	30. Ⓐ Ⓑ Ⓒ Ⓓ Ⓔ
31. Ⓐ Ⓑ Ⓒ Ⓓ Ⓔ	31. Ⓐ Ⓑ Ⓒ Ⓓ Ⓔ
32. Ⓐ Ⓑ Ⓒ Ⓓ Ⓔ	32. Ⓐ Ⓑ Ⓒ Ⓓ Ⓔ
33. Ⓐ Ⓑ Ⓒ Ⓓ Ⓔ	33. Ⓐ Ⓑ Ⓒ Ⓓ Ⓔ
34. Ⓐ Ⓑ Ⓒ Ⓓ Ⓔ	34. Ⓐ Ⓑ Ⓒ Ⓓ Ⓔ
35. Ⓐ Ⓑ Ⓒ Ⓓ Ⓔ	35. Ⓐ Ⓑ Ⓒ Ⓓ Ⓔ
36. Ⓐ Ⓑ Ⓒ Ⓓ Ⓔ	36. Ⓐ Ⓑ Ⓒ Ⓓ Ⓔ
37. Ⓐ Ⓑ Ⓒ Ⓓ Ⓔ	37. Ⓐ Ⓑ Ⓒ Ⓓ Ⓔ
38. Ⓐ Ⓑ Ⓒ Ⓓ Ⓔ	38. Ⓐ Ⓑ Ⓒ Ⓓ Ⓔ

SECTION 5

1. Ⓐ Ⓑ Ⓒ Ⓓ Ⓔ
2. Ⓐ Ⓑ Ⓒ Ⓓ Ⓔ
3. Ⓐ Ⓑ Ⓒ Ⓓ Ⓔ
4. Ⓐ Ⓑ Ⓒ Ⓓ Ⓔ
5. Ⓐ Ⓑ Ⓒ Ⓓ Ⓔ
6. Ⓐ Ⓑ Ⓒ Ⓓ Ⓔ
7. Ⓐ Ⓑ Ⓒ Ⓓ Ⓔ
8. Ⓐ Ⓑ Ⓒ Ⓓ Ⓔ
9. Ⓐ Ⓑ Ⓒ Ⓓ Ⓔ
10. Ⓐ Ⓑ Ⓒ Ⓓ Ⓔ
11. Ⓐ Ⓑ Ⓒ Ⓓ Ⓔ
12. Ⓐ Ⓑ Ⓒ Ⓓ Ⓔ
13. Ⓐ Ⓑ Ⓒ Ⓓ Ⓔ
14. Ⓐ Ⓑ Ⓒ Ⓓ Ⓔ
15. Ⓐ Ⓑ Ⓒ Ⓓ Ⓔ
16. Ⓐ Ⓑ Ⓒ Ⓓ Ⓔ
17. Ⓐ Ⓑ Ⓒ Ⓓ Ⓔ
18. Ⓐ Ⓑ Ⓒ Ⓓ Ⓔ
19. Ⓐ Ⓑ Ⓒ Ⓓ Ⓔ
20. Ⓐ Ⓑ Ⓒ Ⓓ Ⓔ
21. Ⓐ Ⓑ Ⓒ Ⓓ Ⓔ
22. Ⓐ Ⓑ Ⓒ Ⓓ Ⓔ
23. Ⓐ Ⓑ Ⓒ Ⓓ Ⓔ
24. Ⓐ Ⓑ Ⓒ Ⓓ Ⓔ
25. Ⓐ Ⓑ Ⓒ Ⓓ Ⓔ
26. Ⓐ Ⓑ Ⓒ Ⓓ Ⓔ
27. Ⓐ Ⓑ Ⓒ Ⓓ Ⓔ
28. Ⓐ Ⓑ Ⓒ Ⓓ Ⓔ
29. Ⓐ Ⓑ Ⓒ Ⓓ Ⓔ
30. Ⓐ Ⓑ Ⓒ Ⓓ Ⓔ
31. Ⓐ Ⓑ Ⓒ Ⓓ Ⓔ
32. Ⓐ Ⓑ Ⓒ Ⓓ Ⓔ
33. Ⓐ Ⓑ Ⓒ Ⓓ Ⓔ
34. Ⓐ Ⓑ Ⓒ Ⓓ Ⓔ
35. Ⓐ Ⓑ Ⓒ Ⓓ Ⓔ
36. Ⓐ Ⓑ Ⓒ Ⓓ Ⓔ
37. Ⓐ Ⓑ Ⓒ Ⓓ Ⓔ
38. Ⓐ Ⓑ Ⓒ Ⓓ Ⓔ

SECTION 6

1. Ⓐ Ⓑ Ⓒ Ⓓ Ⓔ
2. Ⓐ Ⓑ Ⓒ Ⓓ Ⓔ
3. Ⓐ Ⓑ Ⓒ Ⓓ Ⓔ
4. Ⓐ Ⓑ Ⓒ Ⓓ Ⓔ
5. Ⓐ Ⓑ Ⓒ Ⓓ Ⓔ
6. Ⓐ Ⓑ Ⓒ Ⓓ Ⓔ
7. Ⓐ Ⓑ Ⓒ Ⓓ Ⓔ
8. Ⓐ Ⓑ Ⓒ Ⓓ Ⓔ
9. Ⓐ Ⓑ Ⓒ Ⓓ Ⓔ
10. Ⓐ Ⓑ Ⓒ Ⓓ Ⓔ
11. Ⓐ Ⓑ Ⓒ Ⓓ Ⓔ
12. Ⓐ Ⓑ Ⓒ Ⓓ Ⓔ
13. Ⓐ Ⓑ Ⓒ Ⓓ Ⓔ
14. Ⓐ Ⓑ Ⓒ Ⓓ Ⓔ
15. Ⓐ Ⓑ Ⓒ Ⓓ Ⓔ
16. Ⓐ Ⓑ Ⓒ Ⓓ Ⓔ
17. Ⓐ Ⓑ Ⓒ Ⓓ Ⓔ
18. Ⓐ Ⓑ Ⓒ Ⓓ Ⓔ
19. Ⓐ Ⓑ Ⓒ Ⓓ Ⓔ
20. Ⓐ Ⓑ Ⓒ Ⓓ Ⓔ
21. Ⓐ Ⓑ Ⓒ Ⓓ Ⓔ
22. Ⓐ Ⓑ Ⓒ Ⓓ Ⓔ
23. Ⓐ Ⓑ Ⓒ Ⓓ Ⓔ
24. Ⓐ Ⓑ Ⓒ Ⓓ Ⓔ
25. Ⓐ Ⓑ Ⓒ Ⓓ Ⓔ
26. Ⓐ Ⓑ Ⓒ Ⓓ Ⓔ
27. Ⓐ Ⓑ Ⓒ Ⓓ Ⓔ
28. Ⓐ Ⓑ Ⓒ Ⓓ Ⓔ
29. Ⓐ Ⓑ Ⓒ Ⓓ Ⓔ
30. Ⓐ Ⓑ Ⓒ Ⓓ Ⓔ
31. Ⓐ Ⓑ Ⓒ Ⓓ Ⓔ
32. Ⓐ Ⓑ Ⓒ Ⓓ Ⓔ
33. Ⓐ Ⓑ Ⓒ Ⓓ Ⓔ
34. Ⓐ Ⓑ Ⓒ Ⓓ Ⓔ
35. Ⓐ Ⓑ Ⓒ Ⓓ Ⓔ
36. Ⓐ Ⓑ Ⓒ Ⓓ Ⓔ
37. Ⓐ Ⓑ Ⓒ Ⓓ Ⓔ
38. Ⓐ Ⓑ Ⓒ Ⓓ Ⓔ

GRE General – Test 2
ANSWER SHEET

SECTION 3	SECTION 4
1. Ⓐ Ⓑ Ⓒ Ⓓ Ⓔ	1. Ⓐ Ⓑ Ⓒ Ⓓ Ⓔ
2. Ⓐ Ⓑ Ⓒ Ⓓ Ⓔ	2. Ⓐ Ⓑ Ⓒ Ⓓ Ⓔ
3. Ⓐ Ⓑ Ⓒ Ⓓ Ⓔ	3. Ⓐ Ⓑ Ⓒ Ⓓ Ⓔ
4. Ⓐ Ⓑ Ⓒ Ⓓ Ⓔ	4. Ⓐ Ⓑ Ⓒ Ⓓ Ⓔ
5. Ⓐ Ⓑ Ⓒ Ⓓ Ⓔ	5. Ⓐ Ⓑ Ⓒ Ⓓ Ⓔ
6. Ⓐ Ⓑ Ⓒ Ⓓ Ⓔ	6. Ⓐ Ⓑ Ⓒ Ⓓ Ⓔ
7. Ⓐ Ⓑ Ⓒ Ⓓ Ⓔ	7. Ⓐ Ⓑ Ⓒ Ⓓ Ⓔ
8. Ⓐ Ⓑ Ⓒ Ⓓ Ⓔ	8. Ⓐ Ⓑ Ⓒ Ⓓ Ⓔ
9. Ⓐ Ⓑ Ⓒ Ⓓ Ⓔ	9. Ⓐ Ⓑ Ⓒ Ⓓ Ⓔ
10. Ⓐ Ⓑ Ⓒ Ⓓ Ⓔ	10. Ⓐ Ⓑ Ⓒ Ⓓ Ⓔ
11. Ⓐ Ⓑ Ⓒ Ⓓ Ⓔ	11. Ⓐ Ⓑ Ⓒ Ⓓ Ⓔ
12. Ⓐ Ⓑ Ⓒ Ⓓ Ⓔ	12. Ⓐ Ⓑ Ⓒ Ⓓ Ⓔ
13. Ⓐ Ⓑ Ⓒ Ⓓ Ⓔ	13. Ⓐ Ⓑ Ⓒ Ⓓ Ⓔ
14. Ⓐ Ⓑ Ⓒ Ⓓ Ⓔ	14. Ⓐ Ⓑ Ⓒ Ⓓ Ⓔ
15. Ⓐ Ⓑ Ⓒ Ⓓ Ⓔ	15. Ⓐ Ⓑ Ⓒ Ⓓ Ⓔ
16. Ⓐ Ⓑ Ⓒ Ⓓ Ⓔ	16. Ⓐ Ⓑ Ⓒ Ⓓ Ⓔ
17. Ⓐ Ⓑ Ⓒ Ⓓ Ⓔ	17. Ⓐ Ⓑ Ⓒ Ⓓ Ⓔ
18. Ⓐ Ⓑ Ⓒ Ⓓ Ⓔ	18. Ⓐ Ⓑ Ⓒ Ⓓ Ⓔ
19. Ⓐ Ⓑ Ⓒ Ⓓ Ⓔ	19. Ⓐ Ⓑ Ⓒ Ⓓ Ⓔ
20. Ⓐ Ⓑ Ⓒ Ⓓ Ⓔ	20. Ⓐ Ⓑ Ⓒ Ⓓ Ⓔ
21. Ⓐ Ⓑ Ⓒ Ⓓ Ⓔ	21. Ⓐ Ⓑ Ⓒ Ⓓ Ⓔ
22. Ⓐ Ⓑ Ⓒ Ⓓ Ⓔ	22. Ⓐ Ⓑ Ⓒ Ⓓ Ⓔ
23. Ⓐ Ⓑ Ⓒ Ⓓ Ⓔ	23. Ⓐ Ⓑ Ⓒ Ⓓ Ⓔ
24. Ⓐ Ⓑ Ⓒ Ⓓ Ⓔ	24. Ⓐ Ⓑ Ⓒ Ⓓ Ⓔ
25. Ⓐ Ⓑ Ⓒ Ⓓ Ⓔ	25. Ⓐ Ⓑ Ⓒ Ⓓ Ⓔ
26. Ⓐ Ⓑ Ⓒ Ⓓ Ⓔ	26. Ⓐ Ⓑ Ⓒ Ⓓ Ⓔ
27. Ⓐ Ⓑ Ⓒ Ⓓ Ⓔ	27. Ⓐ Ⓑ Ⓒ Ⓓ Ⓔ
28. Ⓐ Ⓑ Ⓒ Ⓓ Ⓔ	28. Ⓐ Ⓑ Ⓒ Ⓓ Ⓔ
29. Ⓐ Ⓑ Ⓒ Ⓓ Ⓔ	29. Ⓐ Ⓑ Ⓒ Ⓓ Ⓔ
30. Ⓐ Ⓑ Ⓒ Ⓓ Ⓔ	30. Ⓐ Ⓑ Ⓒ Ⓓ Ⓔ
31. Ⓐ Ⓑ Ⓒ Ⓓ Ⓔ	31. Ⓐ Ⓑ Ⓒ Ⓓ Ⓔ
32. Ⓐ Ⓑ Ⓒ Ⓓ Ⓔ	32. Ⓐ Ⓑ Ⓒ Ⓓ Ⓔ
33. Ⓐ Ⓑ Ⓒ Ⓓ Ⓔ	33. Ⓐ Ⓑ Ⓒ Ⓓ Ⓔ
34. Ⓐ Ⓑ Ⓒ Ⓓ Ⓔ	34. Ⓐ Ⓑ Ⓒ Ⓓ Ⓔ
35. Ⓐ Ⓑ Ⓒ Ⓓ Ⓔ	35. Ⓐ Ⓑ Ⓒ Ⓓ Ⓔ
36. Ⓐ Ⓑ Ⓒ Ⓓ Ⓔ	36. Ⓐ Ⓑ Ⓒ Ⓓ Ⓔ
37. Ⓐ Ⓑ Ⓒ Ⓓ Ⓔ	37. Ⓐ Ⓑ Ⓒ Ⓓ Ⓔ
38. Ⓐ Ⓑ Ⓒ Ⓓ Ⓔ	38. Ⓐ Ⓑ Ⓒ Ⓓ Ⓔ

SECTION 5

1. Ⓐ Ⓑ Ⓒ Ⓓ Ⓔ
2. Ⓐ Ⓑ Ⓒ Ⓓ Ⓔ
3. Ⓐ Ⓑ Ⓒ Ⓓ Ⓔ
4. Ⓐ Ⓑ Ⓒ Ⓓ Ⓔ
5. Ⓐ Ⓑ Ⓒ Ⓓ Ⓔ
6. Ⓐ Ⓑ Ⓒ Ⓓ Ⓔ
7. Ⓐ Ⓑ Ⓒ Ⓓ Ⓔ
8. Ⓐ Ⓑ Ⓒ Ⓓ Ⓔ
9. Ⓐ Ⓑ Ⓒ Ⓓ Ⓔ
10. Ⓐ Ⓑ Ⓒ Ⓓ Ⓔ
11. Ⓐ Ⓑ Ⓒ Ⓓ Ⓔ
12. Ⓐ Ⓑ Ⓒ Ⓓ Ⓔ
13. Ⓐ Ⓑ Ⓒ Ⓓ Ⓔ
14. Ⓐ Ⓑ Ⓒ Ⓓ Ⓔ
15. Ⓐ Ⓑ Ⓒ Ⓓ Ⓔ
16. Ⓐ Ⓑ Ⓒ Ⓓ Ⓔ
17. Ⓐ Ⓑ Ⓒ Ⓓ Ⓔ
18. Ⓐ Ⓑ Ⓒ Ⓓ Ⓔ
19. Ⓐ Ⓑ Ⓒ Ⓓ Ⓔ
20. Ⓐ Ⓑ Ⓒ Ⓓ Ⓔ
21. Ⓐ Ⓑ Ⓒ Ⓓ Ⓔ
22. Ⓐ Ⓑ Ⓒ Ⓓ Ⓔ
23. Ⓐ Ⓑ Ⓒ Ⓓ Ⓔ
24. Ⓐ Ⓑ Ⓒ Ⓓ Ⓔ
25. Ⓐ Ⓑ Ⓒ Ⓓ Ⓔ
26. Ⓐ Ⓑ Ⓒ Ⓓ Ⓔ
27. Ⓐ Ⓑ Ⓒ Ⓓ Ⓔ
28. Ⓐ Ⓑ Ⓒ Ⓓ Ⓔ
29. Ⓐ Ⓑ Ⓒ Ⓓ Ⓔ
30. Ⓐ Ⓑ Ⓒ Ⓓ Ⓔ
31. Ⓐ Ⓑ Ⓒ Ⓓ Ⓔ
32. Ⓐ Ⓑ Ⓒ Ⓓ Ⓔ
33. Ⓐ Ⓑ Ⓒ Ⓓ Ⓔ
34. Ⓐ Ⓑ Ⓒ Ⓓ Ⓔ
35. Ⓐ Ⓑ Ⓒ Ⓓ Ⓔ
36. Ⓐ Ⓑ Ⓒ Ⓓ Ⓔ
37. Ⓐ Ⓑ Ⓒ Ⓓ Ⓔ
38. Ⓐ Ⓑ Ⓒ Ⓓ Ⓔ

SECTION 6

1. Ⓐ Ⓑ Ⓒ Ⓓ Ⓔ
2. Ⓐ Ⓑ Ⓒ Ⓓ Ⓔ
3. Ⓐ Ⓑ Ⓒ Ⓓ Ⓔ
4. Ⓐ Ⓑ Ⓒ Ⓓ Ⓔ
5. Ⓐ Ⓑ Ⓒ Ⓓ Ⓔ
6. Ⓐ Ⓑ Ⓒ Ⓓ Ⓔ
7. Ⓐ Ⓑ Ⓒ Ⓓ Ⓔ
8. Ⓐ Ⓑ Ⓒ Ⓓ Ⓔ
9. Ⓐ Ⓑ Ⓒ Ⓓ Ⓔ
10. Ⓐ Ⓑ Ⓒ Ⓓ Ⓔ
11. Ⓐ Ⓑ Ⓒ Ⓓ Ⓔ
12. Ⓐ Ⓑ Ⓒ Ⓓ Ⓔ
13. Ⓐ Ⓑ Ⓒ Ⓓ Ⓔ
14. Ⓐ Ⓑ Ⓒ Ⓓ Ⓔ
15. Ⓐ Ⓑ Ⓒ Ⓓ Ⓔ
16. Ⓐ Ⓑ Ⓒ Ⓓ Ⓔ
17. Ⓐ Ⓑ Ⓒ Ⓓ Ⓔ
18. Ⓐ Ⓑ Ⓒ Ⓓ Ⓔ
19. Ⓐ Ⓑ Ⓒ Ⓓ Ⓔ
20. Ⓐ Ⓑ Ⓒ Ⓓ Ⓔ
21. Ⓐ Ⓑ Ⓒ Ⓓ Ⓔ
22. Ⓐ Ⓑ Ⓒ Ⓓ Ⓔ
23. Ⓐ Ⓑ Ⓒ Ⓓ Ⓔ
24. Ⓐ Ⓑ Ⓒ Ⓓ Ⓔ
25. Ⓐ Ⓑ Ⓒ Ⓓ Ⓔ
26. Ⓐ Ⓑ Ⓒ Ⓓ Ⓔ
27. Ⓐ Ⓑ Ⓒ Ⓓ Ⓔ
28. Ⓐ Ⓑ Ⓒ Ⓓ Ⓔ
29. Ⓐ Ⓑ Ⓒ Ⓓ Ⓔ
30. Ⓐ Ⓑ Ⓒ Ⓓ Ⓔ
31. Ⓐ Ⓑ Ⓒ Ⓓ Ⓔ
32. Ⓐ Ⓑ Ⓒ Ⓓ Ⓔ
33. Ⓐ Ⓑ Ⓒ Ⓓ Ⓔ
34. Ⓐ Ⓑ Ⓒ Ⓓ Ⓔ
35. Ⓐ Ⓑ Ⓒ Ⓓ Ⓔ
36. Ⓐ Ⓑ Ⓒ Ⓓ Ⓔ
37. Ⓐ Ⓑ Ⓒ Ⓓ Ⓔ
38. Ⓐ Ⓑ Ⓒ Ⓓ Ⓔ

GRE General – Test 3
ANSWER SHEET

SECTION 3

1. Ⓐ Ⓑ Ⓒ Ⓓ Ⓔ
2. Ⓐ Ⓑ Ⓒ Ⓓ Ⓔ
3. Ⓐ Ⓑ Ⓒ Ⓓ Ⓔ
4. Ⓐ Ⓑ Ⓒ Ⓓ Ⓔ
5. Ⓐ Ⓑ Ⓒ Ⓓ Ⓔ
6. Ⓐ Ⓑ Ⓒ Ⓓ Ⓔ
7. Ⓐ Ⓑ Ⓒ Ⓓ Ⓔ
8. Ⓐ Ⓑ Ⓒ Ⓓ Ⓔ
9. Ⓐ Ⓑ Ⓒ Ⓓ Ⓔ
10. Ⓐ Ⓑ Ⓒ Ⓓ Ⓔ
11. Ⓐ Ⓑ Ⓒ Ⓓ Ⓔ
12. Ⓐ Ⓑ Ⓒ Ⓓ Ⓔ
13. Ⓐ Ⓑ Ⓒ Ⓓ Ⓔ
14. Ⓐ Ⓑ Ⓒ Ⓓ Ⓔ
15. Ⓐ Ⓑ Ⓒ Ⓓ Ⓔ
16. Ⓐ Ⓑ Ⓒ Ⓓ Ⓔ
17. Ⓐ Ⓑ Ⓒ Ⓓ Ⓔ
18. Ⓐ Ⓑ Ⓒ Ⓓ Ⓔ
19. Ⓐ Ⓑ Ⓒ Ⓓ Ⓔ
20. Ⓐ Ⓑ Ⓒ Ⓓ Ⓔ
21. Ⓐ Ⓑ Ⓒ Ⓓ Ⓔ
22. Ⓐ Ⓑ Ⓒ Ⓓ Ⓔ
23. Ⓐ Ⓑ Ⓒ Ⓓ Ⓔ
24. Ⓐ Ⓑ Ⓒ Ⓓ Ⓔ
25. Ⓐ Ⓑ Ⓒ Ⓓ Ⓔ
26. Ⓐ Ⓑ Ⓒ Ⓓ Ⓔ
27. Ⓐ Ⓑ Ⓒ Ⓓ Ⓔ
28. Ⓐ Ⓑ Ⓒ Ⓓ Ⓔ
29. Ⓐ Ⓑ Ⓒ Ⓓ Ⓔ
30. Ⓐ Ⓑ Ⓒ Ⓓ Ⓔ
31. Ⓐ Ⓑ Ⓒ Ⓓ Ⓔ
32. Ⓐ Ⓑ Ⓒ Ⓓ Ⓔ
33. Ⓐ Ⓑ Ⓒ Ⓓ Ⓔ
34. Ⓐ Ⓑ Ⓒ Ⓓ Ⓔ
35. Ⓐ Ⓑ Ⓒ Ⓓ Ⓔ
36. Ⓐ Ⓑ Ⓒ Ⓓ Ⓔ
37. Ⓐ Ⓑ Ⓒ Ⓓ Ⓔ
38. Ⓐ Ⓑ Ⓒ Ⓓ Ⓔ

SECTION 4

1. Ⓐ Ⓑ Ⓒ Ⓓ Ⓔ
2. Ⓐ Ⓑ Ⓒ Ⓓ Ⓔ
3. Ⓐ Ⓑ Ⓒ Ⓓ Ⓔ
4. Ⓐ Ⓑ Ⓒ Ⓓ Ⓔ
5. Ⓐ Ⓑ Ⓒ Ⓓ Ⓔ
6. Ⓐ Ⓑ Ⓒ Ⓓ Ⓔ
7. Ⓐ Ⓑ Ⓒ Ⓓ Ⓔ
8. Ⓐ Ⓑ Ⓒ Ⓓ Ⓔ
9. Ⓐ Ⓑ Ⓒ Ⓓ Ⓔ
10. Ⓐ Ⓑ Ⓒ Ⓓ Ⓔ
11. Ⓐ Ⓑ Ⓒ Ⓓ Ⓔ
12. Ⓐ Ⓑ Ⓒ Ⓓ Ⓔ
13. Ⓐ Ⓑ Ⓒ Ⓓ Ⓔ
14. Ⓐ Ⓑ Ⓒ Ⓓ Ⓔ
15. Ⓐ Ⓑ Ⓒ Ⓓ Ⓔ
16. Ⓐ Ⓑ Ⓒ Ⓓ Ⓔ
17. Ⓐ Ⓑ Ⓒ Ⓓ Ⓔ
18. Ⓐ Ⓑ Ⓒ Ⓓ Ⓔ
19. Ⓐ Ⓑ Ⓒ Ⓓ Ⓔ
20. Ⓐ Ⓑ Ⓒ Ⓓ Ⓔ
21. Ⓐ Ⓑ Ⓒ Ⓓ Ⓔ
22. Ⓐ Ⓑ Ⓒ Ⓓ Ⓔ
23. Ⓐ Ⓑ Ⓒ Ⓓ Ⓔ
24. Ⓐ Ⓑ Ⓒ Ⓓ Ⓔ
25. Ⓐ Ⓑ Ⓒ Ⓓ Ⓔ
26. Ⓐ Ⓑ Ⓒ Ⓓ Ⓔ
27. Ⓐ Ⓑ Ⓒ Ⓓ Ⓔ
28. Ⓐ Ⓑ Ⓒ Ⓓ Ⓔ
29. Ⓐ Ⓑ Ⓒ Ⓓ Ⓔ
30. Ⓐ Ⓑ Ⓒ Ⓓ Ⓔ
31. Ⓐ Ⓑ Ⓒ Ⓓ Ⓔ
32. Ⓐ Ⓑ Ⓒ Ⓓ Ⓔ
33. Ⓐ Ⓑ Ⓒ Ⓓ Ⓔ
34. Ⓐ Ⓑ Ⓒ Ⓓ Ⓔ
35. Ⓐ Ⓑ Ⓒ Ⓓ Ⓔ
36. Ⓐ Ⓑ Ⓒ Ⓓ Ⓔ
37. Ⓐ Ⓑ Ⓒ Ⓓ Ⓔ
38. Ⓐ Ⓑ Ⓒ Ⓓ Ⓔ

SECTION 5

1. Ⓐ Ⓑ Ⓒ Ⓓ Ⓔ
2. Ⓐ Ⓑ Ⓒ Ⓓ Ⓔ
3. Ⓐ Ⓑ Ⓒ Ⓓ Ⓔ
4. Ⓐ Ⓑ Ⓒ Ⓓ Ⓔ
5. Ⓐ Ⓑ Ⓒ Ⓓ Ⓔ
6. Ⓐ Ⓑ Ⓒ Ⓓ Ⓔ
7. Ⓐ Ⓑ Ⓒ Ⓓ Ⓔ
8. Ⓐ Ⓑ Ⓒ Ⓓ Ⓔ
9. Ⓐ Ⓑ Ⓒ Ⓓ Ⓔ
10. Ⓐ Ⓑ Ⓒ Ⓓ Ⓔ
11. Ⓐ Ⓑ Ⓒ Ⓓ Ⓔ
12. Ⓐ Ⓑ Ⓒ Ⓓ Ⓔ
13. Ⓐ Ⓑ Ⓒ Ⓓ Ⓔ
14. Ⓐ Ⓑ Ⓒ Ⓓ Ⓔ
15. Ⓐ Ⓑ Ⓒ Ⓓ Ⓔ
16. Ⓐ Ⓑ Ⓒ Ⓓ Ⓔ
17. Ⓐ Ⓑ Ⓒ Ⓓ Ⓔ
18. Ⓐ Ⓑ Ⓒ Ⓓ Ⓔ
19. Ⓐ Ⓑ Ⓒ Ⓓ Ⓔ
20. Ⓐ Ⓑ Ⓒ Ⓓ Ⓔ
21. Ⓐ Ⓑ Ⓒ Ⓓ Ⓔ
22. Ⓐ Ⓑ Ⓒ Ⓓ Ⓔ
23. Ⓐ Ⓑ Ⓒ Ⓓ Ⓔ
24. Ⓐ Ⓑ Ⓒ Ⓓ Ⓔ
25. Ⓐ Ⓑ Ⓒ Ⓓ Ⓔ
26. Ⓐ Ⓑ Ⓒ Ⓓ Ⓔ
27. Ⓐ Ⓑ Ⓒ Ⓓ Ⓔ
28. Ⓐ Ⓑ Ⓒ Ⓓ Ⓔ
29. Ⓐ Ⓑ Ⓒ Ⓓ Ⓔ
30. Ⓐ Ⓑ Ⓒ Ⓓ Ⓔ
31. Ⓐ Ⓑ Ⓒ Ⓓ Ⓔ
32. Ⓐ Ⓑ Ⓒ Ⓓ Ⓔ
33. Ⓐ Ⓑ Ⓒ Ⓓ Ⓔ
34. Ⓐ Ⓑ Ⓒ Ⓓ Ⓔ
35. Ⓐ Ⓑ Ⓒ Ⓓ Ⓔ
36. Ⓐ Ⓑ Ⓒ Ⓓ Ⓔ
37. Ⓐ Ⓑ Ⓒ Ⓓ Ⓔ
38. Ⓐ Ⓑ Ⓒ Ⓓ Ⓔ

SECTION 6

1. Ⓐ Ⓑ Ⓒ Ⓓ Ⓔ
2. Ⓐ Ⓑ Ⓒ Ⓓ Ⓔ
3. Ⓐ Ⓑ Ⓒ Ⓓ Ⓔ
4. Ⓐ Ⓑ Ⓒ Ⓓ Ⓔ
5. Ⓐ Ⓑ Ⓒ Ⓓ Ⓔ
6. Ⓐ Ⓑ Ⓒ Ⓓ Ⓔ
7. Ⓐ Ⓑ Ⓒ Ⓓ Ⓔ
8. Ⓐ Ⓑ Ⓒ Ⓓ Ⓔ
9. Ⓐ Ⓑ Ⓒ Ⓓ Ⓔ
10. Ⓐ Ⓑ Ⓒ Ⓓ Ⓔ
11. Ⓐ Ⓑ Ⓒ Ⓓ Ⓔ
12. Ⓐ Ⓑ Ⓒ Ⓓ Ⓔ
13. Ⓐ Ⓑ Ⓒ Ⓓ Ⓔ
14. Ⓐ Ⓑ Ⓒ Ⓓ Ⓔ
15. Ⓐ Ⓑ Ⓒ Ⓓ Ⓔ
16. Ⓐ Ⓑ Ⓒ Ⓓ Ⓔ
17. Ⓐ Ⓑ Ⓒ Ⓓ Ⓔ
18. Ⓐ Ⓑ Ⓒ Ⓓ Ⓔ
19. Ⓐ Ⓑ Ⓒ Ⓓ Ⓔ
20. Ⓐ Ⓑ Ⓒ Ⓓ Ⓔ
21. Ⓐ Ⓑ Ⓒ Ⓓ Ⓔ
22. Ⓐ Ⓑ Ⓒ Ⓓ Ⓔ
23. Ⓐ Ⓑ Ⓒ Ⓓ Ⓔ
24. Ⓐ Ⓑ Ⓒ Ⓓ Ⓔ
25. Ⓐ Ⓑ Ⓒ Ⓓ Ⓔ
26. Ⓐ Ⓑ Ⓒ Ⓓ Ⓔ
27. Ⓐ Ⓑ Ⓒ Ⓓ Ⓔ
28. Ⓐ Ⓑ Ⓒ Ⓓ Ⓔ
29. Ⓐ Ⓑ Ⓒ Ⓓ Ⓔ
30. Ⓐ Ⓑ Ⓒ Ⓓ Ⓔ
31. Ⓐ Ⓑ Ⓒ Ⓓ Ⓔ
32. Ⓐ Ⓑ Ⓒ Ⓓ Ⓔ
33. Ⓐ Ⓑ Ⓒ Ⓓ Ⓔ
34. Ⓐ Ⓑ Ⓒ Ⓓ Ⓔ
35. Ⓐ Ⓑ Ⓒ Ⓓ Ⓔ
36. Ⓐ Ⓑ Ⓒ Ⓓ Ⓔ
37. Ⓐ Ⓑ Ⓒ Ⓓ Ⓔ
38. Ⓐ Ⓑ Ⓒ Ⓓ Ⓔ

GRE General – Test 4
ANSWER SHEET

SECTION 3

1. Ⓐ Ⓑ Ⓒ Ⓓ Ⓔ
2. Ⓐ Ⓑ Ⓒ Ⓓ Ⓔ
3. Ⓐ Ⓑ Ⓒ Ⓓ Ⓔ
4. Ⓐ Ⓑ Ⓒ Ⓓ Ⓔ
5. Ⓐ Ⓑ Ⓒ Ⓓ Ⓔ
6. Ⓐ Ⓑ Ⓒ Ⓓ Ⓔ
7. Ⓐ Ⓑ Ⓒ Ⓓ Ⓔ
8. Ⓐ Ⓑ Ⓒ Ⓓ Ⓔ
9. Ⓐ Ⓑ Ⓒ Ⓓ Ⓔ
10. Ⓐ Ⓑ Ⓒ Ⓓ Ⓔ
11. Ⓐ Ⓑ Ⓒ Ⓓ Ⓔ
12. Ⓐ Ⓑ Ⓒ Ⓓ Ⓔ
13. Ⓐ Ⓑ Ⓒ Ⓓ Ⓔ
14. Ⓐ Ⓑ Ⓒ Ⓓ Ⓔ
15. Ⓐ Ⓑ Ⓒ Ⓓ Ⓔ
16. Ⓐ Ⓑ Ⓒ Ⓓ Ⓔ
17. Ⓐ Ⓑ Ⓒ Ⓓ Ⓔ
18. Ⓐ Ⓑ Ⓒ Ⓓ Ⓔ
19. Ⓐ Ⓑ Ⓒ Ⓓ Ⓔ
20. Ⓐ Ⓑ Ⓒ Ⓓ Ⓔ
21. Ⓐ Ⓑ Ⓒ Ⓓ Ⓔ
22. Ⓐ Ⓑ Ⓒ Ⓓ Ⓔ
23. Ⓐ Ⓑ Ⓒ Ⓓ Ⓔ
24. Ⓐ Ⓑ Ⓒ Ⓓ Ⓔ
25. Ⓐ Ⓑ Ⓒ Ⓓ Ⓔ
26. Ⓐ Ⓑ Ⓒ Ⓓ Ⓔ
27. Ⓐ Ⓑ Ⓒ Ⓓ Ⓔ
28. Ⓐ Ⓑ Ⓒ Ⓓ Ⓔ
29. Ⓐ Ⓑ Ⓒ Ⓓ Ⓔ
30. Ⓐ Ⓑ Ⓒ Ⓓ Ⓔ
31. Ⓐ Ⓑ Ⓒ Ⓓ Ⓔ
32. Ⓐ Ⓑ Ⓒ Ⓓ Ⓔ
33. Ⓐ Ⓑ Ⓒ Ⓓ Ⓔ
34. Ⓐ Ⓑ Ⓒ Ⓓ Ⓔ
35. Ⓐ Ⓑ Ⓒ Ⓓ Ⓔ
36. Ⓐ Ⓑ Ⓒ Ⓓ Ⓔ
37. Ⓐ Ⓑ Ⓒ Ⓓ Ⓔ
38. Ⓐ Ⓑ Ⓒ Ⓓ Ⓔ

SECTION 4

1. Ⓐ Ⓑ Ⓒ Ⓓ Ⓔ
2. Ⓐ Ⓑ Ⓒ Ⓓ Ⓔ
3. Ⓐ Ⓑ Ⓒ Ⓓ Ⓔ
4. Ⓐ Ⓑ Ⓒ Ⓓ Ⓔ
5. Ⓐ Ⓑ Ⓒ Ⓓ Ⓔ
6. Ⓐ Ⓑ Ⓒ Ⓓ Ⓔ
7. Ⓐ Ⓑ Ⓒ Ⓓ Ⓔ
8. Ⓐ Ⓑ Ⓒ Ⓓ Ⓔ
9. Ⓐ Ⓑ Ⓒ Ⓓ Ⓔ
10. Ⓐ Ⓑ Ⓒ Ⓓ Ⓔ
11. Ⓐ Ⓑ Ⓒ Ⓓ Ⓔ
12. Ⓐ Ⓑ Ⓒ Ⓓ Ⓔ
13. Ⓐ Ⓑ Ⓒ Ⓓ Ⓔ
14. Ⓐ Ⓑ Ⓒ Ⓓ Ⓔ
15. Ⓐ Ⓑ Ⓒ Ⓓ Ⓔ
16. Ⓐ Ⓑ Ⓒ Ⓓ Ⓔ
17. Ⓐ Ⓑ Ⓒ Ⓓ Ⓔ
18. Ⓐ Ⓑ Ⓒ Ⓓ Ⓔ
19. Ⓐ Ⓑ Ⓒ Ⓓ Ⓔ
20. Ⓐ Ⓑ Ⓒ Ⓓ Ⓔ
21. Ⓐ Ⓑ Ⓒ Ⓓ Ⓔ
22. Ⓐ Ⓑ Ⓒ Ⓓ Ⓔ
23. Ⓐ Ⓑ Ⓒ Ⓓ Ⓔ
24. Ⓐ Ⓑ Ⓒ Ⓓ Ⓔ
25. Ⓐ Ⓑ Ⓒ Ⓓ Ⓔ
26. Ⓐ Ⓑ Ⓒ Ⓓ Ⓔ
27. Ⓐ Ⓑ Ⓒ Ⓓ Ⓔ
28. Ⓐ Ⓑ Ⓒ Ⓓ Ⓔ
29. Ⓐ Ⓑ Ⓒ Ⓓ Ⓔ
30. Ⓐ Ⓑ Ⓒ Ⓓ Ⓔ
31. Ⓐ Ⓑ Ⓒ Ⓓ Ⓔ
32. Ⓐ Ⓑ Ⓒ Ⓓ Ⓔ
33. Ⓐ Ⓑ Ⓒ Ⓓ Ⓔ
34. Ⓐ Ⓑ Ⓒ Ⓓ Ⓔ
35. Ⓐ Ⓑ Ⓒ Ⓓ Ⓔ
36. Ⓐ Ⓑ Ⓒ Ⓓ Ⓔ
37. Ⓐ Ⓑ Ⓒ Ⓓ Ⓔ
38. Ⓐ Ⓑ Ⓒ Ⓓ Ⓔ

SECTION 5

1. Ⓐ Ⓑ Ⓒ Ⓓ Ⓔ
2. Ⓐ Ⓑ Ⓒ Ⓓ Ⓔ
3. Ⓐ Ⓑ Ⓒ Ⓓ Ⓔ
4. Ⓐ Ⓑ Ⓒ Ⓓ Ⓔ
5. Ⓐ Ⓑ Ⓒ Ⓓ Ⓔ
6. Ⓐ Ⓑ Ⓒ Ⓓ Ⓔ
7. Ⓐ Ⓑ Ⓒ Ⓓ Ⓔ
8. Ⓐ Ⓑ Ⓒ Ⓓ Ⓔ
9. Ⓐ Ⓑ Ⓒ Ⓓ Ⓔ
10. Ⓐ Ⓑ Ⓒ Ⓓ Ⓔ
11. Ⓐ Ⓑ Ⓒ Ⓓ Ⓔ
12. Ⓐ Ⓑ Ⓒ Ⓓ Ⓔ
13. Ⓐ Ⓑ Ⓒ Ⓓ Ⓔ
14. Ⓐ Ⓑ Ⓒ Ⓓ Ⓔ
15. Ⓐ Ⓑ Ⓒ Ⓓ Ⓔ
16. Ⓐ Ⓑ Ⓒ Ⓓ Ⓔ
17. Ⓐ Ⓑ Ⓒ Ⓓ Ⓔ
18. Ⓐ Ⓑ Ⓒ Ⓓ Ⓔ
19. Ⓐ Ⓑ Ⓒ Ⓓ Ⓔ
20. Ⓐ Ⓑ Ⓒ Ⓓ Ⓔ
21. Ⓐ Ⓑ Ⓒ Ⓓ Ⓔ
22. Ⓐ Ⓑ Ⓒ Ⓓ Ⓔ
23. Ⓐ Ⓑ Ⓒ Ⓓ Ⓔ
24. Ⓐ Ⓑ Ⓒ Ⓓ Ⓔ
25. Ⓐ Ⓑ Ⓒ Ⓓ Ⓔ
26. Ⓐ Ⓑ Ⓒ Ⓓ Ⓔ
27. Ⓐ Ⓑ Ⓒ Ⓓ Ⓔ
28. Ⓐ Ⓑ Ⓒ Ⓓ Ⓔ
29. Ⓐ Ⓑ Ⓒ Ⓓ Ⓔ
30. Ⓐ Ⓑ Ⓒ Ⓓ Ⓔ
31. Ⓐ Ⓑ Ⓒ Ⓓ Ⓔ
32. Ⓐ Ⓑ Ⓒ Ⓓ Ⓔ
33. Ⓐ Ⓑ Ⓒ Ⓓ Ⓔ
34. Ⓐ Ⓑ Ⓒ Ⓓ Ⓔ
35. Ⓐ Ⓑ Ⓒ Ⓓ Ⓔ
36. Ⓐ Ⓑ Ⓒ Ⓓ Ⓔ
37. Ⓐ Ⓑ Ⓒ Ⓓ Ⓔ
38. Ⓐ Ⓑ Ⓒ Ⓓ Ⓔ

SECTION 6

1. Ⓐ Ⓑ Ⓒ Ⓓ Ⓔ
2. Ⓐ Ⓑ Ⓒ Ⓓ Ⓔ
3. Ⓐ Ⓑ Ⓒ Ⓓ Ⓔ
4. Ⓐ Ⓑ Ⓒ Ⓓ Ⓔ
5. Ⓐ Ⓑ Ⓒ Ⓓ Ⓔ
6. Ⓐ Ⓑ Ⓒ Ⓓ Ⓔ
7. Ⓐ Ⓑ Ⓒ Ⓓ Ⓔ
8. Ⓐ Ⓑ Ⓒ Ⓓ Ⓔ
9. Ⓐ Ⓑ Ⓒ Ⓓ Ⓔ
10. Ⓐ Ⓑ Ⓒ Ⓓ Ⓔ
11. Ⓐ Ⓑ Ⓒ Ⓓ Ⓔ
12. Ⓐ Ⓑ Ⓒ Ⓓ Ⓔ
13. Ⓐ Ⓑ Ⓒ Ⓓ Ⓔ
14. Ⓐ Ⓑ Ⓒ Ⓓ Ⓔ
15. Ⓐ Ⓑ Ⓒ Ⓓ Ⓔ
16. Ⓐ Ⓑ Ⓒ Ⓓ Ⓔ
17. Ⓐ Ⓑ Ⓒ Ⓓ Ⓔ
18. Ⓐ Ⓑ Ⓒ Ⓓ Ⓔ
19. Ⓐ Ⓑ Ⓒ Ⓓ Ⓔ
20. Ⓐ Ⓑ Ⓒ Ⓓ Ⓔ
21. Ⓐ Ⓑ Ⓒ Ⓓ Ⓔ
22. Ⓐ Ⓑ Ⓒ Ⓓ Ⓔ
23. Ⓐ Ⓑ Ⓒ Ⓓ Ⓔ
24. Ⓐ Ⓑ Ⓒ Ⓓ Ⓔ
25. Ⓐ Ⓑ Ⓒ Ⓓ Ⓔ
26. Ⓐ Ⓑ Ⓒ Ⓓ Ⓔ
27. Ⓐ Ⓑ Ⓒ Ⓓ Ⓔ
28. Ⓐ Ⓑ Ⓒ Ⓓ Ⓔ
29. Ⓐ Ⓑ Ⓒ Ⓓ Ⓔ
30. Ⓐ Ⓑ Ⓒ Ⓓ Ⓔ
31. Ⓐ Ⓑ Ⓒ Ⓓ Ⓔ
32. Ⓐ Ⓑ Ⓒ Ⓓ Ⓔ
33. Ⓐ Ⓑ Ⓒ Ⓓ Ⓔ
34. Ⓐ Ⓑ Ⓒ Ⓓ Ⓔ
35. Ⓐ Ⓑ Ⓒ Ⓓ Ⓔ
36. Ⓐ Ⓑ Ⓒ Ⓓ Ⓔ
37. Ⓐ Ⓑ Ⓒ Ⓓ Ⓔ
38. Ⓐ Ⓑ Ⓒ Ⓓ Ⓔ

GRE General – Test 5
ANSWER SHEET

SECTION 3

1. Ⓐ Ⓑ Ⓒ Ⓓ Ⓔ
2. Ⓐ Ⓑ Ⓒ Ⓓ Ⓔ
3. Ⓐ Ⓑ Ⓒ Ⓓ Ⓔ
4. Ⓐ Ⓑ Ⓒ Ⓓ Ⓔ
5. Ⓐ Ⓑ Ⓒ Ⓓ Ⓔ
6. Ⓐ Ⓑ Ⓒ Ⓓ Ⓔ
7. Ⓐ Ⓑ Ⓒ Ⓓ Ⓔ
8. Ⓐ Ⓑ Ⓒ Ⓓ Ⓔ
9. Ⓐ Ⓑ Ⓒ Ⓓ Ⓔ
10. Ⓐ Ⓑ Ⓒ Ⓓ Ⓔ
11. Ⓐ Ⓑ Ⓒ Ⓓ Ⓔ
12. Ⓐ Ⓑ Ⓒ Ⓓ Ⓔ
13. Ⓐ Ⓑ Ⓒ Ⓓ Ⓔ
14. Ⓐ Ⓑ Ⓒ Ⓓ Ⓔ
15. Ⓐ Ⓑ Ⓒ Ⓓ Ⓔ
16. Ⓐ Ⓑ Ⓒ Ⓓ Ⓔ
17. Ⓐ Ⓑ Ⓒ Ⓓ Ⓔ
18. Ⓐ Ⓑ Ⓒ Ⓓ Ⓔ
19. Ⓐ Ⓑ Ⓒ Ⓓ Ⓔ
20. Ⓐ Ⓑ Ⓒ Ⓓ Ⓔ
21. Ⓐ Ⓑ Ⓒ Ⓓ Ⓔ
22. Ⓐ Ⓑ Ⓒ Ⓓ Ⓔ
23. Ⓐ Ⓑ Ⓒ Ⓓ Ⓔ
24. Ⓐ Ⓑ Ⓒ Ⓓ Ⓔ
25. Ⓐ Ⓑ Ⓒ Ⓓ Ⓔ
26. Ⓐ Ⓑ Ⓒ Ⓓ Ⓔ
27. Ⓐ Ⓑ Ⓒ Ⓓ Ⓔ
28. Ⓐ Ⓑ Ⓒ Ⓓ Ⓔ
29. Ⓐ Ⓑ Ⓒ Ⓓ Ⓔ
30. Ⓐ Ⓑ Ⓒ Ⓓ Ⓔ
31. Ⓐ Ⓑ Ⓒ Ⓓ Ⓔ
32. Ⓐ Ⓑ Ⓒ Ⓓ Ⓔ
33. Ⓐ Ⓑ Ⓒ Ⓓ Ⓔ
34. Ⓐ Ⓑ Ⓒ Ⓓ Ⓔ
35. Ⓐ Ⓑ Ⓒ Ⓓ Ⓔ
36. Ⓐ Ⓑ Ⓒ Ⓓ Ⓔ
37. Ⓐ Ⓑ Ⓒ Ⓓ Ⓔ
38. Ⓐ Ⓑ Ⓒ Ⓓ Ⓔ

SECTION 4

1. Ⓐ Ⓑ Ⓒ Ⓓ Ⓔ
2. Ⓐ Ⓑ Ⓒ Ⓓ Ⓔ
3. Ⓐ Ⓑ Ⓒ Ⓓ Ⓔ
4. Ⓐ Ⓑ Ⓒ Ⓓ Ⓔ
5. Ⓐ Ⓑ Ⓒ Ⓓ Ⓔ
6. Ⓐ Ⓑ Ⓒ Ⓓ Ⓔ
7. Ⓐ Ⓑ Ⓒ Ⓓ Ⓔ
8. Ⓐ Ⓑ Ⓒ Ⓓ Ⓔ
9. Ⓐ Ⓑ Ⓒ Ⓓ Ⓔ
10. Ⓐ Ⓑ Ⓒ Ⓓ Ⓔ
11. Ⓐ Ⓑ Ⓒ Ⓓ Ⓔ
12. Ⓐ Ⓑ Ⓒ Ⓓ Ⓔ
13. Ⓐ Ⓑ Ⓒ Ⓓ Ⓔ
14. Ⓐ Ⓑ Ⓒ Ⓓ Ⓔ
15. Ⓐ Ⓑ Ⓒ Ⓓ Ⓔ
16. Ⓐ Ⓑ Ⓒ Ⓓ Ⓔ
17. Ⓐ Ⓑ Ⓒ Ⓓ Ⓔ
18. Ⓐ Ⓑ Ⓒ Ⓓ Ⓔ
19. Ⓐ Ⓑ Ⓒ Ⓓ Ⓔ
20. Ⓐ Ⓑ Ⓒ Ⓓ Ⓔ
21. Ⓐ Ⓑ Ⓒ Ⓓ Ⓔ
22. Ⓐ Ⓑ Ⓒ Ⓓ Ⓔ
23. Ⓐ Ⓑ Ⓒ Ⓓ Ⓔ
24. Ⓐ Ⓑ Ⓒ Ⓓ Ⓔ
25. Ⓐ Ⓑ Ⓒ Ⓓ Ⓔ
26. Ⓐ Ⓑ Ⓒ Ⓓ Ⓔ
27. Ⓐ Ⓑ Ⓒ Ⓓ Ⓔ
28. Ⓐ Ⓑ Ⓒ Ⓓ Ⓔ
29. Ⓐ Ⓑ Ⓒ Ⓓ Ⓔ
30. Ⓐ Ⓑ Ⓒ Ⓓ Ⓔ
31. Ⓐ Ⓑ Ⓒ Ⓓ Ⓔ
32. Ⓐ Ⓑ Ⓒ Ⓓ Ⓔ
33. Ⓐ Ⓑ Ⓒ Ⓓ Ⓔ
34. Ⓐ Ⓑ Ⓒ Ⓓ Ⓔ
35. Ⓐ Ⓑ Ⓒ Ⓓ Ⓔ
36. Ⓐ Ⓑ Ⓒ Ⓓ Ⓔ
37. Ⓐ Ⓑ Ⓒ Ⓓ Ⓔ
38. Ⓐ Ⓑ Ⓒ Ⓓ Ⓔ

SECTION 5

1. Ⓐ Ⓑ Ⓒ Ⓓ Ⓔ
2. Ⓐ Ⓑ Ⓒ Ⓓ Ⓔ
3. Ⓐ Ⓑ Ⓒ Ⓓ Ⓔ
4. Ⓐ Ⓑ Ⓒ Ⓓ Ⓔ
5. Ⓐ Ⓑ Ⓒ Ⓓ Ⓔ
6. Ⓐ Ⓑ Ⓒ Ⓓ Ⓔ
7. Ⓐ Ⓑ Ⓒ Ⓓ Ⓔ
8. Ⓐ Ⓑ Ⓒ Ⓓ Ⓔ
9. Ⓐ Ⓑ Ⓒ Ⓓ Ⓔ
10. Ⓐ Ⓑ Ⓒ Ⓓ Ⓔ
11. Ⓐ Ⓑ Ⓒ Ⓓ Ⓔ
12. Ⓐ Ⓑ Ⓒ Ⓓ Ⓔ
13. Ⓐ Ⓑ Ⓒ Ⓓ Ⓔ
14. Ⓐ Ⓑ Ⓒ Ⓓ Ⓔ
15. Ⓐ Ⓑ Ⓒ Ⓓ Ⓔ
16. Ⓐ Ⓑ Ⓒ Ⓓ Ⓔ
17. Ⓐ Ⓑ Ⓒ Ⓓ Ⓔ
18. Ⓐ Ⓑ Ⓒ Ⓓ Ⓔ
19. Ⓐ Ⓑ Ⓒ Ⓓ Ⓔ
20. Ⓐ Ⓑ Ⓒ Ⓓ Ⓔ
21. Ⓐ Ⓑ Ⓒ Ⓓ Ⓔ
22. Ⓐ Ⓑ Ⓒ Ⓓ Ⓔ
23. Ⓐ Ⓑ Ⓒ Ⓓ Ⓔ
24. Ⓐ Ⓑ Ⓒ Ⓓ Ⓔ
25. Ⓐ Ⓑ Ⓒ Ⓓ Ⓔ
26. Ⓐ Ⓑ Ⓒ Ⓓ Ⓔ
27. Ⓐ Ⓑ Ⓒ Ⓓ Ⓔ
28. Ⓐ Ⓑ Ⓒ Ⓓ Ⓔ
29. Ⓐ Ⓑ Ⓒ Ⓓ Ⓔ
30. Ⓐ Ⓑ Ⓒ Ⓓ Ⓔ
31. Ⓐ Ⓑ Ⓒ Ⓓ Ⓔ
32. Ⓐ Ⓑ Ⓒ Ⓓ Ⓔ
33. Ⓐ Ⓑ Ⓒ Ⓓ Ⓔ
34. Ⓐ Ⓑ Ⓒ Ⓓ Ⓔ
35. Ⓐ Ⓑ Ⓒ Ⓓ Ⓔ
36. Ⓐ Ⓑ Ⓒ Ⓓ Ⓔ
37. Ⓐ Ⓑ Ⓒ Ⓓ Ⓔ
38. Ⓐ Ⓑ Ⓒ Ⓓ Ⓔ

SECTION 6

1. Ⓐ Ⓑ Ⓒ Ⓓ Ⓔ
2. Ⓐ Ⓑ Ⓒ Ⓓ Ⓔ
3. Ⓐ Ⓑ Ⓒ Ⓓ Ⓔ
4. Ⓐ Ⓑ Ⓒ Ⓓ Ⓔ
5. Ⓐ Ⓑ Ⓒ Ⓓ Ⓔ
6. Ⓐ Ⓑ Ⓒ Ⓓ Ⓔ
7. Ⓐ Ⓑ Ⓒ Ⓓ Ⓔ
8. Ⓐ Ⓑ Ⓒ Ⓓ Ⓔ
9. Ⓐ Ⓑ Ⓒ Ⓓ Ⓔ
10. Ⓐ Ⓑ Ⓒ Ⓓ Ⓔ
11. Ⓐ Ⓑ Ⓒ Ⓓ Ⓔ
12. Ⓐ Ⓑ Ⓒ Ⓓ Ⓔ
13. Ⓐ Ⓑ Ⓒ Ⓓ Ⓔ
14. Ⓐ Ⓑ Ⓒ Ⓓ Ⓔ
15. Ⓐ Ⓑ Ⓒ Ⓓ Ⓔ
16. Ⓐ Ⓑ Ⓒ Ⓓ Ⓔ
17. Ⓐ Ⓑ Ⓒ Ⓓ Ⓔ
18. Ⓐ Ⓑ Ⓒ Ⓓ Ⓔ
19. Ⓐ Ⓑ Ⓒ Ⓓ Ⓔ
20. Ⓐ Ⓑ Ⓒ Ⓓ Ⓔ
21. Ⓐ Ⓑ Ⓒ Ⓓ Ⓔ
22. Ⓐ Ⓑ Ⓒ Ⓓ Ⓔ
23. Ⓐ Ⓑ Ⓒ Ⓓ Ⓔ
24. Ⓐ Ⓑ Ⓒ Ⓓ Ⓔ
25. Ⓐ Ⓑ Ⓒ Ⓓ Ⓔ
26. Ⓐ Ⓑ Ⓒ Ⓓ Ⓔ
27. Ⓐ Ⓑ Ⓒ Ⓓ Ⓔ
28. Ⓐ Ⓑ Ⓒ Ⓓ Ⓔ
29. Ⓐ Ⓑ Ⓒ Ⓓ Ⓔ
30. Ⓐ Ⓑ Ⓒ Ⓓ Ⓔ
31. Ⓐ Ⓑ Ⓒ Ⓓ Ⓔ
32. Ⓐ Ⓑ Ⓒ Ⓓ Ⓔ
33. Ⓐ Ⓑ Ⓒ Ⓓ Ⓔ
34. Ⓐ Ⓑ Ⓒ Ⓓ Ⓔ
35. Ⓐ Ⓑ Ⓒ Ⓓ Ⓔ
36. Ⓐ Ⓑ Ⓒ Ⓓ Ⓔ
37. Ⓐ Ⓑ Ⓒ Ⓓ Ⓔ
38. Ⓐ Ⓑ Ⓒ Ⓓ Ⓔ

GRE General – Test 6
ANSWER SHEET

SECTION 3

1. Ⓐ Ⓑ Ⓒ Ⓓ Ⓔ
2. Ⓐ Ⓑ Ⓒ Ⓓ Ⓔ
3. Ⓐ Ⓑ Ⓒ Ⓓ Ⓔ
4. Ⓐ Ⓑ Ⓒ Ⓓ Ⓔ
5. Ⓐ Ⓑ Ⓒ Ⓓ Ⓔ
6. Ⓐ Ⓑ Ⓒ Ⓓ Ⓔ
7. Ⓐ Ⓑ Ⓒ Ⓓ Ⓔ
8. Ⓐ Ⓑ Ⓒ Ⓓ Ⓔ
9. Ⓐ Ⓑ Ⓒ Ⓓ Ⓔ
10. Ⓐ Ⓑ Ⓒ Ⓓ Ⓔ
11. Ⓐ Ⓑ Ⓒ Ⓓ Ⓔ
12. Ⓐ Ⓑ Ⓒ Ⓓ Ⓔ
13. Ⓐ Ⓑ Ⓒ Ⓓ Ⓔ
14. Ⓐ Ⓑ Ⓒ Ⓓ Ⓔ
15. Ⓐ Ⓑ Ⓒ Ⓓ Ⓔ
16. Ⓐ Ⓑ Ⓒ Ⓓ Ⓔ
17. Ⓐ Ⓑ Ⓒ Ⓓ Ⓔ
18. Ⓐ Ⓑ Ⓒ Ⓓ Ⓔ
19. Ⓐ Ⓑ Ⓒ Ⓓ Ⓔ
20. Ⓐ Ⓑ Ⓒ Ⓓ Ⓔ
21. Ⓐ Ⓑ Ⓒ Ⓓ Ⓔ
22. Ⓐ Ⓑ Ⓒ Ⓓ Ⓔ
23. Ⓐ Ⓑ Ⓒ Ⓓ Ⓔ
24. Ⓐ Ⓑ Ⓒ Ⓓ Ⓔ
25. Ⓐ Ⓑ Ⓒ Ⓓ Ⓔ
26. Ⓐ Ⓑ Ⓒ Ⓓ Ⓔ
27. Ⓐ Ⓑ Ⓒ Ⓓ Ⓔ
28. Ⓐ Ⓑ Ⓒ Ⓓ Ⓔ
29. Ⓐ Ⓑ Ⓒ Ⓓ Ⓔ
30. Ⓐ Ⓑ Ⓒ Ⓓ Ⓔ
31. Ⓐ Ⓑ Ⓒ Ⓓ Ⓔ
32. Ⓐ Ⓑ Ⓒ Ⓓ Ⓔ
33. Ⓐ Ⓑ Ⓒ Ⓓ Ⓔ
34. Ⓐ Ⓑ Ⓒ Ⓓ Ⓔ
35. Ⓐ Ⓑ Ⓒ Ⓓ Ⓔ
36. Ⓐ Ⓑ Ⓒ Ⓓ Ⓔ
37. Ⓐ Ⓑ Ⓒ Ⓓ Ⓔ
38. Ⓐ Ⓑ Ⓒ Ⓓ Ⓔ

SECTION 4

1. Ⓐ Ⓑ Ⓒ Ⓓ Ⓔ
2. Ⓐ Ⓑ Ⓒ Ⓓ Ⓔ
3. Ⓐ Ⓑ Ⓒ Ⓓ Ⓔ
4. Ⓐ Ⓑ Ⓒ Ⓓ Ⓔ
5. Ⓐ Ⓑ Ⓒ Ⓓ Ⓔ
6. Ⓐ Ⓑ Ⓒ Ⓓ Ⓔ
7. Ⓐ Ⓑ Ⓒ Ⓓ Ⓔ
8. Ⓐ Ⓑ Ⓒ Ⓓ Ⓔ
9. Ⓐ Ⓑ Ⓒ Ⓓ Ⓔ
10. Ⓐ Ⓑ Ⓒ Ⓓ Ⓔ
11. Ⓐ Ⓑ Ⓒ Ⓓ Ⓔ
12. Ⓐ Ⓑ Ⓒ Ⓓ Ⓔ
13. Ⓐ Ⓑ Ⓒ Ⓓ Ⓔ
14. Ⓐ Ⓑ Ⓒ Ⓓ Ⓔ
15. Ⓐ Ⓑ Ⓒ Ⓓ Ⓔ
16. Ⓐ Ⓑ Ⓒ Ⓓ Ⓔ
17. Ⓐ Ⓑ Ⓒ Ⓓ Ⓔ
18. Ⓐ Ⓑ Ⓒ Ⓓ Ⓔ
19. Ⓐ Ⓑ Ⓒ Ⓓ Ⓔ
20. Ⓐ Ⓑ Ⓒ Ⓓ Ⓔ
21. Ⓐ Ⓑ Ⓒ Ⓓ Ⓔ
22. Ⓐ Ⓑ Ⓒ Ⓓ Ⓔ
23. Ⓐ Ⓑ Ⓒ Ⓓ Ⓔ
24. Ⓐ Ⓑ Ⓒ Ⓓ Ⓔ
25. Ⓐ Ⓑ Ⓒ Ⓓ Ⓔ
26. Ⓐ Ⓑ Ⓒ Ⓓ Ⓔ
27. Ⓐ Ⓑ Ⓒ Ⓓ Ⓔ
28. Ⓐ Ⓑ Ⓒ Ⓓ Ⓔ
29. Ⓐ Ⓑ Ⓒ Ⓓ Ⓔ
30. Ⓐ Ⓑ Ⓒ Ⓓ Ⓔ
31. Ⓐ Ⓑ Ⓒ Ⓓ Ⓔ
32. Ⓐ Ⓑ Ⓒ Ⓓ Ⓔ
33. Ⓐ Ⓑ Ⓒ Ⓓ Ⓔ
34. Ⓐ Ⓑ Ⓒ Ⓓ Ⓔ
35. Ⓐ Ⓑ Ⓒ Ⓓ Ⓔ
36. Ⓐ Ⓑ Ⓒ Ⓓ Ⓔ
37. Ⓐ Ⓑ Ⓒ Ⓓ Ⓔ
38. Ⓐ Ⓑ Ⓒ Ⓓ Ⓔ

SECTION 5

1. Ⓐ Ⓑ Ⓒ Ⓓ Ⓔ
2. Ⓐ Ⓑ Ⓒ Ⓓ Ⓔ
3. Ⓐ Ⓑ Ⓒ Ⓓ Ⓔ
4. Ⓐ Ⓑ Ⓒ Ⓓ Ⓔ
5. Ⓐ Ⓑ Ⓒ Ⓓ Ⓔ
6. Ⓐ Ⓑ Ⓒ Ⓓ Ⓔ
7. Ⓐ Ⓑ Ⓒ Ⓓ Ⓔ
8. Ⓐ Ⓑ Ⓒ Ⓓ Ⓔ
9. Ⓐ Ⓑ Ⓒ Ⓓ Ⓔ
10. Ⓐ Ⓑ Ⓒ Ⓓ Ⓔ
11. Ⓐ Ⓑ Ⓒ Ⓓ Ⓔ
12. Ⓐ Ⓑ Ⓒ Ⓓ Ⓔ
13. Ⓐ Ⓑ Ⓒ Ⓓ Ⓔ
14. Ⓐ Ⓑ Ⓒ Ⓓ Ⓔ
15. Ⓐ Ⓑ Ⓒ Ⓓ Ⓔ
16. Ⓐ Ⓑ Ⓒ Ⓓ Ⓔ
17. Ⓐ Ⓑ Ⓒ Ⓓ Ⓔ
18. Ⓐ Ⓑ Ⓒ Ⓓ Ⓔ
19. Ⓐ Ⓑ Ⓒ Ⓓ Ⓔ
20. Ⓐ Ⓑ Ⓒ Ⓓ Ⓔ
21. Ⓐ Ⓑ Ⓒ Ⓓ Ⓔ
22. Ⓐ Ⓑ Ⓒ Ⓓ Ⓔ
23. Ⓐ Ⓑ Ⓒ Ⓓ Ⓔ
24. Ⓐ Ⓑ Ⓒ Ⓓ Ⓔ
25. Ⓐ Ⓑ Ⓒ Ⓓ Ⓔ
26. Ⓐ Ⓑ Ⓒ Ⓓ Ⓔ
27. Ⓐ Ⓑ Ⓒ Ⓓ Ⓔ
28. Ⓐ Ⓑ Ⓒ Ⓓ Ⓔ
29. Ⓐ Ⓑ Ⓒ Ⓓ Ⓔ
30. Ⓐ Ⓑ Ⓒ Ⓓ Ⓔ
31. Ⓐ Ⓑ Ⓒ Ⓓ Ⓔ
32. Ⓐ Ⓑ Ⓒ Ⓓ Ⓔ
33. Ⓐ Ⓑ Ⓒ Ⓓ Ⓔ
34. Ⓐ Ⓑ Ⓒ Ⓓ Ⓔ
35. Ⓐ Ⓑ Ⓒ Ⓓ Ⓔ
36. Ⓐ Ⓑ Ⓒ Ⓓ Ⓔ
37. Ⓐ Ⓑ Ⓒ Ⓓ Ⓔ
38. Ⓐ Ⓑ Ⓒ Ⓓ Ⓔ

SECTION 6

1. Ⓐ Ⓑ Ⓒ Ⓓ Ⓔ
2. Ⓐ Ⓑ Ⓒ Ⓓ Ⓔ
3. Ⓐ Ⓑ Ⓒ Ⓓ Ⓔ
4. Ⓐ Ⓑ Ⓒ Ⓓ Ⓔ
5. Ⓐ Ⓑ Ⓒ Ⓓ Ⓔ
6. Ⓐ Ⓑ Ⓒ Ⓓ Ⓔ
7. Ⓐ Ⓑ Ⓒ Ⓓ Ⓔ
8. Ⓐ Ⓑ Ⓒ Ⓓ Ⓔ
9. Ⓐ Ⓑ Ⓒ Ⓓ Ⓔ
10. Ⓐ Ⓑ Ⓒ Ⓓ Ⓔ
11. Ⓐ Ⓑ Ⓒ Ⓓ Ⓔ
12. Ⓐ Ⓑ Ⓒ Ⓓ Ⓔ
13. Ⓐ Ⓑ Ⓒ Ⓓ Ⓔ
14. Ⓐ Ⓑ Ⓒ Ⓓ Ⓔ
15. Ⓐ Ⓑ Ⓒ Ⓓ Ⓔ
16. Ⓐ Ⓑ Ⓒ Ⓓ Ⓔ
17. Ⓐ Ⓑ Ⓒ Ⓓ Ⓔ
18. Ⓐ Ⓑ Ⓒ Ⓓ Ⓔ
19. Ⓐ Ⓑ Ⓒ Ⓓ Ⓔ
20. Ⓐ Ⓑ Ⓒ Ⓓ Ⓔ
21. Ⓐ Ⓑ Ⓒ Ⓓ Ⓔ
22. Ⓐ Ⓑ Ⓒ Ⓓ Ⓔ
23. Ⓐ Ⓑ Ⓒ Ⓓ Ⓔ
24. Ⓐ Ⓑ Ⓒ Ⓓ Ⓔ
25. Ⓐ Ⓑ Ⓒ Ⓓ Ⓔ
26. Ⓐ Ⓑ Ⓒ Ⓓ Ⓔ
27. Ⓐ Ⓑ Ⓒ Ⓓ Ⓔ
28. Ⓐ Ⓑ Ⓒ Ⓓ Ⓔ
29. Ⓐ Ⓑ Ⓒ Ⓓ Ⓔ
30. Ⓐ Ⓑ Ⓒ Ⓓ Ⓔ
31. Ⓐ Ⓑ Ⓒ Ⓓ Ⓔ
32. Ⓐ Ⓑ Ⓒ Ⓓ Ⓔ
33. Ⓐ Ⓑ Ⓒ Ⓓ Ⓔ
34. Ⓐ Ⓑ Ⓒ Ⓓ Ⓔ
35. Ⓐ Ⓑ Ⓒ Ⓓ Ⓔ
36. Ⓐ Ⓑ Ⓒ Ⓓ Ⓔ
37. Ⓐ Ⓑ Ⓒ Ⓓ Ⓔ
38. Ⓐ Ⓑ Ⓒ Ⓓ Ⓔ

Additional
ANSWER SHEET

1. Ⓐ Ⓑ Ⓒ Ⓓ Ⓔ	1. Ⓐ Ⓑ Ⓒ Ⓓ Ⓔ
2. Ⓐ Ⓑ Ⓒ Ⓓ Ⓔ	2. Ⓐ Ⓑ Ⓒ Ⓓ Ⓔ
3. Ⓐ Ⓑ Ⓒ Ⓓ Ⓔ	3. Ⓐ Ⓑ Ⓒ Ⓓ Ⓔ
4. Ⓐ Ⓑ Ⓒ Ⓓ Ⓔ	4. Ⓐ Ⓑ Ⓒ Ⓓ Ⓔ
5. Ⓐ Ⓑ Ⓒ Ⓓ Ⓔ	5. Ⓐ Ⓑ Ⓒ Ⓓ Ⓔ
6. Ⓐ Ⓑ Ⓒ Ⓓ Ⓔ	6. Ⓐ Ⓑ Ⓒ Ⓓ Ⓔ
7. Ⓐ Ⓑ Ⓒ Ⓓ Ⓔ	7. Ⓐ Ⓑ Ⓒ Ⓓ Ⓔ
8. Ⓐ Ⓑ Ⓒ Ⓓ Ⓔ	8. Ⓐ Ⓑ Ⓒ Ⓓ Ⓔ
9. Ⓐ Ⓑ Ⓒ Ⓓ Ⓔ	9. Ⓐ Ⓑ Ⓒ Ⓓ Ⓔ
10. Ⓐ Ⓑ Ⓒ Ⓓ Ⓔ	10. Ⓐ Ⓑ Ⓒ Ⓓ Ⓔ
11. Ⓐ Ⓑ Ⓒ Ⓓ Ⓔ	11. Ⓐ Ⓑ Ⓒ Ⓓ Ⓔ
12. Ⓐ Ⓑ Ⓒ Ⓓ Ⓔ	12. Ⓐ Ⓑ Ⓒ Ⓓ Ⓔ
13. Ⓐ Ⓑ Ⓒ Ⓓ Ⓔ	13. Ⓐ Ⓑ Ⓒ Ⓓ Ⓔ
14. Ⓐ Ⓑ Ⓒ Ⓓ Ⓔ	14. Ⓐ Ⓑ Ⓒ Ⓓ Ⓔ
15. Ⓐ Ⓑ Ⓒ Ⓓ Ⓔ	15. Ⓐ Ⓑ Ⓒ Ⓓ Ⓔ
16. Ⓐ Ⓑ Ⓒ Ⓓ Ⓔ	16. Ⓐ Ⓑ Ⓒ Ⓓ Ⓔ
17. Ⓐ Ⓑ Ⓒ Ⓓ Ⓔ	17. Ⓐ Ⓑ Ⓒ Ⓓ Ⓔ
18. Ⓐ Ⓑ Ⓒ Ⓓ Ⓔ	18. Ⓐ Ⓑ Ⓒ Ⓓ Ⓔ
19. Ⓐ Ⓑ Ⓒ Ⓓ Ⓔ	19. Ⓐ Ⓑ Ⓒ Ⓓ Ⓔ
20. Ⓐ Ⓑ Ⓒ Ⓓ Ⓔ	20. Ⓐ Ⓑ Ⓒ Ⓓ Ⓔ
21. Ⓐ Ⓑ Ⓒ Ⓓ Ⓔ	21. Ⓐ Ⓑ Ⓒ Ⓓ Ⓔ
22. Ⓐ Ⓑ Ⓒ Ⓓ Ⓔ	22. Ⓐ Ⓑ Ⓒ Ⓓ Ⓔ
23. Ⓐ Ⓑ Ⓒ Ⓓ Ⓔ	23. Ⓐ Ⓑ Ⓒ Ⓓ Ⓔ
24. Ⓐ Ⓑ Ⓒ Ⓓ Ⓔ	24. Ⓐ Ⓑ Ⓒ Ⓓ Ⓔ
25. Ⓐ Ⓑ Ⓒ Ⓓ Ⓔ	25. Ⓐ Ⓑ Ⓒ Ⓓ Ⓔ
26. Ⓐ Ⓑ Ⓒ Ⓓ Ⓔ	26. Ⓐ Ⓑ Ⓒ Ⓓ Ⓔ
27. Ⓐ Ⓑ Ⓒ Ⓓ Ⓔ	27. Ⓐ Ⓑ Ⓒ Ⓓ Ⓔ
28. Ⓐ Ⓑ Ⓒ Ⓓ Ⓔ	28. Ⓐ Ⓑ Ⓒ Ⓓ Ⓔ
29. Ⓐ Ⓑ Ⓒ Ⓓ Ⓔ	29. Ⓐ Ⓑ Ⓒ Ⓓ Ⓔ
30. Ⓐ Ⓑ Ⓒ Ⓓ Ⓔ	30. Ⓐ Ⓑ Ⓒ Ⓓ Ⓔ
31. Ⓐ Ⓑ Ⓒ Ⓓ Ⓔ	31. Ⓐ Ⓑ Ⓒ Ⓓ Ⓔ
32. Ⓐ Ⓑ Ⓒ Ⓓ Ⓔ	32. Ⓐ Ⓑ Ⓒ Ⓓ Ⓔ
33. Ⓐ Ⓑ Ⓒ Ⓓ Ⓔ	33. Ⓐ Ⓑ Ⓒ Ⓓ Ⓔ
34. Ⓐ Ⓑ Ⓒ Ⓓ Ⓔ	34. Ⓐ Ⓑ Ⓒ Ⓓ Ⓔ
35. Ⓐ Ⓑ Ⓒ Ⓓ Ⓔ	35. Ⓐ Ⓑ Ⓒ Ⓓ Ⓔ
36. Ⓐ Ⓑ Ⓒ Ⓓ Ⓔ	36. Ⓐ Ⓑ Ⓒ Ⓓ Ⓔ
37. Ⓐ Ⓑ Ⓒ Ⓓ Ⓔ	37. Ⓐ Ⓑ Ⓒ Ⓓ Ⓔ
38. Ⓐ Ⓑ Ⓒ Ⓓ Ⓔ	38. Ⓐ Ⓑ Ⓒ Ⓓ Ⓔ

1.	Ⓐ Ⓑ Ⓒ Ⓓ Ⓔ		1.	Ⓐ Ⓑ Ⓒ Ⓓ Ⓔ
2.	Ⓐ Ⓑ Ⓒ Ⓓ Ⓔ		2.	Ⓐ Ⓑ Ⓒ Ⓓ Ⓔ
3.	Ⓐ Ⓑ Ⓒ Ⓓ Ⓔ		3.	Ⓐ Ⓑ Ⓒ Ⓓ Ⓔ
4.	Ⓐ Ⓑ Ⓒ Ⓓ Ⓔ		4.	Ⓐ Ⓑ Ⓒ Ⓓ Ⓔ
5.	Ⓐ Ⓑ Ⓒ Ⓓ Ⓔ		5.	Ⓐ Ⓑ Ⓒ Ⓓ Ⓔ
6.	Ⓐ Ⓑ Ⓒ Ⓓ Ⓔ		6.	Ⓐ Ⓑ Ⓒ Ⓓ Ⓔ
7.	Ⓐ Ⓑ Ⓒ Ⓓ Ⓔ		7.	Ⓐ Ⓑ Ⓒ Ⓓ Ⓔ
8.	Ⓐ Ⓑ Ⓒ Ⓓ Ⓔ		8.	Ⓐ Ⓑ Ⓒ Ⓓ Ⓔ
9.	Ⓐ Ⓑ Ⓒ Ⓓ Ⓔ		9.	Ⓐ Ⓑ Ⓒ Ⓓ Ⓔ
10.	Ⓐ Ⓑ Ⓒ Ⓓ Ⓔ		10.	Ⓐ Ⓑ Ⓒ Ⓓ Ⓔ
11.	Ⓐ Ⓑ Ⓒ Ⓓ Ⓔ		11.	Ⓐ Ⓑ Ⓒ Ⓓ Ⓔ
12.	Ⓐ Ⓑ Ⓒ Ⓓ Ⓔ		12.	Ⓐ Ⓑ Ⓒ Ⓓ Ⓔ
13.	Ⓐ Ⓑ Ⓒ Ⓓ Ⓔ		13.	Ⓐ Ⓑ Ⓒ Ⓓ Ⓔ
14.	Ⓐ Ⓑ Ⓒ Ⓓ Ⓔ		14.	Ⓐ Ⓑ Ⓒ Ⓓ Ⓔ
15.	Ⓐ Ⓑ Ⓒ Ⓓ Ⓔ		15.	Ⓐ Ⓑ Ⓒ Ⓓ Ⓔ
16.	Ⓐ Ⓑ Ⓒ Ⓓ Ⓔ		16.	Ⓐ Ⓑ Ⓒ Ⓓ Ⓔ
17.	Ⓐ Ⓑ Ⓒ Ⓓ Ⓔ		17.	Ⓐ Ⓑ Ⓒ Ⓓ Ⓔ
18.	Ⓐ Ⓑ Ⓒ Ⓓ Ⓔ		18.	Ⓐ Ⓑ Ⓒ Ⓓ Ⓔ
19.	Ⓐ Ⓑ Ⓒ Ⓓ Ⓔ		19.	Ⓐ Ⓑ Ⓒ Ⓓ Ⓔ
20.	Ⓐ Ⓑ Ⓒ Ⓓ Ⓔ		20.	Ⓐ Ⓑ Ⓒ Ⓓ Ⓔ
21.	Ⓐ Ⓑ Ⓒ Ⓓ Ⓔ		21.	Ⓐ Ⓑ Ⓒ Ⓓ Ⓔ
22.	Ⓐ Ⓑ Ⓒ Ⓓ Ⓔ		22.	Ⓐ Ⓑ Ⓒ Ⓓ Ⓔ
23.	Ⓐ Ⓑ Ⓒ Ⓓ Ⓔ		23.	Ⓐ Ⓑ Ⓒ Ⓓ Ⓔ
24.	Ⓐ Ⓑ Ⓒ Ⓓ Ⓔ		24.	Ⓐ Ⓑ Ⓒ Ⓓ Ⓔ
25.	Ⓐ Ⓑ Ⓒ Ⓓ Ⓔ		25.	Ⓐ Ⓑ Ⓒ Ⓓ Ⓔ
26.	Ⓐ Ⓑ Ⓒ Ⓓ Ⓔ		26.	Ⓐ Ⓑ Ⓒ Ⓓ Ⓔ
27.	Ⓐ Ⓑ Ⓒ Ⓓ Ⓔ		27.	Ⓐ Ⓑ Ⓒ Ⓓ Ⓔ
28.	Ⓐ Ⓑ Ⓒ Ⓓ Ⓔ		28.	Ⓐ Ⓑ Ⓒ Ⓓ Ⓔ
29.	Ⓐ Ⓑ Ⓒ Ⓓ Ⓔ		29.	Ⓐ Ⓑ Ⓒ Ⓓ Ⓔ
30.	Ⓐ Ⓑ Ⓒ Ⓓ Ⓔ		30.	Ⓐ Ⓑ Ⓒ Ⓓ Ⓔ
31.	Ⓐ Ⓑ Ⓒ Ⓓ Ⓔ		31.	Ⓐ Ⓑ Ⓒ Ⓓ Ⓔ
32.	Ⓐ Ⓑ Ⓒ Ⓓ Ⓔ		32.	Ⓐ Ⓑ Ⓒ Ⓓ Ⓔ
33.	Ⓐ Ⓑ Ⓒ Ⓓ Ⓔ		33.	Ⓐ Ⓑ Ⓒ Ⓓ Ⓔ
34.	Ⓐ Ⓑ Ⓒ Ⓓ Ⓔ		34.	Ⓐ Ⓑ Ⓒ Ⓓ Ⓔ
35.	Ⓐ Ⓑ Ⓒ Ⓓ Ⓔ		35.	Ⓐ Ⓑ Ⓒ Ⓓ Ⓔ
36.	Ⓐ Ⓑ Ⓒ Ⓓ Ⓔ		36.	Ⓐ Ⓑ Ⓒ Ⓓ Ⓔ
37.	Ⓐ Ⓑ Ⓒ Ⓓ Ⓔ		37.	Ⓐ Ⓑ Ⓒ Ⓓ Ⓔ
38.	Ⓐ Ⓑ Ⓒ Ⓓ Ⓔ		38.	Ⓐ Ⓑ Ⓒ Ⓓ Ⓔ

ESSAY ANSWER SHEETS

REA's Test Preps
The Best in Test Preparation

- REA "Test Preps" are **far more** comprehensive than any other test preparation series
- Each book contains up to **eight** full-length practice tests based on the most recent exams
- **Every** type of question likely to be given on the exams is included
- Answers are accompanied by **full** and **detailed** explanations

REA publishes over 70 Test Preparation volumes in several series. They include:

Advanced Placement Exams (APs)
Art History
Biology
Calculus AB & BC
Chemistry
Economics
English Language & Composition
English Literature & Composition
European History
French Language
Government & Politics
Latin
Physics B & C
Psychology
Spanish Language
Statistics
United States History
World History

College-Level Examination Program (CLEP)
Analyzing and Interpreting Literature
College Algebra
Freshman College Composition
General Examinations
General Examinations Review
History of the United States I
History of the United States II
Introduction to Educational Psychology
Human Growth and Development
Introductory Psychology
Introductory Sociology
Principles of Management
Principles of Marketing
Spanish
Western Civilization I
Western Civilization II

SAT Subject Tests
Biology E/M
Chemistry
French
German
Literature
Mathematics Level 1, 2
Physics
Spanish
United States History

Graduate Record Exams (GREs)
Biology
Chemistry
Computer Science
General
Literature in English
Mathematics
Physics
Psychology

ACT - ACT Assessment
ASVAB - Armed Services Vocational Aptitude Battery
CBEST - California Basic Educational Skills Test
CDL - Commercial Driver License Exam
CLAST - College Level Academic Skills Test
COOP & HSPT - Catholic High School Admission Tests
ELM - California State University Entry Level Mathematics Exam
FE (EIT) - Fundamentals of Engineering Exams - For Both AM & PM Exams

FTCE - Florida Teacher Certification Examinations
GED - (U.S. Edition)
GMAT - Graduate Management Admission Test
LSAT - Law School Admission Test
MAT - Miller Analogies Test
MCAT - Medical College Admission Test
MTEL - Massachusetts Tests for Educator Licensure
NJ HSPA - New Jersey High School Proficiency Assessment
NYSTCE - New York State Teacher Certification Examinations
PRAXIS PLT - Principles of Learning & Teaching Tests
PRAXIS PPST - Pre-Professional Skills Tests
PSAT/NMSQT
SAT
TExES - Texas Examinations of Educator Standards
THEA - Texas Higher Education Assessment
TOEFL - Test of English as a Foreign Language
TOEIC - Test of English for International Communication
USMLE Steps 1,2,3 - U.S. Medical Licensing Exams

Research & Education Association
61 Ethel Road W., Piscataway, NJ 08854
Phone: (732) 819-8880   **website: www.rea.com**

Please send me more information about your Test Prep books.

Name _____

Address _____

City _____ State _____ Zip _____

MAXnotes®

REA's Literature Study Guides

MAXnotes® are student-friendly. They offer a fresh look at masterpieces of literature, presented in a lively and interesting fashion. **MAXnotes®** offer the essentials of what you should know about the work, including outlines, explanations and discussions of the plot, character lists, analyses, and historical context. **MAXnotes®** are designed to help you think independently about literary works by raising various issues and thought-provoking ideas and questions. Written by literary experts who currently teach the subject, **MAXnotes®** enhance your understanding and enjoyment of the work.

Available **MAXnotes®** include the following:

Absalom, Absalom!	Henry IV, Part I	Othello
The Aeneid of Virgil	Henry V	Paradise
Animal Farm	The House on Mango Street	Paradise Lost
Antony and Cleopatra	Huckleberry Finn	A Passage to India
As I Lay Dying	I Know Why the Caged	Plato's Republic
As You Like It	Bird Sings	Portrait of a Lady
The Autobiography of	The Iliad	A Portrait of the Artist
Malcolm X	Invisible Man	as a Young Man
The Awakening	Jane Eyre	Pride and Prejudice
Beloved	Jazz	A Raisin in the Sun
Beowulf	The Joy Luck Club	Richard II
Billy Budd	Jude the Obscure	Romeo and Juliet
The Bluest Eye, A Novel	Julius Caesar	The Scarlet Letter
Brave New World	King Lear	Sir Gawain and the
The Canterbury Tales	Leaves of Grass	Green Knight
The Catcher in the Rye	Les Misérables	Slaughterhouse-Five
The Color Purple	Lord of the Flies	Song of Solomon
The Crucible	Macbeth	The Sound and the Fury
Death in Venice	The Merchant of Venice	The Stranger
Death of a Salesman	Metamorphoses of Ovid	Sula
Dickens Dictionary	Metamorphosis	The Sun Also Rises
The Divine Comedy I: Inferno	Middlemarch	A Tale of Two Cities
Dubliners	A Midsummer Night's Dream	The Taming of the Shrew
The Edible Woman	Moby-Dick	Tar Baby
Emma	Moll Flanders	The Tempest
Euripides' Medea & Electra	Mrs. Dalloway	Tess of the D'Urbervilles
Frankenstein	Much Ado About Nothing	Their Eyes Were Watching God
Gone with the Wind	Mules and Men	Things Fall Apart
The Grapes of Wrath	My Antonia	To Kill a Mockingbird
Great Expectations	Native Son	To the Lighthouse
The Great Gatsby	1984	Twelfth Night
Gulliver's Travels	The Odyssey	Uncle Tom's Cabin
Handmaid's Tale	Oedipus Trilogy	Waiting for Godot
Hamlet	Of Mice and Men	Wuthering Heights
Hard Times	On the Road	Guide to Literary Terms
Heart of Darkness		

Research & Education Association
61 Ethel Road W., Piscataway, NJ 08854
Phone: (732) 819-8880   **website: www.rea.com**

Please send me more information about your MAXnotes® books.

Name _____

Address _____

City _____ State _____ Zip _____

REA'S
PROBLEM SOLVERS

The PROBLEM SOLVERS® are comprehensive supplemental textbooks designed to save time in finding solutions to problems. Each PROBLEM SOLVER® is the first of its kind ever produced in its field. It is the product of a massive effort to illustrate almost any imaginable problem in exceptional depth, detail, and clarity. Each problem is worked out in detail with a step-by-step solution, and the problems are arranged in order of complexity from elementary to advanced. Each book is fully indexed for locating problems rapidly.

Accounting	Genetics
Advanced Calculus	Geometry
Algebra & Trigonometry	Linear Algebra
Automatic Control Systems/Robotics	Mechanics
Biology	Numerical Analysis
Business, Accounting & Finance	Operations Research
Calculus	Organic Chemistry
Chemistry	Physics
Differential Equations	Pre-Calculus
Economics	Probability
Electrical Machines	Psychology
Electric Circuits	Statistics
Electromagnetics	Technical Design Graphics
Electronics	Thermodynamics
Finite & Discrete Math	Topology
Fluid Mechanics/Dynamics	Transport Phenomena

If you would like more information about any of these books,
complete the coupon below and return it to us or visit your local bookstore.

Research & Education Association
61 Ethel Road W., Piscataway, NJ 08854
Phone: (732) 819-8880   **website: www.rea.com**

Please send me more information about your Problem Solver® books.

Name _____

Address _____

City _____ State _____ Zip _____

REA's Test Prep Books Are The Best!

(a sample of the <u>hundreds of letters</u> REA receives each year)

" I am writing to congratulate you on preparing an exceptional study guide. In five years of teaching this course I have never encountered a more thorough, comprehensive, concise and realistic preparation for this examination. "
Teacher, Davie, FL

" I have found your publications, *The Best Test Preparation...*, to be exactly that. "
Teacher, Aptos, CA

" I used your *CLEP Introductory Sociology* book and rank it 99% — thank you! "
Student, Jerusalem, Israel

" Your *GMAT* book greatly helped me on the test. Thank you. "
Student, Oxford, OH

" I recently got the French *SAT II* Exam book from REA. I congratulate you on first-rate French practice tests."
Instructor, Los Angeles, CA

" Your *AP English Literature and Composition* book is most impressive. "
Student, Montgomery, AL

" Just a short note to say thanks for the great support your book gave me in helping me pass the test... I'm on my way to a B.S. degree because of you! "
Student, Orlando, FL

(more on front page)